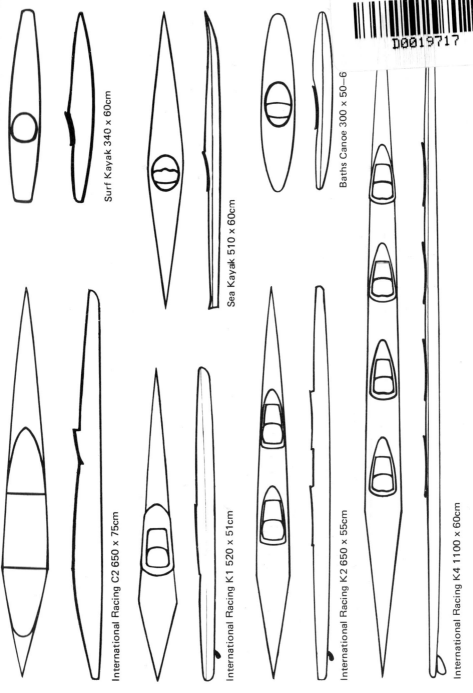

Surf Kayak 340 x 60cm

Sea Kayak 510 x 60cm

Baths Canoe 300 x 50—6

International Racing C2 650 x 75cm

International Racing K1 520 x 51cm

International Racing K2 650 x 55cm

International Racing K4 1100 x 60cm

Types of canoes and kayaks in common use in Great Britain, reproduced to a scale 1:62. Competition boat dimensions are as per ICF regi others are approximations.

'For I am the captain of my craft
My word is law from fore to aft,
I am the cook and the steward too,
I am the passenger and crew.
And though 'tis said I'm hard to please,
I'm not afraid of mutinies;
In fact my complement at sea
Is as perfect as it can be'

From *Canoe Handling* by C Bowyer Vaux
Forest and Stream Publishing Co, New York, 1885

Canoeing Handbook

Edited by Ray Rowe

with contributions by:

Frank Goodman   Ray Rowe   David Train   Mark Attenburrow
Nigel Foster   Derek Hutchinson   Rob Hignell
Graham Lyon   Dave Collins   Geoff Smedley   Dave Ruse
Phil Quill   Geoff Good   Marcus Bailie   Howard Jeffs
Dennis Ball   Carel Quaife   David Gent

illustrations by:

Ron Brown

British Canoe Union
Adbolton Lane, West Bridgford, Nottingham NG2 5AS

First published 1981
Re-print with minor corrections 1982
Re-print with minor corrections 1983

Second Edition 1989
Re-print with minor corrections 1990
Re-print with minor corrections 1991

ISBN 0 900082 04 6

Cover design and photos by courtesy of
The Tickle Group

British Library Cataloguing in Publication Data.
Canoeing handbook: the official handbook of the British Canoe Union.
- 2nd edition.
   1. Canoeing
   I. Rowe, Ray II. British Canoe Union
   797.1'22

   ISBN 0-900082-04-6

Printed in Great Britain by:
The Tickle Group
The Powerhouse, Parker Street, Bury, Lancashire BL9 0RJ

Preface

The sport of canoeing has progressed fast and furiously during the last decade. It is as a response to the developments and trends which have emerged that the *Canoeing Handbook* has been re-written.

Many of the practices, and most of the information recounted in the original book still holds good. This edition provides greater depth in the individual chapters as well as accommodating the expansion in breadth of activities within canoeing.

In essence, however, the book remains as a collection of the vital areas of knowledge in each discipline, as opposed to a manual supplying every last fact required for safe and successful canoeing. It is written with the instructor and potential instructor in mind, but is intended for a wide canoeing audience.

The generic term 'canoeing' continues to be used to describe the activity involved with any small craft propelled by a paddle. The term 'kayak', however, has been employed wherever it is important to distinguish this type of craft.

It is intended that this book should inform and inspire everyone interested in the sport of canoeing, regardless of gender, age or physical ability. The use of the male pronoun has been made purely on the basis of convenience of print and it is most certainly not our intention to imply that canoeing is a sport for males only.

The detailed requirements for the BCU Coaching Scheme tests and awards have deliberately been omitted, since these are subject to periodic review. This information can be obtained in leaflet format through the BCU office.

Ray Rowe
Gwynedd, 1989

Acknowledgements

It is with deep gratitude that I thank the following:

The authors who gave so willingly of time and effort to produce the individual chapters, and allowed me the freedom to interfere with their work; Ron Brown who drew every single piece of artwork with loving care, and remained calm and patient no matter how often I asked him to alter illustrations; Richard Robinson, who spent countless hours on the tedious work of proof-reading; the late Bill Mason, who allowed us to use extracts from *Path of the Paddle* for chapter 7, and to whom this section of our *Canoeing Handbook* shall remain a tribute; and the Royal Life Saving Society for their assistance with parts of the chapter on safety.

Thanks are also due to the contributors to chapter 20: Competition - Brian Barfoot, Alan Edge, Chris Eyre, Brian Greenaway, John Handyside and Alan Ball.

The photographs which illustrate and enhance the text were supplied by Tony Tickle, Jerry Elsmore, Sarah Ashmead, Keith Robinson, Alan Kimber, Richard Robinson, Colin Broadway and Stuart Fisher. Most of the photographs taken specially for the *Canoeing Handbook* are the work of Keith Price.

A great number of individuals have made contributions with little regard to the inconvenience it has caused them, including George Parr, James Bloc, Colin Broadway, George Oliver, Graham Wardle and many others who I hope will not be offended if this list is not extended to include every name.

To Bob Gray, who provided professional support and guidance, and gave untold hours of voluntary time to this project, must go a very special vote of thanks.

Finally, I would like to pay tribute to the Director of Coaching, Geoff Good, who single-handedly compiled the first *Canoeing Handbook*. He gave us the only totally comprehensive work on the sport and pastime of canoeing - an invaluable document for beginner, participant, or coach. Without his unfailing dedication to the BCU and its members this re-write could not have happened.

Ray Rowe

Contents

Introduction

I first began reading the draft of this *Canoeing Handbook* on a train journey, and became so enthralled that I almost missed my stop ! As a canoeist of some twenty-four years' experience I expected to find little that was new to me. The more I read, the more I felt that I needed to read, to fill the gaps in my knowledge, of which I was suddenly becoming aware.

Perhaps this should not have surprised me, because the various chapters are written by paddlers who are active in their specialist field. This has provided for the very latest thinking and practice to be expounded.

The aim was to revise the previous *Canoeing Handbook,* and re-write it where necessary, besides covering in more detail some aspects which it was felt had been given insufficient attention.

The *Canoeing Handbook* should cover the needs of all canoeists, although clearly those who instruct others will find it essential reading. Many of the comments about early publications have been taken into account. To this end I hope that you will find the check lists and summaries useful.

Illustrations are obviously very important to a book of this nature, and very careful consideration has been given as to whether a drawing or a photograph would be most appropriate. Drawings are often a weak aspect of canoeing literature and particular attention has been paid to their accuracy, here.

You will not want to sit down and read this manual from cover to cover, in the way one might read a novel. Rather, it has to be taken a chapter, or even a few pages, at a time. It will be necessary to read certain sections over again with constant reference to the diagrams and illustrations before everything becomes clear. This is inevitable when you deal with a sport in book form, and is particularly so in the case of a varied and complex pastime like canoeing.

Although the *Canoeing Handbook* is intended for paddlers, I am sure that it will be popular with school and other libraries, because it contains a wealth of related information. Sections on river morphology, first aid, and resuscitation will be studied by many a non-canoeist.

The *Canoeing Handbook* has not set out to be a 'teach yourself canoeing' guide, although it may well be used by some in this way. The aim has been to provide a wealth of background knowledge to complement that already gained through experience.

Graham Lyon
Chairman of the BCU Coaching Scheme

1 A Short History of Canoeing in Britain

Compiled by Geoff Good, Bob Gray and Ray Rowe, with acknowledgement to Oliver Cock, MBE for his booklet of the above title, published by the British Canoe Union.

INTRODUCTION

The modern canoeist or kayakist enjoys a primitive battle with a hostile environment, equipped only marginally better than his ancient forebears. For while the latest building materials give the advantage of greater strength, and allow for more sophisticated hydro-dynamic shapes, essentially the craft is still the simplest, most basic form of vessel on which it is possible, efficiently and successfully, to navigate the lakes, rivers, estuaries, coasts and oceans of the world.

Part of the attraction that canoeing holds must be that there is a sympathy with the past, when man first sat astride a log and drifted down-river. This may well have been before the invention of tools, although a branch would have made a crude paddle at an early stage. Logs tied together formed a more stable platform, and then the advantage of shaping points would have been discovered. Finally, the hollowing out of trunks by burning and chiselling, created the dug-out, which was the craft from which all other forms of water transport have evolved.

Dugouts up to 18 metres in length, papyrus or balsa-wood rafts, outrigger canoes, all developed according to the raw materials available, and the type of water on which communities found it advantageous to travel. In North America, the dugout and the timber frame and birch bark river canoes were developed by the Red Indians, while the Eskimos evolved the skin-covered sea-going kayak.

Canoes are still in use for hunting, fishing, trading, journeying and warring in many parts of the world today.

Victorians explored every corner of the globe, playing and refining all forms of games, and developing into recreational sports and pastimes ancient survival skills such as mountaineering and ski-ing. In 1865, one such gentleman, John (Rob Roy) MacGregor, a London Scot who was a barrister by profession, after seeing canoes and kayaks in North America and the Kamschatka, persuaded Searle's of Lambeth to make him a craft based on his observations. Clinker-built (a form of construction whereby timber planks are overlaid rather like a fence) the very first 'Rob Roy' weighed 90lbs (41kg) including doubled-ended paddle, mast and sail. It was 15' (4.4m) in length, 30" (.76m) beam, with oak hull and cedar decks fore and aft. The occupant sat on the floor and propelled the vessel with the double-bladed paddle, although the small lug-sail could be set to take advantage of a following or beam wind.

Rob Roy then began a series of remarkable journeys, covering over 1,000 miles of Continental waterways, after which he built Rob Roy II with length 14' (4.3m) beam 26" (.66m) and all-up weight 60 lbs (27kg). This canoe has been preserved, for display at the National Maritime Museum, Greenwich. Later navigations included the Jordan and Nile, and paddling around the Baltic, besides other voyages. Lecture tours and books of his journeys spread interest in this new sport, besides raising many thousands of pounds which he donated to charity - the plight of London's orphans in particular being of great concern to him. The well known titles by MacGregor are: *A Thousand Miles in the Rob Roy Canoe (1867); The Rob Roy on the Jordan (1869); The Rob Roy on the Baltic (1872)*

The Canoe Club, the first in the world, was founded on the Thames at Twickenham in 1866, the Prince of Wales becoming Commodore in 1867 until his accession to the throne as Edward VII in 1901. By command of Queen Victoria, the name had been changed to the Royal Canoe Club in 1873, and so it is known today. MacGregor's Jordan and Nile tour boat is still preserved there.

Many adherents began to cruise the rivers and coasts of Britain, *The Field, The Boys Own Paper*, other periodicals, and numerous books, attest the rapid growth in canoeing which occurred during that final quarter of the 19th century, spreading to Europe, and even to Australia. For instance, in 1879, using a 'Rob Roy' shipped to him by the designer, the Rev Fred C B Fairey paddled over 300 miles of the coast of Tasmania to visit outlying parishes, performing in the process the first recorded 'loop'.

Other types of kayak began to evolve as various boat builders, some of whom had been making traditional punts and skiffs for 100 years, became interested in this fresh market. The 'Rob Roys' themselves were of varying lengths and beams, and open canoes were also popular. Much reliance was put on the expanding railway system for the transporting of equipment to the start and finish of watery explorations. A pictorial record of a trip by three elegantly dressed ladies on the Warwickshire Avon in 1885 is recorded in *The Field* at that time, culminating in a wait at the station, with all their gear, by the exhausted trio.

Interest in canoeing in Britain appears to have diminished following this first generation of intense activity however, and it is to Germany that we must look, with the invention, before the first World War, of the folding canoe, for the further development of the sport in the early part of this century. It will be easier from then on to follow its evolution through the history of each section separately, for canoeing is a multi-faceted activity. No other form of water transport allows for quite the same feeling of being part of the element. Another of its great attractions is that, once a person is equipped with the basic craft, and is in possession of the fundamental skills to operate it, the proponent of this ancient art can enter so many different realms. From paddling the peaceful solitude of a placid stream, to negotiating the roaring turbulence of raging rapids, or riding the mighty surge of savage surf, the canoeist is able to enjoy the whole spectrum of experiences that the sport has to offer, and to concentrate on that which gives him or her the greatest pleasure, as character or mood dictates.

GENERAL DEVELOPMENT AND ORGANISATION

The British Canoe Association was formed in 1887, primarily for touring canoeists. This organisation quietly died in the 1920s, never having become the governing body for the sport. With the explosion of interest in canoeing on the Continent however, in spite of the set-back of the Great War, an international federation known as the Internationalen Representation fur Kanusport (IRK) was formed by Austria, Germany, Denmark and Sweden in 1924.

Plate 1:a
John MacGregor, MA, the founder of the sport of canoeing in Great Britain.
From Pictorial Chronicles of the Mighty Deep *about 1890*

It was an Austrian, H W Pawlata, who performed the first Eskimo roll achieved by a European in 1927. He learned the art by studying papers about the Eskimos, particularly those by Rasmussen. Gino Watkins, an Englishman, dreamed of an Arctic air route over Greenland, and went there to explore its possibilities in 1930. Whereas Pawlata learnt to roll for the fun of it, Watkins did so to survive and obtain food for his expedition party. Film of Watkins' group in training for Greenland still exists in the BCU film library.

At that time, travellers to Europe began to bring back news of the elegant folding canoes which were to be seen in thousands on German rivers. One of the first manufacturers in this country was Kissner, who started to make the 'Folbot' in London, in about 1933. Another, F O D Hirschfeld, a refugee from Hitler's Germany, started on Tyneside in 1935, creating the firm of Tyne Canoes Ltd.

The early '30s also saw the development of clubs, with Manchester Canoe Club, and the Canoe Camping Club being formed in 1933; so then it became important to establish a national governing body. After correspondence in the national press, the British Canoe Association (Mark II) was formed. It amalgamated with the canoe section of the Camping Club, but remained as a section of the Camping Club of Great Britain, and affiliated to the IRK. A national governing body needs to be entirely independent before it can be affiliated to by other clubs, and so, after much debate, a new national body was formed in March 1936. This was called the British Canoe Union, and it was under the aegis of the BCU, finally that Britain entered a team for the first Olympics to include canoe racing, held in Berlin later that same year.

When Franz Schulhof came to England as manager of the London branch of an Austrian company, significant developments were to take place. He was an experienced canoeist, with seven first descents of Alpine rapid rivers to his credit, and he had invented the 'Schulhof' or 'put across' method of rolling. In 1937 he took parties from the Royal Canoe Club to the French Alps and to the Hampshire and Sussex coasts, where films were made which were the foundation of the BCU library. Franz taught rolling, and in 1938 launched the first BCU Rolling Circus. He anglicised his name to Frank Sutton, and during the war distinguished himself as the first 'enemy alien' to gain a commission in HM Forces, being awarded the Military Cross. The first canoe slalom to be held in Britain in 1939, was organised by Frank Sutton, assisted by Maurice Rothwell, among others.

The Second World War interrupted all development until, in 1946, John Dudderidge represented Britain in the creation of the new International Canoe Federation (ICF) replacing the IRK, whose headquarters had been in Munich.

Kayak skills were dramatically improved in the early '50s by Milo Dufek, a Czechoslovakian canoe paddler who moved to Switzerland, and translated strokes used in the Canadian canoe to the kayak. Thus began the 'basic skills' defined in this book. The British slalom team of 1953 were coached in these new techniques by the German champion, Erik Seidel, who also developed the shaped seat by sitting on a bag of sawdust !

The rapid growth of the sport required different levels of administration, and so technical committees were set up to cater for the needs of alternative disciplines. Paddle racing (sprint) and slalom were the first to be established. Now, committees exist for marathon, wild water racing, sea canoeing, surf, canoe polo, touring, access, coaching, and the Corps of Canoe Lifeguards.

4

Plate 1:b
'Crossing the Sound'
from the book Come Travelling *by WarringtonBadenPowell published in 1871*

Plate 1:c
'Somersault in the surf at Falmouth' (Tasmania) - surely the first 'loop'
From The Boys Own Paper *of 1892.*

The establishment of the BCU Coaching Scheme owes much to the work of John Dudderidge, who travelled extensively in 1959 and 1960 selecting people to organise coaching on a regional basis. The scheme has developed into an effective network of organisers, and recently full time National Coaches have been appointed to train specialist competition coaches. Oliver Cock was appointed as the first full time National Coach in January 1962.

The initial signs of any form of standard qualification appeared in 1949 with the first Proficiency Tests. John Dudderidge produced a set of standards for the Duke of Edinburgh's Award, and later, the Advanced Tests were introduced. Thus the National Coaching Committee was given some groundwork upon which to develop its standards for teaching. After some years with John Dudderidge in the chair, he retired, and in 1966 Geoff Sanders, who had previously been its honorary secretary, took his place.

The Corps of Canoe Lifeguards was first conceived by Rear Admiral (then Captain) Hoare. The serious East Coast floods of 1953 gave him the idea that a properly trained canoeist could render assistance. However, floods are occasional, and the Corps found itself drawn to lifeguard work on the beaches. It was difficult to convince the authorities that a canoe could be anything but a nuisance, and it was a long, hard battle before the Corps became an accepted part of the lifesaving services. Again, John Dudderidge was initially in the chair, until the scheme became established and could stand on its own.

Due to these developments, the day to day administration of the sport by amateurs became impractical, and in 1962 the Union employed a professional secretary. Captain Alec Kennedy RN (Retired) was appointed, and offices were acquired in Central London.

The Scottish Canoe Association was formed in 1939 and became a 'division' of the BCU in 1944. Northern Ireland followed, with an independent association, the Canoe Association of Northern Ireland (1965). Both retained separate membership facilities and rights until 1978, when a move to create separate Associations for all four nations, with the BCU becoming the federal body to which all belonged, was defeated at a special general meeting. A compromise was reached, where the existing Associations, and the newly formed Welsh Canoeing Association, entered into an agreement with the BCU, which recognised them as the governing bodies within their countries. The BCU retained responsibility for federal (United Kingdom) matters, and for England. Reciprocal rights of membership exist between the Associations and the BCU. It was now essential for England to establish a regionally based structure. This was in keeping with the views of the Sports Council, and by the end of 1980 regional BCU committees had been established in accordance with the boundaries recognised by the Sports Council.

It will be noticeable within this chapter that one name persistently appears. The contribution that John Dudderidge has made to the sport, the Union, and the ICF, is immeasurable. His personal involvement in so many different aspects has been greatly responsible for the development of canoeing. The OBE was awarded in 1963 and in 1964 the Award of Honour of the ICF. At the Moscow Olympics in 1950, John was presented by the ICF with a specially struck gold medal in recognition of his devotion and unique service, which has led to the growth in strength and stature of the pastime founded in the 'pleasure of the paddle'.

Plate 1:d
Franz Schulhof on the Bregenzer Ach, Western Austria in 1932

Plate 1:e
A 'Senior Rob Roy Four' of 1926

SPRINT RACING

Sprint racing was the first type of organised canoe competition, with a formal regatta having taken place at The Canoe Club in 1867, when fifteen Rob Roys participated. In 1874 the, by then, Royal Canoe Club instituted the Paddling Challenge Cup, the oldest paddling trophy in the world. Races for this were competed in Rob Roys, which gradually became longer and narrower, and so faster. By the end of the century four-man kayaks had appeared, also clinker-built, known as Rob Roy Fours.

Following the Rob Roy, the 'Single Streak' evolved, constructed from two 'streaks', or planks, one on each side, of cedar, about 3mm thick. The dimensions as to length and beam varied according to the weight of the paddler, but an average size would have been 6m x 56cm, decked fore and aft with a bulkhead cockpit, or 'well', protected by narrow side decks and coaming. The paddler sat on the floorboards, bracing himself against a backboard, and adjustable footrest, or 'stretcher'. The paddle was about 230cm long, spoon-bladed, and unfeathered.

Paddle racing in Britain was carried on mainly in the spring and autumn meetings of the Royal Canoe Club and at a few local regattas on the Thames in the early 1900s, with the emphasis changing to single blade paddling. On the Continent, however, it grew from strength to strength, until the President and Secretary of the IRK, both Germans, were influential in persuading the Olympic Organising Committee of the Berlin Games to put forward canoeing as a new sport for that programme. This led to a great leap forward in international canoe racing. The British Canoe Association immediately made a provisional entry for the 1936 Games, but with little or no idea how to implement it. John Dudderidge became involved in finding and preparing a team following the first British National Championships, at Chertsey, the previous year. In the autumn, canoeists were invited to take up intensive training, and a squad of twenty was gathered. Winter training began on the Tideway, but in the spring of 1936 the base was moved to the Royal Canoe Club, where a 10,000 metre course had been prepared. By this time the squad had fallen to about twelve. At Whitsuntide, with a move to Windermere to gain experience on water more like that which they were going to find in Berlin, the party numbered some half dozen.

The team were to concentrate on the 10,000 metre event. G W Lawton came 8th out of 13 in the Folding Singles, and A R Brearley and J W Dudderidge came 9th in the Folding Pairs. These Olympic Games were an important landmark, in that it was the first time a British team had taken part in an international event.

Although feathered blades were used for kayaks from early times, particularly in America, it was not until the late '20s that they were generally accepted in Europe. By the 1936 Olympics, most nations had adopted them, apart from the Hungarians - who quickly followed suit.

In the spring of 1937 John Dudderidge organised a course at the Royal Canoe Club, and obtained the services of the leading German coach, Geerhard Quandt, who brought over with him the first K1 (international racing single kayak). The enthusiasm engendered was so great that the 'Royal' bought a fleet of racing kayaks from Austria, of three K1s, and three K2s (doubles) which were supplied and delivered in London for £80 the lot !

The first Olympic Games after the war were staged in London, with the canoeing events at Henley-on-Thames. The BCU had no resources for purchasing boats, but Jicwood of Weybridge came to the rescue by building and donating twelve kayaks. Two racing canoes were made by Austin Farrar of Wolverstone Shipyard, and these boats provided the basis for rebuilding British sprint canoeing. At Henley we were represented in all events, including, for the first time, the Ladies' K1.

Eric Farnham took over the coaching of the team in 1950, and the Swedish coach, Hans Berglund, taught the first post-war racing course at Bisham Abbey. New boats, including modern K4s, appeared. Altogether, the scene looked promising for the future, and there was great hope of achievement at Helsinki in 1952. But standards elsewhere had improved, and our placings were not as good as had been hoped. In 1953, we gained a second place in the first West European Championships in Duisburg, followed by a first in K4 at an international regatta at Namur. Also in 1953, the News of the World sponsored the first of the annual Sprint Championships on the Serpentine in London.

In their efforts to encourage others to join in sprint racing, the Paddling Racing Committee introduced the National Chine Kayak, but despite the fact that this exceptional craft could be made easily and cheaply at home, the class did not flourish. By 1957 the number of competitors had dropped to a dangerously low figure and, in an effort to halt the decline, Junior and Senior events were introduced. This decision produced a record number of junior entrants, and so the situation improved. By the time of the 1959 European Championships at Duisburg, Britain was able to enter the largest team yet. For the 1960 Olympic Games in Rome, we obtained better results than ever, and of the four events entered, only in one did our competitors not reach the semi-finals. In the K1 Men's event, Ron Rhodes not only reached the final - the first time in the Union's history - but by producing his best time, secured fifth place, thereby qualifying for an Olympic diploma.

1961 saw the birth of the British Open Youth Championships. It was hoped that, by building up a large group of enthusiastic young people in sprint racing, a sound pyramid of competitors would develop, forming a broad base from which future world champions could be produced. However, due to lack of able administrators, the scheme foundered.

The creation of Holme Pierrepont National Water Sports Centre in 1972 was a significant factor in the development of British racing, for this magnificent nine-lane purpose built course has enabled world class events to be staged with pride and ease. The annual Nottinghamshire International Regatta, established in 1972, attracts the top canoeing nations, with over 500 international athletes competing.

British interest in sprint canoe racing was spasmodic until 1973, when Willy Reichenstein competed in the World Championships. Since then the sport has started to develop, particularly at Junior level. Steven Train and Alan Saunders, from Fladbury Canoe Club, reached the canoe doubles finals at the 1979 Junior European Championships. A renewed attempt to maintain the C7 (7 man canoe) internationally at Junior level arose from Fladbury's interest, and the first ever British crew was entered for the 1981 Junior Championships in Sofia, Bulgaria. This development foundered, however, and the C4 has now been officially adopted instead.

The total domination of international sprint racing by the Eastern bloc nations has lessened throughout the eighties and in the Montreal world Championships in 1987 a greater number of medals in total were won by Western nations. This improvement in performance in the mid-eighties has been attributed to the use of the innovative 'wing' paddle. The modified technique required to get the best out of the paddle was superbly demonstrated by Jeremy West in Montreal where he became World Champion at 500 metres and 1000 metres. No medals were won by British paddlers in the 1980 Olympic games, but there was representation in several finals. Since then, the following notable performances have been achieved in World Championships:

1981 -	Mens K4 10,000m	Bronze	Williams,Canham,Brown,Jackson
1983 -	Mens K2 10.000m	Gold	Williams,Jackson
1984 -	Olympics	Britain in 10 out of 12 finals	
1985 -	C2 10.000m	Silver	Train,Train
1986 -	Mens Kl 500m	Gold	Jeremy West
1986 -	Mens K1 1,000m	Gold	Jeremy West
1987 -	C2 10.000m	Bronze	Train, Train

The Silver Medal won by Steven and Andrew Train, in the double canoe 10,000m event at the 1985 World Championships, was the first ever canoe medal to be won by non-Eastern bloc Europeans.

Strides have been made in the past decade with large increases in competitors, officials, national regattas, sponsorship and media coverage. A full-time coach, Brian Greenaway, was appointed in 1986, supported largely by special funds allocated by the Sports Council as a result of an enquiry into Olympic preparation headed by Sebastian Coe. Whilst like most of British sport we still lack the sophisticated coaching system of the socialist countries, the potential, and the machinery to capitalise on it, now exists.

CANOE SAILING

As already mentioned, John MacGregor employed a small 'lug-sail' to propel Rob Roy whenever there was a following wind. But it was Warrington Baden-Powell, brother of the founder of the Boy Scouts movement, who developed the first canoe which relied quite specifically upon sail power for its propulsion. By the 1870's, the sailing canoe possessed all the equipment which was needed to make a course against as well as with the wind direction - a centreboard, a rudder and a yawl rig. At this stage the canoeist controlled his craft from a seated position inside the cockpit.

In 1874, the Royal Canoe Club presented the Sailing Challenge Cup which has been competed for annually ever since (with the exception of the war years). This and the New York Canoe Club's International Cup (1886) are amongst the oldest sailing trophies in the world.

International competition began when Baden-Powell and Guy Ellington challenged for the New York Cup in 1886. They discovered that the Americans were making their canoes go much faster by sitting up on the windward side deck, using their body weight more effectively to counterbalance the force of the wind on the sails. Upon his return to Britain, Ellington designed and built 'Charm', a lightweight American style canoe which overwhelmed the home competition. However, the Americans were developing their designs and sailing techniques swiftly and Ellington was never able to win the New York Cup.

Plate 1:f
The Train Brothers
PHOTO: TONY TICKLE

In the 90's, Paul Butler, an American, developed the original sliding seat; by sitting entirely outside the canoe he was able to exert tremendous righting force, making it faster in stronger winds. This feature remains the secret of the sailing canoe's phenomenal speed even today.

In the early 1900's the British modified the overall dimensions of the sailing canoe and ultimately settled upon 518 x 106cm - this was known first as the Cruising Canoe and ultimately as the 'B' Class. This sloop rigged sailing vessel was rapidly accepted as the standard and was raced without major change until the 1930's.

In 1932, Uffa Fox, a name which is synonymous with the development of the sailing dinghy, built two canoes which complied with both the British 'B' Class and the current American rule. With his protege, Roger de Quincey, Uffa challenged for and won the New York Cup in 1933. An important result of this meeting was that the Royal Canoe Club and the American Canoe Association forged new International Building Rules which formed the basis of today's International rules.

At this time, a very different sailing canoe was being used on the continent; it carried only 7.5 rather than the 10 square metres of sail which the Americans and British were using. They held their own World Championship under the aegis of the IRK in 1938 and were overwhelmed when they raced their canoes against the British in 1939. In 1946, the 'Anglo-American' rule was adopted as the International 10 Square Metre Sailing Canoe under the newly formed ICF rules and became recognised as a worldwide competitive discipline of the canoeing sport.

At this stage the 'IC' rules allowed for design development of hull shape and rig within certain laid down restrictions; important names in the world of sailboat design such as Jack Holt, Ian Proctor and Austin Farrar all contributed toward the refinement of an already fine design. In 1955 the sliding seat was redesigned so that it now had a curved shape and a ladder structure in its top surface - it allowed the helmsman to climb out right to the end with greater security and a resultant increase in available power. In 1959, with the new technique well practiced, Alan Emus and Bill Kempner won the New York Cup once more for Britain.

The first World Championship for the IC was held at Hayling Island in 1961 with contestants from Britain, USA, Sweden and West Germany. Britain swept the board, taking the first six places. This stimulated other national fleets to greater activity and although Britain still took gold and bronze in 1965 at Lake Constance, the silver went to Sweden. The Swedes won the European Championship on their home waters in 1967 but just failed to wrest the World title from Emus at Grafham Water in 1969.

During this period, the IC was subjected to continuous technical development - hulls were being moulded from wood veneers using glues developed for the aircraft industry and it was not long after the advent of Glass Reinforced Plastics that GRP canoes appeared. Aluminium replaced wood for masts and booms and synthetic fibres were first used in sailcloths and ropes. It was about this time that the mainsail developed its distinctive 'batwing' profile - aerodynamically very efficient and copied ever since by high performance yacht designers.

Sweden took the World crown at the four championships held between 1972 and 1981 and then, in 1984 America stepped in to revive memories of past glories. Finally in 1987, Robin Wood recaptured the championship for Great Britain with

Plate 1g
An International 10 sq metre Sailing Canoe at the National Championships

another Briton, Pat Marshall, taking the bronze. Competitors at Plymouth came from USA, Australia, New Zealand, West Germany, Sweden and Belgium as well as the home country.

In addition to the countries already mentioned, IC's can now be found in Canada, whose representatives won a recent North American Championship, and also in Spain, Japan and the West Indies. This branch of the canoe sport is growing in popularity as it has never done in more than a century's existence.

Under current regulations, the IC has a 'one-design' hullshape but the rig, its driving force, is left open to development within set limitations.

SLALOM

Slalom first appeared on the continent in the late 1920s, where it was linked with skiing. One can imagine the skiers suggesting the hanging of poles over rapid water for a simple, timed run down between them. The first British slalom at Trevor Rocks on the Welsh Dee, in 1939, was followed by one at Ludlow on the Teme, in 1940. Due to the war, the next event was not until 1948, at Taymain Islands, again on the Dee.

A World Championships was held at Geneva in 1949, where British results indicated we were well behind the rest of Europe. The next World Championships were in 1951 at Steyr, Austria, where the 'Steyr' roll was first seen. Although doing somewhat better, it was not until 1953 at Merano in Italy, that the British were sufficiently depressed to consider remedial action. There was a meeting of interested people at the Chalfont Park Canoe Club at Hambleden that autumn, and Oliver Cock took on the job of coaching the British team. Improvements were gradual, until in 1959, once more at Geneva, Paul Farrant won the coveted F1 (folding single) World Championship. Tragically, he died in a road accident the following Easter. It is of interest to note that Paul had to fit his own footrest and knee grips as these were not then universally accepted.

At the end of 1961, having seen the British team win the Bronze Medal at Spittal-auf-dem-Drau in Austria, Oliver retired as the team coach and became the first National Coach for canoeing. British results were not so successful again until 1967, when Dave Mitchell won the World Silver Medal. Two years later, the men's kayak team of John MacLeod, Ray Calverley and Ken Langford took the Silver at Bourg St Maurice. These three names were at the forefront during the decade following the mid-60s, and the success achieved in the 1981 World Championships is in large measure attributable to their expertise and dedication subsequently in the coaching field.

By 1963 the folding and rigid canvas canoes had disappeared from championship events, replaced by glass reinforced plastic boats ('fibreglass' or 'grp') first brought over from the Continent. The skills which Milo Dufek had introduced in the early '50s, allied to the new designs which were now possible, opened up a new and wonderful field of white water canoeing, although discussion was still enjoined as to whether curved blades could be successfully mastered in moving water! With the introduction of grp, the kayak, with its deck already in existence, could be rounded off in cross-section, and it was found that this was an advantage for its performance in rough water, since there was no sharp angle at the gunwale for the water to catch and capsize the craft. In the case of the canoe, there was traditionally no deck, so the craft was decked in, making what looked crudely like a mis-shapen banana with round holes for cockpits.

14

Slalom kayaks and canoes have gradually become lower in profile. In 1965 Klepper introduced the SL5, which was the first designed to turn more efficiently in an upright position than when leaned. This seemed to be ahead of its time for it was not until about 1975 that a totally new concept and set of skills came into being, with boats being built to allow the ends to be 'dipped' or 'ducked' under the poles. This technique had, however, been observed in the late '60s and early '70s, when used by such masters as Dave Mitchell, seven times British Champion besides World Silver Medalist, and Jorgen Bremmer, the East German who was twice World Champion and Olympic Gold Medalist.

Canoes have moved in the same direction - it is now difficult for a non-slalomist to know whether he is looking at a single kayak or a canoe, and for doubles, the seating has moved to a central position, allowing for faster turning, as well as facilitating dipping techniques. A milestone was reached in the canoe classes when, in 1980, Martyn Hedges became the European Champion, and in 1981 Britain won the World C2 Team Gold Medal at Bala, North Wales.

For the 1972 Olympic Games in Munich, a purpose-built slalom course had been designed at Augsburg, which is still used for international competition and is available for general practice. Victoria Brown was the best placed British competitor, coming 6th in the Ladies' K1.

The Welsh Water Authority had made available for canoeing events the River Tryweryn, which flowed into Llyn Tegid (Lake Bala) but was now controlled by the Llyn Celyn Dam, allowing for metered water releases to be made. Through the generous sponsorship of the Sports Council, this was developed for international competition, and was the site of the 1981 World Slalom and Wild Water Championships which, together with the Racing Championships at Nottingham meant that Britain was unique in being the first nation to stage all three canoeing events with World Championships status in the same country in the same year.

At Bala, in 1981, Richard Fox became World Champion while the men's team with Nicky Wain replacing Alan Edge, successfully defended their Gold Medal. The ladies team including Liz Sharman, produced a Silver. The men's double canoes team Gold was an amazing turn-around since no representatives had been considered good enough to be sent to Jonquiere.

Success then increased to an extent that only the outstanding achievements can be noted. Heading these is the successful defence of his World Title in 1983, and again in 1985, by Richard Fox. Richard was undefeated in European and World Championships during this period, amd won back his title in 1989. He established himself as a 'personality', with appearances in the television series 'Paddles Up', 'Rapid Racing', 'Sporting Chance' and the 'Krypton Factor' which he won, besides recognition through the Paul Zetter Award as the most outstanding British Champion assisted by the Sports Aid Foundation in 1985.

Liz Sharman became World Ladies' K1 Champion in 1983, followed by Silver in the European Championships in 1984. With Martyn Hedges having won the European Canoe Championships in 1980, and becoming World Bronze Medallist in 1985, the past decade has seen growing success internationally.

Britain's notable successes in World Championships since 1981 are:

1983	-	Men's individual kayak	Gold	Richard Fox
	-	Women's individual kayak	Gold	Liz Sharman
1985	-	Men's individual kayak	Gold	Richard Fox
	-	Women's individual kayak	Bronze	Gail Allen
	-	Men's individual C1	Bronze	Martyn Hedges
1987	-	Women's individual kayak	Gold	Liz Sharman
	-	Men's Kayak Team event	Gold	Fox, Jones, Smith

Alan Edge was appointed as a full-time coach to the Union for 1986, and with a fundamental change in attitude to the importance of training and coaching in order to maintain our position in world rankings, the prospects for the future are sound.

Significant changes in the rules were agreed by the ICF to take effect in the 1986 season. These brought in minimum weight end profile requirements for boats; shortened the maximum length of course to 600 metres, and did away with the 'team gate' and 'presentation' rule.

The Slalom Committee, faced with a continuing annual increase in demand, and a limit on suitable resources, has increasingly looked to purpose-built sites. In 1967, it was mooted that the opportunity for an artificial white water course existed at the National Water Sports Centre at Holme Pierrepont, Nottingham. A working model was produced, funded by the Sports Council, in 1974. It was not until 1986, however, that water finally flowed down the £2.2 million channel, by-passing Colwick Sluice on the River Trent. HRH The Princess Royal, performed the opening ceremony.

This major facility owes its existence to the vision and continuing guidance of Frank Goodman and George Parr in particular. It provides a dependable slalom and white water training site, and is likely to play a significant part in helping Britain's paddlers to high levels of achievement in the years ahead.

WILD WATER RACING

Meanwhile the idea of just racing straight down rapid rivers had not escaped the minds of many. Here, skill in reading water was just as necessary as in slalom, and stamina became even more important. Several miles down rapids needs nerves of iron as well, and it is not surprising to find that rapid river racing has a dedicated following. The first World Championships White Water Race was held on the Vezere in France in 1959, and a British team consisting of most of the world slalom team from Geneva was entered.

The terms 'white water' and 'wild water' are synonymous, 'wild water' being favoured internationally. In Britain, since the separation of slalom and racing, it has become accepted that 'white water' is used to denote all activities on rapids. Hence, there are two forms of competition held on 'white water': slalom, and wild water racing.

Although the developments have not been so dramatic in wild water racing as for slalom, there has been a continual evolution of boat designs, which now, whilst being very buoyant, are almost as 'tender' for the novice as is a racing K1. The

Plate 1:h
Liz Sharman

Plate 1:i
Richard Fox
PHOTOS: TONY TICKLE

17

tradition of slalomists doubling as wild water racers continued until about 1977, when increasing specialisation and competition led to the BCU agreeing to a separate committee being formed to concentrate on Wild Water Racing. Internationally, there is still a single Slalom and Wild Water Racing Committee governing the two sports.

Success came in the 1970s when at Skopje, in 1975, Hilary Peacock, Pauline Goodwin and Peggy Mitchell, won the Ladies' team event, with Pauline taking the individual Silver, and Hilary the Bronze. In 1979, Robert Campbell won the Silver Medal at Jonquiere, and in 1980, Britain took the first two places in men's kayak at the Bala pre-World's International. In 1981 Ann Plant became the World Bronze Medallist for Ladies' K1, and the British men's kayak team obtained the Silver.

The ladies shone again in 1983, at Merano, obtaining a Silver Medal, and a Bronze in 1985, while at the first official World Junior Wild Water Championships held at Spittal, Austria, in 1986, Neil Stamps won the Silver Medal. Some progress was made in the canoe sections, and when the difficulty of obtaining access to white water is considered against the fact that Britain has no continuous stretch of grade III rapids, at which level wild water racing is pursued, the world class standing of many of our competitors is all the more remarkable.

MARATHON RACING

It may seem somewhat absurd to find the foundations of marathon racing laid in a bet and a double sculling skiff! Owing to a threatened public transport strike in 1920, a group of friends in the Greyhound Public House at Pewsey, fell to discussing other means of conveyance, and ended up with a bet of £5 that they could travel with their skiff via the River Avon from Pewsey to the sea at Mudeford, near Christchurch, in less than three days. They won their bet with twelve hours to spare. Twenty seven years later, three RAF men and a local farmer met a member of the original crew in the same pub. They decided to try their luck, got to Christchurch in 51 hours, and so won a further £5.

Roy Cooke, a member of that 1947 crew, then planned a boat trip from Devizes to Westminster in 100 hours, and although his project fell through, the idea was taken up by the Devizes Rover Scouts. Their object was to reach the sea by way of the Kennet and Avon Canal to Reading, and thence down the Thames to Westminster. The townspeople of Devizes responded to the idea, and put up money to be donated to the Unit in the event of a successful attempt. Thus it was, that at Easter 1948, with news of their progress interrupting cinema programmes in their home town, the first two crews from the Devizes Rovers, paddling cumbersome home-built double kayaks, completed the course with ten hours to spare. At Whitsun that same year, two doubles of the Chippenham Sea Cadet Unit covered the same course in just under 77 hours, and the competition was on.

Without any formal rules, except the broad stipulation that competitors should carry all their food and equipment from the start, and receive no assistance en route, twenty crews set off from Devizes at Easter 1949. The best time that year was 49 hours 32 minutes. Prompted by the growing interest, Frank Luzmore of the Richmond Canoe Club, set up an organising committee, and Easter 1950 saw the first formal race. From these modest beginnings, the event has continued to grow, so that now more than 300 crews regularly take part, and the winning time

Plate 1:j
The artificial white water slalom course at Holme Pierrepont, Nottingham

Plate 1:k
Princess Anne meets Jeremy West at the opening of the artificial white water
slalom course
PHOTOS: TONY TICKLE

19

for the gruelling 125 miles and 76 portages has been cut down to the present record of 15 hrs 35 mins established by Brian Greenham and Tim Cornish in 1979.

Others became inspired by the concept of long distance racing, as it was then called. At first, the Sprint Racing Committee took charge of this new form of competition, and set up a sub-committee in 1955 to administer it. Later, in 1958, when LD had developed further, this sub-committee became an independent specialist committee of the BCU, racing being held in England, Scotland, Ireland, Europe, and now many other parts of the world. Renamed 'marathon racing' in 1978, and thanks largely to the efforts of John Dudderidge, it was recognised by the ICF in 1979. Internationally, it remained under the control of the Paddle Racing Committee until 1984, when a separate Marathon Racing Committee was established.

In the early days, any type of canoe could be raced by anyone in an 'open class', but the impracticalities of this were soon recognised. Various handicap systems were tried, with varying degrees of success. In 1956 a junior class was set up for those between the ages of 15 and 19, and the canoes were also divided into four classes - singles under and over 15' (4.57m) and doubles under and over 17' (5.18m).

The one-design National Chine Kayak was added in 1959. Ladies were given separate status, and 1960 saw further developments, when classes included K1, K2 and NCK1 for seniors only, while others provided for seniors, juniors and ladies, making fifteen in all. Hard skin and soft skin kayaks and canoes were put into different categories, the soft skin group still providing for folding and home built lath and canvas boats. Hence there was an apparent anomaly between the maximum length for a soft skin double at 17'6" (5.3m) since many folding doubles were of this length, and that of its hard skin counterpart at 17' (5.2m). In 1964, junior K1 and K2 events were added to this list, and ladies' NCK1 in 1966.

With the increasingly improved standards in paddling it became apparent that newcomers were discouraged by having to compete against the country's leading competitors and so, in 1971, a separate grouping was approved for the top paddlers. The other senior paddlers were included in an open class with a third for juniors under 18. The Espada Youth K1 was introduced, with competitors racing in three age groups: 12 to 14; 14 to 16; and 16 to 18 which was also agreed for sprint racing.

Previously, in 1957, Lloyds of London had presented the Royal Marines with a beautiful trophy in memory of their raid on Bordeaux by kayak during the Second World War. This, the Hasler Trophy, named after Major 'Blondie' Hasler, the leader of the raid, was handed over by the Royal Marines to the BCU for administration. It is competed for annually by clubs on a points system.

The first National Championships in Long Distance Racing was held at Bradford-on-Avon in 1965. From 1971 to 1980 this event was held annually on the Severn at Worcester.

International success has been remarkable with Britain having won outright the European Grand Prix series every year since its inception in the late '70s, apart from 1985 when we came second to Denmark.

Individual paddlers of note have been Alan Williams, Robin Belcher, and Rhod Kinch, whilst Anne Plant remained unbeaten in ladies' K1 events since winning the World Cup Marathon in 1983 until the World Championships in 1988, where

Plate 1:1
The start of the first ICF World Marathon Canoe Racing Championships at
Holme Pierrepont, Nottingham, 1988
PHOTO: TONY TICKLE

an injury sadly put her out of contention. Nationally, a re-appraisal of the class arrangement took place in 1980, at the instigation of David Train. There is now a 'divisional' system, which allows for all ages and all types of boat to be raced together, promotion from the lower divisions taking place on an ability basis. Once a certain level has been reached, paddlers naturally gravitate to a racing kayak or canoe if they wish to progress, or they can enjoy good competition in this division in a slower type of craft. Britain has always been one of the top nations on the international marathon circuit and has won the Europa Cup more often than any other country. The cup is awarded on the basis of results over three named international marathons.

The International Canoe Federation awarded Great Britain the responsibility of holding the first official World Championships in marathon racing. These took place in Nottingham in 1988, where Train and Train won the Gold medal in the C2 class, and Lawler and Burns gained Silver in mens' K2. Britain won the Nations Cup for most points overall.

CANOE POLO

This game was first mentioned in two books: Noel McNaught's *Canoeing Manual*, and Oliver Cock's *You and Your Canoe*, both published in the mid 1950s. Although the rules differed, the basic objects of the game were to release people from their inhibitions and fears in their canoes. The idea of having fun was dominant, and rules were kept to the barest minimum for safety.

The origins of polo must lie in an event at Hunter's Quay in Scotland, which was illustrated in *The Graphic* of September 1880, whilst in Germany games were played on football-sized pitches on lakes, attracting great numbers of spectators, before the second World War. Today, a one-design small kayak is used, and a regular national league is operated.

Polo in Britain was first demonstrated at the National Canoe Exhibition at Crystal Palace in 1970. This was met with enthusiasm, a competitive structure was soon formed, the first National Championships were held at the next Exhibition, and have taken place annually ever since. In 1979, a national league was formed.

The special boats for use in swimming pools had been developed as early as 1966, when Bert Keeble produced a wooden canoe, short with rounded ends. Alan Byde designed a similar boat in grp, which he dubbed the 'Baths Advanced Trainer' - BAT for short. Canoe polo is therefore often referred to nowadays as 'bat polo'.

Pressure for international recognition has steadily increased, with a number of 'invitation' matches having been played. The British rules have been agreed as a basis for international competition by the ICF working party.

CANOE SURFING

Whilst an early film made by Schulhof prior to the Second World War depicted surfing at Cuckmere Haven, the sport did not become properly established until 1952. Oliver Cock took a small party to Polzeath in Cornwall and initiated an annual event. In 1964 the BCU surfing week moved to Bude, and it was here in 1967 that the first National Championships in canoe surfing took place. The early competitions used mainly slalom or general purpose kayaks, and the rules were adapted from those used for competitive malibu board riding.

In 1970, a new type of craft, the surf kayak, appeared on the scene from California, specially designed for surfing. It had a flat hull, and considerable rocker, which enabled many more manoeuvres to be carried out. At the same time, however, it cut out some of the other tricks which were popular. Therefore a second class had to be allowed in the competitions, as the two craft could not fairly compete against each other. 1970 also saw the idea of competition in surf spread to the North East, when the first local championships were held. With the advent of the specialisation that the new surf kayaks brought, pressure built up for a separate governing body. A compromise was reached, however, and the BCU Surf Committee came into being in 1974. Since then, surf techniques and skill levels have improved considerably, and whilst there are still open classes for mainly slalom boats, the trend is now to skis, which have superseded the surf kayaks.

The Surf Committee are currently pursuing an active policy of promoting the sport internationally and seeking ICF recognition. In 1980 a British team entered an unofficial World Championships in the USA, competing with merit, and unofficial European Championship's have been held since.

CANOE ORIENTEERING

This is a form of competition in canoeing which has got off to a slow start. It first appeared in print in the 'Know the Game' series, *Orienteering,* published in 1965, and has taken place perfunctorily all over the United Kingdom since then. Perhaps one of its strongest centres is at Martham Ferry in Norfolk, where an annual event has been held since 1970. The sport is well suited to almost any piece of water, but especially over old wet gravel pit workings, which have been allowed to run to nature. It is a pity, therefore, that more have not been attracted to what can be a very exciting activity.

TOURING AND EXPEDITIONING

Rob Roy MacGregor undoubtedly undertook expeditions as well as tours, as did many of the pioneer canoeists. The illustrations from some of the early books demonstrate that many outstanding journeys were made. Rob Roy's voyages, and those of the Rev Fred C B Fairey have been mentioned. In 1885, T H Holding, founder Chairman of the Canoe Camping Club, led a group of four in three canoes from the Clyde, through the Kyles of Bute, past Corryvreken into Loch Fyne, and by land to Loch Lomond, paddling its length and back into the Clyde. He makes the interesting observation, 20 years after the beginning of the sport, that 'there had been a sad decline of interest in sea touring' ! Before and immediately after the second World War, there are matter-of-fact accounts of some very enterprising passages, both sea and inland. Frank Sutton, mentioned earlier, paddled the Upper Inn in Switzerland, in the 1930s, not officially recorded since, until the descent in 1969 covered by the *Sunday Telegraph Magazine* which included the late Dr Mike Jones - then a 16 year-old. J L Henderson, a Scottish sprint champion, describes a voyage around Cape Wrath in 1950 in *Kayak to Cape Wrath,* and a number of unassuming Scottish paddlers undertook totally committing passages around the coasts, and out to the Western Isles in the '50s and '60s, often in PBKs (Percy Blandford designed kayaks - these were mainly large-cockpit canvas covered boats, designed for the Scout Movement).

It is not always recognised that the Marine Commandos, using mainly folding canvas doubles, would have to paddle up to 60 miles when carrying out raids on enemy coasts and shipping during World War II. A notable expedition was the first Atlantic crossing by Franz Romer, who, in 1928, sailed across in a specially built 23' single Klepper. Dr Lindemann, in a Klepper folding double, cruised from Las Palmas to the Leeward Islands in 1956.

In more recent times, and probably the commencement of the present interest in major expeditioning, was the 1966 crossing of the Pentland Firth by Joe Reid and Andy Carnduff. This was followed in 1969 by the first crossing of the Irish Sea from Dun Laoghaire to Holyhead.

In 1971 the first British expedition to conquer the Colorado, the mighty river of the Grand Canyon, took place. This included Mike Jones who, the following year, with Mick Hopkinson, paddled down 220 miles of the Blue Nile. He followed this in 1976 with 'Canoeing down Everest'- a descent of the Dudh Khosi from 5,334m, and in 1977 successfully ran the Maipure Rapids on the Orinocco River in South America, reputed to be the world's biggest cataract. Dr Mike Jones, was tragically drowned when trying to effect a rescue at the outset of the attempt in 1978 on the Braldu River, flowing from the Karakoram (K2) in Pakistan.

Meanwhile, the trend developed on the sea when Chris Hare expeditioned in Greenland in 1966, and brought back some Greenland kayaks. In 1969 Geoff Blackford designed the Anas Acuta, a complete glassfibre boat based on these traditional Eskimo types. With interest reawakened in this type of vessel, a number of individuals and manufacturers began to produce other designs, and major voyages followed.

The first attempt on the North Sea failed, and then a successful crossing was completed in 1976. A pinnacle was achieved when, in 1979, Cape Horn was rounded by a group of kayakists totally independent of either land or sea support. Although the entire coast of Britain has been canoed, in sections, with unrecordable frequency for more than a century it was not until 1980 that Paul Caffyn, a New Zealander, in company with Nigel Dennis, an auxiliary Coastguard, achieved a continuous circumnavigation of the whole of mainland Britain. Paul had previously circumnavigated both North and South Island of New Zealand, mainly solo, and has since been right round both Australia and Japan.

Such is the interest and numbers now involved, that the Long River Canoeists Club has come into being, which exists to exchange information internationally on tours and expeditions, and the BCU has established an 'Expeditions Committee' to monitor and vet British expeditions for grant aid and patronage purposes.

ACCESS TO WATER

During recent years the problem of maintaining and improving access to water, particularly the majority of our rivers, has occupied a considerable amount of voluntary and paid officers' time, besides columns of type in the canoeing, angling and the general press. Rivers are created and kept constantly changing by elemental forces over which man has no control. They have been used as natural highways since the stone age. Many people find it difficult to comprehend, therefore, how this part of man's natural heritage can be privately owned. Yet such appears to be the case in Britain.

A part-time National Access Officer was appointed in 1979 when Oliver Cock, MBE, having been honoured for his services to the sport in 1977, retired as Director of Coaching to take up that position. The Access Committee was separated from the Touring Committee in order to give full attention to the problems, and a network of local and regional access officers has been established. If however, it were possible to speak to the characters mentioned in this history, and their peers, who paddled all the presently disputed waterways in days gone by, they will tell of courtesy, friendliness and interest, in the main, from those anglers whom they passed en route.

What has happened ? An obvious factor is the sheer pressure of numbers. There are claimed to be 3 million anglers in Great Britain. Many millions of canoeing days take place annually. This, allied to the extortionate sums of money involved in the buying and selling of 'fishing rights', has led to the present

Plate 1:m
The River Usk near Gliffaes above Crickhowell.
From Rapid Rivers *by William Bliss, published 1935.*

25

unhappy climate. Let us consider then, the words of John Dudderidge OBE, the BCU President of Honour:

> *Canoeing is one of the few sports in which pure amateurism prevails. There are no great vested interests: canoes are quiet, and do not pollute the environment, nor do they have any adverse effect on the ecology of the river. They pass down and away and leave no evidence of their passing. Let us cling to this reputation for sportsmanship in competition, courage in face of danger, oneness with all other creatures living in, on, or by our waterways. Through courtesy we may even win the tolerance of the angling bodies, for we already have many friends amongst individual anglers.*

We hope that in these few pages canoeists and others will have learned something about the beginnings of our sport, one of the oldest, one which brings the participant near to nature and brings pain and fear to no other living creature.

2 Design and Selection of Equipment

Frank R Goodman

Frank Goodman became interested in canoeing in 1965, and after twenty years as a teacher and lecturer in art he founded Valley Canoe Products in 1970 to design and manufacture kayaks.

He was a division 1 slalomist in 1969-70, and has slalomed and surfed in the USA, Australia and Tasmania, as well as paddling white water there, in New Zealand, and in Europe.

He equalled the world record for surfing with a four mile run on the Severn bore in 1974 and made a sixty mile crossing of the Irish Sea from Wicklow to Aberdaron in the same year.

In 1977 he was a member of a four-man team which made the first rounding of Cape Horn by kayak, and after building kayaks with a group of Inuit in 1979, he returned to Baffin Island in '80 to lead an expedition from Frobisher Bay to Allen Island. Other journeys have taken him to Canada, Bermuda, the USA and Alaska.

In January 1986 his Nordkapp sea kayak was placed on permanent display in the Greenwich National Maritime Museum, and in September, the slalom course at Holme Pierrepont, which he had designed nineteen years earlier, was officially opened.

Current Trends, his canoe school and centre at Holme Pierrepont opened in 1987 and he recently became a director of Proper Channels Ltd, a consultancy specialising in hydraulic designs for sport.

He lectures extensively in the States, and spends part of each year exploring the north shore of Lake Superior by kayak.

THE CANOE OR KAYAK

Introduction

Travel on the surface of water is extremely difficult. Even nature, by and large, avoids it. A few unintelligent birds swim on the surface, but the more sensible marine mammals who must come up to breathe do so as quickly as possible, and then continue their travels at depth, thus avoiding the unpleasant consequences of travelling half submerged.

27

Man has been clever enough to overcome partially some of the intractable problems associated with travel on the water. He started many thousands of years ago, and is still learning. The unknown genius who first sharpened the ends of his floating log should have his place in history alongside his colleague who pierced its centre and added an axle.

The problem

The fundamental problem is that waves created on the surface by any moving object create a resistance that grows very rapidly indeed with increasing speed. Other problems are created because design features that enhance one aspect of performance may hinder another. For example, speed and manoeuvrability are mutually incompatible, as are other more subtle aspects of performance; thus a canoe or kayak must, of necessity, be a compromise.

Varying conditions

Further, canoes and kayaks are asked to perform under a wide spectrum of water and weather conditions, and worse, these are often of a very turbulent nature. This means that the normal mathematics that can be applied to problems of performance will often give unsatisfactory results. Most designs, therefore, are the result of experience and intuition - not necessarily any the worse for that, but very often the stated performance becomes a matter of extravagant subjective claims rather than objective reality. *Caveat emptor !*

Performance and hydraulics

Luckily, many of the fundamentals of the underlying mathematics of motion reveal themselves in either the 'feel' of the craft or its effect upon the water surface. This section deliberately avoids the use of mathematics, but wherever possible basic principles will be related to phenomena that a canoeist can experience for himself.

'Performance' is an expression of the total resistance that a canoe or kayak has to the hydrodynamic forces acting upon it. This resistance depends on the size, shape, contour, weight and surface finish. To select a canoe sensibly these attributes must be assessed in relation to the resistance they will create, so that an idea of its potential performance can be obtained. The canoe's resistance to hydrodynamic force implies resistance to motion and can be conveniently divided into two main components -'static' and 'dynamic resistance'.

Basic Resistances of a Canoe			
Static Resistance		Dynamic Resistance	
Inherent Buoyancy	Inherent Stability	Frictional Resistance	Residual Resistance

All static resistances to motion are dependent upon:
o   The magnitude and position of the centre of gravity
o   The magnitude and position of the centre of buoyancy
o   The relationship between them.

In other words they are dependent on the size, shape and weight of a canoe.

Inherent buoyancy

The size of the canoe determines its ability to support weight. More precisely, the volume of the submerged portion of the canoe is a measure of the weight it is supporting. A grounded canoe, floating after the paddler gets out, is a reminder that a floating body displaces its own weight of water. Obviously a canoe must have enough buoyancy to float its occupants and their equipment. Too much buoyancy which may allow a high freeboard to catch the wind may be just as detrimental to performance as a canoe lacking in buoyancy, where the gunwales submerge easily with consequent lack of stability. It is easy to see that an open canadian canoe will be of little value in strong winds, and for completely opposite reasons, a low-profile slalom canoe is also difficult to control in heavy weather. Thus neither craft is effective for journeys on the sea, although both of course, perform extremely well in the correct situation.

Inherent stability

A change in position of the centre of gravity within a craft may cause a change in the centre of buoyancy. If this change helps to return the canoe to its original position, the canoe has some measure of stability. The form of inherent stability most obvious to the canoeist is lateral stability - the 'tippiness' felt by beginners in a canoe. It is clear that the wider the beam, the more stable the canoe, but the actual cross-section shape of the hull is also very important (Fig 2:1a).

More detail of the consequences of hull cross-sections are shown in Fig 2:1b, and it should be noted that freeboard, which does not affect the initial stability of the canoe (when it is upright), becomes important as the boat is heeled over progressively. Once the gunwale is submerged, stability decreases rapidly.

Generally speaking, for a single-seat kayak, any beam width of more than about 60 cm starts to make the boat a bit of a barge. However, no hard and fast rules can be laid down, and as Fig 2:1c shows, varying conditions can alter the 'feel' considerably.

Longitudinal stability

The support given by a canoe or kayak at different points along its length will vary. This variation will correlate with the 'aspect ratio' of the canoe. Aspect ratio is the relationship between the length and beam of the craft. 'High' aspect ratio is long and thin, and will support weight at the ends better than a 'low' aspect boat. The fineness of the bow and stern, and the rocker of the hull, will also affect the longitudinal stability. Because kayaks are often used in turbulent conditions, where bow and stern are submerged, the buoyancy of the deck and hull - the whole boat - must be taken into account.

A low-profile slalom kayak can be looped easily because of its lack of buoyancy, which is so extreme that the bow and stern can be forced under water deliberately by the slalomist himself (Fig 2:2 drawings a and b).

Generally, fine-bowed canoes with rocker will be very wet boats in a sea-way, but in some lengths of wave a straight-keeled kayak can be worse, especially when it has a buoyant stern, since the stern may be lifted just as the bow is plunging into the face of the next wave. This is, of course, a contrary indication to the norm, and shows further that there are no simple answers to canoe design (Fig 2:2 drawing c)!

Generally, a broad beam gives a stable canoe, but the hull shape in cross-section is important.

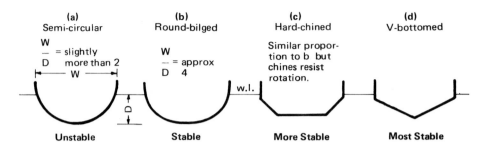

| **(a)** Semi-circular | **(b)** Round-bilged | **(c)** Hard-chined | **(d)** V-bottomed |

$\dfrac{W}{D}$ = slightly more than 2

$\dfrac{W}{D}$ = approx 4

Similar proportion to b but chines resist rotation.

Unstable **Stable** **More Stable** **Most Stable**

Fig 2:1a
(Lateral stability)

Canoe with semi-circular hull (unstable)

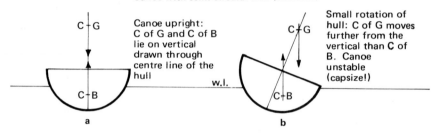

Canoe upright: C of G and C of B lie on vertical drawn through centre line of the hull

Small rotation of hull: C of G moves further from the vertical than C of B. Canoe unstable (capsize!)

Canoe with Round-Bilged Hull (stable)

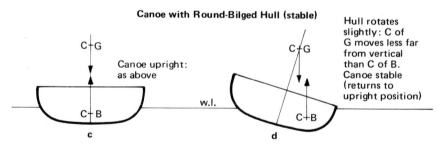

Canoe upright: as above

Hull rotates slightly: C of G moves less far from vertical than C of B. Canoe stable (returns to upright position)

Canoes with low or high gunwales have the same initial stability

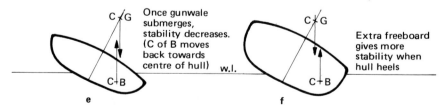

Once gunwale submerges, stability decreases. (C of B moves back towards centre of hull)

Extra freeboard gives more stability when hull heels

Fig 2:1b
(Lateral stability)

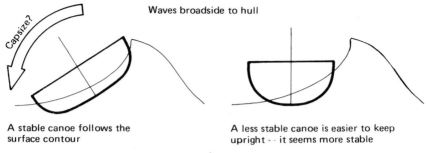

Waves broadside to hull

Capsize?

A stable canoe follows the surface contour

A less stable canoe is easier to keep upright -- it seems more stable

The wave can be surf, sea or stopper

Fig 2:1c
Wave effects on lateral stability

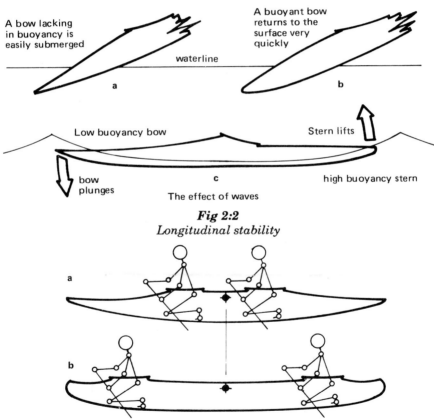

A bow lacking in buoyancy is easily submerged

A buoyant bow returns to the surface very quickly

waterline

a

b

Low buoyancy bow

Stern lifts

bow plunges

c

high buoyancy stern

The effect of waves

Fig 2:2
Longitudinal stability

a

b

Fig 2:3
Longitudinal stability: both centres of gravity are central, but the effect of the weight distribution in 'b' means that the bows here must be fuller in a dynamic situation

Although the stability of a craft is the relationship between the centre of gravity and the centre of buoyancy, in a dynamic situation the distribution of the component weights making up the centre of gravity is important. For example, in double canoes, the farther apart the crew sit, the fuller the bow and stern must be to counteract any pitching movements (Fig 2:3).

Directional stability

A canoe cannot travel in a straight line when the driving force, of necessity, is applied on either side of the centre line. It will yaw slightly from side to side, the amount depending on the resistance to turning of bow and stern. A deep section at the hull extremities will help to keep the canoe running true. Conversely, an increase in the amount of rocker will increase manoeuvrability (Fig 2:4b). This is not the only significant contour, however.

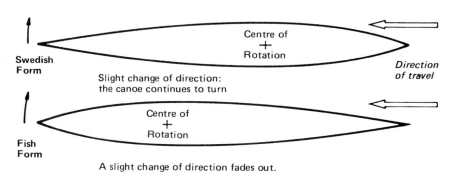

Fig 2:4a
The effect of shape on directional stability

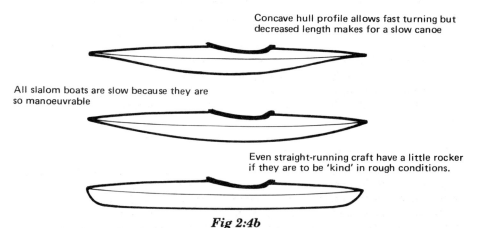

Fig 2:4b
The effects of rocker on directional stability. Increased rocker means more manouevreability but also more drag

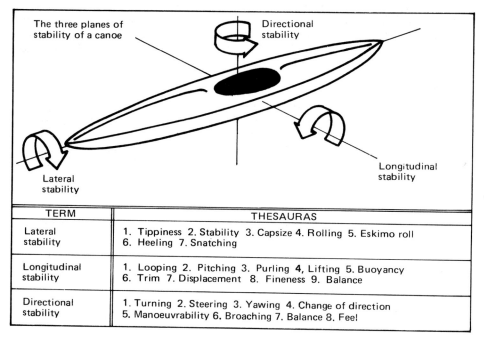

TERM	THESAURAS
Lateral stability	1. Tippiness 2. Stability 3. Capsize 4. Rolling 5. Eskimo roll 6. Heeling 7. Snatching
Longitudinal stability	1. Looping 2. Pitching 3. Purling 4, Lifting 5. Buoyancy 6. Trim 7. Displacement 8. Fineness 9. Balance
Directional stability	1. Turning 2. Steering 3. Yawing 4. Change of direction 5. Manoeuvrability 6. Broaching 7. Balance 8. Feel

Fig 2:5
The three planes of stability of a canoe

A high aspect ratio hull will be more directional than a beamy boat, but the shape in plan will also be important. If the widest section is behind the centre, this will also allow the centre of gravity to be moved aft. In this case, once a turn commences it will continue to grow in magnitude. Boats of this shape are known as 'swedish form' craft. The reverse is true if the centre of gravity is in front of centre - any change of direction will lessen, until the canoe continues on a straight line again. This type of craft has the name 'fish form' (Fig 2:4a).

Leaning the kayak onto its gunwale will alter the underwater contours and produce a turning effect. Usually, round bilge kayaks will turn away from the lean, but those with a hard chine will normally, but not always, turn into the lean (Fig 2:4b).

Obviously it follows that waves will alter the water-line contour and may affect the directional stability of the canoe.

Ease of turning is also a function of weight distribution in relation to the centre of gravity. Weight near the ends will have a much more deleterious effect than weight near the centre. One pint of water in a bottle, pushed to the end of a canoe, has roughly the same effect as a gallon of water in the cockpit area. For the same reason, a C1 slalom canoe will always turn faster than a K1 slalom kayak, simply because the paddler's weight is more compact when kneeling, than when his legs are stretched out in the sitting position.

The static resistance of a canoe can be summarised as its resistance to rotation in three planes. Canoeists and other water users have many expressions to describe the phenomena (Fig 2:5) !

Dynamic resistance

These resistances are the result of water flowing past the hull of the canoe. They are the same, whether the craft is moving through still water, or whether a current or water is flowing past a stationary canoe.

Frictional resistance

As a canoe or kayak moves through water, molecules adhere to the hull, and move along with it, however fast it goes. Because of viscosity, the hull becomes surrounded by a thin layer of water being dragged along by the boat. The outside of the layer is at rest, the inside (in contact with the hull) travels at the speed of the canoe. This is the boundary layer, and within it the forces of friction act to slow the canoe down.

Within the boundary layer the water molecules can move in two ways:

o *Laminar flow*

The molecules slide past one another in orderly fashion, parallel to the hull. The thickness of the boundary layer is in the order of 0.1mm. Frictional losses are small.

o *Turbulent flow*

The molecules cease to flow parallel to the hull, and jostle one another at random. The thickness of this boundary layer depends on the length of the craft, but can be as much as 4cm on a 4m canoe. Frictional losses are large. Do not confuse turbulent flow within the boundary layer with the large eddies seen within the wake of a canoe. To keep frictional losses low, we need to:

1 keep the boundary layer flow laminar.

2 keep the boundary layer itself as small as possible.

Point 2 is the easy one. The least wetted area for a hull is when its shape is hemispherical. Problems ! The best compromise is a semicircular hull tapering at each end. Point 1 seems easy. A good surface finish, with imperfections not bigger than 0.1mm (the thickness of a human hair) is easily achieved. At very low speeds, the boundary layer will remain laminar over virtually the whole of a hull made as smooth as this; friction is minimal, and the canoe will glide forward almost effortlessly. However, as speed increases, flow within the boundary layer becomes turbulent. At best, only about one fifth of the total boundary layer, that part near the bows, retains its laminar flow, however smooth the surface.

To achieve the optimum situation as shown in Fig 2:6, you need:

o Fine bows to part the water as gently as possible

o No imperfections, particularly at the bow, to set up premature turbulence

o A smooth surface finish with no imperfections bigger than 0.1 mm.

o The surface may be polished (buffed) but not waxed, since this will increase friction.

34

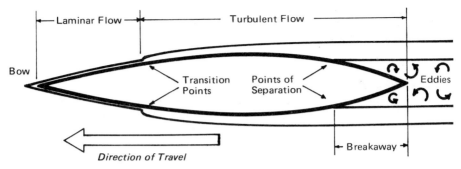

Fig 2:6
Skin friction; the boundary layer

Frictional resistance increases steadily with speed. Up to about 3km/h it accounts for 90% of the total drag on the canoe. Above this speed, although frictional resistance continues to increase, residual resistance becomes more important.

Residual resistance

Waves

Residual resistance causes the formation of waves and eddies. Eddies are so complicated and unpredictable that we shall have to ignore them, but waves are simpler, and knowledge of them will help us to assess a canoe's performance. Certain facts about waves should be remembered. They are listed here without any proof, but many books on oceanography or ship performance will give the mathematics behind these statements.

o   A wave is an oscillation upon the water surface. The water does not move with the wave but traces an orbit as the wave passes. (We are talking about green waves in deep water, not breaking waves). The orbits are circular. It follows that the water molecules move forward at the crest, but backwards in the trough (Fig 2:7).

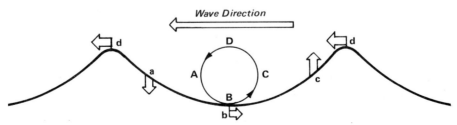

Fig 2:7
The circular orbit ABCD shows the actual movement of the surface water molecules shown on the waves a, b, c, d

o   In deep water, the speed of the wave depends only on its length. The longer the wave, the faster it travels: speed is proportional to length. It is worth noting that the wavelength of a series of standing waves in a deep pool at the tail of a rapid, will give a rough indication of the speed of the water. To be 'deep', the depth must be more than half a wavelength.

o   In shallow water, the speed of the waves depends only on depth. All waves in a given depth of water travel at the same speed; the shallower the water the slower the waves travel. Speed is proportional to depth. To be 'shallow', the water must be less than half a wavelength deep.

o   The height and length together give an indicator of the energy contained in a wave. Energy is proportional to length times height. (A long low wave in deep water slows as it reaches shallows. The energy contained is the same (nearly), since as the wavelength gets shorter, the wave must get higher until eventually it breaks. Result - surf !).

o   The energy within a group of waves travels at half the speed of the individual waves. (If you 'surf' upon wind-blown waves in deep water, you will notice that, if you start on a big wave, it soon decreases in height, and the one behind it grows larger, and so on. This is a measure of the energy contained within a group of waves, and underlies the fact that you can only get intermittent surf rides in a following sea).

Resistance to forward motion

How does wave formation, due to residual resistance, affect the canoe in motion ? Above about 3km/h waves begin to develop, and form the distinct pattern we call the 'wake'. Eventually, the energy drained from the canoe to form the wake accounts for 60% of the total drag. The most conspicuous feature of the wake is the straight-armed 'V' that spreads out from the bow. In deep water, its angle is always 39 degrees regardless of the speed of the canoe. Conspicuous though it is, the energy lost in this divergent wave pattern is not great, but within its arms, another transverse wave pattern is created, and it is these transverse waves that create drag (Fig 2:8).

The wavelength of transverse waves depends upon the speed of the canoe. Thus, a canoe travelling at 5.5km/h will generate a wave 1.5m long, while at 11km/h the wave will be 6m long. (Notice that when the speed is doubled the wave length is quadrupled).

Now let us see how this applies to a canoe of known length - say, a slalom canoe of 4m. At 4.5km/h it must generate a wave 1m long, so there will be four waves passing down the length of the hull at this speed. At twice this speed, the wave must be four times as long. In other words, the kayak is now sitting in the trough of a wave exactly the length of the hull - strictly speaking, the water line length (Fig 2:9).

How can the poor canoeist ever escape from this trough of his own making ? The simple answer is that he cannot. As he paddles faster, the wave created must lengthen; the bow of the canoe remains at the crest of the bow wave, but the centre of the trough moves towards the stern as the wave length increases, and the kayak 'squats'. Not only has the paddler to overcome increasing skin, eddy and wave resistance, but he must literally climb up and out, off the back of the wave. Alas, the best athletes in the world cannot generate the power required for this.

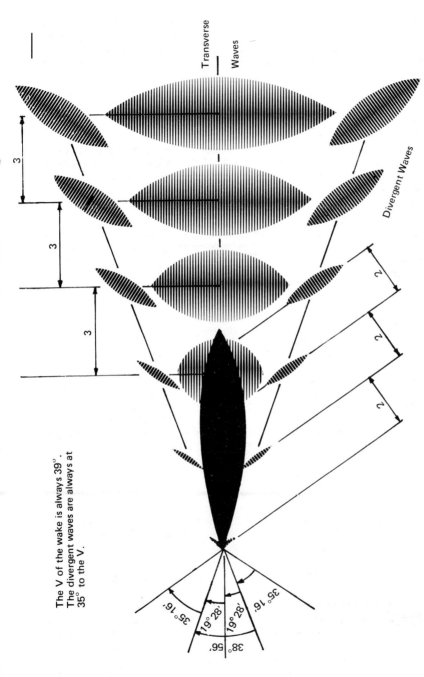

The V of the wake is always 39°.
The divergent waves are always at 35° to the V.

Transverse Waves

Divergent Waves

35° 16'
19° 28'
19° 28'
35° 16'
38° 56'

Fig 2:8 *The canoe wake formed in deep water. The transverse waves always have a wavelength one and a half times the wave length of the divergent train of waves. If this canoe is 5m long, at what speed is it travelling?*

37

(a) SPEED 2.75 m.p.h. WAVELENGTH 1 metre
(EASY PADDLING)

(b) SPEED 5.5 m.p.h. (twice diag. a) WAVELENGTH 4 metres (4 times a)
(HARD WORK)

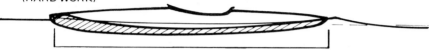

(c) SPEED 7 m.p.h. WAVELENGTH 6.25 metres
(VIRTUALLY UNATTAINABLE)

Fig 2:9

*Waves formed by a slalom canoe at different speeds. At (a) canoe displaces its
own weight of water. At (b) canoe 'sucks' itself deep into the water, thus
displacement increases. (c) The stern lies in the trough and the canoe can never
escape the wave*

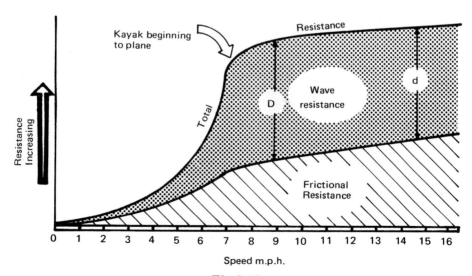

Fig 2:10

Total drag acting on a canoe approximately 4m long

How near a paddler can approach the impossible, depends on several factors. The wave-making resistance of a canoe will depend on its shape. A blunt bow offers more resistance than a fine one, and therefore builds higher waves, as does a rockered hull and a broad beam. Higher waves of similar length mean steeper crests, so the paddler loses twice over; first because the energy needed to create the high wave has come from him originally; and second, because more energy is needed to climb up the steeper angle of slope.

Now another factor must obviously become important. Since the paddler is climbing a slope, the weight that he must pull upwards will determine how successful he is. Displacement is a factor of weight. Therefore, of two canoes with similar shape, the one with the least displacement will make most progress up the back of the wave, and be the fastest. Obviously the paddler's weight is the most important item here, and it is paramount that the canoeist's own power/weight ratio is high. Now we can see the intractable problem of travel at the water surface.

In a slalom kayak 4m long, speeds up to 4.5km/h create skin-friction drag. This drag increases relatively slowly, roughly the square of the speed. (You must paddle four times harder at 2km/h than at 1km/h). Once fewer than about four waves are flowing along the length of the hull, wave-making drag becomes increasingly important, and resistance begins to increase at a higher rate. When there are less than two waves along the hull, wave drag gets really big, and by this time the canoeist is trying to claw his way out of his own trough. A 10% increase in speed may need a 100% increase in power. It cannot be done, and indeed it is this dramatic increase in power needed to increase top speed, that makes the finish of sprint canoe races so much less dramatic than track events. There can be no 'kick off the bend' or sudden explosion of speed. At best the canoeist will only edge forward to victory (Fig 2:10).

Notice that of two canoes of identical proportions and weight, but different lengths, the longest one would always win, since a long canoe makes a longer wave to 'sit in', and a longer wave is necessarily travelling faster. This does not mean that the longest canoe is always faster - there are other factors to take into account as we have seen.

However, another point may be answered here: if the canoe sits in its own wave, which is travelling at the same speed as the canoe, why cannot the canoe surf on its own wake ? The answer is found when it is remembered that the canoe generates a series of transverse waves and their group energy is only travelling at half the speed of the waves in the canoe's wake.

Notice too, that in shallow water, the wake and wave forms change. The wave must travel at a speed related to depth of water, not wavelength. The canoe 'feels the bottom' and slows down to the speed of these waves.

Planing

If the speed of a canoe can be increased beyond the limits already indicated, for instance, by sliding down the face of a steep wave, the pressure of water hitting the hull may be sufficient to raise the craft bodily almost clear of the surface. This dynamic lift is called 'planing', and the boat ceases to displace its own weight of water. Wave resistance decreases, but skin friction increases. Since there is considerable reduction in wetted area, this increase is much less than might be expected. However, a great deal of energy is needed to keep the canoe planing.

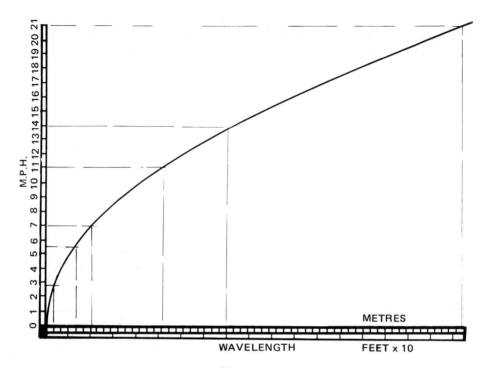

M.P.H.

WAVELENGTH **METRES**

FEET x 10

Fig 2:11
The graph shows the speed of the canoe in relation to the wavelength of wake.
The graph holds true for waves in deep water only. Deep water means water
deeper than half a wavelength; ie 'depth' varies with wavelength and therefore
speed. Use this graph to solve the problem in Fig 2:8

Contrary to popular belief there is no fall in resistance when on the plane, only a
less rapid rise with speed (Fig 2:11).

As we have seen, while solely under paddle power, a canoe can never reach the
point where it begins to plane. In fact, when paddled at speed, a canoe displaces
more than its own weight, as the flow beneath the canoe actually sucks it down.
(The ends of a slalom canoe are often at water level when paddled at speed, yet
when stationary they are well clear of the surface. Also, the effectiveness of self-
balers indicate that there is reduced pressure below the hull).

While most canoe hulls will plane, a completely flat hull, especially at the
stern, will obviously help to force the canoe out of the water and onto the plane.

Rail

High velocities, and high drag owing to friction, suggest that a blemish-free hull
is very important for maximum speed. Another major factor with planing hulls is
the drag created when the water leaves the hull. Because the hull is flat, and the
gunwale line is below the waterline, it is re-named the 'rail'.

40

If the rail is rounded, or 'soft', the water tries to flow around the curve, and high drag is the result. If, however, the rail is 'hard', meeting the hull at a very sharp angle, the water leaves the hull surface with minimum drag.

The rail is also important in preventing the stern of the kayak slipping sideways down the wave front. This is a job often shared by the canoeist's paddle and a skeg. The harder the rail, the better 'grip' the stern has on the wave. To increase this grip, the stern of some boats are bifurcated. While this will increase the grip, the increased length of rail edge will create extra drag, which must have its effect on speed.

In practice, the rail usually has some rounding to give what can only be called 'feel' to the canoe, and, of course, a very sharp edge is vulnerable to chipping.

Movement in other directions

We have so far looked at the forces affecting the canoe when moving forward. It must be remembered that these forces are also generated when the canoe is moved sideways through the water, as when a canoeist uses a draw stroke. The canoe can now be considered as having a length equal to the beam, and a beam equal to its length. Similarly, when a canoe is rotated horizontally by, say, an alternate forward and reverse sweep stroke, the bow and stern halves can be considered separately as hulls of very wide beam, and very short length, moving in opposite directions.

A canoe with forward motion, which is also being turned horizontally, will create forces that lie between two extremes of forward motion and stationary horizontal rotation.

Design compromise

It must now be clear that there is no simple answer to the best design for a canoe. Compromise is needed between all the different possibilities, and for some competition boats design restrictions are also added. Not only are water conditions tremendously varied, but windage can become important and must be allowed for.

Racing canoes and kayaks

Probably the design of a racing canoe needs to have the least compromise built in, since its sole purpose is to go as fast as possible on calm water. Indeed sprint canoes resemble each other closely: all have fine bows, non-rockered hulls, a forward cockpit position to keep the centre of gravity well forward, preventing squatting, and a minimum wetted surface to the hull by means of extremely narrow beam, and a semi-circular cross-section.

The design restriction, of a minimum beam size, and convex curves only, creates the typical diamond shape of the gunwale in plan. This leaves the water line contour as narrow as possible, and moves the widest point of the gunwale to the rear of the cockpit, allowing the paddler to place his paddle in the water as close to the centre-line of the canoe as possible. Even so, the hull section in the water gives a little stability to the paddler, by being very slightly elliptical rather than semi-circular.

The increase in paddle power due to this added stability, overcomes the slight increase in drag thus created, so even here some compromise must be built in. All very fast canoes have such poor turning characteristics that rudders are a necessity, and it is surprising what little thought has gone into these. Generally a flat plate of alloy is used. In fact there is ample evidence that to create the least drag, the front section of the rudder should be parabolic. Sharp edges or even circular leading surfaces, create turbulence, particularly when the rudder is angled. If you want to go faster - look to your rudder !

Slalom kayaks

At the other end of the scale, we can look at slalom canoes. Here we need good control in turbulent water, high manoeuvrability, but, if possible, fast forward speed. Within the design restriction on length and beam, there is tremendous variety of form, as each designer tries yet another set of compromises. A large amount of rocker in the hull means a shorter water line and quicker turning ability. A concave section in the rocker contour near bow and stern shortens the water line even further. Add a very flat cross-section to the hull, and a highly manoeuvrable canoe is the result. To give such a canoe even a modicum of speed, these design features must not be overdone; they must be modified - but by how much ?

Low-profile slalom canoes have such low decks that they can pass beneath slalom poles, and the extremities of the canoe have so little buoyancy that they can be pulled below the surface by weight shift and paddle stroke. Although sinking the ends of a slalom canoe was originated to avoid hitting the slalom pole, theoretical evidence shows that there is some advantage in sinking the bow or stern. Firstly, since part of the canoe is completely submerged, wave-making, and therefore friction is reduced. Secondly, since the canoe is inclined to the horizontal, its total weight moves towards the centre of gravity, and resistance to the rotation is reduced. Thirdly, although energy is used to sink the stern, this energy is in fact stored (water is in-compressible), and the submerged section receives an acceleration which can help the canoeist. It would seem that the forward speed of the canoe through the water when dipping, and the final direction after re-surfacing, would play an important part in deciding whether a sink is advantageous. Certainly, in order to sink the canoe, the gunwales must be lowered to such an extent that lateral stability at high angles is drastically reduced. 'Gunwale snatch' is the observed result. This reduction in water-worthiness seems to be acceptable to slalomists, but it must be remembered that slalom is not conducted on the heaviest of water.

These points underline the fact that canoe design may follow fashions in paddling style and, in the case of slalom, trends in slalom course design. This is not really surprising when it is realised that turbulent water allows little room for serious analysis, and the financial aspects of canoeing do not provide the necessary money anyway ! The empirical approach is fine, but it must always be borne in mind that it cannot divorce performance from the current paddling fashion.

Wild water and sea kayaks

Let us look at one more case where varying conditions alter the design dramatically. Consider a wild water racing kayak, and a sea-going kayak. Both need to move easily through large waves, but speed is paramount to the racer, which works in conditions where wind is of no importance. Speed is not essential for the sea boat, but windage can be a problem.

For a wild water racer to achieve maximum speed, the bows must be kept fine, but they will then plow deep into an approaching wave. To counteract this, the bow section can be extended vertically, so that its buoyancy is increased when submerged, with very little loss of forward speed. The bow will now lift through a wave efficiently. If the same principle is applied to sea boats, the deep bow will catch any cross wind with dire consequences. How can the sea boat have a fine bow for easy paddling, yet resist ploughing into waves without increasing its windage ? One answer is to use 'shape' to resist immersion, rather than 'volume'.

An equilateral triangle with its apex as bow, and base as stern, creates a deal of resistance to water flow. If this shape is incorporated into the bow above the water level, and at the correct angle, it can be used to resist sinking as the bows bury in a steep wave. There need be little increase in volume, and therefore windage, to achieve this, but of course there will be somewhat more resistance to forward motion than in the case of the wild water racer. This time, however, it is acceptable.

With the wild water racer, extra buoyancy provides the answer. For the sea boat, form-drag solves the problem, and of course there are a dozen compromises in between. It is possible to continue in this vein quoting how canoe design problems can be solved, but the main point to remember is that there is no simple answer or single solution. A subtle blending of many features that will give an acceptable compromise is needed. Among the many hundred of different canoe designs available, it is clear that certain basic shapes give certain performance characteristics, and this enables canoes to be grouped into families (Fig 2:12).

General purpose canoes

Obviously, the design of competition canoes receives a great deal of attention to achieve the best possible performance, and the general purpose and touring canoe try to combine many traits, of necessity in conflict with each other, in order to produce characteristics that will tolerate many varying conditions.

Within each category, listed in Fig 2:12, an infinite number of design compromises are possible. Even so, there is no such thing as a genuine 'all-purpose' canoe, and even within the specialist fields it is not easy to discover which set of compromises works best. Whether they are the result of thoughtful design, happy chance, or copying other designs in the field, with utter lack of understanding, is even harder to judge !

Scientific design

It has already been noted that there is very little canoe design that has any serious scientific back-up. As far as can be determined, Jorgen Samson is the only designer in the world who has tank-tested his designs in a methodical way. This is realistic when designing sprint boats for speed on still water, but where turbulent waters are encountered the best test is still the full-sized boat tested in reality by an experienced canoeist. In the USA, some existing sea kayaks have been subjected to limited static tests, but there has been great difficulty relating these results to the paddler's actual experience. There is always a danger that undue importance is given to spurious scientific data, while a mention of computers is also a sure way of making a design appear better !

CANOES									
	KAYAKS – ORIGINATING FROM THE ESKIMO					CANOES – FROM THE BIRCH-BARK CANOE			
	TYPE	SINGLE	DOUBLE				TYPE	SINGLE	DOUBLE
RECREATION	Sea Expedition Sea Touring GP* Touring GP Slalom	X X X X	 X X	TOURING SEA		RECREATION	NOT USED		
RECREATION	GP Touring GP Slalom	X X	X	TOURING INLAND (including flat & white water)		RECREATION	Open Cockpit Also many open cockpit canoes seating from one to four plus	X X	X X Plus
RECREATION	Surf Kayak Surf Ski	X X		SURFING		RECREATION	NOT USED		
RECREATION	GP Slalom GP Touring Baths Boats Competition Boats	X X X X	 X X	TRAINING		RECREATION	ALL TYPES	X	X
COMPETITION	K1, K2, K4	X	X	SPRINT RACING		COMPETITION	OPEN COCKPIT C1, C2, C7	X	X
COMPETITION	† K1, K2,	X	X	MARATHON RACING		COMPETITION	‡ C1, C2	X	X
COMPETITION	K1	X		WILD WATER RACING		COMPETITION	CLOSED COCKPIT C1, C2	X	X
COMPETITION	K1	X		SLALOM		COMPETITION	CLOSED COCKPIT C1, C2	X	X
COMPETITION	K1 SKI	X		SURFING		COMPETITION	NOT USED		
COMPETITION	BATHS BOATS	X		POLO		COMPETITION	NOT USED		

* GP = general purposes. † Any type of Kayak or Canoe may be used, but above certain levels only Racing or Wild Water Racing Boats are likely to be successful. ‡ Consideration of the 'class rules' still underway at the time of publication.

Figure 2:12 *Families of Canoes. In the UK the generic noun 'Canoe' means 'any craft capable of being portaged by its crew'; 'kayak' and 'open Canadian canoe' naming the sub-species. In most other countries, the name 'canoe' is reserved for craft paddled with a single blade, and the term 'kayak' applied to boats propelled with a double paddle*

Design features

If the canoe designer must rely largely on his own experience and intuition, a novice canoeist must indeed be hard pressed to make a sensible choice of craft. Even if it were possible to try out a variety of boats in varying conditions, the canoeist himself may have insufficient skill to assess their performance successfully and, as we have already noted, the interaction between skilled paddler and canoe will depend on individual style.

A chapter such as this, outlining just some of the basic principles of canoe design, cannot possibly take the place of actual canoeing experience, but an understanding of the forces affecting the canoe should help a canoeist to predict more accurately the canoe's performance.

The following table lists basic features and relates them to performance. They only apply if all other things are equal ! For instance, although we have seen from the speed/length ratio principle that all similar canoes of a given water line length have the same theoretical top speed, this will not apply to canoes of the same length but of different proportions. The beam, fineness of bow, cross-section, rocker, wetted area, surface finish and so forth, will affect the final performance.

FACTORS AFFECTING CANOE DESIGN

LATERAL STABILITY

INCREASED BY	DECREASED BY
Wide beam	Narrow beam
Flat curves on hull cross-section	Semi-circular cross-section
V-shaped hull sections	
Hard chine hull	Multiple chine hull
Low centre of gravity (seat close to hull)	High centre of gravity (high seat)
Rounded gunwale	
Extra freeboard	Sharp gunwale
Tumblehome amidships	

LONGITUDINAL STABILITY

INCREASED BY	DECREASED BY
High aspect ratio hull	Low aspect ratio hull
Full bow and stern	Fine bow and stern
Deep bow and stern	Shallow bow and stern
Hogged hull	Rockered hull
Weight in centre	Weight at bow and stern
Tumblehome at bow and stern	

DIRECTIONAL STABILITY

INCREASED BY	DECREASED BY
Narrow beam	Wide beam
V cross-section to hull	Flat cross-section to hull
Deep hull	Shallow hull
Fish-form waterline plan	Swedish-form waterline plan
Straight hull profile	Rockered hull profile
Skeg	Rudder
Weight at bow and stern	Weight in middle

SPEED

INCREASED BY	DECREASED BY
Longer waterline length	Shorter waterline length
Semi-circular cross-section	Increase in total wetted area
Straight hull	Rockered hull
Narrow beam	Broad beam
Fine bows	Blunt bows
Tapering stern	Blunt stern (except planing canoes)
Smooth surface finish	Poor finish especially at bows
Parabolic leading edges to rudder and skeg	Flat plate rudders and skegs
Low weight	Heavy weight
Weight near centre	Weight near bow and stern

Performance is not the only criterion by which design must be judged. The price of a canoe is often the overriding factor in selection, and it can also be a good indicator of quality. While it is true that the brand name of a product can inflate the price of a commodity, it is also true that you get what you pay for.

Construction materials

Although the use to which a canoe is put dictates shape, the material from which it is made also determines form. The traditional eskimo kayak made from driftwood and sealskin could not have a round bilge, although the use of many stringers could give an approximation. In fact, no frame boat, with a stretched skin, albeit seal, canvas or plastic could give any concave shapes to hull or deck. Thus the shape of the boat was a compromise between the best hydraulic shape and the shape dictated by the materials used.

Glass reinforced plastic

The nineteen sixties saw a revolution in building materials when lath and canvas, together with marine plywood, were largely replaced by glass reinforced plastic (grp). Once frames were eliminated and the skin of the boat was strong enough in itself to bear the stress of canoeing, moulds for grp boats could be made to produce almost any shape that the designer could imagine. Grp boats were reasonably cheap and so much stronger than lath and canvas canoes that there was a major change in the nature of canoeing, and new ground was broken in terms of boat handling techniques. This was mainly in the area of white water canoeing where difficult rapids could be tackled in boats that would withstand contact with rocks. However, there was a constant pressure to produce lighter weight boats, and eventually, even with carbon-fibre and so-called exotic composite materials, boats were shattering against rocks or collapsing when thrust deep below the water surface in heavy rapids or surf.

Polyethylene

Just as the sixties saw the advent of grp as a building material with a consequent leap forward in canoe handling, the eighties is proving to be the decade of the polyethylene boat, and once again major steps in canoeing techniques are being advanced. Although grp is not as stiff as timber, it is still liable to shatter on impact. Polyethylene is a much softer, unreinforced plastic that will deform under impact and then regain its previous shape. Thus in the world of white water, there has been another quantum leap forward as canoeists have attacked more difficult rapids and higher vertical falls.

Every material has its disadvantages, and the flexibility of polyethylene which allows it to deform and not shatter under impact, also means that the skin thickness, and therefore the weight, is greater than for grp boats. Thus, competition boats, where weight is of primary importance, are built from grp and not polyethylene. It also means that a flexible boat that folds around its occupant without breaking can be potentially lethal. Many ways have been devised to prevent this wrap-around situation occurring, such as stiff pillar buoyancy supporting the deck of the kayak between the canoeists legs, various types of stiffening frames, including cockpit liners, the prevention of water entry into the kayak by well-fitting air bag buoyancy, helped in some cases by large key hole shaped cockpit coamings that allow easier egress from the kayak.

The softness of polyethylene also means that it is subject to abrasion. Dragging boats overland or continuous scraping over coarse boulders in river beds will do more damage to polyethylene than grp. Similarly, tying polyethylene boats down tightly onto roofracks can leave large dents in the surface. Unlike abrasions, these can easily be removed by relieving the pressure and applying gentle heat - even sunlight - if it is shining !

Choosing a canoe or kayak

With practical experience, some knowledge of hydraulics and the materials used for construction, together with an eye on the price, a canoeist can begin to select the correct craft for himself. He will learn a lot too, by looking closely at the details of the canoe. Are there any fancy shapes that cannot be explained by the constraints of the methods and materials used in manufacture ? Do all the separate parts of the boat flow together into a rational whole ? Unfortunately, the truism 'If it looks right it is right' is true, but only experience will tell the canoeist what looks right !

Check the quality of construction with particular reference to the seat, buoyancy and footrest. The BSI Code of Practice for Canoe Building MA 91 is worth consulting and a knowledgeable friend looking at a possible purchase with you will also help.

Go to a reputable dealer or manufacturer. The non-specialist sports shop is not the best place to purchase, as lack of specific knowledge about canoeing means that there is a dearth of sound advice. Even though there are a few restrictions on the shape of the modern canoe, some designs bear little relation to any of the known facts about efficient motion across the surface of water, which all makes the selection of a canoe to suit you extremely difficult.

When selecting a canoe, this checklist will help you:

o   Decide what type of canoeing you wish to do

o   Study as many different canoes as possible and in particular the family to which your choice of craft belongs

o   Paddle it in varying conditions if possible

o   Assess the performance of the canoe in relation to its shape, contour weight and finish

Plate 2:a (top) Single racing canoe (C1)
(bottom) Double racing canoe (C2)

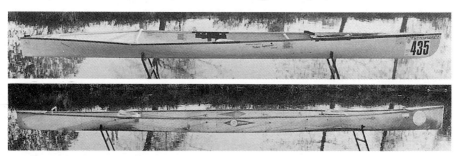

Plate 2:b (top) Single marathon racing canoe (MC1). Seated position
(bottom) Double marathon racing canoe (MC2). Seated paddling position

Plate 2:c Touring canoe

Plate 2:d (top) Single slalom canoe (C1)
(bottom) Double slalom canoe (C2)

Plate 2:e *Single slalom kayak (K1)*

Plate 2:f (top) *Single international racing kayak (K1)*
(centre) *Double international racing kayak (K2)*
(bottom) *4-person international racing kayak (K4)*

Plate 2:g *Single wild water racing kayak (K1)*

Plate 2:h   Single touring kayak

Plate 2:i   Sea touring kayak

Plate 2:j   Single general purpose white water kayak

Plate 2:k   Single white water kayak for use up to 'extreme difficulty'

Plate 2:l   Canoe polo kayak and swimming pool trainer

o   Talk to as many canoeists as possible about the canoe (visit the local canoe club); avoid individual canoeists who may have a bee in their bonnets !

o   Beware of canoes that are 'way out' in design: they are seldom satisfactory

o   Check prices with reputable manufacturers.

PADDLES

Fashion in canoe design changes, and as a consequence, or because of it, paddling styles alter. For instance, over the years, paddles have become shorter, in line with the trend for less beamy canoes.

Few single kayaks have a beam of more than 60cm, and the average paddle length has been reduced from 'height of paddler with arm raised and fingers outstretched' to 'height of paddler with arm raised and fingers curled over paddle blade'. This means that paddle length lies roughly within the range of 204 cm for slalom to 230cm for sea canoeing, with something in between the two for sprint racing.

Since the paddle does not touch the canoe during the normal paddling stroke, there is no fixed fulcrum for the paddle to work against. The arms and body of the paddler form a very complicated series of levers and a moving fulcrum which are beyond the scope of this chapter to analyse.

For the most efficient propulsion, it is important that the blade of the paddle must move along a line parallel to and as near to the centre line of the canoe as possible. This produces the 'high paddling' style of the competition canoeist.

The touring paddler has other problems besides making his canoe move as fast as possible. Apart from the water, windage becomes important, and a low paddling style, to keep the upper blade close to the surface where wind speeds are dramatically reduced, is advocated by many sea canoeists in very windy conditions (Fig 2:13).

An analysis of the function of the paddle blade will give some indication of good paddle design. The blade must perform three functions efficiently. It must :

1   Enter the water
2   Grip the water
3   Exit from the water.

On entry, any splashing or wave-making is wasteful of energy. Immediately, it becomes clear why curved blades are so much more efficient than flat. They can enter the water almost without disturbing the surface, and asymmetrical curved blades will do this even more smoothly. Once the paddle is in the water, any air around the blade will reduce its efficiency. As the paddle enters the water, air is dragged down with it, particularly at the back of the blade. Again the smooth entry of the curved blade is a sign that the minimum amount of air has been taken below the surface. 'Cavitation' is at a minimum (Fig 2:14).

Once in the water, the paddle blade must create drag. All the rules that apply to the motion of a canoe also apply to the blade of a paddle. It is clear that 'form drag' is most important, and that the surface area of the blade is the most important factor here. Spooned blades are most efficient but the amount of curve that gives most effective propulsion is too great to allow the blade to slide in and out of the water without splash. Therefore a compromise must be reached by reducing these curves so that both functions are catered for reasonably well.

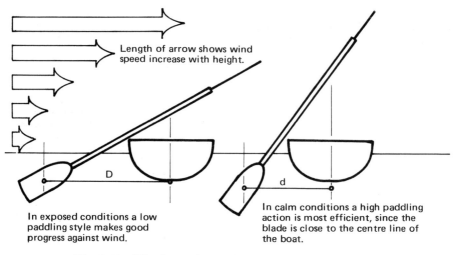

Length of arrow shows wind speed increase with height.

D

d

In exposed conditions a low paddling style makes good progress against wind.

In calm conditions a high paddling action is most efficient, since the blade is close to the centre line of the boat.

Fig 2:13   Wind speed may determine the paddle action

water surface

surface

Flat blade causes large cavitation on entry.

Curved blade reduces cavitation to a minimum.

Fig 2:14   The entry of the paddle through the water surface

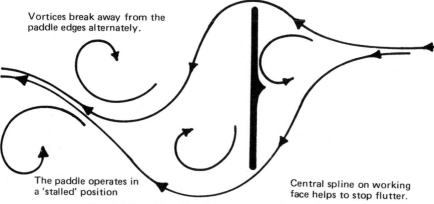

Vortices break away from the paddle edges alternately.

The paddle operates in a 'stalled' position

Central spline on working face helps to stop flutter.

Fig 2:15a   Paddle eddies as seen from above

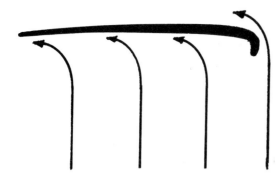

Fig 2:15b
Although the wing paddle is supposed to act like an aircraft wing, creating lift as it moves at an angle to the boat's direction it is difficult to see how the amount of movement involved can make the paddle move in anything other than a 'stalled' position. More likely it is the elimination of 'flutter' that is important. Another possibility is that these blades can be lifted from the water more easily at the end of the stroke

The eddies behind the paddle blade moving through the water form a distinct pattern. Vortices break away from the edges alternately, and it is these that cause pressures on the blade that can result in 'flutter' (Fig 2:15a). Preventing flutter may require considerable effort from the paddler, albeit he is unaware of it.

Recently, the winged blade from Sweden has tackled the problem of flutter by removing the central rib and curling one edge of the blade (see Fig 2:15b. This seems to throw water right across the face of the blade and cut out the alternate vortices that normally form.

Some changes of paddling style are needed and, while there is no doubt that wing blades are only at their best in calm conditions, they win races in the sprint field which is what racers want ! It appears that the extra speed comes from the paddler's energy not being wasted on controlling the flutter caused by the formation of unwanted vortices.

Another way of giving more 'grip' to the blade surface is to add texture or patterns in low relief to the working face of the blade. These are supposed to slow down the water as it slips sideways across the face, but although claims have been made, there seems to be no hard evidence to substantiate them.

Although for most of the time during its travel through the water, the blade is working in a 'stalled' position, there is a short period as it plunges into the water vertically, when the blade acts much like an aircraft wing, creating 'lift' by virtue of its thin section and angle of incidence (Fig 2:16). Again the curved blade will be most efficient at creating 'lift' acting in a forward direction, and it may well be that parabolic sections at the tip of the blade could add to the propelling power.

There is some experimental evidence to show that the downward plunge at the start of the stroke does indeed add considerably to the forward propulsive effort, but at the moment the data are imperfectly understood and more thought will have to be given to this aspect of paddling and paddle design before significant progress is made.

Getting the paddle out of the water without loss of energy is such a huge problem that it is achieved by taking it out prematurely, while the blade is still close to vertical as it passes the canoeist's body. In this way, energy loss is kept to a minimum, in spite of the fact that some of the possible propulsive power from the tail end of stroke is wasted.

It is clear that, on several counts, the superiority of the curved blade is overwhelming. The correct aspect ratio of the blade is related to the angle at which the blade is used. When used vertically, as in a racing stroke, the aspect ratio is

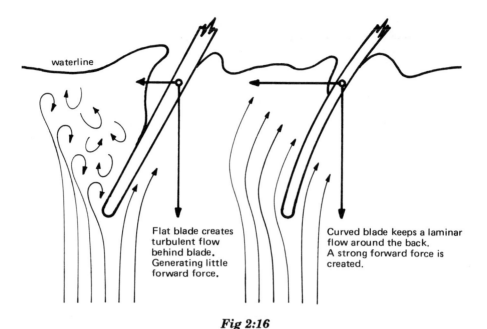

waterline

Flat blade creates
turbulent flow
behind blade.
Generating little
forward force.

Curved blade keeps a laminar
flow around the back.
A strong forward force is
created.

Fig 2:16

*As paddle blades submerge, their downard movement creates 'lift' which pulls
the canoe firward. The figure illustrates the fundamental difference between
flat and curved blades*

low, but if a blade is to be used in strong winds where it is beneficial to keep the
angle of the shaft closer to the horizontal, a high aspect ratio blade is helpful. This
is because, at a low angle, the whole blade can be immersed more easily if it is long
and thin (Fig 2:17).

Present paddling style dictates that paddles shall be feathered. There is
evidence that windage is reduced when paddling forward, but a feathered paddle
may be more severely affected by cross winds. Paddlers prone to tino synovitis in
the wrist have found that unfeathered paddles can give relief, and of course many
of the traditional eskimo paddles are unfeathered.

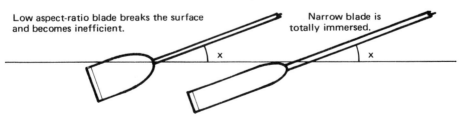

Low aspect-ratio blade breaks the surface
and becomes inefficient.

Narrow blade is
totally immersed.

Angle x is the same in both cases, and both paddle blades have similar areas.

Fig 2:17
Paddle action may determine the blade shape

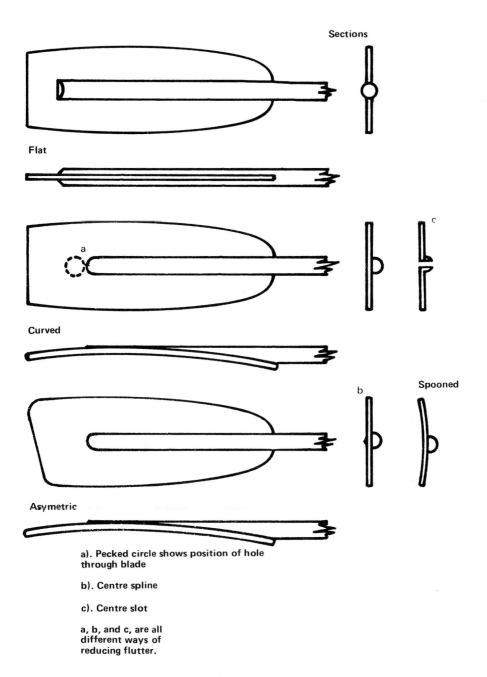

Sections

Flat

Curved

Spooned

Asymetric

a). Pecked circle shows position of hole through blade

b). Centre spline

c). Centre slot

a, b, and c, are all different ways of reducing flutter.

Fig 2:18
Basic paddle blades

One good compromise is to reduce the feather to as low as 60 degrees for those who wish to paddle steadily over long distances. At this angle, the wrist does not need to be flexed at all, as the angle of the upper forearm, with a low elbow position, will easily give the required angle to the blade entering the water. Not only is tino synovitis less likely, but it is very easy to re-adjust to 90 degrees feather for white water paddling if required.

Once paddles are feathered, then the set of the blades for either left and right hand control becomes a factor. Flat blades avoid this issue, and the convenience factor offered by flat blades when a mixed group of paddlers share a set of paddles is, of course, considerable. This fact, together with the point that a flat blade is cheap to produce, are the only points in its favour. The belief that flat blades catch the wind less or are more efficient at a low angle of paddle is unfounded.

Basic types of blade: flat, curved, spooned and asymmetric are shown in Fig 2:18.

The paddle shaft

The action of the blade through the water suggests that, the stiffer the shaft, the more efficient will be the stroke. While it is true that a springy shaft stores the paddler's energy and then releases it later during the stroke, it can be shown that this has no advantageous effects. However, most paddlers feel that a slight spring in the paddle shaft produces better results, and it may well be that there are physiological benefits from this. The use of very stiff carbon fibre shafts seems to have increased the incidence of shoulder injury among sprint paddlers. Diameter of shaft is important. When grasped, the thumb nail should be level with, or overlap the line of the finger nails. A bigger loom than this can cause unnecessary fatigue and even 'tennis elbow'. The ovalling of the shaft, at least under the control hand, is important to give the paddle 'feel', particularly for performing eskimo rolls.

Weight

Since a paddle is entirely supported in the hands, its weight is important. Clearly this must be related to strength, and it must be remembered that the strain placed upon a blade during a sprint start or a rocky slalom run, is tremendous. The strength of any material has an upper limit, and if sections are reduced for lightness, then this limit can be approached quite easily.

All the factors that were noted earlier in relation to the selection of a canoe, apply to the selection of paddles. Shape, size, weight, finish, feel, balance, and, of course, the specific use of which the paddle will be put, and price must be considered. However, the material used for paddle construction is of paramount importance, and plays a very large part in the strength and performance characteristics.

Any combination of shaft and blade material is possible.

Wooden paddles

Wood is an underrated material and can still hold its own against the best artificial material man can devise. Generally, wood for paddles must be laminated to give homogeneous strength. This means that the quality of the water-proof glue is also very important.

Type of timber

Spruce, though soft, is very strong for its weight, and combined with ash in the shaft for added toughness, is probably the best combination possible. Beech is sometimes used as a substitute for ash, but it is definitely inferior, especially when wet, which means the varnishing is particularly important. Waterproof plywoods of various timbers can be used with success. Birch ply with thin laminations seems strongest. Coarse grained timbers are less satisfactory. Points to look for are:

o   The thinner the glue-line between laminates, the stronger
    the join
o   The more laminations the stronger
o   Check for defects such as knots, resin pockets, short grain
    shakes and warping
o   Look for a well-made, long-tapering splice on the shaft
o   Check quality of varnish.

Alloy shafts

These are very cold unless sheathed in plastic - usually pvc. Alloy gives very good service and it is reasonable in price. Points to look for are:

o   Wall thickness not below 18 swg
o   Diameter not above 32 mm
o   Unblemished pvc sheath.

Where there is an inserted blade, a belled end to the alloy tube allows the blade to be fitted without a sharp shoulder, which increases the strength of the neck considerably. This is an expensive operation, and cannot be expected on low-price paddles, where the chief virtue of the paddles is the price.

Several paddle designs made with grp blades have the alloy loom pressed flat so that it can continue down to the tip of the blade. This tends to overcome the weak point at the junction of the blade and loom, but it does mean that if the blade breaks it is impossible to replace it.

Grp shafts

These are very strong, have a nice 'feel' and are lightweight. They need the addition of a fairing to oval them for the control hand.

Since the ends of the glassfibre tubing are liable to split, check that there is some type of collar here to prevent this.

Grp blades

These are strong if made thick enough, but rather heavy and easily abraded. Points to look for are:

o   Thickness of laminate
o   Use of woven roving cloth is important to give tensile strength
o   Check for air bubbles, dry mat
o   Alloy tips are needed for general purpose use.

Cored grp blades

Many blades are now available where a core is sandwiched between two layers of glass reinforced plastic. The core can be:

o   A sheet of non-woven fabric impregnated with minute hollow spheres of polypropylene

o   High density polyurethane foam.

Both materials have drawbacks ! The non-woven fabric absorbs up to 50% of the resin, which makes it reasonably strong, but if the core is starved of resin, it will be very weak. It is difficult to detect dry regions within the core, but small sunken areas on the blade area are an indicator and should be looked for. Polyurethane foam will absorb some water if exposed. Unless the edges of the blade are protected with alloy they can wear away to the core quite quickly and allow water to add weight to the blade. Both these materials produce a light-weight paddle blade, but there is a limit to the strength/weight ratio, and the paddler cannot expect to get the impossible !

3 Canoe Construction: materials and methods

Frank R Goodman

INTRODUCTION

The twentieth century has seen a tremendous leap forward in our understanding of the way small craft move over the water surface, and this in turn has led to the development of more efficient shapes for competitive paddling. It is also fair to claim that safer recreational craft with superior handling characteristics have evolved too, but this has not been a continuous development by any means.

Both the indian canoe and the eskimo kayak, in their traditional forms, appear to have pedigrees stretching back at least five thousand years. It is not surprising therefore that scientific theory, filtering down to our sport for less than a century, has made only a small impact on design compared with the empirical judgements of generations of builders and paddlers, who were not paddling just for fun, but for the serious business of feeding and supplying their communities.

Indeed, much canoe design today is still of an empirical nature, and none the worse for that. The changing needs of the paddler have resulted in developments that cater for those demands, but people who have troubled to recreate traditional designs, have been continually amazed at their degree of sophistication and the quality of their performance. This does not mean that we should invest super-human qualities on those ancient builders. They were limited in ways that no longer affect us. For example, individual builders consciously limited innovation, simply because they felt it unreasonable to insult their ancestors by moving too far away from the traditional designs that had been handed down to them.

Of course, some shapes, then as now, echo the idiosyncrasies of the builder, and have no useful purpose. Present-day students of the eskimo kayak will argue for hours on end, trying to decide the practical use for some of the more bizarre contours to be seen on ancient kayaks. In all probability, they are simply the remnants of magical animal shapes that were needed to ensure success in the hunt, just as surely as a little scientific jargon and an assurance of a kevlar/carbon lay-up will spur on the modern competitor to even higher achievements !

Although we no longer believe in magic and ancestor worship, or so we are told, there is no doubt that tradition plays a dominant role in our choice of construction method, and this in turn depends very much on the building materials that are available. Whatever shapes are used in a design, whether they be traditional proportions, or curves plotted out from a modern computer, these shapes will be modified to some degree not only by the building materials actually selected, but

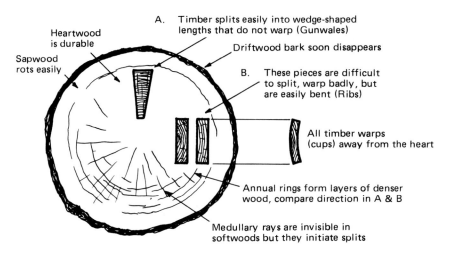

A. Timber splits easily into wedge-shaped lengths that do not warp (Gunwales)

Heartwood is durable

Sapwood rots easily

Driftwood bark soon disappears

B. These pieces are difficult to split, warp badly, but are easily bent (Ribs)

All timber warps (cups) away from the heart

Annual rings form layers of denser wood, compare direction in A & B

Medullary rays are invisible in softwoods but they initiate splits

Fig 3:1

also by the traditional boat-building materials used in the past, and the traditional 'mind set' of the designer. So while this chapter will note the properties of building materials used for kayak and canoe building, it will also record some of the ways different materials and construction methods have affected the shape of the craft.

Until thirty years ago, when modern technology began to make an impact the most radical departure from the traditional shapes of both eskimo kayak and indian canoe was probably when MacGregor and the early Victorian builders chose to build planked hulls in line with the white man's own boat-building tradition rather than use the materials used by native builders.

Even now, surrounded by advanced technology, our traditions make it difficult for us to see the wood for the trees - almost literally ! It is possible, for example, that the widespread medieval method of silviculture - the coppicing of woodland - still continues to affect our thinking. Coppicing was carried out to provide small section timber, and the availability of thin branches for construction affected our tradition . . . for wattle and daub building, lath and canvas canoes or lath and plaster ceilings - both the latter very much in common use fifty years ago. Even present-day features of our landscape can be seen as a direct legacy of our past boat-building activities; hedgerow oaks still abound, many of them planted originally to provide the curved timbers for boat-building that were unobtainable from the straighter growing forest trees.

Closer to canoeing, these half-remembered traditions still affect our thinking. For example, when the perennial arguments are revived with regard to the large modern paddle blade versus the narrow eskimo style. We have difficulty getting rid of the idea that every culture had a plentiful supply of small branches or laths to work with. It has often been stated that the eskimos only used narrow paddle blades because wide timber was not available. Not true ! In fact the reverse is the case. The eskimos' only source of timber was drift-wood, and the log's long journey north inevitably meant some abrasion. By the time the eskimo gathered his building material, all the small branches had disappeared. He started work with large sized logs that had to be split down for his kayak framework.

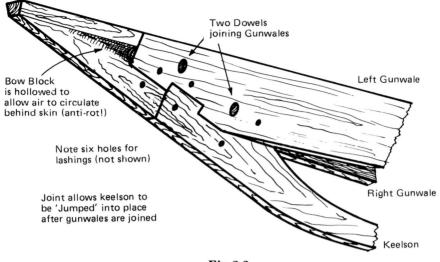

Fig 3:2
Bow of Greenland Kayak (after H C Peterson)

Text inside figure:
- Two Dowels joining Gunwales
- Bow Block is hollowed to allow air to circulate behind skin (anti-rot!)
- Note six holes for lashings (not shown)
- Joint allows keelson to be 'Jumped' into place after gunwales are joined
- Left Gunwale
- Right Gunwale
- Keelson

Actually, splitting produces stronger timbers than sawing, as the grain direction is followed perfectly, and tapered cross-sections that are not prone to warping are easily produced. Modern machinery will turn out 'squared' timber very quickly, but it will be inferior to that produced by the more 'primitive' method.

THE ESKIMO KAYAK

Eskimo kayak designs often incorporate surprisingly wide timbers in their longitudinal framework, with any tapered cross-sections indicating the way they were split from the log (Fig 3:1).

The kayak frame of driftwood was very carefully constructed, with sophisticated mortise and tenon and scarf joints that were held together by pins of wood or bone and bindings of sinew (Fig 3:2). Pine, fir and spruce were used, and willow ribs, soaked and bent to shape were usual. Ribs were sometimes bent by hand and mouth, the eskimo's teeth crushing the inner curve and also preventing the outer fibres from splitting away.

The baidarka

The main strength of a kayak lay in the heavy gunwales, into which all the ribs and transverse frames were fitted. Heavy keelsons were seldom incorporated into the design. This produced a semi-rigid frame that was complete in itself, but was further strengthened by the seal-skin cover that was then sewn on. The Aleut baidarkas were kayaks of this general construction, but generally wider and more buoyant than the Greenland style of kayak. The baidarka was an extremely seaworthy boat often with interesting features: bone rubbing plates between the frames, bone ball and socket joints set into the scarf joints, and bifid bows. The flexible joints were said to increase speed by letting the craft 'sit' onto the moving

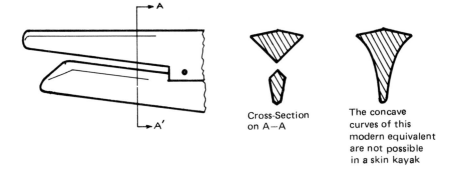

Cross-Section
on A—A

The concave
curves of this
modern equivalent
are not possible
in a skin kayak

Fig 3:3
Bifid bow of Aleut baidarka from Akun island, collected in 1845

sea surface, while the bifid bows, although maybe of 'animal' origin, certainly produced the effect of a concave flare at the bow, which otherwise cannot be formed with a stretched skin (Fig 3:3).

Performance and the double-ended paddle

The speed of the kayak and its 'self-righting' ability amazed the early explorers, as did the load-carrying capacity and shallow draught of the canoe. (Many of the larger canoes were virtually flat-bottomed, which meant that their draught was deceptively small even when loaded). The quality of these traditional craft is not surprising when a comparison is made with the heavy, keeled pinnaces and sluggish sailing characteristics of the white mans' larger ships. The baidarkas were considered particularly fast and sea-worthy, and even today, suggestions

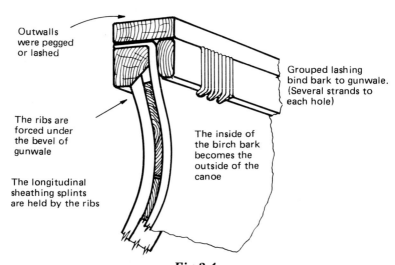

Outwalls
were pegged
or lashed

Grouped lashing
bind bark to gunwale.
(Several strands to
each hole)

The ribs are
forced under
the bevel of
gunwale

The inside of
the birch bark
becomes the
outside of the
canoe

The longitudinal
sheathing splints
are held by the ribs

Fig 3:4
General form of birch-bark canoe (after Adney)

are still made that the flexibility imparted by the ball and socket joints already mentioned, gave the boat a turn of speed surpassing the normal. In fact, the relative narrowness of both canoes and kayaks, coupled with the light weight building materials employed, accounts quite easily for their excellent showing, and it is not reasonable to suppose that the parameters of performance laid out in the previous chapter of this book will be found to be invalid.

One consequence of a flimsy construction was that the forces generated by the paddler needed to be spread over a large area of the boat to prevent high concentrations of stress fracturing its framework. What better than to remove the fulcrum of the oar from the boat altogether and invent the double ended paddle held in the hands only. This unique Inuit achievement, not only allowed the paddler to face the way he was going, which for hunting, was essential in a single seater craft, but also passed the propulsive stresses smoothly and gently into the body of the boat via the paddler's feet, thighs and buttocks. Thus, the invention of the kayak paddle must owe something to the construction of the boat itself, and indeed to the unique shape of the human anatomy !

THE BIRCHBARK CANOE

All kayaks could be made by adze, axe and knife beyond the tree-line, whereas the birch-bark canoe, as its very name indicates, developed further south and depended on a forest culture for its development, the paper birch (betula papyrifera) being the preferred material for the skin. The open canoe was quite different to the kayak in construction, as the skin of the craft was first bent into shape using temporary stakes driven into the ground. The top edge of the bark was sewn to a pre-formed gunwale frame and then the ribs were fitted into the skin. Binding thongs were made from cedar and basswood bark, and the birch bark was sewn, without needles, with the soaked roots of black spruce - although some indian tribes did use rawhide. Seams were sealed with spruce gum tempered by the addition of animal fat and charcoal (Fig 3:4).

DIFFERENCES BETWEEN TRADITIONAL CANOES AND KAYAKS

There seem to be no hybrids between the construction of the traditional canoe and the kayak. Fundamentally, the kayak could be re-skinned, the frame being a unit in itself, whereas the canoe frame would disintegrate if the bark was removed.

BASIC DIFFERENCES BETWEEN TRADITIONAL CANOES AND KAYAKS	
KAYAK	CANOE
Frame of driftwood made as a one-piece unit	Wooden frame held together by pressure of birch-bark skin.
Covering skin of sea mammals, usually seal	Covering skin of bark, usually birch.
Cross-section always chined. bilged.	Cross-section always round-

Deterioration of natural materials

Both types of boat needed great care to prevent the skin from puncture or abrasion. The mammal-skins of the kayak were strong enough to allow careful entry on the beach but the canoe needed to be entered and loaded only when it was afloat.

Whatever the construction of these beautiful boats, they suffered from lack of permanence. The skins of a kayak had to be treated every few weeks with boiled seal-oil, and thongs, wood and gum deteriorate. Freezing winter air contains very little moisture, and therefore decay in the winter was not a problem. However, a seal-skin kayak was a meal for a hungry Husky, and kayaks were stored on poles above leaping height ! Birch-bark canoes need to be stored in the dry if the bark is to be prevented from becoming soft, and prone to warping and, of course, rot is encouraged by higher temperatures and damp. Yet too much drying leads to brittleness - longevity could never be assured !

The demise of the traditional craft

Contact with the white man introduced new materials to both eskimo and indian. Metal tools, nails, canvas and strong twine became available. These were a mixed blessing, and sometimes very strong items in juxtaposition with softer traditional materials created their own problems; nails split timber more easily than wooden dowels, and nylon twine could cut into the softer materials it was supposed to restrain.

Both eskimo and indian seemed to have taken easily to the new materials, and indeed, designs altered because of them. The last Baffin Island kayak to be built in Frobisher Bay in 1980 when the author was there, was to be finished in canvas, because it could be done more quickly than with seal-skins - traditionally always sewn by the women-folk. (It was the last of the line, as the only man in Frobisher who knew the traditional framing methods had recently died). One inuit hunter

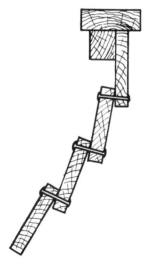

Fig 3:5 (left)
*Section of clinker-built canoe with planking
overlapped and rivetted or clenched nailed*

Fig 3:6 (below)
Waterproof ply made one-piece frames a possibility

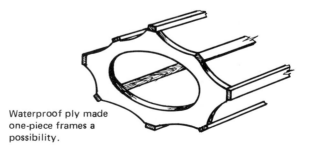

Waterproof ply made
one-piece frames a
possibility.

and carver from Ellesmere Island often glued horn and ivory together, and I had ideas of him using dried Caribou blood, which was the traditional glue of the eskimo . . . 'Krazi-glue from the Hudson Bay Company store is pretty good' was his reply when I questioned him !

The powerful influence of the white man's culture, the longevity of his materials, together with the power of the outboard engine have effectively seen the demise of the traditional kayak and canoe. There has been a flurry of activity in recording these traditional designs, as it became clear that they were doomed to die, and today a handful of inuit, indian and white men continue to build in the traditional way, but it is a labour of love.

DEVELOPMENT OF TRADITIONAL METHODS

MacGregor and the clinker-built kayak

MacGregor returned from North America with the idea of using the kayaks he had seen there as small, light, single-seat craft for personal journeying. This vision must have been greatly modifies at the out-set by the materials and methods of construction that were readily available to him in the London of 1865. The final choice of an oak planked clinker-built vessel immediately put the emphasis on strength rather than lightness, and the distinctive bows of traditional craft were replaced by a shape more easily achieved by planking (Fig 3:5). Also, the inclusion of a small lug-sail probably meant that the overall design was modified somewhat to take this into account. One interesting fact was that the overall length of the second Rob Roy canoe MacGregor had made was reduced from 15' (4.57m) to 14' (4.27m) and it seems that this was directly related to the storage space available in a railway luggage van - 15'. Thus right from the start, the transport arrangements for the return journey affected the shape of the vessel used on the outward leg !

Lapstrake canoes

In North America during the latter part of the nineteenth century, lightweight open canoes were built with cedar planks, similar in construction to the Rob Roy, although in America, clinker-built construction is called lapstrake. The less dense cedar wood produced canoes of half the weight of the Rob Roy, and single seaters of as little as 4.5kg were reliably reported.

Canvas-covered wooden canoes

Canvas covered canoes became popular in the States at this time. They were made on a metal form over which ribs were bent. Longitudinal planks of cedar were added and copper-nailed to the ribs, which clinched automatically against the metal form. The boats were carvel-built, that is the planks were fitted side by side, not overlapped as in clinker-built. The smooth hull was then covered with stretched canvas, filled and painted. Of course similar boats of this type were made much later on with the outer canvas replaced with a layer of glass reinforced plastic. Not only were these stronger, but they were aesthetically very pleasing, with the wood grain clearly visible through the transparent grp.

Lath and canvas kayaks

The development of plywood and waterproof glues after the First World War again brought about changes. All the transverse framing that had previously been made in solid timber such as the ribs and the deck-beams, could be merged into bulkheads cut from a single piece of ply. Each bulkhead was the shape of the appropriate cross-section of both hull and deck combined, and by cutting away the centre of each bulkhead to make a space for both legs and equipment, the frames could be lightened with very little loss of strength. Longitudinal laths were added to the ply and proofed canvas was used to sheathe the frame (Fig 3:6). Although this construction method was very close to the traditional skin boats of the eskimo, the boats retained the shape of their clinker-built predecessors. This type of construction was easy to build at home and, in Britain, the PBK (Percy Blandford Kayak) designs were built in large numbers until the early nineteen sixties.

Folding kayaks

Beyond the scope of the home-builder was the folding kayak, which used essentially the same construction materials but could be partially assembled and then unfolded inside the skin. This stretched the skin and the whole kayak became virtually as rigid as its uncollapsable skin and bone counterpart. Originating in Germany, these boats became very popular, and could be packed into bags for transportation by both road and rail.

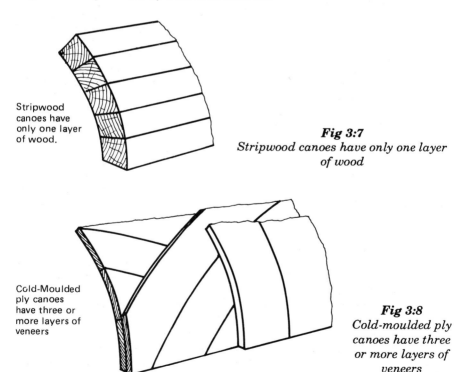

Stripwood canoes have only one layer of wood.

Fig 3:7
Stripwood canoes have only one layer of wood

Cold-Moulded ply canoes have three or more layers of veneers

Fig 3:8
Cold-moulded ply canoes have three or more layers of veneers

Although the basic material of the canvas and its proofing improved dramatically over the years, abrasion was always a problem, especially the unseen attack made by sand within the craft. It was virtually impossible to keep this unwelcome abrasive out of the boat, where it collected between the frames and the inside surface of the skin, wearing away the covering with every movement of the boat. Sharp rocks could tear the covering from end to end of a boat, and needle and thread were an essential part of a repair kit. A heavy blow could break the frame even if it did not puncture the covering and this meant that a wrap-around accident, so much feared by white water paddlers today, was particularly dangerous when splintered batten ends were crushed into the legs of the paddler. In spite of these remarks the lath and canvas kayak was pretty tough. The real problem, especially with the non-collapsible type, was that maintenance of the wooden frame was impossible without removing the covering - a daunting task. A constant building programme was the alternative.

MODERN WOOD AND COMPOSITE METHODS

Stripwood and cold-moulded boats

Waterproof glues were not only used for making plywood, and when chemists synthesized glues capable of bonding at room temperature, many improved methods of construction became possible. Stripwood kayaks and canoes were made, where longitudinal strips the thickness of the boats skin, usually around 6mm thick, were fitted to a temporary frame made to the shape of the *interior* of the hull. These strips are fitted and glued edge to edge and held with staples until the glue set. The finished product was a boat without any internal frames. Only a coat of varnish needed to be applied, although later, a thin outer skin of grp was added to increase the strength and reduce the maintenance requirements (Fig 3:7). This method uses a single thickness of timber, but a stronger variation can be constructed using three layers of veneers, only a couple of millimetres thick, cut into, say, 50mm wide strips. Each layer is stapled into place, but the strips of each layer are fitted in a different direction to give extra strength. As each strip of the subsequent layer is added, the edges are shaped to fit and they are bonded to the under layer. Staples are shot from a hand stapler to hold the strip until the glue hardens. In time, and many thousands of staples later, a shaped piece of three-ply is produced that is the shape of the complete boat (Fig 3:8). This cold-moulded ply construction is generally lighter than the stripwood method, although layers can be added to produce any thickness or weight required.

Wood and epoxy construction

The above-mentioned methods need a minimum of equipment, and boats are readily constructed by the amateur builder. The smooth outer surface of these wooden boats keeps skin friction down to a minimum, and this meant that the racing fraternity were extremely interested, as it meant faster boats. Wood is also a very stiff material - far stiffer than either grp or thermoplastics, and this too meant that very stiff, fast boats could be produced in timber.

In the sprint racing world, wooden canoes and kayaks still reign supreme. In top competition, all K4, C1 and C2 are wood veneer craft, and many K1 and K2 boats are of wood too.

It is remarkable that sprint design has been totally dominated for decades by one person - the Dane, Jorgen Samson. It is not an exaggeration to say that this extraordinary man has been responsible for *all* the sprint kayak designs in current use. Any boats that are not actual copies of his designs, and there are plenty of these, owe so much to his models that it is easy to see that they stem directly from his work. He is the only designer who has undertaken meaningful scientific tank-testing of designs, with the exception of the tests done on the 10 square metre sailing canoe.

There are only two manufacturers of wooden sprint boats in the world. Their premises back onto one another, and they share Jorgen Samson as their designer ! The company of Kajakbyggeriet Struer market for both companies, but they only make sprint K1s and K2s themselves. These are constructed from layers of fine quality veneers, held over a male mould, glued together, vacuum-bagged down into position, held in place by a female mould and then heated in an enclave oven under pressure until the glue has hardened and cured. Obviously this method is beyond the scope of the amateur builder.

Kirk and Storgaard, just around the corner, build all the K4s, C1s and C2s. Again wide sheets of veneer are used, with mahogany selected for the outer layer, but their method of construction, while very similar to that previously described, hold their veneers down into place with steel straps rather than vacuum bag and a female mould. Also, they use glues that cure at room temperature, making the use of an oven redundant.

Some sprint K1 and K2 boats are now made in glass reinforced plastic but it has been the demands of modern athletic preparation that has brought about this change. Training sessions several times a day mean that boats never get a chance to dry out, and therefore wooden boats deteriorate much more quickly than composites. Once again, it is cost and durability that have changed the material used rather than any superior performance gained by the new construction.

It is interesting to note that while sprint paddlers, rowers and dinghy racers recognise that the stiffest craft is the fastest, all other things being equal, there is the opposing idea that flexibility can add to speed in a seaway. It has been noted that the incorporation of ball and socket joints in the frames of some baidarkas imparted greater flexibility, and according to some, an increase in speed. It must be said that the field notes of Langsdorff, 1814; Veniaminov, 1840; and Lantis, 1933; all first-hand observers of these craft, give conflicting evidence. There may be an explanation, but there is no certain proof.

Wood and grp combinations

Although glassfibre reinforced plastic (grp) was invented just before the second world war, like aluminium, it was not until the fifties that it was used for small boats. The quality of some of the early polyesters, and glassfibre for that matter, was quite inferior to the modern material, and it was not until the sixties that it began to replace timber as the ubiquitous boat-building material.

Around this time, there were several hybrids that used both wood and grp. The most successful of these started as a method for building kayaks, but unfortunately, because the invention was not protected, it made money for other boat designers without the inventor reaping his just reward. A range of kayaks, known as the Kayel range (the designer was Ken Littledyke - initials KL) used the system. The kayaks were designed as chined boats, and a shape of its section was drawn out

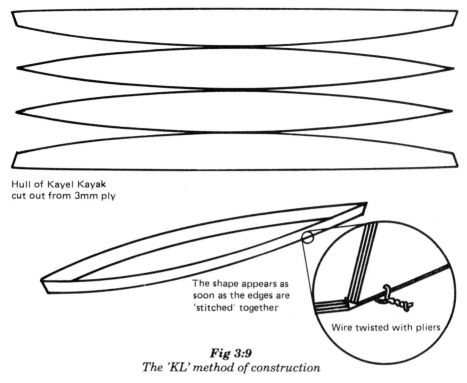

Hull of Kayel Kayak
cut out from 3mm ply

The shape appears as
soon as the edges are
'stitched' together

Wire twisted with pliers

Fig 3:9
The 'KL' method of construction

full-size onto marine ply. These shapes were cut out with a jig saw, and small (approx 1mm diameter) holes were drilled at 100mm intervals all around the edges. Short pieces of copper wire, with ends twisted together with pliers, pulled the edges of the ply together, and as if by magic, and without the use of frames, the overall contour of the kayak could be pulled into shape within minutes (Fig 3:9). The chines themselves were formed by glass tapes about 50mm wide, impregnated with resin. Once the inner chine had cured, the twists of copper wire left on the outside were filed away and an outer chine of grp tape was added. It was a brilliant idea, making excellent use of the properties of a new material to achieve a quick, cheap method of construction.

The inventor was a school teacher who had started canoe building with his pupils. By chance, when his mother was dressmaking, he noticed her tacking together separate pieces of a garment with large stitches prior to sewing it together permanently on a sewing machine. He remembers thinking, 'If it's possible to tack together material to fit a complicated shape like my mother, I'm certain I can do it to make a simple shape like a canoe !' He was right, and Kayel kayaks are still being made today.

Of all the designs using this type of stitched construction, the open canoes were probably the most successful. Here, the superb stiffness of wood could be used to maximum effect. This quick building method removed much of the tedium associated with other types of wooden craft, they were cheap to produce, and results did not depend on a high degree of skill.

ALUMINIUM CANOES

Aluminium had been developed as an aircraft material during the second world war, and in fact it was an executive engineer at the Grumman Aircraft Company in the US who developed the alloy Canadian canoe. During the 1950s and 60s aluminium was the most popular material for open canoes in the States. Alloy sheets, stretch-bent around a male plug were riveted along the keel and the ends, thwarts and fittings added to make a metal boat that could compete in weight with wooden canoes, and also have a cost advantage.

Alloy canoes are noisy and liable to 'stick' to rough rocks when they touch, and for this reason they are not popular on white water rivers. Since alloy is a very good conductor of heat, cold water cools the knees and hot sun can overheat the surface unpleasantly too. There is no doubt that aluminium has limitations as a building material. Maybe for run of the mill open canoes it is satisfactory, but it is doubtful that an alloy kayak could be considered safe on any grade of white water. Bending and consequent entrapment would be a very serious problem indeed. Also, metal fatigue is always a problem - an initial dent can be easily knocked out of an alloy canoe, but subsequent damage similarly dealt with can lead to cracking as the metal-work hardens under the hammer. There is a French double sea-kayak in aluminium which lacks aesthetics and makes it clear that alloy for kayaks is not going to catch on !

THE BASIC PROPERTIES OF WOOD AND METAL

It should be noted that the nature of wood and metal are almost direct opposites - wood is unidirectional in strength, unlike metal, and of course, a non-conductor of electricity. But the most interesting property of timber is its unique ability to resist repeated impact loads that are much higher than those it can sustain for long periods of time. This means that you can hit wood repeatedly without damaging it, even though the force exerted is much higher than the static loading that would normally break it. Metal, on the other hand will eventually fatigue and break under repeated blows that are way below the threshold of a sustained force that would cause it to fracture. Add to this the tactile ' warmth' of wood owing to its low conductivity, and it is easy to see why timber was used in virtually all small boat construction until recently when the advent of plastics introduced properties superior to any natural materials, and with a durability only slightly affected by neglect !

GLASS REINFORCED PLASTIC

Design problems, skills and durability

The basic problems of design in terms of the performance of canoes and kayaks had, of course, been solved thousands of years previously. Different materials and construction methods had come along and influenced design, but the shape of the craft's hull, essentially a simple one, could be built to perform effectively using a variety of materials and methods.

So it was not just a demand for higher performance that sent canoe designers and builders off searching for new materials. While it was always realised that light-weight materials meant lower displacement, and therefore higher top speeds, racing rules often included weight limits which precluded ultra-light boats.

70

The real problems were as follows:

o   The high levels of skill generally required for boat-building
o   The lengthy processes involved in construction
o   The high cost of boat production (linked to the above)
o   The tyranny of essential regular maintenance
o   The rapid deterioration of boats in use and in store. (Although careful maintenance prolonged active life, cosseted kayaks seldom outlived their canine counterparts !)

All of the above points were answered to a large extent by the introduction of grp, and by the early seventies most professional canoe and kayak builders had embraced the new technology, and home workshops were turning out rough and ready, but nevertheless perfectly serviceable craft. The explosion in canoe sport at this time was part of growth throughout the sporting world. While the increase in discretionary spending, the time available for leisure activities and the interest in sport generally (dare we mention television ?) were important ingredients, the increase in the number of individually owned cars, which could easily transport a light-weight kayak on their roofs, was a particularly important development in the case of canoeing. It is also true that the arrival of grp as a construction method had considerable effect, not only on the general increase in the numbers of paddlers who could afford to take up the sport, but also, as we shall see, on the design of the boats themselves.

The nature of the material

Glassfibre reinforced plastic (grp) is an umbrella term that covers a large range of materials, although canoeists are normally only interested in the resins that are particularly resistant to attack by water, and indeed Lloyds give approval to high-grade resins suitable for marine use. These resins are in fact polyesters. They consist of long chains of molecules which produce a treaclely liquid that is thinned with styrene to give a working consistency.

Most resins are sold with an accelerator already incorporated, and it only requires the addition of one ot two percent of a hardener, usually an organic peroxide, to initiate a 'cure' at room temperature. As the chains of molecules form cross-links, the liquid turns into a solid without any heat being applied - in fact, the chemical reaction gives off a considerable amount of heat.

Once the reaction has occurred it is not possible to soften the resin by heating. It is classed as a thermo-setting material, although it does burn, producing dense, toxic smoke, if heated strongly.

The resin is not very strong in tension, and like concrete it needs to be reinforced with strands of a stronger substance. Glass, in thin strands is not only flexible but it is extremely strong in tension. Resin adheres very well to glass threads, and the combination of glass and resin forms a very strong matrix indeed.

Basic method of construction

The combination of polyester resin and glass proved to be ideal for boat-building, especially as the moulds too could be made relatively inexpensively in the same material. First a 'plug' is made in virtually any material - wood, foam, plaster, papier mache, or their combinations, as long as the surface can be satisfactorily filled, polished and treated with release agent so that mould can be taken from the surface. Essentially, a plug is the shape of the kayak required, and the mould is a mirror-image of it but with inbuilt flanges and locators so that any separate parts can be fastened together correctly. Once the mould has been made and its surface treated with a release agent, the boats, which of course are replicas of the original plug, can be laid up within it. Obviously, the simplest and cheapest mould consists of a single shape with no undercuts that will prevent the finished boat from being released. This is ideal for open canoes, and a simple two piece mould, flanged together along the gunwales, is ideal for making kayaks.

Implications for design

There are almost no restraints imposed on the shape of a craft by grp - even undercuts can be coped with at a price. But if there are no constraints and the possibilities are infinite, what does the boat designer actually do ? The hull will obviously have restrictions if he is to make it perform at all well hydrodynamically, but what shapes should he use for decorative purposes ? Of course, as normally happens, he can fall back on decorative elements that have evolved in other materials, but sometimes, very strange configurations appear as designers try to discover appropriate shapes for a new material.

Indeed it is not just superficial decoration that is incongruous. It is still possible to see glassfibre dinghies whose hulls are replicas of clinker-built planked boats. The steps in the surface are poor design hydrodynamically speaking, but can be justified in wooden boats as the outcome of the construction method, which is excellent. Replicated in glassfibre, when in fact the repeated steps are very hard to mould satisfactorily, it is quite ridiculous.

Mercifully, within the canoeing world, where virtually all the boat may be under water at some time or other, and thus needs to be a reasonable hydrodynamic design, these excesses have not developed to any large extent. Kayaks for both competition and recreation, are still produced, however, where even the basic shapes are hard to justify in the cold light of known fact. Certainly, kayaks in grp, and indeed plastic, often exhibit decorative features that have a long way to go before they finally become integrated with the overall design, and are appropriate to the material being used.

In spite of the problems that new materials always bring, glassfibre could produce a lightweight, inexpensive kayak with round bilges, convex and concave surfaces could be bonded into the boat without the use of rivets or bolts, the capital costs were low, and the skills required were not beyond the amateur builder.

Bright colours and exciting patterns could be incorporated into the surface resins of these boats, or translucent pigments could be used. But most importantly, since the moulds were relatively cheap, changes could be made to designs without incurring too much expense. Within a few years of the introduction of glassfibre craft, a handful of manufacturers within the UK were producing a range of well over five hundred designs. It did not make economic sense, but development was very rapid indeed. In particular, the changes that swept through both slalom and white water racing kayak designs were very much the result of a material that allowed very cheap remodelling. It was as easy to work empirically on a full size kayak, test it on the river and if needs be repeat the process, as it was to sit at the drawing board and try to get it right first time from basic principles.

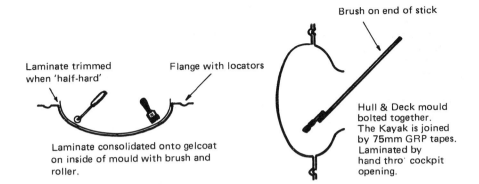

Laminate trimmed when 'half-hard'

Flange with locators

Brush on end of stick

Laminate consolidated onto gelcoat on inside of mould with brush and roller.

Hull & Deck mould bolted together. The Kayak is joined by 75mm GRP tapes. Laminated by hand thro' cockpit opening.

Fig 3:10

Strength and stiffness

The only drawbacks to the material were that it was not very stiff, and it was only moderately resistant to abrasion, as the brightly coloured scrapes left behind in well-used rocky rivers testified. The stiffness problem could be overcome to a considerable extent by curving the surfaces intelligently, but since the stiffness of a material increases by the cube of its thickness, the best way of increasing stiffness was to increase thickness. Even so, it was easy to build a very strong kayak indeed that was no heavier than the lath and canvas craft it replaced.

The standard technique of building kayaks was to lay down a gel-coat in the mould. This was thick unreinforced resin that acted as a barrier against moisture and abrasion for the rest of the laminate. Layers of glass were added, wetted out with laminating resin and consolidated with brush and roller by hand. After trimming the semi-cured gunwale edges the two halves of the mould were bolted together and the kayak was joined by laying in glass tapes across the seams throughout the length of the boat, working by hand through the cockpit opening (Fig 3:10).

The decked kayak was perfect for the material, as the cigar shape was extremely stiff. The open canoe was not quite so successful, as this shape is intrinsically less stiff. However the addition of stiff gunwales, thwarts and some end decking overcame any unwanted flexibility.

In one sense glassfibre was too good for its own good ! It was *so strong*, that demands were made for ever lighter weight boats, and what was good for the competition boys was also good for the less able paddlers. Boats became lighter in weight, thinner skinned, and less strong.

Materials

Demands for higher performance from grp was, as always, met by stronger materials. Originally the standard glass reinforcement was chopped strand mat (csm) - fibres of minute diameter were pulled from a glass furnace, and 120 of them used to form a roving. (Rovings denote fibres lying parallel to each other as distinct from fibres twisted together to form rope and most other threads used for weaving). These rovings were chopped into 50mm lengths and bonded in random

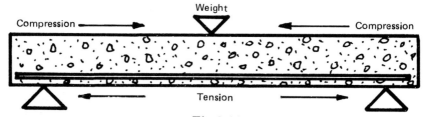

Fig 3:11

Note that the reinforcing bar is placed to resist the tension in lower part of beam

directions into a continuous sheet usually about one metre wide. Various thicknesses were manufactured that were designated by weight, 300g/m² and 450g/m² being common. This produced a rather stiff sheet of non-woven fabric that was easily handled and could be cut with knife or scissors. The bonding agent which held the strands in contact was soluble in resin, so that once the mat was laid into the mould and wetted out, it draped as the strands separated, and was then easily formed to the mould shape with rollers and brush.

Csm produced stiff, but somewhat brittle boats. The solution was to produce a woven cloth from rovings which had a higher tensile strength. In effect, this meant higher resistance to puncture, but somewhat less stiffness. Diolen was used instead of woven glass rovings, this was a cloth woven from specially treated polyester - Terylene in the UK, Dacron in the US. The higher tensile strength increased the impact resistance yet again, but the search for lighter materials continued.

Kevlar was introduced in the early seventies as a light-weight aramid fibre suitable for bullet-proof vests ! It is a petroleum product belonging to the family of nylons. Dramatic reductions in weight of the order of 30% were possible, when it was used for kayak building, but it was prone to delaminate when used with polyester resins. Polyvinyl resins were introduced that were more compatible with kevlar. Epoxies were even better, but expensive !

Reinforcements

One very happy combination was the introduction of carbon fibre into the mix. Often referred to as 'graphite', carbon fibres are heat treated until their altered molecular structure makes them virtually unstretchable. Their stiffness is not an indication of ultimate strength - in fact, carbon fibres are not very strong - but a measure of this lack of stretch.

When any bending takes place, the outer curved surface will be under tension and the inner curved surface will be compressed. If you cannot stretch the outer surface, you cannot bend the material at all, and the inner surface is not compressed either. Obviously, placing carbon fibre close to the outer surface of any potential bend will keep the material stiff. Concrete beams with reinforcing bars close to their bottom edges remind us that the same principles apply in the construction industry too. The problem for boat designers is to decide which way it will bend, and if the answer is 'both ways' then the stiffening must be placed as close as possible to both surfaces (Fig 3:11).

74

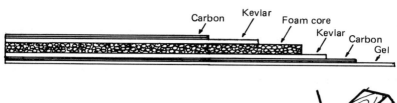

Carbon | Kevlar | Foam core | Kevlar | Carbon | Gel

A blow in direction of arrow often splits
stick lengthways down centre Q.E.D.

Fig 3:12
Sandwich construction
Down the centre of the laminate there is neither tension nor compression. This is called the 'neutral plane'. Beware! This is where shear stress is greatest. Prove it by breaking firewood in half with axe!

We know that thickness means stiffness anyway, so the further apart the two surfaces are, the better. But, we are back to square one, thickness means weight! So why not hold the two surfaces apart by a light-weight material and then let the carbon fibres do their job! Good, but the two surfaces must not move relative to each other, so the centre material must be strong enough to resist the shear forces involved. Without going into the finer points of placing reinforcing fibres, I have dwelt on this a little to show the tip of the complex ice-berg of light-weight construction.

Composites

Light-weight, but strongish materials have been used as cores for years. Block-board in the timber trade is well known, as is corrugated card (!) and balsa wood, polyurethane foam, PVC foam, and 'Coremat' - a proprietary name for thick, non-woven polyester fibres (like thick blotting paper) impregnated with minute hollow plastic spheres. This is not to mention aluminium and stiffened paper honeycombe material, which are all used to stiffen the shells of all manner of light craft including canoes and kayaks (Fig 3:12).

Kevlar does not perform too well under compression, so carbon fibre and kevlar was an ideal combination. Since grp was absent, the term 'composite' was used, and 'sandwich' construction described the use of core material. These terms soon became buzz words among competitors who wanted ever lighter craft, and they filtered down to the recreational canoeists too. Unfortunately, while first-rate competitive craft were produced, the problem of durability was again apparent. Impact damage was bound to be a problem, and delamination was always a spectre. Trapping kevlar between two thin layers of glass helped here, but on went the weight again.

Laying-up

Hand lay-up methods are always preferable for canoes and kayaks as opposed to mechanical spray-up techniques, because the glass/resin ratio can be kept very high - 1:1 compared with the average of twice the weight of resin to glass as in the normal industrial lay-up. A high resin content means good resistance to moisture, not important for canoes and kayaks that are not permanently afloat, but a high glass content means strength. Unskillful hand lamination means dry areas of matt and air bubbles that can spell disaster for the thin skins of light-weight craft, and vacuum-bagging techniques developed to try and prevent these problems.

The idea of vacuum-bagging is to seal the wet lay-up onto the mould with a sheet of plastic that will allow a vacuum-pump to extract the air from the lay-up. The outside surface of the bag is squeegied to spread out the underlying resin, removing some of it along with any entrapped air (Fig 3:13). Stiffer reinforcing materials can be used and better bonding of cores and stiffening ribs can be achieved, but the dark cloud chasing the silver lining is that inexperienced operators can easily create very thin areas starved of resin with little stiffness and strength.

Growth of manufacturers

It has already been noted that the low capital costs of moulding in grp had created a boom in new designs as well as rapid growth in the number of people taking up the sport. Grp also encouraged the amateur builder, and throughout the country, club canoeists, scout leaders, and a host of home builders made their own kayaks in any garage or club hut large enough to harbour a kayak mould.

Here and there, a few individuals in this army of amateurs became hooked; not on the waves of styrene fumes that they inhaled, but on the heady excitement of not only building their own kayaks, but designing them as well. It was not long before there was a thriving cottage industry of builders working from small premises and selling their boats - at first to friends, secondly to local paddlers,

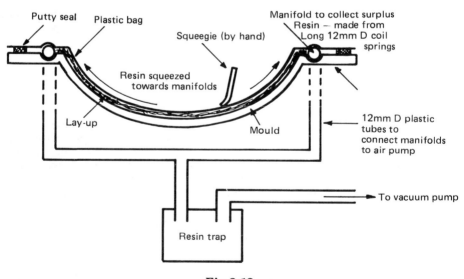

Fig 3:13
Vacuum bagging for grp

then nationally, and finally on an international scale. They did everything themselves - design, manufacture, marketing, and it is still true today that virtually all kayak manufacturers are paddlers who started their businesses when enthusiasm and a commitment to developing their own ideas was more important than a large loan from the bank.

Customising
Because of this flexibility in the basic materials and methods, grp and composite boats are virtually the only type that can be tailor-made for the individual, or indeed that can be customised to any great extent by the paddler once he has purchased his boat.

Competition boats, sea-kayaks and squirt boats, are all types that need to be customised if they are to be ideally suited to the individual paddler, and it is significant that grp and composites still dominate these markets. If you are in line for this type of craft, you need to be able to recognise a good boat when you see one.

Choosing a boat
Unfortunately, just to describe the basic materials and construction in one chapter leaves insufficient space to delve into all the pros and cons of different techniques and materials used in laminating, not to mention the common faults associated with them. Further information for your interest here is provided in the bibliography at the end of the chapter. As a general guide, look for neatness. Go to the annual International Canoe Exhibition, traditionally held at Crystal Palace each February, and look at as many grp or composite kayaks as you can. Check inside particularly for roughness, patchy resin, spikes of glass protruding form the laminate especially where the various pieces have been bonded together, and check for straight seams. Take a flashlight and a small mirror. You'll never know whether the advertising blurb is true or false, so judge yourself after gaining some experience and chose the canoe that will suit your needs from a position of knowledge.

ROTO-MOULDED POLYETHYLENE KAYAKS

Advantages
A visit to the Canoe Exhibition, with its huge choice of kayaks and canoes, will convince you that most general purpose boats are now made in polyethylene. This is the same unreinforced plastic that is used for plastic bags and plastic containers, hence the rather derogatory nick-name of 'Tupperware' boats. Certainly, polyethylene kayaks are not aesthetically pleasing, so as this material has dominated the market during the eighties, it must have other distinct advantages.

It has: first and foremost, comparative cheapness; secondly, freedom from regular maintenance; thirdly, resistance to puncture from impact.

The moulding process
True mass-production was never possible with lath and canvas, timber or grp kayaks, although the speed of lamination with grp construction kept prices low

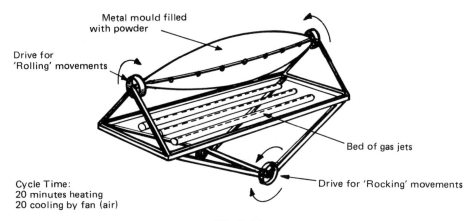

Metal mould filled
with powder

Drive for
'Rolling' movements

Bed of gas jets

Drive for 'Rocking' movements

Cycle Time:
20 minutes heating
20 cooling by fan (air)

Fig 3:14
Schematic drawing shows basic layout for roto-moulding.
There are many variations on this theme

in spite of continually rising labour costs. Polyethylene (Polythene is a trade name) was the material that ensured the success of a mass produced kayak.

The first of this new generation of boats was designed by Tom Johnson of Kernville, California for the Hollowform Company. They produced a boat in polyethylene by roto-moulding, but immediately gave up the idea of specializing in kayaks, so the story goes, because they landed a contract to supply the whole of Phoenix, Arizona with plastic garbage cans ! (dustbins to you and me).

The roto-moulding process had been used for some years to make medium sized, but compact items, and the rather thin proportions of a kayak and its considerable size created some problems.

The basic idea of roto-moulding, is to fill a metal mould with a plastic powder and melt it until it runs over the inside surface. To achieve an even covering over the whole of the interior, the mould must be tilted and rotated while maintaining high temperature, and then cooled to allow the plastic to become rigid enough to be removed. It is a little like pancake making when the frying pan is tilted to allow the mix to run over the surface before it cooks. Polyethylene of course is a thermoplastic material which means that it can be re-softened by heat, whereas the pancake cooking process is a chemical one and is irreversible.

The metal mould can be of beaten steel or of cast aluminium, and are sometimes nickel plated. In the future, developments in the spraying of metal may well offer even better alternatives. Pressed steel moulds are cheap but usually less accurate, and their poor conductivity make them inferior to aluminium.

Heating can be by open flame in the form of gas jets, but it is difficult to control the heat over the awkward shape of a kayak, and this method is normally used on smaller objects that are easier to heat evenly. Ovens that can spread the heat from the gas jets evenly over the mould must be big enough to allow the mould to tilt and rotate within it, or the whole oven must move with the mould. Another approach is to place the mould in an enclave oven and blow hot air onto the mould from a heat-source. Some ovens can control the heat locally by controlling separate banks of gas jets so that the correct temperatures can be achieved in every part of the mould (Fig 3:14).

The correct temperature to melt the plastic and give it its proper physical properties, and the correct frequency and duration of the 'rock and rolls' given to the mould to spread the molten material within it must be carefully controlled. This is done by computer, but as far as can be ascertained no machine yet built has a true positive feed-back system that can monitor the actual temperature on the inside surface of the mould and relay this back to the heat source for correction if necessary. The computer is merely acting like the punched-hole system of a pianola, it can repeat the tune ad infinitum, but the master piano roll has to be made by a pianist first. Clearly it is a trial and error process, and depends on the skill of the person who is in charge of those crucial original settings.

Properties of polyethylene

The use of the name 'polyethylene' gives no more information than to say 'timber' - are you getting balsa or teak? Polyethylene is a generic chemical name for polymers of ethylene and is composed basically of carbon and hydrogen atoms. These molecules can exist together in four separate forms:

o   As random molecules forming amorphous areas.
o   As molecules lying together in regular patterns forming crystalline areas.
o   As long chains wandering at random through both the amorphous and crystalline molecules.
o   As long chains cross-linked together.

It is the proportions of these different forms of the molecule within the material that give it such widely varying properties. These are dependent on minute differences in the chemical processes used in manufacture, and as these also control the molecular weight, it means that polyethylene can vary from the low density associated with those irritating plastic bags that tear so easily to HD (high density) polyethylene that is much harder than the material used for kayaks.

So although there is an on- going argument in canoeing circles revolving around the relative merits of linear and cross-linked polyethylene, it should be remembered that these are merely the two major groups of material, and that there are horrendous kayaks available that bend, warp, split and abrade, depending on the quality of the material purchased in the first place and the quality of the manufacturing process in the second.

Cost of manufacture

Several industrial roto-moulders saw the kayak market as a supplement to their normal income. The results from these people who are not deeply involved with the sport has generally been disastrous.

Once again it must be emphasised that polyethylene is no more the perfect building material for the canoe world than was grp when it was introduced as the panacea for all ills. Of all the thermo-plastics, it is bottom of the list as far as its physical properties are concerned. Its saving grace is that it is cheap.

Building a roto-moulding oven can take you into six figures quite easily, and an alloy mould will set you back five. While this is small beer compared with the capital costs in say the car industry, it is many times higher than the capital required for any other form of kayak construction. These capital costs must be allowed for in the final cost of a boat, so it is not unreasonable to find that only a small proportion of the cost of a plastic boat is spent on materials.

Construction compromise

Apart from its cheapness, the other reason polyethylene is favoured for roto-moulding is its relatively low melting point. An oven temperature of about 300°C will give an internal mould temperature of approximately 200°C in twenty minutes which will be sufficient to melt and cross-link the plastic powder. Materials with better properties than polyethylene tend to have higher melting points. This means higher fuel bills and also shorter mould life, as the constant heating and cooling of the mould over a higher range of temperature causes a more rapid deterioration of the crystalline structure of the metal.

The three most attractive points in favour of polyethylene have been noted: low cost and minimal maintenance have endeared these boats particularly to the outdoor centres who must needs give their craft a very hard time. The third point, resistance to impact, is only achieved at a price - stiffness. Thicker means stiffer and weightier ! Although it is possible to cause the centre of a polyethylene skin to foam, producing a construction akin to the composite boats using a foam core, portaging any polyethylene boat reminds us of the general weightiness of plastic, and careless storage or harsh tying down onto canoe trailers soon exposes its lack of rigidity.

Perhaps the worst feature of polyethylene is its very poor abrasion resistance, which is far worse than grp. Shavings of polythene are stripped from the boat every time it is dragged across a gravel path or scrapes a rough boulder, yet canoeists seem to be content to equate impact resistance with complete imperviousness to damage.

Having said that, there is no doubt that the ability of polyethylene to bounce off rocks that would normally hole almost any other type of boat has given white water canoeing yet another shot in the arm, just as grp did twenty years previously. Sadly, while responsible paddlers have been able to develop their skills in the knowledge that their boats can be more forgiving, the other side of the coin can be seen in the number of unskilled paddlers who are attempting water that is far too advanced for their puny efforts. And worst of all, the fact that people who should know better are encouraging them. In spite of the ongoing development of safety consciousness within both manufacturing and coaching, there are a growing number of people who believe that tough boats are a substitute for skill. A blind run down a river with only the prospect of a rescue with the latest piece of safety equipment does not auger well for longevity ! Well, do not blame the boat !

But this ability to withstand impact is a huge plus, far greater than the sum of the minus marks that we must give it for stiffness, and poor resistance to abrasion. Once again we can see the material affecting the design, the short white water kayaks of the eighties are partly due to the necessity to save weight in the new material. Certainly, larger sea-kayaks amplify the problems. It was said that if you could not carry you sea-boat up the beach, you had paddled too far. With a polyethylene sea-boat, you would be lucky to get it to the water on your own at the beginning of the trip ! Metal bars and plastic stiffeners are common-place in plastic sea boats, and remind us that they are really beyond the critical size for their stiffness.

Another problem with polyethylene is the problem of bonding. At present, parts are bolted or rivetted to the boat. There is a very expensive French 'advanced epoxy' glue (this means it is secret !) that seems capable of bonding to polyethylene, but the method of preparation is tedious, and even then, from personal experience, it seems very difficult to make it work reliably. This means, for instance that bulkheads bonded into sea-boats to provide water-tight compartments are unreliable. One manufacturer claimed that, 'I guarantee my bulkheads will leak within a month'. Until some of these problems are solved there will be some limits to the use of plastics within the wider aspects of canoeing.

Linear and cross-linked

There is no doubt that the physical properties of cross-linked polyethylene are better than those of a linear type. The cross-linked product is stiffer, tougher and less prone to cracking. Unfortunately, it is possible to start with a cross-linked polyethylene formulation, but finish with a poor quality product, because the cross-linking process was not completed in the oven. The correct temperature must be reached and then held for a longer period than is needed for linear polyethylenes.

This costs more of course, and how do you *know* you have a cross-linked boat ? Well there are sophisticated tests that can be made. For instance, you can see if you can dissolve out any non cross-linked portion with xylene, or you can drop a 4.5kg metal dart onto the polyethylene cooled to -40°C and see if it shatters. If it does, it is not fully cross-linked. Too difficult ? Try a simple DIY test. Cut a narrow strip, approximately 20mm wide, from your kayak, and bend it over sharply so that the inside surface of the strip is on the outside of the bend. If there are extensive cracks crazing the surface, it is not fully cross-linked. Properly treated material may show a slight whitening of the surface, but nothing more.

Once you have discovered the nature of the material in your kayak, how do you put it back ?

It has been claimed, apocryphally I am sure, that the following was overheard after an intrepid paddler had performed the test, on his new kayak:

'So the test shows that your suspicions were unfounded - never mind, let's straighten the strip and put it back into the kayak now.

'I'm afraid you cannot weld the strip back into place, because cross-linked material acts like a thermo-setting plastic, and doesn't want to melt again; and even if it was only linear material, it would be a little bit dicey to expect it to be super strong . . . I told you not to cut it out from under the seat where it gets all that flexing during a seal-launch.

'Well, you can use an EVA hot-melt glue. Mind you, you'll have to open up the cuts with a sharp knife so that there are vees on either surface. Then the glue will pass through from side to side and form a rivet. It'll work well on a small split, but I did think you were over-doing it when you cut out a strip half a metre long !

'Try this new French glue. Don't forget, you must flame the surface with a blow torch to oxidize the plastic first. It works all right if you practise, practise, practise.

'Yes, I *do* know what 'merde' means. Well I'm sorry, there was no need to test it anyway, and no need to go on like that !'

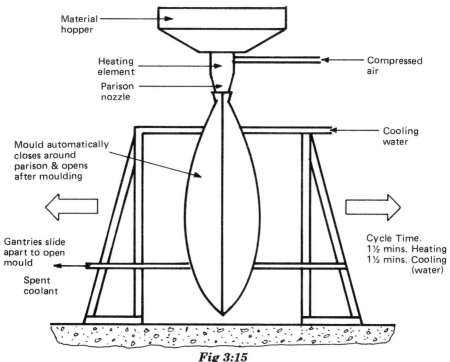

Material hopper

Heating element

Parison nozzle

Compressed air

Cooling water

Mould automatically closes around parison & opens after moulding

Gantries slide apart to open mould

Spent coolant

Cycle Time:
1½ mins. Heating
1½ mins. Cooling
(water)

Fig 3:15
Schematic drawing of blow-moulding

Although this cautionary tale has never been verified, there is no doubt that a large scale repair of polyethylene is considerably more difficult than in grp. Even welding linear polyethylene is beyond most amateurs, partly because they do not get enough practise, and partly because a good heat gun is expensive, and is not worth buying unless you need to use it regularly.

However, splits or holes in either linear or cross-linked polyethylene are rare, and it is the thinning of the skin by abrasion that is the most common damage affecting plastic boats. Unfortunately, if the thickness of the skin is drastically reduced, then repair is usually out of the question.

Blow-moulded kayaks

Polyethylene can also be blow-moulded, which is a process that allows a higher molecular weight of material to be used. This means that the quality, in terms of toughness and stiffness is better than in roto-moulded boats. There are only two companies in the world producing blow-moulded kayaks, compared with a dozen or more roto-moulders. The reason for this is that the blow-moulding process costs much more money !

The HD polyethylene is melted into a 'parison' which Thurber would have described as a 'blob of glup'. The mould is opened mechanically to receive this semi-molten dew-drop of plastic, and it is forced into the mould by compressed air. The parison's thickness is controlled carefully (by what else ?) so that when it is blown into place, it is the correct thickness at the ends of the kayak as well as on the flatter sections. This method seems to be just about as accurate as the thickness control methods used for roto-moulded kayaks. Cooling water floods through tubes in the mould that is rapidly cooled and opens automatically to release the completed kayak (Fig 3:15).

The blow-moulding machine in Chicago that makes a kayak just over 3m long, stands ten metres high ! It is an awe-inspiring sight as it drops out a kayak every three minutes or so ! The cost of moulds that need a complicated cooling system within them is enormous, and to be cost effective they must be kept running twenty-four hours a day. The mind-blowing logistics of shipping these boats before the factory disappears under a pile of colourful boats is daunting, and is reminiscent of the tale of the sorcerers apprentice. The machine in Chicago could take a variety of moulds, and 100,000 trash cans were its next job. There is obviously a strong link between garbage and kayaks - but comment on its significance would be uncalled for !

Vacuum formed polyethylene canoes

Open canoes are made in polyethylene by the roto-moulding process, but the method that finds most favour is called vacuum forming - sucking instead of blowing ! In this process, a sheet of polyethylene is heated until pliable and then sucked down onto a mould and allowed to cool. One US company using this method has registered its polyethylene under the trademark Ram-X. The sales of open canoes in the US are enormous, and the problems of distribution over the continent are formidable. Transport costs can be minimised by delivering boats unassembled and stacked inside one another; the dealer assembling the canoe at its point of sale. Once again we see transportation problems introducing design changes that may not necessarily boost the paddling qualities, but certainly help to lower the price tag on the craft (Fig 3:16).

Vacuum formed ABS composites

Ram-X, a polyethylene, must not be confused with Royalex, another trademark, denoting a sheet of unsupported plastic that is a laminate of vinyl/ABS/vinyl. Best known of the vinyl family is PVC and the initials ABS stand for an unpronounce-able plastic which is styrene-based, and is therefore compatible with polyester resins.

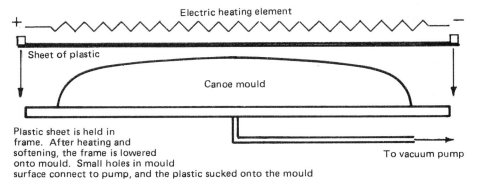

Fig 3:16
Vacuum forming

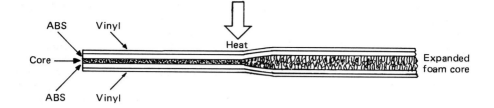

ABS Vinyl Heat Expanded foam core
Core
ABS Vinyl

Fig 3:17
Section of Royalex

What is cunning about Royalex is that an inner core expands with heat and creates a foam during the vacuum-forming process, producing an extremely tough, resilient material that makes a fine open canoe (Fig 3:17). Large dents will usually spring out of their own accord, but it can still tear under severe stress. However, repairs can be easily made with epoxy resin repair kits that include a 'putty' for outside scratches.

The Uniroyal Company that make Royalex also produce other very similar products for various canoe builders under other names. Oltonar and Sawyerlex are examples, and Duralex is the name for a similar material where the outer vinyl skin is replaced by a thick layer of acrylic.

One problem associated with sandwich construction, is that it is difficult to vacuum-form tight curves at bow and stern. Rubbing strips, suitably contoured are sometimes added to this type of canoe to overcome the problem.

The future for plastic boats

Make no mistake, unsupported plastics are in the canoeing world to stay. It is the only material capable of producing a mass-produced boat, and the chemical industry will continue to invent better and better materials that will answer the canoe designer's needs far better than today's products.

We are only at the threshold of this development, and there is little doubt that this is where research efforts will be concentrated, rather than in the development of grp systems, which only lend themselves to relatively short production runs. Grp is becoming the 'hand-crafted' material of the future, just as wood is the present-day material of the boat-building connoisseur.

Although the best qualities of polyethylene have 'memory' and tend to return to their original shape after distortion, tests show that like humans, its memory is not perfect ! In particular, severe stress can leave permanent degradation, and, just like sportsmen, they eventually deteriorate !

Conclusion

This short account of construction methods and materials has had to be very general. The bibliography will give much more detail to those who wish to delve deeper, and after all, the best master is your own experience - why not build your own boat ?

There are always contradictions, and in the end the individual must sift the information from all sources as best he may. For example, this chapter states that sprayed lay-ups are inferior to hand lamination for grp. This is true, yet Graham Sissons, in New Zealand, built a sea-boat for Paul Caffyn that was one layer of kevlar with a thin layer of glass sprayed onto it. It weighed virtually nothing, but Paul paddled over 9,000 miles around Australia in 360 days, including a continuous 112 mile crossing of the Great Australian Bight in 36 hours, without ever repairing the boat or taking on a spot of water ! Again, strong plastic boats are generally considered, in the UK, to be safer for top grade white water than grp. Yet many German paddlers prefer very thick, heavy, but immensely strong grp boats that seem to be capable of taking on the most difficult conditions.

Theory and practice do not always match up, and as we know, fashions in paddling styles and mind-set can alter. But the water remains constant - only our perception of it changes, and this, together with the advent of new materials, affects the way we design and build our boats.

These craft are only vehicles for our own pleasure - enhanced a hundredfold by our skills, and made safe too by the judgement we develop as our knowledge and experience grow. This penultimate paragraph is merely saying that the whole chapter should be taken with a pinch of salt, unless it is added to a sensible diet of first-hand knowledge and practice !

Bibliography

Books

Adney and Chappelle; *The Bark Canoes and Skin Boats of North America;* Smithsonian Institute, Washington DC; 1964

Clark; *Advanced Fabrication Techniques for Whitewater Boats;* W A Clar Associates, Boulder, Colorado; 1977

Penn; *GRP Technology;* MacClaren & Sons, London; 1966

Peterson; *Instruction in Kayak Building;* Greenland Provincial Museum and The Viking ship Museum, Roskilde, Greenland; date unknown

Riviere; *The Open Canoe;* Little, Brown and Co, Boston & Toronto; 1985

Roff and Scott; *Fibres, Films, Plastics and Rubbers;* Butterworth and Co, London; 1971

Walbridge; *Boatbuilders Manual (sixth edition);* Menasha Ridge Press, Birmingham, Alabama; 1987

Zimmerly; *Qajaq: Kayaks of Siberia and Alaska;* Division of State Museums, Juneau, Alaska; 1986

Periodicals

Wooden Canoe; *Wooden Canoe Heritage Association, PO Box 5634 Madison, WN 53705 USA.*

Canoe Focus and *Canoeist* magazines have some articles of interest from time to time.

This chapter has a completely changed emphasis from the chapter in the first edition of the *Canoeing Handbook*. It replaces a chapter that dealt largely with the home-building of a glassfibre kayak, but we recognise that building activity has declined dramatically since the 1970s.

Those who wish to build their own grp kayak will find that the original chapter giving details of building procedures will be available as a separate booklet. Enquiries via the BCU.

4 Safety

Compiled by the Editor

INTRODUCTION

Safety should be a positive, not a negative, concept. It is a matter of adopting a realistic attitude to the inherent risks of the activity, rather than listing a series of 'don'ts'. There must be an interaction of sound knowledge, good equipment and adequate training and technique.

Properly prepared, the canoeist can enter situations which challenge and thrill. He can have fun where the untrained person may drown, and where few other vessels can operate.

Although not all canoeing is undertaken on raging rapids or pounding surf, even placid water can drown, and drowning can damage one's health ! Therefore, it is necessary, at all times, to take the common sense precautions which experience and statistics demonstrate can reduce the risk of fatality in a canoe to almost nil.

KNOWLEDGE

The following golden rules apply:

o   The ability to swim

It is desirable that every person who sits in a canoe should be able to swim at least 50 metres in light clothing. The ability to swim vast distances is not essential, but basic confidence in and under the water without panic are fundamental to safe canoeing.

o   Personal flotation aids

A life jacket or buoyancy aid should always be worn when afloat.

o   Stay with the boat

In the event of a capsize, stay with the boat. A canoe or kayak is more easily spotted than an individual swimmer's head in the water. On a river, it may be necessary to abandon the boat and swim as swiftly as possible across the current to the bank, if you are being carried into danger. Should you ever have to abandon a boat, inform the authorities immediately. Inland, this will be the police; at sea, inform the coastguard. The coastguard service is also on the 999 emergency system, but for routine matters the number of the nearest station can be obtained from the telephone directory.

o   'Less than three there should never be'

Three trained paddlers, working within their experience, should be able to cope with most situations. With three persons available, one can always summon help while one deals with a casualty.

One can of course add other rules. If they are needed you can construct them from the material in this chapter and the safety aspects which appear in the relevant chapters related to specific activities.

The group

The particular areas of knowledge required for the organisation of inland or sea journeys are highlighted within the relevant sections. If one factor is important above all others, it is the necessity to know the limits of one's personal ability, and that of every member of the group. The ability to identify situations which are apparently, but not inherently dangerous, and will thus excite and challenge the novice, yet remain within manageable safety limits, is basic to the art of the instructor.

MOVING WATER

Moving water is a powerful and relentless force. A simple 3-4km/h current can pin a canoe or a person against an obstacle, overcome a 6kg buoyancy aid and hold the paddler under water. The following obstacles in moving water must therefore be avoided: rocks, bridges, posts, buoys, moored boats, and especially trees.

Weirs

Three types of weir commonly exist in the United Kingdom: sharp crested, broad crested (also known as long-base) and triangular profile (or 'crump'). A variation on the triangular profile weir, but not usable on large rivers is the flat-V, or measuring weir (Figs 4:1,4:2,4:3). Weirs exist in order to control levels between various sections of river, to divert water, to create a hydraulic head for power generations, to provide storage, or to facilitate flow measurement.

The main concern of water authorities is to dissipate the energy created by water accelerating over a weir as efficiently as possible. This means that the bigger the hydraulic jump (stopper), and the more it can be contained, the less the speed of the flow downstream of the weir, and consequently less erosion to the banks will occur.

A 'stopper' behaves like a vertical eddy current. Whenever moving water passes an obstruction, there is a low-pressure area created on the down-stream side of that obstruction. This should appear as a hole, but as water must find its own level, and 'nature abhors a vacuum', this hole is filled by water coming back upstream. Therefore, behind any rock, or wherever water flows faster in one place than another, 'eddy' currents will form (Fig 4:4).

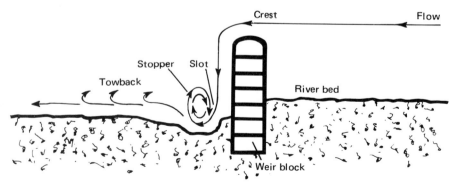

Fig 4:1
Broad crested weir

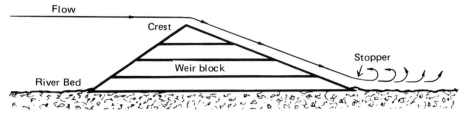

Fig 4:2
Triangular profile or 'crump' weir

In the case of a stopper, water has accelerated over a drop. Whether this is only a couple of centimetres, or the Victoria Falls, the principle is the same. Because the water has accelerated, it does not just stop at river level below the fall, but in fact continues downwards before rising gradually as the velocity diminishes. The 'hole' that is thus left immediately downstream of the drop is filled by water breaking away from the surface, and pouring down into it in the form of tumbling foam. An object failing to break through this foaming wave is therefore pushed down by it, taken under by the water dropping over the fall and, provided it is buoyant, brought back up to the surface again. If this occurs too near the fall, the surface water moving upstream will take it (or him) back to the stopper, and the cycle will be repeated...and repeated...and repeated.

In order to overcome the problems of erosion to the river bed, an undesirable trend has been to build 'anti-scour' weirs, with a concrete step at the bottom (Fig 4:5). This creates a continuous large area of 'back-tow'. The likelihood of anyone

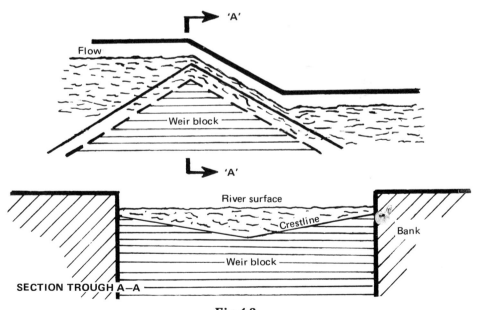

Fig 4:3
Flat-V or 'measuring' weir

89

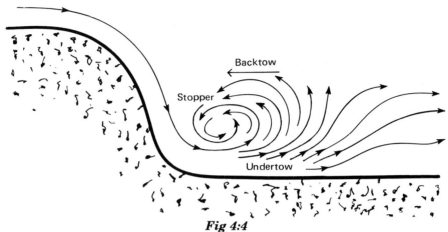

Fig 4:4

Behaviour of water in a 'stopper' wave

escaping from this situation is slight, and this type of weir must be avoided at all costs. The BCU is currently objecting to the building of these on the grounds of the lethal nature of the hazard which they create.

Other methods of dissipating energy include the planting of metal stakes, or the construction of concrete 'dragon's teeth'. Some weirs have wire baskets full of rocks, known as 'gabions', placed on the bed of the river. When the wire breaks, or becomes loose through the stones being moved by the force of the water, bows of canoes can become entrapped.

On natural weirs, and on some that are man-made, there is an erosion problem under the fall. Here, the water can be circulating two ways, and anyone trapped in this situation is probably in an irretrievable position (Fig 4:6).

Novices should never be encouraged to shoot a weir that the instructor does not know from practical experience. Factors that determine whether or not a weir is 'shootable' are:

o Depth of water

o Vertical drop

o Amount of 'back-tow'

o Size of stopper

o Whether there is a natural break in the stopper

o Whether the stopper ends in a natural flow, or is sealed in by walls

o The shape of the weir - a 'horseshoe' shape could mean that everything works into the middle and there is no escape

o The power of the 'back-tow' - a large vertical drop into a deep pool, or a lot of water over a small drop, could produce a giant vertical eddy from which escape may be impossible.

Careful study is required by experts for any unknown weir before an attempt is made to shoot it. If in doubt, portage.

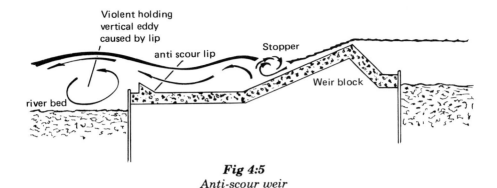

Fig 4:5
Anti-scour weir

HYPOTHERMIA AND COLD WATER IMMERSION

A person is in a state of hypothermia when their 'deep body temperature' is lowered. This deep body or 'core' temperature can only be measured using a special instrument but for us, as canoeists, the signs and symptoms of a hypothermic person are quite clear enough to allow us to recognise the condition as soon as we see it. It is this recognition of hypothermia in its early stages which is the key to successful first aid action. It gives us the chance to arrest the deterioration of a person's level of hypothermia to its potentially deadly conclusion.

What happens to the body when it cools ?

When a person becomes cold his body puts into action automatically a sequence of functions which are aimed at conserving and generating heat. One of the first

Fig 4:6
Two-way stopper caused by erosion under-cutting a fall

of these results in the familiar white face. The skin becomes pale because the circulation of blood to the body's surface has been reduced drastically. This lessens the natural radiator effect of warm blood near the skin, losing heat to surrounding air and wet clothing. A person in this state of cooling is definitely not in danger of dying of hypothermia. Their condition is very mild and merely exercising or putting on more clothing will probably improve things dramatically. Failing to do anything about it will result in further cooling and the body puts into action its next survival reflex: shivering. This reflex is designed to give us exercise whether we want it or not. The rapid contraction of surface muscles all over the body is clearly visible and results in heat being produced. Shivering is a unique form of exercise since we can do it whilst sitting or standing still, so it is possible to sleep and shiver, for example. It can increase the body's heat production by three or four times and can be maintained for long periods, but the price paid in energy expenditure is high.

If a person should continue to cool beyond this stage, their condition becomes very serious and the first aid treatment gets increasingly difficult to make effective. Firstly, the shivering stops and is replaced by rigidity in the muscles making the person look very stiff-limbed in their movements. The ability to balance and coordinate movement is gradually lost and speech becomes increasingly incoherent. At this stage a paddler, no matter how strong and fit, is in grave danger. As the condition worsens, consciousness decreases until eventually there is total heart failure.

How does hypothermia happen to canoeists ?

The ways in which a canoeist can become hypothermic fall into three areas:

o   Immersion in cold water

o   Cooling by exhaustion

o   Combination of these two.

On capsizing and becoming a swimmer, if the water temperature is lower than your body temperature (and it usually is), you will lose heat and, if you are not wearing protective clothing, you will lose it very rapidly indeed. Our bodies lose heat to water 26 times faster than to air at the same temperature. The maximum summer temperature of water around the British Isles is 10°-15°C (50°-60°F). At this temperature, survival time in the water without insulated clothing could be as little as one hour.

River and white water paddlers often work in water much cooler than this and are arguably more likely to take a swim than canoeists on the sea. They must therefore be careful to use canoeing clothing which will effectively reduce heat loss to the water on immersion.

The hard, physical work of canoeing combined with the need for keeping our bodies warm in the cold weather in which we frequently paddle, places high demands on our body's energy stores. None of us has an unlimited supply of energy and so it is possible to use it up beyond the limit of the body's resources. The result is exhaustion. This can be caused by all kinds of circumstances such as: too long on the water, insufficient rest or not fuelling the body's engine with food. If we bear in mind the fact that paddlers are in wet clothing for most of their canoeing time and losing heat constantly because of this, you can see how easily an exhausted paddler can rapidly reach a point where he can no longer produce enough energy to maintain his normal body temperature. From this point onwards he is a victim of hypothermia and only quick, effective action on his part, or on the part of his friends, will save him from sinking deeper into its grip.

How do we treat a paddler who has become hypothermic ?

Treating hypothermia requires you to have an understanding of the condition itself and is based on the simple principle of preventing further heat loss by whatever means possible.

The first thing to remember is that the two methods of cooling (immersion and exhaustion) happen at different rates. In immersion, the canoeist is cooled rapidly, and in the case of exhaustion the heat leaks away slowly. It is important to know which of these applies when you are dealing with a hypothermia victim and deciding on your course of action.

For a number of medical reasons a person whose core temperature has dropped gradually over a period of time, say during a whole day's paddle, must be re-warmed slowly and treated so that no further body heat is lost. This means using additional dry insulating clothing, sleeping bags, etc, to lag his body and preserve the little heat which he is slowly and naturally generating. Shelter must be provided, preferably in an atmosphere which is warm. The casualty may be given fluids to drink, since hypothermia causes body fluid levels to drop, but very cold drinks should be avoided for obvious reasons. Very hot drinks offer no advantages and can cause scalds. When wrapped in as much insulation as you can get and at rest, the casualty will re-warm himself from the core outwards.

When a person's core temperature sinks to below 32°C they are in a state of profound hypothermia. This is an advanced stage and the casualty is usually semi-conscious or comatose. It might still be possible to save them at this stage by applying the principles of preventing further heat loss but it is absolutely essential to cause the minimum of disturbance to their state of rest. The reason for this is that the heart is in a delicate balance at this point and a dangerous rhythm (ventricular fibrillation) can be triggered off by the slightest stress, resulting in heart failure. You should do your best to insulate and then see that their airway is kept clear. The urgency to hospitalise the casualty should not override the priority for minimum of disturbance, and evacuation should be carried out with great care.

If a paddler has become mildly hypothermic through short term immersion alone and he is conscious and shivering, in other words rapidly cooled and not profoundly hypothermic, then he can be re-warmed quickly in a hot bath. The bath temperature should be hand-hot and the casualty immersed totally to the neck. There is no need to remove canoeing clothing but the water should be re-heated and stirred to maintain its temperature. The speed of recovery from this treatment is usually remarkably quick but it would be wise not to paddle for the rest of the day.

How do we prevent hypothermia ?

The following actions will help to reduce the risk of becoming hypothermic:

o   Avoid multiple capsizes

o   Use good insulating clothing including wet or dry suits if you are going to be immersed or soaked

o   Plan journeys which are within your ability and fitness level

o   Avoid standing or sitting in the wind when you get out of your boat since windchill will take your body heat away very quickly.

o   If you run short of food or cannot eat be aware of this when you make plans for paddling

o   Be practised in your rescue techniques so that you are quick to get swimmers out of the water

o   Be constantly aware of your own temperature-level warning signs and be prepared to take action no matter how inconvenient it might be for others

o   Learn to recognise the signs of hypothermia in other paddlers and do not rely on people in your party telling you when they feel cold.

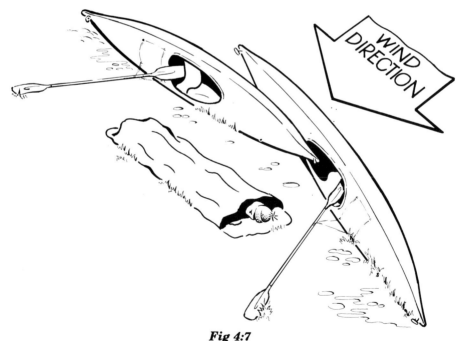

Fig 4:7
If a dangerously cooled person has to be put into an exposure bag, take every action possible to shelter the bag from wind

Signs of hypothermia

The following signs of hypothermia should be watched for in paddlers:

o   Abnormal and irrational behaviour

o   Slowing down, stumbling and uncoordinated movements

o   Uncontrollable shivering

o   Vague, slow, slurred speech

o   Memory lapses or incoherence

o   Drowsiness.

Hyperventilation

Often when a paddler capsizes in cold water he surfaces and gasps desperately for air even though his head is clearly above the surface of the water. This can be a very frightening experience. It is caused by a reflex action in the throat which is set off by cold water contacting the top of the windpipe. It is best described as a 'cough reflex', which shuts off the airway to the lungs in order to prevent anything undesirable such as water from entering. It is the partial closure of the airway which causes the croaking gasps for air which most of us have experienced at some stage whilst canoeing. Although there is little anyone can do to suppress the reflex and the resulting gasping, we can adjust our behaviour to make life a little easier when it does happen. It is important not to struggle or swim hard whilst in the throes of gasping since this only adds to the distressed breathing and, indeed, this action has been the likely cause of several drownings of strong swimmers. Research shows that it is better to let the gasping subside (and it always does) before starting to swim. If you have a good buoyancy aid or lifejacket then allow yourself to float in it, or hold onto your boat, for the few moments that it takes for your body to adjust to the sudden immersion.

Several cases have been reported where children have continued to hyperventilate after having been removed from the water. The condition is associated with panic and an instructor confronted with this should try to calm the child down. Getting the victim to breathe into a paper bag can assist in restoring a normal breathing rhythm.

Windchill

The windchill chart shows that air which is moving feels colder and has a greater cooling effect than still air at the same temperature. One important way of preventing heat loss, therefore, is to use clothing which is windproof and to ensure that emergency, temporary or overnight shelters are good wind barriers.

DROWNING

Drowning is death caused by asphyxia following immersion in water. The term 'near-drowning' is used if the casualty survives. Although the final cause of death is failure to get air into the lungs, there are often other factors which lead up to this and may therefore be considered causes of drowning: hypothermia, heart attack, alcohol intoxication are the ones which figure most highly in accident statistics for Britain.

In most cases of drowning, relatively small quantities of water enter the lungs, but this is enough to interfere with the normal transfer of oxygen from the inspired air to the blood. The water also causes irritation, and results in an outpouring of fluid into the alveoli (air sacs) which further impairs oxygen

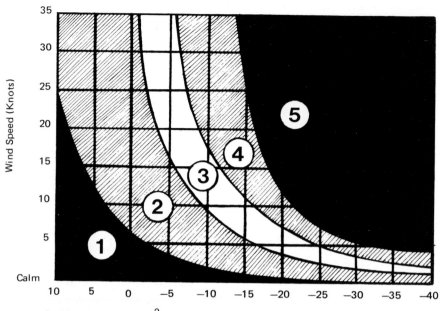

1 Comfort with normal precautions

2 Very cold, travel becomes uncomfortable on overcast days

3 Bitterly cold, travel becomes uncomfortable even on clear sunny days

4 Freezing of human flesh begins. Travel and life in temporary shelter becomes disagreeable

5 Exposed flesh will freeze in less than one minute

Fig 4:8

The body cools much more quickly in moving air (wind) than in still air. The wind chill chart shows this effect clearly. The importance of sheltering cooled victims from wind must always be remembered

transfer. This 'secondary drowning' can be delayed for up to 72 hours, so it is important to watch any immersion victim carefully, even if he appears to have recovered fully.

There is little difference between the effects of inhaling small amounts of fresh water or sea water. On the other hand, if the quantity reaching the lungs is large, fresh water leads to more rapid drowning because it is absorbed into the blood stream and damages the red cells.

In about 10% of cases of drowning, water does not reach the lungs because of a muscle spasm in the region of the larynx (so called 'dry drowning'). This spasm also cuts off the air supply and asphyxia results.

During prolonged immersion, the water has a 'squeezing' effect on the body causing loss of fluid (including blood plasma) through the kidneys. When the casualty is rescued, his body expands but there is now insufficient blood and fluid

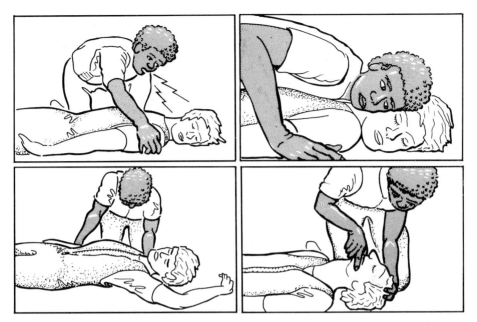

Fig 4:9 (top left) *Check for consciousness;* ***(top right)*** *Check for breathing*
(bottom left) *Turn casualty onto back;* ***(right)*** *Obtain a clear airway*

to fill the restored volume. As a result, blood circulation is inadequate and signs of shock may appear. This condition is known as 'post-immersion collapse'. The first aid treatment is as for shock and medical help should be sought.

Treatment of drowning

The priority of first aid treatment is cardiopulmonary resuscitation (CPR):

o If possible keep the casualty horizontal during rescue to counteract shock due to post-immersion collapse

o Turn the casualty on to his back, clear obvious debris, seaweed, etc. from the mouth, and if necessary start expired air resuscitation (EAR); continue with combined EAR and external chest compression

o Drowning casualties often vomit or have froth around their mouths; this makes EAR unpleasant and you must be prepared to continue resuscitation under these conditions

o Do not stop CPR even in apparently hopeless cases; complete recovery has been reported after prolonged resuscitation even when the casualty has initially appeared dead

o Keep the casualty lying flat with his feet raised to prevent the effects of shock

o All near-drowned casualties and those who have been successfully resuscitated, and in whom aspiration of water is even suspected, must be taken to hospital, however complete their apparent recovery, because of the risk of secondary drowning.

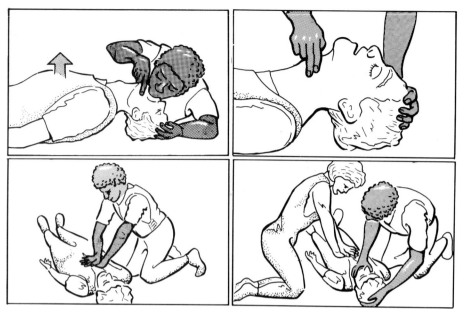

Fig 4:10 (top left) Maintain chin lift and neck extension. Breathe steadily into the mouth, watching from the corner of your eye for the chest to rise (top right) Check for pulse; (bottom left) Start chest compression (bottom right) After 15 compressions, lift chin, extend neck, give two breaths

Expired air resuscitation

The sequence of action is as follows:

1 Check whether casualty is conscious

2 Check whether casualty is breathing

Look for movement of the chest. Feel and listen at the mouth for breathing, which should be quiet - a wheeze or rattle indicates an obstruction. Look for cyanosis - this is a bluish discolouration of the face ears and nails which shows that blood contains very little oxygen.

3 Turn casualty onto his back

It is important to turn the casualty over as quickly as possible, whilst exercising great care, particularly not to injure his head.

4 Obtain a clear airway

With the casualty on his back, quickly remove any debris from the mouth - leave well-fitting dentures in place. Remove helmet chinstraps and loosen tight clothing around his neck. Lift his chin with the fingers of one hand placed under the bony part of the jaw, near the point of the chin. At the same time extend his neck by pressing downwards, just above his forehead, with your other hand; this will often allow breathing to re-start, or obstructed breathing to improve. If breathing does not become normal, then continue to next stage.

5   Start expired air resuscitation

Maintain chin lift and neck extension. Pinch the soft part of his nose closed with finger and thumb. Allow the casualty's mouth to open a little, but maintain chin lift. Take a full deep breath and place your lips around his mouth making sure you have a good seal. Breath steadily into his mouth, watching from the corner of your eye for his chest to rise. Maintaining chin lift and neck extension, take your mouth away from the casualty, take another full breath and repeat the sequence. Do this for a total of four full breaths to ensure that the casualty's lungs are fully expanded. If breathing does not re-start, then continue to next stage.

6   Check casualty's pulse

The best pulse to feel in an emergency is the carotid, which is found in the neck. Ensure that the casualty's neck is extended. Feel for the 'adams apple' - a hard piece of cartilage in the midlle of the neck about halfway between chin and upper part of the chest. Slide two fingers from the 'adams apple' sideways until they meet a strap-like muscle. Just beneath this can be felt the pulse. If the pulse is present, maintain chin lift and neck extension and repeat EAR at the rate of one breath every five seconds. If the pulse is absent, assume that cardiac arrest has occurred provided the casualty is: still unconscious; making no movement; deathly pale or blue.

7   Start external chest compression

Ensure that the casualty is on a flat, firm surface. Feel for the lower borders of the rib cage, removing outer clothing if necessary. Identify the lower end of the breast bone, which is where the two rib borders meet. Place the heel of one hand on the centre of the lower half of the breast bone, with your other hand on top. Keep your arms straight and your fingers interlocked and raised to ensure that pressure is not applied over the ribs. Rock forwards until your arms are vertical, compressing the breast bone. Release the pressure, then repeat at a rate of one compression per second (60 per minute).

Notes:

o   In an unconscious adult you should aim to press down approximately 4-5 cm and apply only enough pressure to achieve this

o   At all times, the pressure should be firm, controlled and applied vertically. Erratic or violent action is dangerous

o   Try and spend the same time in the 'compressed' as the 'released' phase.

The combination of expired air resuscitation (EAR) and external chest compression (ECC) is termed cardiopulmonary resuscitation (CPR). If you are on your own:

o   After 15 compressions of ECC immediately lift the chin and extend the neck

o   Give two full breaths of EAR

o   Return immediately to ECC

o   With an assistant: quickly decide who is to undertake EAR. This rescuer should obtain a good airway and give a full breath after each fifth compression of ECC.

99

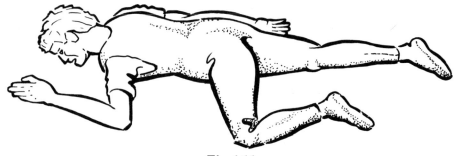

Fig 4:11
The recovery position

The recovery position

Any unconscious or semi-conscious casualty must be placed in the recovery position. This ensures that breathing remains unobstructed and yet can be observed closely. Once a drowned person starts to breathe, kneel at his side and roll him towards you. Place his upper arm and thigh at right angles to his body. This supports his chest and abdomen and keeps them clear of the ground, making it easier for him to breath. Adjust his lower arm so that it is back, holding the jaw forward and mouth open. Be prepared to re-start resuscitation if necessary.

WEIL'S DISEASE

Weil's disease (or leptospirosis icterohaemorrhagiae) is an infection caused by bacteria carried in rats' urine, which contaminates water and wet river banks. The bacteria does not survive long in dry conditions. It can occur in any water, including swift streams and rivers. The likelihood of becoming infected is greater from stagnant or slow moving waterways.

Weil's disease is rare, but it can be a serious illness requiring hospital treatment and can lead to kidney or liver failure. One patient in 19 dies with it. The disease is a notifiable illness.

It is caught by absorbing the bacteria through the skin and the mucous membranes of the mouth and eyes. The bacteria gets into the bloodstream more easily if you have a cut on your skin or feet, or if you do capsize drill or rolling.

Should you fall ill with the symptoms after canoeing, particularly within a period of 3-19 days, then see your doctor immediately. The most common symptoms are: temperature, an influenza-like illness, and joint and muscle pains (pains in the calf muscles are often particularly noticeable). Tell your doctor you have been canoeing and where, and show him the information on the back page of the BCU members' Year Book. It is important that antibiotics are administered straight away if there is any chance of your having contracted Weil's disease. A blood test is usually taken to confirm the illness. A local laboratory using an ELISA test can supply a result to a medical practitioner within 2-3 hours of the commencement of the test.

In summary:

o Avoid capsize drill or rolling in stagnant or slow moving water, particularly in areas of obvious rat infestation

o Inform the district council and insist upon rodent control should you suspect a significant rat population exists on your local waters

o Wash or shower after canoeing

o Cover minor scratches on exposed parts of the body with waterproof plaster

o Use footwear to avoid cutting feet

o If you have a flu-like illness after canoeing go to your GP early - tell him/her you are a canoeist

o Let the BCU know, if you are unlucky enough to contract the disease.

FIRST AID

First aid is largely a matter of common-sense, but it needs to be enlightened common-sense. Total competence is only achieved through pursuing a course of training, and studying the manual of one of the first aid services. The basic principles should be known by all:

o Keep calm

o Do not move the patient unless absolutely essential

o Seek professional help

o Deal with priorities

o Do not give food or drink

o Be firm but gentle - reassure the patient.

Minor accidents that require professional assistance should be dealt with by the nearest hospital with an accident and emergency department. For a serious accident dial 999. Speak slowly, clearly and briefly. Give your location, name and address, the type of accident, and the number of casualties.

Dealing with priorities

In an emergency situation it is vital to establish the correct order of priorities. These are:

1 Breathing/heart stopped
2 Bleeding
3 Injuries
4 Shock

Treatment of wounds

In any case of external haemorrhage, cover the wound with a dressing, apply pressure directly on to it for at least 10 minutes. Do not remove the original dressing, but add further ones if necessary. Tie with a tight bandage, but do not tourniquet. The limb below the bandage should be warm and pink. Reduce blood flow by raising the limb and/or keeping it cool.

If there is a foreign body in the wound, do not use direct pressure, but stop the flow of blood at a pressure point between the heart and the wound, as close to the latter as possible. Do not attempt to remove large foreign bodies as a massive haemorrhage may ensue.

Treatment for shock

Shock is a factor in all cases of injury or sudden collapse.

o   Treat the cause if possible; stop any external bleeding; dress burns; reassure the casualty

o   Lay the casualty flat with legs raised, unless he is unconscious when he should be placed in the recovery position

o   Keep him warm enough to prevent heat loss

o   Give nothing by mouth because of the possibility that surgery and hence anaesthetics, will be needed; if the stomach is full, anaesthesia often produces vomiting and, in the unconscious casualty, inhalation of vomit into the lungs

o   Get the casualty to hospital as a matter of urgency.

If you cannot move the casualty (eg if spinal injury is suspected) watch his respiration carefully. Close the mouth and hold the jaw closed. Pull very slightly on the lower jaw to keep the tongue held forward. Do not leave a casualty alone in this position.

Other and minor accidents

Bites

From animals - clean the wound, stop the bleeding, visit the doctor or hospital casualty unit

From snakes - do not make an incision; kill the snake so it can be identified, make the casualty lie down, keep him cool and raise the limb to slow down the blood-flow to the heart; remove to a doctor or hospital, but do not exert the patient

From insects - apply a soothing cream or calamine lotion.

Burns or scalds

Do not remove clothing adhering to the burn, or cover with ointment or spirits. Do not burst the blisters. For superficial burns wash immediately under cold, running water. Dry without rubbing. Cover with a dry sterile dressing. For extensive burns roll the casualty very gently, still clothed, into a clean sheet. Medical help must be obtained directly.

Foreign bodies

In the nose - do not meddle with tweezers or pointed objects; ask casualty to take a deep breath, block the other nostril, and breathe out hard; do not try this with small children - get to a doctor

In the ear - a live insect can be rendered harmless with a few drops of castor oil; do not use tweezers or anything similar, but let the doctor remove the foreign body

In the eye - do not let casualty rub the eye; keep the eye protected, preferably closed and free from movement, and get to a hospital casualty department.

Fractures

Immobilise the joint. Legs can be tied together with triangular bandages, ties, belts or scarves. Tie the knots on the unaffected side, padded with handkerchiefs or something similar.

Hyperthermia (heatstroke)

Victims usually have a pale face with a pinched and worried expression, and a high temperature (but possibly not sweating), a racing pulse, and shallow breathing. Cool the casualty by uncovering him; sponge him and give lots of cool fluids. Keep in the shade and give well salted crisps to eat if he feels like it.

A death occurred in France due to a paddler climbing out of a gorge after losing his canoe on a hot day, still wearing his wet suit. It is advisable to remove wet suits or excessive clothing in such situations.

Cramp

Cramp and 'pins and needles' are often confused. Cramp is a painful spasm of the muscles, especially when the circulation is impaired in cold conditions. The pain may be so severe as to completely immobilise the victim. Normal treatment is to stretch the muscle out, against its contracting spasm, and to pummel or massage it firmly towards the heart. Cramp usually occurs in the sole of the foot or the calf muscle, but any muscle of the body may suffer.

Pins and needles

These are caused by pressure on a nerve causing its temporary 'death' and the consequent loss of any feeling or control of the part of the body normally controlled by that nerve. The commonest form of pins and needles amongst canoeists is in the legs, nearly always caused through faulty design in the seat of the canoe, when pressure on the pelvic bone will cause the nerves of the legs to 'die'. The sensation is an aching limb, but is nothing like as painful as cramp. The cure is movement.

Head injuries

Anyone suffering a severe blow on the head, whether or not they become unconscious, should be seen by a doctor because of the danger of a haemorrhage. Signs to watch for are drowsiness, vomiting and unequal dilation of pupils.

Anti-tetanus protection

Canoeists, due to the nature of their activity, should consider maintaining the anti-tetanus course of injections. These can be arranged through your own doctor.

EQUIPMENT

The term 'equipment' does not imply 'lucky charm'. Criticism has been levelled at the departure of kayaks from our coasts, festooned like the proverbial Christmas tree, but with a consequential increased call upon the rescue services ! Safety is a total concept. It is only when the right gear is used by a trained person, that risk is minimised.

Personal flotation aids

As will be deduced from the facts surrounding hypothermia, apart from preventing drowning, a buoyancy aid or lifejacket prolongs survival time in water by allowing the victim to conserve body heat through not expending energy in the effort to stay afloat.

Buoyancy aids

Some aids are made to no particular standard, and are therefore to be avoided. Buoyancy aids particularly suitable for canoeing are made to the specification agreed jointly between the British Canoe Union and the British Canoe Manufacturers Association: BCU/BCMA BA 83. This ensures a standard protection and a minimum inherent buoyancy of 6 kg which conforms to the International Canoe Federation (ICF) rules for competition. Other aids which may be suitable, depending upon the design of the particular model, are those which are produced to the specification of the Ship and Boat Builders National Federation (SBBNF/ 79), or its more recent name, 'BMIF Standard'.

In so far as it adds to one's own buoyancy, a buoyancy aid helps a person to remain on the surface and facilitates working whilst there. It will not, however, float the wearer face uppermost and support him in that position, should he become unconscious.

Good buoyancy aids are particularly necessary for competition, surfing (which should only be undertaken in kayaks or canoes by competent canoeists) and rapid rivers. The types most popular for canoeing are either the one-piece, or zipped, waistcoat variety. Some are available with pockets for touring canoeists.

Lifejackets

Lifejackets made to British Standards Institution (BSI) specification 3595/81 are made to guaranteed standards of manufacture, and are also designed to do their best to save the wearer's life should the victim become incapacitated. They are particularly applicable to sea or open water touring.

The BSI has recommended different types of lifejacket for different uses. The BCU considers that only one of the six types available is suitable for canoeing. This is the one with two stages of buoyancy: an 'inherent' stage, which brings the wearer to the surface and has all the advantages of the buoyancy aid, and an inflatable stage which will do its best to keep the wearer afloat, on his back, at the correct angle, and with the best presentation to the waves, even if the victim becomes unconscious. The inherent stage gives 6 kg of buoyancy. When fully inflated (orally), the lifejacket has 16 kg buoyancy. 'Inherent buoyancy' comprises closed cell plastic foam.

The current BCU recommendation on the wearing of personal flotation aids is:

'It is recommended that buoyancy aids to BCU/BCMA Standard BA 83 be worn by novices for all canoeing activities, and for white water paddling at all levels.

Life jackets to BSI 3595/81 or buoyancy aids to SBBNF (now known as BMIF) standard are normally suitable alternatives, but are not permitted for BCU ranking competitions. For canoe polo additional body protection may be required'.

The leaflet *BCU/BCMA BA-83: A Standard for Buoyancy Aids* is available from BCU headquarters and explains the specifications and construction for canoeing buoyancy aids.

Faced with a choice between wearing a buoyancy aid or a lifejacket, most canoeists will choose the buoyancy aid because, overall, it is a more functional piece of equipment. The thick flotation foam fits snugly around the trunk providing superb insulation of the body core and forming flexible body armour against rocks, trees, etc. This alone sets the buoyancy aid ahead as a piece of canoeing equipment. It also allows a canoeist who has accidentally become a swimmer to choose whether to swim on his front or his back. In surf or in wide rapids this kind of flexibility in the body's attitude in the water can improve the chances of survival dramatically. The simple comfort and fit of a buoyancy aid means that it offers the minimum of interference to the paddling movements whereas the bulky front loading of a lifejacket is a great hindrance.

A lifejacket is designed to float an unconscious body in deep water but this is a very uncommon accident scenario in canoeing. It is cold water or rocks in a shallow river which most often cause problems and therefore the versatility of the buoyancy aid makes it a more useful piece of equipment.

Whatever type of flotation aid is worn, it will be useless unless properly fitted. Careful attention must always be paid to the manufacturer's instructions. A leader must check the wearing of flotation by those under his supervision.

Crash helmets

The wearing of a helmet for white water paddlers in kayak or canoe is absolutely essential. Even in wide, deep stretches of rapids, there is a risk of hitting your head against other boats or even against your own. Other aspects of canoeing which involve the wearing of a helmet are canoe polo, surf kayaking, slalom, river racing and sea touring when making a landing through waves onto a rocky shore.

A canoeing helmet must have an outer shell which is resistant to both impact and abrasion. It should be made from light weight materials and have a strong chin strap. Research has shown that chin cups are not advisable. A helmet should fit snugly onto your head and, with the chin strap secured, it should not be possible to rock the helmet backwards by pulling upwards on the front rim. The best helmets have impact absorbing foam liners which also improve the grip of the helmet on your head. You should ensure that your helmet protects your forehead and temples; always check this in a mirror before buying one. Remember that a proper fit is just as important as the quality.

Kayakers working in extreme white water are at greatest risk to head impact and abrasion. Many use full face helmets or face guards and substantial foam liners inside the helmet shells.

Clothing for the canoeist

It is important that clothing should protect the body, keep it warm and yet not interfere with its movements. This always presents problems in a water based sport, and canoeing makes special demands on your body. The equipment you need depends on the type of canoe you are paddling, the weather and your resistance to cold.

Conditions are seldom constant during the day. Temperatures rise and fall; wind force and direction change; sunshine varies in intensity and direction. The paddler's activity also varies during the course of a days canoeing. Competition canoeists warm up, race, then cool down. Recreational canoeists paddle at varying speeds and may then stop to rest, eat, or enjoy the scenery. Thus, basic clothing sense means suiting clothing to the varying needs of insulation required by changes in weather and activity.

In the warmest conditions, a pair of shorts, tee-shirt and some form of footwear will prove suitable. The worst fabric when wet is cotton and should be avoided. In the cold, the problem of body insulation assumes great importance. Therefore you will require two basic layers of clothing:

o   An insulating layer

o   A water/windproof layer.

Insulation is better from several layers of garments rather than a single layer of the same total thickness. This is because more dead air is trapped in and between thin layers than in one thick layer. Multiple layers also allow the use of special purpose garments, each fulfilling a particular clothing need.

A whole host of firms now produce base-layer garments known as 'thermal wear' from man-made polyfibres. Worn on the torso and/or legs, these need to be thin, close fitting, comfortable and designed to transport perspiration outwards, away from the skin.

The intermediate layer needs to be thicker than that of the base. 'Fibrepile' or 'fleece', which are 'fur'-like fabrics made from polyester, nylon or acrylic are ideal. These fabrics warm quickly by trapping air to provide a thermal barrier. They are warm when damp/wet and are

Two popular clothing systems for paddlers

Plate 4:a (top)
The basic paddling jacket or 'cag'. There should be no restriction to arm movement. Wrist and neck seals made from neoprene are well worth having

Plate 4:b (bottom)
The 'dry cag' is a more expensive garment. Efficient latex seals at wrists and neck make this appeal to the white water paddler

106

Plate 4:c
Fibre pile suit (above); hard wearing, quick drying and warm, is worn underneath, with windproof, water repellant cag and trousers on top (left). In colder conditions, a polypropylene, long sleeved vest worn against the body, can also be added

available in different thicknesses for use in different layers; but they are not windproof. As canoeing is a wet sport, the water/windproof layer (the shell) will protect the insulation layer from the majority of external moisture, and counteract the windchill effect.

For canoeists there are specially cut and shaped 'paddling jackets' sometimes called 'canoe cags'. These are made from coated nylon and have close fitting wrist and neck seals to stop water penetration.

A pair of overtrousers made from the same material is very useful. Such trousers need to be held up very securely when paddling in rough water otherwise in the event of a swim they can be torn from the waist to form a lethal binding around the legs. Shoulder straps or a strong waist-tie cord are the safest methods.

Wet suits are very popular with non-competitive paddlers. They are uniquely functional in that they can provide the innermost insulating layer and also form a very practical outer layer. Wet suits come in all kinds of garment shapes, but the most common design used by paddlers is the one piece, sleeveless suit with full length legs, often referred to as the 'long john'. This, combined with a synthetic or light woollen, long sleeved under garment, with a paddling jacket on top of the lot, gives a good, versatile clothing system. Bearing in mind that British rivers and coastal waters are cold all year round, the 'long john' wet suit is a very sensible piece of real safety clothing for canoeists. In addition to its superb heat retaining

Plate 4:d
Sleeveless one-piece wet suit with an
appropriate long sleeved insulating
vest or sweater underneath. This
system is superior if prolonged
immersion in water is a possibility.
The wet suit also gives greater leg
protection for a paddler likely to be
taking a swim in white water.

qualities (especially in immersion) a wet suit provides considerable flotation. In the event of a swim in serious white water the distribution of this extra flotation around the hips and legs is a big advantage. The padding provided by the suit in such a situation is second to none.

For beginners, the availability and relatively low cost of wet suits has taken canoeing beyond the summer-only activity that it would otherwise have been. Many outdoor centres would have much more limited canoeing programmes were it not for their supply of wet suits.

Wet suits are made from material called neoprene. This is essentially a synthetic rubber filled with bubbles and is available in several thicknesses starting at around 2mm and going up to 6 or 7mm. The thin suits of around 2 to 3mm are most suitable for canoeing. Paddlers are rarely immersed for long periods of time and so the rather restricting thicker neoprene is unnecessary. Modern neoprene is extremely flexible and yet retains its hard wearing qualities. Suits with an outer and inner lining of nylon are especially durable. The outer nylon coating however, holds a little water and through the process of evaporation can be cool to wear when standing around on a windy day. A simple way to overcome this is to wear light waterproofs on top of the suit.

In recent years, the dry suit and dry cagoule have become popular, especially with paddlers whose canoeing involves frequent dousings in very cold water. The

Plate 4:e
Paddle mitts. Simple nylon sleeves which
fit around the paddle shaft and keep the
wind off. A remarkably simple way to keep
the hands warm

dry suit is made from waterproof nylon fabric with rubber seals at the wrists, neck and ankles. The wearer gets into the full suit through a rather expensive watertight zip. The dry cagoule seals at the wrist, neck and waist. Suitable insulating clothing is worn under the dry suit making it a more comfortable system than the wet suit to wear for long periods. Sea expedition paddlers in Arctic waters and white water paddlers in very cold rivers are finding the comfort and flexibility of a dry suit a distinct advantage.

The choice of footwear is a matter of personal preference. An old pair of training shoes is sufficient for summer paddling and can be uprated by wearing woolen socks during the colder months. Stiff soled training shoes which have the sole rolled over at the toe at the front should be treated with caution as there has been a case of a paddler being trapped in his low-volume slalom kayak by such a shoe becoming wedged. It is also sensible to keep laces short to prevent snagging on the inside of the canoe. For white water or winter paddling, a pair of purpose made wet suit boots is ideal. You can also make or buy neoprene socks which are worn inside polythene sandals or over-sized training shoes. Choose a sole pattern which gives good grip for walking along the river bank.

A great amount of heat is lost through the head so a woollen ski hat is useful in winter paddling.

Keeping hands warm whilst canoeing is important but not always easy. The most popular and serviceable system is paddle mitts. These are cuff-like gauntlets made from proofed nylon which attach around the paddle shaft. The hands grip the shaft inside the loose-fitting mitts. Mitts lined with synthetic insulating fabric are available for Arctic weather. You can easily design and construct your own paddle mitts by using material saved from an old spray cover or overtrousers.

Canoes and kayaks

There is no such thing as a 'safe' canoe. This is an absolutely true statement: it is the canoeist who must be safe. Safety comes through training, experience and developing safe attitudes. In Britain, boats marked with the British Canoe Manufacturers Association (now British Association of Canoe Traders) label are constructed to a high standard.

Specialised kayaks and canoes for specific aspects of the sport vary enormously in their construction characteristics. However, the following basic safety features should be looked for.

Internal flotation

The canoe should be fitted with a buoyant material on the inside which will keep it afloat when completely full of water. This requires 25kg of flotation positioned evenly in front and rear as the minimum for safety. The buoyancy should be secure inside the boat so that turbulence cannot flush it out. Most canoes use a closed cell foam for this purpose and this provides the added advantage of strengthening the boat. For safety, you cannot have too much internal buoyancy and an excellent system is to use air bags to supplement the standard flotation provided by the manufacturer. Air bags are very adaptable and allow you either to use storage space inside the boat or fill it with the fully inflated air bags. It has been shown that, in white water, a boat with maximum internal flotation has many safety advantages. The much feared pinning of a kayak against an obstacle by the force of the current is considerably less serious if the swamped boat floats high on the surface. With minimum flotation it sinks deep into the current and increases significantly the forces exerted on the boat and its occupant.

Footrests

A kayak without a footrest is a danger to its paddler, especially in rough water. The footrest also provides an important base for the paddling action; travelling any distance without one is very tiring. Footrests are dangerous if they can trap the paddler's feet. Most manufacturers have taken this into account in the design of their footrests and there are now several very good types available. In surf and white water paddling, the footrest is likely to be subjected to considerable impact forces. It follows, therefore, that footrests used in these circumstances must be very strong and it is also important that the whole foot is supported. This reduces the possibility of foot and ankle damage. A full plate footrest covered with a foam shock absorbing pad is the best arrangement so far developed for this kind of paddling. See Plate 4:f.

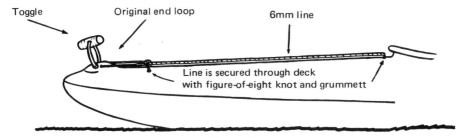

Toggle   Original end loop   6mm line

Line is secured through deck
with figure-of-eight knot and grummett

Fig 4:12

*Fitting decklines. Anchor the cockpit end through a hole in the deck with a
tight-fitting neoprene washer. Tie the other end into the boat's original grab
loop with a secure knot. Keep the line taught by re-tying this knot when
necessary. A simple toggle can also be threaded into the original grab loop*

End toggles, grab handles and deck lines

If you take a swim in rough water, it usually makes sense to keep hold of your boat.
The plastic skin of modern kayaks is extremely slippery making some form of
handle attachments essential. Once again there are several very functional
systems used, each with its own special advantages. For white water and sea
canoeing uses, these grab handles, toggles or decklines are especially important
and you need to give careful thought to your own system before attempting
anything but the simplest of journeys. This process of thinking about and refining
your own personal equipment so that you are comfortable and happy with it is
very much a part of the sport. Adapting equipment is not difficult and both
instructors and manufacturers will be keen to advise and help you.

There are two particular traps with regard to safety. One is to beware of loops
threaded through the ends of boats. They can crush fingers if the boat spins whilst
you are holding on. The other is much more serious and it is to do with fitting
decklines. These must not run past the cockpit, ie, the full length of the boat, if
there is any possibility of using the boat in white water. They can trap you if the
boat folds around an obstacle. Decklines are invaluable in any situation where the
boat has to be manhandled. They extend your grip on the slippery boat to its whole
length instead of only the ends and the cockpit area. In deep water rescues at sea
this can speed up the rescue dramatically and therefore can be a determining
factor in surviving a capsize emergency. In the same way, decklines are an
advantage in an entrapment situation on white water. Some paddlers, however,
feel that the risk of entangling decklines in trees is too great to justify their use
in white water. The way to reduce this risk is to ensure that the lines remain tight.
A suggestion for fitting decklines to a kayak to be used for sea and/or white water
paddling is shown in Fig. 4:12. The lines are fitted centrally extending from each
end grab handle to the cockpit.

Cockpit

Many modern kayaks, including those used in white water, have large cockpit
openings making it very easy to get in or out of the boat. In a few special cases
there are good reasons for keeping cockpits small but, for most purposes, a large

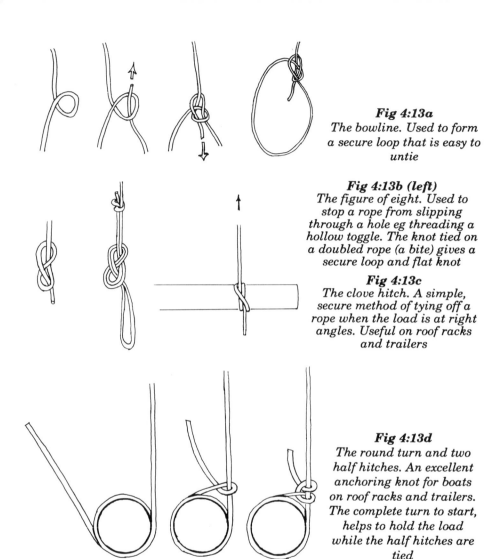

Fig 4:13a
The bowline. Used to form a secure loop that is easy to untie

Fig 4:13b (left)
The figure of eight. Used to stop a rope from slipping through a hole eg threading a hollow toggle. The knot tied on a doubled rope (a bite) gives a secure loop and flat knot

Fig 4:13c
The clove hitch. A simple, secure method of tying off a rope when the load is at right angles. Useful on roof racks and trailers

Fig 4:13d
The round turn and two half hitches. An excellent anchoring knot for boats on roof racks and trailers. The complete turn to start, helps to hold the load while the half hitches are tied

cockpit opening is very useful and, especially with beginners, helps to reduce the feeling of being trapped inside the boat. Many white water paddlers also believe that these large cockpits are safer for paddling rapids. Fast touring and racing kayaks are fitted with even larger cockpits. This, combined with the fast, easy cruising characteristics of this type of craft makes it a very suitable way of introducing people to canoeing. See Chapter 5.

For paddlers specifically interested in white water kayaking, the BCU produce a booklet called *A Standard for Kayaks Designed for use in White Water*. This gives useful guidance on boat design with special reference to safety.

Spray decks

A spray deck keeps the water out and the heat in. The cheapest is made from nylon and the most expensive from wet suit material (neoprene). A better quality spray deck gives you a superior seal both around the cockpit rim and around your trunk. The flexibility of neoprene means that it has a greater tolerance to different shapes and sizes of cockpit. The rougher and more committing the piece of water you are attempting to paddle in, the more important will be the quality of the spray deck.

A spray deck should always be fitted with a release strap of some kind. This is the means by which the spray deck skirt is released from the cockpit rim so it must be in good condition and be positioned as soon as you fix on the spray deck.

Spare paddles

Kayak paddles are carried as spares in split form; ie, the shaft is jointed at the mid-point. This makes it possible to store them inside the boat until they are needed. On the sea, the ability to hand out a paddle swiftly to a capsized canoeist, who has let go of his in heavy seas, can be a significant factor in preventing a situation from worsening and, for this reason, it is recommended that the leader and his competent helpers carry split paddles strapped to the stern decks of their boats.

Canoeist's knife

A folding knife with sharp blade is a useful tool for both sea and white water canoeists. The uses are wide and varied and in some white water emergencies not being able to cut a rope could result in a fatal accident. Only a stainless steel knife will stand up to the corrosive action of sea water. The knife should be simple and have a blade which can be opened with cold hands.

Paddle park

In any situation where the canoeist is likely to have to carry out deep water rescues, especially in difficult conditions, a paddle park is necessary. This can be a 5 or 7mm diameter marine elastic stretched across the fore or stern-deck, but is basically a means of retaining the paddle(s) when left floating alongside the canoe. Commercially produced systems are available. A short length of 3 mm line, or marine elastic, attached to the canoe, is adequate. This can have either a loop through which a paddle blade will just pass, or a plastic hook on the end, which clips on to the line after it has been taken round the shaft.

Repair kit

A minimum repair kit is a roll of good quality 5cm wide insulating tape and a knife. For open water canoeing, however, where it may be necessary to apply a patch to a wet boat, a quantity of mastic tape, available from hardware stores, is advised. This non-hardening tape is messy to handle so it is worth cutting it up into 20cm lengths and carrying it inside a polythene bag.

First aid kit

Basic items which should be included in a first aid kit are:

o One triangular bandage
o Two medium wound dressings
o A crepe bandage
o A strip of plaster or six plasters
o Box of matches
o Pair of fine tweezers
o Pencil and paper
o Small pair of pliers
o Pair of scissors
o Headache tablets such as those containing paracetamol.

This list would obviously need to be enlarged upon depending upon the size of the party, the duration of the journey and the particular hazards of the country involved. There is currently concern over the implications of administering medication such as headache tablets, and instructors are advised to act cautiously in this respect. It is is not an illegal act to do so, but a claim for damages could be made in the civil court if a person, particularly a juvenile, suffered a harmful reaction. On the other hand, where a group is operating far from qualified help, it is unlikely that the prudent administering of simple medication to relieve unnecessary suffering from headache and similar ailment, would be cause for an action. If in doubt, an instructor should obtain parental consent with regard to the use of particular drugs in such instances.

TRAINING

A programme for learning canoeing skills is outlined elsewhere. If 'wild' or open water canoeing is the aim, be it sea or inland, then a gradual progression is vital, learning to cope with increasingly difficult conditions, but in controlled situations.

When things do go wrong, however, remember first principles. It is the maintenance of the safety of those who are not yet in trouble that must normally be given priority. There is no point in rushing to perform a heroic rescue on one person, only to discover, having effected it, that six others are now in jeopardy. This is easy to say, but not so easy to carry out in an emergency. Those who lead must cultivate a habit of thinking ahead, and delegating to other competent paddlers initial responsibility to rescue or tow when incidents occur, ensuring that someone is always giving consideration to the total safety of the group.

Capsize drill

Statistics show that an ability to swim, allied to the wearing of a personal flotation aid, and undertaking a basic course, virtually preclude any likelihood of drowning from a canoe in normal circumstances. Most 'canoeing' fatalities occur to non-swimmers, or poor swimmers who are invariably not wearing a buoyancy aid or lifejacket. Whatever type of canoeing is being pursued, the ability to cope with a capsize should be part of basic training. This does not mean that capsize drill must be carried out at the beginning of the first session, or even necessarily

Fig 4:14 *Short tow*   **Fig 4:15** *Rafted tow*

during that session, but must be practised at some stage. Where small cockpit, decked kayaks or canoes are involved, this should be earlier, rather than later, in a course.

Not everyone enjoys constantly falling out of boats, particularly in mid-winter, and the degree of emphasis put on capsize and rescue drills should be adapted to the type of canoeing that the individual wishes to pursue. It is a far more vital factor for the white water and surf paddler, or the sea tourist, than for others. Where a swimming pool is used for initial training, great emphasis must be put on grabbing and maintaining a hold on the canoe immediately on surfacing, and the routine practised out of doors at the first suitable opportunity.

Towing

The ability to attach a tow-line swiftly can play a significant part in preventing any 'incident' from developing into an 'epic'. In any situation, apart from the most sheltered of conditions, where beginners are involved, a leader needs to be able to pull a canoeist to safety efficiently, either away from danger out of the path of an oncoming vessel, or back to land. If the group is drifting too far away from the bank or the shore, the one student who cannot control his or her direction at this time, is a potential disaster. Once a group is journeying down river or on the sea, then the ability to tow one another is vital.

There is no single 'right' way of towing, but there are some basic principles that can be stated, and some ideas that can be incorporated. For simple situations, a small loop just aft of the cockpit allows a toggle to be threaded through, and a quick efficient tow effected.

It is possible to 'tow' the paddler in difficulties by merely rafting on, facing the rescuer by leaning across his boat and holding on, keeping the bow of his own canoe in close to the rescuer, and assisting the steering by pulling with the knees.

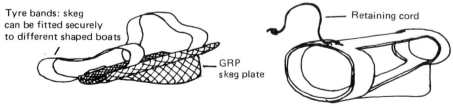

Tyre bands: skeg can be fitted securely to different shaped boats

GRP skeg plate

Retaining cord

Fig 4:16
Two designs of skeg. Many improvised versions are possible

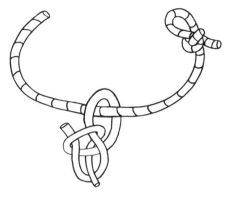

Fig 4:17 (left)

A cam cleat provides an excellent towing attachment (fitted to the rear deck, close to the cockpit). The towing paddler is unhindered, and can release the tow rope with a single action

Fig 4:18

An improvised waist-attached towing system. The waist belt is joined by trapping one end in the noose of a slip knot. The tow line is attached to the waist belt by a small loop formed with a bowline. Keep the waist belt short and use floating rope

There is then the simple means of assisting a beginner who cannot control his or her own direction, by nudging the stern with your bow. This will apply where there is a beam or quartering wind, and where the novice is constantly letting the boat turn up into the wind. (All kayaks have this tendency once they are being propelled forwards). The experienced paddler merely has to sit down-wind, at the beginner's stern, and prevent it from skating away.

In this situation, unless conditions have deteriorated beyond the ability of the whole group, the individual who is having difficulty with steering needs help with technique. The most common cause of a sweep stroke failing to correct a boat that is turning off course because of the wind, is that the paddle blade is taken from the water too soon. It needs to drive in close to the stern, to correct the 'skating' movement that occurs with slalom-type hulls. The use of a detachable 'skeg' is advised for the person in a general purpose or slalom boat who really cannot cope, and two types are illustrated (Fig 4:16). These can be carried by the leader and fitted as necessary.

A full length tow-line should permit another canoe to be pulled about a metre astern of the rescuer. If this distance is too great, a considerable amount of 'veering' will occur to the boat being towed. If it is too short, there will be constant collisions. For long craft, such as the eskimo kayak, the line can pass through the stern loop, which avoids it 'sweeping' the rear deck, and keeps the distance between towing point and casualty short, minimising the 'veering off' effect. Most prefer to tow from a point just behind the cockpit, or from the body. A 'cam cleat',

Fig 4:19
This kind of snap link, made from stainless steel, is suitable for the clipping on and off of a tow line. Choose a size that you can handle with numb fingers

available from dinghy chandlers, is most suitable as a towing point. A bridge (metal hoop through which the line passes) is necessary to avoid the rope jerking free. 'Funnel cleats', 'jamming cleats' and similar, are best avoided as stones can become wedged in them.

The cleat does not need to be fixed exactly in the middle of the canoe, and is best not so positioned, as this makes for very tricky attachment and release - especially in difficult conditions with cold fingers ! About a hand's width in from the gunnel on the control-hand side, is a useful position.

Some do not like to have fixtures and fittings on the boat unless absolutely necessary and consequently prefer to tow with the line attached around the waist. This is an efficient system, and allows the body to act as an additional 'shock absorber'. When towing at sea, for instance, there will be times when the rescuer is 'surfing' down a wave, and the casualty is climbing up the back of another one. It is then that a 'shock-cord' incorporated into the tow-line comes into effect, and when using the body as the towing point can also have an advantage. It is obviously vital that there is a foolproof quick release system if the line is attached around the waist. A method of achieving this is shown. Another method, favoured by some, is to use a belt, to which the tow line is attached in the middle of the back, and which secures with a velcro strip, or other quick-release mechanism, on the stomach side.

Shock-absorption has been mentioned, and it is worthwhile incorporating a short length of 5 or 7mm marine shock-cord into the system. Keep the line intact, so that should the shock-cord break, the tow-line does not part.

The final piece of equipment for efficient towing, is the snap link. There are a number on the market. Again, visit your local canoe supplier or dinghy chandler. Climbing karabiners are popular. Beware of 'fiddly' fittings, such as small brass shackles which need two fingernails to lift a tiny 'sprung' head. The shackle should be of stainless steel, and a reliable type for the job is shown. 4-6mm diameter polypropylene line, which floats, is ideal for tow-lines. If terylene or nylon is used, then a small float needs to be attached near the shackle.

Towing in white water

Attaching yourself or your boat to another boat in white water is something which must be done with extreme caution. It endangers your own life because of the possibility of the towing line snagging and even in wide, deep rapids your ability to manoeuvre and accelerate will be seriously hampered. It is best to let swamped kayaks wash out of rapids before attempting to pick them up. If the river is wide, towing with a quick release system, mounted onto the rear deck is best.

RAFTING

Forming a group of canoeists into a raft can make an ideal platform to effect repairs or rescues, to gather together for instructional purposes, to have tea, or to have fun. Choose an anchor man, and build the raft up from both sides, all facing in the same direction. Each person holding onto both partners' cockpit coaming is probably the most effective way of keeping the raft together.

A three-man raft can rescue an unconscious patient from the water. Assuming the patient is on the left, the middle man grabs the patient's arms and pulls up, while the man next to the patient capsizes to his right. The middle man hands the patient's arms to the right man who pulls the patient across the deck, while the middle man pulls up the left man in a clockwise eskimo rescue.

Canoeists will generally need to raft should a helicopter rescue be necessary because of the considerable down-draught from the rotor blades. Should the victim be in an exposure bag on a raft, it is vital that the bag is tightly secured. If it flies free as the casualty is winched away, it could seriously interfere with the aircraft.

SAFETY ON THE ROAD

Purpose-made webbing straps, with quick-release buckles, can be purchased and are ideal for attaching canoes and kayaks to roofracks.

Boats must be secured with a final rope at bow and stern onto the bumper of the car, for insurance purposes, and out of responsibility for the well-being of other road users, rather than reliance being placed on elastic straps alone. Where elastics are used on trailers, a rope through the toggle lines should be standard practice.

The following projections are permitted:

o   Up to .305m (1ft) on either side with a maximum load width 2.9m (9'6")
o   Up to 1.07m (3'6") forward or rearward.

Distinctive flags at the ends are required when there are forward or rearward projections of more than 1.07m (3'6") but less than 3.05m (10'). This is a dispensation for 'racing boats propelled solely by oars'. The normal load limit is 1.83m (6ft). For overhangs between 1.83m (6ft) and 3.05m (10ft) red and white striped triangular boards are required, plus a light at night. For projections over 3.05m (10ft) to front or rear prior notice to the police is required.

The AA publish *The Law and Vehicle Loads, The Law and Trailers,* and *The Law and Dual Purpose Vehicles.* It is an offence to tow a trailer in the outside lane of a 3-lane motorway.

Plate 4:g (i-iii)
A simple method for securing a boat to a roof rack or trailer. Tension the rope and make a round turn on a secure post. Finish off with a round turn and two half hitches. Seat the half hitches well down on themselves

Plate 4:h (i-iv)
For a load which requires more tension on the rope: form a small loop. Take the rope around the post and back through the loop. Tension, taking care not to crush the boats, and tie off at the loop with two half hitches

Plate 4:i (above)

Using tapes with self-locking buckles. Run the tape under the bar on the other side of the boat and adjust the buckle position to give you about 20cm above the bar. Take a turn around the bar and then tension through the buckle. Finish off with a couple of half-hitches and tuck surplus tape away

Plate 4:j (left)

Bolt-on uprights help to stabilise boats on the roof. They enable the carrying of boats on their sides, which lessens compression damage

5 Placid Water: Getting Started

David Train

David Train commenced paddling as a family man on the canals and slow moving rivers of the Midlands. He moved to Bedford, joined Viking Kayak Club and became interested in marathon racing. In 1972, he moved to Fladbury, a small village situated on the placid river Avon in Worcestershire. There he established a club which, in five short years, became and has remained a major force in the marathon and sprint racing world. His sons Stephen and Andrew are Britain's leading canoe racing paddlers, finalists in the Los Angeles Olympics and gold medallists at the 1988 Marathon World Championships. Involved at the top as Olympic Squad Canoe Coach, David has also been deeply committed as a member of the Coaching Scheme, teaching people of all ages and levels of ability. He is the architect of both the Marathon Racing and Placid Water Coaching Schemes.

INTRODUCTION

The Placid Water Teacher Award is a base teaching award of the Coaching Scheme. The Award is an ideal starting point for the leader, whether in a school, scout or guide group, or in a canoe club. This chapter covers part of the course. It traces the evolution of canoeing and the place in it of the Placid Water Award, the teaching philosophy, the base skills for single and double bladed paddling and points the way into where next to go. Basic safety, an essential element of the Teacher Award, is covered in another chapter.

THE EVOLVING CANOEING CULTURE

Canoeing is a fascinating and wide ranging activity. Rough water canoeing, placid water canoeing, sea canoeing, pool canoeing, slalom and racing, each with different canoes and kayaks, present the newcomer with a bewildering choice. Yet, this seemingly complicated array is based on two very ancient and simple craft - the kayak of the eskimo (Fig. 5:1) and the canoe of the indian (Fig. 5:2).

Around the world, canoeing as a sport and recreation has evolved in different ways, with each country developing its own canoeing culture, and within it the type of craft used. In America, the main interest has been centred around the Canadian canoe; in Germany and Scandinavia, both canoes and kayaks have traditionally formed the base of the sport. In all three, the canoe type used has been the same, but the kayaks are rather different. In Germany, the touring kayaks are bulky, whilst in Scandinavia slim designs for fast touring predominate. Some might say these differences occur because of the type of water available, but

Fig 5:1 and 5:2

The origins of the sport - the eskimo kayak (above) and the indian canoe (below)

a look at the evolution of British canoeing culture during the past one hundred and twenty years would suggest that the major changes are due to those who have written and taught, coupled with the availability of the canoes or kayaks.

The first period between 1865 and 1930 evolved from the founder of British canoeing, John McGregor. His book, *A Thousand Miles in the Rob Roy Canoe,* fired the imagination of the Victorians. The 'Rob Roy' was a stable kayak, went in a straight line and had a large cockpit (Fig. 5:3). Made of wood, it was easy to handle and a boat in which any beginner would have felt safe. In this period, wooden canoes were imported and were used for family outings and touring. The limitation to the growth was the cost of the wooden craft.

The second period from the 1930's to the 1950's is identified with the wooden frame and canvas kayaks and the start of the BCU Coaching Scheme. Percy Blandford wrote books and produced a host of designs for the Scout movement, which brought canoeing to a much wider number of people. The low cost, make-it-yourself PBK (Percy Blandford Kayak) designs, were, like the 'Rob Roy', stable, went in a straight line, and had large cockpits. The BCU Coaching Scheme was

Fig 5:3
The Rob Roy canoe on tour on an English canal

started in the 1950's by John Dudderidge. The original proficiency tests were designed around the use of the open cockpit straight line kayak.

The third period which had a massive impact on both the expansion and the change in direction of British canoeing culture started around the early 1960's. The BCU appointed its first Director of Coaching, Oliver Cock, in 1962, giving added drive to what was to become a very powerful teaching scheme. For various reasons, the Coaching Scheme became more and more interested in rough water canoeing. At the same time, glass reinforced plastic became available. Moulds were produced for the home builder and the designs reflected the interest in rough water. Thousands of kayaks were produced with rockered hulls and small cockpits. By 1980, the Coaching Scheme had 3,000 members almost all teaching in the close fitting cockpit kayak. So powerful had that culture become that, if the word 'canoeing' be mentioned to almost anyone in Britain, their immediate image would be that of a young man or woman strapped into a kayak, wearing a crash helmet and wetsuit, performing turns and rolls on rapidly moving rivers. This was a great image for the adventurous teenager but daunting for many others who might wish to paddle. Indeed, a far, far cry from the canoeing of McGregor.

In the late 1970's, new forces were emerging and promoting the use of open cockpit canoe and kayak. In 1981, Geoff Good, the new Director of Coaching edited the *Canoeing Handbook* and included chapters on 'Canadian Canoeing' and one on 'A Club Based on Flat Water'. In 1984, an awards system for the Canadian canoe was introduced and my small book *Canoeing the Fladbury Way* was published, becoming the catalyst for the introduction of the Placid Water Scheme. In 1987, the Placid Water Canoe Awards and the Canoe Star Tests were merged. As with the previous major changes, it has coincided with craft made of a different material - this time, polyethylene.

In essence, this fourth major change in British canoeing culture has completed the circle, teaching canoeing at the base in the canoes and kayaks of the founder of the sport, John McGregor. It is putting the bottom rung back in the ladder, making it possible for many more people to get started. It is indeed a very exciting time for anyone teaching canoeing in this age of leisure.

We have a teaching scheme that is within the reach of all non-specialist leaders, in education, scouts, guides, and so forth, as well as providing the base for the specialists. The canoes and kayaks can be produced in huge volume, and we have 4,000 miles of easy waterway available for people to get started on.

THE TEACHING PHILOSOPHY

I first started canoeing in PBK touring kayaks. These were stable, open cockpit, and were easy to paddle in a straight line. It was a family activity and with our three young sons we would go for a paddle and a picnic on a warm day. We would use the canoe on our holidays and occasionally go for a longer tour on placid water. I had read about marathon racing, thought I would like to have a go, and joined a canoe club.

After five years of paddling on top of the water I soon discovered how to get wet. There were two distinct factions in the club. The first, put me into a close-fitting-cockpit kayak, complete with a spray deck, turned me upside-down in the murky river Ouse, and told me to bang on the hull when I wished to be brought upright again. This was called 'drownproofing'.

The second faction put me in a very slim racing kayak, and were greatly amused each time I fell out. Despite this, I persevered, found myself a stable racing kayak and starting racing. When I first taught at Fladbury, I had become a Senior Instructor and used the close-fitting-cockpit, slalom type kayaks, that were generally favoured by the Coaching Scheme. I found that many of the people I was encouraging to 'have a go' were put off by the emphasis on capsize, and so I started to use my old touring kayaks to get people started. As a result, I was able to teach people of all ages, sizes and levels of ability. The club became a success, not only because of the youngsters, but also because adults started to take part. The 'Fladbury Philosophy' was born, and that is the teaching system which is now embodied in the Placid Water Scheme.

By using stable, open-cockpit canoes and kayaks such as those featured in Plates 5:a i-iii the fear of being trapped is removed, and we are able to teach anyone how to canoe; that should be the aim of every teacher.

When I say canoeing is for all, I really do mean all. Because of their stability, straight line running, and open cockpit, touring kayaks can be paddled by people with a wide range of handicaps, without the need to invent special equipment or activities. The totally blind are quickly able to kayak in a straight line, and paddlers with leg disabilities compete on equal terms with the able bodied. Those who cannot swim because of a fear of water, can gain confidence in a double, with an experienced paddler.

'Canoeing is for fun, it's for fitness, it's for the family. Canoeing is for ALL.'

The method of teaching can be very simple. In the first session, the following points should be covered:

o   A brief session on safety

o   Wearing of a buoyancy aid

o   Danger of weirs

Plate 5:a(i)
The stable touring single

Plate 5:a(ii)
The stable touring double

Plate 5:a(iii)
The open canoe

o No wellington boots - they are dangerous
o What to do in the event of a capsize
o Importance of dressing in accordance with conditions
o How to use the paddle
o How to paddle forwards, stop, reverse
o How to get into the kayak
o Stress that everything must be done gently at first
o Steering the kayak with paddle.

Once your pupils are on the water, let them get a feel of how the canoe responds to the paddle. As they experiment, help them but do not 'overteach'. To most people being on the water is an experience in itself, so let them enjoy it. You do not have to be teaching something new every minute. Relax and enjoy it yourself; that way, both you and your pupils will continue.

Having mastered the few simple skills in this chapter you will be able to give many others their first taste of canoeing. If you do not push them too hard, then many will canoe for a lifetime. Some may only go for a gentle paddle on a warm day; others will become dedicated canoeists. Your success as a teacher is simply that they have carried on.

BASIC SKILLS

Whenever possible, the kayak and canoe skills are shown together. Apart from steering, the strokes and principles are the same.

When you are first learning, do not get too worried about knowing all of the strokes. Canoeing and kayaking are really very easy to begin with. Remember, 'doing' is the best means of learning.

125

Fig 5:4
The paddle grip

The width of grip on the paddle is fairly wide, as shown in Fig 5:4. As you become used to paddling, you will modify the grip but to get started, the position shown is good enough. Once you have experimented and found your best grip, it is a good idea to wrap a few layers of tape at the outside and inside of your hand positions on the paddle. If your hands move along the shaft, you will feel the tape and will readjust quickly.

The blades on most kayak paddles are feathered to cut down on wind resistance. This means that the shaft must be rotated by one or the other hand during each paddle stroke. It does not matter which hand is used to control the

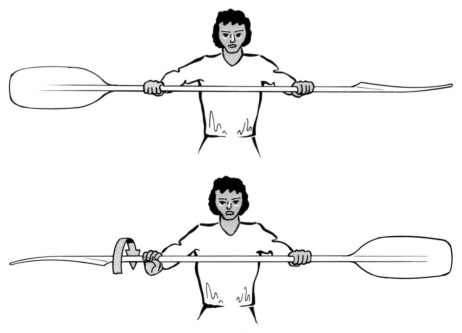

Fig 5:5
Feathering the blade of a kayak paddle

Figs 5:6a, b
Putting the boat into the water

paddle, this being determined by personal choice - or perhaps by the feathering of the particular paddle borrowed when first going afloat.

If a club is just starting, it is better economically if all are taught to use the same feather, so that paddles can be readily passed around.

Before going afloat for the first time, practise the feathering of the blade. It is quite easy. The paddler in Fig. 5:5 is using the left hand for control.

Canoeing is a sport that is quite gentle and results in few problems with injuries. Almost all the injuries which do occur are due to lifting, carrying, or falling over - so be careful when lifting.

Keep a straight back and lift with your legs, as shown in Figs. 5:6.

Getting in and out

With open cockpit boats this is very easy, as shown in Figs. 5:7 abc and 5:8.

The paddler can simply sit on the seat or, for more control, can kneel. Most beginners will prefer to sit.

Forwards, backwards and stopping strokes

Forwards stroke

Fig 5:9 shows the start of the canoe and kayak stroke.

The important points to remember at this stage are:

Fig 5:7
Getting into the open canoe

o The paddle is placed gently in the water as though through a narrow slot. There should be no power on and no splash. The lower arm should be 'straight' and the top hand well back near the ear.

o Once the paddle is fully immersed in the water it becomes fixed. It will slip a little but not too much.

o The power is then applied using the back muscles and pulling the canoe or kayak past the paddle blade. The pull is transmitted through the lower arm. The top arm guides and does not push.

o When the hips are level with the blade, it should be flicked out of the water and then it will be ready for the next stroke.

Reverse stroke

The starting point of the stroke is shown below. The paddle grip is not changed. The back of the blade is used, not the driving face. A common fault with beginners is to rotate the blade so that the drive face is used. The best practice initially is to sit in the kayak or canoe, put the paddle in the water just in front of the body, and gently pull and push without changing the position of the hands on the shaft. The boat will move forwards, stop, then backwards.

Fig 5:9 (below)
The start of the canoe and kayak forward stroke

Fig 5:10
The reverse stroke

When paddling backwards, remember to look over your shoulder so that you can see where you are going, as shown in Fig 5:10.

Stopping

This is very simple. If you are moving forwards then do a reverse stroke. If you are going backwards then do a forwards stroke. Remember not to change the position of your hands on the paddle. Practise stopping very gently at first. As your skill develops, try it at higher speeds.

Steering

The previous sections have described forwards and reverse strokes. Steering strokes differ between canoe and kayak. Placid water kayaks are normally controlled with a rudder.

Sweep stroke

The canoes and kayaks used on placid water are flat along the keel and tend to run in a straight line. The sweep stroke (Fig 5:11) is used to turn the craft and can be applied when stationary or travelling.

Fig 5:11
The sweep stroke

Fig 5:12
The 'J' stroke

'J' stroke

Whilst steering a kayak can be carried out using sweep strokes on either side of the boat, for a Canadian canoe a different stroke has to be used to bring the bow round to the side on which the canoe is being paddled. This is called the 'J' stroke. With the canoe moving, it is used whenever necessary to steer without disturbing the paddling rhythm.

The beginning of the stroke is the same as for the forwards stroke but, as the lower arm comes level with the hip, the blade is turned by the action of the upper wrist (Fig. 5:12). The drive face of the blade is then pushed away from the canoe, which brings the bow around.

Stern rudder

Another steering stroke is used for both canoe and kayak whilst the craft is in motion. The blade is taken to the rear of the paddler and trailed in the water as shown in Fig. 5:13. The bow will then turn towards that side.

Fig 5:13
The stern rudder

Fig 5:14
The draw

Moving sideways

At times you will need to be able to move the kayak or canoe sideways. This may be when you are coming in to the landing stage or lining up for a fun race. To move sideways, we use a draw stroke. There are various types of stroke but, for this chapter, we will only describe the simple draw

The start of the draw is shown in Fig 5:14. You are simply stretching out to pull yourself towards the paddle.

When the canoe or kayak reaches to within about 15cm of the paddle, the paddle is turned 90 degrees and sliced away from the canoe. It is then turned again and the boat pulled towards it, and so on.

At first it is easier to pull the blade right out of the water, rather than turning through 90degrees, and then place it back in the position for the next stroke.

Support stroke

Although, throughout this chapter, we have made the point that we use canoes and kayaks of a stability that match the paddler and limit the possibility of a capsize, there are strokes which are used to stop a capsize if it is about to happen. These are called support strokes and are best practised on a warm summers day.

In the stationary position, the blade is laid flat on the water and a downward push will be enough to right a capsizing canoe (Fig 5:15). Be careful taking the blade out of the water. Go gently and then you will not pull yourself in.

When moving, the blade is also placed flat on the water, as shown, but with the leading edge raised. This gives a very powerful 'lift' and can be leant on quite heavily. If the leading edge of the blade is low then the opposite effect will occur and a very powerful lever will capsize the canoe. Make sure the leading edge is raised.

Fig 5:15
The support stroke

Emptying the kayak or canoe

If you have followed the advice in this chapter, then this should be a rare experience - but, just in case, here is how to empty the boat. With the canoe it is very easy. Just lift one side of the canoe slowly and let the water pour out of the other. The sequence for emptying a kayak is shown in Plates 5:bi, 5:bii, 5:biii. Be careful not to strain your back.

Throughout the skills section of this chapter, the traditional canoe has been shown to demonstrate single bladed paddling. Some kayaks, such as that in Plate 5:ai, can be adapted to teach with the single blade, while others have been designed specifically for the purpose.

Plate 5:b (i-iii)
Emptying the kayak

132

Plate 5:c
A junior racing single. Dimensions have been reduced to make the boat more suitable for young paddlers

WHAT NEXT ?

Within the Placid Water Scheme, the teacher can teach basic skills, introduce racing skills and organise 'achieving marathons'. For most teachers this will be enough but, for those who wish to go further, what are the next steps ? There are four main avenues within the Coaching Scheme; rough water kayak, sea kayaking, Canadian canoeing, and fast touring or racing in both canoe and kayak. From this teaching base spring the wide range of canoeing activities.

The limitation on the numbers who canoe used to be the way we taught, and the supply of canoes and kayaks. This is no longer the case. The main limiting factor in the future will be the availability of water to paddle on. With rough water being such a scarce resource in Britain, the future for most must be based on placid water. I hope this chapter, and what we teach, encourages, indeed inspires people, to use this great resource.

6 The Basic Strokes of Kayaking

Ray Rowe was, for several years, Head of Canoeing at the Sports Council's National Centre for Mountain Activities at Plas y Brenin in North Wales. He then worked on behalf of the BCU as Special Projects Officer.

He has considerable experience in the teaching of beginners, and has given particular thought to the analysis and breaking down of the basic skills.

Hailing from Northern Ireland, with a sprint racing background, Ray has canoed extensively on the sea and in white water. Latterly, he has undertaken the shooting of numerous falls in North Wales - several of them 'firsts'.

CONTENTS

THE MEANING OF 'BASIC STROKES'

Good technique

The term 'basic strokes' can be confusing. It implies that there are more advanced strokes to follow. This is not so. They are called 'basic' because they are the simplest way of causing and responding to movement of the kayak in the water. Complete beginners, top competitors and world wide adventurers propel and manoeuvre their kayaks with this same collection of basic strokes. What makes a skilful paddler is the ability to do two things. These are:

o Waste little energy by making each basic stroke work to its maximum effect; in other words, be efficient

o Connect the basic strokes and fine tune the movements to give the best handling for the kind of paddling undertaken.

It is difficult to identify individual basic strokes when we watch a skilful paddler at work because there is no clear separation of stroke positions; they are somehow neatly linked. Practice has given him an acute feel for what he can make the boat do and paddle movements are more of a flow of energy than a series of successive actions. To reach this level of performance the paddler must break down his technique into the original building blocks, or basic strokes.

Learning progression

The concept of learning progression is fundamental to acquiring kayak handling skills. It means that the paddler learns and improves technique by proceeding through a series of quite naturally connected steps or 'progressions'. This idea is based on the principle of developing good habits which lead onwards, never interfering with each other. Habits require no conscious effort and leave the mind free to continue learning. If a paddler works with the guidance of an instructor or coach, this foundation of good habits will form quickly and safely, and the result will be good technique and skilful kayak handling.

THE PRE-SESSION CHECK

Before any technique training begins the paddler and his equipment should be matched so that he is not hindered by some simple physical problem such as the poor fit of a cockpit. Paddlers should try to do their own pre-session check after initial guidance from an instructor.

Footrest

The footrest determines the whole of the lower body position in the boat. No paddler, no matter how skilful, can have full control of his kayak if he cannot hold himself securely against a good footrest. Start off by setting the footrest position roughly and then make finer adjustments forwards and backwards during paddling sessions until it feels comfortable and secure.

Paddle length

Determine the correct length of paddle for your height and canoeing purpose. It is best to get advice on this. A basic rule is longer shaft for touring; shorter for rough water.

Paddle shaft

Use paddles with ovalled shafts or moulded grips. Good paddling technique relies on feel. Only shafts like this will help you to acquire this feel.

Hand position

Your hands must be evenly spaced on the paddle shaft. The width of the grip is important and should leave your hands just outside of your shoulder width when you hold the paddle shaft against your chest.

Clothing

Your clothing, spraydeck and buoyancy aid should impose the minimum of restriction to body movement. You need to be free to rotate your trunk and lean forwards and backwards.

Kayak fit

The boat itself should allow freedom of movement. 'Feeling part of the boat' applies especially to paddlers working in rough water. This is achieved with knee braces which make contact without moving the legs, and hip pads which bring the hips into contact with the seat sides.

GROUPING OF THE BASIC STROKES

The basic strokes fall into three groups:

o   Basic control
o   Turning and steering on the move
o   Sculling.

Basic control
o   Forward paddling
o   Reverse paddling
o   Stopping
o   Sweep stroke - forward/reverse
o   Draw stroke
o   Recovery stroke.
  These strokes start or cancel out movement in the boat.

Turning and steering on the move
o   Stern rudder
o   Low brace turn
o   Bow rudder.
  These strokes change direction and require the boat to be moving in order to be effective.

Sculling
o   Sculling draw
o   Sculling for support.
  These are refinements of the first group 'draw and recovery' and permit continuous pressure to be applied.

STROKE DEFINITIONS

Forward paddling

A more detailed breakdown of the racing stroke, which is the ultimate in efficient kayak propulsion is best seen through the eyes of a racing coach and is contained in another chapter.

A paddler in a closed cockpit kayak built for slalom or white water touring can never reach this ultimate performance of the stroke. The immobility of his legs under the deck, tight fit of the cockpit on his hips and open leg position together with the width of the boat where the blade enters the water, all limit good forward paddling movement.

It is, however, in every paddler's interests to achieve the maximum efficiency within these limits.

Good forward paddling technique is essentially composed of three elements:

o   Trunk rotation

o   Arm extension

o   Coordination.

Trunk rotation

Trunk rotation is easily seen and felt when we are sawing through a thick log. The shoulder of the sawing arm is clearly driving forwards and backwards with each saw cut.

The movement is much the same as the 'pull through the water' phase of the paddling cycle. In both cases it is heavy work and the body needs to employ more muscle than the relatively short, spindly ones which bend the arms. So we draw upon the considerable collective power of the *torso musculature* to help pull the shoulder backwards in the 'pull' phase.

To make use of this power from the rotation of the trunk it must be transmitted through the pelvis to the thighs and then to the footrest of the kayak. To achieve full rotation of the trunk and to use it effectively takes time and practice. The canoeist must develop flexibility of the hips and back, and build strength in parts of his torso which might otherwise be unused.

Remember that trunk rotation plays a major part in nearly every paddling skill and so it must be developed conscientiously from early days.

Practise notes

The following notes are to help paddlers and instructors to understand and perfect trunk rotation:

o   Practise in a boat which does not give steering problems

o   Exaggerate your natural rotation - it is almost impossible to over-rotate

o   Practise on flat water, sometimes wearing very light clothing so that your movements are completely unrestricted; remember and recall this freedom in future paddling

- o Use trunk rotation exercises to warm up before paddling or training sessions (sit upright in the boat with the paddle shaft held at chest height - keep your head steady and swing the trunk in rotation to face alternate sides)
- o Reverse paddling is impossible without considerable trunk rotation - use it to develop a feel for good rotation in forward paddling
- o Practise accelerating from slow paddling - when your rotation is good you will feel alternate pressure on the soles of your feet as the footrest pushes in.

Arm extension

The start of the kayak paddling cycle is called the 'catch'. The paddle blade has just 'bitten' into the water. In this position the trunk is fully rotated, and the lower arm is extended. This 'extension' has to be cultivated as it does not always come naturally to paddlers. Its purpose is simply to increase the length of the 'pull through' which is the next phase in the cycle. This starting position is exactly the same in the sweep stroke.

Practise notes

- o Imagine that you can see through the deck to your feet - try to begin each stroke at that point - reach it by rotation not by bending forward
- o Allow the paddle shaft to move away from your chest - if you like, imagine it has some foul smelling yuck on it - hold it away from your nose
- o Think only about the start of each stroke and let the end of the stroke take care of itself.

See Fig 6:1

Fig 6:1a
Forward paddling
The extended arm and rotated trunk
can be seen as the paddle locks into
the water

Fig 6:1b
As you drive forwards past the left
blade you should feel pressure on the
sole of the left foot; proof that the
trunk rotation is working.

Plate 6:a
This time lapse photograph of a racing paddler shows full trunk rotation and arm extension coming together as the blade is about to dip into the water.

Co-ordination

Trunk rotation, arm extension and the recovery of the blade through the air are parts of a cycle. Forward paddling is only efficient when the whole cycle is happening smoothly and without thinking. This is CO-ORDINATION. It lies within the mind and body of the paddler. To achieve it canoeists and instructors must perceive the forward paddling stroke as a whole and not as a collection of still images. We are seeking a continuous, flowing motion, not a procession of separate movements.

Practise notes

o   Watch paddlers who have good technique and copy them

o   Try to see yourself on film or video tape and watch for extension and rotation

o   Think about your technique often

o   Try to arrange to do some practising in an open cockpit kayak.

Reverse paddling

The reverse stroke involves even more trunk rotation than the forward stroke. To gain the 'catch' in reverse the trunk is cranked into a fully rotated position and unwinds as the hips are driven past the blade. The stroke feels like a pushing action. The paddler who has complete control in reverse will choose one shoulder only to look over. Good flexibility in the trunk rotation makes this much easier. The beginner, however, might find it easier to alternate glances over each shoulder.

The build of the human body means that reverse paddling is less powerful than forward, and steering is slightly more difficult. A paddler can adjust his

140

reversing technique to emphasise controlling and steering, or power and acceleration. Holding the paddle shaft low and using wide strokes helps the paddler to line
up the rear of the kayak very accurately. This might be necessary when the boat
is spun accidentally in the middle of a rapid and the next couple of moves have to
be made in reverse, or when backing into the narrow entrance of a cave. Where
the priority is power, the blade is taken close to the side of the boat and driven
deep into the water. These kind of reverse thrusts are needed to reverse out of a
stopper, for example, or to back quickly off a dumping wave whilst approaching
the shore. See Fig 6:2.

Stopping
A kayak and paddler on the move have momentum which is the product of mass
and velocity. Velocity might be small but the combined mass of the paddler and
his boat may be considerable and the resulting momentum is often more than

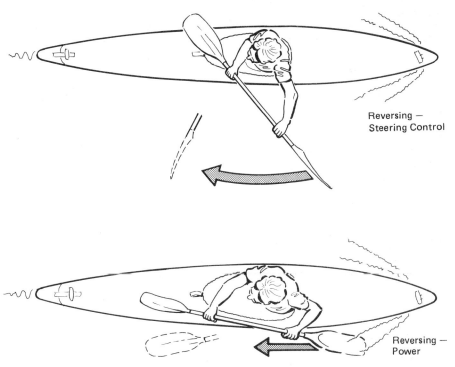

Reversing —
Steering Control

Reversing —
Power

Fig 6:2a (top)
Reverse paddling. Where control and steering are required the reversing stroke
is wide with a low paddle shaft.

Fig 6:2b
Where power in reverse is required the blade travels close to the side of the
kayak. A position mid-way between a and b is the one for beginners to learn.

expected. This momentum must be overcome to stop a boat running and this requires considerable effort.

Short strokes are used to minimise any turning effect which might be generated.

Using only partly immersed blades in the first few strokes lessens the overbalancing feeling.

It might be necessary to use a reference point for stopping practice as it is not always clear when a boat is completely stopped.

Sweep stroke

The sweep stroke, shown in Fig 6:3, is the most fundamental of turning strokes. Its most important function is to cause the boat to spin. It is also used to:

o   take the boat in a new direction

o   slow the boat down as it enters an eddy

It is vital to perfect good sweep stroke technique for two reasons. The first is that fewer strokes are required to make a turn with good technique and this means energy saved and more time to concentrate on thinking ahead. The second reason is that the sweep is frequently used as an 'initiating stroke' in a sequence of strokes. In this context the success and efficiency of a manoeuvre depends on the quality of the first sweep.

Just like every other stroke in kayaking the sweep has its own unique feel. Paddlers need to spend time learning this feel and understanding the mechanics involved.

In the forward sweep the blade is fixed in the water, level with the feet. The blade is completely immersed, the arm operating it is straight and the trunk is fully rotated. This is the starting position which is the same for forward paddling.

Fig 6:3
The forward sweep. The blade is fully immersed, the trunk rotates, and the kayak is driven around with feet and knees

142

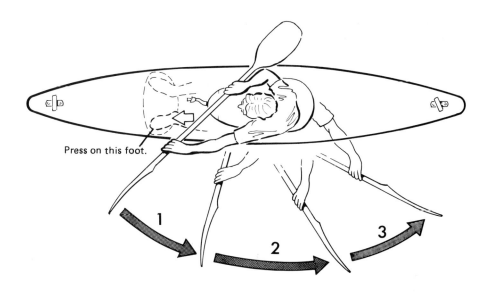

Press on this foot.

Fig 6:4
The three sectors of the sweep stroke. The same applies to the reverse sweep.

The paddler should now imagine that the boat is not there. By levering off the paddle he swings his legs away from the blade, across the water so that the soles of his feet point in a new direction. The paddler moves the boat in the same way by locking into the seat, knee braces and footrest. *Trunk rotation* causes the boat to spin and not the pulling of the paddle blade through the water.

For the reverse sweep exactly the same principles apply. Once again the arm working the immersed blade is kept straight throughout the sweep and the trunk unwinds from full rearward rotation.

The paddler should aim to keep the boat level throughout the turn so that no drag is set up by edges cutting into the water. It is worth remembering that every kayak has an optimum speed for spinning. This is determined by hull shape, buoyancy and friction. To exceed this optimum speed requires disproportionate amounts of energy and is therefore wasteful. Good sweep stroke technique is built up in flat water practice where the boats response can most easily be felt.

In both forward and reverse sweeps the path of the paddle is that of an arc with the paddle shaft forming a radius. The radius line can be drawn back to its origin, the paddler's spine, and so the shoulder and arm become part of this radius. See Fig 6:4.

The arc has three sectors. In the case of the forward sweep:

  Sector 1 moves the bow away from the blade
  Sector 2 maintains the spin and can shoot the boat forward if required
  Sector 3 draws the stern towards the blade

Counting through these sectors when practising helps the paddler to appreciate the subtle timing of the sweep stroke.

Sweep on the move

When a sweep stroke is applied to a boat which is moving the amount of time which the blade spends in each sector changes. The boat's movement over the water appears to pull the blade more quickly through the whole arc. Once familiar with the stroke in the non-moving boat the paddler must learn the new feel of the sweep applied to a boat on the move.

The next stage is to learn to make full use of the three sectors. If the situation requires simply a very powerful, fast spin then the paddler applies pressure evenly throughout the arc. He might decide at the last minute to push the boat deeper into an eddy in which case the emphasis is on Sector 2. The third sector is the one most often seen in use. It is an excellent steering position because after the initial draw in to the stern, the paddle can be left in place to give further control as the boat glides. This position is often added on to the end of a forward power stroke when the boat is swung slightly off course by a wave for example.

Draw stroke

The purpose of the draw is to fix the blade in the water and side slip the boat towards it. The position of the paddle shaft is critical and can be illustrated by pulling alongside a vertical post sticking high out of the water. Catch the post with the nearside hand just above the water and reach across the top of your head to grasp the post with the other hand. Once again this position requires flexibility in the trunk and shoulders, as shown in Fig 6:5.

To give the greatest amount of purchase on the water the blade and sometimes part of the shaft are held deep for the whole sideslip. If the paddler wants to cover a lot of ground sideways he must recover the paddle to the starting position each time. This recovery can be made through the air or by slicing back through the water. It is useful to practise both as different water conditions demand different tactics. The slice recovery is made by wrist-rolling the blade through ninety degrees so that its driving face looks rearward; the blade can then easily be knifed

Fig 6:5
The draw stroke. The blade is fully immersed, the trunk is slightly rotated, and the top arm 'frames' the face

Plate 6:b

This demonstration shows how the top arm acts as a 'hanger'. This position is the key to getting the best possible grip on the water with the drawing blade

Plate 6:c

Emergency stops. Two paddlers aim for the nose of each others boat. At the last moment, the one who has been agreed upon as 'the caller' shouts 'stop'

away from the hip to restart the stroke. Another method of recovery is to combine these two. At the end of the pull the blade is sliced out of the water rearward without being rotated and then a through-the-air recovery is made. This system is often used to introduce beginners to the draw but is also used at times by proficient slalom and river paddlers in shallow water or when they feel they might need to convert the draw to a stern steering stroke.

The trunk position for a draw stroke is upright with some rotation towards the direction of the sideslip. This rotation gives a greater range of movement to both arms, allowing the paddler to make alterations to the angle of pull on the paddle shaft. This keeps the boat running true in the sideslip and not slewing off course.

The job of the top arm in the draw is to act as a hanger for the paddle on the drawing side of the boat. This arm remains high, (forearm no lower than forehead) throughout the pull and recovery. The reason for this position is that the blade in the water must be kept vertical as much as possible to minimise 'spilling water' off the end of the blade during the pull.

145

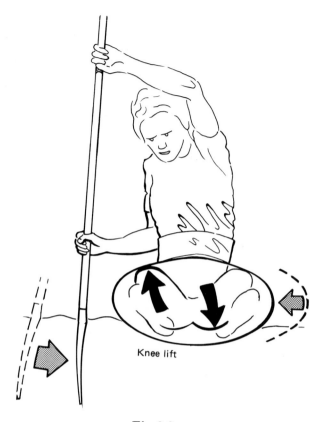

Fig 6:6
During the side-slip use knee-lift to ensure that all the water slips under the hull

The paddler's vision forwards and sideways must remain unobstructed by the top arm. A quick draw stroke is often used to avoid an obstruction or to make a last minute 'nudge' to line a boat up for a narrow shoot on a rapid. Watch a paddler in difficult water and you will see as many draws as forward strokes.

It is absolutely essential that paddlers learn to draw stroke without hindering vision.

The sideslip

As the boat moves sideways any water which is scooped onto the deck will slow it down and unbalance the paddler. To avoid this the paddler must apply lift to the edge of the boat which is leading the sideslip. The amount of lift required is minimal and determined by the speed of the boat, its volume and shape. It is done by lifting the knee or thigh but remember that it is only enough to allow water to pass under the hull. To an observer the boat will appear to remain level as in Fig 6:6.

146

Recovery stroke

The instant a beginner recognises that he is in danger of overbalancing his boat he abandons the paddle and reaches for the surface of the water. This action is a reflex designed to protect the body when it stumbles. It is precisely this reflex which we want to utilise for recovery strokes. The response, however, must be adapted so that the paddler perceives the paddle blades as his hands or at least extensions of them. The greater area of the paddle blade provides sufficient purchase on the water to prevent the stumble. Good use is therefore made of the body's automatic reaction system.

The total recovery of the paddler's balance is only complete if the support from the paddle is transmitted into the lower body, knees and hips to exert righting action in the boat. This action is essentially a rotation of the pelvis causing the knees and thighs to give lift to one side of the boat. See Fig 6:7.

The paddler has the choice of two arm positions in his recovery. These are the 'low recovery' and the 'high recovery'.

The high recovery

The high position, shown in Fig 6:8, allows the paddler to recover from extreme capsize angles if he is well practised. The action is basically one of striking the surface of the water with the driving face of the blade. It is a natural pulling movement and it is often seen incorporated into a forward paddling stroke when a paddler senses a sudden overbalancing force.

After the recovery the paddle is retrieved from the depths by slicing it vertically upwards. This slice is made by a wrist roll which should already be familiar to paddlers from the draw stroke. This is shown in Fig 6:9.

The paddler lifts his elbow as soon as the wrist roll occurs.

The low recovery

The low recovery, shown in Fig 6.10, resembles a reverse paddle stroke but exerted vertically downward, again onto the surface of the water. It is a pushing action. The paddle shaft is kept horizontal with the paddler's weight over it rather than under as in the high recovery. To reach this position the paddlers arms form the classic 'elbows up' shape. This method of recovery has many applications.

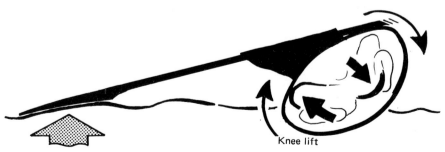

Knee lift

Fig 6:7
In any recovery stroke, knee lift and hip rotation ruturn the boat to the level

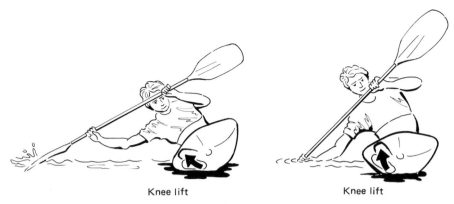

Knee lift   Knee lift

Fig 6:8

The high recovery stroke is vitally imporant to any padlder in a rough water situation. The subtle timing between instinctively striking the water with the blade and applying knee lift and hip rotation needs concentrated practise

The support

The slice out

Fig 6:9a (top)   *The wrist position for the high recovery stroke*
Fig 6:9b (bottom)   *The wrist roll and slice out of the blade*

148

Fig 6:10
The low recovery position. If the position is held for more than an instant, it is known as a low brace

These are all in cases where the paddling position is high. Some examples of the low recovery in use are:

o Paddler in racing kayak steadying himself on start or resting

o Holding a boat steady to take a swimmer onto the deck

o River paddler in a stopper with relatively small wave

o Canoe games . . . 'not all in it' game; paddler on rear deck with feet in boat.

Fig 6:11
The stern rudder. Trailing blade is fully immersed, trunk is rotated and the paddle shaft is held low

The low recovery becomes a low brace when the paddle rides on the surface giving support for more than just the instant of the strike of the blade on to the surface.

Retrieving the paddle after a low recovery begins with a wrist roll (knuckles move upwards) and a slice to the surface follows. The wrist roll action is the same as accelerating a motor bike through the twist grip.

Stern rudder

The stern rudder is a steering stroke which permits very fine control of the direction. Like any rudder it requires the boat to be moving to be effective. The paddler trails a blade to the rear of the kayak and controls the glide by ruddering. The trailing blade is most

149

effective when completely submerged, upright and well to the rear of the boat. This is all much easier to achieve if the paddler has rotated his trunk towards the ruddering blade leaving him virtually looking over one shoulder as in Fig 6:11.

With the steering blade positioned on the right side of the kayak, the paddler has three options (Fig 6:12):

Blade Action		Result
Push blade away from side of boat	-	Boat steers to right
Trail only; no push or pull	-	Straight ahead
Pull blade towards canoe	-	Boat steers to left. Range of steering limited.

Some paddlers improve on the basic stern rudder by adding refinements to it. Two commonly used are:

o Wrist rolling whilst applying the push and pull. This is called 'changing the pitch of the blade' in the water and gives a very fine feel to steering control.

o Tillering. Here the rear hand is fixed and the forward hand operates the push and pull. The theory is that greater leverage is achieved enabling greater effort to be applied to a turn.

Each paddler will develop his own style in every stroke to suit his own unique physique and canoeing requirements. Developing good technique does not exclude individuality.

When it comes to making a steering correction the paddler has a choice of sides for the stern rudder. Making the correct choice is sometimes vital. Where powerful corrections are needed the paddler changes the stern rudder side as often as necessary to make use of the pushing position (number one position). Crossing a wave would be an example of this. On the other hand a paddler steering into a narrow cave or manoeuvreing through an overhanging tree would try to keep the rudder on one side only, guiding the boat with delicate pushing and pulling movements.

The stern rudder is used in a wide range of canoeing applications but the aim is always the same - steering with the minimum loss of speed. The following examples illustrate its use:

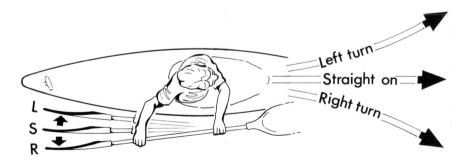

Fig 6:12
A stern rudder on the right permits extensive turning to the right and very limited turning to the left

Plate 6:d
The low brace turn. The kayak must be running forwards and tilted onto the inside edge. The bracing blade skids but does not sweep

o   Complete beginner in a non-directional kayak: stern rudders to hold straight course.

o   Kayak running on a green wave: stern rudders bring about changes in direction of run. A stern rudder is used to hold a diagonal run. Placed on the shoreward side it acts as a fin preventing the boat from turning into the wave

o   Crossing a standing wave on a river: the kayak, facing upstream, surfs across the wave. The rudder is placed on the upstream side.

o   At sea with the kayak running downwind: constant slewing of the boat is countered by stern rudders neatly incorporated into forward paddling.

o   Paddler passing under low bridge or tree: with speed built up beforehand, paddler folds forward at the waist and trails a stern rudder to steer. The leading blade is used to break or deflect small branches.

Low brace turn

This is a slow, safe turn where the boat tracks in a gentle arc through the water. This movement of the kayak is sometimes referred to as 'carving'. It describes perfectly the non-skidding nature of this flowing turn. It is illustrated in Fig 6:13.

The paddle position is shown in Fig 6:14 and is much the same as that for the low recovery but the leading edge of the blade is raised very slightly to ensure that it does not cut underwater. The blade is in line with the paddler's shoulder in a position to give most support and the kayak is set onto its edge. The function of the blade is to give support as it skids across the water with the movement of the boat and not to act as a break by biting into the water.

The edging of the kayak in the turn is essential. It is done by rotating the pelvis to lift the knee. This raises the edge of the boat opposite the working blade.

Edging and leaning

At this stage it is useful for paddlers to recognise the difference in these two terms, as shown in Fig 6:15.

Leaning is where the paddler actually moves his upper body mass. It is similar to the way that a cyclist leans to the inside of a bend. Leaning is used mostly in canoeing for the same reason, ie: to compensate for the forces in a fast turn.

Knee lift

Fig 6:13 (left) *The low brace turn is simply a low brace applied whilst the kayak is running forwards and set on its edge*
Fig 6:14 *This gives a long, wide turn. The altered hull shape caused by the edging creates a natural track through the water. The low brace emphasizes security - not speed - through the turn*

Edging is the action of setting the boat on its side. It starts in the pelvis and results in the lifting of one buttock. This depresses the boat on one side while the thigh and knee on the other side lift the boat's edge. The better the paddlers fit in the kayak's knee braces and hip pads the easier and more precise will be the edging. Notice that it is possible to edge without leaning.

In the low brace turn it is edging which is emphasised and this is best learnt during flat water training before moving on to turns in the flow. Paddlers should aim to apply the minimum of weight to the skidding paddle blade, edge the boat and use only the amount of lean required to balance the turn.

Leaning

Edging

Knee lift

Fig 6:15a (left) *Leaning. Movement of body weight, as in cornering on a bike*
Fig 6:15b *Edging. Movement of the kayak, as in sitting on one buttock*

152

Plate 6:e

Edging. Sitting on one buttock whilst remaining in-balance is a useful exercise to help paddlers learn how the technique feels in the boat

The low brace turn is a security stroke. It gives the paddler a handrail on which to hang when he is not feeling confident. It is usually applied when the energy for the turn is supplied by a current as in eddy turns in a river or strong tideway, or even by a powerful sweep stroke on the opposite side. In a white water river situation the use of the low brace turn characterises defensive paddling which is slow but safe. Certain technically difficult rapids do not lend themselves to this style of paddling but generally it is a very good strategy for beginners in moving water or nervous experts finding themselves close to their limit !

Bow rudder

The bow rudder is the fastest, most attacking turning stroke in the whole of the paddler's repertoire. Energy gathered from the kayak's forward speed is stored momentarily by the paddler and then released in a powerful surge in a new direction. The bow rudder, with the kayak in mid flight has become the hallmark of dynamic white water technique demanding commitment, flexibility, strength and timing from the paddler.

It must first be emphasised that the bow rudder is a compound stroke. This is to say it is not a simple, single movement, but rather a collection of pushes, pulls and slices. Each of these components can be varied in duration and in the amount of pressure applied. It can cause the boat to spin in an instant or power through a long, carved turn.

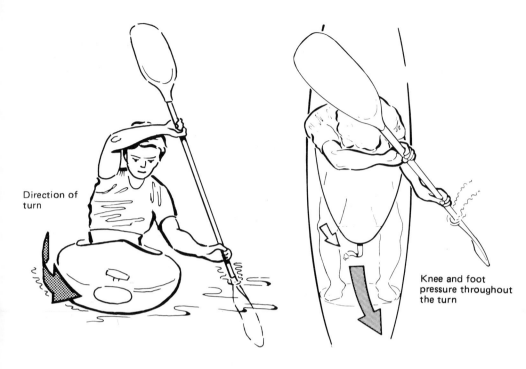

Direction of turn

Knee and foot pressure throughout the turn

Fig 6:16 (left)
Bow rudder - a compound stroke. The position is very similar to the draw. High top arm, fully immersed blade. The lower arm has many possible positions according to the characteristics of the turn required

Fig 6:17 (right)
It is important to feel the outside knee and foot driving the kayak around the turn

The bow rudder on still water

The bow rudder is only applied when a kayak has already started to turn. When there is no current the energy for this turn comes from a good forward sweep. The paddler then wrist rolls (motor cycle throttle) and plants the opposite blade level with his knee. The open angle of this blade appears to slow or even stop the boat on that side and a turn occurs around the paddle shaft. The top arm crosses the top of the head in the same position as for the draw stroke. The lower arm is flexed and positions the blade deeply and slightly off the side of the boat. The trunk is rotated with the paddler facing the new direction before the blade is planted. It is the powerful unwinding of this trunk rotation that forces the boat through the turn. The knee on the side opposite the working blade is felt to lift and drive the boat around the paddle shaft. With the turn of the boat comes a natural unwinding of the wrist roll and the paddler is poised to make a forward driving stroke. The stroke is illustrated in Figs 6:16 and 6:17.

154

The bow rudder in eddy turns

If the paddler is accurate with his boat placement and has mastered boat balance then the moving water bow rudder is easy. The energy of the flow gets the boat turning and the function of the bow rudder is to position the boat correctly for what comes next.

Here are two break-out situations:

o   Gain the eddy and stop

The bow rudder blade position looks like a draw stroke, ie parallel to the side of the boat. When the turn is completed the bow rudder becomes a forward driving stroke to check backwards drift.

o   Gain the eddy and re-enter current immediately

Blade position as for draw. During the turn it is sliced forward to leave the lower arm fully extended and the blade deep, ready to apply a long, forward driving stroke which will shoot the boat back into the flow.

In both cases the blade is placed in the eddy water. In the case of breaking into the flow the blade is planted into the downstream flow.

Bow rudders in eddy turns demand commitment. Half hearted attempts are risky because of the uncertainty in the boat's movements. The paddle position offers little support to a nervous paddler who is tempted to lower the top arm so that it crosses below the chin. The lower arm is often held too far away from the kayak side. Both of these actions are unhelpful as they make it impossible to achieve the wrist roll and also reduce the depth of the blade.

The following examples show some bow rudder variations and their uses:

o   The blade is positioned wide of the side of the boat

This gives a slower turn and lets the boat 'carve'. It is common on flat water where the paddler wishes to maintain forward speed or to penetrate deeply into a wide eddy. Mostly it is used in break-ins where the flow is very powerful. Much less trunk rotation is used in this version.

o   Excessive edging during the turn

It is possible to control the speed of the turn by varying the degree of edging. Lifting the edge up high increases the spin but has a stalling effect on the speed of the boat. Conversely flattening the boat off in mid turn allows the paddler to cover more ground in the eddy and therefore slows the turn. This is a subtle technique and demands a lot of kayaking skill.

o   Use of the trunk and weight shift

Kayaks which are sensitive to shifts in the paddlers weight such as slalom boats and 'squirt' boats can improve the boats bite in the eddy or flow. By leaning forward the paddler depresses the front of the boat causing it to snatch the piece of water into which it is moving and consequently turn earlier and faster. This is often combined with a powerful forward thrust of the hips which shoots the kayak forward.

o   The bow pull

In this case the paddler's lower arm is extended so that the paddle shaft slopes towards the front of the kayak in a reach towards the feet. The blade is parallel to the boat's side and the pull is towards the feet. This causes the front of the kayak to sideslip into a turn. This version is used to add a little extra usually when the boat has lost its speed. It is shown in Fig 6:18.

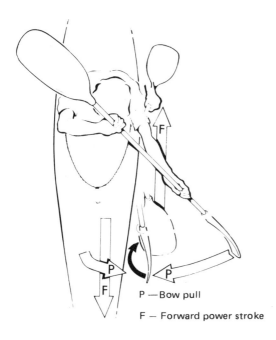

P — Bow pull

F — Forward power stroke

Fig 6:18
One variation of the bow rudder is the bow pull. The lower arm pushes towards the front of the kayak and then draws the bow towards the blade. It is often converted into a forward power stroke (as illustrated) when it is necessary to maintain forward speed

The 'compound' nature of the bow rudder should now be obvious. Combinations of these variations are seen linked into the same turn. The paddler needs a lot of practice to build the strength, mobility and feel that is necessary to make full use of the bow rudder.

Plate 6:f
The bow pull. Slice the blade forwards and outwards; then pull in towards feet

Sculling draw

This stroke makes it possible to apply sideslip to the kayak for a prolonged period. There is no recovery phase in the movement. The paddle blade is always gaining purchase on the water.

With the shaft in the same upright position as described in the draw stroke, the working blade is sliced forwards and angled so that the blade tries to pull away from the side of the boat. The paddler resists this and gains purchase to pull the boat sideways. The blade is then sliced rearward with opposite angling and another sideways pull is gained. A smooth back and forth action is maintained with the lower arm, and both wrists work hard to make the sculling action possible. The paddler rotates his trunk so that his chest is facing the direction of travel. This rotation is important as it gives the lower arm a greater range of movement and brings the torso musculature into a more powerful working position.

Notice that this is not so much a single stroke but more of a series of linked paddle movements. It is good to practise sculling without looking at the blade in the water.

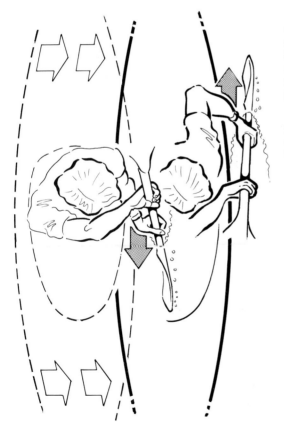

Knowing what the paddle is doing without looking at it is called 'paddle awareness'. Sculling is excellent practice for developing this very important mind-hand-paddle linkage. It is illustrated in Fig 6:19.

Remember that the sculling draw requires the same subtle knee lift which was used in the simple draw stroke.

Fig 6:19
The sculling draw.
Subtle feathering of the blade as it knifes forwards and rearwards provides continuous sideslip pressure. The top hand is held high, as for a draw stroke

Direction of sideslip

157

Sculling for support

Not all capsizing forces last for an instant. Some, like a strong wind or stopper wave, go on for longer than can be coped with by a single recovery stroke. The sculling support stroke allows the paddler to resist a capsize or alter the boats balance over a prolonged period and is shown in Fig 6:20.

The emphasis is on controlling the boat with knees, thighs and hips. The paddle movement is simple. The aim is to keep the blade on the move across the water surface. To do this it is sliced flat but with the leading edge raised slightly to cause it to track on the surface. The forwards and rearward sculling action uses wrist movements to lift the leading edge alternately. The paddle shaft is held low, almost parallel to the water. This is important as it ensures maximum contact with the sculling blade. The paddler has the feeling of hanging from the paddle shaft.

Knee lift

The kayak is controlled essentially by knee lift. If you are practising sculling support on flat water the knee opposite the sculling side will be supplying the lift. When you use sculling to resist a capsize you are trying to keep the boat level and so the lift comes from the knee nearest the sculling blade.

Fig 6:20
Sculling for support, or the sculling brace, as it is sometimes called, is a continuous high brace. The raised leading edge of the blade gives it lift as it sculls forwards and rearwards

The following examples show sculling for support put to use:

o   Stopper wave holding a paddler sideways on.

The priority here is to keep the upstream edge clear of the descending water. The scull is on the downstream side but the knee lift is on the upstream side.

o   A paddler at sea is hit by a sudden squall.

Initially the scull and the knee lift are on the down wind side as a response to the capsizing force of the wind. The aim, however, is to change the scull quickly to the windward side so that the paddler is leaning into the wind.

Practise exercises and progressions for basic strokes

The aim of practice exercises is threefold:

o   To help a paddler to learn a new stroke

o   To improve existing stroke technique by concentrating on its constituent parts

o   To show the use of a stroke in a wider canoeing context.

Good instructors should have an extensive range of exercises up their sleeves. Some of these are used often, others are pulled out like tools from a box to solve a particular problem. Improving paddling performance and teaching new skills is frequently a problem solving task as individual paddlers present unique movements which result in varying degrees of success. Recognising what is good in a performance and drawing attention to it are important qualities in coaching.

The following are samples of exercises and progressions which could be used to introduce or improve paddlers basic technique.

Developing trunk rotation:

o Paddle forwards with arms locked out straight: this forces the action of trunk rotation since it is physically impossible to make the boat move without it

o Exaggerate rotation so much that the boat swings wildly from side to side; now control the swinging by shortening the stroke at the rear and pulling close to side of the boat

o Get someone to watch you from side-on; they should see your back, then your chest, then your back and so on

o Use stretching exercises to improve mobility: sit in the boat on land and rotate to full extent and hold for ten seconds; use other land based trunk, back and shoulder girdle stretching exercises

o Practise lots of reverse paddling.

Developing arm extension:

o *Punch* the top arm forwards and slightly downward on each recovery; once full extension is learnt, this emphasis on punching should be removed

o Mark the boat with tape at the point of blade entry; be careful to avoid excessive body lean forwards and rearward

o Paddle holding shaft further away from chest than usual

o Allow the grip of the top hand to loosen each time; this allows the paddle shaft to pull slightly out of the grip and gives greater reach.

Plate 6:h
Cross-deck paddling. The kayak is being 'paddled' sideways. This is a good exercise for helping tyros to appreciate the full range of their trunk rotation

Plate 6:i

Two exercises which fix the blade firmly, allowing the paddler to concentrate on feeling that the sweep is about moving the kayak away from the blade, and not vice versa. In 6:j the instructor holds the blade and the paddler swings the boat away and then towards it

Plate 6:j

Stopping:

o Change direction: forward, reverse, forward,...

o Paddle towards soft bank and stop just before colliding with it

o Paddle towards partner; stop when he shouts

o Paddle down stream; stop and hold position at a bank marker.

Sweep stroke:

o Blade positioned as for sweep (arm straight) make forward and reverse swings on same side keeping the blade immersed; notice how the blade remains 'fixed' in the water

o Start with the boat stationary; spin boat with forward or reverse sweeps; count 1, 2, 3 for each sector of the sweep

o Practise fixing the arm at the shoulder in order to transmit trunk rotation directly to the paddle; the shoulder joint should be solid

o Combination sweeps: spin using forward, reverse, forward . . . sweeps

o Practise not looking at sweeping blade,but looking forward

o Sweep on the move: paddle along a straight course and make a 180 degree turn to the left, paddle straight back and make a 180 degree turn to the right.

Plate 6:k
Using a partner to increase the resistance of the side-slip. This helps the paddler to feel the grip of the blade in the water. It is also a useful way to get the instructor in close to help sort out problems with the 'slice'

Plate 6:l (top)
Paddlers must eventually learn to draw without looking at the blade. Here the instructor has chosen a coaching position which makes the canoeist look at her. This also underlines the importance of not obstructing vision with the top arm

Plate 6:m (left)
In this draw stroke on the move exercise, the paddlers aim for each other. At the last moment the caller shouts and they side-slip and pass

Draw:
o Allow beginners to hold paddle shaft at blade neck with the lower hand; this makes control and sensation of the blade movement easier
o Start beginners with rearward slice out recovery
o Move to wrist roll, slice out
o Experiment with angle of pull to control sideslip
o Partner forms a raft alongside; draw stroke the whole raft
o Practise not looking at the working blade, but looking forwards.

Plate 6:n
A good test of the low recovery stroke is 'not-all-in-it' paddling. Feet in the water to start with and then inside the cockpit for the more adventurous

Recovery strokes:
o   Start with paddle in low recovery position; push downward to feel the resistance
o   Partner supports paddle blade; practise the knee and hip movement
o   Consecutive low recovery strokes, alternating sides
o   Sit on rear deck with feet in the cockpit; the low recovery is completely natural from this position
o   Move to high recovery and practise on alternate sides which comes easily since it resembles forward paddling
o   Hold paddle shaft at eye height; overbalance onto high recovery
o   Gradually increase the height of the shaft starting position.

Stern rudder:
o   Practise the position with the boat at a standstill
o   Apply stern rudder after a slow glide using push-away steering only at first
o   After fast glide change rudder side to run a zig-zag course
o   Zig-zag ruddering one side only: this uses the push and pull system
o   Practise neutral position in glide
o   Long diagonal run on green wave using control position with rudder on down wave side only

o Raise down wave edge at same time
o As above but on a standing wave in a river; rudder on upstream side - lift upstream edge.

Plate 6:o
Learning to steer with a stern rudder. Here the paddler gets the blade positioned at the rear and then the instructor sets the kayak running with a push from the bank

Low brace turn:
o Rehearse position of the blade
o Practise the turn from a slow glide
o Use a forward sweep to start the turn
o Work on flat water and experiment with differing degrees of edging
o Experiment with the distance that the bracing blade sits from the side of the boat
o When momentum of turn has gone, slice blade forward, convert to forward stroke
o Practise the turn with blade held just off the water; this develops sensitivity to edging and boat balance.

Bow rudder:
o Dig paddle upright into mud on river bed; spin boat around it as for bow rudder
o Perform low brace turn with blade on drive face; gradually raise the height of the top arm until it forms a bow rudder

165

Plate 6:p

Low braces are much easier to perform on the water, because you don't have to lift so much of the kayak's weight. The exercise, however, is worthwhile for developing strength in the abdominal muscles

o Practise moving the paddle into bow rudder position with the boat at rest

o Always start the boat turning with a forward sweep

o Finish the turn by slicing the blade forward and converting to forward driving stroke

o Set markers on flat water which require both fast turns and long carve turns.

Plate 6:q

One way to introduce the bow rudder is to let the paddler position the blade with the boat standing still. The instructor then pushes the kayak gently forwards

Plate 6:r

Using a post anchored to the bottom to help paddlers to feel the knees and feet driving the boat around the turn. Especially useful to reproduce tight turns, where the boat pivots around the blade

Plate 6:s

A good way to inccrease confidence in sculling for support is to use an extended paddle grip

Sculling: (see Plate 6:s)

o Rehearse sculling movements with boat held securely so that it can not overbalance
o Practise sculling draw with lower hand on neck of the blade
o To emphasise trunk rotation in sculling draw, look towards direction of travel
o Experiment with length of scull and speed in both strokes
o Scull for support using an extended paddle grip.

LINKING STROKES

Whatever the paddler chooses to do with his boat, be it running rapids, touring, or riding waves, he will be drawing upon the range of basic kayaking strokes. The greater the requirement to manoeuvre the boat the more diverse and complex will become the amalgam of strokes used. Paddling white water, for example, is an activity which is intense in demanding differing strokes.

As paddlers learn the basics they naturally acquire the art of combining strokes. This is called stroke linking. It is possible to help paddlers to develop stroke linking simply by building up confidence with practice on easy or even flat water. Establishing a firm grounding in basic strokes and at the same time practising the many different ways that they can be linked should form the basis of kayak control teaching at beginner level and upwards.

The benefits of developing good stroke linking are:

o Economy of effort

    Time is not wasted in moving between strokes because the paddler has already established and learnt the pathways that join them

o Emphasises effective basic strokes.

    The smooth links lead into strokes performed technically; the result is fewer overall strokes and conservation of energy

o Assists further learning

    The paddler becomes better at learning; new movements can be integrated into the paddler's routine easily because he has developed a sense of making connections

o Dispels hesitation

    White water paddlers are sometimes caught out by momentary hesitation; good linking develops a sense of timing and rhythm which helps to overcome this.

Two main areas are involved in stroke linking work:

o Stroke sequence practice

    Paddlers are given set manoeuvres to carry out; they must follow a predetermined stroke sequence

o Slicing

    Strokes on the same side of the boat are linked through the water by knifing the blade into its new position; another form of slicing is to skid the blade flat across the water surface

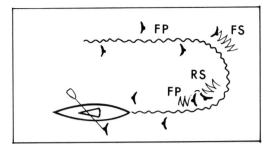

Fig 6:21

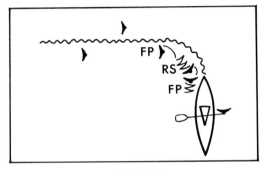

Fig 6:22

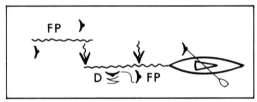

Fig 6:23

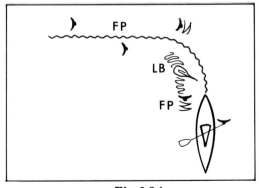

Fig 6:24

Stroke sequence practice is not intended to restrict a paddler in any way. It is based on forming habits which are efficient.

The following are examples of stroke linking exercises. Good technique in the basic strokes must be emphasised. In most cases the exercises are integrated with forward paddling, helping to develop a sense of rhythm:

o Forward paddling - forward sweep - reverse sweep - forward paddling (Fig 6:21)

After the reverse sweep the blade is left in the water; the opposite arm is raised and the forward stroke begins

o Forward paddling stroke - reverse sweep - forward paddling stroke (Fig 6:22)

The strokes are all on the same side

o Forward paddling - draw - forward paddling (Fig 6:23)

When the drawing blade is close to the boat the wrist is rolled and a forward driving stroke takes over

o Forward paddling - sweep - low brace turn - slice to forward paddling (Fig 6:24)

The slice is across the surface. Now try the same angle of turn using this sequence.

o Forward sweep - bow rudder - slice to forward paddling

A long slice with full arm extension gives a 'slow in, fast out' turn

o Forward paddling - draw - slice to bow rudder - forward paddling (Fig 6:25)

The slice is taken forward and slightly away from the side of the boat

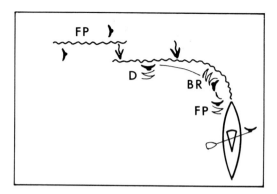

Fig 6:25

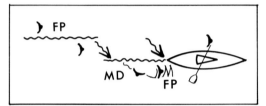

Fig 6:26

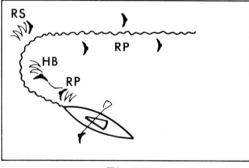

Fig 6:27

o Forward paddling - moving draw - slice to forward paddling (Fig 6:26)

A moving draw is needed to prolong side slipping when the boat is moving faster than the water; the blade is positioned further back than in the normal draw and is opened slightly to pull the water in towards the boat; it is easiest to do if the last stroke before the draw is done on the same side as the draw

o Sculling support - forward power stroke

The blade is sculled, driving face down, across the surface towards the bow; from where it is converted into a forward power stroke; this sequence would be used to shoot a boat out of the end of a stopper since it combines forward propulsion and support

o Sculling - reverse power stroke

This is used when a paddler reverses out of a stopper slot using one of two systems

- Change from scull to low brace; slice paddle to rear and reverse power from there

- Scull to high brace and lean back; rotate trunk to face blade then use a 're-versing draw' to pull stern towards blade: this position is very 'off-balanced' !

o Reverse paddling - right sweep - high brace - slice to reverse paddling

This is the stroke sequence for a reverse break out: the high brace position is as for high recovery; in flat water the paddle shaft is held low but the driving face of the blade is always used; the slice is rearward and converted to reverse power (Fig 6:27).

The following comments apply to slicing:

o   Slices through the water need depth: in shallow water either avoid slicing or lift the paddle high so that it is only partially immersed

o   Some paddle blades slice easier than others: good quality competition slalom blades are best because of their wafer thin edges (their flimsiness, however, makes them unsuitable for white water touring); spooned racing blades and some sea touring paddles have minds of their own in a slice

o   Paddle awareness goes hand in hand with slicing; paddlers must learn to slice without having to look at the blade.

TECHNIQUE CHECKLIST FOR BASIC STROKES

Forward paddling

Trunk:

o   Full rotation - use torso not arms

o   Sit upright or slightly forward - do not lean back

o   Body steady - no bobbing.

Arms:

o   Extend arm at 'catch' phase

o   Pull close to boat for power

o   Elbows held high when paddling in very rough water

o   Hands relax in recovery phase.

Lower body:

o   Thrust is transmitted to feet and knees

o   Where maximum rotation is possible there is some movement of the hips.

Head:

o   Hold steady

o   Occasionally raise chin to release neck tension

Reverse paddling

Trunk:

o   Emphasis on rearward rotation

o   Upright or slightly inclined rearward.

Arms:

o   Pull-through close to boat for power

o   Wide for control

Lower body:

o   Drive transmitted through backstrap and/or seat pan

o   Relax knee grip unless in rough water.

Head:

o   Try to sight over one shoulder only for accuracy

o   Must be able to see rearmost point of kayak.

Stopping

o   Apply maximum effort

o   Short strokes

o   Quick strokes

o   Partially covered blade if work is too heavy

o   Be aware of any current which might carry the boat onwards.

Sweep stroke

Arms:

o Working arm straight until lift out

o Other arm in comfortable working position but not higher than shoulder

o Three phases in pull:
  1 Away from boat
  2 Parallel
  3 Towards stern
  Make use of all three phases.

Trunk:

o Rotate shoulder in line with paddle shaft

o Use slight amount of forwards and rearward lean to extend rotation.

Paddle:

o Completely cover blade

o Blades square to surface.

Lower body:

o Use knees, feet and hips to transmit spin to boat.

Shoulders:

o Drop shoulder slightly on sweep side to help lock it in position

o Especially useful at 'catch' in forward sweep.

Head:

o Look forward in forward sweep

o Look towards intended direction of travel in reverse sweep.

Boat:

o Keep level.

Draw stroke

Paddle:

o Shaft upright for as much of the stroke as possible

o Whole paddle on draw side of boat

o Blade totally submerged.

Arms:

o Top arm high (no lower than forehead)
  - Leave forward visibility clear
  - Top arm elbow points skyward
  - Good shoulder flexibility required
  - Slight movement of top arm is sometimes necessary - in line with lower arm

o Lower (draw) arm
  - Fully extends to catch water
  - Does most of the work
  - Pulls to hip
  - Controls direction in sideslip by pulling to front or stern.

Trunk:

o Slight rotation in direction of sideslip

o Body upright

o Flexibility in lateral bending required.

Lower body:

o Knee lift on side slip of boat

o Hip flexibility required.

Head:

o Look towards the boat's overall direction of movement, forwards, sideways and backwards.

Boat:

o Keep level to avoid water being scooped onto deck.

Feel:

o Boat moves towards blade.

Low recovery

Paddle:
o   Back of blade on water surface
o   Shaft held low and horizontal (about stomach height).

Arms:
o   Pushing action on shaft
o   Elbows high
o   Reach away from boat on recovery side
o   Recover paddle with 'motor cycle wrist roll' and slice to   surface.

Lower Body:
o   Pelvis rotation to bring boat upright
o   Hips and knees also used
o   In open cockpit boats the righting is achieved by pressure on opposite buttock.

Trunk:
o   Remains upright.

High recovery

Paddle:
o   Driving face of blade faces downwards
o   Shaft held high (chest height or above).

Arms:
o   Hanging/pulling action on shaft.
o   Reach slightly away from boat on recovery side
o   Arms remain flexed at all times.

Lower body:
o   Powerful hip action as soon as blade makes contact with water
o   Hip rotation is delivered to boat through knee braces, hip pads and seat
o   The hip action is fast.

Trunk:
o   Stays low to keep body weight close to kayak
o   Trunk is raised from water after hip action has been applied
o   Flexibility in all planes is required.

Head:
o   In extreme recovery the head falls onto shoulder on recovery side.

Blade recovery:
o   Wrist roll and slice out vertically.

Stern rudder

Paddle:
o   Aligned alongside boat
o   Trailing blade deep and square
o   Blade positioned well to rear.

Trunk:
o   Rotated towards trailing blade
o   Forwards and backwards lean to shift weight and trim boat when running on waves.

Arms:
o   Rear arm almost straight
o   Push, pull and neutral positions for steering
o   Wrist roll to assist steering
o   Tillering with forward arm to gain more powerful pressure on trailing blade.

Lower body:
o   Imparts steering forces to boat
o   On surf wave the down-wave edge is raised
o   On river wave the upstream edge is raised.

Boat:
o   Not a fast turn.

Low brace turn

Boat:

o A carving slow turn

o Boat sits on inside edge

o The boat is allowed to glide.

Paddle:

o Back of blade used

o Blade remains in brace position unless there is a sudden demand to increase speed of turn

o Blade as flat as possible

o Shaft low, close to horizontal

o Blade held away from side of boat

o Blade position in line with near shoulder

o Leading edge of blade slightly raised.

Arms:

o Elbows up

o Arms flexed, absorbing surface roughness.

Trunk:

o Slight rotation towards blade

o Upright sitting position

o Lean forwards to increase grip in eddy turns.

o Lean slightly rearward for softer, slower turn.

Head:

o Look towards new direction of travel.

Lower body:

o Knee and hips lift outside edge

o Degree of edging varied according to speed of turn and power of current.

Bow rudder

Blade:

o Deep blade grips the water

o Blade angle determined by nature of turn required and the amount of turning energy which the boat has already developed - in flat water the blade forms a shallow 'V' with side of boat, open and facing forwards

o Blade position

   - forwards to pull bow around

   - level with knees for a fast spin

o Wrist roll blade and slice to forward power stroke.

Shaft:

o Upright - viewed from front

o Upright or sloping to bow viewed from side

o All of shaft on rudder side of boat.

Trunk:

o Rotation towards blade

o Rotation unwinds throughout turn

o Body upright, changing to a forward lean if the rear of the boat sinks or is sucked under during the turn.

Lower body:

o Hips and opposite knee pull the boat around in the turn

o Control boat edging

   - Hard edging for fast turns and break-ins

   - Softer edging (more level boat) for longer turns and covering ground in break-outs and break-ins.

Arms:

o Top arm high - no lower than forehead

- Elbow points skyward
- Top hand helps set blade angle
o   Lower arm
- Flexed for strength
- Limit of outward wrist roll determines maximum blade angle
- Arms extends in slice to forward power stroke
- Elbow may be pulled into chest if very powerful turning forces are generated
- This helps to hold the paddle in position.

Head:

o   Look towards anticipated direction of travel.

Sculling draw:

Paddle:

o   Shaft vertical
o   Blade deep
o   Blade angled in each scull
o   Path of blade is straight line.

Arms

o   Top arm high
o   Top arm supports paddle and hand assists with blade feathering
o   Lower arm operates scull
o   Lower arm is flexed to give strong pull.

Trunk:

o   Full rotation towards sideslip
o   Body upright.

Lower body:

o   Knee lift on sideslip to prevent water being scooped onto deck
o   Otherwise boat sits level.

Head:

o   Face direction of sideslip or downstream if skirting around obstruction.

Sculling for support

Paddle:

o   Horizontal shaft
o   Driving face of blade downwards
o   Leading edge of blade raised on each scull
o   Keep blade moving.

Arms:

o   Keep flexed
o   Elbows under paddle shaft.

Trunk:

o   Hang under paddle shaft
o   Lateral flexibility required
o   Amount of body weight transferred to paddle shaft is variable according to circumstances
- Boat sits on edge, body upright (stopper surfing)
- Boat almost level, body towards water (brace against wind or wave).

Plate 7:a

7　Reading Water

Bill Mason

Bill Mason was the author of the very excellent, comprehensive manual on paddling the open canoe, The Path of the Paddle, *from which this chapter has been drawn. He had a lifetimes experience of wilderness paddling on which to draw, and directed several films on canoeing techniques for the National Film Board of Canada.*

Modification of Bill's original text has been undertaken to translate Canadian terms such as 'souse hole' for British paddlers, and to emphasise the relevance of this statement to kayakers.

Bill Mason sadly died in October 1988. We are grateful to Key Porter Books for permission to use this chapter, and pay tribute to one who gave so much to the sport from which he obtained a lifetime of fulfillment.

MODERN RAPID RUNNING TECHNIQUES

You've probably heard the old saying 'only fools run rapids'. I don't know who said it: probably the saying originated with the same guy who said you should never stand in a canoe. Whoever it was, I feel sorry for him. He never knew what he was missing.

The rapids and falls that break up the free flow of most of the world's rivers can be regarded in two ways. You either love them or you hate them. Most of the earlier travellers along North America's inland waterways hated them because they were a barrier. A falls meant transporting tons of furs and other goods around them by means of an excruciatingly difficult portage. More often rapids were feared because of the high risk to the heavily laden, fragile canoes in the seething whitewater. The bounty of ancient trade goods that divers dredge up at the base of many rapids along the old routes is evidence of many disasters. And an upset in those days really was a disaster, since it could mean losing a year of many men's labour, not to mention losing lives.

As we cavort in these same rapids in our small, tough, lightly loaded canoes and kayaks, it is well to remember those travellers of long ago. Today the risks we take are by choice, not of necessity. Improved equipment and paddling techniques have enabled modern canoeists to attempt rapids that never would have been run when life on the river was a serious business. In spite of these improvements, the risks, though they are different, have not diminished. The almost indestructible canoes and kayaks of today can cover a multitude of sins, all of them perpetrated in the name of whitewater canoeing. But it is well to remember that the dangers to a paddler who wipes out are just as great now as they ever were.

Rapids are much more than a place to play. It is because of these rapids and waterfalls that great islands of wilderness exist in many parts of the world today.

These barriers to navigation have cut off all the modern forms of transportation, and with them development along large stretches of rivers and lakes. It is true that here and there a railway intrudes to follow the river, but as soon as the river curves away from the desired direction, the river is once again left to go its own way. One portage in these areas puts the traveller beyond the reach of motorised transport.

The rapids and falls always have been the lock and bar to this secret world beyond the whitewater and portages, to be enjoyed only by those who acquire the skills and are willing to expend the effort to get there. It can be strenuous work, even arduous, but the wilderness traveller knows that the greater the difficulty, the greater the sense of stepping back into a time when life was simpler and basic. Not easier, just simpler. Out there it is possible to re-discover the joy to be derived from just looking, listening and thinking.

In those times, professional canoeists, such as trappers or prospectors, would have run rapids of moderate difficulty, but there was too much at stake to fool around in rapids just for the fun of it. They could not go off to the store to purchase another canoe and outfit. Nor could they return home and save up enough money to start over, since the lost outfit was the means by which their livings were earned.

Today recreational paddlers, with not so much at stake, have developed the skills of whitewater paddling to an amazing degree. People run rapids that a few years ago would have been considered suicidal. Whitewater racing is to a large extent responsible for this high level of skill that has blossomed in recent years.

The object of racing techniques is to get to the end of the rapids as quickly as possible without touching or missing a gate. These races take place within easy access of a road and with rescue crews standing by, so the price of failure doesn't come too high. Kayaks and decked-over whitewater canoes are commonly used. In open-canoe wilderness cruising, the object is to get to the end of the rapids with as little water in the canoe as possible, without regard to how long it takes.

With the open canoe, the canoeist descends slowly, allowing the canoe to ride high on the waves rather than powering through them. The recreational wilderness cruiser loves a fast, turbulent rapid but must always keep in mind the price of failure in a remote area.

WHAT IS A RAPID ?

To understand rapids and really get to know what they are and how they work, it helps to think of them as a living, breathing organism, like a wild animal. A stretch of rapids can be as gentle as a lamb or as wild as a rampaging rhinoceros, as playful as a kitten one moment and as deadly as a man-eating tiger the next.

Many times I have broken out of a gentle current above a tight corner to check out what's ahead to find that certain death was waiting around that bend. I've seen rapids that, given the choice between the rapids and a cage of Bengal tigers, I think I would take my chance with the tigers.

Most of the recent books on whitewater canoeing talk about vectors, kinetic energy, hydraulics, current differentials, and so on. I have avoided the use of such scientific terminology for the sake of simplicity. However, the science of flowing water is a fascinating study if you want to get into it. I have rendered the illustrations in a very realistic technique so you can more easily associate the diagrams on these pages with the rapids you will confront out there.

178

It's easy to talk about upstream and downstream Vs, but when you actually get out there and attempt to read a rapid they are not always as clearly defined as they are in a simple diagram. One V merges into another, creating a very complex conglomeration of whitewater patterns.

I have attempted here to give you all the information you need to understand fully what happens under the water's surface, how to avoid the dangerous elements that make up a rapid, and how to take advantage of its weaknesses to get through it safely. The most important aspect of running rapids is to be able to predict the degree of difficulty from shore, instead of finding out from an overturned or swamped canoe or kayak.

RIVER MORPHOLOGY

I must confess that the first time I heard the word morphology it sounded pretty awful, but it simply means the workings of a river. How water flows downhill on its journey to the sea is a very important subject for the whitewater canoeist.

Study the photographs carefully and see if you can figure out where all the rocks are, how close they are to the water's surface, and where the deep water channels are.

An experienced canoeist knows exactly what's under the surface and how the surging currents will affect the boat, even before the run begins. This is possible because every wave, every disturbance, is caused by the bed of the river. By learning what it is that causes haystacks, downstream Vs, upstream Vs, eddies, rollers and stoppers, you can formulate a mental picture of the river bed. You will know exactly where the rocks lay, how far beneath the surface they are, and whether or not they will present a problem. But what is even more important, you can tell with reasonable certainty where the rocks aren't. Now you are probably saying to yourself 'That's what I want to know. Who cares where they are as long as I don't hit them'.

The canoeist must learn to read the rapids from shore to appraise the degree of difficulty and choose a course if the rapid is to be run. Rapids also must be read from the canoe or kayak during the descent, far enough ahead to give time to make all the right moves to avoid the problem areas. It is quite possible to run easy rapids without knowing much about what's going on by allowing the current to carry you along. If you keep the canoe aligned with the current, it will tend to follow the deep-water channel.

But in a rapid of even moderate difficulty, canoeists must choose the course and position their canoes where they want them to go. Anything less is not running rapids under control. It is not only dangerous but much of the fun of running rapids cannot be fully experienced. There is very little merit in getting through a rapid on a hope and prayer. It's a lot safer and much more enjoyable to put some effort into acquiring the knowledge and skill to do it under complete control.

VARYING WATER-FLOW RATES

The rate at which water flows down a river varies across the width and depth. It is very important to understand how these variations in current affect the behaviour of the canoe. The canoeist not only must learn how to cope with these differentials, but also how to use them to advantage. For example, if you are drifting downstream, the canoe or kayak can spin right around at the most

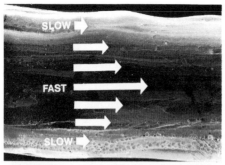

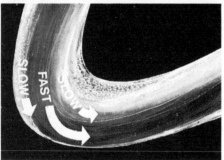

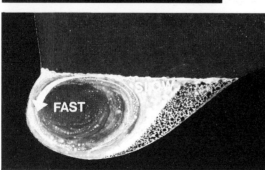

Figs 7:1, 7:2, 7:3, 7:4

inopportune moment, perhaps above a dangerous rapid or falls. On the other hand, an understanding of flow rates can enable you to exit from the main stream quickly under complete control.

Let us assume you are canoeing a straight stretch of river with a straight shoreline and a relatively smooth river bed. The slowest water flow is along the banks and bottom of the river because of friction. The water flows progressively faster toward the middle of the river (see Fig 7:1) with the fastest current right in the centre (Fig 7:2). To understand how these current differentials can affect the canoe, let's imagine you are paddling downstream close to shore for reasons of safety. If you let the front of the boat get into the slower water by the shore, your rear, which is in the swifter water further from the shore, will start to swing around, putting you broadside to the current. If a rock happens to come along at this moment, it's wipeout time. Otherwise the rear will keep moving downstream until you end up facing upstream by the shore.

Varying flow rate around a bend

Now let's imagine we come to a bend in our river. The deep water channel moves to the outside of the bend as it sweeps around the corner (Fig 7:3). The water on the inside of the turn moves very slowly, like the hub of a wheel. The outside of the turn is always deep, while the inside corner is always shallow.

A secondary current develops as the water on the surface is carried toward the outside of the turn and downward like an undertow (Fig 7:4). This can be seen in

180

Fig 7:4 looking upstream. In a white water river, where the irregular shape of its edge and bottom causes waves, sheer flows and stoppers, however, these secondary currents are insignificant.

Sharp bends in a river

A situation where currents can present a real problem is to be found on a sharp corner. As the water flows toward the corner, abruptness of the required change in direction prevents the river flowing smoothly round the bend. As the water bashes against the bank, it piles up, sinks and boils. The severity and extent of this turbulence will depend on the speed of the flow, the depth of the water and the shape of the bank.

As you attempt to hug the inside of the corner, you have to overcome the tendency of the current to carry you into the rock face, where you will be swamped and maybe pinned. In extremely swift, deep water, the turbulence could be strong enough to pull you under. The trick is knowing how strong a current you can contend with. The currents coming out of the corner are very confused and disoriented. Not far downstream, however, the river gets itself back together, and the current becomes predictable once again.

Rock gardens

In high water conditions, boulders are rolled along the bottom and dumped at the base of the rapids, where the river usually widens out, forming an apron of rubble stretching from shore-to-shore and curving downstream. It's called a rock garden and it creates a riffle that is difficult to get through in low water without hitting rocks. The deepwater channel, if there is one, is usually very hard to find. In low water, rock gardens usually make it necessary to get out and wade.

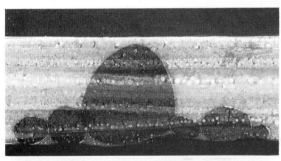

Fig 7:5 (top)   Plate 7:b
Rock in still water

READING RAPIDS

Rocks in current cause turbulence

The next thing one must know about rapids is how a rock located in swiftly flowing water can affect the surface. While the canoeist is concerned only with the surface of the water, it is important to understand what's going on along the bottom. Knowing where the rocks are, recognizing the

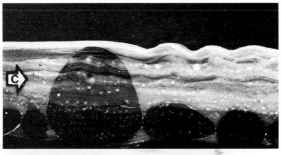

Fig 7:6 (top)   Plate 7:c
Rock in slow current

Fig 7:7 (top)   Plate 7:d
Rock in deeper, faster current

deepwater channel, and putting your canoe or kayak exactly where you want it is what running rapids is all about.

Rock in still water

In deep, quiet, or slow-moving water, the surface tells you nothing about the bottom of the river. Even a rock only a couple of inches under the surface gives no sign of its presence unless the water is clear. But river water is often dark or reflections make it difficult to see beneath the surface. As a result, it's quite common to run aground in the slow water above and below a rapid.

Rock in slow current

As the speed of the river increases, the rocks near the surface cause disturbances just downstream, usually in the form of a wave curling upstream. The wave isn't much of a problem, but the rock in front of it sure is.

Rock in deeper, faster current

An increase in the depth of the water and the speed of the current causes a corresponding increase in the size of the wave. If the rock is deep enough and the wave isn't too large, you can run right over the rock without hitting it.

Rock in deep, very fast current

With a further increase in water depth and velocity of

current, the curling wave builds in height and power and is capable of giving a beginner in a kayak a good shaking.

Stoppers

Stoppers are caused by water pouring abruptly or vertically over a large rock, ledge or weir. The fast-moving water seems to scoop out a deep hole filled with foaming aerated water that rolls back upstream. There is a definite tendency for floating objects, be they canoe or kayak, swimmer or plastic bottle, to be held in this hole. If a canoe is allowed to float freely into a stopper the returning wave will grip it and turn it side on to the current. If the paddler still takes no action the boat will be quickly flipped over towards the upstream side. The secret to not getting caught is to power directly through the stopper when you see it coming and to maintain this power whilst the boat is engulfed by the wave.

Stoppers which have water circulating well below the surface with a clear current returning upstream are potentially lethal. Such stoppers are commonly found on vertical or near-vertical man-made weirs. Swimmers held in the returning water or back tow are pushed under, then carried a few feet downstream and drawn back into the weir face as they surface. It is very difficult and risky for anyone to render assistance.

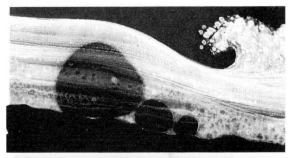

Fig 7:8(top)   Plate 7:e
Rock in deep, very fast current

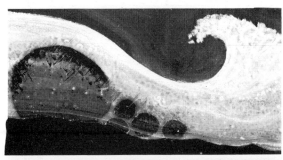

Fig 7:9   Plate 7:f
Large rock in very fast, deep current

Fig 7:10 (top)   Plate 7:g
A hole with its accompanying stopper

Fig 7:11   Plate 7:h
Large rock in very fast, deep current

Dangerous stoppers are not always obvious. Caution is the key, especially with rivers in high spate. See also Chapter 9.

Diagonal curling wave

Another thing which occurs in rivers in spate or those with naturally high volumes of water is a diagonal curling wave which is often hard to avoid. The wave is created when the whole river funnels into one large V, ending in a stopper. The sides of the V, which extend all the way from the shore, consist of a wave curling diagonally. Only a very strong brace into the wave as you shoot through it can keep you upright. Fig. 7:14.

Eddies

In a rapid it's the rocks that cause all the problems and obviously are to be avoided. However, they aren't all bad. Hiding just downstream of the bigger rocks and rocks that protrude above the surface, you will find eddies of flatwater. Water can't flow through the rock, so it is forced to go around or over it. If the rock is sufficiently near the surface, very little water is going over it and a pool of relatively still water is created behind the rock. These areas of flat water provide a haven in the midst of the worst of the rapids - if you can get into them without hitting the rock or upsetting. The eddies are an escape route that can be used to avoid a dangerous area downstream or to rest and plan your next move.

Downstream and upstream Vs

You want to look for the deep-water channel between the rocks. The water flowing between the rocks forms a dark V pointing downstream (Fig. 7:16). If these dark Vs are clearly defined and aligned in such a way that you can follow them throughout the entire length of the rapid, the rapid can be considered easily runnable. A V that is pointing upstream is pointing directly at a rock. Whether or not you can see the rock beneath the surface, you can be sure it's there.

Standing waves and haystacks

'Standing wave' is the generic term for any wave created by a local increase in the rate of flow of water (Fig. 7:17). A glassy dip on the water surface with a broad, rounded crest which is smooth and unbroken is a standing wave. A steep pointed wave with an exploding, cascading top is also a standing wave. Indeed, technically speaking the wave which forms a rolling, surface-circulating stopper is a form of standing wave. Canoeists distinguish between some of these forms of wave because their affects on the boat are quite different; hence the term 'stopper'. Waves which rise steeply to a turbulent crest are referred to as 'haystacks' and the less broken, rounded forms remain 'standing waves'.

Fig 7:12 (top)   Plate 7:i
An eddy, downstream of a boulder

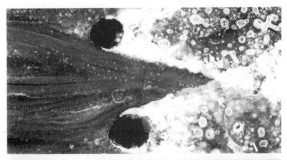

Fig 7:13   Plate 7:j
Downstream and upstream Vs

185

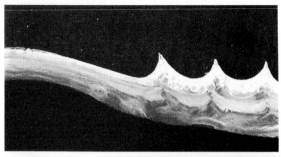

Fig 7:14 (top)   Plate 7:k
Standing waves

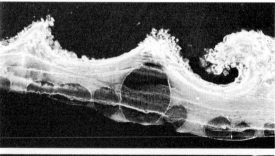

Fig 7:15   Plate 7:l
Haystacks with rocks

Standing waves and haystacks are usually found at the apex of the downstream Vs. They are friendly deepwater waves caused by fast water racing down the V and hitting the deep, slower-moving water. There is usually a series of these waves aligned downstream like a roller coaster. Haystacks are what make a rapid fun and white water kayak paddlers often spend hours surfing and somersaulting on the upstream faces of well formed waves.

It is of course important to learn to tell the difference between a deep water haystack and an upstream curling wave caused by a rock. The two formations do, however, merge - especially in difficult rapids.

It's one of the hardest things to read in a rapid. Sometimes you can actually catch a glimpse of the rock if you study the wave closely.

Rock in the path of a downstream V

If the rock is located right in the main path of a fast V after a sharp drop, water can spray in all directions. You also will see a hump of water downstream of the turbulence. Remember that when the water flows over a rock, the curling wave is located downstream of the rock. In this case, the fast water hits the rock and causes turbulence in front of it. You will want to stay well away from this area. Hitting the rock will cause severe damage because of the speed of the current. Many a hidden haystack rock has spoiled a nice run down a fast V. A rock in a fast V is of great danger to a swimming canoeist. As you will see from the illustration (Fig 7:15, Plate 7:l) it is not easy to see if the rocks are close enough to the surface to cause a problem to a passing canoe or kayak.

Fast-water narrows, haystacks

The easiest form of rapids is found where a narrowing in the river causes an increase in the speed of the current. Haystacks usually result as the water surges through the gap (Fig. 7:19).

Fast water with a few rocks

In a rapid with a few rocks, the upstream Vs indicate the presence of the rocks, making them easy to see and to avoid (Fig. 7:20).

Fast water with many rocks but clearly defined downstream Vs

Despite the presence of many upstream Vs, the downstream Vs are clearly discernable and are aligned in such a way that they can be easily followed. The haystacks at the end of each downstream V are of moderate size (Fig. 7:21).

Fast water with unaligned Vs

When running a rapid involves the connecting up of

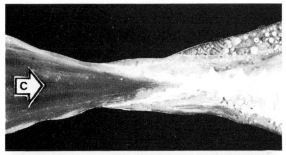

Fig 7:16 (top)   Plate 7:m
Fast water narrows and haystack waves

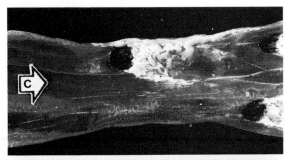

Fig 7:17   Plate 7:n
Fast water with a few rocks

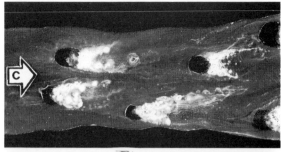

Fig 7:18 (top)   Plate 7:o
Fast water with many rocks but obvious Vs

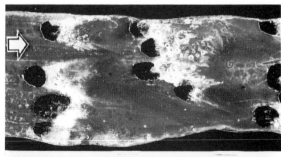

Fig 7:19   Plate 7:p
Fast water with unaligned Vs

unaligned Vs you are getting into the realms of more difficult grades. Often in such rapids the paddler has to reverse ferry glide into position before letting the boat slip through each V. An alternative is to 'eddy hop' from break-out to break-out, giving you time to get a good look at each move before committing yourself to it (Fig. 7:22).

Rapids with unaligned Vs, stoppers and drops

The existence of serious stoppers, and drops, renders a rapid a lot more difficult because failure to avoid them can send you swimming Whether or not the rapid should be attempted depends on many factors. Can the obstacles be avoided with your present level of skill ? Do the drops or ledges have a clearly defined V ? The most important factor is the length of the rapids. What would be the price of a capsize and swim ?

Another factor that determines the danger of rapids is the distance between rapids. Is there sufficient distance between rapids to recover before being swept into the next. You just can't appraise the difficulty of a rapid by looking at it. What lies downstream should have a lot to do with your decision.

Ledges

Ledges sometimes extend all the way across a river. A good example is the one below Pont Agog bridge on the

Tryweryn in Wales. They can be dangerous if the drop is abrupt because of the stopper at the bottom. Even a drop of only 30 to 60cm can cause enough of a backtow to hold a canoe or kayak.

A ledge becomes easily runnable if there is a clearly defined V anywhere along its length. The main problem is locating the V as you approach from upstream.

Weirs

Weirs are man-made ledges. They are found in abundance on British rivers, often providing the only white water in an otherwise slow-moving length of river. The fabric of these artificial ledges can be wood, stone, reinforced concrete or even steel. As these construction materials break down through time, deadly traps for the canoeist and swimmer start to appear, in the form of spikes, holes and edges. To make matters worse, these hazards are often totally invisible to the paddler inspecting from the river bank. The only way to be certain that a weir is clear is to see it in dry conditions, but remember that it is at the base of a weir that the most erosion takes place and therefore this is the place you most want to see.

The Safety chapter in this Handbook describes the common types of weir to be found in Britain.

The geometric symmetry of weir shape is often perfect for causing dangerous, deeply circulating stoppers. There are many cases throughout Europe of people drowning in weirs as a result of being

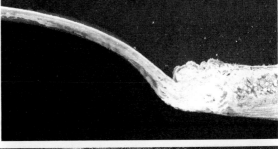

Fig 7:20 (top)   Plate 7:q
Rapids with unaligned Vs, stoppers and drops

Fig 7:21   Plate 7:r
A ledge in low water

189

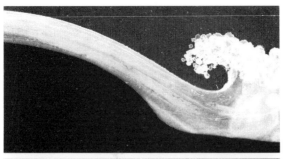

Fig 7:22(top)   Plate 7:s
A ledge in high water

trapped by the circulation of a stopper,

Unfortunately, it is not easy to look at the formation of water at the base of a weir and say with confidence that a swimmer will escape from it easily. Even experienced white water paddlers find it difficult to appraise the danger of such places accurately. To complicate the matter, variations in water level can radically change the characteristics of the formation. It is therefore dangerous to make any assumptions about the degree of safety of a weir on the basis of seeing it at one water level only.

The only safe rule is to stay well clear (above and below) if there is any doubt. Remember that a paddler in a kayak getting through a stopper offers no guarantee that a swimmer, as a result of a capsize, will also get through. See also White Water Safety and Rescue chapter.

Plate 7:t
A typical weir on a British river in high water. The water pouring over the lip is smooth, and this makes it hard to see from upstream

Plate 7:u
The water formation below a small vertical weir in high water. The stopper is circulating deeply and the surface water, pouring back into the stopper slot is clearly visible. To further add to the hazard, there is no clear downstream V running through the stopper

8 Kayaking: White Water Technique

Ray Rowe

INTRODUCTION

To appreciate this chapter fully, the Basic Strokes need to be understood. Good white water technique can only be built upon a foundation of well practised, efficient basic strokes. Although some of the information might be useful to competitors, it is not primarily aimed at any form of competitive canoesport. Its purpose is to help paddlers and coaches to raise the level of satisfaction gained from white water paddling by examining efficient boat handling technique and showing how it can be enhanced by practice, training and coaching.

BASIC MANOEUVRES

The basic manoeuvres on white water can be grouped into:

o Eddy turns - where the paddler uses the energy of the river to turn by taking advantage of current and eddy interaction

o Cross current moves - where the kayak crosses the current using the combined efforts of the paddler and the flow.

These manoeuvres allow the paddler to leave and regain the current and to position himself accurately in the flow. They are essential skills for negotiating all but the very simplest of rivers. In each case they use power from the river to move the boat. It is part of the paddler's job to make the best use of this power.

Fig 8:1 shows the basic terminology applied to parts of a rapid.

The break-in

The aim of a break-in is to enter the current from an eddy or from the slack water at the river's edge. The kayak, pointing upstream, is driven forwards and then across the eddy line so that it enters the flow. From the moment its bow touches the powerful downstream current, the kayak starts to turn downstream and its forward momentum takes it clear across the eddy line and away down the river.

The eddy line is an important reference point in a break-in. The paddler must decide on the speed at which he is going to cross it and also on the angle. The angle is relatively easy to work out because, if the boat cuts it at too fine an angle, it will

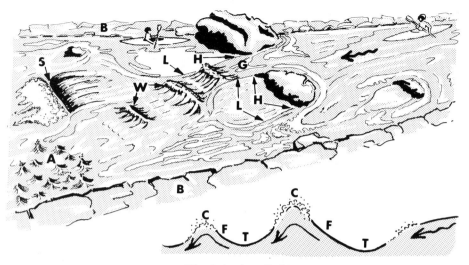

Fig 8:1a (top left)

White water terminology. A rapid

A: Irregular spraying waves - haystacks; B: River bank; G: 'Tongue' or 'jet'; H: Head of the eddy, with the slack water of the eddy directly downstream; L: Eddy lines - the boundaries where eddy water meets the downstream flow; S: stopper, with the deep trough of the stopper slot running across; W: Standing waves

Fig 8:1b (bottom right)

Profile of standing waves

C: Wave crest; F: Face; T: Trough

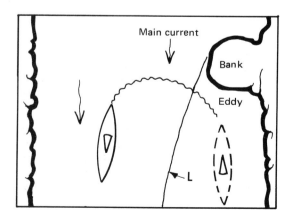

Fig 8:2
Breaking-in
L indicates the eddy line

194

Plates 8:a(i) and 8:a(ii)
When breaking in, seek a smooth turn downstream, with the kayak constantly moving forwards. Here, the low brace turn gives a sluggish but safe manoeuvre. The alternative is to pull out into the current with a bow rudder - much faster, but more difficult for the novice

merely enter the current and point upstream; too wide an angle will result in failure to cross the line and the kayak will remain in the slack eddy water; around 45 degrees is right. The speed at which the kayak should cross the eddy line will be determined by the speed of the current. The rule is, the faster the current, the harder you have to hit it with the bow of the kayak. If you try to enter a fast current with little speed, you will bounce straight back into the eddy and feel very unstable in the process.

Edging
The paddler must raise the kayak's upstream edge before the bow breaks the eddy line. This has to be done because it deflects the current under the kayak's hull and prevents the build up of water pressure on the upstream edge which would cause the boat to flip.

Paddle action
The low brace turn forms the basis of a break-in. It is for precisely this purpose that it is learnt as a basic stroke. The wide bracing paddle forms a good 'handrail' for the paddler whilst he applies the edging. A more experienced paddler, who has learnt to balance the kayak throughout the turn, could choose to use a bow rudder in preference to the low brace. This lets him pull the kayak very quickly through the turn, but offers considerably less stability.

Figs 8:3, 8:4, 8:5 show three different break-in situations and the strokes sequences which could be used with them. In Fig 8:3, the paddler wishes to make a safe break-in with no concern for the speed of the turn. In Fig 8:4, the break-in takes the kayak into a narrow jet of current. To avoid overshooting the jet, the turn must be assisted by the paddler applying a reverse sweep. In Fig 8:5, the paddler wants to break-in fast and pull away fast.

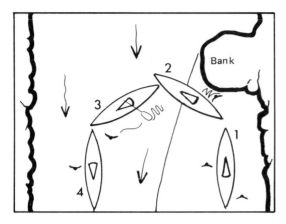

Fig 8:3
For a slow, but safe, break-in

Boat position	Paddle action	Balance
1 moves forwards	forward paddling	level
2 set angle	forward sweep	lift upstream edge
3 turns downstream	low brace turn	maintain edging
4 runs downstream	forward paddling	level

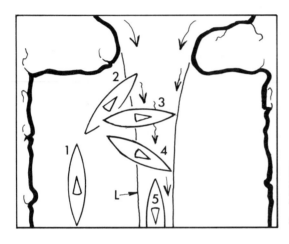

Fig 8:4
For a slow break-in to a narrow jet

Boat position	Paddle action	Balance
1 moves forward	forward paddling	level
2 set angle	forward sweep	lift upstream edge
3 crosses eddy line	low brace turn	maintain edging
4 turning speed increases	low brace to reverse sweep	level off slowly
5 runs downstream	forward paddling	level

Fig 8:5
Fast break-in - fast away

Boat position	Paddle action	Balance
1 accelerates forward	forward paddling	level
2 set angle	start forward sweep	lift upstream edge
3 crosses eddy line	finish forward sweep	maintain edging
4 turns downstream	bow rudder	maintain edging
5 turns downstream	bow rudder	maintain edging
6 runs down stream	slice to forward paddling	level off

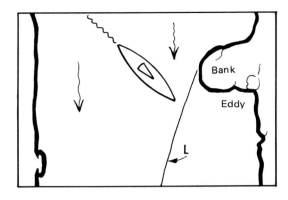

Fig 8:6
Breaking out. Driving out of
the main current into an eddy.
Positioning the boat on the
approach to the eddy is called
'lining up'

The break-out

The aim of a break-out is to enter an eddy from the current. Once again, the paddler is required to cross the eddy line, this time tucking the kayak into the slack water. This manoeuvre has particular significance because it is the surest and safest method by which a paddler removes himself from the current. When the river is thundering along and you are going with it, making a break- out lets you freeze the action whilst you get your breath back or inspect the next section.

The break-out sequence has three parts:

o   Positioning the boat

o   Balancing the turn

o   Use of an appropriate stroke sequence.

Positioning the boat

The planning for a break-out starts well in advance when the paddler adjusts his position across the river so that he is on the correct line. This is called 'lining up'. It is common for a paddler to line up before he actually has the eddy in sight. He might know of the eddy position through being familiar with the area, or he might have decided that the features which he can see will cause an eddy. Once he spots the eddy he should:

Plate 8:b
The forward sweep is a vital
trigger in the break-out
sequence, pushing the boat
across the eddy line and
setting up a rhythm for the hip
and trunk movements to
follow. Applying a forward
sweep that generates drive and
spin whilst in rough water,
takes considerable confidence

197

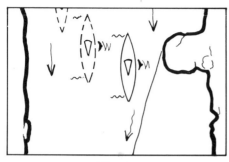

Fig 8:7
Lining up by using draw strokes to side-slip the boat into position

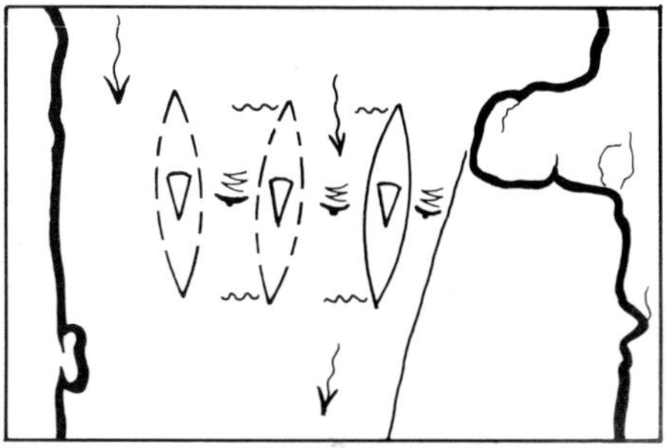

Fig 8:8
Using reverse ferry gliding to line the boat up

o   Keep it in view
o   Notice its length and breadth
o   Be decisive: make up his mind to go for it or leave it alone
o   Continue to line up by moving towards the eddy.

The paddler in Fig 8:6 finds himself across the river from the eddy. He has a choice of three tactics to line up:

o   Sprint across the river
o   Draw stroke the boat into position (Fig 8:7)
o   Reverse ferry glide across (Fig 8:8)

Sprinting works well providing the move is made early. In very fast water, you need a lot of warning and it is difficult to hit small eddies accurately. The draw stroke technique allows the boat to drift downstream whilst the paddler puts all his effort into moving sideways. This is an excellent method but is strenuous if large distances have to be covered. The ferry glide would be used when the line-up has been overshot and the boat has almost drawn level with the eddy. Where the route to the eddy is a long way across a wide river, the paddler sprints to cover most of the ground and then incorporates more and more draws into the paddling to make fine adjustments to his position.

The eddy line 'target'

The paddler should imagine a target on the eddy line. The target represents the point at which he would like to cross that line. He should position the target to take best advantage of the slack water in the eddy. This is normally quite close to the source of the eddy, but allowing enough room to take the whole boat.

With experience, the paddler learns to place the target according to what his intentions will be after making the eddy. If he intends to break-in immediately after he gains the eddy, then he sets the target a little further downstream to allow himself room to accelerate up the eddy before re-entering the current. If he wishes to pause in the eddy then he moves the target close to the source, where he finds a good parking space.

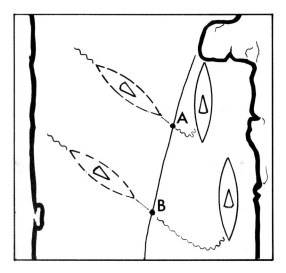

Fig 8:9
*The eddy line target - the point
on the eddy line where you
decide to cross. Choosing
position A gives different
results from position B,
because the eddy line becomes
less defined as you follow it
downstream*

POSITION A In this position, the target takes the boat into the area of the eddy which has slackest water. The turn is very fast.

POSITION B In this position, the target allows the boat to penetrate deep into the eddy. The turn is much slower and there is a greater risk of missing the eddy completely.

The angle at which the boat initially cuts the eddy line is called the *angle of approach*. The paddler's mental computer tells him what this angle should be. The optimum angle will be one which takes the boat across the eddy line and smoothly into the turn (Fig 8:10).

A paddler must set a wide angle of approach if the eddy he is attempting to enter is very narrow, say alongside a wall or a very thin strip of slack water behind a small boulder. The turning strokes must be made very quickly (Fig 8:11).

A narrow angle of approach may be imposed by a narrow shoot which the paddler is forced to take immediately above the eddy. A very powerful sweep is required to take the kayak across the eddy line and only a strong bow rudder will hold it in the eddy (Fig 8:12).

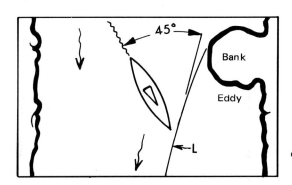

Fig 8:10
*The angle of approach to the
eddy line. The optimum would
be about 45 degrees*

199

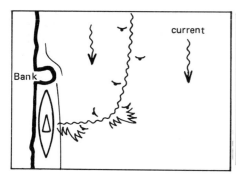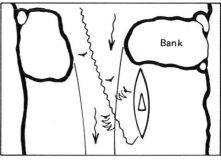

Fig 8:11
Where the eddy is very narrow, the paddler must set a wide angle of approach. It is important with this tactic to keep the boat moving forwards

Fig 8:12
Rivers with tight channels and gulleys often force a narrow break-out angle. The paddler needs to think ahead as very fast stroke timing is necessary

Balancing the boat in the turn

When the kayak crosses the eddy line, it is felt to bite into the still water while its stern is driven around. As a consequence of this turning momentum which builds up in the boat, the paddler must:

o   Lean to the inside of the turn

o   Lift the outside edge of the kayak (edging)

Remember the distinction between edging and leaning (see Basic Strokes chapter). Lean involves dropping the body weight into the turn, like rounding a corner on a bicycle. Edging involves raising one edge of the boat using lift from the thigh an knee, and depressing the opposite buttock. The faster the turn, the more lean is required.

Edging

When a boat crosses the eddy line, its front inside edge digs in while its rear outside edge skids across the surface.

Kayaks which have very sharp edges and low decks need to be tilted a lot to keep the rear edge from catching in a turn. A skilful paddler in a low-decked boat deliberately allows the stern edge to catch in a manoeuvre known as a 'pivot turn'. The sunken rear edge drags the boat's stern deep under water. This causes the bow to rise clear of the water so that the boat can be spun to land pointing in a new direction. The pivot turn only works in very low volume boats.

Higher volume boats with more rounded sides are less prone to accidentally catching edges but do not grip the water as well in break-outs. The paddler can get away with a smaller range of edging but can only extract the greatest performance from his boat if he masters edging control completely.

Plate 8:c(i-iv)
Setting a wide angle of approach to gain a narrow, mid-stream eddy

Stroke sequence

The paddle can be used during the break-out for the following purposes:

o   To control the distance the boat travels into the eddy
o   To act as a handrail to the paddler for balance
o   To speed the turn up
o   To finish off the turn

The paddler selects a sequence of linked strokes which will allow him to place emphasis on whichever of these functions he requires.

Here are two typical examples of stroke sequences.

Example A.   A novice paddler learning break-out technique.

BOAT POSITION	STROKE SEQUENCE	BALANCE
1 line up and set angle of approach	forward paddling	level
2 cross eddy line	forward sweep	begin edging
3 turns in eddy	low brace turn	hold edging
4 turn ends	surface slice to forward paddling	level

In this example the emphasis is on safety and stability throughout the turn; hence, use of the low brace turn. This is a simple and easy to remember sequence. The final stroke (No.4) is called a 'checking stroke'. Its purpose is to cancel the tendency for the boat to slip backwards down the eddy after the turn. It is, in effect, a single forward power stroke.

Example B.   A competent paddler taking a mid stream break-out into a small, narrow eddy.

BOAT POSITION	STROKE SEQUENCE	BALANCE
1 line up	forward paddling + draw strokes	level
2 set wide angle of approach	forward paddle stroke to last half of forward sweep	level
3 cross eddy line	powerful forward sweep	begin edging
4 fast turn	bow rudder then slice to bow draw	hold edging
5 turn ends	checking stroke	level

Plate 8:d(i)
The paddler is entering an eddy (current moving right to left) using a low brace turn break-out. Useful for beginners

Plate 8:d(ii)
(Current moving left to right) Using a bow rudder to break out offers much greater accuracy. In more difficult water, with a faster current and smaller eddies, the break-out is likely to be impossible without the use of the bow rudder

The bow rudder is placed deep and with the blade fully opened. This causes the boat to stall, and the slice to the bow pull prevents the bow overshooting the eddy.

The strokes which are used in a break-out and the methods of their use are widely variable. Clearly there is no one, perfect stroke sequence since every break- out is unique in its form and in the strength of current passing it. The presence of overhanging trees, shallow ground or other paddlers in the eddy add further complications. The skilful paddler has a range of stroke sequences at his finger tips and is quick to select or construct the most suitable one. Being able to interrupt a sequence to create a different result is also the mark of good paddler.

This flexibility and variability should be built into training programmes for paddlers. Many different eddies should be used and instructors should be imaginative in creating problems for paddlers by restricting angles of approach, limiting the length of eddy water etc, so that paddlers are forced to improvise and adapt their strokes.

Summary of break-out techniques for paddlers

o   Plan ahead; know your movements for lining up, approach angle and boat speed well in advance

o   Commitment; decide and then go; hesitating will only give you problems

o   Initiating stroke; develop a powerful and positive forward sweep so that the boat leaps into the eddy !

o   Bow rudder; remember that the blade is placed in the slack water; it should be deep and upright

o   Edging; develop power and flexibility in your edging; if you are using a heavy kayak it will take time to develop the abdominal strength to edge it fully

o   Checking stroke; get into the habit of always using this and be prepared to use two or even three

Speed across the eddy line

An eddy line forms the boundary between water in two quite different states of motion. If we watch a piece of free floating debris, we will see that the eddy line is a substantial barrier keeping the floating object firmly on one side. Similarly a kayak will not merely drift across the eddy line and, if the paddler tries this, he is simply bounced back into the water that he started from. Momentum as a result of speed across the water is needed to overcome the invisible force-field that exists on the eddy boundary. The more powerful the current, the greater is the penetration speed required.

The need for speed across the eddy line applies to both break-outs and break-ins. The message here for the pupil is very simple. Cross the eddy line with speed on the kayak and the eddy turns will be smooth and steady.

Reverse eddy turns

A paddler should perfect *reversing* into and out of eddies for two reasons:

o   It develops orientation and awareness of the boat's position in the water

o   Paddlers often find themselves accidentally spun around in a rapid and the fastest way to get back on course is to break-out in reverse.

Reverse break out stroke sequence

The priority for the paddler in reverse turns, apart from lining up, is to give stability.

A simple stroke sequence that can be rehearsed on flat water first is:

STROKE SEQUENCE	BOAT POSITION
1 reverse paddling and draw 2 reverse sweep 3 reverse brace 4 slice to reverse paddle stroke	lining up cross eddy line, begin edging boat turns

The 'reverse brace' is a stroke which is unique to reverse eddy turns. It could be described as a high brace with a low paddle shaft, ie the blade has its driving face down and the shaft is about shoulder height. The leading edge of the blade is very slightly raised to prevent it from diving under and it skids across the surface exactly as it would in a low brace turn. The blade is positioned level with the near shoulder. This is a natural and comfortable angle at which that arm can work. If the paddler wants to increase the speed of the turn, he can convert the reverse brace to the last half of a reverse sweep and this, in turn, can be taken into

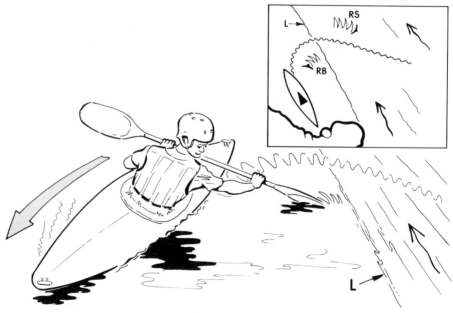

Fig 8:13
The reverse brace - a position peculiar to reverse eddy turns - which provides stability (L: eddy line; RS: reverse sweep; RB: reverse brace)

a reverse paddling stroke. A good tip for the reverse break-out is to look over the shoulder of the bracing arm as you make the turn. This helps in two ways:

o   It sets the boat onto the correct edge

o   It gives a better view of the piece of water coming up (Fig 8:13).

Finally, paddlers who are feeling tippy can usually be found to be holding the bracing blade too close to the side of the boat. This reduces the platform of stability drastically.

Exactly the same principles apply to the reverse break-in.

The ferry glide

A ferry glide is the simplest way of crossing a current so that the boat does not lose ground downstream. The forward ferry glide is the easiest to carry out as the paddler faces upstream and paddles forwards. The reverse ferry glide is more strenuous and harder to control because the paddler is holding the boat by reverse paddling.

The forward ferry glide

Picture a paddler in the middle of a wide, even-flowing current. He is holding his ground by paddling steadily into the current. To cross to the right he swings the bow of the boat gradually towards the right bank and continues to paddle forwards. He slides sideways across the current until he reaches the bank (Fig 8:14).

To change the speed with which you cross in a ferry glide, two things must be altered:

o   Speed of paddling

o   Angle of boat to current.

To speed up a ferry glide, a paddler increases his paddling speed and the angle of the boat to the current, ie points more towards the bank. The limiting factor on the speed of a ferry glide is the paddler's top speed in the boat. If he sets too wide an angle for his top speed, he will slip away downstream (Fig 8:15).

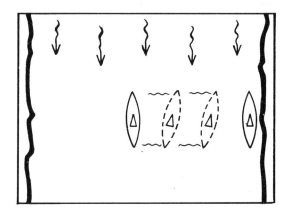

Fig 8:14
Ferry gliding across the current in an evenly flowing stretch of river

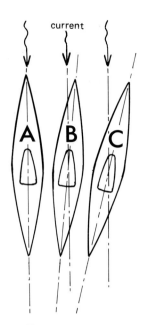

Fig 8:15
Setting the angle of the ferry glide
Position A gives no sideways movement
Position B. When the current is very fast the paddler
must set a narrow angle and adjust the paddling
speed accordingly
Position C. When the current is weak or a fast ferry
glide is required a wider angle can be set

Beginners often have difficulty with leaving the slack water at the bank to start a ferry glide. Here are two ways to leave the bank safely:

o Set a very small angle to the current and use powerful forward paddling strokes which take the boat upstream slightly - this gets you into the current where you can then set the correct angle

o Draw stroke into the current and quickly start paddling forwards to check the downstream drift; set ferry glide angle.

The reverse ferry glide

The ability to make a good reverse ferry glide is essential in white water paddling. Most paddlers can recall a time when it proved the only means of escape and many rivers have sections which can only be negotiated by a succession of reverse ferry glide moves. The same relationship of boat speed and angle to current applies as for the forward ferry glide, and it must be remembered that all paddlers have a lower top speed in reverse and less boat control. This means that the boat angle to the current must be kept well within that which can be matched by comfortable paddling speed.

The paddler looks over the downstream shoulder and controls the boat angle with reverse sweeps. If the boat suddenly swings widely off course, he can use a quick forward sweep to regain the angle. The reverse paddling style is usually a compromise between low, wide sweeping strokes which give good steering, and deep strokes, close to the boat, which give acceleration.

Reverse ferry gliding should be introduced on wide, even currents where paddlers can acquire feel for the technique without the interference of sudden changes in current.

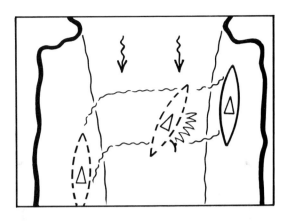

Fig 8:16
The cross. A high speed ferry glide on a jet

Summary of ferry gliding:

o Try to use good basic stroke technique

o Flexibility in the trunk is needed

o Be determined and take control of the boat

o Learn to feel the boat angle to the current

o Know the current you are about to cross; notice variations in strength and allow for them.

o Be aware of the boat's movement with respect to the bank; it is easy to lose track of your drift.

The cross

Moving from one eddy across a fast, narrow jet to another is called a 'cross'. It is in fact a high speed ferry glide. The boat is accelerated up the eddy and penetrates the eddy line at a very narrow ferry glide angle. The paddler edges hard downstream and the boat's forward momentum shoots it smoothly across the jet and into the new eddy. A change of edging occurs as the boat enters the new eddy. If the boat looses momentum on the cross, a forward power stroke or two can be applied on the downstream side (Fig 8:16).

Plate 8:e
Mid-way on a cross.
The mid-sector of a forward sweep is used to provide the power to assist the cross

207

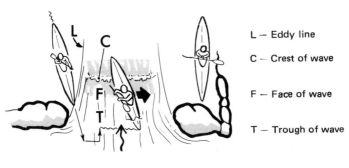

L — Eddy line

C — Crest of wave

F — Face of wave

T — Trough of wave

Fig 8:17

Crossing on a wave. The boat runs across the wave face as if on a surf wave.
Even the faintest of depressions on the surface of the flow will help the kayak to
cross. The upstream stern rudder is important, on longer crosses, to hold the
position on the wave

Crossing on a wave

A second method of crossing a current is to take advantage of waves which form
on the surface. The waves are known as 'standing waves' and they are in two
forms:

o Pyramid shaped, sometimes with a cascading top, in which case they are
termed 'haystacks'

o Long and straight topped like a surf wave.

The top of the wave is the 'crest', the ramp facing upstream is the 'face' and the
base in front of the ramp is called the 'trough'.

The paddler approaches the wave from downstream and to its side. The boat
is dropped onto the wave face with the bow in the trough. The ramp of the wave
face shoots the boat forward and across the current. A skilful paddler searches out
waves when he wants to make a cross and even the tiniest wave which shows as
merely a dip on the surface can give a lot of help (Fig 8:17).

Just like the ferry glide, a cross requires the paddler to set exactly the correct
angle to the current. Facing straight upstream on a wave will cause the boat to
surf momentarily, then run into the trough and finally shoot backwards off the
wave. Maintaining the angle on the wave can be done in two ways:

208

o Having a lot of forward speed as the boat hits the wave helps it to stay on course by virtue of its momentum

o The paddler gains the wave carefully and gets on to the face; he trails a stern rudder on the upstream side which locks the boat onto its diagonal run across the face.

Edging

On the wave cross, it is necessary to raise the upstream edge to allow water to pass underneath it. This also causes the downstream edge to bite into the wave which helps the kayak to hold the wave. Combined with a stern rudder, this edging can give superb rides on long crosses.

S-cross

Steep 'haystack' waves are often found between two well-defined eddies and a conventional wave cross in this situation often poses the problem of shooting the paddler too far upstream so that he ends up above the eddy. The aim is to cross and land in the security of the eddy and not in a no-mans land around the eddy source. The manoeuvre required is called an 'S-cross'.

The boat is driven hard across the eddy line at a wide angle to the current. The paddler aims to get his seat to pass over the crest of the haystack as he makes the cross. Considerable speed in approaching the wave is needed to do this (Fig 8:18).

Plate 8:f(i) (top left)
Leave the eddy on a course that will let the boat rise broadside, over the haystack

Plate 8:f(ii) (top left)
As it passes through the haytstack, apply a powerful forward sweep

Plate 8:f(iii) (left)
Transfer edging; quickly and aggressively change to a bow rudder

209

Plate 8:g
Positioning the kayak for the S-cross. The haystack peak can be seen at the apex
of the black tongue (Current from left to right)

S-cross stroke sequence

STROKE	BOAT POSITION	BALANCE
1 forward paddling to accelerate	cross eddy line	raise upstream edge
2 high brace	rises to wave	hold edging
3 convert to forward sweep	off wave, across eddy line	change to opposite edge raised
4 bow rudder	complete the turn	reduce edging
5 checking stroke	straight in eddy	level

This is a fast and wet manoeuvre and the paddler often finds himself having to work 'blind'. For this reason, he relies very much on the feel of the boat's movements to know where he is in the cross. The timing of strokes and weight transfer is critical and it is useful for paddlers to rehearse mentally, ie: imagine themselves doing the cross before they go. A common fault, resulting in a capsize in the S-cross, is to be late with the transfer of edging.

Stopper technique

Stoppers present themselves in three ways:

o   Surface circulating; a cascading wave on the surface with water immediately underneath it escaping downstream

o   Weir stoppers; circulation is below the surface; usually offers a long towback.

o   Holes; slot behind a boulder where the water has poured over and formed a deep circulation.

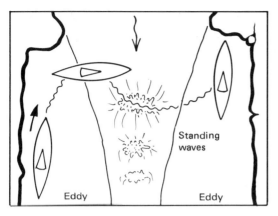

Fig 8:18
The S-cross is used where the
wave is a pronounced hump or
peak. The boat is allowed to
rise to the wave top and then
run off it into the eddy

The second two categories are the most dangerous as their powerful back tow can cause kayaks and swimmers to be re-circulated.

When a paddler is confronted with a stopper downstream, which he cannot avoid, there is only one choice of action at his disposal regardless of the stopper type:

o   Accelerate, with high revving strokes

o   Reach over the top of the wave as the boat drops into the slot and dig deep for the next power stroke

o   Keep the boat pointing square downstream and keep the power on.

Applying this power stroke as soon as possible after landing in the slot, and not removing it is usually the key to success. It is all too easy to be intimidated by the approaching wave, but to give up paddling and lean back is asking for trouble (Fig 8:l9).

Weirs

Overcoming the deep, re-circulating stopper which forms below a vertical weir face can be nerve racking and frequently life-threatening. The back tow from such a weir can easily extend beyond the length of a boat, making it virtually impossible to paddle out of its influence. Weirs like this should be avoided.

Plate 8:h
Penetrating stoppers demands
a sense of acceleration. Use
deep, fast, short strokes. Get
mean ! Keep the power on
until you are through

211

Plate 8:i
A sideways 'ride' in a stopper (current from right to left). A clearly raised upstream edge, sitting upright, and steadying himself on a low brace shows this paddler is balanced yet relaxed.

Plate 8:j
Where the stopper slot is deep, and the downsteam wave high, a high brace is needed for support

If you do have to run the weir, then you will need every ounce of speed that you can muster as you approach the lip. If the water is shallow on the lip, you might get a push off the shelf itself. The aim is to cover as much distance in the air as possible. This is called 'jumping the stopper' and it helps you to land flatter and offer less grip for the back tow.

Riding surface stoppers
People sit sideways and 'ride' surface stoppers because they have been drawn in by accident, or simply because it is good fun. Providing the stopper is safe to escape from, this is a practice very much to be recommended.

Once the boat is held sideways, the paddler raises the upstream edge and uses a paddle brace on the breaking wave on his downstream side. The boat bounces and jumps, sometimes wildly! Getting the paddle brace position correct is important and affects how comfortable you feel in the slot. When the circulating wave is high, a high brace is most comfortable, otherwise, a low brace works well. One of the most common errors in stopper surfing technique is to use a very high

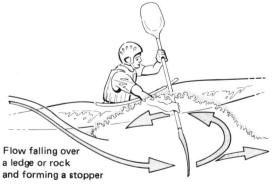

Flow falling over
a ledge or rock
and forming a stopper

Fig 8:19
Keep the power on to penetrate the stopper. When the curling wave hits your chest, drop the next paddle stroke in deep and keep firm pressure on it as the boat climbs out

212

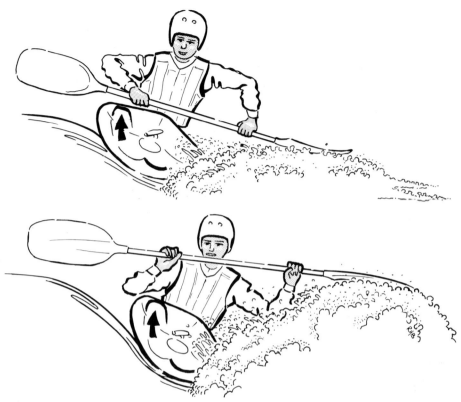

Fig 8:20a, b
Bracing in a stopper, either by accident or for fun is about keeping the
upstream edge clear of descending water and using as little energy as possible
to do it. Fig 8:20a (top) shows the low brace: good for getting in balance and
unweighting the paddle. 8:20b shows the high brace which is necessary when
the slot is deep and the curling wave high

brace position and then to lie back with all of the body weight coming on the paddle shaft. This leads to two problems: one is that the paddler very quickly exhausts himself and the other is that it increases risk of the shoulder dislocation. The ideal position is with the body upright with the weight balanced over the downstream buttock and very little weight on the arms (Fig 8:20).

Escaping from surface stoppers
Stoppers which are easy to ride are not necessarily easy to escape from without taking to swimming. There are three possibilities for escape once you are locked sideways into a stopper:

o   Capsize
o   Out of the end of the stopper
o   Skyrocket

Capsize

The paddler takes a breath and capsizes on the downstream side. The additional drag of his body in the water pulls the boat clear and he rolls up. The signal to roll up is when the buffeting of the boat stops. Some paddlers increase this drag effect by opening up underwater and holding their paddles at arms length.

Out of end

The boat is driven along to the end of the stopper or to where a jet of water is pouring through. This downstream flow is used to prise the boat from the grip of the stopper. To move the boat along the slot, the high or low brace is pushed forwards towards the feet and then converted to a forward power stroke.

As many of these strokes are taken as is necessary to get into position. They are short strokes and are connected by a paddle brace in the form of a slice. When the exit point is reached, a final forward power stroke is applied deeply and with the shaft almost upright. The blade will be in the downstream flow beneath the surface and it is the pressure on this that gives the purchase to drive the boat out into the current.

It is not uncommon for a paddler to have to reverse along the stopper slot to reach a suitable exit tongue. This is, in fact, no more difficult than pulling forwards and it is often possible to apply more power to the reversing stroke because you can get your body weight behind it.

Out of a sky rocket

Fig 8:21

(Inset) Exiting from the end of a stopper by pulling into the smooth flowing current. The main figure shows the paddler using the end of the stopper to turn and then allowing the rear to drop deeply into the slot., Hold the boat square and it will leap out of the slot (sky rocket)

Plate 8:k (left)
Out of the end. The paddler has slid the kayak to the limit of the stopper and pulled clear of it, into the main current.

Plate 8:l (below)
Sky rocketing. Allow the rear end to be pulled deep into the stopper slot and let the natural buoyancy of the kayak in contact with the deep undertow squirt you out. A deep pull with the paddle might also be required

Practising moving the kayak forwards and backwards along a stopper slot should form a major part of white water training. Paddlers develop their sense of balance and also strength and endurance by working and playing in safe stopper slots. The white water course at Holme Pierrepont is ideal for this.

Skyrocket

This is a variation on the previous technique which is often used in short stoppers. The downstream water at the stopper end is used to turn the boat downstream, but the paddler allows the boat to be sucked straight back into the stopper. The rear end of the boat digs deep into the slot, suddenly hits the rush of downstream water and shoots the boat skywards out of the stopper. Both of the last two techniques work equally well with the boat moving in reverse (Fig 8:21).

Stopper paddling summary

o   Stay clear of stoppers with long back tows.

o   Avoid vertical weirs.

o   Avoid any weir in exceptionally high spate conditions. Lethal stoppers do not need big drops, they can form on small weirs just as easily.

o   Practise only in surface stoppers which you know are safe to escape from.

o   If you have to paddle through deep stoppers, look for a weakness in its back tow.

o   Always accelerate into stoppers and keep the power on as you come out.

o   Think about and practise rescue procedures.

215

WHITE WATER COACHING

To understand the work of a white water coach, we must answer three questions:

o   Why do we want a coach ?
o   What exactly will we coach ?
o   How will we coach ?

The first question is about what is called your coaching philosophy. It asks if you have aims or a purpose for coaching as well as a code of ethics. Here are some examples of coaching objectives:

o   To help the paddlers to have fun
o   To help the paddlers to have fun, to grow and develop as individuals
o   To help the paddlers to have fun and to improve their performance
o   To help the paddlers to have fun and to develop as safe, efficient and responsible canoeists

One of the nice things about non-competitive white water coaching is that there is no concept of 'winning' which could easily come to dominate our work. Our primary responsibility to our paddlers is to recognise them as *individuals*. This means that they must be allowed to make their own decisions about their paddling and particularly about the degree of difficulty which they choose to tackle. It is the coach's duty to provide the guidance and education for them to make decisions wisely.

The role of the coach is diverse, taking in many areas of experience but, in the main, the work comes down to:

o   Instructing - directing actions and drills
o   Teaching - new skills and concepts
o   Training - improving all round performance

Effective coaching requires you to 'wear many hats' and there is always scope to improve your own performance.

Exactly what you coach will depend very much upon the level of paddlers with whom you are working. Naturally, you will be dealing mainly with the skills and techniques of white water paddling and, therefore, you will need to understand thoroughly the mechanics involved and have a personal feel for them. This is not to say that you must be able to out-perform your paddlers. Your skill is in your ability to sort out faults, grade learning and motivate. This skill will very quickly be recognised and respected by your paddlers, but you must practise it constantly.

How we coach is a matter of method and style. It is here that you bring your personality to bear. Your own coaching methods will be built up from working with other coaches, from your understanding of the sport and from your knowledge of human nature. You communicate your methods through your own unique style and it will evolve as you assess your own performance and improve it.

A coach should:

o   be enthusiastic and appear enthusiastic
o   be status free
o   use language appropriate to his paddlers and avoid jargon
o   listen to what the paddlers have to say
o   give plenty of sincere praise
o   know his paddlers or get to know them
o   give a purpose to every session
o   keep up to date with developments in the sport.

216

It is useful to break a day or weekend up into structured coaching sessions Here are two sample programmes for two-day white water training courses aimed at introductory and intermediate level paddlers.

Introductory

DAY 1
o Warm up and stretching
o Coaching session: sweep strokes
o Coaching session: low brace turn, flat water stroke sequences (flat water)
o Free practice: all basic strokes (flat water)
o Theory: reading rivers (flat water)
o Coaching session: break-ins,low brace turn (moving water)
o Coaching session: breaking-out,low brace turn (moving water)
o Coaching session: forward ferry glide (moving water).

DAY 2
o Warm up and stretching
o Practice: eddy turns (low brace turn)
o Coaching session: bow rudder, flat water sequence
o Coaching session: bow rudder break-out
o Free practice: ferry glides and S-turns
o Coaching session: draw on the move
o Final practice exercises: multiple eddy turns

Intermediate

DAY 1
o Warm up and stretching
o Practice: eddy turns (low brace turn sequence)
o Coaching sessions: bow rudder break-out
o Coaching session: turning on standing waves
o Theory session: types of waves, eddies, stoppers
o Practice: forward ferry glide
o Coaching session: crossing on waves
o Practice exercises: eddy spins, continuous S-turns

DAY 2
o Warm up and stretching
o Practice:
o Coaching session: bow rudder break-in
o Coaching session: reverse ferry glide
o Coaching session: surfing stoppers
o Practice exercises: circuits and crosses, small break-outs
o Rescue training

Plate 8:m(i) (below)
A rope through the end grab can help a coach stay in touch with a paddler training in a simple stopper

Plate 8:m(ii) (right)
The attachment must be easy to release. Push the unknotted end of a throw rope through the handle and check that it can run freely. Floating rope only should be used. If a loop is not attached, clip on and thread through a karabiner

'BAT'

One easy way to break down eddy turns for the purposes of technique coaching is under the following headings:

o Balance

o Accuracy

o Timing.

Balance is to do with how the boat sits on the water. Leaning and edging are skills which relate directly to balance. Paddlers who are having balance problems in eddy turns can be given the following exercises:

o Edging the kayak on dry land

o Paddle kayak on flat water whilst holding it on edge

o Alternating hard edging and levelling off

o Break-outs/break-ins with eyes closed

o Bow rudder turns experimenting with degrees of edging

o Low brace turn break-outs with blade held off surface; also with break-ins.

These exercises develop strength in the hips and groin and make the paddler aware of degrees of edging and lean.

Accuracy is the overall positioning of the kayak in an eddy turn sequence. It includes the lining up and angle of approach to an eddy line. Accuracy awareness is improved by encouraging the paddler to visualise the water from a birds eye view and to plan moves with this in mind. As he paddles, he should have an image of the aerial view of his position on the rapid, as though he were watching himself on a TV screen.

Accuracy exercises:
o   Experimenting with angles of approach
o   Experimenting with speed of approach
o   Forcing the paddler to use narrow or short eddies
o   Placing restrictions in width in the approach to a break-out
o   Eddy line spins on the spot and moving downstream
o   Holding the boat on the eddy line so that it points along the line.

Timing is the coordination of paddle strokes with the other aspects, ie balance and accuracy. The paddler mostly teaches himself about timing but the following exercises help the learning process:
o   Flat water stroke linking practise
o   Transfer to easy moving water site
o   Study the rhythm of the stroke sequences
o   Say the sequence as it is performed
o   Use extra words and phrases to help get the rhythm, for example: 'sweep-bite-bow rudder-slice-power' or 'sweep-two-three-low brace-glide-power'.

Basic practice exercises
The exercises in Fig 8:22 are simple manoeuvres which can be given to groups of paddlers. Once learnt by the paddlers, the exercises or routines are carried out and the coach is spared the wasteful duty of traffic control. Using combinations of these on groups of eddies, the coach can set paddling tasks of whatever duration he chooses. Fig 8:22 shows white water training exercises involving the use of a single tongue with two eddies.

The coach's position
Some coaches like to work from their boats, while other prefer to stand. There are advantages in both positions but, often, safety considerations force you one way or the other. The best rescue position is rarely the best coaching position and it is sometimes necessary to compromise providing the danger is not too great. Ideally the coach will have an assistant for safety cover or perhaps could use one of his paddlers to share the job. Standing on the bank is an excellent position to see everything and makes it easy for the paddlers to see you. If you do this, you need to know who will perform the demonstrations.

Adaptability, imagination and preparation are the important things here. The coach's clothing must allow him to spend an hour on the bank followed by ten minutes in the boat. He will need a first aid kit, throw line and emergency clothing. One moment he may be operating a video camera on the bank, the next he might be swimming to retrieve a boat tangled in rocks. The ability to do all this and remain sympathetic and enthusiastic towards his paddlers is why a coach is good value for money !

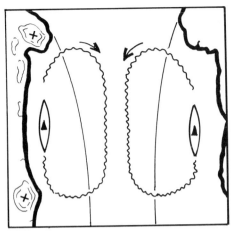

Fig 8:22a
Basic circuits, right and left. Involves a break-in followed by a break-out. The crosses are markers on the water's edge indicating where the paddler should make the eddy turn. It is important to vary the training which paddlers are given. Try altering the distance between the markers

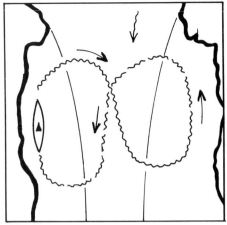

Fig 8:22b
The S-turn. Break in: cross and descend the current; break out. Continuous S-turns, even on easy water, are excellent endurance training and test the paddlers' skill under pressure. Introduce variation by using break-out targets, other paddlers, rolls in the current, reversing, eddy width restrictions, paddling with a missing blade, imaginary low branches on the eddy line

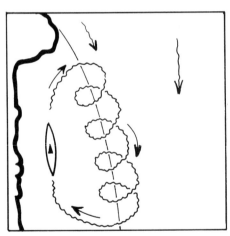

Fig 8:22c
Eddy line spin. This exercise helps the paddler to feel the turning energy available to him as the boat is set across the eddy line. There are two forms: the first is performed in one spot - usually the head of the eddy. In the second the boat is allowed to slip downstream. A well defined eddy line is essential

Fig 8:22d
The basic cross is a good training exercise. Inexperienced paddlers need lots of practise to get happy with the subtle transfer of edging. Once again there is scope for varying the tasks so that paddlers are being challenged by different crossing situations

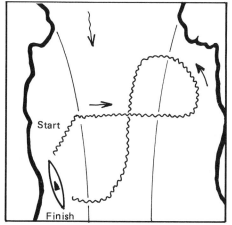

Fig 8:23a
Set paddlers combinations of basic exercises and let them get on with it. This is a cross, followed by an S-turn. Notice that only the simplest of moving water formations is needed; multiple jets and eddies offer even more interesting possibilities for training exercises

Fig 8:23b
An example of a training task using a single tongue
1 Enter the current and cross
2 Stop the cross
3 Reverse down the current
4 Eddy line spin to point bow downstream, followed by break-out
5 Break-in and forward downstream
6 Stop, and reverse ferry glide
7 Forward and break-out

Plate 8:n
Setting off on an S-turn. The paddler is about to apply a sweep stroke whilst raising the kayak edge on that (upstream) side. This combination of actions is indicative of a skilful paddler

Plate 8:o
Increasing the speed and power on the entry to the S-turn allows the paddler to compress the turn until there is practically no travel downstream. The number of paddle movements required can also be trimmed down

9 White Water Safety and Rescue

Mark Attenburrow

As a youth, Mark Attenburrow paddled for the Great Britain Junior Slalom Team. He became interested in the coaching of kayaking techniques at an early stage in his paddling career, and qualified as an Inland and Slalom Coach whilst studying physical education. He has led expeditions on white water and sea in Europe and further afield. Through his experience as rescue co-ordinator with the Arctic Canoe Race, he has accumulated a wealth of knowledge on the prevention of accidents, and dealing with problems that arise, on white water.

INTRODUCTION

The excitement of white water paddling and its dangers are linked to the fact that the sport is immediate in its nature. Once you start your descent you are committed in a very real sense. All decisions have to be made instantly and a bad decision can lead quickly to problems. This is true of a novice, paddling down Grade II, or an experienced and skilled paddler on Grade IV/V or above.

As technology brings us new materials and equipment, so our horizons are extended. It is important, however, that with new developments in equipment we also keep pace with our understanding of the dangers of our sport and methods of rescue so that we and others can enjoy white water paddling more safely.

The information which follows is intended to provide a foundation of knowledge from which a white water paddler can draw and hopefully add to.

If we are to investigate 'white water safety', first we must understand the white water environment and its potential dangers. White water is caused by water falling over an uneven river bed, the variables being:

o   The rate of fall of the water

o   Volume of water

o   The nature of the river bed.

It should not be forgotten that where white water exists, there is power, and to navigate successfully on white water, paddlers must learn to recognise and use its power and not fight against it. To underestimate water power is to underestimate what the river can do to you ! It would be a mistake to think only big water conditions are dangerous. A number of white water paddlers have died, and will probably continue to die, on low grade, low volume water. It takes a surprisingly small flow rate to pin or wrap a canoe around a rock, or hold a canoeist against a wall or in the branches of a tree.

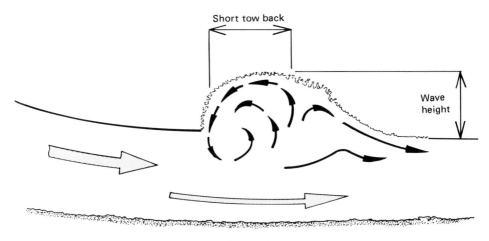

Fig 9:1
The principles of flow within a stopper wave. The deep water passes downstream whilst on the surface there is a characteristic returning flow, known as 'tow back'

WAVE FORMATIONS

Stoppers

Stoppers vary in their form tremendously: some are 'safe' and some are 'not safe'. As a guideline, the following points should be considered.

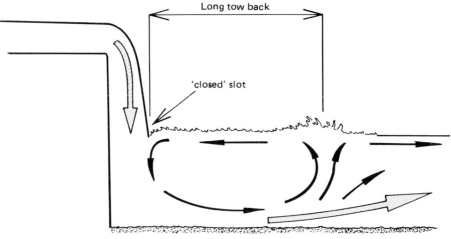

Fig 9:2
The stopper formed when the river falls over a steep drop, such as a vertical weir face, holds the greatest danger for swimmers. The vertical circulation of water is deep and the tow-back extensive

Is there a wave ?

Is there a 'wave' with tumbling foam, or is the water rushing back horizontally towards the jet ? As a rough guide, if a wave exists above river level and the tow-back is less than half a metre, the stopper will normally release a swimmer, or canoe. If there is no wave, and the tow-back comes from more than one metre behind the fall, the water formation is potentially dangerous.

Is the fall vertical ?

Is the water falling vertically, or off a steep ramp (45 degrees or more) ? Water falling vertically normally forms dangerous stoppers (depending on the volume of flow) as the horizontal tow-back is extremely powerful. The problems for the canoeist who gets caught side-on in this type of stopper are:

o There is no 'slot' to sit in

o Water falls powerfully on the upper gunwale of the canoe, causing a violent capsizing action into the sill or rock ledge

o Due to the water rushing back horizontally, it is almost impossible to get any support from the paddle blade

o The only exit by kayak is out from the ends of the stopper or, should these be blocked, by swimming (Fig 9:3)

o The swimmer will have to get out by using the deep fast jet into which he must swim and hope he is forced down and under the stopper's tow-back the first time, otherwise he will have to try again, but this time with less air in the lungs !

When canoeing over a vertical drop, speed of approach will not always lead to the boat jumping the fall and landing in a horizontal position. The canoe normally follows the line of the fall quite closely. Most of the speed will be lost in vertical penetration causing the canoe to plummet deeply into the pool. All, or most, of the forward momentum will be lost, resulting in a strong likelihood of the canoe being caught by the stopper. This is especially true for 'short' slalom-length boats.

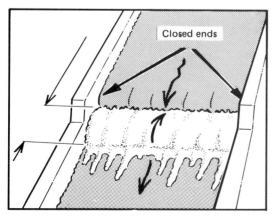

Closed ends

Fig 9:3
A vertical weir with its stopper blocked at each end. A potentially very dangerous place to be

Paddling hard at the stopper and punching through at 90 degrees to the wave normally avoids the risk of being held. However, if a canoeist is held either voluntarily or involuntarily, exit can normally be executed by one of the following:

o   Digging the paddle deep into the wave to catch the jet.

o   Paddling along the wave and out of an end or point where the stopper is worked out.

o   Capsizing and catching the deep jet with the paddle blade; body drag can also assist exit.

o   Looping by placing the bow or stern in the main jet at the bottom of the slot with the canoe at 90 degrees to the wave face.

o   Swimming

   Advice to swimmers: It is felt that the removal of a buoyancy aid is not necessary. A swimmer with or without a buoyancy aid will sink as he hits the jet, if he has not done so already in the less buoyant white water of the tow-back. On entering the jet it is probably advisable to curl up. This prevents you swimming up and out of the 'jet' which is a natural reaction to being pulled down. It also reduces the chance of clothing being caught by underwater obstructions. Exit will be achieved by coming up to the surface on the downstream side of the point where the water divides and the tow-back starts. At this point you will need the buoyancy aid !

o   Rescue (this is covered later in this chapter).

Standing waves

These are not dangerous in normal situations, although in big standing waves the combination of water power - steep face, collapsing crest - may cause the canoe to reverse loop. In large volume water these waves can also throw the kayak around violently, but once the canoeist capsizes he is normally swept out quite quickly. This is due to the water flow, which moves through the wave, catching the body and pulling the canoeist and the kayak downstream (Fig 9:4).

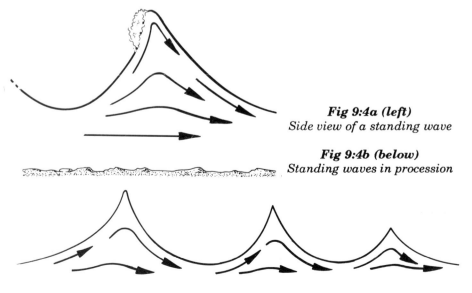

Fig 9:4a (left)
Side view of a standing wave

Fig 9:4b (below)
Standing waves in procession

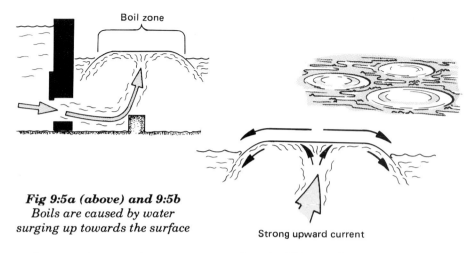

Fig 9:5a (above) and 9:5b
Boils are caused by water
surging up towards the surface

Strong upward current

In normal water volumes experienced in the UK, standing waves present no problem, and will not hold or loop a canoe, unless deliberately manoeuvred to do so.

Boils

Boils are caused by a surge of water to the surface (Fig 9:5).

Boils can be caused by man-made structures or may occur naturally in a river where water is forced upwards.

Boils only become dangerous with the presence of large hydraulic forces. As the water jets to the surface it flows out from the middle and down under the surrounding water. Risk from capsize from water catching a gunwale occurs and in large boils swimmers can be pulled under.

Holes

By definition, a 'hole' suggests that something is missing: the water is either being sucked down by a jet falling at great speed, or is being caused to circulate in a manner which results in a vortex forming.

With such forces present it can be seen that 'holes' form a problem to white water canoeists. The degree of problem and seriousness are related to the energy involved. The greater the hydraulic forces the more dangerous the hole.

If you paddle into a 'hole' which is caused by water falling vertically, you will normally be thrown totally out of control and submerged with some violence, which may easily cause injury. Should you paddle into a 'hole' caused by circulating jets, the movement is slower and not violent. The kayak may disappear under water and tend to spin slightly. It is unusual for the boat or body to submerge, and normally the kayak is released after a few seconds. Unlike the 'holes' caused by vertically falling water, which are constant, and normally have horizontal stoppers, 'holes' caused by circulating jets tend to appear, fill and disappear at intervals. Vortex formations tend to occur close beside fast jets which have more than usual power - eg: sluice releases, or jets formed by constructions or bends in a river.

Eddies

Eddies vary tremendously according to the character of the jet, rock bed and depth of water. They can be placid refuges within a large rapid, or bouncy and lively, being as interesting to sit in as the main rapid ! The basic form of an eddy is a circulating, flat, non-white movement.

Normally, eddies are placid, causing no problems of instability to a paddler, unless near the eddy line (point where fast jet and eddy meet).

Diagonal waves

This wave type occurs mainly on large volume rapids, and is caused by water jetting around the side of large rocks. The sudden increase in water volume and force of water beside the rock results in a strong wave formation which is normally diagonal in direction to the main flow. Its characteristics are similar to those of a standing wave.

Diagonal waves create problems for any swimmer who is unfortunate enough to take the 'wet line' as these waves constantly wash the swimmer back into the main jet. The problem is the same for a rescuer trying to rescue a kayak.

Geological effects

The following geological features will affect wave formations:

o   Resistant bands of rock crossing the river bed cause short rapids, normally with few boulders, eg: Llangollen Town Fall, North Wales.

o   The high gradient of the early stage of a river, regardless of river bed type, normally produces continuous rapids, eg: river Tryweryn, North Wales

o   A 'kick point' is a site of active erosion which results in waterfalls and gorge formation, eg: Swallow Falls. river Conway, North Wales. These areas are normally characterised by big rapids and committing canoeing.

o   Boulder strewn river beds are caused by glacial outwash material made up of finely ground sand and much larger boulders. If at a subsequent date the river is rejuvenated due to the land mass being uplifted, active erosion occurs and the rivers are normally fast flowing, brown coloured, and boulder strewn, eg: Karakoram Rivers.

o   Plunge pools occur below steep natural falls, eg: waterfalls such as Swallow Falls. These pools are caused by the increased erosional force of falling water, ever-deepening the river bed.

WHITE WATER DANGERS

Weirs

Weirs are complex in design and the hydraulic forces also vary. As a guideline the following aspects make a weir dangerous:

o   Closed stopper - walls either end

o   Stanchions supporting weir

o   Weirs where the water falls vertically, eg: Horse Shoe Weir above Ludlow, on the Teme in Warwickshire, or Horse Shoe Weir above Serpents Tail, on the Dee at Llangollen.

o   Horse-shoe shaped weirs or other such shapes which results in a 'slot' that a canoeist cannot sit in.
o   A powerful tow-back from the 'stopper', especially if the tow-back is some distance behind the 'slot' (one metre or more)
o   Shallow sills
o   Hidden obstructions.

If there is any sign of the weir having been modified, collapsing or visible obstructions existing in the stopper great care should be taken. Better still, the weir should be avoided.

Current setting under trees

In this situation, the danger of becoming snarled up is very high and rescue is very difficult.

Strainer

This term refers to water flowing through small holes or passages normally caused by boulders. The danger from this situation is large and rescue difficult.

Rocky bed

The chances of 'hogging', 'sagging' or 'lodging end-on' are greatly increased where the river bed is rocky. The speed and volume of water are obviously crucial variables.

Large hydraulic forces

Where these occur, stoppers, jets, surges and under-tow make capsize likely and rolling difficult.

Long rapids

The longer the rapid the more difficult it is to get a swimmer out. Long swims increase the chances of injury to the swimmer due to fatigue and may result in water entering the lungs.

Undercut ledges

Great care should be taken where there is evidence of an undercut ledge. A swimmer or kayak out of control will follow the water flow, and so there is a real danger of being swept under a ledge and becoming trapped.

Vertical drops

Whenever the canoeist plummets vertically nose-down, there is a danger from two sources:
o   Hitting the bottom causing leg/hip damage
o   Entrapment.

Trees

The branches of a tree which are in the water are a real danger to canoeists and their equipment, as once caught in the branches they are easily pinned. Rescue is difficult and may be dangerous. If a main river jet passes through tree debris, such as on the outside of a bend, great care must be taken.

Bridges

Upstream bases of bridge pillars are designed to split the water flow. If caught on the stanchions in fast moving water, wrap-around will be extremely quick.

Immersion

Cold water affects respiration. If you try standing under a cold shower or sit in a cold bath, you will soon discover that sudden immersion in cold water (15°C or less) has a profound effect on you. One of the first noticeable effects will be uncontrollable gasping, which can last for several seconds: the cold water 'takes your breath away'. The implications of this gasping for the canoeist are:

o   He may take in water, leading to choking, especially in confused white water conditions

o   The hyperventilation may lead to dizziness or in some cases unconsciousness, due to high oxygen levels in the blood.

Whole body immersion also causes a sudden rise in blood pressure due to the squeezing effect of the water pressure. This can be dangerous if a person has a heart complaint, or is very unfit or old, and could lead to a heart attack or stroke. For this reason, care should be taken when pulling a person out of the water, as if he/she is pulled too rapidly from the water there will be a sudden drop in blood pressure(see chapter 4 - Safety - for more information on cold water immersion).

OTHER FACTORS OF POTENTIAL DANGER ON WHITE WATER

Personal

Inexperience can lead to great danger because the lack of a foundation of knowledge prevents a balanced judgement from being made.

Solo attempts on difficult rapids or falls should only be contemplated by extremely experienced and practised white water paddlers and then only after the consequences have been weighed up. Solo attempts exclude the chance of outside help, and greatly increase the risk factor.

Equipment

Poorly designed craft which are supposedly built for white water but fall well short in terms of choice of material, buoyancy, end grabs, design of cockpit, and so forth, clearly present dangers for the white water canoeist.

Poor workmanship such as poorly fitted footrest, seams, cockpit, end grabs, and weaknesses in fibreglass (grp) boats also present hazards.

Some craft are not designed to be used on white water and such use may be dangerous. Other craft built for top class competition may be dangerous in the hands of novices, eg: an all-kevlar kayak.

Age of equipment is important because materials often have a life span which is linked to:

o Exposure to direct light

o Amount of usage

o Type of usage.

The equipment should be chosen with the environment in mind. Care needs to be taken not only with the choice of kayaks but also in the correct clothing and buoyancy aid(s) to meet environmental demands.

River grading

A river grading system exists to help pass on information about any given, naturally formed, rapid or fall. The scale ranges from Grade I to VI.

Although the grading system is helpful when planning a trip, its main limitations are:

o Grading is subjective (what some may call Grade III, others will call a Grade IV, and vice versa).

o No information is given by the grading about the volume of water: there is a big difference between a technical Grade IV and a large volume Grade IV fall.

o No information is given on the rapid's length, or its width. Therefore, although 'gradings' are very helpful, their limitations should be remembered.

FORMULATING A RESCUE PLAN

Emergency situations on white water demand that the person on the spot decides on the best technique, or course for action, to effect a safe rescue, taking into account all the variables involved. The following principles are designed to help any would-be rescuer in decision-making, and formulating a successful rescue plan:

o Is the victim's head above water ? If not, this is obviously the first priority.

o Is the situation stable or does it look as if it may change for the worse, eg, head slipping under ? In some rescue situations, a canoeist may be trapped but be in no danger so long as the situation remains stable. If a canoeist is trapped in this way, head above water and stable, you have more time to plan, and effect the rescue.

o Speed of rescue is important but, 'panic actions' by the rescuers are positively dangerous. Remember, you, the rescuer, have the benefit of air in your lungs, and hopefully clear thought; the person you are going to rescue may not. His or her life will be in your hands and depend on what you do.

o If there is more than one person involved in the rescue, someone must take charge in a positive way. A strong lead should be taken by the group leader or the most experienced white water paddler present.

o If a kayak is lodged end-on with the canoeist entrapped, the ideal force to apply is one which is as close to 180 degrees to the angle of attack, as possible, see Fig. 9:6. If other de-stabilising forces are applied, consider the consequences. Sideways forces or downstream forces may lead to a collapse of the kayak, causing the legs to become jammed with the head under water.

231

Table One   Wild Water – Grades of Difficulty

Grade I *Not Difficult*	Grade II *Moderately Difficult*	Grade III *Difficult*	Grade IV *Very Difficult*	Grade V *Extremely Difficult*	Grade VI *Limit of Practicability*
	passage free	route recognisable	route not always recognisable. Inspection mostly necessary	inspection essential	generally speaking impossible
regular stream	irregular stream	high, irregular waves	heavy continuous rapids	extreme rapids	possibly navigable at particular water levels
regular waves	irregular waves	larger rapids	heavy stoppers whirlpools and pressure areas	stoppers, whirlpools and pressure areas	high risk
small rapids	medium rapids small stoppers, eddies/whirlpools and pressure areas*	stoppers, eddies and whirlpools and pressure areas			
simple obstructions	simple obstructions in stream	isolated boulders, drops and numerous obstructions in stream	boulders obstructing stream, big with undertow	narrow passages, steep gradients and drops with difficult access and landing	
	small drops				

* 'Pressure areas' refers to water piling up against a rock or other obstacle (sometimes called 'cushions' in this country).
N.B. Weirs are not classified as wild water and as such are not evaluated. They are (either) easily navigable or (very) dangerous.

o If a kayak is stuck side-on in a rapid on any obstruction it can be thought of as in a stable condition. *To dislodge it, de-stabilising forces are required.* Always try to use the environment to help you. For example, an empty canoe dropped side-on into a fast water jet can produce a large force on a rope which can be used to help you.

o In any rescue situation always think of the degree of risk to the rescuers. It goes without saying that you should always try to develop a rescue plan which has the smallest risk factor. If the risk factor is very high, an extremely difficult decision will need to be made. Two casualties are worse than one. Also, if the risk factor is extremely high to the rescuer, it also tends to suggest that the choice of rescue methods is limited, and should the rescuer get into trouble, help may not be available.

o It is generally recommended that a canoeist should not put a tow line between himself and a kayak on a rapid. Rope lines on rapids can be dangerous as they can wrap around rocks or trees, or generate large forces due to drag caused by strong jets. If a person is connected to a line in a rapid, a quick-release device is essential at all times.

o Approach wrap-around situations from downstream. Approaching a canoeist wrapped around a rock or stuck in a tree or strainer from the upstream side has a high risk factor and should be avoided.

RESCUE EQUIPMENT

It is possible to carry all manner of rescue equipment. It is strongly advised that each paddler should carry a throw-bag with a 'soft rope' of minimum diameter 8mm, two karabiners and a sling.

It is possible to take quick-release chest harnesses, axes, pulley systems, hooks that fit onto a paddle blade and other devices. The equipment carried should depend upon the nature of the challenge. If the party is, for example, attempting a first time descent down a narrow, fast flowing stream, with several vertical drops and a danger from trees, it would be advisable to consider carrying most of the items listed.

Throw bag

This should contain 8 mm rope and be easy to deploy. It is important to practise using the line; just carrying one is not enough.

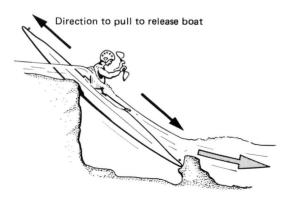

Direction to pull to release boat

Fig 9:6
The ideal force to release a trapped boat is in a direction exactly opposite to that in which it entered

Slings

A sling is a webbing loop which can be bought at any climbing shop. It can be used in a number of different ways in a rescue situation, and allows the rescuer more flexibility in rope attachments, etc.

Karabiners

These are available from climbing shops. They are strong snap-closure devices allowing quick and easy attachment.

Quick-release chest harness

A quick-release harness is an excellent piece of equipment to carry in case you have to enter the water on a line. However, this is a piece of equipment which should only be used by people who have practised with it before hand, and realise the full implications of having a rope attached to them. Some very rocky rapid water conditions do not allow safe use of harness and line. Some buoyancy aids now available include a quick release harness as standard.

Important

It should be remembered that equipment can never be a substitute for experience. Equipment may help in a rescue situation, if the rescuer is experienced enough to use it, but in some situations it will be useless, eg: on wide, big volume rivers.

GENERAL RESCUE TECHNIQUES

The type of rescue possible for any given situation will depend upon the nature of the bank and river conditions, equipment available and the experience and number of the rescuer(s).

Rescues can be divided into three basic types:

Water based
o   Kayak(s) to swimmer at the end of the rapid
o   Kayak to swimmer on the rapid
o   Kayak to kayak

Land based
o   Throw line to swimmer
o   Assist in helping to pull man and equipment out of the river

Combination techniques
o   Line to entrapped paddler or kayak
o   Diver (man on line).

Water based

Kayak to swimmer

The swimmer should pull his torso onto your back deck if possible as this reduces drag considerably and allows you to make headway.

Fig 9:7
Retrieving an abandoned
kayak using the 'piggy back'
method

Kayak to swimmer in rapid

The kayak should be thought of as a buoyancy bag which you can position on a rapid, but once the swimmer has made contact, do not expect to do any more than support him as you float downstream. Sideways movement is difficult, and requires a lot of power. It can be seen that this type of rescue in a 'rock garden' or large volume river would be a mistake.

Kayak to kayak

It is strongly advised that a tow-line attached to you or your kayak is not used in extracting a capsized kayak from a rapid. Instead, use the 'piggy back' method of paddling your kayak up onto the capsized kayak and pushing it to the bank, and into an eddy (Fig 9:7). In wide deep stretches of river where there is no risk of entanglement a boat-attached quick-release towing system works very well.

The 'piggy back' method has the advantages that:

o   You are not attached to a heavy free floating object

o   You can start the rescue immediately you arrive on the scene without having to stop, take at least one hand off the paddle, and take your eyes off the hazards downstream, which you would do if you attached a tow-line.

If you do decide to use a tow-line, it is essential that you have a quick-release device which can be activated quickly, using action from one hand only and with the rope under tension.

A kayak can also be used to get to the site of the problem where, for instance, a canoeist is jammed in his cockpit, or where a kayak is trapped (Fig 9:8).

Fig 9:8
Paddling a kayak into position
to assist a trapped paddler

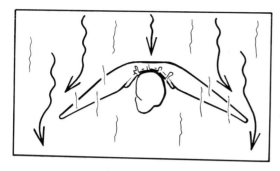

Fig 9:9
A wrap-around situation where the obstruction is centrally located - sometimes referred to as 'hogging'

'Hogging' wrap-arounds

If you can get to the trapped boat before it really starts to bend, it can normally be dislodged by paddling your kayak into one end (Figs 9:9 and 9:10). This results in a de-stabilising effect and the kayak floating off the rock.

Once the kayak has bent, and the paddler is trapped, the problems are far greater. It is possible in some situations to paddle into the eddy behind the rock around which the kayak is wrapped, exit from your kayak, leaving it the right way up for re-entry later, and lift one end of the wrapped kayak up and out of the flow by placing a shoulder under one end. This action normally allows the paddler to escape. Depending on the degree of bend, the kayak should also float free.

These techniques are only possible in low volume rivers.

It may be necessary, if the above methods fail, to use a rope (see combination techniques), or cut the kayak, to either extract the paddler, or de-stabilize it, eg: cut the back off.

'Sagging' wrap-arounds

Once again, if you can get to the scene before the kayak bends, it can often be dislodged by lifting one end off the rock (Figs 9:11 and 9:12).

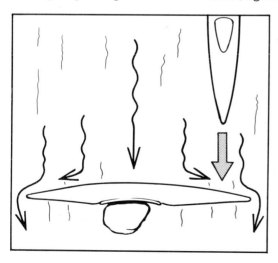

Fig 9:10
A passing paddler can often prevent the kayak from wrapping by guiding one end downstream as the boulder approaches

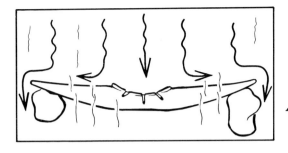

Fig 9:11
*A wrap-around situation where
the kayak is held by its ends -
sometimes known as 'sagging'*

If the kayak has bent, entrapping the paddler, it may be necessary to get out of your kayak and bounce or smash the rear end to allow the kayak to float free. Due to the hydraulic forces involved, it is normally impossible to lift or push one end clear once the kayak has bent. Work with the water if possible.

Land based

Throw Lines

Throw lines can have several uses, and it is strongly advised that every white water canoeist carries one. Just carrying a throw line is not enough however. Practise in its use is essential.

To throw the line:

1   Grip the top of the bag with your throwing hand. Pull the rope loop at the top out of the bag and keep hold of it with the other hand.
2   Throw the bag beyond the victim.
3   Aim to lay the rope across the swimmers body.
4   Shout 'rope'
5   Brace yourself securely against the jerk of the rope. If possible, hold the rope around a rock or tree so that you have a friction brake. A force of 50kg or more can be expected on the rope, and this is strong enough to pull the thrower in. The size of the force is greater if the strain is taken all at once, with the swimmer downstream of the thrower. It is lower if the line can start to be hauled in with the swimmer level or slightly upstream of the thrower.

Fig 9:12
*Where the obstructions are low
boulders, it is possible to lift an
end clear*

To pull the victim in to the bank:

1 When the victim grabs the rope there will be a sudden jerk on it. In a strong current this may pull the victim under water. The victim should try and float on his back.

2 Be ready to ease the rope, so that the victim is not forced to let go.

3 After this initial 'snatch' on the rope, the pull normally stabilises as the victim surfs in to the bank.

4 Pull the victim in steadily; play him like a big fish. Be ready to ease the rope, or let go of it, or change your position if necessary.

If you miss:

o Do not waste time trying to re-stow the rope. Simply pull the bag in, leaving the rope neatly lying on the ground at your feet, and throw the bag full of water.

TIPS

In strong or gale force winds, undo the top of the bag and, with the rope still in it, fill it with water before you throw. This gives the bag the necessary extra weight without hurting the victim.

Try to keep your throw nice and smooth so that the bag does not tumble through the air. After a few throws you should be quite accurate.

Some people prefer to use one arm by looping the top end around their throwing wrist.

Do not tie or clip yourself to the rope.

If the rope is not long enough, tie the top ends of two ropes together. Hold one bag open in one hand so that the rope from it can pay out freely. Throw the other bag, having first filled it with water to give it the extra weight necessary to throw further.

To re-stow the rope, place it in the bag one handful at a time, so that it is flanked down neatly. Obviously, do not try to coil it into the bag or try any short cuts. This needs a few minutes of care, and is very important.

Safety cover and rescue from the bank

Try to set up safety cover on both banks. As a general rule, do not use the throw-bag in the middle of a rapid or if there is a danger from trees along the bank. It is normally safer for the capsized paddler to be washed down the main chute.

Try to station yourself a little distance downstream from where you expect trouble; leave the capsized paddler enough space and time to roll up or bail out and surface.

If possible, choose a stance next to an eddy so that the current will help swing the victim into the bank. The person will pendulum into the shore. It is therefore important that the area and bank immediately downstream must be clear of danger, eg: overhanging trees (Fig 9:13).

If possible, belay yourself to the bank (tree or rock) separately from the throw-line. This avoids the embarrassment of you joining the swimmer, due to the 'jerk' force of the swimmer on the line.

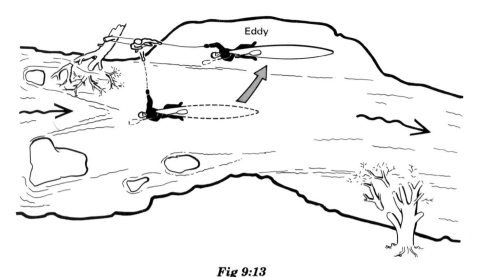

Fig 9:13

Position rescuers with throw bags where the swimmer will swing out of the fast current into safe water

Make sure that all members of your party know that they should hold the rope and not the bag, and that they should not attempt to tie or wrap the rope around themselves.

Rescue from trees

Where a canoeist is trapped against a fallen tree, try to approach the victim by wading into the water below the tree or by climbing out along it. The throw bag may prove useful to support the victim above water, to pull the boat clear, or to pull or break the branch of the tree.

Any approach from upstream is normally very hazardous to the rescuer, and should not be attempted unless there is no alternative, and then with great care.

It may be possible to tie a buoyancy aid and/or a kayak to your throw-line, and float it down to the trapped person from upstream.

Rescue from a stopper

The buoyancy in a throw bag is not really sufficient for a stopper rescue. It is better to tie a buoyancy aid to the rope.

The following approach may be used:

1   Throw the buoyancy aid to land downstream of the stopper, in the back-tow, so that it gets carried back upstream towards the victim.

2   Stand downstream of the stopper and try to keep the rope taut, so that it does not get carried to the bottom of the river and risk becoming entangled.

3   Pull the victim sideways along the stopper to the bank. Pulling a swimmer through the back-tow requires a large force - 2 or 3 men, depending on the strength of the tow back.

Fig 9:14
Recovering a trapped kayak
Pulling vertically upwards is
ideal, but rarely possible
Try to find a direction of pull
which is not against the
current

Salvage of a trapped boat
This is not a life or death situation. Spend time to think out the easiest and safest way of freeing the boat (Fig 9:14).

If wading out seems the best way:

1 Consider carefully the risks of foot entrapment
2 Use the rope for support and face upstream
3 Cross diagonally downstream towards the trapped boat
4 Tie a second throw bag to the boat
5 Ensure you are not knocked over when the boat is pulled free

Paddler trapped in midstream
If you encounter this situation, the first question to ask is: can you reach the victim by wading ?

If the person obviously cannot breath you should immediately consider a swimming rescue from upstream to break them loose, but ensure you have an escape route and/or back up.

If the person can grab a rope, consider throwing him one, preferably two; the first to pull and hold him against the current, the second to pull him to the shore. In some cases, a better idea is to throw the rope across to a partner on the far bank. Both people can then walk upstream on each bank with the rope stretched between them. The victim can then grasp the middle of the rope.

If the victim is only marooned, rather then entrapped, it is usually safer for the victim to swim the rest of the rapid or be rescued by kayak, rather than risk a rope entanglement in the middle of a rapid.

Teamwork
If you are paddling as one of a group and have a capsize and a swimmer, whilst the others in the party look after the immediate safety needs of the swimmer, boat salvage, etc, consider paddling ahead (with another) so that you can get on the shore with the throw bag to render assistance. Getting the victim the last few metres to the shore is often the hardest part of a rescue by kayak.

Do not tie yourself to the rope because:

o The rope can become snagged under a rock or other obstruction, trapping you with it
o The rope can hold you trapped at full stretch against the current, probably under water !

240

Possible exceptions to this are:

o If you have a quick release harness

o If it is a life or death situation but have a second rope ready to pull you to shore, and also a knife handy; remember, two deaths are not better than one (Fig 9:15).

Practise improves performance

The following should be practised to improve performance:

o Practise with your throw rope in safe situations with competent partners

o Try out some of the simple rescue systems described

o Discuss possible incidents and how you might deal with them

o Think about your own local hazards

Combination techniques

Most rescues involve a degree of land and water support, but rescues which depend upon both teams working together are infrequent. When necessary, this is often due to the seriousness of the situation.

A crucial factor in all rescues is time. By definition, a two-part effort requires a degree of organisation. A forceful lead is required if time is not to be lost.

Serious entrapment

This may involve the use of a rope being taken out by a swimmer or kayak and attaching it to part of the kayak which is 'wrapped around' an obstruction. This is extremely difficult, and the drag on a rope is considerable when put across a flow. For this reason the rope may need to be thrown.

In hogging and sagging situations the rescuer(s) should try to dislodge the kayak, if at all possible, using the forces available from the water flow. A partially collapsed kayak in a hogging situation can be lifted if the rescuers are reasonably strong and the environment allows the rescuers to position themselves with their shoulders under a collapsed end. A rope attached to the end loop will increase the possibility of success.

In situations which are seen to be critical, think before you act. For example, if a kayak has lodged end-first onto an unseen obstruction and the canoeist is trapped, remember to stick to the following principles:

o Is the victim's head above water ?
o Is the situation stable, or does it look like it might change for the worse - head slipping under ?
o If possible, the kayak will require pulling back at the angle it went down. The closer you can apply force to the angle of attack the better. Is it possible to rig a line up from a tree upstream ? If not, what is the best angle you can get ?
o If other de-stabilising forces are to be applied think of the consequences. Sideways or downstream forces, for example, may lead to a collapse of the kayak and legs being jammed with the head under water.
o Attaching a hauling line to an end loop, or flaps of fibreglass, has to be done in the safest manner for the rescuer and victim.

The following variables will influence your actions in an entrapment situation:

o Experience of rescue team
o Equipment carried
o Position of the trapped canoeist in the rapid
o Type of rapid
o Nature of the bank (eg cliff, thick undergrowth, rocky)
o Size of group

Basic principles

It is dangerous for a swimmer entering water to assist with a rescue. If anyone is going to enter the water, they should be attached by a rope and harness and they must know what they are doing. The equipment must be designed for white water and include quick release, rope attachment at rear and high up on the back.

o The line should be downstream of the entry point.
o Great care must be taken not to get the line between rescuer and land team wrapped up around a rock or around the swimmer's neck ! If it does, the swimmer must quick release.

Stopper rescues

The following examples show the different ways in which rescue from a stopper may be attempted. The type of rescue method used will depend upon the type of stopper, the forces involved and the tow-back. The following notes may help you in making your decision.

When a swimmer is trapped:

o If using a throw line, attach a buoyancy aid to end to help (Fig 9:16).
o Use a paddle or branch to reach
o If the tow-back is small offer the bow or stern of your kayak
o The method shown in Figs 9:18 and 9:19 is recommended, provided conditions allow, as the person on the bank can help in pulling the swimmer out. They also help keep the kayak from broadsiding or being caught in the tow-back. The man on the bank must be downstream as shown and not level with kayak
o Another kayak can be used to stop the rescue kayak being caught
o A rope (with floats attached if possible) can be used.

242

Fig 9:16 (top left)
Swimmer trapped in a stopper - using a throw line

Fig 9:17 (top right)
Reaching with a paddle or branch

Fig 9:18 , 9:19 (above)
Using a paddler on a line

Fig 9:20
A spanning rope with floats

243

Fig 9:21

Where the paddler in the stopper has remained upright, but cannot get clear of the stopper

Fig 9:22

A means of creating extra drag on the rescuer's kayak

When both the kayak and paddler are stuck:

o   As shown in Fig 9:21, B first tries to pull A from the stopper in his kayak. If this fails the following procedure is recommended: A stays in his kayak until B gets into position where A can grab the rescue kayak. A then bails out and B pulls him from the stopper

o   An additional kayak can be positioned to create drag on B's kayak, so helping to pull A out of the stopper. It is possible to add to this situation with further kayaks

o   In Fig 9:23, B floats into stopper from upstream side. As B enters the stopper he will tend to push A out. This is known to work but would only be attempted when B feels he can get out of the stopper un-aided.

Direction of river flow

Fig 9:23

o   In cases where an experienced paddler is caught and unable to move to safety, it is possible for the rescuer B to pull A along a slot to safety. Pushing is not advised as it will tend to lead to you joining A (Fig 9:24).

o   If you are caught and unable to get out by normal paddling skills, a possible option to be considered before swimming is to remove the spray deck. The kayak will sink and as it does so, it is far more likely to 'catch' the fast jet and get swept out. If not, nothing is lost, swimming is the next option anyway !

Fig 9:24

LEADING

Before you go, here are some thought-provoking questions to ask yourself:

o Is your standard of paddling appropriate to leading on the stretch of water you have chosen ?

o Is the group ready for the challenge of this grade of water ?

o Is the group equipment safe and appropriate ?

o What do you, the leader, know about the stretch of river to be paddled ?

o What grade of rapids are there on the river, and where are they ?

o Have you got a map of the area ?

o What equipment are you going to carry ?

o What equipment are the group members carrying ?

o Is your equipment appropriate to the challenge ?

o What temperatures do you expect ?

o What type of clothing are you and your group members wearing and carrying as spare ?

o What is the ratio of competent to less competent paddlers ? instructors to students ?

o Is the ratio a safe one ?

o What is the weather forecast ?

o What is access like, and do you need permission ?

o Where can you leave the river in emergencies ?

Leading on white water

It is presumed that all leaders are:

o suitably qualified

o suitably experienced to lead on the chosen white water grade and type.

Although it is possible to adopt several different systems of leadership, it is strongly recommended that the following points are considered by group leaders:

o The leader should be in a position to see every rapid (potential danger) before any group member descends.

o Rapids should be inspected for dangers - eg logs jammed. A competent canoeist, who does not have to be the leader, should descend by an agreed route. This paddler signals back to another competent paddler at the top of the fall whether the route is OK or not. The competent paddler at the top of the fall organises group members to descend one at a time giving simple instructions, if necessary, to help the paddlers make their descent safely.

o   In the event of a capsize, the competent paddler at the bottom, rescues whilst the competent paddler at the top of the fall stops further descents. Should the swimmer encounter problems on the rapid, the competent paddler at the top signals the group to get off the water, and then goes to the aid of the swimmer.

o   Where applicable, throw lines should be positioned along the rapid to provide 'rescue cover' for anyone who takes a swim.

o   On wide rapids it may be necessary to have someone on the bank to help signal to the canoeist making the descent. This is sometimes necessary where the start point for the line (route) down is crucial for a safe descent.

FACTS AND FORCES

The following notes are taken from research carried out by various people. It is recommended that the 'papers' on these and other aspects of white water safety are read fully (after: Peter Reithmaier, Austria).

Water speed

Measurements of water speed showed that the fastest current a canoeist is likely to encounter in the Alps is 17.5km/h. Sections of rivers where canoeists thought the water moved extremely fast only measured 12km/h).

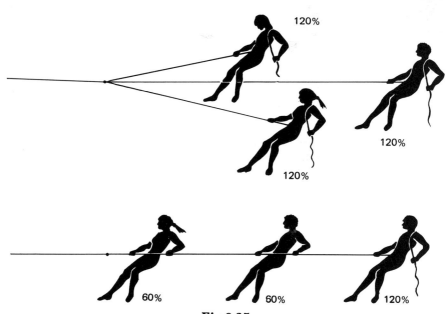

Fig 9:25
Those using a shoulder belay can each exert a pull equivalent to 120% of their body weight. Without the belay, this falls to 60%.
Further advantage can be gained by each person pulling at an angle of about 30° as illustrated in the top picture

246

Velocity and force

Doubling the velocity of the current results in a quadrupling of force exerted on a trapped boat; half the speed results in ¼ force.

Forces available to rescuers

Peter Reithmaier followed up his research on the forces that work against us, with an investigation of what forces we can apply in a rescue situation. His findings showed that one of the most important factors was that the maximum pull on a horizontal rope depends upon the weight of a person, and not on their strength:

o   Maximum jerk pull on a horizontal rope of 8mm diameter, using a shoulder belay is 120% of bodyweight when exerted by a single person. Using a 6mm rope this figure fell to 110% of bodyweight.

o   When pulling on a rope, if a shoulder belay is not used, only 60% of bodyweight can be exerted (Fig 9:25).

Plate 10:a
Sea kayaking: a special kind of freedom

10 Sea Kayaking

Nigel Foster

Nigel Foster is one of our most eminent Sea Coaches. He has made many outstanding sea kayaking journeys including the first circumnavigation of Iceland, early exploration of the Faroe Islands and a section of the Labrador coast. His solo voyage from Baffin Island across the Hudson Straits to the North Canadian mainland is arguably the most impressive of any sea kayaking adventure in the world.

He has been an innovator in sea kayak design and has a deep interest in the whole natural marine environment.

Nigel now runs his own canoeing school in North Wales.

INTRODUCTION

Sea kayaking in Britain is a rapidly expanding branch of the sport. One of the great attractions is that the British coastline is vast, varied and beautiful, lending itself to both short and long journeys. Short journeys may take the paddler beyond the holiday beaches to sea cliffs and stacks alive with myriads of sea birds, and to offshore rocks where seals wallow in the swell. Longer journeys enable the paddler to return to an almost timeless nomadic existence, cruising from island to island, camping on hidden beaches and exploring wherever the mood and weather permits. Sea kayaking is a complex art, and the artist must be master of many things to extract the greatest amount of pleasure.

This chapter only scratches the surface of the many subtle techniques and tricks of the trade and points briefly towards the wild exhilaration of riding through a big tide race, or to the beauty of cutting silently across a sea so glassy that every cloud is mirrored in a deep blue sea below, creating an illusion of flying.

EQUIPMENT

Kayaks

There are many designs available today, ranging from 'day-boats' through a mid-range to the more specialist expedition kayaks. In addition, many general purpose kayaks are suitable for use on the sea, and both single and double sea kayaks are used.

General purpose kayaks

Many people use this type of kayak on the sea both for surfing and for short excursions. Their great manoeuvrability makes them a good choice for exploring among rocks and narrow caves, but in windy conditions they will broach persistently. The addition of a detachable skeg will improve the directional performance significantly. As much buoyancy as possible should be included, as well as deck lines and provision for the use of compass and chart.

249

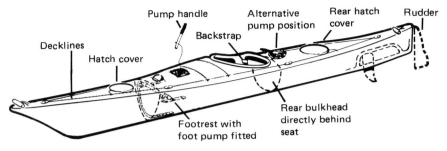

Fig 10:1
A typical sea touring kayak

Sea kayaks

There are a number of good 'day boats' available for those who are mainly interested in day trips. These are generally fairly flat-bottomed, stable and manoeuvrable, and are roomy enough to carry equipment for weekend expeditions. As they are designed to be stable when paddled empty, they make good kayaks for beginners.

In the mid range, there are several kayaks which retain a fair amount of stability, but are larger and run straighter than day boats; they also have a full expedition capacity. The initial stability, however, usually means that in stronger winds there is more difficulty with directional stability, so these kayaks are ideal for those not intending to expedition in rougher waters.

At the high performance end of the scale, there are expedition kayaks designed for speed and directional stability even in strong winds and rough conditions. These kayaks however are much less stable and require a much greater level of handling skill.

Sea kayaks in general are between about 4.5m and 5.5m long, have a little or no rocker and have bows designed to keep the paddler fairly dry. The cockpit is usually fairly small and the degree of stability varies between that of a slalom kayak and that of a white water racer. They are straight running, giving them a longer paddling range than a general purpose kayak.

Double sea kayaks

Although these have been in continuous use for several decades in Scotland on a small scale, and are now very popular in North America, they are just beginning to make a tentative return to other parts of Britain. Doubles tend to be stable, longer than singles (often longer than 6 metres) and fast. It is an advantage to have well separated cockpits in order to avoid the clashing of paddles, although this leads to the bow being less responsive to steep seas. They are ideal for couples with different abilities, when the more experienced paddler takes the rear seat to enable him or her to make allowances for the other paddler without needing to look behind.

Bulkheads and hatches

Nowadays bulkheads and hatches are usually fitted to sea kayaks. Bulkheads are usually made either of glass reinforced plastic or polyethylene foam. Damage to the hull often occurs at the inflexible point of a rigid bulkhead, so polyethylene foam, being compressible, provides a less vulnerable form of construction.

The position of the bulkheads is important. To make best use of the storage space the front bulkhead should be close to the footrest, and the rear bulkhead should be immediately behind the seat. This also makes good safety sense as there is then minimum available space for water in the event of a capsize; all of the water can be drained by raising only the bow of the kayak. In the past, the rear bulkhead has often been placed as much as a foot behind the cockpit in order to house a hand pump and leave room for equipment too large to fit through the hatch. Since then, it has been realised that a forward and backward action pump mounted on the front deck, with a removable handle, or a high volume foot pump, together with the larger sized hatches that arc now available, make this unnecessary.

Hatch covers should be tied to the kayak and it is advisable to fill an otherwise empty compartment with air bags in case of damage to the kayak or loss of a hatch cover, which could otherwise fill the compartment with water.

Pumps

These now come in a number of shapes and sizes. For rescue purposes, a high volume hand or foot pump or electrically operated pump is needed, but for draining out the seepage of water that comes through spraydeck or down the neck, the addition of a low volume foot pump greatly increases comfort.

Outlet holes for pumps should be positioned low down on the deck. My first ever pump outlet was on the top of the rear deck and used to provide me with a cold shower every time I used it. As I happened to be circumnavigating Iceland at the time, this was a mistake that I never repeated.

Deck lines

These are essential grab points for use primarily when launching and landing, and for manoeuvring the kayak in awkward places on land. They also provide something to hold on to when rafted or when swimming, and for attaching the end of tow lines. They should have anchor points that are strong enough to lift the loaded kayak. I prefer a series of short individual sections rather than one continuous line running around the kayak that gathers all its slack into one piece.

Toggles should also be fitted, using strong rope. The addition of a loop of elastic from the deck line will prevent it from constantly battering the boat.

Paddles

Most expedition paddlers use asymmetric paddles, curved with a slight spoon for reasons of efficiency. For manoeuvring around rocks in a general purpose kayak or day boat, a slalom type symmetrical curved blade is perfectly adequate. Some paddlers use long flat bladed paddles on the sea, more in the style of many Eskimo paddles. Whereas I personally choose on the basis of efficiency, the choice is very much up to the individual. There is a definite advantage to a lighter weight paddle, especially for longer distances, as this means less work.

251

Whatever the choice, your paddles should be well maintained and looked after. Throwing your paddles up the beach, using them to brace on barnacled rocks when getting in and out of your kayak, and using them for HI rescues will shorten their life.

Rudders

The use of rudders is currently returning to popularity, providing a simple alternative to many of the turning and steering skills described later. Kayaks susceptible to broaching in winds may be controlled more easily by the addition of a rudder or an adjustable skeg.

Clothing

Nowadays we are spoilt for choice. The wet-suit long johns designed especially for canoeing and board sailing are supple enough to be comfortable, and often have additional thickness on the knees. These, worn with a couple of sweaters and topped with waterproof anorak, buoyancy aid and woolly hat, make good winter paddling wear. On the feet, neoprene boots with a strong thick sole worn with or without socks are probably the most comfortable in cold conditions, but wool socks with trainers provide a good alternative. Footwear must be sufficient for scrambling over sharp stones and slippery weed so the choice of sole is important. The heel is in contact with the floor of the kayak, so a sole that curves a little way up the heel is an advantage. Sailing wellington boots that are close fitting to the legs are also often worn, but will not keep the feet dry.

A hood on a waterproof anorak is a good idea as you will always have that extra warmth and protection from the elements readily at hand. Neoprene wrists on anoraks prevent a lot of the water from entering your sleeve, however, you will get evaporation and heat loss from the neoprene, so your hands will get colder. A sleeve that extends over a neoprene wrist seal is the best of both worlds. An alternative to a wet suit long john is a fibre pile long john. Both forms of clothing will lose heat rapidly once you are out of your kayak, so waterproof trousers should be carried for use at these times.

For very cold conditions or if you intend to practise techniques that will involve long periods in the water, a fibre pile suit covered by a dry suit is ideal.

A spray deck is a part of your clothing. You should always wear a spray deck when on the sea, or have one ready to put on while afloat.

Always bear in mind that it will probably be colder on the sea than on land and that the weather may well turn for the worse. Make certain that your clothing is adequate for that eventuality.

Backstraps may be attached to either side of the seat and held up by shock cord or nylon tape to a loop glassed behind the inside of the cockpit coaming. The strap itself should be broad and well padded. If your bulkhead is immediately behind your cockpit, then a few layers of 'karrimat' glued onto the bulkhead will make an excellent back support. The support should prevent your back from resting on the cockpit coaming even when you relax, as this can lead to back problems.

For coastal work it is advisable to carry a simple compass, and one that is fluid-filled and designed for orienteering is quite adequate. If your paddling will take you further offshore, where the compass will be used for longer navigation rather than just the safe return to shore in event of poor visibility, then a larger

Plates 10:b, c
The paddler feels close to the ever changing moods of the sea

domed compass fitted further towards the bow of the kayak is a worthwhile investment. The compass will be easier to use if it is further away from you as it is difficult to follow a compass course and paddle properly whilst looking down at your lap.

Charts should be placed in a transparent waterproof covering and secured on the deck where they can be easily referred to.

Emergency equipment

Careful thought needs to be given to emergency equipment. It is no use carrying a tow line if you have to land first to dig it out from the depths of your kayak. The following equipment should be readily available:

o   tow line

o   compass

o   flares

o   spare paddles

o   basic repair kit (eg plumbers tape which can be applied onto wet surfaces, cut into rectangles ready for use and rigid polythene to cover larger holes)

o   first aid kit

o   whistle

o   spare food

o   hot drink

o   exposure bag

o   anorak and hat if not worn.

The following equipment should also be carried:

o   packed lunch

o   dry clothing and towel (including shoes)

o   comprehensive repair kit

o   money for phone, ice creams, public transport, etc.

All the equipment should be secured so that it cannot escape in event of capsize, and those items that need to be kept dry must be stored in waterproof containers or bags. As few serious paddlers can boast that they have never found water in the hatches of their sea kayaks, it is advisable always to waterproof equipment before stowing to avoid what could at best be disappointing and at worst dangerous.

For multi-day trips camping gear would normally also be carried. There is no standard way to load a kayak as this will depend very much on the handling characteristics of the particular craft but, in principle, the heaviest items would normally be carried nearest to the cockpit and the kayak, when loaded, should sit a little lower in the water as when unladen but at the same angle.

Flares

Flares are a normal part of the sea kayaker's equipment. A range is now produced in waterproof casings. Flares must be readily accessible for emergency use on the water and you must be familiar with the firing procedure. They have a limited useful lifespan, indicated by an expiry date stamped on the flare.

Red flares are for distress use only. Their use will not guarantee a rescue as they may not be seen by anyone who would know what to do. Even if the coastguard is notified immediately it may be a considerable time before searchers reach your area. If searchers are spotted, a further flare will probably be needed to pinpoint your position.

Parachute flares, which rise by rocket to about 300 metres and float down as a red flare on a parachute, are recommended as a first line of seeking attention. For pinpointing your position, a hand held orange smoke flare for daytime use or a red hand held flare at night-time should be used. Mini-flares, which have limited range and a short duration, may be used to pinpoint your position, and their loud bang may help to attract attention.

White flares are not distress flares and may be used to warn other craft against collision if it becomes apparent that you have not been noticed.

Radios

Radio telephones and emergency pinpointing beacons are carried by some paddlers, especially when involved in long open crossings in busy sea areas, but are not in common use at present.

TECHNIQUES

Launching

Sheltered launch from a rock
As a basic principle, the kayak should be afloat before you embark if possible. This will protect the hull from unnecessary abrasion. With care, the kayak can be placed in the water alongside a low rock and the paddler can embark with dry feet.

Seal launch
If conditions are unsuitable for a sheltered launch, then a seal launch from a beach or even a rock may be appropriate. Sit in the kayak at the water's edge pointing into the oncoming waves, secure the spray cover then, with the paddles held in one hand in the manner of a punt pole and with the other hand on the beach or rock, shunt yourself and the kayak forwards into the water. If the direction of the wind is going to turn the kayak as soon as the bow is afloat, then the paddle is best held on the downwind side for extra directional control. Once afloat, paddle out through the break keeping the kayak pointing into the waves. Balance is maintained by paddling through crests rather than lifting the paddles from the water.

Seal launching from steep beaches or rocks can be more tricky. Sea kayaks with little rocker will experience a moment of instability when the bow is afloat but the stern is still supported by the beach. Readiness for a paddle brace at this point will help. Another problem relates to kayaks having a pronounced skeg. A steep launch forwards can damage this comparatively fragile structure, so a backward launch may be necessary. The greater the degree of rocker, the easier will be a launch from a steep beach.

When launching through surf or small dumpers, it is important to watch the pattern of waves and to time your launch to coincide with a lull in the larger

Fig 10:2
Launching from a beach

waves, preferably launching soon after a larger set of waves. In awkward situations, the most experienced in the group may need to help launch the rest of the group before launching himself.

Fig 10:3
Seal launching from steep or rocky shore

Fig 10:4
Awaiting a lull in the waves in which to launch

Landing

With planning and observation, it is usually possible to avoid the roughest landings and to gain shelter behind a headland or rock, or at least to find a spot where the waves are at their smallest.

If you are landing a sea kayak through surf onto a beach, then a controlled landing is preferable. A 'bongo slide' in a 5 metre long sea kayak can be somewhat hazardous to other water users. If the kayak is paddled backwards when the stern begins to rise to meet the steepest and the broken waves, then forwards as the stern drops again towards the following trough, progress may be made to the beach without surfing. Even quite large breaking waves may be backed through in this manner, although heavily laden kayaks are easier to control than empty ones.

Dumpers can be approached in a similar way, taking care to stall until the wave breaks in front of you before sprinting up the beach behind it and leaping out before being caught by the back wash. Dumpers can be extremely dangerous and should be avoided if possible but, if a landing is necessary, the most experienced should normally land first. He should prepare a long throw line, maybe using his tow line with a buoyancy aid as a float, and then signal the others in one at a time during suitable lulls. As each kayak arrives, it should be hauled up the beach beyond the back wash and held secure while the paddler scrambles out. Speed is important.

In the event of a capsize in these conditions, the victim should get clear of his kayak as quickly as possible to avoid injury. This is one of the few situations where you are safer when separated from your kayak. It is often impossible to escape from the back wash without assistance and, without help, drowning may follow, so the swift use of the throw line may be called for. Unfortunately, the explosive power of dumpers may not leave your kayak unscathed, so avoid dumpers when possible and always treat them with respect.

A seal landing onto rock can be made in a similar way, after first choosing a ledge or sheltered pool into which the waves wash and drain away without too much violence. The kayak is eased forwards on the back of the wave rather than the front, which would tend to plough you into the rock, and then held in position until the wave has subsided sufficiently to make a timely exit and to move the kayak to safety before the next wave.

With all of these landings, it may be necessary to wait and watch for a wave of a suitable size before landing.

Forward paddling

The sea paddler spends more time paddling forwards than performing any other stroke, so it is vitally important that he masters this subtle technique. Ideally the style will emulate that of a racing paddler, with blade close to the kayak, full use being made of body rotation. A low paddle action, in which the paddler performs a series of sweep strokes, is usually unnecessary even in strong winds. A slight lean of the body into the wind should normally suffice. It is important to use a footrest. With many modern sea kayaks, the knees may be brought together comfortably to enable a direct brace against the footrest, but can be spread outwards when bracing is needed for stability. Also of importance for longer times afloat is some form of back support. Ideally this should support the back low down so as to enable an unhindered rotation above the hips.

Taking advantage of a following sea can greatly increase your speed whilst economising on effort. Even a general purpose kayak can hitch a ride in suitable conditions, but kayaks with a longer keel line benefit most. With a short sea (waves close together), the stern of the kayak will start to rise on the following wave when the crest of the previous wave is approaching the bow. Two or three vigorous paddle strokes will give the kayak enough speed to run down the face of the following wave. This is the time to relax, steer if necessary and to wait until the wave drops you. Then, watching the passing crest as it nears your bow, prepare for a couple more paddle strokes. It should not be necessary to look behind you to anticipate the position of the next wave. With greater wavelength, forward paddling will need to start as the kayak becomes level in the trough, or even as the kayak is inclined upwards towards the passing crest because, the greater the wavelength, the faster the wave and the faster you will need to paddle in order to get a ride. There comes a point when the waves are too fast to be able to take advantage of them unless they are steepening towards breaking. At the smaller end of the scale, quite tiny waves can be used, even waves reflected from cliffs which may be travelling against the wind. Timing is all important but, with practice, running on a following sea will become rapid and almost effortless.

Steering on a following sea in some kayaks is hard work. Often a forward sweep stroke ending in a stern rudder with the top of the blade angled towards the kayak will maintain your course and speed, where a reverse sweep stroke will lose your position on the wave.

Turning techniques

Beginners in sea kayaks often prefer to keep their craft upright and to turn using an ordinary sweep stroke. With the longer and straighter keeled kayaks, this requires time and effort, so many sea kayaks suitable for beginners have quite a flat bottom to facilitate this type of turn. Edging or leaning the kayak, which effectively increases the rocker, will make turning easier. Modifying the sweep stroke by angling the paddle blade will provide the necessary support. Kayaks with prominent skegs will turn more easily when the kayak is edged so that the skeg slides across the surface, rather than digging in.

A moving kayak can be turned easily through a few degrees by using a forward sweep stroke and edging the kayak towards the blade (ie tilting the kayak on the opposite side to the required turn). The body remains upright whilst the leg on the side of the turn is pressed upwards and the other knee is held straight. This permits minor corrections in course without loss of speed or of paddling rhythm. Edging is maintained while the paddle is returned to the bow for repeated sweeps by skimming it over the surface in a low brace position so that it can provide support if necessary.

Forward sweep

Direction of turn

Fig 10:5
Tilting the kayak to aid a turn

259

Reverse sweep

Direction of turn

Fig 10:6
Tilt towards the turn and reverse sweep to get a tight turn

If a more radical turn is needed, the moving kayak is edged into the turn using a vigorous reverse sweep stroke, with the blade angled to give support. This is almost a low brace turn, but there is much more emphasis on the reverse sweep. The greater the edging, the more effective the turn, as the effective rocker will be at its greatest when the kayak is tilted right onto its side.

In strong winds, some sea kayaks become difficult to turn. To add to this, the paddler often feels reluctant to commit himself to leaning sufficiently. One way to overcome this problem is to extend the paddle to gain a wider and more powerful sweep. This technique can also be used with beginners in calmer conditions to speed up a turn.

Doubles

Doubles, for their length, will turn more readily than singles, because the paddlers are closer to the ends of the kayak. The bow paddler uses the part of a sweep stroke that is forward of his cockpit and the stern paddler uses the part of a sweep stroke that is behind his cockpit.

When leaning or edging is used to assist a turn, the bow man performs a powerful bow draw angled slightly, if necessary, to provide extra support. The stern man performs a stern push/rear half of a reverse sweep stroke, with the paddle slightly angled for support. This same manoeuvre can be performed at speed.

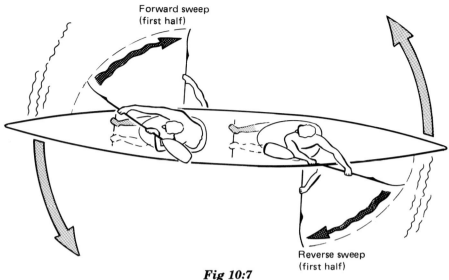

Fig 10:7
Turning a double

The stern rudder

The stern rudder is used to control a kayak in a following sea. It is used more often with the more manoeuvrable kayaks, and may be introduced to beginners as soon as required. When the kayak begins to broach or turn broadside to the waves, a stern rudder may be applied to the downwind side of the kayak with the paddle blade held close to the kayak well to the stern, and with the uppermost edge of the trailing blade angled away from the kayak. Unfortunately, although this is the easiest technique to master, it carries the risk of capsize due to the kayak being swept over the paddler.

It is better to apply the stern rudder on the upwind side with the upper edge of the trailing blade angled in towards the kayak. This makes it easier for the paddler to lean slightly into the wind while using the stern rudder to correct his

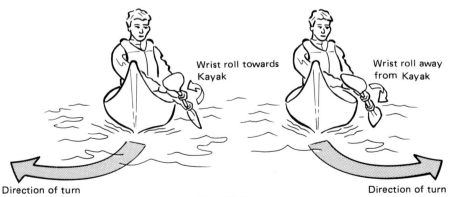

Wrist roll towards Kayak

Wrist roll away from Kayak

Direction of turn

Direction of turn

Fig 10:8
Stern rudder showing the 'wrist roll'

Plate 10:d
Sea kayaking may be enjoyed in conventional kayaks built for white water

course. This is a more subtle skill to master. It is usually applied at the end of a forward sweep stroke when the paddle is kept in the water for a moment or two longer with the uppermost edge angled towards the kayak.

Sea kayaks do not broach as readily as general purpose kayaks, but need more active correction strokes when they do, although the sweep followed by stern rudder is frequently used when riding waves with a following sea (see forward paddling).

The paddle brace

The paddle brace can be used to maintain balance whilst broadside or nearly broadside to steep or breaking waves. The paddle blade is placed on the wave, either drive face uppermost (low brace) or drive face downwards (high brace). The arm should not be extended fully and the paddle should be horizontal or inclined upwards towards the wave crest. This means that, in the event of the wave carrying the kayak sideways, the blade will plane across the water providing support rather than digging in. A fully extended arm together with a steeply angled blade is a recipe for a dislocated shoulder.

When caught sideways by a breaking crest, forward travel may be continued by moving the paddle brace towards the stern of the kayak. This will allow the bow to drop and the kayak will move along the wave at the same time as travelling sideways. Considerable acceleration may be gained in this way, giving speed that lasts well after the passing of the crest.

When paddling into steep waves, a low brace may be used to follow a forward paddle stroke to maintain balance as the kayak lurches through the crest and drops into the following trough.

In a following sea, a low brace is a valuable aid to confidence and balance when the back of a paddle blade is flat on the water behind the cockpit and a little away from the kayak. This can be used to negotiate steep waves on which the paddler is nervous of surfing forward and, because the blade is flat on the water under very little pressure, steering is not affected.

The paddle brace is also useful when seal launching from a steep beach or rock, as described in the section on launching, when a moment of instability is often experienced.

RESCUE TECHNIQUES

There are a number of ways to return a capsized victim to this kayak and these are described in detail in the chapter on Deep Water Rescues. Obviously a kayak may be emptied on the beach, but when the capsize is further from the shore a 'deep water rescue' is far more suitable. Whereas you may favour one particular rescue, it is advisable to familiarise yourself with and practise a range of techniques as different rescues may lend themselves to different situations.

The capsize

On the sea, it is essential that you hold onto your kayak and paddle throughout a capsize. A kayak will be blown across the water much faster than a swimmer can swim even if the wind is only light. The resulting rescue will be more time consuming and traumatic, and may be dangerous. A lost kayak must be pursued by one rescuer. Once the drifting kayak is reached, it must be either righted and towed back to the victim before emptying, or emptied first, depending on the circumstances. This takes much more time than a straight forward rescue so, in the event of a capsize, hold onto the kayak.

The basic procedures for deep water rescues are covered in Chapter 11 of this Handbook. In dealing with sea kayaks fitted with bulkheads close behind the seat or cockpits pods, the draining process in a rescue is greatly simplified. It is necessary only to raise the bow. In these cases the victim should always make his way to the bow of his kayak so that the approaching rescuer can clearly see which end to aim for. Many sea kayaks float on their sides when swamped. This is caused by the shape of the bow section and when it comes to raising the bows in a rescue, it is often possible to make the lift directly from this position without having to roll the boat completely upside down.

The H rescue

This is a difficult rescue to coordinate in single kayaks, but it is probably the best rescue for doubles.

A rescue kayak is positioned across each end of the capsized kayak, forming the shape of the letter H. The victim's kayak is rolled onto its side and raised simultaneously from each end. The ends are then drawn across the decks of the two rescue kayaks and the craft is inverted for final draining, lifting one end at a time. When the rescuers are in doubles, one paddler in each kayak maintains position while the other rescues.

Fig 10:9
A deep water rescue of a double kayak

Rescue with pump

When a pump is fitted to a bulkheaded kayak, or one well packed with buoyancy, the rescuer may simply turn the kayak upright and assist the victim to re-enter and to secure his spray deck. The kayak may then be pumped dry. This is a particularly useful technique for fully laden kayaks and for inexperienced rescuers. The time taken pumping dry by hand or foot makes this less popular than it might otherwise be, but it does get the victim out of the water with the greatest speed. This is where the electric pump is particularly effective.

Other techniques

A waterlogged kayak may be drained by the rescuer lifting the cockpit gradually so that the water steadily drains out until the kayak may be pivoted straight into an X rescue. The victim may assist by holding the end to ensure that the kayak remains level during initial draining.

Fig 10:10
With a heavy kayak the swimmer can assist emptying by getting his feet onto the rescuer's kayak and using leg power to haul the boat

Fig 10:11
Spilling water from a heavily swamped kayak by raising it on its side. Lift slowly and use the swimmer to keep it level

Fig 10:12
Hauling out an inert paddler into a position for resuscitation

Another method, the 'curl', relies on the victim doing most of the work. The victim reaches across the rescuer's kayak close to the cockpit and grasps his own cockpit with his palms uppermost and his elbows locked against the deck of the rescue kayak. The rescuer ensures that the victim's kayak remains level. As the water drains out, the rescuer can progressively lean away from the victim's kayak which lifts his elbows and helps to raise his kayak. Final draining may be by the X method.

The problem of fully waterlogged kayaks and kayaks floating on end (Cleopatra's needle) are avoidable by the use of sufficient buoyancy. A reasonable guide to sufficient buoyancy is to see how easy it is for one person to drain a completely waterlogged kayak unaided. If it is difficult, then more buoyancy is needed.

Cleopatra's needle can occur in an empty sea kayak with bulkheads if no other buoyancy is carried and the stern becomes holed. The victim holds onto another kayak for support and brings his own kayak to a level position on the surface by working his other hand along his deck lines, or by lifting the cockpit with a foot. Once level, the kayak may be drained as described for a waterlogged kayak although, in the case of a kayak with bulkheads, the kayak will need to be repaired, perhaps with rigid polythene and plumbers tape, which can be applied even when the surface is wet.

All-in rescue

In the event of a whole party ending up in the water, one remedy is for victims to pair up for rescue. Provided the kayaks are fitted with sufficient buoyancy, the end of one kayak may be lifted onto the middle of the upturned hull of the other. The two swimmers place their feet against the opposite gunnels of the lower kayak whilst holding the upper kayak. This keeps the two kayaks at right angles and keeps the lower one upside down. By straightening bent knees, the kayak can be pulled across the lower one to the point of balance, and drained by see-sawing each way. This kayak is then righted and manoeuvred alongside the other. The first paddler then re-enters across the upturned hull, whilst the remaining swimmer leans across it to stabilise the empty kayak. Once re-entry is completed, then the second kayak is treated as waterlogged and rescued in the manner described earlier.

Methods of re-entry

There are three commonly used methods of re-entry:

Face up from stern

The swimmer positions himself between his own and the rescuer's kayak, close to his own cockpit. Grasping both kayaks, he drops head and shoulders back into the water whilst raising his legs into the cockpit. By pulling the two kayaks together he can then easily raise himself from the water to the back of his kayak, from which position he can slide into the cockpit. Some people find this method difficult, especially in rougher conditions.

Side entry

The victim climbs across his own kayak from level with the cockpit. The rescuer may assist by grasping the buoyancy aid of the victim, which is an advantage of this method re-entry.

Face down from the stern (crawl)

The victim drags himself onto the rear deck. He can be aided by the rescuers pulling on the buoyancy aid, especially if there are two rescuers, one on either side.

THE ESKIMO RESCUE

This is a method of rescue which may be used on capsize victims who are confident enough to stay in their kayaks. It is possible to swim in a kayak, and to raise the head enough to gain a quick breath of air. The rescuer on hearing either the banging of hands on the upturned kayak, or seeing the upturned hull, approaches quickly but carefully alongside. There are then three courses open to him.

The bow rescue

If the victim's hands are visible above the water on either side of the kayak, then the bow may gently be presented to a hand, and the victim flicks up on this. The rescuer needs to push forwards slightly to assist.

266

The paddle rescue

The paddles are placed across both the rescuer's boat and the upturned hull and the victim's hand is guided onto the part of the paddle between the kayaks on which he flicks up. There is a possibility here that the victim will make contact with the end of the paddle and try to pull on that, resulting in failure.

The side rescue

The rescuer leans over for support onto the upturned hull, reaches for the near hand of the victim and places it on the deckline on his foredeck, on which the victim pulls up, aided if necessary by the free hand of the rescuer.

ROLLING A SEA KAYAK

Despite their size, sea kayaks are generally surprisingly easy to roll, especially when laden. However, there are one or two quirks which you may discover. The first is that on calm water a sea kayak will often rest on its side instead or completely capsizing. The paddler, on finding himself supported just under the surface, will find it easier to return on the side he fell in. Secondly, in windy conditions, the larger size of the kayak will catch the wind, making it easier to roll up into the wind. Thirdly, in tide races, your body will be carried down-tide of the kayak, making a roll on this side much easier, and in surf you will need to leave the water on the seaward side of the kayak. It is a good idea to practise rolling in a variety of conditions, with the kayak laden and unladen, with a proficient rescuer at hand.

Double sea kayaks, perhaps surprisingly, roll quite easily, and if the front person lies flat forward then the back paddler can right the kayak alone.

SELF RESCUES

A self rescue can range from a quick method of saving time following a capsize in straightforward conditions as a beginner, to an advanced technique to be used when things are going badly.

At its simplest, a kayak well fitted with buoyancy may be more or less drained by turning it onto its side and depressing the stern to allow most of the water to drain from the cockpit. The kayak may then be flipped upright and the paddler can re-enter by hauling himself across the kayak, swinging one leg across to sit astride close behind the cockpit, and then sliding himself into the seat. Any remaining water may be sponged or bailed out. This type of self rescue will only work well with a fairly stable kayak packed with buoyancy, or with a kayak fitted with a pod.

The use of a 'paddle wing' may assist in the re-entry. For this, the paddle is held across the kayak with one blade lying flat in the water, preferably just submerged, increasing stability.

To increase stability still further, an inflatable mitten may be pulled over the blade. One such device is available under the name 'paddle float'. This is an American device in the form of an inflatable platform from which to perform a rescue and re-entry. It seems too time and energy-consuming for most applications in our waters and with our kayaks.

267

Plate 10:e
An almost timeless nomadic existence

The most effective self rescue in rough conditions is a re-entry and roll. Even the most experienced paddlers occasionally exit from their kayaks and this is often in committing conditions where a conventional rescue may present more danger to the swimmer and boat than a prolonged swim or tow out of the danger area. A self rescue can speed up the rescue process. The swimmer holds the kayak by the cockpit and rolls it onto its side, with the cockpit towards the oncoming waves. With the cockpit grasped with hands either side the legs are manoeuvred into position in the cockpit. The body will not normally sink below the surface until seating is almost completed when a support stroke or roll will right the kayak. An extended paddle roll will increase confidence and reliability, as the kayak will contain water. Once the kayak is upright, usually without the spray deck in place, the kayak can be gently paddled away, although it will be tippier than usual.

Recent developments have been made into different ways of using spare paddles as outriggers to increase stability of a waterlogged craft and these will facilitate replacement of the spray deck and pumping out, which until now has usually been done whilst rafted up.

One of these ideas is to incorporate a tube into each side of the kayak, into which the split paddles are pushed, each blade being set at an angle into the water for maximum stability. A second method, which is less drastic for the kayak, is to carry an angled tube into which the two parts of a split paddle can be fitted. The paddles are restrained by two loops of tape through which the paddles are passed prior to docking with the tube. My own idea is to use a swivelling device similar to a cam cleat into which the split paddles are permanently stored. When required for extra stability, the blades are swivelled out into position in the water on either side, and when their help is no longer required they are simply swung back to lock into their storage position. The same device may be used whilst taking photographs or removing or replacing clothing, instead of having to raft up.

The additional buoyancy of an inflatable life jacket over a buoyancy aid makes it possible to perform a re-entry and roll without the face being submerged. This reduces anxiety, especially when learning the technique.

Self rescue may be performed in doubles in gentle conditions by righting the kayak, one paddler climbing aboard and bailing whilst the other steadies the kayak. The second re-embarks while the first steadies the kayak with his paddles. The ease of this operation depends on the presence of sufficient buoyancy, especially in the centre section of the kayak which may otherwise contain considerable water.

KAYAK RESCUES FOR SWIMMERS

If a swimmer is in difficulty, he may be returned to safety by clasping your kayak with arms and legs from underneath, with his head close to one side of the bow. Alternatively, he may simply lie flat face downwards on your rear deck, holding around your waist or onto the rear deck lines and with feet gripping either side of the kayak at the stern. This is more suitable in calmer waters. A small passenger may sit astride immediately behind you providing that you are able to keep the kayak upright. When coming in through surf, the best technique seems simply to keep the swimmer in the water holding onto your rear toggle, although a firm grip will be needed.

Raft assisted resuscitation

Although it may sometimes be necessary to get out of your kayak to support and resuscitate a non-breathing person, whenever practical, resuscitation should be carried out across a raft of kayaks. In this way, it will be possible to continue for longer and it may be possible for the raft to be towed to shore. The patient is turned to face the raft, his wrists are grasped by the paddler in the further kayak and hauled across the decks. He is then turned over and prepared for resuscitation.

A non-breathing capsize victim may be treated by a single rescuer in a similar way by using the victim's kayak as a roller over which he can be hauled, and if breathing is successfully re-started, he may be taken to shore using one hand to secure the patient across the decks whilst operating the paddle with the other, using the shoulder as a second contact point. This is an extremely tiring procedure, but one which I have used successfully in an emergency.

TOWING

Towing on the sea presents different problems from towing on rivers and both equipment and techniques differ.

On the sea, a tow line may be needed when conditions are getting rougher to prevent the capsize of a weaker paddler. In this case, a rafted tow may be used to assist a paddler with directional control, or to help increase the speed of the party. In more serious circumstances, it may be used to evacuate a casualty, or to safeguard the rescue of a capsize victim from drifting downwind onto rocks. It may be used by an instructor to prevent the drift of a rafted group, or to tow a capsize victim from an area of danger prior to a deep water rescue.

To cope with such a variety of circumstances requires a towing system that is strong, easily attached and detached, and usable with the rescuer's kayak facing either forwards or backwards. In addition, it is advisable to have a system that floats, and one that is adjustable in length. In choppy conditions, it becomes difficult to even catch hold of the end of a kayak, let alone attach a line, so the fastening clip must be large enough for easy attachment. It must also be usable with cold hands (a good guide here is to try to operate it beforehand with mittens on). Many plastic clips are not strong enough to cope with the huge forces which can operate, and alloy climbing karabiners tend to corrode and seize up unless constantly maintained. Stainless steel is better but, whilst trouble free, is rather heavy when of sufficient size.

Lines must be strong. A loaded sea kayak with some water and a paddler may weigh in excess of 150kg and, with two kayaks rafted on the end of a tow line, a sharp jolt may be enough to snap a weak line. I have seen this happen in a potentially hazardous situation. Six millimetre diameter braided polypropylene 'floating' line is satisfactory. It does not retain much water and is therefore light to carry. Some form of float, sufficient to float the fastening clip, should it be dropped, can save time. Attachment to the rescuer's boat may be by means of a cam cleat, in which case a restraining loop must be present to stop the rise and fall of the rope from lifting it from the cleat. For short distances, manoeuvring, and anchoring rescues, I often prefer a waist tow. My preference is for a broad waist belt fastened by a quick release diver's buckle and with the line attached in such a way that it is free to travel around the belt without moving the release buckle. The line may be stored simply by fastening the clip to the belt for easy access and stuffing the line up under the buoyancy aid. For longer distances, towing from a cleat on the deck is more comfortable.

A length of shock cord elastic fastened across a loop of the rope will absorb the jarring and snatching experienced on a choppy sea. The rope should not be cut, and the elastic should be tied in such a way that the rope takes the full strain before the elastic reaches full stretch, otherwise the elastic will soon fail.

Sea kayaks need fairly long tow lines, about 8m being a minimum, leaving about a boat length between the two kayaks. An even longer line can sometimes be an advantage.

Tow lines to be used only from the kayak may be stored neatly on the deck behind the paddler in a bag fastened to the deck by velcro. One end can be placed ready in position in the cleat and the other end clipped onto an accessible deck loop. Whatever your chosen system, it should be available for use in the shortest possible time.

Rafted tow

A stabled platform can be created by two or more paddlers rafting up and fastening the ends of their kayaks together. This can be towed without fear of the raft breaking up.

Fan tow

For this method, two or more paddlers attach their tow lines to the kayak(s) to be towed and paddle more or less parallel to one another. Kayaks towing to either side need to tow from a point close to the centre of turning of their own kayak, but may attach to a deck line nearer the cockpit of the kayak being towed. This is a very efficient system of towing, but tow lines must be long.

Tandem tow

In order to make steering easy in awkward conditions, several paddlers can attach their tow lines to one another's kayaks with the victim on the end.

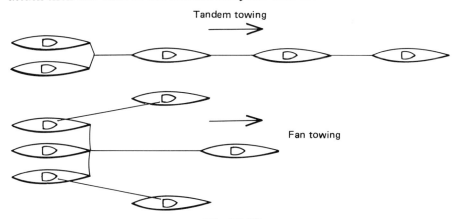

Fig 10:13
Tandem towing (top) maintains direction easily in poor conditions
Fan towing is useful for moving rafts of kayaks

Anchor man

Fig 10:14
Using an anchor man to hold an X-rescue away from danger

Anchor man

During a deep water rescue, and at any time when two or more kayaks are rafted together, an 'anchor man' with a tow line attached to the raft can assist the situation by pointing the kayaks head or tail to wind or tide. He may also check the drift down-wind or down-tide. An X rescue in rough conditions can be held by an anchor man with the rescue kayak tail to wind. If the victim then holds onto the rescue kayak by the cockpit, the victim's kayak cannot be swept onto either person by a breaking wave. In these conditions a long tow line is best.

An anchor man can also prevent the kayaks being towed from surfing forwards onto the towing kayak when landing through surf or in a steep following sea. This is difficult and requires skill and practice to do well.

Tow lines are important safety aids and their use should be practised. They should clear the end of the towing kayak and not prevent it turning freely. Care must be taken with any loading of the rear deck to avoid fouling the line around equipment, or lifting of the rear hatch cover.

REPAIRS

Repairs may be carried out on kayaks whilst at sea. Plumbers tape, resembling grease-impregnated cloth, with or without a foil finish, together with rigid polythene which may be cut from a plastic bottle, makes a good emergency kit. The tape may be cut into rectangles, the backing film peeled off, and the sticky surface set against a strip of heavy polythene ready for use. The polythene strip may then be rolled and carried in an accessible place. A couple of polythene bags to protect the hands from the sticky surfaces when the tape is peeled off make a useful addition.

If the paddler in the damaged kayak leans across another kayak, the damaged hull will be revealed to a third paddler who may locate and repair the hole. If there are only two paddlers, a support stroke will be needed or else the victim's kayak will need to be upturned across the other and repaired there whilst the victim sits astride the rescuer's kayak.

NIGHT PADDLING

This can be a magical experience, especially on a dark night when the bioluminescence paints a moving snake-like line of green light from either side of your bows, and your deck is awash with gleaming sparks of green at each breaking wave. The stirring of the water with the paddles creates whirlpools of light and the passage of a shoal of fish resembles some weird underwater searchlight. On a moonlit night, the effect is different, with a corridor of reflected pale light pointing to the moon and with objects bathed in its gentle light.

Night paddling can also have its more sinister aspects. The roar of an approaching overfall, where the indistinct shapes of dancing white water menace at an uncertain distance and size, or the approach of an unknown coastline beset with dangers that need to be identified before a landing may be found. My most terrifying paddling experience to date was at night on the sea.

Certain precautions need to be taken for night paddling. Every paddler must carry a powerful white light with which to show his presence and position to other craft to prevent collision. Ideally, your first few excursions should be on water that is utterly familiar, as even the familiar seems very different in the dark. A gentle light should be used for reference to the chart, and this should be used as sparingly as possible, so as not to destroy night vision. Distances are hard to gauge, so paddling pace should be kept constant so that distances may be measured in time. Direction can be maintained by compass, although there are many lighthouses and beacons, shown on the chart, each with its own special sequence of flashes and/or colour that may be used to pinpoint your position. Try to plan your journey thoroughly beforehand, taking the tide into consideration, and noting places where two lights in transit will confirm your progress. Allow a little more time than you would expect to need in day-time.

The leader of a group at night has the difficult task of keeping track of each paddler. One way of doing this is to divide the group into threes, each with a leader, who displays a chemical light stick in a prominent position, such as on his head or on the end of his kayak. Other sources of gentle light will serve. His two partners then paddle close on either side, remaining within talking distance. Each leader then follows the light of the previous trio with the front one navigating. The overall leader is then free to ensure that the different groups remain close enough together and that the navigation is correct.

An alternative is for everybody to display a light all of the time so that a count may be made of the lights.

Practise at night is the key, with which you will open the strange world of night paddling.

TIDES

Tides are a result of the gravitational pull of the moon and the sun. When the moon, sun and earth are in line (at full and at new moon), the pull is in a straight line resulting in a large tidal range, known as a spring tide. When the sun and moon form a right angle with the earth (at half moon), the tidal range is at its least and this is known as a neap tide. Thus there are two spring tides and two neap tides in every lunar month.

The times of high and low tide as predicted according to the paths of the sun and moon are published in tide tables. The following format is quite common. This one refers to Dover but separate tables are produced for ports all around the coast.

273

Date	MORNING		AFTERNOON	
	Time Hr Min	Height Metres	Time Hr Min	Height Metres
1 SA	0148	6.6	1406	6.3
2 SU	0229	6.4	1453	6.1
3 M	0318	6.1	1548	5.7
4 TU	0417	5.7	1655	5.3

Times are usually presented in Greenwich Mean Time, so during British Summer Time, you will need to add one hour to the time given. Other places around the country will differ in the time of high water (HW) from Dover by a constant amount. For example, the time of HW for London Bridge you simply look up the time of HW Dover, add one hour if it is British Summertime and add a further two hours 52 minutes to correct for London Bridge.

Included with the Dover Tide Tables would normally be a list of Tidal Differences on Dover for places all around Britain. The + or - sign tells you whether you need to add or subtract the constant from the Dover time.

The height of the tide, also given in the tables, will tell you where you are in relation to spring or neap tides. The highest figures represent spring tides, whereas the smallest figures represent neap tides. When you study the tables, you will find that at certain times of the year, the spring tides have a greater range than at others, giving an indication of the greatest strength of the tidal streams in those months.

There is a general rule applying to the rate of rise or fall of the tide with respect to high and low water. This is known as the Twelfths Rule. Simply, this states that if the height difference between low and high water is divided into twelve equal units, then during the first hour after low water, there will be a rise of one unit, during the second a further two units, during the third and fourth three units each, during the fifth another two units and in the last hour to high water, the final single unit. This rule may help you to decide how far up the beach to carry your kayaks for a lunch stop, or help you calculate the time at which a sandbar or rock may become covered or uncovered. Unfortunately, it does not always bear any relation to the speed or direction of tide streams.

CHARTS AND MAPS

The Admiralty produce charts of various scales covering all our coasts and seas. These charts display the same degree of information about the sea as the Ordnance Survey maps show for the land.

Admiralty charts have a key in the form of a booklet, published as chart 5011, which in its introduction explains clearly about terms such as chart datum, drying heights and sea miles. In its text, it includes the full range of symbols used on our modern metric charts, which in this country have replaced the older fathom charts. Abbreviations and symbols used on fathom charts still in use for some areas of the world are also included. Admiralty charts and publications are available in many yacht chandlers.

Metric charts are coloured for ease of use, with yellow for land, white for sea, with shallower water highlight in blue and green representing land covered by water at some point by the tide and uncovered at others. Magenta is used for some important information such as lights and shipping lanes, and places to which the tabulated tidal information refers.

Admiralty charts show only limited information about the land, so many people also carry an OS map for road access points, and for other useful information such as the positions of telephones and public houses. Some merely transfer the relevant information onto the chart.

In addition to the charts produced by the Admiralty are a number produced for yachtsmen for popular yachting areas, and these are also perfectly suitable for navigation.

Pilots and cruising guides

These are publications containing detailed information about the coast including helpful navigation tips, historical and geographical connections, tidal information, etc. They are invaluable planning aids although often expensive, but can be obtained through your local library. Pilots are produced by the Admiralty in a comprehensive series, and there are an increasing number of yachting pilots of varying quality available for certain areas.

TIDE STREAMS

When the tide rises from low to high water, there is a flow of water along our coasts which in the main is reversed when the tide falls. These water movements are known as tide streams. The speed of these streams increases from neap tides to a maximum at spring tides. The directions and strengths of these streams have been carefully measured at a number of places around our coasts, hour by hour from low water through high and back to low water.

This information is tabulated on Admiralty charts referring to specific points on the chart (see Fig 10:16), and presented on tidal flow diagrams in tide stream atlases. In these atlases, the direction of the stream is shown by an arrow, the boldness and size of which increases with the speed of the tide. Speeds representing mean springs and mean neaps and also present beside some of the arrows.

These documents, used in conjunction with tide tables, are a valuable aid to planning as they indicate not only when the tide will be moving in your favour, but how fast it will carry you, enabling you to calculate a good time to depart on a trip and an estimated time of arrival at your destination.

TIDE RACES AND OVERFALLS

The characteristics of tidal streams resemble those of rivers. When the stream is constricted in depth and/or width, it will increase in speed. When the restriction is in depth and the water is pushed over a ledge or bank, this is known as an 'overfall'. Where the restriction is in width, and the water is forced around a prominent headland, or squeezed between an island and the shore, this causes a 'tide race'.

Both tide races and overfalls are potentially hazardous places requiring a certain amount of care, especially when there is any swell, or wind. When a wind

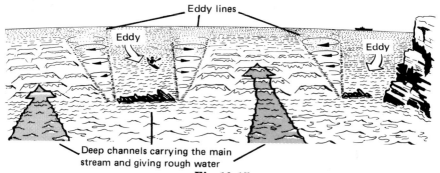

Fig 10:15

Overfalls. The broad arrows show the direction of flow

blows against the tide, the sea will be much rougher than would normally be expected for that wind strength whilst, when the wind blows in the same direction as the tide, the waves will be less steep. This holds for any tidal stream, but is particularly noticeable in tide races and overfalls, where a light breeze can produce a violent sea. When planning a journey through such areas, careful consideration must be taken of the wind direction in relation to the exact direction of the stream in the race, which may differ from that of the general tidal direction. Also of concern should be the wind speed, the presence of swell, and the ability of the group. Rescues in the rough water of a tide race can be difficult.

Many tide races and overfalls may be largely avoided by either hugging the shore to avoid the strength of the tide, or by passing them well out to sea, where the stream may be much weaker. Study of the local 'pilot', together with obtaining local knowledge, may help.

Where a tide stream runs between two islands or past a headland, chutes of water are formed, similar in pattern to those caused on a smaller scale between rocks on a river. Eddies will form behind islands and headlands and, as on rivers, there will be a narrow, clearly defined eddy line close behind the obstruction dividing the main stream from the eddy. Further downstream, however, the eddy line widens into a broad band of turbulence which in strong tides will make a sea kayak weave and spin quite violently.

As the water leading into a race may be quite smooth and very fast flowing, the speed of approach and the scale of these first waves can be quite intimidating. Conversely, it can be startling to be surfing upstream through a race amidst huge crashing waves and to suddenly come upon the head of the race, with almost flat water ahead.

In overfalls, the water running over ledges can produce stoppers, with considerable tow backs and powerful boils. Sometimes it is difficult to distinguish between safe waves breaking as a result of the fast water, and waves breaking onto exposed rock.

The ferocity of tide races and overfalls will vary from spring tide to neap, and will also depend on the amount of swell and wind. They will be calmest at slack water, and roughest when the water is at its fastest. Even small headlands may produce local tide races which are suitable for training purposes, although they are often not marked on the chart. A good training site will have a clearly defined area of fast rough water, with an eddy that is easily gained for resting and for regaining the race further upstream, or for rescue purposes. It is essential to establish some means of preventing a group from becoming too spread out. An easily visible transit on shore beyond which a return must be made to the eddy, is one way of achieving this.

Paddling out on tidal races and overfalls can be very tiring. Do not overestimate the stamina of the group, particularly if you may need to paddle some distance to your egress point.

WEATHER

Before setting out on the sea, it is important to obtain a weather forecast. In order to interpret a forecast, you will need to understand a certain amount about the weather. There are several very good books on the subject and the following are particularly recommended:

Practical Weather Forecasting - Frank Mitchell-Christie

Outlook - G. W. White

Wind

Wind is moving air. It is referred to by the direction of origin, so a west wind comes from the west. The speed of the wind is usually expressed as a number on the Beaufort Scale or as a speed in knots.

The wind speed is determined by the pressure gradient: the closer together the isobars (lines joining points of equal air pressure), the stronger the wind. If the wind 'veers', then its change of direction is clockwise, eg from south to south west; if it 'backs', it changes in an anti-clockwise direction, eg from south to south east.

The wind blowing over the open sea will take time to produce its maximum sea state, but in tidal waters, it may produce a rough sea in minutes. If the fetch, the distance over which the wind can blow across the water before reaching land, is small, then the waves will never attain much height. A gale blowing offshore may produce a bit of spray from the water, but the sea will be quite calm close to the shore. The further out to sea, the larger the waves. A capsize victim here would be blown into rougher and rougher conditions. This type of shore is known as a weather short. Care should be taken with offshore winds as the apparent calmness close in is deceptive. With an onshort wind (a lee shore), the waves will be at their greatest, but a capsize victim will find himself carried back towards the shore.

The local effect of mountains can be dramatic. Storm force offshore winds may be produced by the funnelling effect caused by mountains when wind strengths fairly close to the area affected may be quite acceptable to the paddler. General wind directions may be modified locally by coastal mountains. These local effects are often referred to in the local Admiralty Pilot when of significance.

The sky

The state of the sky is described in four ways: fine - where no more than one quarter of the sky is obscured by cloud; fair - one quarter to one half cloud cover; cloudy - one half to three quarters cloud cover; and overcast - more than three quarters of the sky hidden by cloud.

Plate 10:f
Exposed Scottish Western Isles (Rhum in the background)

Precipitation

This falls from clouds as drizzle, rain, snow, sleet or hail. It can be light, moderate or heavy, and intermittent or continuous.

Visibility

Haze is caused by dust particles and usually permits a visibility of at least 2,000 metres, though it can be less. Mist is water vapour causing a visibility of less than 2,000 metres, although if the visibility drops below 1,000 metres it is described as fog. Otherwise, visibility in weather reports may be described as excellent (over 30 nautical miles), very good (up to 30 miles), good (up to 10 miles), moderate (up to 5 miles), or poor (up to 2 miles).

Depressions

These are areas of low pressure around which the wind swirls in an anti-clockwise direction in the northern hemisphere. They normally have an associated warm sector, containing warm tropical air. The leading edge of this sector is called a warm front, and usually carries moisture which falls as rain when it mixes with the cold air which has a much lower saturation point. Surrounding this warm sector is colder polar air, the front of which, when following the warm sector, is known as a cold front. This usually swings in from the west behind depressions and carries a shorter period of heavy rain. The cold front is often accompanied by a sudden increase in wind speed, and change in its direction.

THE BEAUFORT WIND SCALE

Force	Knots	Called	Sea Conditions	Sea State	Canoeists
0	1 or less	calm	like a mirror	smooth	
1	1-3	light air	ripples like scales	calm	suitable for beginners
2	4-6	light breeze	small wavelets, glassy crests, not breaking	calm	under instruction
3	7-10	gentle breeze	large wavelets, crests begin to break, glassy foam	calm	proficiency standard
4	11-16	moderate breeze	small waves, becoming longer, fairly frequent white horses,	slight	paddlers should be OK
5	17-21	fresh breeze	moderate waves, more pronounced long form, many white horses, possibly some spray.	moderate	over proficiency standard
6	22-27	strong breeze	large waves begin to form, white crests more extensive everywhere. probably some spray	rather rough	advanced paddlers only
7	28-33	near gale	sea heaps up with white foam from breaking waves.	rather rough	advanced paddlers probably wishing they had got a forecast
8	34-40	gale	moderately high waves of greater length, much foam	rough	
9	41-47	strong gale	high waves, dense streaks of foam along the direction of wind	very rough	
10	48-55	storm			
11	56-65	severe storm			
12	66+	hurricane			

Anticyclones
Anticyclones are areas of high pressure where the wind circulates in a clockwise direction in the northern hemisphere.

Weather forecasts
These have become increasingly accurate over the past few years. There are several sources of weather forecast and some of the more significant follow:

Telephone
There are pre-recorded local and 'marine-call' forecasts. The marine-call forecast usually carries an outlook for the following couple of days, and goes into reasonable detail about the coastal weather for the area. It is prepared specifically for water users. The general local forecast is not so detailed and is more applicable to the family wishing to go to the seaside and wanting to know whether or not it will be sunny or not, although it does contain a wind forecast.

These two services are pre-recorded which give the advantage that you can use them at any time.

Television
There are now some fairly detailed forecasts, showing simulated satellite photographs displaying the progress of weather systems across the British Isles.

Although these are displayed in an easily understood manner, there is little time to give much detail for any one area and the forecast is only given at certain times. The Oracle service does carry a summary of the shipping forecast from the radio, which can be referred to at any time.

Radio

There are shipping forecasts broadcast at advertised times. These carry detailed information such as a general synopsis of the weather, forecasts for each sea area, weather reports from weather stations around the country and warnings of gales when appropriate. These forecasts are the ones most used by sea paddlers on multi-day trips as they require only a small transistor radio, and can be heard from the comfort of a tent. They do take a bit of getting used to, as the information is given very quickly, and specific terminology is used. Most weather books will help with the interpretation and recording of shipping forecasts, and these are skills that may be practised at home on winter evenings.

Local radio forecasts are sometimes very good, but others are inadequate for the needs of the sea paddler.

Newspapers

Some papers carry a forecast, but these are usually very brief and, where a map is included, it often covers a vast area in a tiny space. They have limited use.

Personal observation

With practise and regular observation, you should be able to recognise approaching weather systems and forecast the probable sequence of changes. By looking to see which way the clouds are moving, you can watch for the weather in the distance that will affect you later, and be able to be more specific than merely saying 'I don't like the look of the weather'.

PLANNING A JOURNEY

There are many ways of planning a journey, but certain factors should always be considered. First, assess the level of your party by the ability of the weakest person. A journey may be measured more realistically by time afloat than by distance and, for beginners, two to three hours afloat, broken by lunch and maybe by other landings for coffee, sunbathing, etc may be sufficient. On an interesting section of coast with nooks and crannies to explore and maybe the occasional cave, a distance of 5 kilometres may be realistic. There is a danger of equating enjoyment and achievement with a long distance paddled.

At proficiency level in general purpose kayaks, a time afloat of four hours will allow a distance of, say, 12 km to be accomplished. In sea kayaks, this distance could be increased to about 18 km. However, with the assistance of a simple three knot tide, a distance of 18 km may be covered in two hours and, after a wait for the tide to change direction, a further two hours return journey may complete a 36 km round trip within those four hours afloat. Such a journey might qualify towards the BCU Advanced Proficiency Test.

Having established a reasonable time afloat, a reasonable paddling pace for the group, and a possible area in which to paddle, the next stage if the area is unfamiliar to you is to study both the Admiralty chart and a land map (eg OS map) to check for possible dangers, launching and landing places, a sheltered spot for lunch and other places of interest. Next, work out the time of high water, the direction of the tidal streams, and the strength of the streams throughout the period you may be afloat. Finally, plan your day to take advantage of the tide in a way that would suit your group.

Before setting off on your journey, obtain a weather forecast for the area, and consider how it would affect your plans. Let somebody who is not coming with you know where and when you intend to paddle, who is with you in the group, their level of ability, what safety gear you are carrying, including the number and type of flares, and leave them with the telephone number of the local coastguard, whom they should contact if you have not returned by a specified time. Make certain that this return time leaves plenty of allowance for eventualities that may arise during your trip. You will not want your journey marred by a frantic rush to be back on time when an extra half-hour of leeway would have meant a pleasant end to the day.

Finally, before setting off, check the suitability of all the equipment in the group from kayaks and paddles to clothing, lunches and emergency gear. Do not be afraid of cancelling or altering your plans if the equipment is not of sufficient standard, conditions are worse than you expected, or if the group proves to be less able than you expected.

Controlling the group on the water

There should be no doubt in the minds of the group members as to who is the leader. The ratio of leaders to participants should not be less than one to eight. If the conditions ahead are questionable or the route uncertain, the leader should be at the front. In less serious conditions, the leader might choose to move within the group offering advice and encouragement to anyone who needs it. Train your group to be aware of each other, show them how to brace with the paddle blade whilst they turn around to look behind.

Knowing how much a group should be allowed to spread out on the sea is something you can only learn from working with experienced instructors. In rough seas and big swells, you rapidly loose sight of individuals and so you will want to pull them in close together. There comes a point, however, when, in very rough conditions, the group pose a collision threat to each other as the boats surf off the steep wave crests.

Leaders should be careful during 'rock dodging' exercises close inshore not to let paddlers get behind rocks or into caves where they can be out of sight. Remember also that helmets are essential for this activity.

Do not take untried novices into situations where they have to cope with steep following seas a long way off shore until they have done some simple forward running exercises close inshore.

Coping with 'incidents'

When any incident occurs, such as a capsize, everyone should turn and face the oncoming waves, holding their position close to the 'action', but not knocking into one another or impeding those involved in sorting out the problem. There will be a constant tendency for someone to start paddling off, and the rest to follow. It

Plate 10:g
The east coast of Iceland

is vital, therefore, that the leader ensures that this does not happen, and it is better that he or she is not personally involved in the rescue, repair, or tow, etc. There could be times when speed will be of the essence, however, and it is then that the leader must keep constant watch on the rest of the group, whilst dealing with the matter in hand.

'Rafting up' the rest of the party in this situation is not a desirable practice. The 'raft' will drift more quickly than an individual canoeist and, in particular will drift away from someone in the water holding onto a boat. It will be extremely difficult in waves for the raft to be maintained, and there will be considerable danger of capsize on splitting up.

If you must form a raft, keeping it head to wind by means of an anchor-man on a towing line is a useful idea.

Should a situation ever have got so out of control that help is needed, and individual paddlers are in danger of capsize, then rafting in pairs, facing one another, would be a way of containing matters until help arrived. In breezy conditions, paddlers will be carried in the direction of the wind whereas swimmers and waterlogged kayaks will not; they will be taken in the direction of the tide.

Navigation

The main principle of kayak navigation is to use the tide to your advantage. On coastal trips, this usually means planning your trip to go with the main tide stream, although in some instances you may wish to make use of a series of eddies in order to explore close in. On trips with cross-tides, the main principle is to attempt to minimise the effect of the tide by cancelling out a period of flood tide against a period of ebb tide, or by careful choice of starting point. I always try to visualise the simplest possibilities before starting any calculations.

Coastal planning

Let us follow the process by means of a simple hypothetical example. I wish to take a group of relatively inexperienced paddlers for a morning paddle in my own area, starting at Tan Bay.

Refer to the Tide Tables
Let us say High Water Dover is 1300 and tides at present are on springs.

Adjust to British Summer Time if necessary.
Let us say that it is summer. We need to add one hour, so HW Dover is 1400.

		53º 10.0'N	
		4º 6.2'W	
		Rate (kn)	
Hours	Dir	Sp	Np
6	080	0.4	0.2
5	085	0.9	0.5
4	090	1.5	0.8
3	090	1.5	0.8
2	090	0.8	0.4
1	090	0.3	0.2
HW	265	0.2	0.1
1	270	0.6	0.2
2	270	0.7	0.3
3	270	0.9	0.4
4	270	0.9	0.5
5	270	0.6	0.3
6	260	0.2	0.1

(Before HW: hours 6 to 1; After HW: hours 1 to 6. Position Ⓐ)

Fig 10:16
The format of a tidal information table as it would appear on an Admiralty Chart. It relates to position Ⓐ on the chart

Refer to Chart
The tidal information on the chart states 'Tidal Streams referred to HW at Tan Bay', so it is necessary to convert from HW Dover to HW Tan Bay from the Dover tide tables we discover that the tidal constant for Tan Bay is - 2 hours. HW Dover is 1400, so HW Tan Bay is 1400 minus 2 hours = 12 noon.

Find direction of tide stream
I would like to be afloat at about 9 am. The tidal diamond A is the closest to Tan Bay. 9 am will be three hours before HW Tan Bay. Referring to the tidal information (Fig 10:16) the direction of the stream 3 hours before HW Tan Bay will be 90 degrees, (easterly) and will continue in this direction until mid-day, so it will be preferable to paddle east with the tide in the morning.

Find the speed of the tide
Tides are on springs, so the rate of the tide in the first hour afloat will be 1.5 knots.

Calculate travelling speed
This will vary from hour to hour depending on the speed of the tide. Our estimated paddling speed is 2 knots. In our first hour afloat, the tide will carry us 1.5 miles to the east, while we paddle 2 miles to the east. Our total distance covered will be 2 + 1.5 = 3.5 miles. If we were to paddle west against the tide we would cover a distance of 2 - 1.5 = 0.5 miles.

283

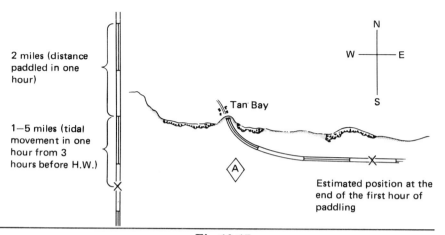

2 miles (distance paddled in one hour)

1—5 miles (tidal movement in one hour from 3 hours before H.W.)

N

W —|— E

S

Tan Bay

Estimated position at the end of the first hour of paddling

Fig 10:17
Plotting distance on a chart

Plot the distance on the chart

Referring to the side of the chart at the same latitude as Tan Bay for accurate measurement of distance, 3.5 minutes of latitude represents a distance of 3.5 nautical miles. Transfer this across to the chart to plot the expected position of the group at the end of one hour of paddling.

Check

Repeat the process checking the tidal stream information for direction and speed of the tide, but this time for 2 hours before HW Tan Bay in order to calculate the travelled distance for the second hour afloat, and for a third hour if required. Now we will need to choose a landing place that can reasonably be reached comfortably before the tide changes direction, whilst allowing a little spare time to cover any eventualities.

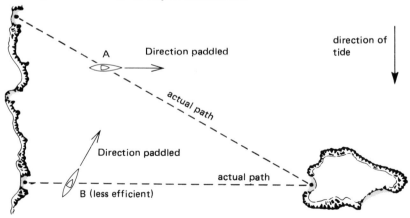

A   Direction paddled

direction of tide

actual path

Direction paddled

actual path

B (less efficient)

Fig 10:18
Crossing the tide

284

Open crossings

A short crossing may be timed to coincide with a slack period of tide, but otherwise it is preferable to start up-tide of your destination in order to side-slip down onto it (A on diagram). This is preferable to the 'ferry glide' shown by B on the diagram as the distance actually paddled is shorter.

Similarly, on a longer crossing, it is preferable to offset the tide stream in one direction against the tide stream in the opposite direction. In this way, the paddled distance is again kept to the minimum. Any element of ferry gliding will increase the distance paddled.

In Fig 10:19, we assume that the paddler reaches his half-way point, C, at the end of the northerly tide stream, and is taken south to his destination, E, during the second half of his paddle. The paddled distance will be the straight-line distance from D to E, whereas the actual path will follow a longer route.

This technique is used successfully to plan longer open crossings involving more than one change in the tide. However, in order to be accurate, you will need to take note of all the tidal information available to you in terms of the direction and strength of the tide in different places. It may be discovered, for example, that the tide is stronger in the vicinity of your destination than at your starting point. You may find that you need to balance out 3 hours of flood tide against only two hours of ebb tide in order to get neutral a effect.

'Aiming off'

Where assumptions have to be made because lack of tidal stream information, it is preferable to aim for a point that will be up-tide of your destination. If all goes to plan, you can cruise down-tide with confidence onto your target at the end of the crossing. The error of a kilometre either way on a long crossing will then be perfectly acceptable for, if visibility is poor, you will still know in which direction your destination lies, if not exactly how far, and it will be easier

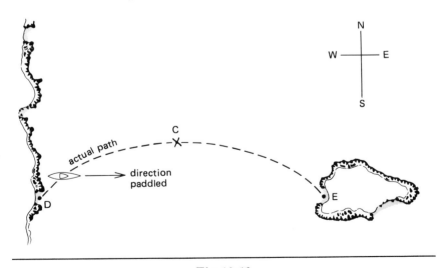

Fig 10:19
Allowing the tide to carry the kayak northwards and then southwards

paddling down-tide at the end of the journey than paddling up-tide. 'Aiming off' is also a useful technique for windy weather.

Allowance for wind

Unfortunately there is no simple rule for this. Different kayaks and different paddlers will be affected by wind to different degrees and in different ways. By experience it may be seen that your own craft behaves in a particular way in certain wind conditions, and it may be necessary to make an allowance of time or direction. Generally, a faster paddling speed may be maintained on flat water than on choppy water, and a much faster paddling speed may be maintained down-wind than into the wind. Where timing may be questionable because of weather conditions, then aiming off up-wind is recommended on crossings with a cross-wind (tides having been considered first) and extra time will need to be allowed for any journey into the wind.

Ferry gliding using transits

Using transits, you can navigate precisely. If you approach an island, keeping two prominent points in line, then your path will be a straight line. If the rear object appears to be moving to your left, then you are moving to the left, and you will need to angle more to the right to correct your course. A check on a transit to your side will confirm that you are travelling forwards. I have watched people paddling into a strong tide stream, blissfully unaware that they were being swept slowly backwards by the tide, when a glance at the nearest land and reference to a couple of transit points would have warned them instantly of their predicament. Any points will do: a shoreline rock in line with a crack in the cliff behind, or a house against a hillside on the skyline. With constant reference to transits, you will find that you will be aware automatically of how the tide and wind are affecting you, without really thinking about it.

Ferry gliding using transits is a useful method of crossing a tide when the stream is not too strong. In good visibility the use of transits enables a perfect

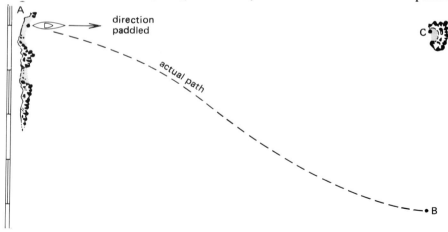

Fig 10:20

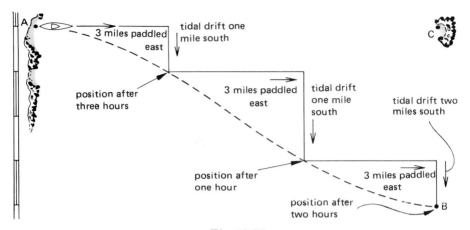

Fig 10:21

line to be followed. Two prominent features of your target are lined up, for example a vertical crack in a cliff with a building on a hill behind, and by adjusting the angle of the kayak against the tide they are kept in line throughout the crossing. Compensation is made automatically for irregularities in the speed and direction of the tide. The distance paddled is greater than in the other methods described.

Ferry gliding by compass

Paddling on a compass bearing, especially on a rough sea, can be difficult, so it is a good idea to practise on journeys where you are not dependent on the compass. The kayak will often swing quite wildly to either side of the course

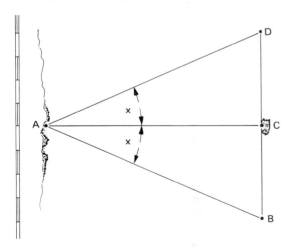

Fig 10:22

you wish to follow but, despite this, you will find it possible to follow a course with surprising accuracy.

When using a compass, the bearing used must take into consideration the direction and distance that the tide will carry the paddler during the estimated time for the crossing.

For example, if a paddler starts at A (Fig 21) and paddles due east, the southerly tide carries him to point B. Position B can be worked out using the following tidal information. If the distance A-C is 9 nautical miles, and the paddling speed is 3 knots, then the estimated time A to C is 3 hours. If, during the first hour the tide speed is 1 knot south; during the second hour: tide 2 knots south; and during the third hour: tide 1 knot south then the distance C-B can be determined (Fig 10:21).

If the angle between B, A and C is taken, and is carried onto the up-tide side of C, then the point at which the paddler will need to aim from A in order to reach C may be found. (Fig 10:22). This direction may be measured on the chart and adjusted to give a magnetic bearing for a compass.

Now, a single bearing AD will take the paddler to C, but he will not follow the straight line AC because the tide is seen to increase and then decrease during the time of this crossing. Therefore, the use of this compass bearing will not tally with the use of transits as described earlier.

BUOYS

A knowledge of buoyage is important to the sea paddler. Buoys often mark areas of water dangerous to shipping, such as shoals, isolated rocks and overfalls. They are also used to indicate channels used by shipping, the position of which may not otherwise be obvious to the paddler. Others may be used to indicate areas of danger in the vicinity of firing ranges, or the position of sewage outfalls. Buoys are identified by shape, colour and by their top-marks.

The system of buoyage now in use around the UK is known as the International Association of Lighthouse Authorities (IALA) Buoyage System 'A'. Under the IALA system A, there are five types of mark, which may be used in any combination:

Lateral marks

These are either red (port-hand) can-shaped buoys with a single red can as a top-mark (where fitted), and a red light of any rhythm (when fitted); or green (starboard-hand) conical or spar shaped, with a single green cone top-mark, pointed upwards (where fitted), and a green light of any rhythm (where fitted). These are generally still laid from seaward inward in rivers and estuaries, marking well-defined channels. They follow a clock-wise direction around land masses when used in open water.

Basically, a canoeist should not cruise in a narrow channel marked by these buoys, and should, where necessary, cross such a channel at right angles.

Cardinal marks

These are placed to the north, south, east or west of an area of danger such as a rock or shoal. A north cardinal mark, for example, will be placed to the north of the hazard. Whilst shipping keeps out of the indicated area, the danger to canoeists is often much less.

North cardinal mark:

Top-mark	-	2 black cones, one above the other, points upwards
Colour	-	Black above yellow
Shape	-	Pillar or spar
Light (when fitted)	-	White, VQkFl or QkFl. (Very quick flashing or quick flashing)

288

East cardinal mark:

Top-mark	-	2 black cones, one above the other, base to base
Colour	-	Black with a single broad horizontal yellow band
Shape	-	Pillar or spar
Light (when fitted)	-	White, VQFl(3) every 5 sec or QkFl(3) every 10 sec.

South cardinal mark:

Topmark	-	2 black cones, one above the other, points downward
Colour	-	Yellow above black
Shape	-	Pillar or spar
Light (when fitted)	-	White, VQFl(6) + long flash every 10 sec or QkFl(6) + long flash every 15 sec.

West cardinal mark:

Top-mark	-	2 black cones, one above the other, point to point
Colour	-	Yellow with a single broad horizontal black band
Shape	-	Pillar or spar
Light (when fitted)	-	White, VQkFl(9) every 10 sec or QkFl(9) every 15 sec.

There is an easy way to remember the colours and top-marks of cardinal buoys. The points on the cones confirm the position of the black band on the buoys. Top-marks with point towards point (westerly mark) for example indicate that the black band is in the middle with yellow above and below. Both points uppermost (North Mark) indicate black is uppermost with yellow below.

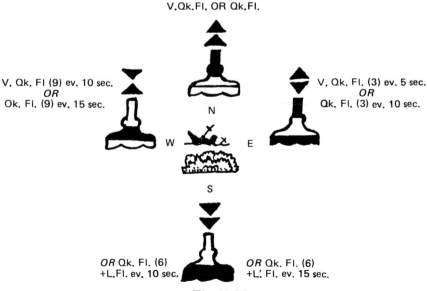

Fig 10:23

The flashing sequences are also logical. The Northerly mark (12 o'clock position) is continuously flashing, the easterly mark (3 o'clock) flashes 3 times then pauses, the southerly flashes 6 times then pauses and the westerly flashes 9 times between pauses. The choice between quick or very quick flashing is used to distinguish between buoys in close proximity.

Isolated danger marks

An isolated danger mark is a mark over an isolated danger which has navigable water all around it:

Top-mark	-	2 black spheres, one above the other
Colour	-	Black with one or more broad horizontal red bands
Shape	-	Pillar or spar
Light (when fitted) -		White, GpFl(2). (Group flashing in sets of 2).

Safe water marks

Safe water marks indicate that there is navigable water all around the mark; they include mid-channel and landfall marks.

Colour	-	Red and white vertical stripes
Shape	-	Spherical, pillar with spherical topmark or spar
Top-mark (if any)	-	Single red sphere
Light (when fitted) -		White, isophase, occulting or one long flash every 10 sec. (The terms isophase, occulting and other abbreviations for lights are explained in Chart 5011).

Special marks

Special marks are not primarily of assistance to navigation but are used to indicate special features such as sewage outfalls.

Colour	-	Yellow
Shape	-	Optional
Top-mark	-	Yellow cross (optional)
Light if fitted	-	Yellow

Beware of the danger of becoming pinned against a buoy in a fast tidal stream. This could well be a drowning situation. This applies to any fixed object in fast moving water such as a moored boat. Allow for the drift, and always aim to go behind the obstruction if there is any shadow of doubt. Never attempt to race across in front of a large vessel. 'Steam' has right of way in narrow channels and, quite apart from the personal danger involved, there is the risk to the ship should the pilot feel he has to try to take avoiding action. In any case, the chances of his being able to make a significant adjustment will often be nil.

As a ship turns, the stern sweeps round in a wide arc. Never wait within the marked channel for a large vessel that is going to turn on a buoy opposite. It is extremely difficult to judge the path the stern will take.

Plate 10:h
The grey seal is a frequent companion to sea kayakists around the British coast

CAMPING

For many paddlers,this is an integral part of sea kayaking, giving them a flexibility of planning, and a greater range than day trips will allow. A good site will have fresh water, enough flat ground for a tent, shelter from the wind, and a good view. It must also have a reasonable landing. Whether you wish to have a driftwood fire is your own choice, but when you move on, you should leave the area with no signs of your passing. Litter should be carried with you. Camping is described in more detail in the chapter 'From camps to expeditions'.

NATURE CONSERVATION

A major part of the enjoyment of sea kayaking for many people is observing the wild-life. There is something magic about sitting patiently in a kayak and watching an inquisitive seal venture closer and closer, or to drift through a raft of several thousand shearwaters without disturbing them into flight.

There are areas however where a certain amount of care is needed if we are to continue to enjoy the wildlife. One of these is sea-bird nesting sites. Try to avoid landing near nesting birds as this will obviously disturb them, as will paddling too close. If you are not out specifically to watch the nesting birds, then give nesting areas a wide berth. You will still see plenty of activity with birds around you in the air and on the water. If, however, you are particularly wishing to observe the nesting, try to avoid paddling in a large group, and be quiet and gentle in your movements. You will be able to observe more closely without disturbing the birds if the weather is calm.

Most birds will show signs of anxiety, looking nervously around them, maybe a special noise or standing up, before finally taking flight. These are signs that you are too close and you should gently retreat to avoid frightening the bird from its nest. If there are birds standing on the rocks close to the water, use these as your indicators. If they are showing signs of anxiety, you are too close.

Finally ,some species are much more sensitive to disturbance than others. Guillemots, which often nest together in large numbers on the ledges, will fly off while other species such as fulmars and shags will be sitting tight. Guillemots incubate their eggs on top of their feet, so a mass exodus may result in the loss of eggs from the cliff. The remaining eggs or chicks are vulnerable to marauding gulls which quickly take advantage of such a situation. Each disturbance will obviously lessen their chances of successfully rearing their young. Be particularly sensible, therefore, when approaching cliffs where guillemots, and also their relative the razorbill, are nesting.

As a general guide, if in doubt, stay further out. If you would like to learn more about sea-birds, the RSPB have a number of coastal reserves with information centres and wardens who will help you to recognise and understand the birds. Why not encourage your local warden to join you on the sea to help you identify the birds from the water ?

11 Deep Water Rescues

Derek C Hutchinson

Derek Hutchinson lives in South Shields where he earned his living as a teacher from 1961. He is renowned throughout the world as a sea kayakist, author of widely acclaimed books on sea kayaking and eskimo rolling, designer of sea kayaks, and leader of several major expeditions. His contribution to the sport has played a major formative part in the evolution of adventuring on the sea in kayaks.

His journeys in wild and remote areas, include the Aleutian Islands and Prince William Sound, both in Alaska. In 1975 he organised the first attempt to cross the North Sea in unescorted solo eskimo kayaks, followed by a successful attempt in June 1976 when, with two others in kayaks of his own design, he made the non-stop crossing in 31 hours.

He is deeply interested in Eskimo culture, especially their use of kayaks in hunting, travel and recreation. His latest book, Eskimo Rolling For Survival *reflects this interest. Derek is a BCU Senior Coach, travelling the country lecturing and teaching, and is Vice-Chairman of the BCU Coaching Committee.*

INTRODUCTION

Capsizing is part of training for white water and sea canoeing, at least during the early learning stages. The best remedy for a capsize is undoubtedly the Eskimo roll. It matters little, however, which method you use so long as you arrive on the surface, still sitting in your kayak at the end of it all.

Not everyone can Eskimo roll and some boats are almost impossible to roll due to excessive beam or poor deck design. There is always the possibility of failure, and so over the years various methods have been developed of putting people back into their canoes from the water. The water does not have to be very deep to merit this type of emergency procedure, in spite of the term 'Deep Water Rescues'. The water, in fact, need only be as deep as the tallest member of your group.

Since I began canoeing I have seen many methods of rescue tried with varying degrees of success. This ranged from group rescues, with as many as six people working out a complicated sequence, involving an ingenious system of levers and pulleys, brought about by the careful positioning of canoes and paddles before hand, to solo rescues - with a purple-faced man desperately trying to tread water, while at the same time blowing down a large 'U' tube which vanished up inside his inverted cockpit. This was an effort to expel the water and raise the kayak. Both methods had only limited support.

The methods of rescue and re-entry which follow should be practised in the calm waters of swimming pools or sheltered bays. It can be dangerous to practise in very cold or rough conditions without suitable clothing. Remember always that it is vital for the capsized canoeist to grab hold, and maintain a grasp of the canoe, immediately upon surfacing. This should be drilled into paddlers from the very first capsize practise, and particularly emphasised when initial training is taking place in a swimming pool, where the canoe does not immediately drift away as it does in most open air situations.

Beginners should also be trained to retain the paddle where possible, and to swim with the boat to the paddle, if it has been dropped.

All equipment should be securely stowed whether it is inside the boat or on the deck. After your rescue practise is finished, the surface of the water should not be littered with floating debris such as flare containers, broken vacuum flasks, the contents of first aid and repair kits, sandwich, or pieces of bloodstained polythene foam.

It is dangerous to perform any deep water rescue in surf. It is far safer to tow both paddler and kayak out of the danger area, whether it is amongst breaking waves or against rocks.

Rough water practise may be made safer by wearing crash helmets.

Learning to Eskimo roll successfully is a sign of success. Once learned, having to roll is a sign of failure.

'HI' RESCUE - ALSO KNOWN AS THE 'IPSWICH' (Figs 11:1a and 11:1b)

The rescue raft with paddles across forms the letter 'H', and when all three boats are in line, this becomes an 'I'.

1 A and B position their boats quickly, collect C's paddle, and then raft up facing him. C guides the bow of his upturned kayak between the two rescuing craft. A and B now lift the bow of C's kayak up and over the paddles which are positioned as shown, as quickly as possible, to allow the minimum amount of water to enter.

   Make sure the cockpit is clear of the water before you start to pull the kayak over the paddles.

2 The upturned kayak now rests and pivots on the paddles. A and B hold the boat steady. If you are careful, you should not damage the paddle looms as you lift the boat over. As C see-saws his end of the kayak up and down, the water drains out. As soon as the boat is empty, the two rescuers turn it over into its upright position and slide it forward off the paddles, to be in a position for C to re-enter by one of the methods described in Figure 11:6.

Fig 11:1a
'HI' rescue - the initial lift

2

Fig 11:1b
'HI' rescue - rocking the boat over the paddles

With practise, this rescue should be completed in under a minute. At no time must the man in the water let go of one of the rescuer's boats, as the wind will blow the two rescuers and the upturned boat away faster than it is possible to swim after them.

Some prefer that the rescuers come together facing in opposite directions, so that should the boat have to be emptied stern first, one of the rescuers is the best way round to assist with the re-entry.

In the event of the capsized boat being very heavily waterlogged, C can move to the other side of the paddles, either going around the outside of B's boat, holding on all the time, or coming between, and ducking under. He can then wrap one arm around a rescuer's boat, and with the other push up on his to take the weight. This will allow A and B to continue threading it along until the cockpit is over the paddles. C is then well placed to apply maximum leverage by pulling down to commence the see-saw.

It should never be necessary to 'swim'. The person in the water should always pull the boats around him. In essence, he stays still and manoeuvres the raft, or his own boat, as necessary. This is not what usually happens, where people naturally tend to pull themselves around the boats. There is a different action involved, which needs to be identified, thought about, and learned.

THE 'X' RESCUE (Figs 11:2a and 11:2b)

It is important that all leaders and instructors are able to recover and empty a kayak without assistance. Two canoeists paddling together should also be able to rescue each other if the need arises. Both these requirements are met by the 'X' Rescue, so called because when the boat is pulled across the other, the raft forms the letter 'X'.

1   B lifts the kayak as quickly as he can so as to allow as little water as possible into the cockpit of the capsized kayak. Using his fore deck as a pivot B pulls the kayak across his boat until the cockpit rests near his own cockpit.

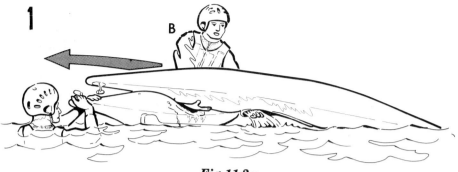

Fig 11:2a
The 'X' rescue

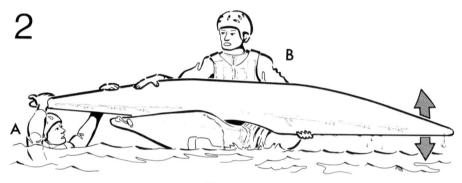

Fig 11:2b
The 'X' rescue - emptying the kayak

2   B see-saws the kayak by leaning his own boat from side to side. He is assisted by A in the water who helps to control the emptying movement by holding the bow. Once the boat is empty it is turned the right way up and A re-enters by method illustrated in Fig 11:6.

It is easy for B to damage his spray cover as he tries to drag the partially waterlogged kayak across his own cockpit. It is as well to wear two spray covers, the oldest underneath, so that the top one can be removed before the rescue starts.

It is important that B looks after both pairs of paddles, this is when the paddle park is useful. If there is too much water in the capsized boat, its excessive weight will compress one or both of the decks during the see-sawing operation. It would be prudent to remove the worst of the water by The Curl (Fig 11:4) before attempting the 'X' rescue.

It is possible for two boats to empty a third in what would become a Rafted 'X' Rescue. In case of difficulty also, A can assist by placing both feet against B's hull, and straightening his body to pull the capsized boat across. He needs to push up as he does so, rather than pull down, which puts too great a strain on the foredecks.

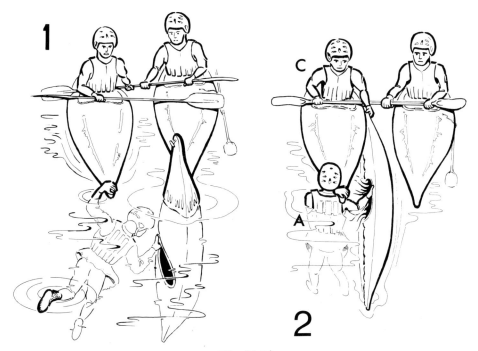

Fig 11:3
Rescuing a 'Cleopatra's needle'

CLEOPATRA'S NEEDLE (Fig 11:3)

Not a pretty sight - and hardly a situation a careful leader should get himself into if he has checked the buoyancy of all the kayaks in his group before setting off. It is possible, however, that on your travels you may come across some lone canoeist whose boat is floating like this, either because of no buoyancy at all, or because what little it has is badly distributed.

It will be your responsibility to instruct the man in the water what to do.

1 First the boat must be manoeuvred to the surface. This can be done by hooking the foot under the cockpit, or diving down and grabbing the coaming by hand and then lifting. Once the boat is level with the surface emptying can begin.

2 A supports the cockpit coaming on his shoulder. As he slowly lifts, he watches the water draining out. While A does this, C holds the kayak LEVEL. As soon as most of the water is out, the boat is flipped over so it is floating in the upright position. Any further water can be emptied out by the 'HI' method.

This method of emptying a swamped canoe can be difficult, especially for people of limited strength and experience. After a great deal of experimenting I found a method which seemed to work every time and did not require an enormous amount of energy from the person in the water. This method is called 'The Curl'.

THE CURL (Figs 11:4a, 11:4b)

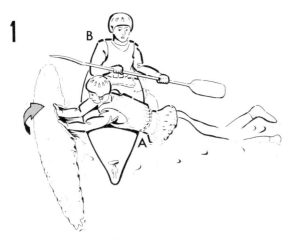

Fig 11:4a
Emptying a swamped kayak using the 'curl'

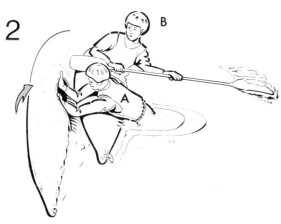

Fig 11:4b
The rescuer assists by leaning his kayak to empty the water

1 The swamped boat lies alongside the boat of man B, its deck completely awash. A pulls himself over B's foredeck, as near as he can to B's cockpit without getting in the way of B's paddle, and then hooks his hands under the cockpit coaming of the swamped boat, his palms uppermost.

2 A rests his elbows on B's deck, pulling the swamped kayak towards him and tilts the cockpit so that the water begins to drain out. Once his elbows are jammed against the deck by the weight of his kayak, B can then increase the draining angle by leaning over and sculling for support. Apart from making sure that the draining kayak is held firmly and perfectly level, no further effort is required on the part of A.

This method of rescue does not require exceptional strength, and as long as A can get his kayak on its side and hold it level, the water will drain out as B controls the angle of the lean.

The 'TX' rescue can also be used for a swamped boat. Here, the cockpit is turned towards the rescuer, who paddles his bow into it, thus forming the letter 'T'. The swimmer reaches under his own boat with both arms and joins his hands on the rescuer's bow, gradually levering up with his shoulders until the capsized boat is across the rescuer's. From there it is pushed along the deck, until the 'X' rescue described earlier can be completed.

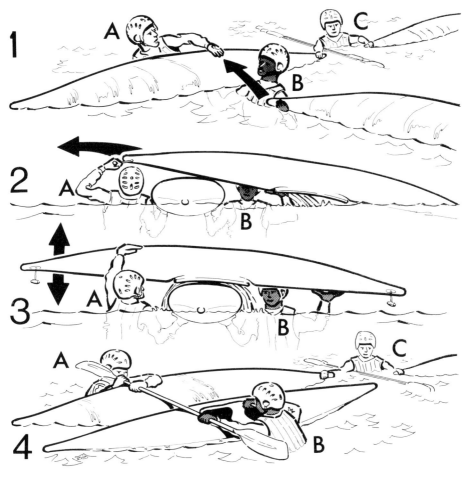

Fig 11:5
All-in-rescue

ALL-IN RESCUE (Fig 10:5)

Weather conditions which are going to capsize all three members of a canoeing group at the same time, are bound to be bad. The remedy is tiring and the participants will have their anxious moments, even if they are only practising this in a swimming pool - especially if all the boats have had their buoyancy removed just to make things difficult.

1   C holds onto his kayak and looks after the paddles. If he wished he could hold the paddles between his legs, leaving his arms free. He must on no account become separated from the main rescue. A and B hold onto the upturned cockpit coaming facing in opposite directions. B lifts the bow of the kayak as high and as quickly as he can so that the cockpit clears the water. As B does this he will automatically pull down on his right hand. Any tilting of the pivot

boat is counteracted by A, who holds onto the other side of the coaming. The less buoyancy the pivot boat has, the more important it is for both men to hold it perfectly level and still, otherwise the air inside will escape and the boat will fill up and sink.

2   B passes the kayak over the pivot boat to A, who continues taking it across until its cockpit rests on the upturned hull.

3   A and B see-saw the kayak until it is empty. Once this is done, it is turned onto its right side and placed alongside the pivot canoe. B who wants to get in first, positions himself next to his cockpit.

4   The re-entry can be tricky in a rough sea. B passes his paddle across the middle of the pivot canoe. To gain entry, B will place his right hand at the rear of his cockpit and in the centre, whilst he holds the paddle and the front of the cockpit with his left hand. He enters the cockpit by kicking out with his feet, pushing down with his weight upon his arms. To counteract any unsteadiness caused by B's re-entry, A pulls downwards on his end of the paddle loom.

As soon as B is secure in his boat, A's kayak can be emptied by a 'TX' Rescue, and C is finally put back in his kayak by the 'HI' method.

The order of leaving the water is important, and the leader will have to make some decisions before the rescue commences. The most scantily dressed should hardly be the last out of the water, but if the weakest is put into his boat first, he might not be able to undertake the 'TX' Rescue which follows next.

OTHER METHODS

A number of other methods of emptying a capsized canoe exist, but those described are the most universally acclaimed and used. The most popular formerly was the 'H' method, whereby two canoeists positioned themselves on each end of the upturned boat, at right angles, forming a large letter 'H'. The capsized boat was then turned onto its side, kept level, and a gradual, even lift applied from each end. The problem with this method was that it is necessary to keep at right angles, and this involves a constant adjustment, the action of wind and waves tending to move the boats around. It also requires an equal effort to be applied at each end, otherwise one person ends up with all the weight, and an impossible task.

Other experiments, with paddles locked across shoulders, and the rescuers lifting the upturned boat (which is lying between them) with the opposite hands, and so forth, have been tried, but have not been generally adopted. The H method should nevertheless be remembered because there are certain special cases such as in the rescue of doubles or racing kayaks when it works extremely well.

Self-rescue techniques, such as strapping the lifejacket to the paddle-blade, re-entering the inverted canoe, and rolling up with the benefit of the extra buoyancy on the paddle, are also advocated by some. These are not to be deprecated if they work for a given individual, but there is sufficient doubt about the wisdom of removing a lifejacket or buoyancy aid in serious circumstances, and insufficient support generally for such innovations, for this book to give them approval.

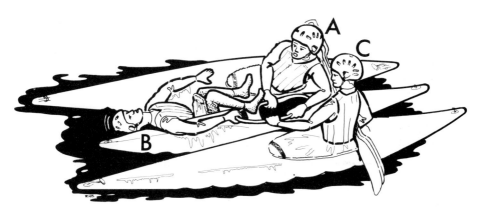

Fig 11:6a
Re-entry face up from the stern

METHODS OF RE-ENTRY

Face up from the stern (Fig 11:6a)

This is probably the most widely used method of re-entry. The paddles are made secure and both A and C have a firm hold on the centre kayak with both hands. If they wished for an even firmer grip they could hold that side of the coaming farthest away thereby crossing their arms. B does not have to use a great deal of energy to get back into his boat, but he may feel slightly undignified.

It is important that the 'victim' lies back in the water, letting the lifejacket or buoyancy aid take his body weight, and puts his legs in first. The arms must reach right across the rescuer's boat and his own, and his push down applied to the outside of the boats, in order to keep them together. Occasionally, a less well co-ordinated person will have extreme difficulty in finally bringing his or her body weight in. It is then necessary that the rescuer C lies firmly across the victim's canoe, with near arm wrapped around, far hand gripping the centre of the

Fig 11:6b
Re-entry face down from the stern

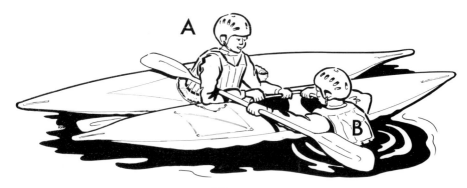

Fig 11:6c
Re-entry over the side of the canoe

coaming at the front, body-weight on the empty boat, and knees pulling strongly to keep his own boat close. If the paddles are across in front of the rescuer the person re-entering can put one leg into his boat, hook the other over the paddle shafts, and thereby gain some added leverage by pulling down with that leg.

Face down from the stern (Figure 11:6b)

Some people prefer to get in like this but in rough seas many people finish up like this anyway, even though they may start differently. This method can be uncomfortable if the rear deck is carrying spare paddles, flares and perhaps a fishing-line, especially as you start hitching forwards towards the cockpit. It is as well to remember where you put the fish hooks.

Over the side re-entry (Figure 11:6c)

I settled on this method some years ago as a good method of re-entry involving only two people. A has one arm under the paddle loom and is gripping the coaming with both hands. This will keep the raft stable, and as B exerts his weight down onto the paddle it will increase stability. If B needed assistance, A could quite easily take his left hand off the cockpit coaming and grasp the others life-jacket without any loss of stability.

ESKIMO RESCUES (FIGURE 11:7)

This type of rescue requires a patient who has water confidence and faith in those around him and a rescuer who can position his canoe quickly and carefully.

The Side Rescue

1 This is the most useful method. The capsized man bangs on his upturned hull with both hands to attract attention of those nearest to him and then moves his hands to and fro in an arc. This will save unnecessary manoeuvring on the part of the rescuer.

2 Once alongside, the rescuer puts the patient's nearest upright hand onto the paddle loom which is placed across the two boats. If the rescuer does not locate

the hand on the loom, the distraught victim may try to pull himself up to the surface on the side farthest away, with disastrous results.

3 As the patient hip-flicks, and then pulls his body to the surface, he must change his hand grip position when he reaches the half up stage.

4 It will be seen that it it possible to give assistance by presenting the bow of the rescuing kayak to the patient, but this can be dangerous. If the rescuer approaches too fast, and there is a collison, an arm can be crushed or a skull cracked. It would be safer for the rescuer to execute a quick turn and come in from the side. During training, the rescuer must paddle forward as the patient, holding his bow, pushes himself up, otherwise the rescuing craft tends to be pushed away by the patient, who will then fall back into the water.

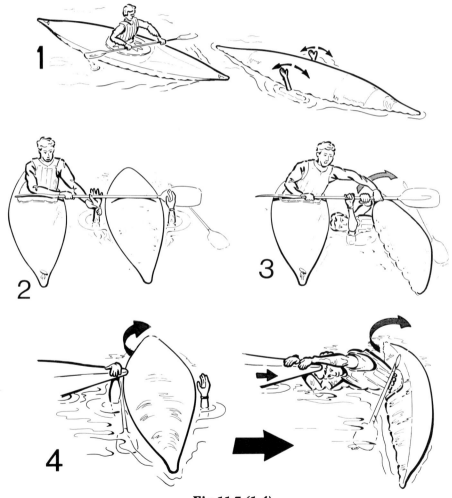

Fig 11:7 (1-4)
Eskimo rescues 1, 2 and 3 demonstrate the side rescue; 4 shows bow presentation

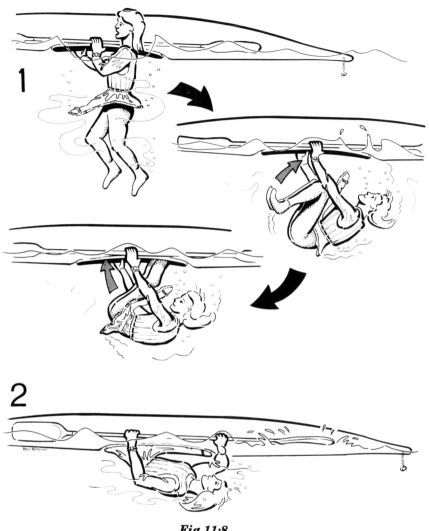

Fig 11:8
Self-rescue; re-entry and roll

R & R RESCUE (Figure 11:8)

(Re-entry and Roll H &H - Hutchinson's Horror)

The golden rule is 'less than three there should never be'. The reason is that in case of accident or illness, one person can stay with the casualty while the third can go and seek help. If a tow is needed, support is usually essential, and a unit of three competent canoeists is as safe as it is possible to be in small boats on the sea. With the advent of single-handed rescue techniques, however, many canoeists have happily operated in pairs, and with the development of bulkheaded boats and efficient pumping, more and more people are seeking adventure by going out to sea alone. I wrote elsewhere 'To condemn the adventurous is pointless; it is more important to develop rescue techniques which enable them to pursue their own particular road to Valhalla with at least some margin of safety'. If a man is a competent eskimo roller it is going to be a rough sea or some unfortunate circumstance which forces him out of his boat and into the water. Any subsequent re-entry balancing act which requires a man to sit on top of his deck and start hitching about in that same rough sea is out of the question. It was for this reason that I introduced the R & R Rescue into print. It takes nerve and needs practice for it to be successful - but then doesn't everything ?

1   The canoeist faces the stern of his boat holding the cockpit coaming with both hands. He holds the paddle ready on the side on which he intends to roll up. In the illustration he is preparing to 'wind up' on his left hand side. He then takes a deep breath, throws his head back and then swings his legs and feet upwards and into the cockpit.

2   Once back in the cockpit, the man can now roll up. With practise even the spray cover can be put back on upside down, but it is hardly necessary, as the amount of water taken into the kayak is not a great deal if it is fitted with bulkheads. A small pump takes care of the rest.

Once upright, the canoeist should put on his spray cover immediately, to stop any breaking seas filling the boat further. If the kayak feels unstable due to the water inside, it is possible to scull for support, resting the extended paddle over one shoulder, while pumping out with the other hand. A foot operated pump has been designed and this can be fitted instead of, or as well as, the hand operated type.

REPAIRS AT SEA (FIG 11:9)

Undertake any of the rescues mentioned previously in anything but calm water and you'll find it all too easy to damage a kayak. As the boats swing about, cracks across the head will not be a rarity. Most serious damage to boats seems to occur when the group is running before a following sea. Kayaks in the hands of novices tend to run out of control and harpoon each other. Until a few years ago, it was recommended that the occupant of a damaged kayak got out of his boat and took to the water while his boat was being repaired. This seemed a little silly to me, so I encouraged all my students to keep dry during the time it took to do the repair, by sitting astride the rescuer's boat.

If the patient is nervous it would be better to choose the rear deck to sit astride. He could use both hands to hold onto the rescuers life jacket, or he could scull for support on one side with the extended paddle. Unfortunately, in this position the patient is unable to assist with the repair. Sitting on the fore-deck however, the patient can hold the kayak or help with the repair. He can also hold the paddles against the side of the boat with his leg, in the absence of a paddle park.

It is in the best interests of the leader if all the members of his group carry their repair kits in a position which is easily accessible. Then the person doing the repair can use the kit from the damaged boat, which when it is across the other boat acts as an outrigger and stabilizes the whole operation.

Fig 11:9
Repairing a damaged kayak at sea

RESCUES TO NON-CANOEISTS

The sea canoeist, with his speed and skill through surf, offers a fast method of rescuing anyone who is in difficulties. They might not be canoeists and their physical condition may vary from normal fatigue to complete unconciousness.

It is a prerequisite of the coaching awards that candidates have a specified life-saving qualification. The BCU Lifesaving Test incorporates certain specialised rescues which are also used by the Corps of Canoe Life Guards.

Stern Carry (Fig 11:10)

If the patient is co-operative and not completely paralysed with fear, carry him on the rear deck. It is probably about the best way to carry anyone as the bow does not dig in, nor is the paddler retarded by the man in the water. The patient however, must keep his body low onto the deck, so that the balance of the boat is not affected. It is possible to carry in through surf, but it takes practise, and a patient who is determined to hang on tight.

If the person being rescued is fairly small, it might be better to carry them in pillion style. In this way, the child will feel more secure and if their body is close to you, as well as having their arms wrapped around, there is less chance of them becoming dislodged. You will also find the kayak easier to control this way (Fig 11:10b).

Fig11:10a
Rescuing a swimmer using the stern carry

Fig 11:10b
The 'pillion' carry

Bow Carry (Fig 11:11)

This method is ideal for someone who is tired and nervous, because in their position on the bow you can watch and encourage them as you paddle them in to shore. If you must come in through surf, it would be better to approach the shore backwards. It could be distressing for the patient to have the rescue canoe loop on top of him.

Always ensure that the bow of the canoe is over the swimmer's shoulder, so that his teeth are not likely to act as shock-absorbers.

If the surf is large and you think there may be a chance that your exhausted patient will be washed off the boat, stay outside the surf line, send up a distress rocket and wait until help arrives.

Panicking swimmers should be approached with caution. If they make a wild grab and clutch your kayak in a way which may cause you to capsize, use your paddle and push their hands off the deck swiftly and firmly with the blade. Talk to the patient and calm him down, then direct him as to what is best to do. In your enthusiasm to escape his clutches do not break his fingers or beat him about the head.

Fig 11:11
The 'bow carry' rescue method

Raft assisted resuscitation (Fig 11:12)

Using kayaks rafted together, expired air resuscitation (EAR) can be carried out successfully on the water. Probably the best way to go about this, is for the rescuer in the boat nearest to the patient to turn round so that he is facing in towards the raft. The canoeist in the boat farthest away from the unconscious person then reaches across his partner's boat, grasps the patient's wrists and with a concentrated heave, pulls him over and across the raft. The patient is then turned over and resuscitation can begin.

It is possible for the two man raft to be towed to shore by a third canoeist, but it is far more prudent to send up a distress rocket the moment the unconscious person is sighted. Thus professional help can be on the way whilst resuscitation is in progress. Remember that anyone who has been unconscious for any reason should be examined by a doctor as soon as possible.

Fig 11:12
EAR being carried out across the decks of kayaks

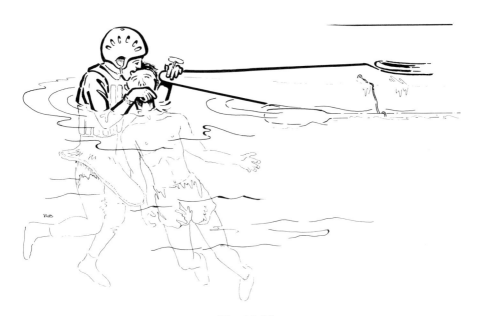

Fig 11:13

EAR being carried out in the water, using the bow of the kayak for support

Resuscitation in the water - Kayak support (Figure 11:13)

To do this you must first jump out of your boat, but be careful not to capsize it, and don't forget to put your paddle in the paddle park. Hold onto the front of your kayak by its lifting toggle. Using this as a support, bend the patient's head well back over your arm (keep your hand off his throat) and start EAR. This is not easy, and you will find it awkward and exhausting work.

DEPENDENT FACTORS

The success of the rescues illustrated depend very much on a number of factors:

o   The age and physical condition of the participants.
o   Their level of competence and their general morale.
o   The type of personal buoyancy and the clothing they are wearing.
o   The distance between group members at the time of the capsize.
o   The skill level of the group and the speed they can manoeuvre.
o   The condition of the sea and the strength of the wind.
o   The distance from shore and the proximity of rocks.
o   The temperature of the water.
o   The weight of the equipment inside the upturned boat.
o   The amount of equipment carried on the deck and how secure it is.
o   The time of day.
o   The prevalence of shipping.
o   The amount of buoyancy inside the kayaks.
o   The personal qualities and experience of the leader.

Capsizes can be infectious, causing others to follow suit, and your attention may be split between calamities. If a rescue lacks supervision, it is possible that the sense of urgency may be lost, which is so important in getting people out of cold water as quickly as possible. You may often find it necessary to use a combination of rescue techniques to solve a difficult capsize situation.

The key to success is plenty of practise against the clock in controlled choppy conditions, even if it means doing it artifically in a swimming pool. Any practise is better than no practise at all.

12 Rolling

Rob Hignell and Martyn Hedges

Rob Hignell paddled for the Great Britain slalom youth team with whom he had many international successes. He was also a member of a league-winning canoe polo team. During his service in the RAF he combined sea paddling abroad with coaching of the GB slalom juniors. In 1986 he qualified as an Inland Coach and is presently Director of the Canterbury Canoe Centre.

Martyn Hedges is respected throughout the world as a canoe slalom athlete. His remarkable flare in handling a C1 has been an inspiration to many paddlers and he has contributed enormously to the coaching of salom canoe technique. He now runs his own business making canoeing equipment.

INTRODUCTION

Rolling is an important skill for paddlers of closed-cockpit kayaks and canoes. Without it many of the benefits of being sealed into the boat by a spray cover are lost. For the advanced sea, surf or white water paddler, an awkward, tiring or dangerous swim may be prevented, and in the competitive disciplines much time may be saved by an efficient and reliable roll. Intermediate paddlers can learn and practise off-balance manoeuvres more confidently if they know that a roll will recover them from their errors and beginners will develop good water confidence and three-dimensional thinking if they learn to roll early.

Rolling is normally learnt in a swimming pool. Calm, warm water, good visibility and the confidence engendered by a controlled and safe environment all help to make this the preferred situation, but if a pool is not available it is not difficult to learn in open water, although the approach is different. If rolling is learnt in a pool, it must in any case be proved in the real situation before any claim to competence can be made.

This chapter outlines the history and principles of rolling before going on to explain how to perform and teach various types of kayak roll. A separate section explains canoe rolling techniques. The section on principles does not need to be understood before rolling is attempted but some pupils and teachers may find it useful in sorting out problems or refining technique.

HISTORY

Eskimos have been rolling their kayaks for many centuries; for them, the ability to roll was a basic survival technique. A missionary, writing in 1765, described ten methods by which an eskimo righted his craft, including full and half-paddle rolls,

311

and rolls using the harpoon or just the hands. A significant observation in the account is that once the paddle was positioned, the kayaker applied 'a flick of the hips' to recover. The first non-eskimo known to have learnt to roll was the Austrian, Edi Pawlata, who taught himself in 1927 after reading accounts by the explorers Nansen and Jophansen. An English explorer, Gino Watkins, learnt directly from the eskimos in 1930, but unfortunately he disappeared on a trip to the Arctic soon afterwards. These early European rolls involved levering the body upright from the water with little or no hip flick. It was not until about 1965 that the hip-flick was re-discovered, and it was this, together with the revolution in boat design and construction caused by the advent of rigid plastic boats, that led to rolling becoming a valid technique for white water paddlers.

PRINCIPLES

Consider the paddler sitting or kneeling in his boat (Fig 12:1). The combined weight, W, acting at the centre of gravity, CG, pulls the boat down into the water until the buoyancy force, BB, generated by the submerged part of the boat, increases sufficiently just to balance the weight. The buoyancy force can be assumed to act at a point at the centre of the submerged part called the centre of buoyancy, CB.

If the boat is tipped to one side the shape of the submerged part of the hull changes and the centre of buoyancy moves as shown in Fig 12:2. The effect of the two forces, now out of line, is to return the boat to the stable position shown in Fig 12:1, and so for small angles of tip the boat is stable.

If the angle of tip is increased further, as in Fig 12:3, then the movement of the centre of buoyancy is insufficient to compensate for the movement of the centre of gravity and the boat will capsize.

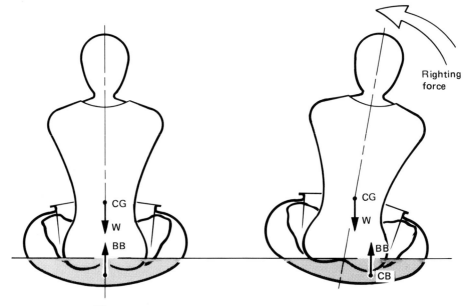

Righting force

Fig 12:1
Basic stability

Fig 12:2
Movement of the centre of buoyancy

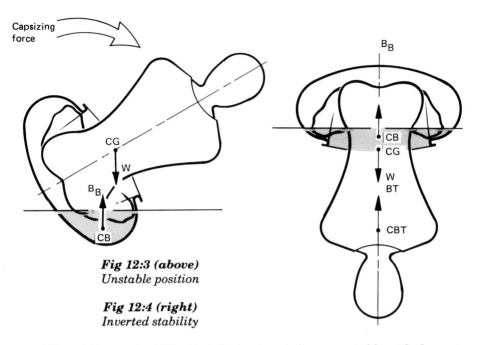

Capsizing force

CG

W

B_B

CB

B_B

CB
CG
W
BT

CBT

Fig 12:3 (above)
Unstable position

Fig 12:4 (right)
Inverted stability

When fully capsized (Fig 12:4) the boat again becomes stable with the centre of buoyancy and the centre of gravity in line. An additional buoyancy force also acts on the torso from the moment it becomes immersed and this is shown as BT, acting at the centre of buoyancy.

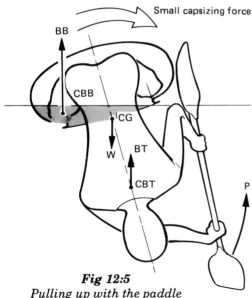

Small capsizing force

BB

CBB

CG

W

BT

CBT

P

Fig 12:5
Pulling up with the paddle

The stiff roll

So far we have considered the paddler as being rigidly fixed in his boat, with no movement at the waist or hips. The roll starts with the submerged paddler reaching for the surface with the paddle. A force, P, is generated which attempts to lift the body. As the boat begins to roll, the centre of buoyancy moves away from the side nearest the surface and increases the resistance of the boat to being righted (Fig 12:5). By the time the rigidly held body is clearing the surface the buoyancy force generated by the torso, which has until then been assisting the roll, rapidly decreases to zero. The weight of the body is then too far from the roll axis

313

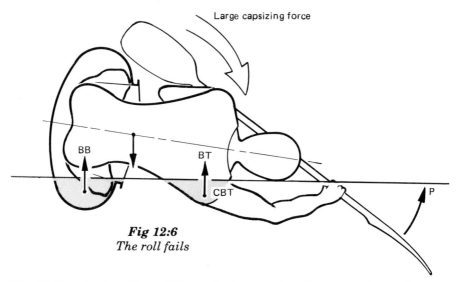

Fig 12:6
The roll fails

(Fig 12:6) and unless the paddle stroke is exceptionally strong, the combination of these two effects causes the roll to fail. They must be minimised by improvements in technique - the first by a movement known as the 'hip flick', and the second by bringing the centre of gravity of the upper body much closer to the roll axis.

The hip flick

The principal aim of the hip flick is to roll the boat far enough upright that its buoyancy force begins to assist the righting action before the body is lifted out of the water (Fig 12:7). The body is twisted at the waist, facing up towards the

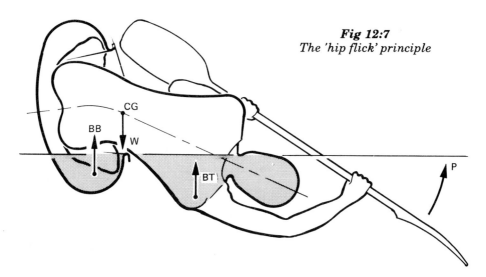

Fig 12:7
The 'hip flick' principle

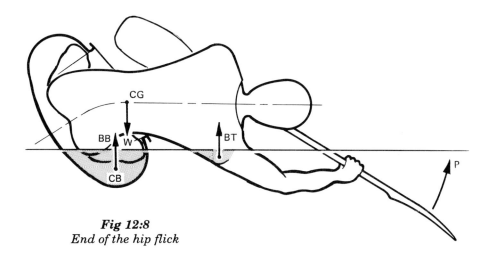

Fig 12:8
End of the hip flick

surface and bending forward for pawlata-type rolls, and towards the bottom, with the back arched, for steyr types. It is allowed to remain there, supported by the water, while the boat is righted with a rolling action of the hips. This is the hip flick. One knee pulls the boat towards the body while the opposite hip pushes it away. In the rolls involving a sweep-type stroke, the waist behaves like a universal joint, converting the twisting action of the upper body into a rolling action of the pelvis and boat. The net result is to roll the boat almost upright while the body remains in the water. During this action the body is pushed further under the surface and so this tendency is resisted by the buoyancy force that acts on the torso, assisted by the paddle if necessary.

The 'flick' part of the hip flick is a refinement of the basic technique, in which the boat is turned upright with a fast driving action of the lower body. Momentum is thereby gained, so that at the end of the flick the boat pulls the body out of the water and helps to restore it to the upright position.

Retracting the centre of gravity - the follow through

When the position shown in Fig 12:8 is reached the boat has been rolled up far enough with the hips so that the action of the boat's buoyancy force changes from resisting the roll to helping it, and the centre of gravity must be pulled close to the boat to enable the body to be lifted out of the water. As it does so, the action of the body must change from resisting the downward force caused by the rolling action of the boat (when the centre of buoyancy of the torso needs to be as far away from boat as possible) to that of reducing the capsizing moment by bringing the centre of gravity towards the roll axis. This can be done in a number of ways: by lying along the back or front decks, or by folding the body over the side of the boat.

If the body lies along the front or rear decks too early then the hip flick is curtailed and the benefit of keeping the buoyancy force acting on the torso is lost (Fig 12:9).

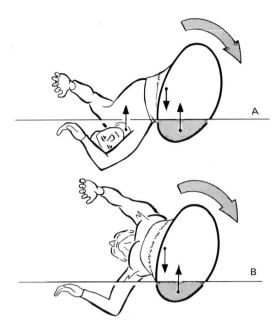

Fig 12:9
Leaning back too soon.
In position A the body is still
generating buoyancy.
In B the lean back is too early,
the body clears the water, and
buoyancy is consequently lost

KAYAK ROLLS

Teaching kayak rolling

The hip flick and associated follow through are so vitally important to good rolling that they must be taught and mastered thoroughly at an early stage. Superficial ability is not enough as the stress of concentrating on body position or paddle movement may cause the pupil to forget to carry out the hip flick actions. As a result, he lifts his head out of the water first, loses power and the roll fails.

The first exercise is to sit in the canoe and feel that it is held firmly by pushing forwards with the feet on the footrest, upwards and inward with the knees and thighs against suitable fittings, downwards with the backside into the seat and perhaps backwards against the backstrap. Many beginners find it hard to remain locked into even a well fitting boat, so it is important that the equipment is adjusted as well as possible. The paddle is then held horizontally above the head and the boat rocked from side to side by lifting the knee and hip, first on one side and then the other; the body remains vertical throughout the exercise (Fig 12:10). The angle of tip and the speed of movement can be progressively increased until the boat is being tilted as far in each direction as the movement of the waist joint allows.

The exercise is repeated next with the body in a face-down horizontal position with the hands holding palm-down on to the side of the pool, the bow of the teacher's boat, or any other reasonably firm support at water level (Fig 12:11). To reach this position a right-handed paddler must first rotate at the waist fully to the right, then hold the support and capsize to the right. It is important for the learner to realise that the face and body must be in the water for the exercise to be effective; again the range of movement should be built up until the paddler is

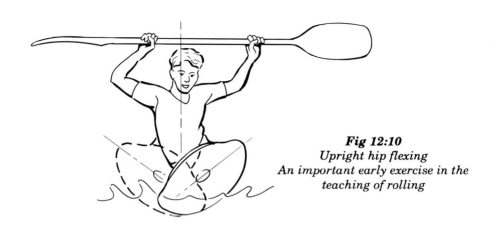

Fig 12:10
Upright hip flexing
An important early exercise in the
teaching of rolling

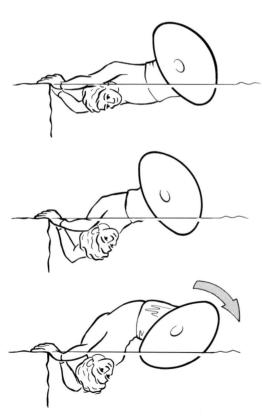

Fig 12:11
Hip flick drill

stretching the waist in each direction as far as possible. Initially this should be repeated several times with the body lying passively at the surface; no attempt should be made to bring the body out of the water until the hip flick can be performed almost without thinking. Once the hip flick can be done consistently with both hands providing support, it should be practised again using only the control hand, since only one hand actually pulls downwards during the paddle rolls.

The body follow through

The next stage in developing the complete action is to add to the hip flick (just described) the recovery from the water: as the boat passes through the on-edge position the spine starts to bend forwards from the base; this keeps the head and shoulders in the water, generating buoyancy, until as late as possible in the recovery; the shoulders and face leave the water last, with the face close to the middle of

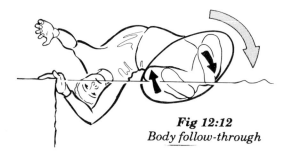

Fig 12:12
Body follow-through

the thigh. This exercise, too, should be repeated a number of times (Fig 12:12).

If the pupil has difficulty in achieving this flexibility of the spine, then alternative methods of lifting the body from the water can be tried. Many kayak rollers finish by lying along the back deck with no rotation at the waist (Fig 12:13); this causes less strain to the beginner, but is less effective for two reasons. Firstly, the body clears the water and the torso buoyancy force is lost much earlier in the movement; secondly, the laid back position is a very poor one for resuming paddling on rough water since the paddler is disorientated, looking up at the sky, and is in a weak position to brace with the paddle. If the roll fails when he is in this position then his face is very exposed to rocks and other obstacles. From this position, he has to pull himself upright with the stomach muscles, expending valuable time and energy, before he can do anything else. If this is the only method learnt for kayak rolling, then in some boats with high rear decks the body is prevented from leaning very far back, and so finishing the roll is difficult. One possible way round this for the stiff-waisted paddler is to lean forward. Particularly in large-cockpit boats the face lies close to the front of the spray cover, and the centre of gravity can be brought very close to the axis of rotation. If the boat has a small cockpit, then the head ends up on the raised part of the foredeck and again the centre of gravity is forced further out. The forward position is better than the laid back position because the paddlers face is much better protected and he can sit up into a strong paddling position quickly after rolling.

Fig 12:13
The back-deck finish

Using the paddle - the teaching rolls

Only when the pupil has a reasonable proficiency in the hip flick and body follow through is it wise to introduce the use of the paddle. Most beginners want to start with the paddle immediately, but its use too soon can lead to the development of bad habits, such as the flick-free or stiff roll, or simply to a discouraging lack of success. Most beginners find it easiest to start by learning either the 'pawlata' or the 'put across' rolls. The former is the most commonly taught, and seems to work very

Fig 12:14a (left) and b (right)
Pawlata starting position. Look closely at how the rear-most hand grips the blade in 12:4b

well for the confident paddler; the latter has the benefit of being simpler and of encouraging a better hip flick. Teachers of rolling should experiment with both methods so that they can use whichever suits their pupil best.

The pawlata roll

The pawlata is a good roll to learn initially. It is directly related to the screw roll which is probably the most useful roll of all, but it is a little easier to perform and more forgiving of failures in hip flick or follow through technique. The aim of teacher and pupil should be to progress to the screw roll as soon as possible after the pawlata has been learnt.

The starting position is shown in Fig 12:14. The paddler sits upright in the boat, with his back curved slightly forward and his body twisted towards the side on which he wants to capsize. A right-hand-control paddler will normally capsize to the left and vice versa. The control hand is then the forward hand and this holds the centre of the shaft. In rolling, as in other strokes, it is important that the hand maintains it normal orientation to the blade, and is not allowed to slip around the shaft. The control of the blade angle during the roll must be carried out by this

Fig 12:15a and 12:15b
'Wind up' with instructor standing by

319

hand. The rear hand holds the centre of the tip of the rear blade as shown, thumb pointing down across the face, and fingers wrapped around the tip (Fig 12:14b). To start the wind-up the control hand rotates the front blade outward through an angle of about 30 degrees. In this position it lines up with the angle of the front of the deck (Fig 12:15a). The instructor should then stand in the water next to his pupil on the opposite side to the paddle. He supports the boat to allow the pupil to complete the wind-up. In the fully-wound position the pupil is twisted at the waist towards the paddle and bent forward over the side of the boat, with the chin near the middle of the thigh. The paddle is parallel to its initial position with the front blade still held at the same angle, but it is now under water. The arms are locked tightly against the side of the boat to make sure that the paddle is not carried out of position by the water flow past it during capsize (Fig 12:15b). The instructor tells the paddler to hold the position when he has capsized, wait until the boat settles, and then sweep the paddle in a wide arc along the surface. An exercise sometimes found useful at this stage is for the instructor to tip the pupil away from the paddle (the 'wrong direction') to a position where the instructor can support the body or boat to enable the pupil to practise the sweeping action. Whether this exercise is used or not, eventually the pupil has to make his first solo attempt.

The instructor should support the pupil so that he can achieve a good tight wind-up with the paddle locked in to the side of the boat. The pupil can then be lowered into the water when he is ready; the instructor reaches under the boat to help hold the paddle in place as it travels through the water, under the boat and back to the surface. He should then move to the bow of the boat, where he is then in a good position to counter one of the most common mistakes, which is for the paddler to pull down instead of sweeping out along the surface. This commonly happens because the back hand is not pushed sufficiently far underneath the pupil's backside during the wind-up, so it is blocked by the gunwhale as it tries to follow through with the body twist. The paddle can not continue with its outward sweep, so pulls down instead (Fig 12:16). The instructor can reset the paddle position or blade angle, walk the paddle round in the correct path, he can give it a push in the right direction, or move in and support it to give the paddler something to pull up on, If necessary he can right the boat by placing a hand on each gunwhale and ducking underneath.

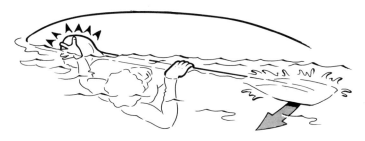

Fig 12:16
Rearmost hand 'blocked' by boat edge. Make sure rearmost hand is pushed well below the backside during the wind up

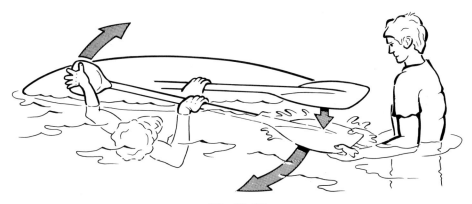

Fig 12:17
Feeling for the surface. Instructor assisting the start of the sweep

The hip flick action in the pawlata has an additional feature to that already practised - during the course of the roll the body must rotate from a face-up position to a face-down position. In doing so the waist and upper body twist in a similar way to the action of a conventional forward sweep stroke. The waist and hips act as a universal joint converting the rotation of the body into a rolling action of the boat, incorporating the hip flick already learned. It is this body rotation that also drives the paddle around in a wide sculling sweep along the surface. The sequence is shown in Figs 12:18-12:20. If the lie-back style of rolling is used as shown in Fig 12:13, then the rotation stops when the paddle blade is level with the body and the hip flick is half-complete; the body then simply hinges at the waist until the paddler is laying along the back deck. The paddle is driven by the waist action and then by the arms. For the hinged-forward recovery shown in Fig 12:20, the action is carried out completely by the arms with virtually no hip flick. This variation only works if the centre of gravity is brought very close to the roll axis.

Once a good pawlata has been achieved and refined, the pupil should be encouraged to try the screw roll. Provided that the hip flick is effective and that the back hand is pushed clear of the hull to give space for the extended rear paddle, the progression can be effected with little difficulty.

In its own right, the pawlata should still be practised by all paddlers from time to time, as occasions can arise where the paddle must be used from an unusual position or extra power must be generated.

The put across roll
The second of the principal teaching rolls is the put across roll. It seems to have fallen out of favour in recent years, but it has one major advantage over the pawlata in that the hip flick action is almost identical to the initial drill. For pupils who have trouble putting all the components of the roll together, particularly those who lose the hip flick while trying to master the paddle action, it offers a valuable intermediate step. In particular, once the eskimo rescue technique has been learnt, the put across offers a method of learning that can be used on open water with a high degree of success. In its own right, it is particularly useful if the paddle has been let go, as it can be performed very quickly after the blade has been

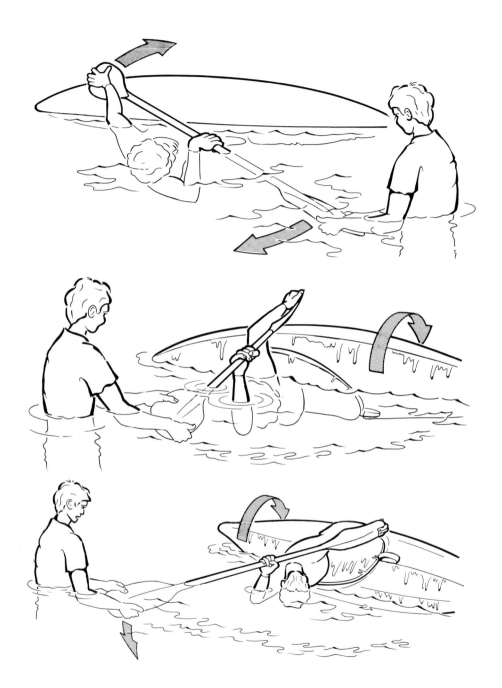

Figs 12:18, 12:19 ,12:20
The complete roll in sequence

Fig 12:21
The Queen's salute.
A way of introducing the put across roll

regained. It is unusual in that the paddle is not carried down on one side during capsize and brought up on the other, but is left at the surface while the body does all the movement.

One way of introducing the roll after the hip flick drills is via the 'Queens Salute' position (Fig 12:21). In this case capsize should be towards the control side. The top hand is the control hand and holds the paddle just above the lower blade, maintaining the correct register with respect to the upper blade. (This may cause a little confusion at first if the hand grips are ovalled since the hand feels the wrong oval). The lower hand holds the edge of the blade as shown, ready to apply upward pressure. The boat is capsized and the position held until the upper blade touches the water. (If the pupil attempts to cheat by lowering the paddle using the arms the blade cuts into the water end first and sinks). Once the blade is flat on the water the paddler pulls down with the control hand and rolls the boat upright, exactly as he did in early hip flick exercises. The other hand prevents the inner blade sinking. The action is much stronger if both elbows remain in the same vertical plane as the shaft and inner blade. The sequence of actions is shown in Fig 12:22. The roll may also be approached by floating the paddle on the water next to and perpendicular to the centre of the boat with the closer blade vertical. The blade hand can easily reach across the body to hold the paddle, and the other hand can move into position during capsize. Care should be taken to ensure that the paddle is not pushed under the surface as the pupil capsizes on to it.

A common problem with this roll is pulling down with both hands, resulting in the near blade knifing very quickly towards the bottom and giving no support. It is corrected by emphasising the upward pressure with the blade hand. (It is possible to roll from a near blade that is horizontal, using a downwards push with one or both hands, but this is really a variety of hand roll and is much harder). Once the basic sequence has been mastered, the hands are moved into position

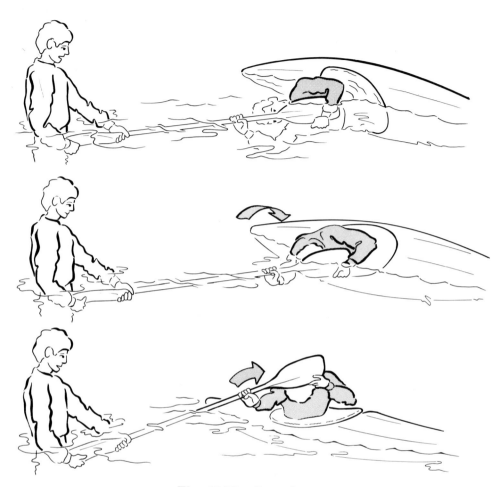

Figs 12:22 a, b, and c
The put across roll

Fig 12:23
The screw roll starting position

later and later in the capsize, until the pupil can swim a few strokes to the blade, find the position, and then roll up. He can finally complete the roll by capsizing on one side and reaching for the paddle on the other.

Many 'real' rolls use elements of the put across, often without the paddler being aware of it. It is, for example, quite common to see a screw roll finished with the downward pull of the put across - this can sometimes leave the paddler in a much stronger position than continuing the sweep to the rear of the boat.

Screw roll

The screw roll is the most commonly used roll of all because it is reliable, easy to learn and works in most circumstances. Most paddlers use a screw roll or some variant of it as their standard survival roll. The sequence of movements is identical to the pawlata described above except that hands remain in the normal paddling position on the shaft. The sequence is as shown in Fig 12:24. The hip flick must be more effective than for the pawlata, since less support is available from the shorter paddle lever, and it is even more important that the back hand is pushed clear of the hull to give the back blade space to move. Like all rolls that are intended to be used in difficult situations, it should be learnt on both sides. It is the basis for a whole family of rolls that can all be performed without moving the hands along the shaft. Some beginners find it easier to learn the screw directly rather than pass through the pawlata sequence.

Steyr roll

The steyr roll is a reverse pawlata. The paddle sweeps across the surface from the rear of the boat to the front and, in order to do this, the wind-up is performed differently. From the pawlata position the paddle is raised to the vertical; as it continues past the vertical it must be turned outward with the wrists until the position shown in Fig 12:25 is reached. To capsize, the paddle is pushed down towards the water and the body follows, arched backwards and to the side. The waist and hips act as a universal joint in a similar way to the pawlata but, in this case, the body rotation is in the opposite direction to that of the boat, because the paddle is carrying out a reverse sculling sweep. The full sequence is shown in Fig 12:26 a and b. The steyr is used as a training roll for the reverse screw in the same way that the pawlata is used for the screw.

Reverse screw roll

The reverse screw is used when for any reason the paddler has capsized and been pushed on to the back deck, or the paddle blade is at the back of the boat; typically this occurs if the boat capsizes over the paddle during a bow stroke. The wind-up position is reached in the same way as the wind-up for the steyr. The roll can be particularly useful as a follow-on to a screw roll which does not quite bring the paddler back into balance: the blade position is quickly reversed and a reverse screw follows. More commonly, a screw backs up a reverse screw which fails. The roll is shown part way through the sequence in Fig 12:27.

Fig 12:24 a-f
The screw roll sequence

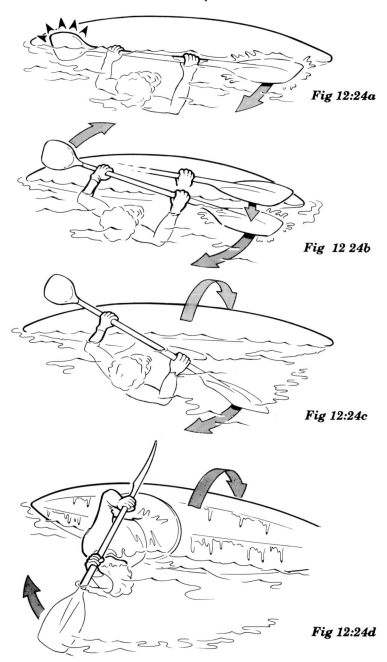

Fig 12:24a

Fig 12 24b

Fig 12:24c

Fig 12:24d

Fig 12:24e

Fig 12:24f

Fig 12:25
Steyr starting position. Notice the 'turned out' wrists

Fig 12:26 a (top) and b (below)
Steyr rolling sequence

Fig 12:27
The reverse screw roll

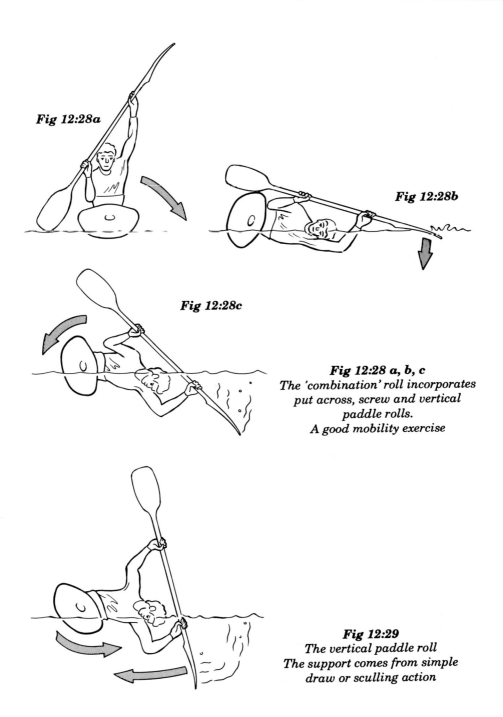

Fig 12:28a

Fig 12:28b

Fig 12:28c

Fig 12:28 a, b, c
*The 'combination' roll incorporates put across, screw and vertical paddle rolls.
A good mobility exercise*

Fig 12:29
*The vertical paddle roll
The support comes from simple draw or sculling action*

Vertical paddle roll

A number of rolls are possible using a vertical instead of a horizontal paddle. The hip flick action in this case pulls the boat underneath the body and the paddle provides the resistance. At first it seems impossible for a vertical paddle to provide the necessary support, but the principle becomes clearer if the boat is thought of as rolling around the hips and under the body (Fig 12:29). Both a simple draw or sculling draw action can be used. A combination of put across, screw and vertical paddle roll can be used as a good mobility exercise, as shown in Fig 12:28 a,b,c. The paddler starts sitting upright in his boat, with his paddle horizontally above his head. For a recovery on the right the right arm is pushed up to full extension and the left arm retracted to the shoulder, until the paddler shaft is almost vertical. The paddler capsizes to the right, holding this position until the blade touches the water. As the blade touches the water a reverse hip flick keeps the paddle and upper body near the surface while the boat completes the capsize. The boat is then hip flicked up while, at the same time, the right arm is pulled in towards the hip and the left arm extended to full stretch.

Storm roll

The storm roll may be performed as a pawlata or as a screw roll. The wind-up positions are the same except that in each case the edge of the forward blade is angled in towards rather than away from the boat. After capsize, the blade is pulled in a vertical arc from bow to stern and becomes a long vertical sculling draw rather than a horizontal sculling sweep. The storm roll is to the vertical paddle roll what the pawlata is to the put across. It is impractical on rivers because of the depth needed for the paddle, but a study of film taken in Greenland shows that it is the preferred roll of the Angmassalik Eskimos. The observer can recognise a storm roll by the pronounced lift of the bow as the roll begins.

Hand roll

If a good hip flick is developed then the boat can be rolled upright using the hands. The flick action becomes important as enough momentum must be given to the boat to lift the body clear after it breaks surface. The top hand is often thrown across to increase the momentum. One sequence is shown in Fig 12:30 a-f. As with the paddle rolls, the body recovery can be in forward or backward positions. Many paddlers can perform one-handed rolls, with the other hand held inside the spray cover, and stories are even told of rolls performed without any use of the hands at all. The ability to hand roll can be more than a stunt: in canoe polo players often lose their paddles and capsize when shooting for goal, and even on the roughest rivers a hand-roll will sometimes buy enough of a respite to enable the bank to be reached. Training to hand roll is progressive, with less and less buoyant or resistant objects being used as the support for the hip flick until, finally, the hands alone are needed.

Other rolls

The experienced roller uses a variety of techniques and combinations of moves to right the boat. The position and feel of his paddle following capsize and his knowledge of the water conditions tell him what he must do in order to bring himself upright. In general he pulls his body to the surface using the waist, knees and hips and then uses the paddle to prevent the body from sinking during the hip flick. This movement enables the body to be brought back over the boat during the follow through. The rolls listed here are merely some of the separately identifiable types that may be used to achieve this.

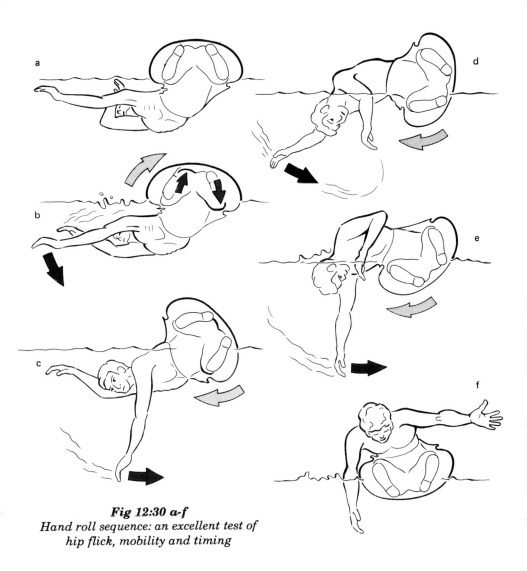

Fig 12:30 a-f
Hand roll sequence: an excellent test of
hip flick, mobility and timing

SPECIAL CIRCUMSTANCES

In certain circumstances the information given in the preceding paragraphs may need to be modified. The possibilities for rolling situations are infinite but a few are readily identifiable.

Rolling in stoppers and breaking waves

In stoppers or when 'bongo-sliding' in surf, there is so much turbulence and power in the water that normal techniques are impossible. Instead the body is braced with the paddle in such a position that the drive of the water turns the boat

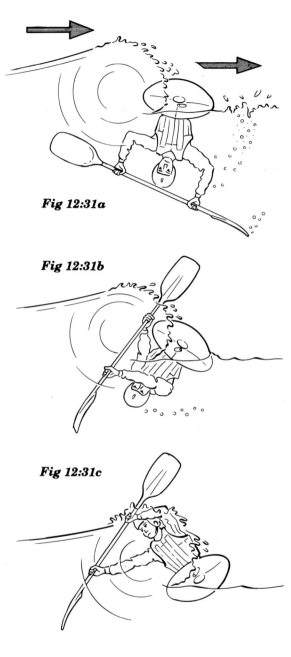

Fig 12:31a

Fig 12:31b

Fig 12:31c

Fig 12:31 a, b, c
Rolling in a breaking wave

upright, and the body position is then adjusted to ensure stability. As an example, a brace roll in surf is shown in Fig 12:31 a-c.

Rolling in shallow water

In shallow water, especially if it is relatively slow moving, pushing off the bottom with a vertical paddle can be very effective. A good hip flick is important, and care must be taken to ensure that the shaft is truly vertical before the roll is attempted. In very shallow water it may be impossible to find clearance to do a normal roll and levering against the bottom may be the only option. In shallow, rough water rivers any use of the paddle to roll may be impossible, and a hand roll off the bottom or passing rock is worth attempting; speed and success in this may save the paddler from bruises and scrapes as he tries to eject.

Re-entry and roll

There may be occasions, particularly when sea paddling, that an attempt at rolling fails and the paddler finds himself in the water alongside his boat but a long way from any safe landing. It may not be possible for his colleagues to come and rescue him, so he is on his own. One option he has is the re-entry and roll. He comes alongside his kayak which has hopefully remained upside-down and is not too full of water, turns himself upside down, gets in and rolls up. Once clear of immediate danger the boat can be emptied by pump or conventional rescue techniques. This technique is discussed further in the chapter on Sea Kayaking.

Stunt rolls

These rolls are used for entertainment and building water confidence.

Clock roll

The paddle acts as the hand of a clock. Wind-up is as for a pawlata roll but turn the wrists outward as for the steyr. During capsize sweep the paddle over the head to the steyr start position. Roll up using the steyr. For a clockwise clock the sequence must be performed left-handed. Repeat as often as desired.

Rotary roll

The boat capsizes. The paddle remains under water, parallel to the surface. It is extended so that the near blade is held horizontally while the far blade is vertical. An action similar to the sweep stroke will cause the boat to spin round and round on the surface. The paddler rolls up when he runs out of breath.

Top hat roll

This can be performed with any prop, but a top hat is traditional. The paddler must be able to roll one-handed. For a right-handed roll he removes the top hat from his head with his right hand and capsizes to the left. As the boat settles upside-down the still-dry hat is placed on the upturned hull with the right hand. It is retrieved with the left hand as the roll is completed with the right hand and placed, still dry, back on the head.

Cross bow roll

Wind up and capsize is as for a normal screw roll. Under water the paddle is crossed over the bow and swept out in the opposite direction. The paddle finishes under the boat, so it must be released as the roll finishes. Many variations are possible.

THE CANOE ROLL

For anyone learning to paddle canoes in rough water the need to be able to roll becomes important very quickly. The use of a single blade, coupled with the high centre of gravity of the boats can lead to frequent capsizes. While the single blade simplifies the mechanics of the stroke, the high centre of gravity and wide beam couple together to make this roll a challenging prospect.

Fittings

Whatever fittings the canoe possesses, whether aluminium or webbing straps, they must enable the paddler to grip tightly in the canoe when capsized. They must be positioned in such a way that exit from the canoe in an emergency is a quick and easy task, not requiring any unbuckling of straps by hand. It is essential that before paddling a Canadian canoe for the first time, capsize drills be performed. The dangers connected with over-tight, badly positioned fittings are very real. Never cross your legs beneath the seat in a Canadian canoe.

Terminology

Throughout this chapter, the expression 'top hand' refers to the hand holding the handle of the paddle. 'Lower hand' means the hand nearest to the blade. 'Drive face' indicates the side of the paddle blade which is pulled against the water *when paddling forward*. The 'back' of the blade is the opposite face.

Drills

Initial drills that can be practised by the paddler to acquaint himself with the roll are as follows:

o Capsize practise to overcome the fear of being trapped and ensure a quick release from the boat.

o Swimming in the canoe to the bank after a capsize, lean back in the canoe and slightly to one side, swim with hands (breast stroke or dog paddle) and the head will break surface. In this position it is possible to swim along whilst breathing satisfactorily. Practise on both sides and swapping over.

o Righting the canoe by use of the bank or a partner. Capsize onto partner's arm or side of pool and use arm strength in conjunction with hip flick to right the canoe. The hip flick is the most important part of the Canadian roll and practise is essential.

The two main rolls practiced today have their origins in the kayak screw and steyr rolls. A third - the cross-bow - is advanced, and peculiar to the decked canoe.

Rolling methods

Screw roll

Hold the blade in the normal manner. Place the shaft parallel to the side of the boat on the side that you wish to roll with the blade stretching out in front of you. The top hand should be positioned slightly to the rear of the hip. Lean forward and ensure that the wrists are bent, so that the outward edge of the blade turns towards the surface of the water (Fig 12:32a).

Capsize towards the paddle and allow boat to turn over fully. Leaning forward, thrust the blade towards the surface, ensuring that the top hand is clear of the deck, or in a comfortable position. Keep both wrists bent, so that the outboard edge of the blade is slightly turned towards the surface (Fig 12:32b).

Keeping the lower arm straight, sweep in an arc form the bow, pulling firmly down. The action should be swift, and a sharp hip flick introduced when the paddle passes through 45 degrees. Keep the body low until the boat is almost fully righted. This is of great importance, due to the amount of body which is out of the boat (Figs 12:32c and d).

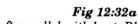

The canoe screw roll sequence

Fig 12:32a
*Shaft parallel with boat. Blade out in front.
Top hand slightly to rear of hip. Lean forward.
Rotate wrists outwards. Capsize towards
paddle*

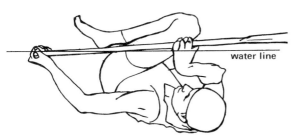

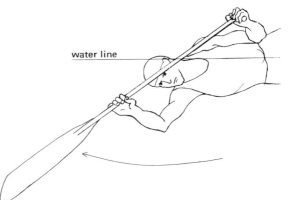

Fig 12:32b
*Give canoe time to steady.
Paddle and both wrists to
surface. Control blade
angle with top hand - too
much 'bite' and canoe will
turn; too little, the blade
will slice*

Fig 12:32c
*Keep body just below
surface. Top hand fairly
close to gunwale and
following as it begins to
lift. Blade, lower hand
and torso sweep out in
wide flat arc. Keep face
and chest down towards
bottom of pool. Use hip
flick to thrust hull
upright*

Fig 12:32d
*Keep body weight
as low as possible.
Reverse sweep
(see Fig 12.32e)
if necessary to
complete recovery*

Fig 12:32e
*Relax wrist on lower hand. Use top
hand to change blade face and sweep
forward using back of blade, pushing
hard down with lower hand*

If difficulty is encountered in this procedure the following addition should be made. As the blade has passed the centre of the boat, say about 130 degrees during the initial sweep, drop the both wrists to reverse the blade and push down hard while moving forwards (Fig 12:32e). Whilst pushing down, the hip flick should come into operation. Keep the body low as outlined before. This addition allows more strength to be used to ensure success. However, in competition, the first method is preferred, due to speed and superior finishing position.

Steyr roll

Many canoe paddlers prefer this method, as it offers stronger leverage, which aids success.

Hold the paddle as normal, lean back, and bring the blade upwards and over the head into the steyr position but rotate the wrists as for a screw roll - the drive face should be flat against the canoe, so that the back of the blade is presented to the surface when you are upside down. Capsize towards the paddle and allow the boat to turn over fully. Ensure that the outward edge of the blade is uppermost on the surface by moving the lower hand towards the surface and thrusting the wrist upwards (Figs 12:33a and b).

Begin the sweep by arcing the paddle from the stern with a straight arm, pushing down using the back of the blade. Maximum downward thrust and hip flick would begin when the blade passes through 45 degrees (Fig 12:33c). As the boat rises, ensure that the body position is kept low, and this will assist in the success of the roll (Fig 12:33d).

In contrast with the screw roll, where the thrust for the roll comes from a downward *pulling* action using the drive face, the steyr relies on the more powerful *pushing* action using the back of the blade.

Cross-bow roll

This is an advanced roll, shown in Fig 12:34a-c, which enables C1 paddlers to roll on their wrong side without changing hands, and C2 paddlers to roll without one partner changing sides. It is awkward to execute, with the additional disadvantage of a very unstable finishing position.

Hold the paddle as normal, but feather it so that the drive face is towards the canoe, parallel to the gunwale. Place it in a vertical position, blade in the water on the paddling side beside the body, top hand shoulder height. The bottom hand should be in the water. Capsize either side (practice will be required in capsizing both ways) holding the paddle firmly in the starting position until the boat has turned over fully. In this position the blade will be in the air pointing vertically upwards. Now the hand nearest the blade pushes out, as the other hand pulls inward towards the body. When the blade meets the water, resistance is felt. Push violently down with the hand nearest the blade. The other hand will continue moving towards the body. At the same time, hip flick. As the boat is righted, the body must be kept low until stability is reached. This is the most difficult stage of the roll as it is so unstable.

336

Fig 12:33a
*Take paddle up and over head. Shaft parallel
with arm on non-paddling side. Lie well back.
Capsize towards that side. Keep blade close to
gunwale and steady while canoe settles. Top
arm relaxed. Lower forearm across face.
Knuckles of blade hand near ear. Torso roughly
in line with stern deck so that the back of head,
both hands and paddle are just under the
surface when capsized, with face and chest
turned towards bottom of pool for as long as
possible*

Fig 12:33c
*Relax grip on lower hand. Use top hand to
set blade angle. Leading edge slightly
raised. Strong pushing action required as
blade is swept forwards. Top hand fairly
still, close to gunwale and following as it
lifts. Push blade hand away, and follow
with body. Keep face and chest turned
towards bottom of pool. Use hip-flick to
thrust hull upright*

Fig 12:33d *Boat should be upright before paddle is at 90 degrees to keel line.
Keep chest and face turned towards bottom of pool as much as possible*

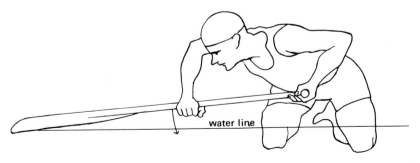

Fig 12:33d *Keep body weight low. Top hand acts as pivot and controls blade
angle. Do not get it higher than necessary or support will be lost*

337

The cross bow roll sequence

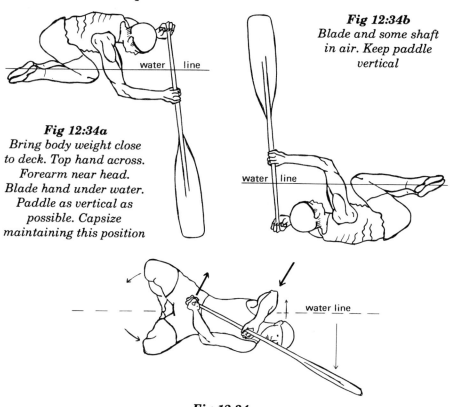

Fig 12:34a
Bring body weight close
to deck. Top hand across.
Forearm near head.
Blade hand under water.
Paddle as vertical as
possible. Capsize
maintaining this position

Fig 12:34b
Blade and some shaft
in air. Keep paddle
vertical

Fig 12:34c
Push out with lower (blade) hand. Pull top hand in across body. After blade
has smacked surface keep pushing down hard with blade hand and pull
inwards across thighs with top hand. Apply hip flick

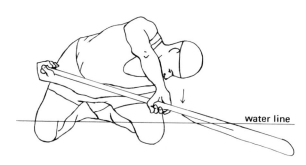

Fig 12:34d
Push down with blade hand. Keep body low until stability is achieved

Rolling the C2

C2 paddling is all about coordination between two individuals, and this is never illustrated better than during a roll. The methods used are based on the C1 rolls, screw, steyr or cross-bow. If one paddler does not use the cross-bow, then the partner must change hands to roll.

When capsized and ready, both paddlers must act together. The one who will take the longest to get into position must signal. Two or three regular hits on the boat with the paddle is the signal to start - the pair rolling up on what would be the third, or fourth 'hit'. This works reasonably well initially, but the following faster sequence should be encouraged. As before, the slowest paddler into position should initiate the roll. In this case, however, the 'signal' is the beginning of the roll itself. When the other partner feels this initial pressure causing the boat to begin to roll up, he joins in to produce the maximum force. This is a subtle advanced method dependent on a good sense of 'feel' for the boat, which works very neatly between paddlers who are well coordinated. With one partner using the cross-bow drill, the return to the surface can be remarkably fast. Practise in a C1 is invaluable for achieving good results in a C2.

CONCLUSION

This list of rolls is not complete, and many other ways can be found of bringing boats upright. It is fun to experiment, and to see what can be achieved. In the end, it is not what the roll is called that matters, but whether it works in difficult situations. Newcomers to rolling should realise that there is a world of difference between a simple screw roll in a swimming pool and a complex recovery stroke performed on the weak side in cold rough water when they are tired and frightened. Only practise in realistic situations can make rolling better and more consistent.

13 Teaching Techniques and Group Leadership

Graham Lyon and Dave Collins

An unfinished Moonraker, left in his school workshop, was the start of Graham Lyon's canoeing career in 1964 and led to his helping a local youth club to build lath and canvas and later, glassfibre canoes. Although failing his Proficiency Test at the first attempt (!), Graham later became an Instructor and founder member of Shrewsbury Canoe Club, leading journeys on many well known white water rivers.

From Local Coaching Organiser, he was elected Regional Coaching Organiser for West Midlands in 1976, appointed a National Coaching and Development Officer a year later and is currently Chairman of the National Coaching Committee.

Dave Collins is a lecturer in Physical Education in London. He is a widely respected sports' psychologist with a flare for helping coaches to bridge the gap between scientific theory and actual practice. His canoeing interests are in white water and racing. In his copious free time he also plays American football, rugby and knock-down karate.

INTRODUCTION TO TEACHING TECHNIQUES

Plate 13:a
What we teach, and the approach we take to teaching it, depends entirely on whom we are teaching
PHOTO: GERRY ELSMORE

341

It is not uncommon to hear stories of pupils struggling in a subject and then a change of teacher produces a dramatic breakthrough. Sometimes it is a personality problem but usually a different personality has a different or slightly different method of putting things over. If we look at the world of sport then we find a variety of coaching methods employed, all of which would seem to be effectively used by somebody.

However, in canoeing terms, most methods have a few things in common that need to be right before the method has any chance of success.

Firstly we need to check that the equipment that we shall use is correct. This is an important aspect of the job not only from the safety point of view but it also helps to establish the instructor or coach as being competent in the eyes of the individual or a group. If the equipment is all there on time, in the right place and suitable for the group, the session is off to a good start. How often are sessions started with problems with the boat fittings, hunting for an extra buoyancy aid or a problem with a helmet fixing just as you are about to get on the water ?

Secondly some thought needs to be given to the content of the session. It is always worth jotting down a few notes to help focus your mind. Start by deciding what is the main objective of the session. It might be part of a straight forward course on learning to paddle a kayak, in which case the teaching of canoeing skills will make up the main part of the session. However, canoeing is used as a vehicle to help develop a great range of other qualities. This might be management skills or social skills, in which case the main thrust of the session might be presenting

Plate 13:b
Youngsters thrive on variety and plenty of activity
PHOTO: GERRY ELSMORE

Plate 13:c
A calm but fairly relaxed, businesslike atmosphere is required, with the instructor quite obviously controlling events when he needs to
PHOTO:GERRY ELSMORE

problems of group organisation or cooperation, and the actual canoeing takes a secondary role. The objective might be one of trying to raise the self-esteem of an individual or a group, and the carefully controlled challenge which is rewarded by success becomes the main theme of the session. However, whatever the objective, when the actual skills of canoeing become relevant, they should be taught properly.

Once you have identified what it is that you are hoping to achieve, then you can sort out the detail and the methods to be used. It is obviously very useful to have some idea at this stage of the canoeing experience of the individuals in the group.

Consideration needs to be given as to how to ensure the success of the session. It is easier to plan if you know the group, but certain factors should always be borne in mind. A good start has been made by prior planning and obviously the enthusiasm of the instructor plays an important part. Sometimes it is hard to drum up your enthusiasm on a cold wet day, so a little thought about your own motivation is important. I always try to build into each session something that I particularly like doing, or something that is amusing or brings almost instant success. Youngsters seem to thrive on variety and plenty of activity, and whilst these are also important ingredients for adults, they like to see that they have learnt something new.

At the end of a session, it is a good idea to make a written comment about things that went well and things that were less successful. The total disaster is usually remembered.

Lastly, it is important that the instructor is in control of the group. This is an essential learning and safety factor and it must be remembered that not all individuals arrive at canoeing sessions of their own choice, or with the wish to learn.

Control should not be gained through a domineering, authoritarian approach since this produces tension and stress which can be counter-productive to gaining the best performance. A calm and fairly relaxed but businesslike atmosphere is required, with the instructor quite obviously controlling events when he needs to. There are a few points which can help achieve this.

On meeting a group you need to behave in a confident and efficient manner, because such an approach reflects knowledge, authority and experience. When you wish to talk to the group, organise them so that you can establish easy eye contact with everybody. If possible point them away from other distractions, not looking into the sun, and avoid situations where it is necessary to shout for any length of time. Try to pitch the volume of your voice so that it places the responsibility on the group to listen. Having drawn the group together for the first time, make sure that you have silence and everybody's attention. Pause for a moment savouring the silence before you begin to talk. The mid-sentence pause is a good way of gaining the attention of anybody who has let his concentration slip. Humorous instructions can come once you feel that your authority has been established within the group. Some people have a natural presence and, for them, this moment arrives very quickly.

It has already been mentioned that the group is likely to respond well to the instructor who has enthusiasm for the task in hand. It is perhaps worth looking at how we know that somebody is enthusiastic. The news reader attempting to give an unbiased presentation is the opposite of the enthusiast. When somebody is enthusiastic then there is a great deal of arm and body movement which fits in with the rhythm of their speech. A stream of facial expressions is evident; the pace and volume of their speech varies to emphasise points. Whilst it is not suggested that you force it, do not feel inhibited. Give your natural body language free rein. A little acting can usually be cultivated as your confidence and experience grow.

No matter how well planned or interesting you have tried to make a session, there will come a day when a reprimand becomes necessary. It is worth considering what makes an effective reprimand. Your reprimand needs to be clear, brief and direct. Avoid using words like 'please'. 'Please don't do that' is rather like imploring someone to stop, and you are less likely to be obeyed. It is better to use the lower register of your voice. This gives the impression of self-control, whereas a high pitched outburst suggests the reverse. They have you rattled and you have become insecure and vulnerable. The reprimand can be upgraded by moving closer, into their personal space. This move needs to be in a direct and immediate manner. You have a particular advantage once on the water since they are in a less familiar environment. Gripping their boat with your hand to maintain contact adds weight to your authority. Pointing is another way of re-enforcing a reprimand since this action indicates somebody of a higher status. Sarcasm is best avoided since it invites the clever reply from the more difficult customer.

Unfortunately the sight of you 'losing your cool' with one of the group may be of great interest to the rest. Even if the majority are really motivated, your reprimand is unavoidably distracting, causing them to forget your instructions or coaching points. Where possible therefore, address your negative comments quietly to the individual concerned whilst the rest of the group are working.

Before looking at different teaching or coaching methods it is worth reminding ourselves of the old 'golden rule' which is true for most situations:

o   Most of what you hear, you forget

o   Some of what you see you remember

o   What you do sticks.

THE COACHING SEQUENCE

A useful way to remember the basic structure of any teaching session is :

I D E A S

This stands for :

       o   Introduction

       o   Demonstration

       o   Explanation

       o   Activity

       o   Summary

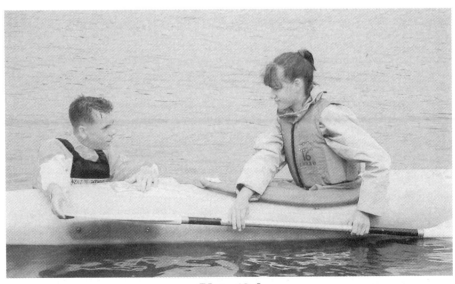

Plate 13:d
Keep explanations short and simple; don't be tempted to elaborate
PHOTO: GERRY ELSMORE

Plate 13:e
If you are in doubt about how well you have communicated, then get the group,
or an individual, to repeat what they are looking for
PHOTO: GERRY ELSMORE

Thousands of people have been successfully taught canoeing by this teaching sequence. The instructor gives an introduction of what the skill is used for. The skill is then demonstrated to the group and the key points are explained. They then attempt to imitate the instructor's demonstration. Whilst this is in progress the instructor goes around and tries to correct faults that individuals are making. Once the skill has been correctly mastered, the aim is to repeat it many times so that it becomes second nature. This is a good sound technique, has scope for variation, but also a contains a number of pitfalls of which we need to be aware.

A verbal *introduction* is important, particularly at the early stages of learning a skill. The eye is not like a camera, and may focus on all the wrong aspects of a demonstration. The observer might be impressed with the wave that the boat made, whereas the instructor at that moment was demonstrating the path of the paddle. The problem is that, at best, we can only hold between five and six facts in our 'short term memory' if there is no rehearsal. Related facts however are more easily remembered. The message to the instructor is then clear: the introduction before the demonstration must be short, and the parts linked. If you are in doubt as to how well you have communicated, then get the group or an individual to repeat what they are looking for (Rehearsal). The message KISS (Keep It Simple, Stupid) could well be added to our IDEAS.

The demonstration which follows can also be a problem, although a visual demonstration would seem to be the most effective method of teaching a skill. It has been suggested that we can only handle one 'stimulus event' at a time. A second stimulus is either disregarded or held up to wait its turn. We do not perceive all the various stimuli coming from all our receptors. We must select certain ones from among all the possibilities. I am therefore suggesting that we attempt to remove as much 'clutter' from the demonstration as possible. Avoid any verbal explanation during the demonstration, except where you are sure it is necessary.

After the demonstration you will give an explanation of the skill's components before releasing the group to practise. Don't forget to summarise these points before they leave. Learners (in fact all of us) have problems remembering lots of new facts especially in the highly distracting environment of a river Try remembering four or five telephone numbers (new ones) for a few minutes whilst you exercise. Your 'key points' must therefore be kept to the minimum.

An additional problem is caused by our tendency to avoid difficult skills and practise easy ones so as to look as good as possible. Set a group of intermediate paddlers to work on their rolls and watch how quickly they commence lengthy discussion of the finer points; all except those who are already proficient, who will display their skills by spinning like tops. Avoid this problem and maintain your control of the group by setting a goal for the practise. This procedure will also encourage the students to practise the skill on both sides: an important point, as you will see later.

The technique for setting paddlers off to practise would sound like this:

EXPLANATION
o Recap key points
o Set a goal
o Start the group working

ACTIVITY

An example, from the first session on breaking-in might go:
EXPLANATION - detailed explanation of the skill
"So remember, paddle hard, sweep stroke, raise upstream edge, brace on the downstream side".
"I want you to try at least four break-ins from this eddy, then four from that one. Any questions . . . ?"
"Go"
ACTIVITY

The Demonstration, Explanation, Activity sequence can now be repeated as many times as necessary. At the end of the session a summary of the content, and how it is applied will help the group remember the details until next time.

The skill that you wish the group to perform should be something that they are able to achieve. If you give a demonstration of a complex skill then most, if not all the group, will produce a copy which is far from perfect. For example, if the instructor gives the explanation and then performs a break-out into the top of an eddy, using a bow rudder, when the group try this many of them may miss the eddy. They have been unable to imitate the instructor because the model is beyond

Plate 13:f
Complex skills need to be broken down into simple stages which are within the
ability of the individual
PHOTO: GERRY ELSMORE

their ability. The successful break-out by that method demands timing, judgement of speed, balance, a feel for the interaction between the boat and current, and so forth. Their system was completely overloaded and they were unable to cope successfully. You can see the puzzled look on their faces, and they frequently have no idea why they were unsuccessful.

The answer to the problem is simple, although it is in practice difficult to achieve, and requires much careful thought on the part of the instructor. The complex skill needs to be broken down into simple stages which are within the ability of an individual. To help us do this, it is useful to have a 'model' to explain how a skill is organised.

We can think of a skill as being organised into an 'executive programme', 'routines' and 'sub-routines'. The executive programme is the overall plan of the skill. Routines represent the movements of the major body parts of the skill. Each of these movements is made up of small units called sub-routines. This is shown diagrammatically in Fig 13:1. For a novice, the draw stroke is a complex sequence of movements which must be carefully coordinated and performed. The little movements or sub-routines which form the components of this skill, however, are relatively simple and the novice knows how to do them.

In the early stages of learning the novice spends a great deal of time thinking about the way in which the various sub-routines are organised. Performance will be highly variable as the learner experiments both physically and mentally. The coach can help by providing a 'running order' (like the key points recap mentioned earlier) or by use of progressive practices in which one element of the skill is added at a time.

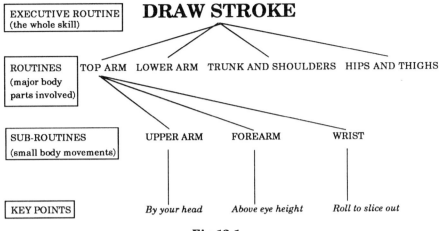

Fig 13:1

In the intermediate stage, the learner gets the various components arranged correctly more of the time. Performance becomes increasingly consistent as the sequence becomes second nature. The coach must ensure that the order which the beginner uses is the correct one since, once acquired, such habits are hard to break. Encourage the student to think through what he did straight after a correct performance of the skill. Paying attention to the 'feel' of the movement is particularly useful at this stage.

At the final stage the skill is performed almost identically every time with little conscious mental effort. The paddler can now take in the sights, worry about the line through the rapid or, of course, move on to a more complex situation in which the original skill is used as a sub-routine itself. The 'expert' is now back at the novice stage again, albeit at a higher level of performance. A compound stroke like the bow rudder is a good example. First the draw stroke is taught, and then incorporated into the new skill. Eventually the bow rudder itself is performed automatically. The paddler's concern is now when to do the stroke, not how.

In summary therefore, the learner must:

o Choose the right sub-routines from his movement library

o Mentally and physically experiment to get them in the correct order

o Work to perfect this sequence and eliminate unnecessary movements

o Practise the now established sequence until it is automatic

o Learn when to use the skill.

Returning to the earlier example, the break-out can now be broken down into as many sub-routines as necessary to suit the abilities of an individual or group. The actual bow rudder might be broken down into sub-routines controlled by an executive programme, and practised on still water until the stroke has reached the final 'autonomic' stage. The sweep stroke might be sufficiently good mechanically, but might need practising in a series of exercises on moving water. Some work on balance and body position related to edging or carving might be necessary. Acceleration and deceleration exercises in a straight line on moving water might help in the judgement of the effects that the current has on the boat. Turning exercises between the eddy and the current will help develop the 'feel' for the movement. When sufficient practice has taken place, an executive programme can be given to organise the sequence of sub-routines. (Some exercises or sub-routines will be missed out since they should happen automatically). The programme might be:

o Paddle at the eddy

o Sweep stroke

o Edge the boat

o Bow rudder

o Correct your position.

You might wish to use only: sweep, lean, bow rudder. It is essential to give a demonstration of a good break-out before all this work is done, since it helps make the exercises more meaningful.

Now let us look at the correction of faults. Firstly, there is a tendency to interfere too soon. Beginners fare better by actual, uninterrupted practice, i.e. practice during which the only feedback is from the pupil's own feelings and observations. If the instructor tries to correct too soon the beginner cannot sort out what is relevant, and we are back with the 'overload' situation.

Don't leave it too late though The old adage 'Practise makes Perfect' should read 'Practise makes Permanent'. Too many repetitions of the wrong skill results in a well learnt but wrong performance. Only perfect practise makes perfect so keep a careful eye on your tyros, especially at the intermediate stage.

Wherever possible, the instructor should, when trying to correct a fault, get the beginner to discover the 'correct' style through his own feedback. So instead of pointing out that the blade is at the wrong angle, it is better to say, 'Move the blade at this angle and compare the result with the angle that you have it at now'. The analysis of the individual's own performance through feedback and discussion becomes an important skill in itself when we are trying to refine the skill still further. The earlier we start to develop this skill, the better. I accept that this technique is not always possible and that it is sometimes inefficient, but it has another advantage. The individuals themselves are deciding what is the correct technique for them. I believe that we should be aiming at teaching the accepted correct technique and, in most individuals, we should except to see most of the components of that technique. However, we do not have a standard person to work with, and people's mental and physical abilities vary. The correct technique therefore is the one that produces the best performance for an individual at that particular stage of their development.

There are things that we recognise as common faults and instructors become very good at picking them up and sorting them out. The question that we should ask ourselves is, 'What do I do that causes my groups to have these common faults ?'

If we return to our model, there are a few points worth remembering. Children are always learning new sub-routines but adults tend to learn by reorganising or re-patterning existing sub-routines in new sequences. This is one reason why children need a variety of movement experiences when they are young to provide them with the resource of sub-routines for later use.

The ACTIVITY part of IDEAS is fairly straightforward, except that people tend to practise the things that they are good at if left to their own devices. Ensure that the strokes are practised on both sides and in a variety of ways. Practising a skill in one way is the best way to learn a skill which you will only perform in one way: eg a rowing stroke. Canoeing strokes must be adaptable to a variety of situations and demands. Sometimes strokes must be adopted very quickly indeed. The ability to apply your basic skill, say a draw stroke, in a variety of situations is only developed by variety in practice. Be imaginative and do not forget to maintain, or even increase, the variety for better performers.

Unfortunately, in practice, not everyone responds well to having things broken down into small units and then re-assembled. They would prefer to take the skill in as one complete unit. This may be characteristic of the way that they always learn, or something that they prefer at a particular stage of their learning. Certainly at the more advanced stages of coaching (refining the techniques) it is either impossible or inappropriate to break the complete skill down. In these situations, different techniques need to be employed.

VISUALISATION

Some individuals are naturally good at visualisation, but most people, with a little practice, can achieve sufficient competence to derive benefit from it. When you can see yourself performing a physical skill, the muscles actually move. In the brain the various connections are being made. The more refined your mental organisation, the better will be your physical skill. This 'mental rehearsal' is now used in a wide variety of sports.

Before looking at what can be achieved with visualisation techniques, let us look at ways of helping an individual visualise well. You need to do it regularly. You should enjoy it. Relax before starting but remain alert throughout. Try to use as many senses as possible. Aim to control the images, and set yourself realistic goals to visualise. You need to decide on your point of view. Are you running through the movement from inside, or are you outside watching your performance ? The executive programme is very useful to help organise the sequence of images. It is also worth persuading paddlers to talk about what they are doing, as verbalisation may help the visualisation process.

Most people tend to be very sceptical of visualisation techniques until they become aware of the extent to which they have been used to solve problems. If an athlete becomes injured and cannot practise, then his performance deteriorates. Once he has recovered, it takes time to make up for lack of training. Many sports have used mental rehearsal to help. For example, a high jumper with a leg injury and unable to train physically can mentally run through his technique. There is sufficient evidence to suggest that if mental rehearsal is used it will take less physical training to restore previous performance.

The slalom paddler has a problem when only one practise run on the course is allowed. It is obviously better if you have several runs and if you cannot do it physically then the next best thing is to do it mentally. This has been used in slalom training with some encouraging results.

However, it is not just at the top level that the technique is relevant. It could be used, for example, to help the learning of the eskimo roll. During the 'struggling-up' stage an almost effortless roll is often performed. If the paddler is stopped immediately after a good roll and asked to go through it mentally several times, good technique is being reinforced. One of the problems of rolling is that paddlers are frequently practising, and therefore learning unsuitable techniques. The wrong technique becomes ingrained, and it can become difficult to break out of this vicious circle.

Also we find that persons proficient at rolling in a pool forget to roll in the river situation. If you are practising some white water exercises in a situation where a capsize is likely, then to mentally rehearse the roll several times before starting your practice could be very worth while.

You may remember the memory problems faced by the learner - hence the need for a recap of key points before practice. These problems are often magnified on the river where the novice must wait his turn for a chance to attempt the skill. Visualisation can help to keep the key points fresh in the tyro's memory until he reaches the front of the queue. Even reciting the sequence of instructions is effective in bridging the gap between demonstration and first attempt.

It is possible to work the opposite way round and ask the paddlers to run through an unsuccessful attempt, so that they can compare it with the model that they are aiming at. Running through a skill in slow motion is possible mentally, and this aids analysis.

To summarise: visualisation techniques can be used as 'instant pre-play' (going through a skill just prior to doing it), 'instant replay' (looking at a skill once it has been performed) and to provide practice when it is not physically possible. Visualisation techniques are mainly concerned with refining skills rather than with basic learning.

A technique which relies on visualisation which is worth a brief mention, is the 'as if' technique.

An example of this technique might be linked in with film or video. Once the paddler has watched the video, the coach asks him to paddle 'as if' he were the world champion seen on the film. The paddler can visualise elements which make up the style of the champion and this can improve his own technique.

Having come this far with an adaptation of a visualisation technique, you may have realised that we have entered the world of the 'inner game'.

THE INNER GAME

This method is based on the idea that to every game there are two parts: an outer game and an inner game. The outer game is played against an external opponent, or obstacles, and the method of achieving this is through the coaching of physical movements. The inner game is the game that takes place in the mind of the player, and is played against such obstacles as lapses in concentration, nervousness, self-doubt, and self-condemnation. Developing the mental skills to deal with these factors is the subject of the inner game.

In his book, *The Inner Game of Tennis,* Timothy Gallwey refers to the discovery of the two selves he calls self 1 and self 2. I can remember times, particularly when I was competing, mentally scolding myself for a mistake. 'You stupid thing Now you have some time to make up. Keep the next break-out really tight'. This raises the question of who is 'I' and who is 'myself' ? The inner game identifies these two selves as the conscious teller, self 1, and the unconscious automatic doer, self 2. The relationship between self 1 and self 2 is critical and self 1 does not trust self 2 even though the unconscious, automatic self is extremely competent. By thinking too hard, self 1 produces tension and muscle conflict within the body. He is responsible for the error, but heaps the blame on self 2. Then, by condemning it further, undermines his own confidence in self 2. Perhaps you have started a slalom run and suddenly found yourself ten gates down the course going fast and clear. Suddenly you think, 'this cannot go on, I will hit a gate soon.' A few moments later this happens. The run has been spoilt because the self-doubt has crept in. If this has happened to you, or something similar has occurred in a different situation, then you can identify with the idea, even if you find the notion of self 1 and self 2 difficult to comprehend.

The inner game concept incorporates a number of techniques to help prevent self 1 from interfering with self 2 in a detrimental way. To stop thinking would be ideal, but this is difficult to do, so the next best thing is to find something interesting to occupy self 1. I remember some years ago a paddler who fell in every time he broke into the current. He could describe exactly what he should be doing, but no matter what I did, he continued to fall in. Was self 1 interfering with self 2 ? Feeling that neither of us had anything to lose, I decided to give self 1 something to concentrate on. I told him for the moment to forget everything he had been taught, because there was one way round the problem, but it would require his full concentration on the new technique. What he had to do when he reached the moving water, was to reach out with the paddle on the downstream side and hold it flat above the surface. The blade had to remain within 10 to 15 cm off the surface of the water at all times It was, therefore, necessary to move it up and down over the waves. We were rewarded with instant success, and were soon working towards the normal method from a position of confidence. I have since used the method successfully on other occasions.

However, self 1 can be of use to self 2 if the relationship is the right one. You do not want the analytical powers of self 1 to view the performance critically, but rather to observe what has happened in a non-judgmental way. Perhaps an example will help to clarify this.

A competitor on a slalom run down a course hits a pole, and he judges it as a disaster. A close rival on the bank observes the same incident and judges it as the best thing that has happened all day ! The gate judge observes what has happened and writes down the appropriate penalty, making some notes in case he is asked about it later. You need to learn to look at your own performance in the same non-judgmental way as the gate judge.

This might be achieved by asking the performer to rate the pressure on the blade of the paddle on a scale of one to ten, whilst performing a particular skill. The blade angle might then be changed, the skill repeated, and the results compared.

One of the main aims of the inner game is to increase the performer's awareness of what is happening. Develop the 'feel' of the kayak, body, paddle and water. This might involve performing a skill with the eyes closed to cut out unwanted visual signals, so that the performer can concentrate on the feel of the movement, or the paddle might be moved by the instructor in the required way and the canoeist who still holds the paddle asked to concentrate on how the movement feels.

In fact, we soon discover that many instructors have used techniques employed in the inner game. Most have used a game of tag to liven up a session, knowing that it rapidly improves canoeing skills. However, they have not consciously set out to find a game to occupy self 1, and so allow self 2 to get on unhindered.

DISCOVERY LEARNING

This method is based on allowing the beginner to discover the knowledge and skill that he or she already possesses. Many of the skills needed to be able to canoe have been previously acquired. Beginners often find a perfectly acceptable method of launching a kayak, sorting out the feathered paddle, and can manoeuvre to a given spot. So it is argued that it is unnecessary, and a waste of time, to teach some of these skills, particularly when there is a danger of giving too much information, which causes confusion. It is the task of the instructor to direct the discovery process. Can you stop ? Can you go backwards ? Free activity and games are an important part of the discovery process.

The method has many obvious advantages. Beginners are quickly on the water, likely to be well motivated and it maximises the transfer to canoeing of previously acquired skills. The beginner does not have to compare himself with the unattainable model produced by the instructor, and this helps to reduce frustration. The number of new variables are kept to a minimum.

However, there are limitations, and the time comes when certain basic skills need to be introduced. The most effective way would be for the instructor to build upon what has already been discovered by each individual. This requires considerable skill, and a good memory on the part of the instructor. It is possible to ensure a 'base level' of discovery for the group as a whole and then build on that common knowledge.

There are a number of other approaches to teaching canoeing, some of which we have looked at, but they are referred to by a different name. We need to familiarise ourselves with these terms.

WHOLE OR PART LEARNING

We have discussed this when we looked at IDEAS. The 'whole' method consists of a full demonstration of the whole stroke with added verbal instruction, followed by practise of the whole action. The 'part' method usually starts with a demonstration of the whole, and is then broken down into simple stages (sub-routines). The stroke is gradually built up to the whole through a series of logical progressions (executive programme).

Plate 13:g
Free activity and games are an important part of the discovery process
PHOTO: GERRY ELSMORE

354

There are individuals who can see a demonstration of a stroke and then produce a good copy. In this case the whole method is quick and efficient. It is, however, unlikely that everyone in the group will succeed, and then it becomes a question of sorting out the individual's faults in technique. Sometimes the reason for failing to achieve the desired result is clear and can easily be corrected. In a complex stroke there may be several faults, and correction requires considerable skill on the part of the instructor.

The part method requires the instructor to have the skill to break down the stroke into parts and then build them up into a logical progression. This requires a thorough understanding of each stroke, but once the progression has been worked out, errors are more easily spotted and corrected. Most people make good progress with this technique and the method is usually better for the more complex skills.

There is the danger that when a skill is broken down, something of the fundamental 'wholeness' is lost, and the instructor needs to be aware of this. Also, when breaking a stroke down, we slow the movement down. Speed is often an essential feature of a skill, and needs to be built back as soon as possible.

CHAINING AND SHAPING

Chaining is, in fact, the same as the part method of learning. The individual parts of a skill are thought of as links in a chain. The links are practised and built up into a complete chain.

The shaping technique is a variation of this method. It consists of taking a complex skill and simplifying it by leaving out some of the parts. It is practised in its simple form, and parts added as success is achieved. So the skill is shaped into the desired final performance.

The aim of the first part of this chapter has been to give some factual information, and to suggest some possible answers, but above all to provoke some thought which will help you develop your own techniques and style. Most of the examples that I have used are based on moving water, but the techniques could apply to teaching on placid water, swimming pools or the sea.

TEACHING CHECK LIST

When planning your teaching or coaching session, it is worth asking a series of questions:

o   What experience has the group or individual ?
o   What are my objectives ?
o   What teaching/coaching techniques will I use ?
o   What will be the content of the session ?
o   Will they enjoy the session ?
o   Will I enjoy the session ?
o   What equipment shall I need ?
o   Where shall I do it ?
o   Have I kept periods of learning short ?
o   Have I kept it simple ?
o   Have I planned for quality rather than quantity of practice ?
o   Have I made provision for making notes of the good and bad features of the session ?

The Star Tests provide good goals to work towards, and help to provide evaluation for the instructor, and a sense of achievement for the performer.

PRACTICAL SESSIONS

Putting the theory into practice requires us to get the group on the water. This could be just confined to one place or it could involve a journey. However, before we start we need to know something about the group and the general situation.

Background knowledge

The previous experience and expectations of the group will enable you to plan your session and choose a suitable stretch of water.

Clearly you need to be aware of any medical problems that individuals might have, and this may entail special precautions being taken. Also, an increasing number of people with physical difficulties are enjoying canoeing, and this can be a challenging and rewarding experience for the instructor.

Whilst it is desirable that all the group should not only be able to swim, but be confident and happy in the water, the non swimmer need not be excluded. We should like to see everyone become swimmers and so an enjoyable canoeing session for the non-swimmer might just provide him with the necessary motivation to learn to swim.

Plate 13:h
Whilst it is desirable that canoeists should be able to swim, an enjoyable session for the non-swimmer might just provide the necessary incentive to learn. A good flotation aid is essential
PHOTO: GERRY ELSMORE

Plate 13:i
Getting the group afloat. The instructor steadies a young beginner in her first attempt to get into a kayak

However, the instructor must ensure that there is close supervision, that everyone is wearing a buoyancy aid, that they are on placid water, and that the canoe or kayak used will allow easy exit in the event of a capsize.

The question of when and where to insist on a practise capsize has always created much debate. My personal preference is to have a group in a heated swimming pool for an introductory session, give a brief explanation or demonstration of how to get out, and then for the capsize to arise naturally out of the work being covered. Having done it once and fairly easily if not particularly cleanly, a deliberate and controlled capsize is usually perfectly acceptable. However, this is an ideal situation, and we are frequently faced with a novice group, no heated swimming pool, dirty cold water, and a cool windy day. To capsize your group, especially at the beginning of the session, puts people off, and creates other problems. We therefore have to content ourselves with an explanation, or perhaps dry land demonstration, and then be prepared to come quickly to the assistance of a capsized person. Practising a capsize is appropriate to certain craft, but if it is to be effective, the conditions and the instructor's approach need to be right. I have known instructors who were capable of creating such tension in the group through their build up to the capsize grown men have gone pale with fear !

On the subject of suitable clothing and other articles that individuals need to bring with them, it is a good idea to issue a written checklist. Frequently people new to the sport are given so much information on the subject that they forget an important item such as footwear. Times, venue and transport arrangements could well go down on this list.

You will need to be aware of any special requirements that the authority for which you are working has with regard to parental permission for those under 18 years of age. Written permission is a good idea, and you can include on the form space for medical information and swimming ability. Avoid, where possible, the situation where the form is brought in on the day. If forgotten, it can cause problems, and there might be information on the form that you require to plan for in advance.

It is important that you satisfy yourself that the equipment is in good order. It is your responsibility to check these items before you start, and obviously you need to be particularly careful if it is equipment that you do not normally use. Your own gear needs to be in good order, and remember to set a sound example, because future instructors may be modelling their approach on you.

Background knowledge checklist:
o What previous experience have members of the group ?
o What are they expecting from the session ?
o Are there any mental or physical problems with individuals in the group ?
o Are there any non swimmers in the group ?
o Does everyone know what clothing to bring with them ?
o If under 18, do they have parents' permission ?
o Do you have sufficient suitable equipment for the group ?
o What are the transport arrangements ?

Getting afloat
When talking to the group you need their undivided attention, and you will achieve this more easily by avoiding other distractions. Try to ensure that you are not talking over other noises, or competing with other visual distractions. Take the group out of the wind, make sure that the sun is not in their eyes, establish eye contact, and make sure that they can all see you clearly. Once on the water, pick a spot where they will not constantly drift downstream and where they can hold on easily to a fixed object. To have the group rafted, with the sterns on the bank, is a good way of organising things.

When you define the operating limits make sure that the group understands, that you can make yourself heard and that you can see all the group in the defined area.

Once on the water keep everybody active. Try to avoid the situation where just one person is working and the rest are watching and waiting for their turn. Although some people will require more help than others, make sure that you get round the whole group, helping and encouraging them all.

Capsizes need to be dealt with quickly and efficiently. Whilst you are dealing with a situation, the group should either cease activity, go to the nearest safe bank, or raft up. The course of action will depend on the circumstances.

If you remain in one place for the session it is not necessary for you to carry your safety kit with you. However, it should be close by - not ten minutes walk away in a car park.

Plate 13:j
When working with beginners, ensure that the canoes or kayaks used will allow easy exit in the event of a capsize
PHOTO: JERRY ELSMORE

Getting the group on the water:

o   Gather the group round for a quick introduction and briefing on the programme
o   Allocate canoes and equipment;   check the condition of both and that equipment is fitted correctly
o   Define the limits within which the group will operate once on the water
o   Explain the procedure for the group in the event of a capsize or other emergency
o   Keep any land drill short
o   The instructor is usually the first on and the last off the water.

PLANNING A JOURNEY

There are many more factors that come into play when planning a river trip, be it a short one day journey or a camping expedition. Determination of the strength and ability of the group acts as the starting point. Consideration must also be given to the time of year, the prevailing conditions of the water, the weather, the equipment available, the presence or absence of a land support party and the ability and experience of the instructor in charge. The aims and objectives of the trip are also important. Having taken these factors into account, the planning can start: where, when and for how long ?

Once a decision is made, carefully study the maps, sort out any access arrangements through local river advisers, check out lunch stops and campsites, plan the distance to be covered each day, and of course look for suitable places to abort the trip should an emergency arise. It is desirable, but not essential, that the leader has canoed the route before.

Plate 13:k(i) (top left)
Getting into a kayak. Have your paddle within reach and crouch low at a point where the cockpit is against the bank

Plate 13:k(ii) (top right)
Keep your weight on the arm and leg on the bank and step a foot into the kayak

Plate 13:k(iii) (left)
Sit on the rear deck and then drop your bottom onto the seat as your legs slide in. Maintain contact with the bank

Plate 13:l(i) (left)
When getting out, if you can raise your knees before lifting your weight off the seat it will be much easier

Plate 13:l(ii) (right)
If it is not possible, then raise your bottom onto the back of the cockpit by placing your hands behind as though you were sitting up in bed

Plate 13:m
People who are less agile can get in easily and safely from sitting on the bank with their feet in the boat, and simply swinging their weight across. Having the bank and the cockpit at the same height is useful here

Plate 13:n(i) (top left)
Getting in from knee-deep water

Plate 13:n(ii) (top right)
Straddle the boat and drop your bottom onto seat

Plate 13:n(iii) (left)
If your knees will not go in easily, raise yourself with equal pressure onto your arms, until the knees slip in

Plate 13:o (bottom)
The seal launch can be useful at times. It lets the paddler get the spray cover in place whilst sitting at ease. Remember, however, that this method can damage river banks

A journey is far more committing than a teaching session at one site, and the background details of those taking part assume greater importance. The same is true of the equipment. A slightly damaged spray deck may cause little problem in a two hour session, but may become of much greater significance at the end of a week's canoeing. These items need checking carefully.

Similarly, the information that you supply to those taking part needs to be well worked out. Make sure that all members have an equipment list, know the transport arrangements and times and what to expect en route. Depending on the nature of the journey this could require just a phone call, a duplicated sheet, or a full evening meeting. The less that you know about the group, the more thorough you need to be with the briefing. You may well wish to take a strange group on the water beforehand so that you can check their canoeing ability and get to know them.

Transporting the canoes, paddles and other equipment to the start, and collecting them at the finish, needs to be well programmed. The ideal situation is to have a land support crew. Various access points en route can be planned in advance and the group's progress monitored, besides help being at hand should an emergency arise. The support driver can then ferry any other drivers back to the start at the end of the trip. This prevents delays at the commencement of the journey, where otherwise cars have to be driven back to the finish and drivers returned in one car, before the trip can begin.

Before getting on the water, the instructor should give details of the system of control and how communication will be made. You may well need to establish a system of signals to deal with certain situations. This would be hand signals, paddle signals or, in an emergency, a whistle signal.

Clearly, the group should remain fairly compact so that you can gather them together quickly in an emergency, or if you wish to talk to them. If there is no competent person in the group who can lead, and the instructor is not familiar with the route, then he may lead himself. This is usually the best position from which to spot hazards, but has the disadvantage that it is not easy to keep an eye on the group. Some instructors favour bringing up the rear. For most of the time, you can see all the group, but spotting hazards is not so simple and communication can be difficult. I have always preferred to adopt a roving approach. You are then in a position to go and talk to and help members of your group. It gives you the freedom to move up to the front and inspect a possible hazard, or drop back to the rear to encourage a timid paddler. It is still a good idea, if possible, to have a competent paddler at the front whom nobody passes, and a tail-end charlie at the rear whom nobody slips behind. Within this sandwich I have generally let the group move about unless some situation dictates a more compact or single file approach. The 'buddy' system is also used, where the group is paired off and you are responsible for keeping an eye on each others' welfare.

Courtesy to other river users is expected. Where there is traffic, it is usual to keep to the right hand side, but watch for anglers, and move out away from lines. In fast flowing streams, pass on the far side or wait until the angler indicates that it is convenient to go through.

When approaching weirs or rapids, everyone should pull into the bank until the leader has inspected. If necessary, explain the route and make any necessary safety arrangements. Then organise the party through one at a time. For easy rapids or 'safe' weirs known to the leader, it may simply be a matter of sending a competent paddler down to show the route. Everybody then follows down in single file, ensuring that there is sufficient space between paddlers to allow for mistakes. For larger groups it is advisable to intersperse the tyros with competent paddlers, as the route tends to become lost by novices following one another.

The leader must not only look to the safety of the group, but to their enjoyment of the sport as well. Sheltered lunch spots, individual encouragement, pointing out things of interest, coaching individuals, spotting potential hazards well in advance and a cheerful presence, all contribute to a safe enjoyable trip.

Stay alert, because there can be potential hazards on even the simplest of journeys. Examples would be overhanging trees, rapids, weirs, shallows, mud banks, difficult access and egress points, anglers and fishing lines, bridges, islands in the river, repair and maintenance work, reeds, river weeds, other river users, pollution or floating objects such as logs and swans.

In addition, the elements themselves can cause problems. Cold weather and strong gusting winds can play havoc with a group. Tackling a rapid with the sun in the eyes is difficult. When rivers are in spate their character can change dramatically. The speed of the stream increases, canoeable weirs become places of danger, or for the expert only, and rapids increase their grading. Any obstruction in the water such as a tree, bridge, or rocks, poses a great threat to the paddler creating a potentially lethal trap with the powerful current acting on its upstream side. If, therefore, it is, or has been raining hard, the river is muddy, swirling along and up to the top of the banks, great caution must be exercised.

On large lakes and reservoirs winds create 'sea canoeing' hazards. In mountain areas, the water temperature is often very low even in mid summer. It would be advisable, if there is any doubt about even a single member of the group, that canoeing be restricted to the shore onto which the wind is blowing. Provided that the waves are not of a height to be dangerous, and this would be unlikely, and can be assessed visually, the worst that could then happen is a few capsizes with everyone blown ashore.

No matter how well the basic preparation has been carried out, in the final analysis it is the conditions prevailing on the day that decide whether or not the plan is to be put into operation, curtailed or cancelled.

Even after everyone is safely home, the leader's job is not necessarily done. There may be letters of thanks to write where appropriate, and possibly arrangements to be made for the maintenance and return of equipment. If there have been any access problems you will need to contact the river adviser.

Journey planning check-list

By asking yourself a few questions, it is possible to check that you have thoroughly planned your trip:

o What is the strength and ability of the group ?

o What are the aims and objectives of the trip ?

o Will there be a support party ?

o What equipment is available ?

o What are the transport and ferrying arrangements ?

o Are there sufficient maps and information on the route ?

o Are any permissions necessary ?

364

o   Have the campsites, access and egress points and other details been checked ?
o   Is an emergency plan required ?
o   What will need to be covered in the group's briefing ?
o   How will the group be organised on the water ?
o   Has the leader sufficient experience and ability for the journey ?
o   What arrangements will be necessary at the end of the trip ?
o   How will the prevailing water and weather conditions be checked ?

EQUIPMENT

Many a potentially dangerous situation has been rendered harmless because the leader has had the necessary emergency equipment to hand.

The risk of hypothermia (exposure) is always prevalent in United Kingdom, even in midsummer, and must be guarded against. The minimum requirement is to carry an exposure bag. For colder conditions the addition of substantial, high-insulation spare clothing and in some cases, a sleeping bag, is advised. A method of providing a hot drink is essential. There are some very good single-skin survival units, which for a group that does a lot of expedition work in cold conditions, would be worthwhile. All can climb inside for lunch, or whilst waiting during the 'ferry' arrangements.

On the Continent, whilst hypothermia must still be allowed for, there can also be a risk of dehydration and hyperthermia (heatstroke).

It is advisable when planning a journey on the Continent in midsummer, to take plenty of drink along. Often there is not easy access to shops once a journey is underway.

In early summer particularly, Continental rivers are often composed of melted snow, with a consequent contrast between air and water temperature. This is difficult to allow for, and speed of rescue is vital.

A first aid kit, suitable for the time of year and the journey being undertaken is essential. Obviously the longer the trip, the more remote the area, the more comprehensive the kit needs to be. The most common complaints are : blisters, splinters, cuts, headaches, insect bites and sunburn in the summer. However, you may have to deal with a dislocation or a broken bone.

Another requirement is a repair kit, and wonders have been performed with adhesive plastic tape. The most difficult conditions in which to repair a canoe are when it is very cold, raining and with a gusty wind. Tape will not stick well to a cold, wet boat, so you will need some method of drying and warming the area to be taped. This can be done by pouring on methylated spirits and lighting it, with interesting results on occasions ! A safer and more effective method of drying a damaged canoe is a small gas blow lamp, but you will need to carry matches which must be kept dry. A cigarette lighter is a handy way around this problem.

Plastic boats have become very popular, but they do present certain safety problems. There is a danger of the kayak folding, not splitting and thus trapping the canoeist. Some paddlers carry a cutting tool such as a serrated-edged diver's knife or a folding saw to deal with such emergencies.

For a member of the party to break a paddle is not uncommon, so you will need a spare pair of paddles in your boat. One pair to every four paddlers should be sufficient. Split paddles fit nicely in the rear compartment of most boats.

There are occasions when a tow line can be a very useful piece of equipment. It must have a quick release mechanism attached to the person performing the tow. The line might get caught, or some other emergency might arise requiring the instructor to break free instantly.

When rescuing on white water or very fast water, there is a greatly enhanced danger of a tow line becoming snagged. Should the quick release mechanism fail, or the paddler be unable to reach it, there is considerable peril. Caution, and careful consideration of the whole situation is necessary, therefore, before a tow line is used in these circumstances.

A throw line is a handy tool to carry in every leadership situation. Commercially available throw bags are the best system but it is quite possible to make your own. Use only floating rope of a thickness that will not cut your hands and between 15m and 20m in length, depending on the area in which you are going to be working.

An ordnance survey 1:50,000 map of the area is invaluable should an emergency arise, and help be needed quickly. A torch is a useful addition, particularly in the winter, together with a whistle.

All the kit in the world is only as good as the leader's ability to use it, and so practice is essential. Keep all emergency equipment packed and together when it is not in use, and in this way nothing is forgotten. Check for deterioration from time to time, and always take the opportunity to see what others have, as canoeists are wonderfully inventive people. Encourage an attitude of self-sufficiency in all those who look like making canoeing a lasting hobby.

Leaders equipment checklist:

o   Exposure bag/sleeping bag
o   Hot drink
o   First aid kit
o   Repair kit
o   Knife
o   Spare paddle
o   Throw line
o   Map
o   Torch
o   Whistle
o   Tow line.
o   Flares if at sea or on very large lakes.

14 Canoeists with special needs

Geoff Smedley

Geoff Smedley is the headteacher of a secondary school for children with special educational needs. He has worked with 'special needs' people of all ages for over twenty years, both in education and in the community. Geoff was Local Coaching Organiser for Warwickshire until he decided to direct his administrative and training experience towards giving other instructors an awareness of both the problems and potential for canoeing with people with special needs. He has been actively involved in the establishment of BCU Endorsement Courses for Instructors and Helpers and has written A Guide to Canoeing with Disabled Persons *published by the BCU.*

INTRODUCTION

The words 'disabled', 'handicapped' and 'special needs' are often used interchangeably and, as a result, there is often some confusion about the meaning of, or difference between, them. In these notes the words will have these meanings:

Disability is the condition or ailment that an individual may have.

Special needs: if we can meet a person's special needs effectively then we can reduce the potential limitations imposed by their disability.

Introducing people with special needs

Introducing people with special needs to the sport of canoeing involves two disciplines. It requires both the expertise of teaching the skills of canoeing and an understanding of the effects of specific disabilities on the potential canoeist. The special need often has implications for the development of canoeing skills when seen through the eyes of the canoeing instructor. Perhaps more important, however, is the concern shown by parents, medical and care staff regarding the effects, good or bad, that canoeing has upon the person.

The breadth of knowledge necessary to understand the implications of all disabilities is beyond the ability of any one individual; in fact this chapter is a series of condensed extracts taken from the more complete *A guide to canoeing with disabled persons.*

Liaison is the key word to success. By fully utilising the experience of the two disciplines, canoe sport and the education and care of people with special needs, there is an increased possibility that a programme will be successful. Thus the canoeist with special needs will realise his or her full potential in the sport with the minimum of risk and the maximum pleasure and satisfaction.

Plate 14:a

When considering the needs and capabilities of people with special needs, it is more helpful to examine what the individual can and cannot do, with an emphasis on what he or she can do, rather than make assumptions based on a label or category. Each person with special needs is an individual with individual needs.

The following general guidelines assist the understanding of special needs:

o   Get to know the person with special needs and, where applicable, those people who provide his or her day to day support and care.

o   Familiarise yourself with his or her disability. Find out what particular problems each individual faces and how he or she comes to terms with them.

o   Have a clear idea of the individual's special needs in relation to the programme you are offering. Take into account transport, access conditions, need for instructor support, equipment, water conditions, temperature and weather.

o   Have a well thought out strategy for dealing with emergencies, ie capsize, muscular spasm, incontinence, and so forth.

o   Know what drugs or medical aids (eg 'Spinhalers') may be necessary and under what conditions they are to be administered.

o   Have the Medical Enquiry Form at hand to refer to.

A positive attitude by the instructor to the person's special needs and ability to take part in the programme is essential to reassure the person and his or her parents, teachers, care staff, physiotherapist or doctor.

Always keep an open mind. Your aim should be to enable persons who are disabled to participate with standard equipment and with the same programme objectives as for an able-bodied person. You should only modify equipment or programmes if it is the only means by which you can meet the person's special needs.

Plate 14:b

MEDICAL ADVICE

Within the book *A guide to canoeing with disabled persons,* mentioned earlier, is an appendix with notes for a number of medical conditions and the implications they have for a canoeist. However, this is not the complete answer and I believe an instructor can do no better than to heed the advice given by the late Ron Moore who had considerable experience of canoeing with persons with special needs.

'The leader must first seek medical advice. Everyone should be free to decide whether the pleasure derived from an activity is worth the risks involved and an objective medical report will be an important factor in making this decision. It is unfair to ask a doctor to sign a form indicating that a disabled person is fit for canoeing, especially if he is not familiar with the standards of care and protective equipment which may be available. Ideally, a medically qualified person will be closely associated with the club or group and will be someone with the insight to distinguish between temporary problems caused by lack of exercise and real disabilities which will be more long-lasting or permanent'.

It is important that you use an enquiry form for each individual disabled person that you take canoeing. If the medical adviser for that person says something on the form that you do not understand, get a clear explanation so that you know how you must react to any misadventure.

There is a suggested format for a Medical Enquiry Form at the end of this chapter.

AWARENESS

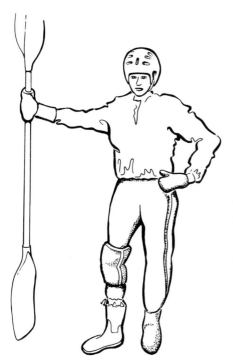

Physical disabilities

Several conditions such as cerebral palsy, spina bifida, muscular dystrophy and polio, etc, may result in a lack of sensation and poor circulation. Such canoeists are, therefore, more susceptible than most canoeists to injury from abrasions and bruises caused by bumps and scrapes and to the effects of being cold and wet.

Many canoeists with a physical disability, such as arthritis, also tire easily and when they get tired their disability is exaggerated. When you consider clothing for these canoeists, extra warmth and more protection may be necessary.

On the whole physical disabilities are usually clearly seen and appropriate

Fig 14:1
Give special attention to clothing.
Extra warmth and more protection
may be necessary

Fig 14:2
*Visually impaired
paddlers can participate
in kayak journeys in
doubles. In a double fitted
with a rudder the sighted
paddler would use the
front cockpit; otherwise he
would sit in the rear
where he could best
control the steering*

action can be taken according to the special needs. Some disabilities are less easily seen and care must be taken to see that the implications of the disability are identified and understood.

Sensory disabilities

Hearing or visual impairment can vary according to the severity. Some canoeists will need one-to-one supervision, both on and off the water, whilst others can cope within a larger group as long as someone is aware of their special needs.

Diabetes, asthma and epilepsy

These are 'hidden' disabilities and it is very important that the group leader is aware of any canoeists with these disabilities so that he can be prepared to meet their special needs, and not underestimate the implications of such problems. For canoeists with epilepsy the advice of the medical consultant must be sought particularly with regard to the situation and the programme the canoeist may undertake.

Multiple Disabilities

Some canoeists may have more than one disability. For example, the leader could be aware of a persons diabetes but have overlooked the fact that the same person is deaf.

Communication

With the majority of these disabilities, and allowing for speech problems, the person involved is usually able to communicate with you in an intelligent way and respond accordingly to any canoeing programme. For a person with a mental disability these assumptions cannot be made and so special consideration will need to be given to their problems.

Mental disability

Whilst learning is limited to some degree, most mentally retarded persons can acquire basic skills if they are given time and sufficient frequent prompts to their learning.

Problems faced by the instructor will be those of generating a suitable learning programme, concerns about the ability of the mentally retarded person's ability to judge situations and by 'disturbed' behaviour patterns.

When the impairment of the ability to understand or perceive danger is a concern then the best solution is to use a 'buddy' system. This is a pairing of the mentally retarded person with a competent person. If the buddy can be someone who knows the mentally retarded person, this is all the better. Ideally you should aim to train your helpers to be canoeing buddies !

With some forethought and general consideration you can avoid most of the situations that create problems for mentally retarded persons and in doing so you will increase the level of their achievement. The following should be considered:

o   Treat them as normally as you treat other persons in the group.

o   Allow for their difficulties in comprehension by giving instructions in a simple straightforward way. Lack of understanding leads to frustration. It is generally better for mentally retarded persons if you use practical demonstration as the main teaching aid.

o   Mentally retarded persons generally take longer to learn skills than other persons. By breaking the skill down into easily learnt stages there is more likelihood of success. Each new skill should be drawn from existing skills and once learnt should be linked into the next skill. Within your coaching programme remember that a little training and a lot of play makes a good recipe for both enjoyment and success.

o   Be prepared for fear and timidity that if not met sympathetically will put the mentally retarded person off canoeing. Give careful consideration to the type of canoe so as to give maximum stability. Encourage clothing that is comfortable. Seek an environment that is safe and reassuring. The key words for success and confidence are familiarity and security. Build these two concepts into your programme from the beginning. The use of open canadian canoes with a competent canoeist as 'captain' can often introduce even the most fearful to the canoeing programme. As the mentally retarded person grows in confidence then canoes such as the Caranoe, Beaver and Rob Roy can be introduced. Eventually many will paddle conventional kayaks or canoes. Be prepared though for those who will not go beyond being a passenger in an open canadian canoe. This in itself is a valid experience giving a tremendous sense of achievement and a source of great pleasure to a person who is mentally retarded.

o   The instructor needs to be very conscious of the mentally retarded person's often apparent disregard for danger. This is more likely to be a lack of awareness of either the situation, or the consequences of a particular course of action that leads to danger. The instructor must draw the attention of the mentally retarded person to impending risk situations in such a way that the pupil will be able to recognise such situations himself in time.

o   The attitude of the instructor and the buddy is paramount to a successful relationship. It must be based on a balance between:
  o   sensitivity and firmness
  o   friendliness and authority
  o   enthusiasm and security
  o   small steps yet not boredom, and
  o   challenge that is not frustrating.

Finally, the emotions of the mentally retarded persons are often closer to the surface and are more easily aroused than with other disabilities. When a mentally retarded person gets upset, often the only person who can resolve their problem is someone who knows them well. A simple matter such as a forgotten towel or the 'wrong' paddle can create a situation. The outcome may be tears, sulks, a bout of swearing or a temper tantrum. To be able to get to the root of the problem quickly is essential. The help of the parent, care assistant or teacher is often invaluable in such situations, but do bear in mind that the instructor and buddy will gain the confidence of the mentally retarded person eventually and so will themselves become just as capable. Given time, a little patience and understanding, it surprising what the mentally retarded person - and their instructors - can achieve !

GETTING STARTED
The process of developing a suitable programme requires three basic stages:
o   Preparation
o   Education
o   Participation.

Preparation

Accessibility
Can participants get:
o   To the site
o   Into the changing rooms/toilets
o   Into the canoes
o   Out of the water ?

Physical needs
Are the participants:
o   Confident in the water
o   Suitably dressed
o   Suitably equipped ?

Is the course:
o   Adequately staffed *
o   Resourced for emergencies and first aid ?

Can participants and staff communicate? In some disabilities the person may have considerable speech difficulties. Always be aware that a number of these people are very intelligent and respond accordingly.

Will it be necessary to provide a preparation programme to develop strength and fitness etc?

Social needs

o   Is a 'confidence' session required?

o   Does everyone know what are the nature and aims of the programme?

Risk

Risk is a variable factor for everyone but it is often exaggerated by disability. For some, the element of risk is the adventurous edge to the sport that gives the participant the sense of satisfaction and raises their self esteem. The element of risk must be determined according to the needs of the individual but careful planning will ensure that there is no undue risk.

Safety

Safety will be featured in all aspects of preparation but it does no harm to keep it as a separate heading to double check. In particular it is necessary to bear in mind:

o   Confidence in the water

o   Proper clothing and suitable equipment

o   Adequate experienced supervision

o   The physical and mental 'readiness' of the individual

o   Emergency and first aid procedures

o   An acceptable level of risk

Education

The participant

Start by considering the question 'why canoe?'. It could be said that many people with special needs have already a number of problems that create difficulties and discomfort in their lives so why add to these by taking up a sport that may add further risks and discomfort. The same basic argument, however, can be used in another way. It is because people with special needs have problems associated with their disability which create a reduced quality of life, that an activity such as canoeing can be so important. Why should these people be denied the same fun, sport, adventure and sense of personal achievement from canoeing as the able-bodied enjoy? A discussion with the individual about the nature and extent of the sport, what he or she might realistically hope to achieve and an honest appraisal of the risks involved might precede any programme.

Participation

Participation can be at a number of levels and can be either as an integrated activity within a canoe club or group, or it can be segregated as a special group for people with special needs. There can be no steadfast rule, except that it should be our aim to give people with special needs the same opportunities as every other canoeist wherever possible.

Experience has shown that some people with special needs can engage in sports as though they had no handicap. They are capable of competing alongside the able-bodied and should have the opportunity to do so. Disabilities in themselves must not cause any person needlessly to be denied opportunities.

EQUIPMENT

Clothes

Bear in mind what has already been mentioned about the need for warmth and protection for some special needs. An alternative to neoprene wet suits, and much easier to take on and off, are the clothes made of thermal pile fabric. Such clothing offers virtually the same insulation as neoprene and whilst it may not be quite as efficient for shock absorption or pressure resistance, some protection is offered with considerably more comfort and ease of movement. Thermal pile clothing can also be easily adapted or even tailor-made with 'velcro' fastenings and non-standard proportions for ease of dressing and undressing.

It is generally advisable to remove calipers when canoeing. However, providing that they will come to no harm by immersion in water, it has now been shown by disabled canoeists who paddle wearing their callipers that the additional support that they get more than offsets the problems of drying them out after use. Do take advice from the physiotherapist, however. You must satisfy yourself that safe capsizes are possible and that the weight of the callipers still allows the person to float and swim safely in their buoyancy aid or lifejacket.

Buoyancy aids and lifejackets

The wearing of some form of buoyancy is essential, but the wearing of any flotation device seriously affects the swimmer's attitude in the water. It requires the swimmer to modify his technique to enable him to swim effectively. For people

Plates 14:c (left) and 14:d
Two paddlers with the illness cerebral palsy. Both are using the type of hand splint shown in Fig 14:7c
PHOTO: SARAH ASHMEAD

375

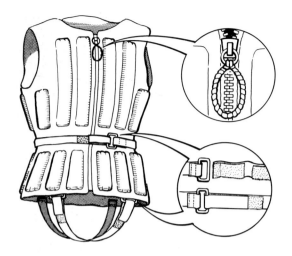

Fig 14:3
*Simple modifications to a
buoyancy aid: tab on zipper
slide; waist belt secured with
velcro to help the jacket fit
snugly; and crutch straps to
keep the jacket in position
during flotation*

with special needs, who have to adapt the skills and techniques of swimming anyway to enable themselves to find propulsion, the addition of a flotation device adds further complications. Practice, therefore, is essential to develop the correct technique to give people confidence in their own ability in the water.

Whichever aid is decided upon certain basic modifications can be made to enable the canoeist to put the aid on, take it off or make it more secure. Zips are easier to use if larger than usual tabs are fitted to the zipper foot and the bottom of the zip to give increased purchase. Jackets that are fastened together using tapes can be secured instead by using either the double ring type of fastening or by using 'velcro'. To help the buoyancy aid or lifejacket to fit the wearer more snugly and to prevent it from riding up on the body when the wearer is in the water, crutch straps can be fitted. Support for canoeists who have back problems can be built into the buoyancy aid. In some cases just the positioning of a pad of closed cell foam inside the back of the aid can be very beneficial.

Consideration can be given to the need for extra buoyancy. Whilst it is undoubtedly necessary for some disabled persons, especially people suffering from epileptic seizure, it may not be the most desirable for others. Bear in mind that the standard buoyancy aid will support even an unconscious person in the water, and that the life jacket is only sure to support an unconscious person face up in the water when it is fully inflated and when the person is not wearing clothing (such as wet suit trousers) that will unbalance the effect of the life jacket.

Helmets

Helmets should be worn whenever the canoeing conditions and the experience of the canoeist dictate that they are necessary. You may consider that helmets should be worn all the time for the purposes of additional safety. Be careful, however, that in adopting this policy you do not make canoeists with special needs more conspicuous by insisting on wearing helmets when no other canoeist is wearing one. You must strike a balance between safety and over-protectiveness.

376

Plate 14:e
A Caranoe with spray cover secured by velcro

Spray decks

Spray decks are very useful for keeping the canoeist dry and subsequently warmer. They do, of course, make exiting from the canoe that much more difficult. This can be offset by ensuring that the elastic holding the spray deck in place is only as tight as it needs to be. There are some spray decks that have an adjuster to allow the tension on this elastic to be varied. Pull-off tags can be made bigger and easier to get at. Finally the spray deck can be made and attached using 'velcro' so that it will pull away in the event of a capsize and yet be quite effective in keeping most of the water out in normal use. 'Velcro' is also used to keep spray decks in place when the canoe does not have the traditional cockpit rim as on the Caranoe. This practice is adaptable for use with other craft but always fix the 'loop' side of the 'velcro' to the deck since this is less abrasive than the 'hook' side and so less likely to injure the paddler.

Canoes and kayaks

Although the aim should be to use the conventional canoes or kayaks there are a number of craft available that can facilitate an introduction to canoeing for people with special needs.

A developmental kayak, which is sat on rather than in, is the Rob Roy made by Pyranha. The construction is in roto-moulded plastic. This material is warm and soft edged thus preventing many of the abrasive problems encountered with the grp kayak or canoe.

A kayak designed principally for the leisure market is the Caranoe from Valley Canoe Products. This craft is also gaining in popularity as a kayak for use by disabled persons. The Caranoe has a fluted hull giving it great stability yet through careful design it still manages to stay reasonably manoeuvrable. Although it is more like a conventional kayak in that it has a closed deck and the paddler

377

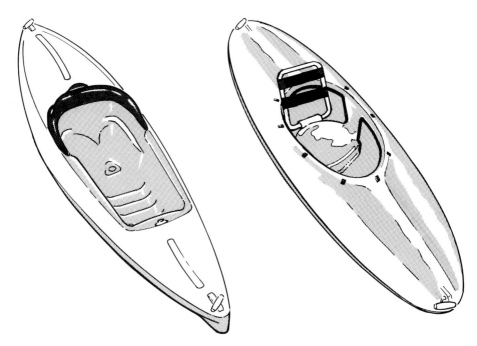

Fig 14:4a (left) and b
The Pyranha Rob Roy (left) and the Valley Canoe Products Caranoe

Plate14:f

sits in a cockpit, the cockpit is very large and its edges are rolled in to give it a very smooth edge.

A spray deck can be fitted with 'velcro' tabs and is quite effective in keeping the canoeist dry although it is not as watertight as a conventional spray deck. A backrest is also available for the Caranoe although fitting a back rest to any kayak or canoe is possible.

With the advent of the Placid Water Scheme, kayaks such as the Poly Pippin from Fladbury Canoeing are now becoming available. As well as being ideal for introducing novices to canoeing they are also very suitable for canoeists with special needs. These placid water kayaks have large open cockpits, are very stable and require only a minimum effort to propel in a straight line.

An alternative to the kayak is the open canoe. This offers a wide variety of usage with disabled persons. The canoe can be paddled by one, two, or even three persons. It is capable of carrying passive passengers without difficulty. With a sighted paddler a visually disabled paddler can complete a canoe team that can progress safely.

AIDS AND MODIFICATIONS

Support

Backrests and protective padding can be fitted without difficulty. The illustrations show some back rests for canoes and kayaks although many other possibilities exist. Even the insertion of a block of rigid foam between between the back of the seat and the cockpit can give quite a substantial degree of support. Care must be taken to ensure that such back supports do not impede the exit of the paddler especially during a capsize.

Strapping the paddler into the canoe or kayak has been used successfully for some canoeists with special needs. This strategy has even enabled canoeists with no control over their lower body to eskimo roll a kayak successfully. If not

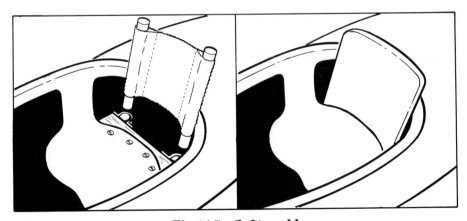

Fig 14:5a (left) and b
Two types of home-made backrests for kayak cockpits. Type b could be wood, foam, or even a swimming float

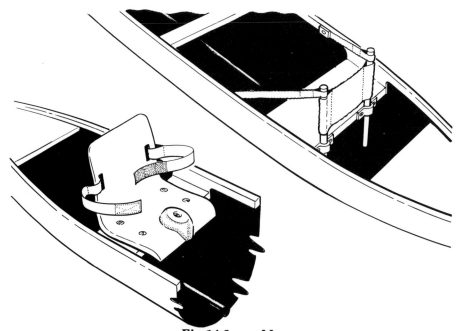

Fig 14:6a and b
Seats and backrests for open canoes

strapped in, paddlers with this disability would fall out of their kayaks when they turned over. This type of strapping must have some form of quick release and must only be used by a canoeist who is proficient and confident in his or her kayak. It is also essential that the technique for escaping from the canoe when capsized is practised fully in the security of the swimming pool before venturing onto open water. Effective straps for this purpose can be constructed from car seats belts.

Paddles

Common sense says use whichever paddle is best suited to the individual and his or her needs according to the disability. Aids that assist in the grip on the paddle are illustrated (Fig 14:7). The simplest is a loop of webbing that is fixed to the paddle and through which the paddler puts his or her hand. Another system is to fix a strip of 'velcro' to the paddle shaft. The corresponding strip of 'velcro' is sewn to a glove or mitten. Once the paddler has gripped the paddle the 'velcro' keeps the grip firm. This system will not work of course with a feathered paddle since it prohibits the necessary rotation.

Double bladed paddles usually come with a 90 degree feather. Whilst most paddlers can use these successfully, there will be some who will need unfeathered paddles. It is possible to buy paddles with a shaft split in the middle so that the blade can be set either feathered or unfeathered. This type of paddle can be very useful for the disabled paddler since it allows him or her to experiment with and without the feather.

Paddles are also made with a thin lightweight shaft. It is also possible to modify a standard paddle to give a thinner grip. A wooden shaft can be shaved down or an alloy shaft can be split and a piece of wood or grip with a thinner cross-section can be inserted. It is also possible to purchase, or adapt, paddles with grips or textured patches on the shaft that enable the paddler to determine the angle of the paddle by feel. These grips can be made quite easily with foam pads and

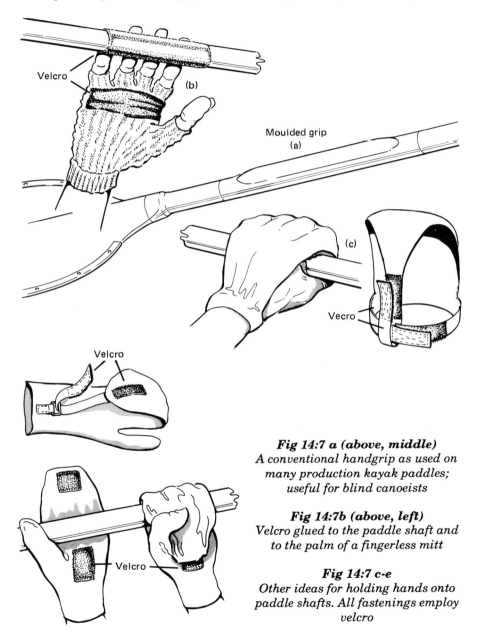

Fig 14:7 a (above, middle)
A conventional handgrip as used on many production kayak paddles; useful for blind canoeists

Fig 14:7b (above, left)
Velcro glued to the paddle shaft and to the palm of a fingerless mitt

Fig 14:7 c-e
Other ideas for holding hands onto paddle shafts. All fastenings employ velcro

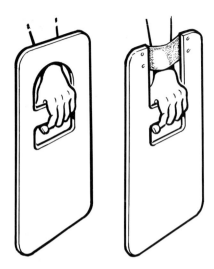

Fig 14:8 a and b
Some canoeists find it easier to use a small hand paddle. Version b has a leather or canvas strap added for comfort at the wrist

Velcro or D-ring fastening

Fig 14:9 a and b
A one-armed paddling aid which allows the use of both blades of a kayak paddle. B (left) shows an alternative fixing system for the forearm using D-rings which, once threaded up, may be tightened by mouth

Plate 14:g
PHOTO: GERRY ELSMORE

adhesive tape. Paddles that are very light are often necessary for canoeists with special needs who have weak muscles.

Some canoeists with special needs find it easier to use a small paddle blade that they hold in their hands, or even just use their hands to propel themselves along. One-armed paddlers can paddle a kayak using a double paddle quite successfully using the aid illustrated, which was designed by the late Paul van der Molen.

Instructors and helpers

Of all the resources you will need, these are the most valuable. They will need to be selected carefully and once you have found the right people they will need careful and thorough training. They must be sympathetic to the needs of the disabled persons without being sentimental. Above all they must be committed to the idea of helping canoeists with special needs and be prepared to meet both the tears and the joys that such an involvement implies.

There is an Endorsement Course for instructors and helpers for canoeing with disabled persons. Its purpose is to give leaders an awareness of the needs of disabled persons and the relationships between disabilities and canoeing, and to give them knowledge and skills to enable them to widen the scope of their existing leader qualification so that they may feel capable of introducing disabled persons to canoeing. Courses usually take place over a weekend and details may be found in the Coaching Calendar published annually by the BCU.

Creative problem-solving between instructor and canoeist can lead to the devising of strategies designed to serve both parties. For example, the person who can describe how much use he has in his legs or how much vision he has will enable the instructor to determine how much help that person needs and what form his coaching programme might take.

HELPING DISABLED PERSONS

Communication

Never speak down to a disabled person. It happens frequently that questions are directed not to the disabled person but to the parent or care assistant. The majority of disabled persons can speak for themselves and so direct your conversation to them personally.

Some disabled persons have speech problems: they know what they want to say but cannot articulate clearly. Be patient, listen carefully and you will probably 'tune in' to what they are saying. Do not be afraid to ask them to repeat what they have said, this is better than making a guess at what has been said and perhaps getting it wrong. Care staff and helpers often understand what the disabled person is saying through their familiarity with the person. Use this expertise to establish communication but, even though someone else may be interpreting responses to help you understand, always direct your conversation toward the disabled person.

When talking to someone in a wheelchair you will both find it more comfortable if you assume the same height to obtain eye level contact. Find a chair, or kneel beside the disabled person's wheelchair.

When to help

Always respect the desire of disabled persons for independence. It is often better to direct your attention to the problems of making access and removing obstacles that will then allow disabled persons to get about unhindered by themselves.

Plate 14:h

Fig 14:i

Fig 14:j (i)

Fig 14:j (ii)

PHOTO: SARAH ASHMEAD

With young persons and children you may feel sometimes that it would be easier, perhaps even kinder, to help them rather than stand and watch their slow painful progress. It is part of the young person's development, however, to learn how to get about. Today's child is tomorrow's adult, and as an adult he or she will almost certainly want to be as independent as possible.

In the main, disabled persons know when they want to be helped. When they do want assistance they will usually ask for it. The disabled persons themselves are also the best persons to tell you how to help them. They know which limbs they can and cannot control and the degree to which they can manoeuvre themselves, or how much they can see or hear. If a disabled person asks you to help you might then ask him or her, 'what do you want me to do ?'

Mobility

Blind or partially sighted persons do not have problems of physical mobility but they may need help to negotiate in certain situations when there may be a number of unusual or unexpected hazards.

If a disabled person needs to be helped by being lifted in or out of their wheelchair or canoe, bear in mind that whilst they may sometimes be a dead weight they are persons not sacks of coal. Give them the respect and dignity that being a person demands. Think about what you are doing, and if you have not had some training in lifting, leave it to the experienced helper

385

until you have been given some lifting advice. Correct training is important if the lifters and carriers are not to become disabled persons themselves! Many disabled persons have lack of sensation in some areas of their bodies. If, through careless handling the skin is bruised or grazed in these areas the injury often takes longer to heal than a similar injury to a healthy body. Lack of preparation may, therefore, result in someone who is disabled being prevented from taking part in the canoeing programme for weeks or even months because of one careless moment.

THE PROGRAMME

In essence, this should be no different to a programme devised for the able-bodied canoeist. In detail, however, some skills will have more or less importance depending upon the degree of disability. If possible an indoor swimming pool is the ideal environment in which to introduce people with special needs to canoeing.

It can be argued quite strongly that a 'placid water' type of programme is more advisable and appropriate to the initial needs of canoeists with special needs. Certainly by following such a programme the need for capsize drills and rescue procedures is greatly reduced if not in the number of occurrences at least in the level of risks incurred.

Swimming

The requirement to be able to swim cannot be applied to canoeists with special needs with the same conviction as it can to the able-bodied. Whilst it is desirable for all canoeists to be able to swim the inability to do this should not, in itself, stop any person with a disability from learning to canoe. Of more importance is the confidence of the person in the water. It is worthwhile trying out different types of buoyancy aids and lifejackets to see if a particular one is more suitable than another. This can only be tried with those canoeists for whom the choice of aid is not specific. A person who has epileptic seizures, for example, should be in an inflated lifejacket all the time.

Capsize

Capsize drill needs only to be introduced to students who are paddling the type of kayak from which there is the need to escape. The use of canoes, and open cockpit kayaks reduces the need for capsize 'drills' since paddlers will be able to extricate themselves from these boats quite easily. However, in the event of a canoeist falling out of, or off, the canoe or kayak it is advisable to have established some procedure for the rescue which is explained to all concerned.

Basic paddle skills

At this point the instructor falls back onto his training and experience of coaching the Star Tests, Placid Water Test, or the Proficiency skills since these are the basics for all canoeists with or without special needs.

Rescues

Towing is a skill frequently used by instructors with all kinds of students. It is a skill that needs to be practised since a poor towing technique can result in exhaustion for the person towing and a state of nervous distress for the person being towed. A towing technique that has proved very effective with disabled paddlers is the short tow. The aim is to pull the bow of the canoe to be towed close to the cockpit of the towing canoe and connect the bow loop or toggle to the tow line. The person in the towed canoe can lean on the rear of the towing canoe for support. This system of towing keeps the two canoes in close contact and prevents the usual yawing and slewing that occurs with other towing systems.

A further advantage of this system is that a canoe can be pushed. The canoe is attached by the bow in the usual way but the canoe to be towed is in front of the rescuer and the person being towed leans on the fore deck of the towing canoe. In this way the person being rescued is under the rescuers observation all the time. Canoeists with special needs may be taken into situations that can result in the need for deep water rescues. If this is planned for, then obviously these procedures should be practised. Extreme care should be taken, however, since as has been previously mentioned, some canoeists with special needs are very susceptible to the effects of cold water and can easily be hurt if they are knocked.

Extension activities
Depending on the skills and confidence of the students there are a number of activities to which they can aspire.

Rolling is within the capabilities of most canoeists and some with special needs have mastered this art within the winter training months spent in the swimming pool. Many students who have little or no strength below the waist develop extremely strong upper bodies and arms.

The wiggle and wriggle tests around a slalom gate are comparatively easy to set up in the pool and give students practice in a number of canoeing skills in what can be either a fun or a competitive situation.

Open water
Canoeists with special needs have tackled virtually all the branches of canoe sport: touring, white water, slalom, marathon and surfing have all been conquered. Everyone has to start somewhere but that somewhere, if ill considered, can discourage all but the most dedicated canoeist for ever. Choose your first outing, therefore, with some care. The weather should be warm and fine. The site should be sheltered. There should be good access to the water. The students should have equipment and canoes with which they are familiar, and therefore confident to use. You should have sufficient support staff for all your students to be instructed and supervised.

The emphasis should be on fun and the gaining of confidence.

Programme development
Having fun and enjoying oneself is a legitimate exercise. The tests and awards are there for all those who wish to work for them, but they should not be presented as the be-all and end-all of canoe sport.

Given the opportunity to enjoy 'messing about in boats' many students will, in fact, want to improve their skills. You will find the students achieve more if the motivation to work toward the Award Scheme comes from the students themselves.

The BCU supports the promotion of canoeing with people with special needs and encourages them to take the Award Scheme tests. The Union's policy is to

Plate 14:k
A deep water re-entry. Some of the instructors in this picture are themselves disabled

Plate 14:l
Support stroke practise. Notice the jointed paddle to allow for unfeathering of the blades

PHOTOS: SARAH ASHMEAD

avoid a separate system. Where a specific disability prevents a candidate from completing a particular part of a test the examiner may give the award with a suitable endorsement setting out the part of the test not completed. Approached in this way, awards help give canoeists with special needs confidence and improved self esteem.

MEDICAL ENQUIRY FORM

INFORMATION TO BE COMPLETED BY THE PARTICIPANT

Name_____ Age _____

Address _____ Tel _____

NHS No _____Emergency contact _____ Tel _____

Ambulant __ Partially ambulant __ Non ambulant __ Can propel wheelchair Y/N

Swimming Ability _____

General Nature of Disability _____

_____(Please refer also to chart overleaf)

Other relevant disabilities (eg: Asthma, epilepsy, diabetes)_____

DRUGS USED   Regularly_____ Dose _____

                    Emergency _____ Dose _____

NFORMATION TO BE COMPLETED BY THE COURSE ORGANISER

Description of Activity _____

_____

Duration _____ Dates _____

Access conditions _____

Site Conditions _____

Support Available Generally (State Qualifications) _____

Signed (Organiser)   Date

TO BE SIGNED BY THE PARTICIPANT'S DOCTOR (If considered appropriate)

This person is, in my opinion, fit to attend this course as described.

Doctor's signature _____ Date _____

Address _____ Tel _____

PLEASE DETAIL DISABILITY

Areas of Muscular Weakness _____

Areas Where Control May Be Poor or Weak _____

Any Limb Liable to Spasm _____

Areas Where Sensation May be Deficient _____

Indicate any Disability of a Sensory Nature _____

If you feel that it may be of help to the course staff, please add any comments about,: temperament, endurance, ability to follow instructions, particular likes or dislikes, speech, incontinence, appliances, etc.

TO BE SIGNED BY PARTICIPANT OR GUARDIAN (if participant is under 16)

All the information that I have given on this form is complete and correct. I know that there are risks of physical injury to my body present in the activities as defined. I consent to any medical treatment that may be necessary. I note that the course organisers cannot be held liable in the event of any accident involving death or personal injury, or for any property damaged or lost, unless it can be shown that the course organisers have been negligent.

Signed _____ Status_____ Date_____

Plate 14:m
PHOTO: SARAH ASHMEAD

FURTHER READING

BCU 1989; *Canoeing for Disabled Persons;* GEOFF SMEDLEY

BSAD (Watersports 1983); *Water Sports for the Disabled;* EP Publishing

Canadian Recreational Canoeing Association, Ontario; *A Resource Manual on Canoeing for Disabled People;* M ARTHUR M & S ACKROYD-TOLARZ

Coventry LEA, Coventry; *Childhood Illness and Disabilities;* J JOYCE (ED)

Croom Helm, London; *Handicapping Conditions in Children;* B GILHAM (ED)

Disabled Living Foundation, London; *Give us the chance* ; K LATTO

Disabled Living Foundation, London; *Outdoor Pursuits for Disabled People;* N CROUCHER

National Co-ordinating Committee on Swimming for the Disabled - Sports Council, London; *2: Lifting and Handling; 5: Medical Considerations*

15 Use of the Swimming Pool

Dave Ruse and Phil Quill

Dave Ruse is a lecturer in watersports with the inner London Education Authority. His imaginative enthusiasm has taken canoeing into the heart of large cities where it might least be expected to take place, and turned dull, and unattractive basins and waterways into exciting places for youngsters. He is the author of two books, one on canoeing games and the other about urban adventuring He has also been a top competition paddler, representing Great Britain in two World Championships in wild water racing C1.

Phil Quill is the warden of Woodmill canoeing and outdoor education centre in Hampshire. He has competed at the highest level in almost every aspect of canoe sport from slalom to marathon racing, and recently finished 5th in the K1 section of the gruelling Devizes to Westminster race Phil is a BCU Inland Coach and has led successful white water trips to the European Alps. He is one of a very active group of southern paddlers whose thinking and innovation has made an enormous contribution to coaching in canoeing.

INTRODUCTION

The swimming pool is an invaluable resource for canoeists. The clear, calm water dispels many of the beginner's fears giving him confidence to practise skills and safety drills, and to discover more about behaviour of the boat. More experienced paddlers benefit also from the pleasant atmosphere of the pool, as protected from the adversity of weather and cold water, they can concentrate on the improving of rolling or other advanced techniques. The teaching and analysis of eskimo rolling is covered in Chapter 12 of this Handbook, whilst Canoe Polo, a popular team game, is discussed in chapter 20.

The purpose of this chapter is to provide guidance to canoeists organising pool sessions, to encourage an imaginative approach to selecting activities, and to stress the safety considerations implicit in using pools for canoeing.

TYPES OF POOL

Few pools in this country have been built with canoe training specifically in mind, since the vast majority exist to provide a facility for swimming. Outdoor pools have never been entirely successful in Britain, simply because of our cool climate, but the few which are still in use are giving good service to paddlers. Indoor heated pools are most sought after by canoeists and, increasingly, they come in all shapes and sizes. Many authorities are now installing unusually shaped pools aimed at

391

the recreational and family swimmer in preference to the traditional rectangular shape. For most canoeing purposes, shallow water is preferable because instructors or partners can stand comfortably beside the person in the boat. A standard depth of about one metre is perfectly adequate for rolling and stroke practice, and is ideal for confidence building exercises.

If you are starting with the problem of teaching people to swim, it is well worth travelling to a special shallow training pool. These are built with toddlers and children in mind, but are also excellent for nervous adults.

All pools must be fitted with a handrail of some description. Those which use a tubular steel rail are especially good for canoeing sessions because of the similarity in feel to a paddle shaft. This type also provides good anchor points for ropes.

POOL CARE

It is important for every canoeist using a pool to develop a caring attitude towards it. Once damaged, the fabric of the pool itself can be very expensive to repair and might well mean the loss of the whole facility to the community for the period of the repair work. If we behave responsibly and are aware of the kind of problems which can be caused by canoes in and around the pool, then paddlers are more likely to be accepted as routine users. The following points are important:

o Boats must be scrupulously clean, inside and out

o Do not use metal edged paddles

o Polystyrene flotation block should not be used as it crumbles

o Make yourself known to the pool manager; establish a rapport so that he is aware of your concern for the pool

o Obtain a copy of the leaflet *The Swimming Pool and the Canoeist* from the BCU, which provides comprehensive guidelines for the use of pools.

SAFETY

It is a worthwhile exercise to watch a pool session in action and try to imagine the accidents which could happen. Take everything into account, from the moment people get changed, to getting the boats out of the pool.

Many coaches are of the opinion that the swimming pool is potentially just as hazardous an environment as any outdoor canoeing location. The apparent lack of danger, the familiar surroundings, and the holiday atmosphere, can easily lead to careless behaviour. This, combined with people, boats and equipment all in close proximity to each other, poses considerable real danger. Someone must be in overall control - aware of the false sense of security, and keeping a check on the euphoria. Accidents, however simple, need to be avoided: they spoil the fun, and interfere with valuable pool time.

The instructor in charge of any pool session should be familiar with lifesaving principles and techniques, and this includes a thorough working knowledge of expired air resuscitation and external cardiac massage.

Swimming and canoeing groups should never be allowed to mix, except when separated by a floating rope lane-marker.

Pool equipment, such as slides and diving board, can be a danger to a canoeist. Warn paddlers about these projections, and be prepared to rope the areas off, if necessary.

Plate 15:a
Wooden blades are best, and bows should be padded

A policy regarding non-swimmers needs to be established. Providing the water is shallow and there is adequate supervision, it should be possible to deal with small numbers of non-swimmers. As a simple precaution, they could wear buoyancy aids but these must fit properly and be well secured.

The instructor in charge needs to be able to see the whole pool area for which he is responsible at all times. This is essential, because pool sessions involve so much activity below the water surface. A person in difficulty needs to be spotted very quickly. Helmets should be insisted on for canoe polo, or any activity where a fall into the water might result in head injury.

The interior of all boats need to be checked for sharp projections which could cut bare feet. The location of first aid equipment and the telephone must be known. A first aid kit must be provided if not readily available on site.

Pupils must declare any medical problems before participating. Without prior planning and organisation, bedlam can ensue.

PLANNING AND ORGANISATION

Not every swimming pool manager will permit canoeing to take place, but it is always worth seeking an interview with the management to show that you are aware of the importance of pool hygiene and care. Be adventurous in your search for a facility. Many hospitals and universities have pools, as do schools and military establishments, and even some prisons permit use by outside groups in the evenings. The importance of establishing direct personal contact with the management cannot be over-emphasised. Those in charge will need to see that you are a responsible person, preferably a trained member of the Coaching Scheme, and a good organiser.

The following needs to be established once permission has been obtained:

o Insurance requirement
o Instructor/student ratios and so forth
o The minimum lifesaving requirement for the person in charge
o Whether the pool has its own fleet of boats and accessories
o The route for bringing boats in from outside, and the availability of a hose
o If there is a storage room, to allow the canoes to stay on the pool site between sessions
o The hire charge and system of payment (some pools are publicly owned, whilst others are private - the rates may vary considerably)
o The times that the pool is available for hire.

Some instructors have negotiated free pool time for their groups in exchange for running a few coaching sessions for others, and so it pays to be alert to opportunities for negotiation.

The size of the pool and the kind of course, or activity, being run, dictates the maximum number of pupils. This is determined by the total number of boats that can be practically fitted into the available space. A good rule is to use two students per boat. An excess of people standing around becomes a hindrance.

A basic skills session, a rolling course, or polo or slalom training, all require differing allocations of space per boat. Those responsible must ensure that the number of craft used is kept to a sensible maximum.

It cannot be emphasised enough that the success of swimming pool sessions depends on them being well organised from start to finish, and this includes planning the programme of activities, be it for a single session or a series.

Plate 15:b
A great deal of useful activity can be successfully undertaken in the relatively small area of a pool, but it must be planned and supervised thoroughly

EQUIPMENT

Boats

The best system for boats is to use a set which is kept exclusively for the pool and never allowed on any other water. Pool managers prefer this system and many pools own such a fleet. Kayaks made for pool use (often called 'Bats') are short: three metres or less, and have broad, rounded ends. Those made from polyethylene are the most popular as they are very durable, do not splinter and are kinder to the pool edges. Such boats have to take a considerable amount of rough treatment, so they must be of strong construction with the minimum of moving or breakable parts. Footrests are necessary, especially if rolling is being taught, but they must be of the simplest type. The chlorinated pool water is corrosive and will quickly render moving parts useless.

Boats with non-rounded ends require padding. This is not a simple job; holding something onto the smooth, tapering end of a boat so that it stays firmly in position is quite a design challenge. Just about every form of padding has been tried from wellington boots to sponge bals. A good solution is to use the polyurethane nose cones, which manufacturers of plastic canoes are producing, fixed on with tape or, more securely, with self tapping screws and washers. Do not forget that both ends of the canoe needs protecting.

Non-pool boats should be washed thoroughly, inside and out, before they touch the water. A hose is best for the inside so that loose material can be flushed out of corners. Any boat which has been used out of doors will require at least three or four good rinsings. A sponge or mop is useful to help move dirt from the outside. However well they are washed, some things always get through and turn up in the pool water. A small net, such as the kind used for collecting pond specimens, is useful for scooping out these floating or partially floating bits.

During rolling sessions, it is useful to have a full size kayak padded up and washed out on standby. This can be used to help people make the transition from the pool training kayak to their own boats. Some instructors keep a canadian single and paddle handy to entertain students who have mastered the kayak roll.

Paddles

Wood or plastic bladed paddles are best for pool use, but any sharp edges that could cut someone should be well taped up.

There is a lot of scope for experimentation with pool paddles. For example, much smaller blades can be used to slow down boat movements and make rolling a little harder. Larger or more buoyant blades can be used to make rolling easier. Shorter shafts reduce the danger of flying blades and are much more user friendly for children. Hand paddles are useful for sculling practice. If paddlers are attending sessions with their own paddles, provide a roll of tape to cover the edges where necessary.

Spray covers

Spray covers provide the pool organiser with the biggest headache of all. Paddlers who have their own neoprene spray decks should be encouraged to use them. For complete beginners, simple nylon decks with adjustable waist bands give greatest flexibility. Although they do not seal well, beginners feel happier with the looser fit around the cockpit.

Other equipment

A few nose clips and a diver's face mask could also be regarded as essential equipment for a pool session. Fit each nose clip with a neck string or they will become lost.

The following equipment can be used in pool sessions as an aid to teaching or to help with activities:

o Slalom poles
o Balls of all shapes and sizes
o Surf ski with lapstrap
o Wet suits, dry suits, buoyancy aids, helmets
o Swim floats
o Plastic buckets
o Strong shock cord and floating rope
o Blackboard or white dry marker board
o Video camera.

Dress

The temperature of the water and of the air surrounding the pool will determine how both the instructor, and students should need to dress. It is likely that everyone in the pool session will be standing around at some stage. Tee shirts are handy unless it is very warm, and that is unlikely. If the water is very cool, wetsuits should be considered. Shivering people make poor pupils and shivering instructors are rather difficult to understand ! Check with the pool manager before using wet suits and show that the need for them to be spotlessly clean is understood.

Clothing also protects students from abrasion or bruising caused by the inside of cockpits. Wet suit trousers are especially good for this. Tracksuit bottoms will also provide some protection, and a pair with a waist draw cord should be used. The pool provides an opportunity for beginners to experience swimming in full canoeing clothing, including buoyancy aids and helmets. More experienced paddlers can also practise rolling wearing full equipment. Remember to wash everything in the shower beforehand.

POOL ACTIVITIES

The following types of session are typical of those that can be run in swimming pools:

o Introduction to the canoe for the complete beginner
o Introduction to rolling
o Rolling technique improvement
o Weekly club sessions for all levels of paddlers
o 'Come and try it'; very short 'taster' session
o Displays and demonstrations; money raising or general interest events for public entertainment
o Lifesaving and rescue training
o Canoe polo training, competitions or leagues
o Indoor slalom competition

Some of these could take the form of a course running for, say, one night per week for six weeks.

The following games, exercises and progressions are listed to help the planning of pool activities (rolling is not included). Further experiment will result in many others being discussed which will help paddlers to learn and have fun.

Games and exercises to give water confidence:

o   Ducking for coins or objects on the bottom

o   Experiment with goggles or face mask, people are often reassured when they can see underwater

o   Somersaults and headstands underwater

o   Ducking under floating canoe

o   Hold the cockpit rim of a capsized boat; duck under and breath inside the cockpit; this is a popular exercise, but needs close supervision

o   Fix the spray deck on an empty canoe and seal it by drawing the waist cord; try to sit astride the upturned hull and paddle it along with two swim floats; now try paddling with your feet resting on the hull.

Capsizing

o   Try climbing into the cockpit of an upright canoe from waist deep water.

o   'Upright Capsizing': the paddler is in the kayak without a spray deck; the instructor fills the boat by pushing it under and the paddler exits as the water rises

o   'Kissing the water': try this from sitting normally in the cockpit; if you end up 'hugging' the water, you have failed !

o   'Toggle touching'. Start in the cockpit, now touch the toggle without getting wet

o   Perform a capsize and make a clean, controlled exit after seeing a demonstration by the instructor

o   Capsize with the spray deck in place, remove it and exit

o   As above, but knock ten times on hull before exiting

o   Partner rescue: capsize and stay leaning forward, arms wrapped around hull; your partner (standing) pulls you upright

o   Stand beside an upturned canoe, take a breath and duck under to wriggle into the cockpit; partner rescue again (the instructor should demonstrate this first, showing how to hold the cockpit rim, face the rear of the boat and backwards somersault underwater into the seat).

o   Same again but this time put the spray deck on underwater !

o   Swimming in the canoe (this is best demonstrated first) the secret is to relax the upper body but maintain a grip with the legs; lie back and let your face rise to the surface; turn the head sideways to breath; students can have a partner stand in beside them and use a partner rescue when they have had enough.

Safety note: Paddlers trying these games need to be held away from the pool sides and clear of other boats. Have a partner stand by to keep the boat in position.

Plate 15:c
The warm, clean water of the pool is the ideal place to let learners explore the boat's flotation and balance

Controlling and paddling the boat
o   Moving the boat around with hands only: try alternate hand strokes (like normal paddling) and experiment with sweeping, draw strokes and stopping
o   Paddle yourself around the pool with paddle but no boat
o   Resistance paddling: tie the boat off with some strong shock cord: there are two possible tasks: one is to see how far you can stretch the cord and the other is to paddle to a mark and see how long you can hold your position
o   Follow my leader
o   Figure paddling: follow an exact course or pattern around the pool
o   Wiggle and wriggle test using slalom poles (single gate) or buoys
o   Mini-slalom: only three or four gates can give an excellent competition; have a video camera running for each run
o   Recovery strokes: get a partner to stand at the rear and try to capsize you
o   Sculling support
o   Edge control and hip action whilst holding handrail
o   Eskimo rescues
o   'The knee-grip challenge': try and stay in the canoe as it is lifted from each end; if all goes well, the lifters can try to jiggle you out
o   Stopper bracing: each end of the boat is tied to a rope so that two people can drag it sideways down the pool; raise the 'upstream' edge of the kayak and brace on the 'downstream' side
o   Relay races, obstacle courses, team challenges and many other games are possible; be imaginative, try out your ideas, but think about safety.

Plate 15:d (i)
Chlorinated water can cause considerable discomfort to the lining of the nose and sinuses. Nose clips, of the kind used by synchro-swimmers, provide a simple solution to the problem

Fig 15:d (ii)
Inexpensive goggles and divers' face masks are useful in confidence building with some individuals. They are also used to help orientation while learning to roll

Rescues

All deep water rescues can be practised in the pool. Use the deep end or insist that feet are kept off the bottom. Use the time to think through problems that occur in open water and practise systems and techniques to overcome them. Experiment with paddle parks, tows and methods of getting exhausted paddlers back into a boat. Rehearse 'all in' rescues.

Time deep water rescues and analyse the movements to determine how they can be speeded up ? Try deep water rescues of open canoes, sea kayaks, doubles. Add interest to rescues by creating a 'storm' with flying water and waves provided by other paddlers.

GOOD INSTRUCTIONAL TECHNIQUE

The principles of good instructing apply just as much in the pool as outside. Here are some guidelines:

o   Get to know students as individuals: know their names
o   Set the tone for behaviour, etc, in the first session and be firm with everyone
o   People learn quickly if they are having fun and are more likely to turn up at the next session
o   Pool sessions can become boring, especially over prolonged periods: always plan the activity, but be prepared to experiment and develop ideas
o   Provide for variety of work in sessions
o   Make students aware of your aim(s) in each session and find out if they are getting what they wanted from it
o   Roping the pool off into sections can be helpful if you are working on differing activities
o   Make use of the more experienced paddlers as assistants; people love to teach and, if supervised, will learn a great deal by doing so
o   Think constantly about safety.

Plate 15:e
There is no limit to the number of simple confidence exercises which can be invented to help learners to overcome their fear of being under water. Partners should be encouraged to assist one another

400

Plate 15:f
Paddlers gain enormous confidence by learning to roll in a pool in the early stages of acquiring boat handling skills. The instructor must nurture this confidence, but never assume the transition to successful rolling in cold water to be automatic

16 The Canoe

An introduction to the open canoe compiled by Geoff Good

INTRODUCTION

Canoeing is a much neglected pastime in Great Britain, when compared with kayaking which has boomed and is invariably the activity that is taught in the hundreds of centres, schools, scout units and clubs where 'canoeing' is a main, or subsidiary pastime.

A trend is discernable, however, in that more and more centres and clubs are now involving 'open canoe' work, while some commercial concerns, which use canoes on camping cruise holidays, and some specialist canoe suppliers, have increasingly established themselves. Many of the British manufacturers have, in fact, been making canoes by the hundred over the years, but these have largely been exported to the continent.

The difficulty in dealing with canoeing in this manual, is that in spite of the comparatively small following at home, in total it is a far more complex sport than is kayaking.

Plate 16:a
PHOTO: MOBILE ADVENTURE

The repertoire and application of skills is more diverse. Most of the kayak techniques described earlier are in fact borrowed from canoeing - the recovery stroke being the only one that was invented by kayakists and is now used in canoes. There is a different application of the strokes for solo or doubles technique. Trim has to be adjusted by the paddlers themselves deciding on the most advantageous position for a particular circumstance. Poling is a separate art, and is reckoned to be canoeing's fastest way to ascend a stream by human power. The craft lends itself to being sailed, as well as allowing for the successful attachment and use of outboard motors. It can also be rowed. All these outlets should be explored by those who would truly call themselves 'canoeists.'

We would need to go back many centuries to discover the beginnings of the paddling skills that Milo Duffek successfully translated to kayaks in the early 1950's, and the canoe to which they relate. This originated in North America, which includes, most importantly for our purposes, Canada.

The indian 'birch bark' canoe has caught the popular imagination. It comprised a timber frame which was moulded into shape by heating the laths over an open fire, and covered with bark from the birch, or other suitable tree. This construction method was related generally to the north east of the continent, however. To the west the more primitive 'dugout' evolved into a plank construction, and it is this tradition which was probably the greater influence on development.

Early explorers, missionaries and traders, obtained these craft from the Indians, and used them as a major means of transport. Often the canoes were large, crewed by many paddlers. Some early settlers who were trappers, hunters and traders, became the 'voyageurs' of the 17th and 18th centuries, obtaining their living by transporting goods and passengers in native-built canoes hundreds of miles across the network of waterways that comprise much of Canada. Their journeys, and ability to cover vast distances, living off a hostile land and 'portaging' heavy loads from one river or lake system to another, are legendary.

It was not until about 1870 that a modern canoe building trade became established by whites, and all-timber, and then lath and canvas construction methods developed. These were followed eventually by boats made of aluminium, grp, and now ABS and other substances which are even more resilient. Currently there are over 600 designs of open canoe available, serving a canoeing population estimated at around 2.5 million. Over 100,000 craft are sold annually.

Besides sailing their canoes, poling was a skill developed by the voyageurs that was largely lost with the advent of down-river recreational canoeing. In recent times there has been a resurgence of interest, with contests in poling canoes up rapids being staged. Many will be surprised to learn that in England there are canoe poling races held at boating club regattas on the Thames, today, pursuing a tradition dating from the early 1900s.

Five different designs of 'shoe' or 'spike' exist for poles, which themselves are made of wood, aluminium or grp. It is not necessary to be able to reach the bottom, however, as poles can be used as paddles, and another repertoire and application of skills is then involved. On long down-river trips, a period of poling can bring relief by allowing for a changed position, and utilising different muscles.

In the light of this brief summary, it will be appreciated that the treatise is necessarily superficial, and that the adaptation that has been made for 'British' purposes of the open canoe skills, which developed in a wilderness context, is less than comprehensive. It is beyond the scope of this chapter to develop further the areas of poling, sailing and powered canoeing. Those who are interested are urged to study the American Red Cross manual, *Canoeing*, available from BCU Supplies.

An attempt has been made to set out the basic skills applicable to the competent handling of canoes logical progressions as an aid to learning. A good demonstration of all these arts makes for a proficient canoeist, able to take charge of his or her craft on an extended journey. A system of canoe handling tests, and tests of touring proficiency, are administered by the BCU.

Camping is dealt with in Chapter 18. The open canoe, is purpose-built for this activity. It is a substantial load carrier, allowing greater ease of packing and unpacking, and keeping its occupants much drier than does a kayak.

The system that follows has been based on the Canadian Recreational Canoe Association's Standard Tests of Achievement in Canoeing, and the very fine film: 'Path of the Paddle: Solo Basic', now in the BCU film library, together with advice from George Steed and Colin Broadway.

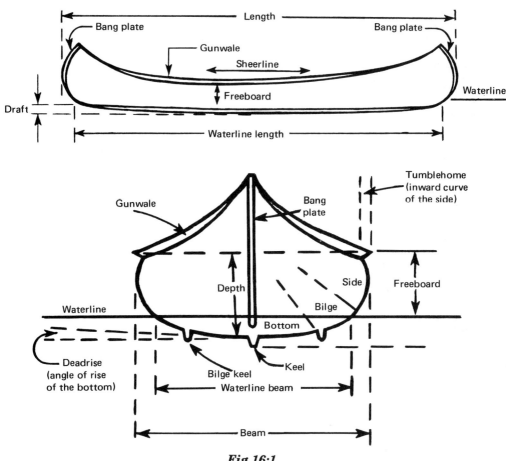

Fig 16:1
The parts of a canoe

CHOICE OF BOAT

For mainly solo work, a length of about 5m is ideal, and about 5.5m for solo or doubles. If doubles use is paramount, then about 6m should be considered, with the longer (or even greater) length being applicable if the carrying of large loads, or extra paddlers on long cruises, is to be the norm.

With the bewildering array of designs available, only general guidelines can be given. The boat should be light enough to be lifted comfortably by an adult crew; have modest tumblehome - an excess makes the boat difficult to empty; be slightly rockered (if manoeuvrability is important); have no keel strip if manoeuvrability on white water is the biggest factor; or a shoe keel (very flat, single strake, wider than it is deep) if a compromise is required; for touring in a straight line, a conventional keel, or keel supplemented by bilge keels, is recommended; wide, flat-bottomed boats are stable, but more cumbersome for solo paddling; narrow bows and stern however will cause the canoe to 'knife' into

405

waves and so ship water; the fullness of the bottom needs therefore to be carried well fore and aft, for general purpose boats; the sheerline should not have excessive rise at bow and stern, nor an excessive dip in the middle.

For canoes up to about 5.5m in length, there should be three thwarts (or seats) and the centre thwart can be 35cm off-set from the centre of the canoe. The distance between the middle thwart so positioned and the beginning of the deck at the far end, divided by two, is the distance that the bow and stern thwarts should be located from the centre thwart. In this way, the stern thwart is nearer its end of the canoe, than is the bow thwart, and the best combination of paddling positions is allowed for.

For lakes and placid river canoeing a painter (up to 5m of 6mm line - preferably floatable) should be located at each end. These are always kept loosely coiled in the bottom, clear of the paddlers. They are not recommended for white water because of the danger of snagging. Buoyancy (minimum 12kg each end) is essential. For running Grade III white water, or above, buoyancy should fill most of the free space. This detracts from the ability to trim and load the canoe, however. The desire to tackle ever harder grades of white water, whilst providing fun and excitement for some, is not compatible with the basic philosophy of the canoe as a vessel for self contained journeying in the wilderness.

Closed cell foam pads glued to the floor for kneeling, complete the fittings, except that where rapid rivers are to be run by competent paddlers, a system of quick-release thigh straps should be incorporated.

MATERIALS

Canoes are mainly available in wood, grp, aluminium, ABS or polyethylene. The processes and qualities of these materials are discussed in greater detail in Chapter 3.

Kits exist for chine-built wooden boats, which are comparatively cheap. A cold moulded veneer canoe, whilst being a joy to behold, is very expensive and requires a degree of loving care.

Grp canoes are comparatively cheap but can be heavy when additional layers, ribs or false floors are used for strengthening. Those incorporating kevlar, diolen or similar materials, using coremat stiffening, attain both strength and lightness.

The Grumman Aircraft Company revolutionized the canoe industry at the end of the second world war, by mass producing aluminium canoes. It did make the canoe affordable, durable and it turned a generation into white water enthusiasts. Purists often dislike aluminium canoes as they bang and clunk their way down rapids. They are cold in winter, and hot in summer, but are durable, and can take most of the abuse a paddler can give.

Various combinations of sandwich construction, or roto-moulded with a foam core, are available, providing tough boats, which are able to recover from considerable distortion. The canoe which provides strength and rigidity, with comparative lightness, at a price you can afford, is the choice to go for.

CHOICE OF PADDLE

Basically paddle choice falls into four categories.

o A traditional blade, usually made from one piece of wood based on the backwoods-man's style of paddle: he would cut down a tree and shape a new paddle whenever it was needed

o A square tipped paddle, usually laminated from wood strips for quality paddles, or made from plastic at the cheaper end of the range: this is also a traditional shape of paddle that was favoured by the Sugar Island Indians

o A modern elbow with a bent shaft, or 'crooked' paddle, developed by Eugene Jenson for the 'sit and switch' style of paddling, now gaining in popularity with many touring canoeists: Eugene Jenson claims that he and his partner were the first to call 'hut' as the cue to switch paddling sides: this developed in 1948, while they were training for the 800km Bemidji to Minneapolis race

o A competition blade.

The choice of these involves personal preference. A wide cross section should be tried before purchase is made.

The decked slalom canoe paddler usually prefers a short paddle to assist in cross deck strokes, the sprint canoeist needs a longer paddle and the bent-shaft paddler a shorter blade. For those starting, however, the following applies.

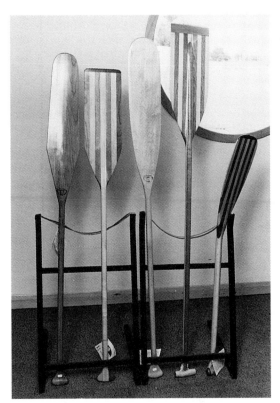

Correct length is the most important factor. The handle should be level with the forehead when the blade is just buried in the water, with the paddler kneeling on the bottom of the canoe, posterior resting on the thwart. A rough gauge is to stand, holding the paddle with the blade on the ground. The top of the handle should be at eye-level. The blade itself should not be too long, and it is best to avoid the very wide blades, used by white water canoeists, in the early stages. Choice of grip is a matter of personal preference, although the T-grip is the more positive.

Plate 16:b
A selection of paddles

HANDLING SKILLS - PROGRESSION I

Paddling position

To commence the paddler should kneel on the bottom of the canoe, with the knees spaced comfortably apart, resting on the pads, his posterior supported on the thwart. It is better, for learning, that the beginner first adopts the bow position in a double, with a competent paddler in the stern. Once a 'J stroke' is performed successfully, however, there is no reason, provided the wind is not blowing too strongly, why the beginner cannot learn to paddle solo. Obviously, the opportunities that canoes give for twice as many people to be afloat in half the number of boats, to have plenty of fun, and yet still be fully occupied, will be exploited by most.

Launching and embarking

Remember always to lift the bulk of any object using the muscles of the legs, rather than the back. Squat, rather than bend over to pick up a heavy weight. There are various efficient methods of carrying a canoe. It can be balanced above the head, with the thwart resting on the shoulders, held against a hip or hung over one shoulder. One person at each end, or on each side can share the load.

The canoe can be placed on the water, either by a straight lift down, or feeding it in end first, and bringing it parallel to the bank once afloat. Where two crew are concerned, the bow-man normally enters first. Facing the bow, the outer foot is placed on the keel-line and both hands grasp the gunwales, with the paddle held across so that the blade is on, or towards, the shore. The other foot is then brought across and the paddling position adopted.

'Forward' or 'power' stroke

The choice of paddling side will depend on the individual's preference, remembering that generally strokes are performed on one side only. A recreational canoeist should, however, aim to be ambidextrous, able to control the boat from all four stations. A double is paddled with bow and stern man working on opposite sides, the stern man being responsible for the general steering.

A method of determining the position for the hands on the paddle is to place the grip well up into the arm-pit and hold with the bottom hand where the fingers lie when the arm is stretched along the shaft.

Place the paddle blade in the water with the blade at right angles to the keel line by extending the lower arm and reaching forward with the body, but not producing an exaggerated lean. Throughout the stroke the top arm guides, in order to keep the paddle upright, and an equal distance from the keel line. The trunk should be rotated about the spine and it unwinds, with the body coming back to the upright position, as the lower arm pulls the blade through the water. Remember that in theory the blade should remain still, by gripping the water, and the boat is levered past it.

When the bottom hand is level with the hips, the blade is lifted cleanly sideways out of the water, and taken forwards to recommence the stroke by the top arm dropping, and the top wrist feathering the blade with the thumb pushing forwards. The blade should be feathered with the top edge high to avoid catching a wave.

408

Plate 16:c
The canoe is the ideal vessel for watery exploration

Plate 16:d
Bivouacking: the versatile canoe serves as a second home

409

Backwater stroke

In order to stop a canoe, or go backwards, a backwater stroke is applied. This uses the non-drive face of the blade - the 'drive' face being the side of the blade that is pulled against the water in a forward power stroke. Commence where the power stroke finishes, by leaning slightly back, inserting the paddle blade, and pushing away with the bottom arm, again using the powerful abdominal muscles. Recovery is the reverse of the forward stroke recovery process.

Cross-deck backwater stroke

When paddling solo, the application of a backwater stroke on one side of the canoe will cause it to turn. This can be countered by the use of the 'reverse J stroke' described later.

A more effective stop, or reverse of direction, can be obtained by applying the 'cross deck backwater stroke'. Having applied the first 'backwater stroke', as described above, on the paddling side, the blade will be towards the bow. Lift the paddle from the water and take it across the boat to place it in the water behind your body, on the opposite side of the canoe. The 'drive face' must be towards the bow, and at right angles to the keel line. The thumb of the top hand, therefore is turned away from the canoe. In order to achieve this position, the trunk and shoulders must be fully rotated.

The stroke is applied by pulling the paddle towards the bow, lifting it from the water and rotating to place it in again on the paddling side ready for a normal 'backwater stroke' as described above. Strokes are repeated on alternate sides until the canoe has stopped or the desired distance has been travelled in the reverse direction.

'J' stroke (Fig 16:2)

A solo paddler, or the stern man in a double, will have to control the direction of the canoe by using 'J' strokes and sweep strokes as necessary.

If the boat is turning away from the steering side, as will inevitably be the case with solo paddling - for power is being applied to one side only - a steering element needs to be introduced to the power stroke, to bring the canoe back on course.

When the paddle blade reaches a point level with the canoeist's hips, instead of lifting it from the water, the blade is turned through 45° and gradually pulled away from the side of the boat. It must remain fully immersed, whilst being pulled, until the canoe's direction has been corrected. In the early stages, the gunwale may well be used for leverage.

To turn the blade through 45°, the wrists are rotated so that the wrist of the top arm is turned with the thumb pushing *forwards* and the *drive face* of the blade turns out away from the side of the canoe. As will be seen, this forms the shape of the letter 'J' when performed on the left, and it is the tail of the 'J' - the blade gripping the water and pushing sideways - that gives the correcting moment.

'Goon' stroke

The 'goon' stroke is the method of steering a canoe that is most likely to be adopted by those left to their own devices. It is performed in exactly the same way as the 'J' stroke, except that the paddle is rotated so that the drive-face of the blade is

Fig 16:2 (above)
The 'J' stroke sequence

Fig 16:3 (left)
The draw stroke

411

turned towards the canoe during the steerage part. It is less efficient than the 'J' stroke because of the 'drag' that is caused by the angle of the blade, but it does allow for more support.

Draw stroke (Fig 16:3)

This is used to move the canoe sideways or to turn it. At this level, the emphasis should be on a simple, functional draw-stroke. Kneeling in the normal paddling position, first turn the head through 90°, then turn the shoulders - rotating at the waist - and reach the paddle well out, with the forearm of the lower arm at right angles to the shaft. The drive face of the blade is towards the canoe. Pull the blade in, keeping the paddle upright, until about 15cm from the side of the canoe, when it is lifted out, and the action repeated.

When some measure of competence and confidence is achieved, the blade should be kept in the water after each stroke, and rotated through 90° by the wrists bending out. The paddle is then returned to the start of the stroke without the blade being lifted from the water. A canoe can be turned in a circle by a doubles pair each performing a draw stroke on his or her paddling side. The blade needs to be deep in the water.

Forward sweep stroke

To turn a canoe away from the paddling side, or to correct its course if it is turning *towards* the paddling side, a forward sweep stroke is used. Remember that, when operated solo, a canoe will rotate around the paddler, and for doubles, will rotate in an arc that passes through the shoulders of the bow and stern man. The maximum effort should be applied along this circle in order to achieve the most efficient turning. Reach well forward, with the top arm low. The bottom hand can be brought up nearer the grip to allow the paddle blade to be inserted further forward, and achieve a wider sweep. The paddle shaft will be at about 45° and body rotation used to achieve power.

For solo paddling, the blade is inserted near the bow and continues in a wide arc, with the blade just covered, until reaching the stern. Once the blade reaches the stern quarter,the top arm pushes across to drive it into the stern. For doubles, the blade's arc is 90° only. The bow man reaches almost directly ahead, and rotates until the blade is at right angles to his body. The stern man commences the stroke from right angles to his body and finishes with the blade well astern.

Recovery is as for the forward power stroke, with the blade feathered and kept close to the water, except that the top hand will remain close to the paddler's waist.

Reverse sweep stroke

Sweep strokes can be applied in reverse by doing the opposite of that necessary for the forward sweep stroke. The non-drive face of the blade is used.

Stern rudder

This is similar to the stern-ruddering described under kayak skills in Chapter 6. The paddle is trailed using the 'goon stroke' with driving face towards the canoe.

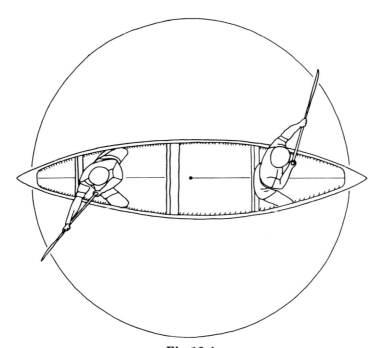

Fig 16:4
A canoe rotates around its axis. Force is only effective when it is applied on this arc.

Fig 16:5
The recovery stroke

Recovery stroke (low brace) (Fig 16:4)

The non-drive face of the blade is presented to the surface, with the paddle held as near horizontal as possible. Lean the canoe towards the paddle, and recover with a sharp push down onto the blade. The skill can be effectively practised 'dry' as shown. In doubles, try it one at a time !

Coming alongside

The canoe is turned into the current, or wind, depending on which has the greater influence, and the upstream (or up-wind) paddler disembarks first. The paddle can be used as a brace by holding it across both gunwales and resting the blade on the bank. Stand, but remain in crouched position, and place the near foot on to the bank, maintaining balance by holding both gunwales. Then bring the far foot ashore. Once ashore, the boat is positioned and held to enable the other paddler to disembark.

The canoe can be lifted out sideways, with the crew's toes protruding over the bank to prevent damage' Alternatively, one end can be lifted ashore first, allowing the water to support most of the weight.

Capsize, swim ashore and empty the canoe

A swamped canoe should be swum to the shore by holding on with one hand and swimming using the other arm and legs. Rest as often as necessary. Where two paddlers are involved hold onto opposite sides.

When emptying, remember that there is no point at all in lifting water. When two people are present, the simplest method is to stand at each end of a canoe that is swamped, turn it the right way up under water, and merely lift with a continuous rolling action until it is upside down above the water, empty. Then turn it the right way up and place it back on the water.

For situations where access is more difficult, there are several possible methods, including the gradual lifting of one end. This will expel water over the other. Gradually bring the end ashore, until two people can turn the canoe over and then lift it out.

A way to empty a canoe solo from a bank is to grasp the far gunwale near midships as the swamped canoe lies alongside, and gently roll the canoe towards the bank. Then, standing up, lift the canoe just enough to let the end of the bow and the stern overlap the edge. Resume rolling the canoe until it is out of the water and upon the bank.

Rescuing a swimmer

A swimmer can be brought aboard by the crew sitting low in the boat, and balancing by holding both gunwales, while instructing the swimmer to grasp the far gunwale, or a thwart beyond the mid-way point. The swimmer must then get his feet near the surface, and keep them there with a strong kick. The canoe must then be pulled under the body by continuing vigorous kicking and exerting pressure on the far arm. When a point of balance is reached, roll backwards and sit in the canoe.

414

PROGRESSION II

Balance

Learn to stand solo, with feet shoulder width apart, and separated fore and aft. The body should face diagonally forwards with the knees slightly bent. Keep the tip of the paddle blade in the water.

Paddler positions and trim

Alternative stances should be learnt and adopted to relieve the stress on the knees. In the early stages, only short periods of kneeling on two knees should be tried. The one-knee cruising position can be adopted, with the bulk of the weight on the thwart. Kneel on the knee that is on the paddling side, and brace the forward foot in some way. Alternatively, it is possible to kneel in a fully upright position on both knees, away from the thwart. The thwarts may be used as seats when there is no rough water to be negotiated. The high-kneeling position is the most dynamic, and is the one used for flat-water racing - see Chapter 14.

A comfortable flat-water cruising position for solo paddling is to kneel off-set on the paddling side of the canoe, with the knees closer together than before, and with the paddler located ahead of the stern thwart. When this stance is adopted, the canoe will be tilted to the paddler's side, and the bow will be high.

Where two or more paddlers are involved, the canoe should sit evenly on the water. It is important that the bow should not be lower in the water than the stern.

Pitch stroke

This is an alternative to the 'J' stroke, having a more delicate application for situations where minimal correction only is required. When the blade is half way through the power stroke, the angle is gradually altered to about 45° and the stroke continued so that the blade remains at a constant distance from the keel-line throughout. The drive face is rotated outwards, as for the 'J' stroke, but the blade is clipped smartly out of the water towards the stern.

Bow cut

The skill described here is the ancestor of the modern kayak bow rudder, which used to be applied with the blade near the front of the boat. The blade is taken forward and out from the side of the canoe by the lower arm. It is turned with the wrists - top thumb pointing back towards you - so that the drive face of the blade is towards the canoe, but the leading edge and tip is angled out away from the boat. The shaft should be at about 45° with the top hand just above the shoulder. Both wrists will need to be pushed well forward to achieve the correct angle on the paddle.

For the stroke to be effective, the canoe must be making good speed. A solo paddler or bow man then places the rudder firmly in the water, and holds the paddle in position, resisting it solidly. The bow will be drawn towards the bow rudder, and the turn can be assisted by the stern man sweeping or drawing. The position of the top hand as described is important, as if it is held in front of the face there is a danger of injury should the blade strike an obstruction (Fig 16:6).

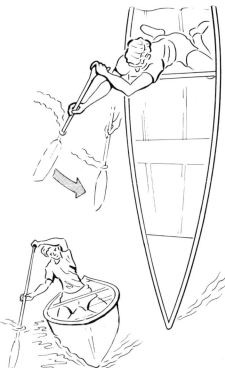

Fig 16:6 (top)
The compound back stroke

Fig 16:7 (left)
The bow cut

Fig 16:8 (below)
The pry - the gunwale is used for leverage

Reverse 'J' stroke

In order to maintain a straight course when paddling backwards, the direction of the canoe will need to be controlled by a reverse sweep, or a reverse 'J' stroke, depending on which way it is veering.

The paddle is taken through the water as for a simple backwater stroke, and the blade rotated through a right angle with the non-drive face turning away from the canoe - the top thumb will be pointing backwards. The effort is applied in the same way as for the 'J' stroke.

Sculling draw

Turn the head, then the shoulders. With an upright paddle, inserted ahead of you towards the bow, the blade is set to 45° from the keel-line - the drive face towards you - and moved as far as is comfortable from fore to aft. At the end of the stroke, the blade is turned so that the drive face remains towards you, but the opposite edge is now leading and the blade set at 45° as before. Move the paddle from aft to fore, when the angle is again reversed, synchronising exactly with the change of direction.

Ensure that the paddle remains the same distance from the keel-line throughout the stroke. This action will draw the boat sideways through the water. The relative position of the bow or stern can be corrected by adjusting the angle of the blade, or extending the length or strength of the pull.

Pry or push-away (Fig 16:7)

To move the boat sideways away from the paddling side, a push-away or a pry stroke may be used.

For the push-away, the paddle is placed upright in the water, near the canoe, with the body turned as for the draw stroke. The bottom arm pushes out, using the non-drive face of the blade. Start with the lower elbow close to the hip, and wrist and forearm lined up behind the heel of the hand. The recovery is made by flattening the blade through 90° and returning to the starting position.

The pry does the same job, but is more powerful as the bilge and side of the canoe are used for leverage. Place the paddle blade in the water under the canoe, with the shaft angled comfortably away from the gunwale - the drive face towards the canoe. The lower hand holds the gunwale and the shaft, while the top arm pulls to lever the blade out. When the effective range of the stroke has been applied, the blade can be feathered by turning the wrists out - top thumb pointing away from the canoe - and sliced back in under the canoe, where it is turned again to repeat the stroke.

The pry can be used as a recovery stroke if the canoe is capsizing away from the paddling side. A pry can be combined with a power or sweep stroke, and is best applied towards the end of the effective part of the stroke. It should not be used on the down-stream side in shallow water, as it may capsize the canoe if it catches a rock or hits the bottom.

Inside pivot turn

This is a modified sweep for solo paddling. Reach out as far aft as possible on the paddling side, and by using the non-drive face of the blade begin an extra-wide reverse sweep stroke. When the mid point of the sweep is reached, turn the paddle over by pushing the wrists forward so that the power face of the blade completes the arc. Do not change your paddle grip.

Recovery stroke (low)

The canoeist should, by now, be able to take the canoe over until the gunwale is on the water line, and recover effectively.

Draw strokes on the move

The draw stroke learned at level I should now be used to ease the canoe to one side whilst it is travelling forwards. For doubles, the partner uses a pry.

Cross-bow draw

The draw stroke can be applied on the opposite side, without changing the paddle grip, by dint of efficient trunk rotation.

Changing positions

By holding on to both gunwales and keeping the body weight low, paddlers should be able to shift to various positions in the canoe whilst moving.

Balance

Balance is demonstrated by holding onto both gunwales near the centre, moving the feet up on to the gunwales, and then standing upright. Conditions should be calm !

Jump out and climb in unaided

With help near at hand, a canoeist should be able to jump out, retaining contact with the canoe, and re-enter by employing the method explained for collecting a swimmer.

Capsize and paddle a swamped boat ashore

Place both hands in the bottom, and raise the legs to the surface behind you. By kicking and pressing down gently with the hands, half drag and half swim your way over the near gunwale until your chin reaches the far gunwale. Keeping your body in the water, roll over on the back of your neck, spreading your arms along the gunwale and resting your legs in an extended position over the opposite gunwale, producing an outrigger type of balance. Gently sit down into the bottom and slowly pivot around to a position where both legs are under the midship thwart, with your thighs (just above the knees) pressing firmly up against the thwart near each gunwale. The arms and legs may be extended sideways, and sculling may be done as necessary to maintain stability. Then hand paddle, or paddle the canoe ashore.

418

PROGRESSION III

Trimming the canoe to cope with varying wind conditions

Remembering that the canoe pivots around the position of the paddlers, it is necessary to alter the trim according to wind and water conditions. For a doubles pair, it will be necessary in waves to move close together in the middle, lightening the bow and stern, thus allowing the canoe to ride up and not ship water. In this instance, the canoe should be turned around so that the bow man kneels ahead of the centre thwart, and the stern man ahead of the stern thwart.

When paddling into a wind solo, it is necessary to move forward in order to keep the bow in the water, and allow the stern to pivot down-wind. For a following wind, the weight should be shifted back. A beam wind is best counteracted by paddling on the opposite side to the wind, and trimming the canoe so that the bow is blown down-wind sufficiently to counteract the paddling effort. In this way, the wind is providing the steerage, and no 'J' stroke should be necessary. If you have to paddle on the windward side, then move forward so that the stern is light.

Canadian stroke

This is also called 'the knifing J' and provides another variation on the forward steering cycle. The paddle is pulled through the water using the normal 'J' stroke, but instead of lifting the blade out of the water at the end, it is carried forwards and out from the side while still under water. The drive face should be upwards with the trailing edge slightly high. Pull up on the paddle as it is knifed forwards.

Indian stroke

This is a complex stroke in which the paddle is rotated through 180° and kept in the water throughout the cycle. It has the advantage that control can be exerted over the canoe throughout the stroke. At the end of the J-stroke, the top hand is rotated (thumb down to thumb up) and the paddle sliced forwards so that a bow draw can be applied if required before the next power stroke, which will be made with the back of the blade.

'C' stroke

In order to maintain steerage in certain conditions, particularly when it is windy, it is sometimes necessary to commence the power stroke with a draw. The paddle is inserted forwards and out from the canoe, and drawn in, so that the movement blends into the formal power stroke. End with a 'J', or canadian recovery.

Compound back stroke (Fig 16:8)

For efficient paddling in reverse, the compound back stroke is used. To commence, the paddler turns his head, looking back over his shoulder, then turns the shoulders and rotates the trunk for maximum effect. The drive face is used until the paddle is level with the body, when it is reversed, and the non-drive face of the blade pushed forwards, as for a normal back-water stroke, The stroke is finished with a reverse 'J', if necessary.

Sculling over the stern

The paddler should be able to reverse his canoe, with diagonal displacement, by applying a sculling draw at the stern, utilising the initial position described for the compound back stroke.

Box stroke

The stroke commences with a bow draw as described for the 'C' stroke, but at the end of the power stroke the blade is turned through a right angle and a push-away applied,, using the non-drive face of the blade. Recovery is through the water, keeping the blade set at that angle, in order to go straight back into the bow draw.

Outside pivot turn (Fig 16:9)

Using the drive face of the blade throughout, the turn commences with a cross bow draw, with the paddle being carried smoothly across the bow and continuing in a sweep as previously described. Recovery is as for the power stroke, but the paddle has to be taken back across the bow and twisted so as to initiate the cross-bow draw as near abeam of the paddling position as possible.

Pry on the move

With the canoe under-way, slice the paddle into the water alongside your paddling position with the blade slightly under the canoe. Using the gunwale as a fulcrum, lever the blade outwards using the non-drive face.

The pry can be used to move the canoe sideways, to initiate a turn, or to lever one end of the boat across the stream.

Recovery stroke (high brace)

The technique is the same as for low brace, but the drive face of the blade is presented to the water, with the paddler 'hanging' -wrists under the paddle shaft.

Reverse sculling

As the name implies, this is the sculling draw used in the opposite way, and moves the boat away from the paddle instead of towards it. The drive face of the blade, set at an angle of 45° from the centre line, remains towards the canoe throughout, but the non-drive face does the work. Commencing forward of your position, with an upright paddle, the drive face of the blade is towards the bow, and the paddle is drawn through the water towards the stern, being kept an equal distance from the centre-line throughout, so that the non-drive face is working against the water. The stroke is continued, synchronizing the change of angle and direction.

Hanging draw

The North-American term for this skill is 'stationary draw', in that the paddle is kept stationary, but the movement of the boat and/or the water cause a diagonal displacement of the canoe.

With the canoe moving at reasonable speed, the paddle is placed upright in the water, well out from the side, with the drive face parallel and towards the canoe.

420

Fig 16:9
Outside pivot turn. This is also the starting position for the cross-bow cut and the cross-bow draw. The 'drive' face of the blade is used throughout

Fig 16:10
Canoe over canoe rescue

Turn the leading edge about 30° outwards, and firmly resist the force on the paddle. The canoe should be drawn sideways across the water whilst the partner prys.

Cross bow cut

This enables the solo paddler or bow man to turn the canoe safely away from his paddling side. The paddle is lifted across to the opposite side without altering the hand positions, and by employing good trunk rotation (see Fig 13:10). The drive face of the blade needs to be towards the canoe, but the top edge should be further away than the lower edge. The paddle shaft is at about 45°. Forward sweeps or draw strokes from the stern man assist the turn, which is occasioned by the paddler holding the position as the bow draws round.

Canoe over canoe rescue (Fig 16:10)

Direct the capsized canoeist(s) to hold on to the end(s) of your canoe while latching onto the capsized canoe with your paddle. If the capsized canoe is upside down, roll it slowly towards you, and place any loose gear in the bottom of your boat. Move your canoe to one end of the capsized boat, maintaining a hold at all times. Grasp the end and lift it slowly onto your canoe, but not more than about a metre across your canoe. Roll the canoe bottom-up and draw it across your gunwales until it is resting empty in a balanced position. Then roll it upright, and slide it back onto the water. Hold both canoes tightly together while the victims climb back in one at a time.

Balance (solo demonstration)

'Gunwale bobbing' is a means of propelling the canoe without paddling ! Stand near the stern deck, with one foot on each gunwale. Sink the stern by bending the knees, and kicking the legs downwards. The canoe will shoot forwards and, as the stern rises again, allow the legs to bend and repeat the driving downwards action. You should be able to travel 25 metres without falling off. Alternatively a 'gunwale walk' on all fours, jumping over a thwart, or a headstand is acceptable !

PROFICIENCY

The canoe is the simplest yet most efficient vehicle designed by mankind for travelling under his own power on nature's highway of unspoiled rivers and lakes. The repertoire of skills so far described, are those necessary for a person to master before tackling open lake crossings, or venturing on to rapid rivers. In order to be competent in these situations, an ability to achieve good technique and a knowledge of other factors is necessary.

Switching

Marathon racing canoeists invariably use a technique called 'switching' which avoids the necessity for the stem paddler to apply constant correction strokes. Their forward paddling technique itself differs, in that the crew are seated, with their legs braced forwards, and they maintain a fast strike rate (the number of strokes per minute), using short paddles. The paddle itself is likely to be 'cranked' - that is, the blade bent at an angle to the shaft - usually between 12° and 18° - so that it maintains a more upright posture in the water for the duration of the stroke. To 'switch', the crew need to decide on a set number of paddle strokes - say 10 - after which they swap the paddle over to the opposite side. To do this efficiently, the paddler in the stern calls 'hut' on the 10th stroke and, as the paddle is lifted from the water on that stroke the top hand grasps the paddle shaft directly underneath the bottom hand, and the bottom hand then slides up to become the top hand. This is accomplished whilst the paddle is being taken across the boat, ready for the first stroke on the other side. There should be no break in the paddling rhythm.

Break-out and break-in

The stern man must control the direction of the canoe so that the bow will slice into the eddy behind a rock. The bow paddler uses a bow, or cross-bow draw in the eddy to hold the bow and pull it into the slack water, allowing the stern to sweep around. The stern man will be bracing, and both paddlers will allow the canoe to be leaned upstream so that the hull is presented to the eddy.

An alternative method is to reverse ferry glide across the stream, ensuring that the stern of the canoe can be slipped into the eddy immediately behind the rock.

To break into the fast current and out of the slack water in order to continue downstream, the canoe is driven into the fast water, aiming for a crest or downsteam face of a wave when possible. The lean must be down-stream onto a low brace.

The ferry glide and 'setting'

As for a kayak, the ferry glide is an essential part of river running. It is more used with canadians however, particularly in the case of reverse glide, which is used to 'set' the canoe across the stream. Unlike a kayak, the canoe should be slowed down on moderate rapids, which allows for a good measure of control. A crew must be able to take the boat across a flow, maintaining the angle of the canoe to the current, in order to move in a straight line across the river relative to the banks.

When running down a rapid, the stern man still supplies the main steering effort, but the bow man takes avoiding action as necessary. He will draw or pry to avoid a rock, and the stern man merely matches this action to keep the canoe running straight. In order to control the general direction in the rapid, the stern man shouts commands such as: 'OK' - do nothing; 'forward' - paddle on; 'back' - reverse paddle; 'left' - do what is necessary in the circumstances to move the boat to the left; 'right' - opposite of 'left'.

To initiate a reverse ferry glide, the stern man first shouts 'back', and both paddlers check the speed. At the right moment, the stern paddler, using a draw or a pry, swings the stern in the direction in which he wants the canoe to move. The stern will be pointing towards the bank toward which the canoe is moving, and the bow will be pointing towards the far bank, at an angle of around 30°. Both paddlers work to maintain this situation.

Lining and tracking

Lining is the art of letting a canoe down a section of rapid that is too difficult to run. Tracking is the art of towing the canoe up against the current. The upstream line in both cases must be attached to the forefoot of the canoe, and a second line to the downstream thwart. One or two paddlers, by keeping the upstream end of the canoe further out from the bank than the downstream end, in both cases, can control the direction and descent.

Capistrano flip

Once a canoe is capsized and swamped, it can be rescued in the following way by two swimmers:

1 Turn the canoe upside down over yourselves
2 Trap as much air under the hull as possible
3 Lift one gunwale slightly to break the suction
4 Give a strong kick up and push on the gunwales
5 At the top of the thrust, push harder with one arm than the other, thus causing the canoe to be flipped over in mid-air, landing alongside you. Properly done, the flip will land the canoe almost empty, and ready for re-boarding.

Portaging

The paddles (there should always be a spare) can be used as a 'yoke' for carrying the canoe on the back by tieing them length-wise between the middle and bow thwarts.

Plate 16:e
PHOTO: MOBILE ADVENTURE

17 Into Fast Touring and Racing

David Train

INTRODUCTION

There are thousands of kilometres of canal and rivers, tens of thousand of hectares of lakes and large areas of estuary in Britain that can be used for touring and racing. I have included 'fast touring' in the title to try and get the message across that touring is not only about expeditions in general purpose kayaks, but can be about travelling at much greater speed in faster canoes and kayaks. Some people feel that touring on canals and slow moving rivers is somewhat boring, and of course it is when using a so-called general purpose boat that is quite unsuitable for the job. Change the craft to one that has some speed, and the boredom turns to real pleasure. This chapter describes the kayaks and canoes used for fast touring and racing, with some comments on introducing paddlers to the faster and more unstable craft. It covers paddling techniques for canoe and kayak, some step-by-step teaching of canoe racing and a description of the competitive events.

THE KAYAKS

Four kayaks are used to provide a progressive system of teaching. The base teaching kayak is the tourer. For those who wish to go faster, the progression is the fast tourer, the stable racer and finally the latest design of racing kayaks. The faster kayaks are, however, less stable and in the case of the racing kayak, extremely unstable. It is very important to realise that speed is a combination of the paddler and the kayak. Most people, trying to start from scratch in a racing kayak, will simply fall in. Their speed will be zero. It is no good having a theoretically fast boat, if the paddler cannot stay upright in it ! The rate at which paddlers can progress depends on age, height, weight and sense of balance.

Most adults will be able to paddle the fast tourer, and many will be able to master the stable racing kayak. Whilst youngsters can quickly move to the racing kayak, most adult newcomers will find their fastest craft is the fast tourer or the stable racer.

Seat, Footrest and Rudder

The layout of a single kayak is shown below.

For comfortable paddling, the seat needs to be at least 5cm high - but the higher the seat the less stable is the kayak. Beginners in racing kayaks can start without a seat, then move to low, medium and high seats as confidence increases. When the paddler feels stable with the high seat in a stage one boat, he or she should be ready to progress to a stage two boat, and so on.

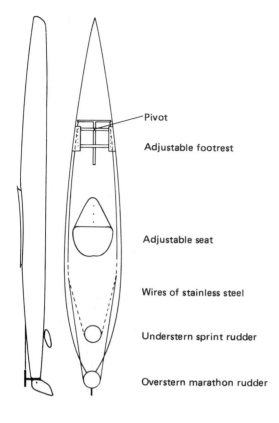

Pivot

Adjustable footrest

Adjustable seat

Wires of stainless steel

Understern sprint rudder

Overstern marathon rudder

Fig 17:1

A rudder is not needed on kayaks up to about 5m long, but for longer boats it is. Once the very basic strokes have been learnt, a kayak with a rudder is much easier to paddle whatever its length.

Rudders are operated by the feet moving a tiller bar. Wires pass along the kayak and are connected to the 'rudder wheel' at the stern. The kayak is turned by moving the tiller bar: right to go right; left to go left.

There are two types of rudder; under-stern and over-stern. The under-stern is used for deep water. The over-stern is designed to lift over anything it touches and is used on shallow or rocky waters.

Buoyancy

All canoes and kayaks should have enough buoyancy fitted in them to support the boat and paddler. The buoyancy should be fixed in such a way that it cannot come loose in the event of a capsize.

The four single kayaks used for the Placid Water progression are shown below. Fast touring doubles and racing doubles are also available. The only four seater kayak which is used is the racing K4.

This figure shows from left to right:

1 The touring kayak. 425cm long, 63.5cm beam. The hull is a flat 'D' shape. It is very stable and because there is little rocker it is easy to paddle in a straight line.

2 The fast tourer. 500cm long, 58cm beam. The hull is 'V' shaped giving reasonable stability. The hull shape and length make it faster than the touring kayak. A rudder is needed.

3 The stable racer. 500cm long, 51cm beam. The hull is 'V' shaped in cross-section, giving some stability, despite the narrow beam.

4 The racing kayak. 500cm long, 51cm beam. The hull is semi-circular in cross-section, giving little stability.

Plate 17:a

Whatever their age, some people have natural balance and will be relaxed whereas others are tense and will sit stiffly. The instructor will soon identify those who are ready to try the more unstable kayaks. It is important to get a lot of practice in the kayak in which the paddler feels most stable. Less stable kayaks should be introduced at the end of a session when, if the tyro gets wet, the training session is not wasted.

THE KAYAK PADDLE

Paddles come in a wide variety of materials and designs: wooden, plastic, flat and curved blades, grp or alloy shafts. Because we are only interested in flat or slow moving water the choice, fortunately, is less. Good paddles make an enormous difference to the paddler and so the best advice is to obtain a good set. Curved and asymmetric blades are essential. The area on each side of the centre line of an asymmetric blade is the same, so that when the paddle is in the water, the blade is balanced and does not flutter.

Whether to use wooden, alloy, grp or carbon-fibre shafts is more a matter of personal choice. Wood and grp have more 'spring' and are not cold on the hands for winter training. For most people they are adequate. Carbon shafts are stiffer and should only be used by stronger and fitter paddlers.

Stiff paddle shafts should not be used by youngsters and only with care by adults. They impose greatly increased shock loads on the arms and have caused lasting injuries to paddlers.

Adults should buy the best paddles they can afford. Growing youngsters should have curved and asymmetric blades but, because they will need a number of sets whilst growing, should purchase cheaper sets or kits.

In 1985 the Swedes introduced a new 'wing' paddle blade into racing, and since then it has started to gain acceptance by many top paddlers. The principle of this paddle is described later.

Paddle feather

All kayak blades used for racing are feathered. Until recently, most were feathered at 90 degrees. During the last few years measurements have been carried out on the wrist rotation of many paddlers, including our top racers, showing that they rotate far less than 90 degrees. As a result, paddle angles have changed to a norm of 80 degrees but with some paddlers using 70 degrees.

Length of paddle

For beginners, the appropriate length of paddle can be found using the following general rule: stand the paddle vertically, reach up with the hand and, without stretching, curl the first joint of the fingers over the blade. As paddlers become more experienced they discover the best length for themselves. The general range is between 218-222cm for men, 210-216cm for women. Ladies' and childrens' blades are also reduced in width. Using the correct paddle for youngsters is very important for the development of good technique.

Paddle grip

The grip on the paddle should be fairly wide as shown in the photograph. Experience will cause this to be modified, but to get started the position shown is good enough. Once the best grip is found it is a good idea to wrap a few layers of tape at the outside and inside of where the hands are located on the paddle. If the hands inadvertently move along the shaft, they will feel the tape and re-adjust quickly.

Plate 17:b
Kayak and canoe paddle grip

SPRAY DECK

A spray deck is a cover which fits around the cockpit of the kayak covering up the legs. In the initial stages spray decks should not be used since, if they are too tight, the paddler may find it difficult to get out in the event of a capsize. Young children may find that removing a spray deck is particularly difficult.

KAYAK FORWARD PADDLING TECHNIQUE

Racing and large cockpit kayaks need to have a comfortable seat and firm footrest, with the hips just above the cockpit coaming. The knees are held lightly together, not too high or too low. Sit fairly upright with chin up and shoulders relaxed.

The sequence which follows commences before the left hand blade enters the water, with the paddler in a confident but relaxed position. The blade is held above the water. The left arm and shoulder are fully extended, with the body straight, but inclined slightly and turned outwards a few degrees from the waist. The right hand is held at shoulder height with the elbow low. In this attitude, a paddler is positioned for maximum exploitation of his strength.

1 The 'catch'. The blade should be placed cleanly into the water at boat speed, as near the boat as possible, by dropping the leading arm.

2 The 'pull'. As the left forearm is drawn back smoothly and parallel to the water, the body is turned from the waist, the boat being drawn to the paddle

Fig 17:c (i)

Fig 17:c (ii)

Fig 17:c (iii)

Fig 17:c (iv)

until the left elbow reaches the hip. At this point, the stroke is at minimum efficiency and should finish. Make sure the paddle blade remains at 90 degrees to the keel line, and equidistant from it, throughout the stroke. The right arm and shoulder have balanced this movement by moving forward in a line parallel to the centre line of the kayak. As the left elbow reaches the hip, the right arm and shoulder are extended in a similar manner to that which were taken by the left arm and shoulder at the beginning of the stroke.

3   The 'lift'. The cycle is continued by the left hand clipping the blade from the water at right angles to the boat, taking the hand close to the shoulder and just above it, leaving the elbow low.

4   This lifting action automatically dips the right blade down into the water. From there on the cycle is continuous. The coordination of the movements being produced smoothly will result in a continuous flowing action, with the arms, shoulders and body making their maximum contributions.

Additional comment

The top arm does not push, but obviously does have to resist the pressure on it, and extend forward smoothly with a straight wrist, the hand relaxed, and the fingers opening. The correct position of the top arm is a most important factor in the early teaching of technique.

The main concentration at first should be on ensuring that the lower, pulling arm, is fully extended before the blade is dropped into the water. Trunk rotation should develop naturally from this.

It is impossible to overemphasize the importance and effectiveness of the body rotation movement. Lack of attention to this means that the powerful muscles in the back are not fully utilised, with a consequent reduction in performance. Concentration is necessary, therefore, on ensuring that this body rotation movement is timed to take its most advantageous phase in the cycle - at the moment the blade is fully immersed in the water, and not before. Leaning forward in an attempt to lengthen the stroke prevents the use of body rotation. Avoid all semi-circular movement of the blade which is usually caused when the arms are held too low. Once the pulling elbow has reached the hip, any further pulling on the blade will merely lift water.

The movement is supported by corresponding leg work. The leg on the same side as the pulling arm is braced by the foot being pressed against the footrest in time with the stroke.

Remember that, within the limits of technical and mechanical efficiency, the stroke will be adapted to the physical qualities possessed by the paddler. The adoption of the various paddling styles that may be observed at all levels of competition have resulted from the mechanically efficient stroke being adjusted to the individual physiological make-up of the paddler. The various styles are not necessarily wrong in themselves. It is vital, however, that the correct ingredients and principles are established at the outset; otherwise, when establishing their personal style, an individual will develop habits to compensate for poor technique, rather than to adapt good technique to their advantage. Without the inculcation of sound basic technique at the early learning stage, a paddler is never likely to achieve his true potential.

To summarise:

o The blade must be fully in the water when the back muscles are in their strongest position

o The blade should present its maximum area to the direction of pull at this point

o The paddle should be pulled straight back as close to the side of the boat as possible

o The leg on the same side as the pulling arm should push against the footrest to impart the pull onto the boat

o The bottom hand pulls, the top hand guides

o The head must be quiet

o The paddler must sit comfortably and fairly upright

Common faults

o The top hand is not straightened

o The top hand grips too tightly

o The top hand drops below shoulder level towards the end of the stroke

o The hand pushes forward above the line of the elbow

o The top hand wrist is bent

o The trunk is 'unwound' before the paddle is fully immersed

o The paddle is angled to the direction of pull

o The paddle is pulled wide of the boat

o The top hand 'crosses over' excessively at the end of the stroke

o The legs are not pressed against the footrest and the reaction goes through the seat only

o The canoe wobbles, possibly due to the lack of pressure on the footrest

o Knees too high or too low

o The head is held on one side or forward

o The head is constantly moved

o The canoe is not evenly balanced

o The paddle is pulled through too far.

Points for observation

Study the technique described. These notes are intended to help observers to identify the important ingredients of the skill, and suggest ways in which improvement can be achieved.

o Is the blade entering cleanly, as far forward as is comfortably possible, with the body upright (or a slight forward lean), the paddle held correctly, the lower arm fully extended and the trunk fully rotated ? If not:

o Is the paddle the right length ? The paddle is the correct length when the blade can be just fully immersed as close to the boat as comfortably possible.

o Is the paddler unwinding before the 'catch' ? Get the canoeist to concentrate on entering the blade into the water by his feet. A piece of tape stuck on the deck as an aiming mark may be useful in some cases. Make sure this does not lead to the body pivoting forwards and backwards. The paddler should concentrate on the blade entering the water cleanly.

o As the boat is pulled past the paddle as closely as possible, does the blade keep 90 degrees and remain the same distance from the keel line throughout ? If not:

o Check body/arm action to ascertain reason. Is the grip of the upper hand too tight, causing the top arm to be forced across unnecessarily ? Persuade the paddler to concentrate on paddling with a relaxed grip, opening the fingers of the top hand and keeping the wrist straight.

o Is the paddle the right length ?

o Is the top, guiding hand, moving forward at shoulder height ?

o Is the blade entering the water, without splashing at boat speed ? Concentrate on the 'catch'.

o Is the blade exiting cleanly when the drawing elbow is level with the waist ? The blade should be lifted out at right angles by the hand, leaving the elbow as low as possible.

o Is the canoe running level ? It should not rock unduly from side to side. If it does, the rocking is most probably caused by the trunk unwinding before the paddle has been dropped into the water.

o Is the foot on the same side as the pulling arm moving against the footrest ? There should be a cycling action with the legs - the knees should move up and down 2-4cm.

o Is the head quiet ? When paddling, the head should remain relatively still.

o Is the canoe upright ? Ensure the paddler is not sitting to one side.

General remarks

Do not attempt to improve or emphasise more than one factor at a time, and do not pursue any concentration on technique to the point of boredom. Involve work on a particular aspect of paddling style at various stages throughout a trip or session. It may be helpful to make a paddler concentrate on a particular movement with his eyes closed.

A few minutes dry land work at the start of each session should reinforce these points. Sit the pupils on a bench, or something similar, in a natural paddling position. A plank on a float over the water is a useful paddling practice aid.

Plate 17d (i)
The wing paddle blade

Paddling technique with the wing paddle

The Swedish wing paddle is shown in Plate 17:d i-iv. The paddle has a shape in cross-section like an aircraft wing. With a conventional paddle the kayak is pulled past the paddle with a force parallel to the centreline of the kayak while the blade stays in a fixed position in the water. The technique with the wing blade is to allow the blade to sweep sideways, creating forward lift from the low pressure area created by its shape. The blade follows this path

Plate 17:d (ii) (top left)
Wing paddle technique. Notice that the non-pulling arm is held high. This is essential to keep the wing blade's leading edge in the correct position

Plate 17:d (iii) (top right)
As the paddler pulls, the blade takes itself away from the side of the kayak

Plate 17:d (iv) (left)
Trunk rotation remains important, as with conventional blades

naturally and once paddlers have adjusted they seem to have no difficulty in what at first seems a strange action. As well as providing forward movement of the paddle, the sweeping out means the back muscles are used at the back end of the stroke.

THE CANOES

There are four categories, as for kayaks, covering the range of activities for the canoe: tourer, fast tourer, stable racing and racing. There are differences in teaching because of the different positions used by the canoe paddler. Whilst the kayak paddler is always sitting, the canoe paddler may sit, low kneel or high kneel. The position of the paddler has a much greater effect on stability than does the inherent stability of the canoe. The touring canoe can be used to teach all positions and there is now a touring kayak which can also be used as a training craft for teaching single bladed paddling in both the high and low kneeling positions.

The types of canoe are shown in Figs 17e-g. Singles and doubles are used for marathon racing while, for sprint racing, singles, doubles and fours are involved.

CANOE PADDLES

There is a wide ranging choice of paddles. All the blades are flat although shapes vary. There are also raked blades which are used for marathon racing and touring. Most top paddlers use wooden paddles, but for beginners the alloy shafted plastic paddles are suitable.

Plate 17:e
Touring canoe: 488cm long, 88cm beam. Bow and stern paddlers in sitting position, centre paddler in low kneeling position
PHOTO: 'CANOEIST' MAGAZINE

Fig 17:f
Marathon racing double. 615cm long, 76cm beam. A reasonably stable canoe; paddled from a sitting position with cranked paddles

Paddle length

This varies depending on the kneeling position, and type of paddle. There will be individual preferences, but as a guide:

General touring

Straight shaft; the total length is the chin height of paddler when standing.

Marathon touring

Bent shaft: the shaft length is the nose height of the paddler when sitting erect and cross legged on the floor.

Racing

For singles, the paddle length is mid-forehead height; for doubles it is eyebrow height of the paddler when standing.

CANOE PADDLING TECHNIQUE FOR SPRINT RACING

The basic principles are:

o Imagine you are kneeling in your canoe and in front of one side of you are a series of stakes coming up from the river bed, at intervals of about a metre, just above river level.

o Reach for the first stake with the pulling arm by leaning forward and rotating the body around the spine.

o Get hold and pull back by lifting the body and rotating back. The canoe will move past the stake. Your pulling arm is straight.

o When the hand reaches a point just in front of the hips leave go and reach for the next stake.

The paddle is simply a convenient way of carrying the stake. The essential principles of the stroke are:

o The boat moves past the stake (paddle)

o The power is provided by the back muscles which, through the lower arm, pull

o The top arm guides only - it does not push

o The blade should go into the water without power, as though into a slot with no splash; the power is applied afterwards.

Steering the racing Cl (single canoe)

Assuming the canoeist is paddling on the right hand side, to steer to the left is simple - just use a sweep stroke.

To steer to the right, or keep the boat straight, is more complicated. To the experience paddler, steering becomes part of the normal forward stroke. For the beginner, the following points are essential. When the bottom hand is at a point just in front of the hips, the blade is kept deep and turned through 90 degrees by

435

Plate 17:h (i)

Paddling the racing C1. The body rotates as the paddle catches the water. Straight lower arm throughout the pull. The head is visible under the top arm which is coming towards the body. The kneeling leg should be forward or at 90°, never back. There is no weight on the forward leg

Plate 17:h (ii)

Clean entry of the blade. Good body rotation. Relaxed upper arm. Remember, power is provided by the back muscles with lower arm pulling. Do not push with the top arm

the top hand with the thumb forwards as for the 'J' stroke (see Chapter 16). The top arm has moved inwards and dropped in a continuous smooth movement, and the blade grips the water for steerage as it is lifted clear by the action of the top arm, as described, together with the bottom arm pulling the paddle away from the side of the boat.

Teaching racing Cl to youngsters

Questions are asked about the danger of one-sided development in people taking up Cl paddling. Many sports are one-sided, such as tennis, squash, golf and so forth. Paddlers should not train too hard when they are young, and all should do other activities such as running and swimming and weight training when old enough. So, for kayaks and canoe, if you train people, give them a balanced programme.

SPECIAL INJURIES

Most sports have specific problems if there is over-indulgence at an early stage. With kayaks, there are wrist problems; with canoes, it is the knees that could suffer damage. If sufficient time is given to adapt, then the risk is removed. When starting beginners off do not allow them to paddle for too long before a rest. Make sure they have an adequate kneeling block - a cushion will do at first. Do not let paddlers kneel in the boat without some support.

PADDLING TECHNIQUE FOR MARATHON/TOURING WITH BENT SHAFT PADDLES

Bent shaft paddles are used so that the blade is vertical during the latter part of the stroke. This allows for thrust right along the canoe, and stops the tendency to lift water. It is more efficient, and steering is made easier, as the paddle more naturally flows into the 'J' stroke, or steering is maintained by 'switching' .

The paddling sequence is:

o The 'catch'

The blade should be placed cleanly in the water at boat speed. The blade is close to the canoe. The lower arm is extended for maximum reach and the trunk is rotated forward.

o The pull

The arm is kept fairly straight whilst the trunk rotates, pulling the canoe past the blade. Unlike the sprint racing stroke, the top arm is driven through using the shoulders and upper back muscles.

o The exit

The blade is sliced from the water by dropping the top hand and lifting the lower. The lower hand does not pull past the hip.

o The recovery

The blade is kept close to the water as it moves to the catch.

Paddling rate

In racing the stroke rate can vary between 55 to 80 strokes per minute. The rate will depend on the type of canoe and depth of water. The more 'racey' the canoe the more it will glide, allowing a longer and more powerful stroke at a lower rate. On shallow water the stroke is shortened and the rate increased.

Switching

Switching the paddle is a more efficient way of keeping a canoe going in a straight line than using a steering stroke. Whilst frowned upon by the 'traditionalist' it is the stroke for the marathon racer and, when perfected, it can be done as quickly as a normal recovery. It also equalises the use of muscles on both sides of the body.

The sequence is:

o After the paddle is lifted from the water the top hand is released completely. The paddle is lifted towards the other side of the canoe with the lower hand.

o The top hand is moved to grasp the paddle below the bottom hand. The paddle is now in a vertical position with both hands on the shaft.

o The top hand has now become the bottom. The hand on the top slides up to the top whilst the arms are continuing to move into position for the next entry.

Switching is carried out as and when necessary. For touring it would be every 10-20 strokes. Racers switch every 5-8 strokes.

In a double the stern paddler signals when to switch by calling out at the beginning of the stroke. At the end of the stroke paddlers switch sides. The code signal used is 'Hut' or 'Hup'.

CLUB AND COMPETITIVE ACTIVITY

Rambling, jogging and running on water is perhaps the best way to describe the activities of a club based on flat water. The Placid Water Coaching Scheme Awards in themselves provide a great range of activity. Schools and youth groups will find enough within the scheme to satisfy their needs. For those who wish to go further there is a step by step range of activities which takes them from 'rambling on water' to racing at Olympic level.

Plate 17:k (i) (left)
Using the touring kayak to teach canoe paddling. The low kneeling position is shown here

Plate 17:k (ii) (top right)
High kneeling on both legs. Youngsters will move naturally to this position. After practise get the paddler to concentrate on kneeling with the weight on one knee (same knee as paddling side) while remaining in this position

Plate 17:k (iii) (bottom right)
High kneeling in the racing position. The final position in the touring kayak. Allow the paddler to develop thigh musculature gradually with short play sessions. Slowly increase the distances paddled

Canoeing, unlike some other sports, has a weak club structure. There are, of course a few notable exceptions. A great number of popular and successful activities such as golf, sailing, squash, tennis, cricket and football, revolve around a club base, where people meet and take part in their sport. Why then is canoeing different ? Many reasons are suggested, but proof exists that a successful club can be established with only a few kilometres of flat water available to it.

With the shortage in this country of white water sites the thousands of kilometres of placid water that are available provide the only real expansion for canoeing.

The club handicap race

The event which binds the club together is the weekly club handicap race. This one activity alone can be the basis of a successful club. The principles are:

o   That each paddler has a standard time for the course based on previous performance

o   That the race is run with the slowest off first and the fastest last; if the handicapping is correct, then all will cross the finishing line together !

This type of race provides something for everyone in the club. All can improve. The beginner competes with the top paddler. The fastest canoeist always has another boat to try and overtake. A safety factor is built in, because competent paddlers are always coming up behind, able to sort out a problem, should one occur.

How is it done ?

o   Hold your club handicap race every week. Club members will then know that if they turn up there will be an activity. It is vital that it is run even if most of the club are away at a national competition.

o   Plan a course suitable to your river or canal. You may wish to have more than one distance, eg: 3km, 5km, 7km. Out and back is easiest to organise.

o   Set standard times. To initiate the system, take a rough guess at each paddler's time and base the handicap on that.

o   Recruit a starter, finishers, someone to work out the results, and someone to provide a cup of coffee at the end. In cold weather a safety boat may be desirable to pick up any stragglers.

o   Having calculated the standard times from the previous race, list the competitors' names, starting with the slowest and ending with the fastest.

o   The start time for each paddler is calculated by subtracting their standard time from the slowest competitor.

eg: slowest time was 55 minutes   -   start time 00.00 minutes,

next was 47 minutes   -   start time 08.00 minutes,

next was 44.15 minutes   -   start time 10.45 minutes.

o   Each paddler is started at the appropriate time, and at the end of the race his or her finish time is recorded. The actual time taken can then be worked out.

o   If the paddler's actual time is faster than his or her standard (previous) time, the standard time will be reduced, giving a greater handicap.

After the race, a chart showing start times, finish time, position, and the new standard on which future handicaps will be based, should be displayed in the clubhouse. This is shown in Table 17.1 and can be paramount in providing interest and motivation.

The BCU Marathon Committee's Open Racing Scheme certificates can be used, so that all competitors have a chance of a good prize with a benefit to the club. Details of this are obtainable from the BCU. The scheme allows for competition within the club for Division 8 and 9 marathon racing events. If there are enough of these paddlers in a club handicap race, it is permissible to promote individual paddlers on a time basis, to a higher division.

Table 17.1 - Weekly Handicap Race

Name	Boat	Std. Time	Start Time	Finish	Position	New Time Calculated
Fred	C1	55	00	53.30	2	53.30
Jack	Touring K1	44	11	54.00	3	43.00
Susan	K1	40	15	55.00	7	40.00
Bill	C1	36	19	54.45	6	35.45
Roger/Phil	C2	35	20	53.30	1	33.00
Stephen	K1	34	31	54.30	5	33.00
Andy	K1	32	23	54.15	4	31.45

Marathon racing and the Open Racing Scheme

It was stressed that the club handicap race should be the regular activity of the club. Racing within the club however can lead to national competition. The Open Racing Scheme provides a very natural extension of the club handicap race. This scheme provides canoeing competition that enables all to join in, and the progressive structure allows people of all abilities to develop to their potential. The competition for the premier team prize in marathon racing, the Hasler Trophy, has rules which make it possible for small and large clubs throughout the country to have a chance of winning. Do not be put off by the word 'marathon'. The lower divisions cover only 5 or 6km.

Ultra long marathons

The best known of these is the Devizes to Westminster race. It takes place every year at Easter. The course on the Kennet and Avon Canal and River Thames is 200km long with 76 portages. Senior Singles, together with all Junior Doubles, can race over four one-day stages, although some doubles race straight through. The record for the Doubles event is 15 hours 45 minutes. The aim of many of the paddlers is to finish the course, this being a great achievement in itself. There are other 'achieving' marathons including the Leeds to Liverpool, also 200km long, the Birmingham Century and the 65km Stratford Stage.

Sprint racing

Sprint Racing is the 'track event' of the canoeing scene and it has been in the Olympic Games since 1936. The top paddlers have to be extremely dedicated. The National Watersports Centre at Holme Pierrepont, Nottingham, is the main centre of racing in Britain. Before competing there, paddlers have to reach a standard based on times over 500m. Members of the BCU Coaching Scheme may test paddlers and issue the necessary certificate.

Triathlon and quadrathlon events.

There are a growing number of triathlon and quadrathlon events which include canoeing. The other sports are swimming, cycling and running. The distances vary considerably. The canoes and kayaks described in this chapter are ideal for this type of event. The non-canoeist can quickly master the touring kayak or the double canoe. It is an ideal event for promoting canoeing to other sports people.

Training for competition
If the flat water canoe club is to gravitate towards competition, then supplementary activities are important, particularly in the winter. Whilst not within the scope of this chapter, such activities that may be considered are:

o Weight training for muscular strength

o Circuit training for muscular endurance

o Flexibility exercises

o Running, football, basketball and similar team games for cardio-vascular efficiency.

'Fun' or 'rag' regattas
Not everyone in a flat water canoe or kayak aspires to be a national champion. The provision of 'fun' activities, where all can participate, is important to a balanced programme. Mini sprints over, say, 100 metres can prove interesting whilst K2 races - parents with child - can provide a diversion that involves the family. Standing-up races in K1s will give the smallest junior a chance to shine, or a tug-of-war between two K2s, or land based teams on opposite sides of the river, can be hilarious. To the imaginative mind, the combinations are endless.

Whilst a barbecue, disco, or cheese and wine party can be the perfect end to an enjoyable day's canoeing, remember that it is the sport that the club is all about. The social side used properly, can complement the canoeing, but it should never become the main function of the club.

CONCLUSION
There is considerable opportunity for everyone involved in canoeing to show thousands of people of all ages and levels of ability how to use and enjoy the waterways of Britain. The water is available, the canoes and kayaks are readily available and there is a Coaching Scheme. Now is your chance and your challenge. Start to use your flat water, teach your paddlers, form your club and enjoy a great sport and recreation.

18 From Camps to Expeditions

Marcus Bailie

Marcus Bailie has a vast amount of experience as an expedition canoeist. This includes white water trips in Mexico, the Grand Canyon, Alaska and the Himalayas. His open canoe journey on the White Nile in 1978 was the longest ever undertaken at that time at 3,126 miles. He has also worked for the Sports Council on the training of Mountain Walking Leaders and is held in high regard by the outdoor education world as a pioneer of new ideas.

AN INTRODUCTION OF SORTS

'. . . with mountainous waves crashing on our heads we battled on through the torrent, narrowly avoiding rocks at every turn, and courting death at every stroke of our frail paddles. This was our 35th day on the river; our porters were either lost or had deserted us in this inhospitable terrain; our kayaks and our bodies were at the limit of endurance; our food had run out a week ago; Archie still had The Fever, but our hearts were true and our spirits were high . . . !'

'. . . It was spectacular to watch the games the sky would play. We stopped paddling for a while and watched as the sky changed from the silver-grey of night to the silver-blue of morning. The east filled with array upon array of reds and golds and crimsons as the early morning sun edged above the skyline, immense and shimmering. Bright orange light caught the tops of the tiny ripples which ran out from our boats, out over the otherwise perfectly still water. It was hard to realise that this time yesterday, and probably this time tomorrow I had been and would be safely tucked up in bed; four walls and a ceiling to keep all this from view, and the noise of traffic replacing the stillness . . .'

JOURNEYS LARGE AND SMALL

The length, difficulty and commitment of an expedition is determined largely by the experience and the imagination of the individual paddlers, and the shortest expedition is a one-night camp. Moreover the basic requirements of a one-night camp are essentially the same as for a three month expedition: food, shelter and a suitable craft. Beyond that, it is all a matter of degree.

Sea journeys

Journeys on the sea are probably best undertaken in a specialist sea kayak. These usually have storage hatches, pumps and a variety of useful deck fittings designed for the job. However, a general purpose kayak, especially if fitted with a skeg, will do almost as well for everything other than very long trips.

River journeys (kayak)

Again, there are specialised expedition kayaks on the market. These tend to be large volume, and some have safety deck lines, and other fittings. Once more, though, a general purpose kayak will do the job. If the kayak has a central rear buoyancy pillar, this will reduce carrying capacity, and to remove it will reduce the strength of the kayak by a dangerous amount. If there is a similar pillar at the front and 'pedal' foot rests, loading the bow is quite awkward. A bulkhead foot rest is much better, for once you have mastered the dexterous skills for removing and replacing it easily, you have access to a substantial and well shaped space.

River journeys (canoe)

For long fairly easy rivers (including Grade III) open canoes are excellent. They have plenty of carrying capacity which is easily accessible, although extra care is necessary when packing to make sure that in the event of a capsize all the gear is not lost ! Open canoes have the additional advantage that it is easy to move your body position: classic position (one knee up, one down); kneeling on both knees; sitting with legs under the seat; sitting with legs stretched in front and braced against gear. You can even stand up and stretch ! If you are at all susceptible to a sore back the canoe must offer the best way to travel. Some designs have cockpit rims so that an enormous two-person spray deck can be fitted. For rougher water, closed cockpit designs have been used although the average paddler with reasonably conventional legs finds the confined position of decked C2s rather uncomfortable after a while.

Getting there and back

Transport arrangements can make or destroy any journey. For some sea trips, for example, things can be very simple. If you plan a circumnavigation, or a 'there-and-back', you end up at your starting point - provided you get the tides right. Similarly, lake journeys need not involve a transport shuffle.

Point to point ventures by sea or river, are a little more complicated. The implication of a journey lasting two or more days is that the distances are longer, possibly to the extent that a normal vehicle shuffle becomes impracticable. Hiring a car at the end may be financially viable, as might the coercing of friends or bribing wives and loved ones. Public transport should not be ruled out. Even in Britain, you can usually get a kayak on a train, though sea kayaks can present more of a problem. For journeys in more distant locations, most third-world buses will also take kayaks on the roof, alongside the chickens, goats and fourth class passengers.

Gear

Try to keep arrangements as simple as possible, especially if you are going to be using trains and other forms of transport (including aeroplanes for the more

Plate 18:b

ambitious). If you have to unpack your boat to travel, make sure you can cope with carrying all the bits. Arms full of dry-bags make a notoriously awkward load. Carrying a lightweight roll- up ruck-sack for the purpose may help to solve the problem.

A better idea is to keep everything inside the boat, especially if it is a kayak. Leave your normal paddles at home, and just travel with split paddles since these will fit right inside the average kayak. Top paddle manufacturers now make really reliable splits, and so their reliability is not in question. A spare spray deck, tied or sewn at the waist hole,fitted to the cockpit, means that you can travel with just one piece of luggage which is completely sealed.

Guides, maps and additional information

Written information exists on most suitable rivers in Britain and Europe. Similarly, all areas of the coast will be covered, even if it is only by the appropriate volume of the Admiralty Pilot. For more serious expeditions, information can be obtained from such organisations as the BCU Expeditions Committee, The Long River Canoe Club, and The Advanced Sea Kayak Club. Details of all these can be obtained from the BCU.

Food

Whether on a one-night journey or an extended expedition, food rapidly becomes more than a mere fuel or an energy source; anticipation of it lasts all day, time is measured by it (it is either one hour after breakfast,or an hour before lunch), and eating places are often remembered better than rapids or sections of sea cliffs - 'Remember that lunch spot on the Spey ?'. In fact, the longer the trip, the more importance food assumes until it becomes almost the sole reason for living. It pervades everything: minds, bodies and conversations alike. Marriages and friendships have foundered under its awesome dominance.

The paddler is at a considerable advantage over foot travellers, for neither weight nor bulk is as critical. This does not mean that we can take what we like . . . but it almost does ! The criteria governing choice of food have more to do with quality than quantity. As long as there is at least two pounds (dry weight) of food per person per day, then reasonable digestive satisfaction can be achieved. Now this may seem a little flippant, but it is a figure which has emerged independently from a number of people on successful major expeditions throughout the world.

Exactly what food to take will depend on a number of factors. Obviously things like the time of year, the expected weather, personal likes and dislikes, the means or otherwise of cooking and the number of pots you are prepared to clean, will all have to be considered. In addition, much thought should be given to the individual and collective cooking expertise within the group. If in doubt, keep it simple. A tin of Irish stew with a couple of mince pies to follow for dessert, may well please many. Personally, I prefer spaghetti with some fresh onions, fresh green pepper, a small tin of tuna fish, a handful of peanuts from the following day's packed lunch supply, and a packet of mushroom soup. I cook it all together in one pot to create a rather splendid little risotto which requires only one heat source and leaves me with only one pot to clean.

For pot cleaning reasons also, I refrain from bacon for breakfast, and lunch is usually of the nibbles variety: fruit, chocolate, nuts. Copious cups of tea and coffee while away the evening hours, and sachets of hot chocolate are simply wonderful with early morning muesli.

Some may prefer the simplicity of dehydrated meals or the more modern freeze dried dishes stocked by supermarkets and a number of camping shops. The choice is quite varied and the result quite palatable. Be careful to avoid those which need to be simmered for 20 minutes, as most are quite fast to prepare. In

Plate 18:c
River Alsek, Alaska

446

addition, there is often less packaging to carry out or dispose of after the meal, though it should be remembered that aluminium foil does not burn. On some long journeys, if a great deal of food needs to be carried, then considerations of bulk may lead the paddler to take at least some dehydrated or freeze dried meals. They are expensive, however, and partly for this reason I prefer to make re-supply stops if possible, rather than live off 'plastic' food.

For journeys occupying less than a week, considerations of nutrition need hardly be a worry, provided your menu is reasonably varied; the expedition needs to be for considerably longer than a week for vitamin deficiencies to become apparent unless the fare is extremely basic.

Some foods travel well, others do not. Tinned foods are comparatively easy to deal with as they do not even need to be kept waterproof. Jars of honey get messy very quickly, and large packets of margarine are a 'nightmare'. Fresh melons are a bit tricky too ! Anything which is decanted into plastic bags needs to be marked clearly, and the bag should be capable of being sealed and re-sealed easily. Those nifty little plastic bottles can be very useful for sugar takers and salt sprinklers, and their convenience, especially on those longer trips, compensates amply for their bulk.

The camp kitchen can be very simple, and the contents very few. A small nylon pan cleaner is useful but, since I generally avoid greasy food, I do not usually take washing up liquid. Two cooking pots are usually sufficient, their size depending on the number of people involved and/or their appetites. A special container is necessary for fresh water, and remember that you may have to carry your drinking water with you, particularly on sea journeys. I also like to carry a sharp knife. Taking a little tin opener as well means that my sharp knife lasts longer !

Finally, camp cleanliness should be scrupulous. I am really quite fussy about this and am very careful not to put cooking utensils on the ground, that my hands are clean when eating, and that pan lids are put on the ground upside-down. Cleaning up the site prior to departure should also be undertaken scrupulously. Once you have vacated a site, there should be no indication left behind to indicate that you have ever been there.

Stoves

There is a wide range of excellent camping stoves on the market and most of them are suitable for canoeing purposes. Usually, one single-burner stove is sufficient for two or three people. We can look at some of the basic operating principles by considering first the fuel they burn.

Paraffin

A number of well established stoves exist which burn paraffin under pressure. The stoves need careful maintenance and operation, and the fuel is really quite smelly and all-pervading. People have sworn by them for years, however, and when burning they give a very good source of controllable heat. Fuel consumption: 0.15-0.25 litres per person per day, depending on the amount of cooking, and number of evening hot drinks !

Petrol

There are a number of designs available, which are almost identical to paraffin stoves, and have many similar problems. The additional danger is that any spilt fuel is highly inflammable. Fuel consumption: 0.15-0.25 litres per person per day.

Plate 18:d (i)
'Primus' pressure
stove, fuelled by
paraffin

Plate 18:d (ii)
Methylated
spirits stove:
'Trangia'

Plate 18:d (iii)
Simple solid fuel
stove

Plate 18:d (iv)
Gas stove with
disposable
cylinder

There is also a new generation of stoves which burn a petrol product called 'white gas', which is usually sold under its trade name of 'Coleman fuel'. These stoves are different in principle to petrol stoves, are much easier to use, yet still give a hot variable flame. The danger of accidentally spilt fuel remains. Fuel consumption is a little less than for paraffin or petrol stoves.

Methylated spirits

There has been something of a revival in 'meths' stoves resulting in a variety of very efficient designs. The most common of these, the 'Trangia', is simple to use, very stable and, comes with its own two cooking pots. It works well in the wind and gives a hot flame. Moreover, only the small burner need be kept dry when being carried in the canoe or kayak. The flame, however, is a little fiddly to adjust, the fuel if spilt is highly inflammable, and extreme care is necessary when re-filling the stove which needs to be done regularly during cooking. Other stoves now exist which give a more variable flame. Fuel consumption: 0.2-0.25 litres per person per day.

Gas

Gas stoves are probably the easiest to use and when the bottles are full

Plate 18:d (v)
Alternative gas system with removable, self
sealing cylinder

are very fast. However, as they begin to empty they become slower and you are left with empty canisters to carry out. Some designs are very unstable. They are also quite expensive. Danger exists when changing canisters anywhere near a naked flame, and leaking gas, which is poisonous, will settle in the bottom of the tent. Some canisters are self sealing when the stove is dismantled, while others must only be separated from the stove when empty, which makes them more fragile during transportation. There are different types of gas available and the canisters are not generally interchangeable. Propane/butane mix is somewhat better in very cold conditions. Fuel consumption: a 165g canister will last two people for approximately three days cooking; however, since it is difficult to tell how full a partially used canister is, it is better always to carry a spare.

Solid fuel
This is generally solid paraffin and it is burnt on a fairly primitive design of stove. It is smelly, slow and the heat is difficult to regulate. It makes a useful emergency stove, but not much else.

Wood fires
In the United Kingdom, the use of wood fires is generally applicable only to sea journeys when drift wood is available, and a suitable fire site can be organised without damage or danger of spreading. In less populated countries, a wood fire may easily be the better alternative and in many third-world countries, it is the only reliably available fuel ! However, fires are dirty and smelly, and considerable expertise is required to produce a good meal on one. They also make an evil mess of cooking pots ! Even if you do not intend to cook on one, however, they make a magnificent focal point to any camp. Fuel consumption: 'Indian make small fire: keep warm. White-man make big fire: keep warm getting wood !'

Fuel abroad
You can have some real epics trying to get fuel abroad. Even if it is available,it will be called something totally obscure or confusing. Be particularly careful with the names for petro-fuels.

British	European	American	Third World
petrol	essence gasoline benzin	gasoline gas	gasoline gas
Coleman paraffin	whitegas petroleum petrole	whitegas kerosene	not usually available - petrol may do kerosene petroleum
gas	butane propane	butane propane	not available
methylated spirits	alcool-a- bruler brennspiritus	methanol	methanol if available
diesel	derv	gas-oil	gas-oil

Do you see what I mean about wood fires ?

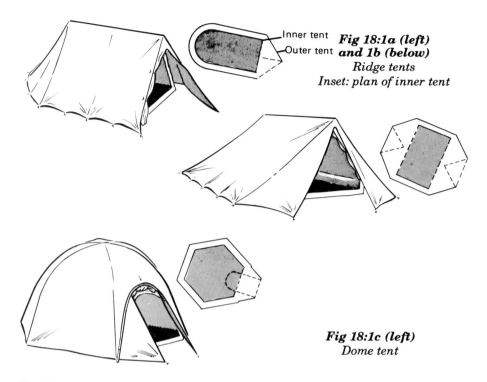

Inner tent
Outer tent

Fig 18:1a (left)
and 1b (below)
Ridge tents
Inset: plan of inner tent

Fig 18:1c (left)
Dome tent

Tents

Just as food on a trip assumes a role far in excess of its original function, so your tent, or whatever means of shelter you choose, will become your ultimate security: a pleasure dome (literally in some cases) of warmth and safety. Storm, stress and Grade VI are left outside; while within you have the illusion of complete immunity from attack from grizzly bears and the collectors of camping fees.

Fortunately, the choice of a suitable tent is easier to deal with than are stoves, although you may get just a little confused by the sheer variety available. It is likely to be your most expensive camping item so careful consideration is necessary.

You may be tempted to opt for the most expensive up-market model you can afford, after all, since it was advertised to withstand the rigours of high mountain expeditions, surely it will cope with low level work. Of course it will, but you may end up using a £275 model when a £50 one would have done just as well. If you already have a reasonable small tent, the chances are it will do for canoe or kayak camping. Bulk can be a problem, so we will be looking at small back-packing tents rather than large frame tents. Again, instead of considering specific models, we will look at a few design features.

Sewn-in ground sheet

Nearly all modern tents now have the ground sheet attached to the walls of the tent. This almost essential feature helps keep the weather out and warmth in.

450

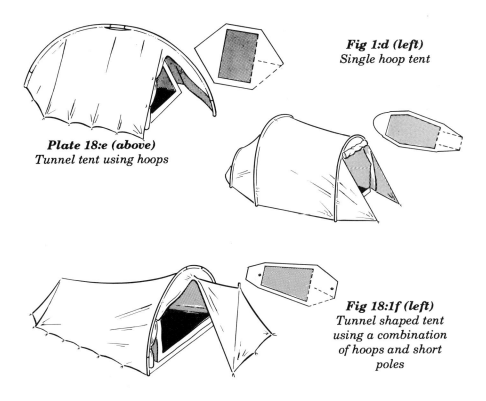

Fig 1:d (left)
Single hoop tent

Plate 18:e (above)
Tunnel tent using hoops

Fig 18:1f (left)
Tunnel shaped tent
using a combination
of hoops and short
poles

Single skin or double skin ?

Most modern tents are double skin. That is, they have an inner tent made of a lightweight breathable material, and an outer shell made of a waterproof material. This prevents condensation inside the tent, and the resulting air-space provides additional thermal insulation. Many designs extend the outer shell at the front and back to provide space for cooking, and for storing wet canoeing kit and other equipment. Some designs permit the outer to be erected first. This is often a bit complicated, but it has the advantage that the inner can then be kept dry when it, in turn, is being erected.

Most single skin tents either leak, are made of gortex, or a similar breathable waterproof material which is very expensive, or both. Very few of the advantages of single skin tents apply to the paddling camper.

Ridge tents

This is the conventional shape for a tent, though the ridge can either be horizontal or sloping. Transverse ridge tents require the direction of the sleeping occupants to change. Rather than lying in line with the ridge pole, they lie across the line of it. The long side wall then becomes the door, so that storage and cooking space is greatly increased.

Dome tents

Tent design went through its revolution with the introduction of 'flexible' tent poles. The various designs of dome require two or more poles which are fed through sleeves in the tent, thus pulling it into shape. There is less space wasted in these designs and often there is more headroom. They usually need fewer if any pegs since most are self-supporting - well almost ! However, they are often quite expensive and can sometimes be a little complicated to erect.

Tunnel tents

Another application of the flexible poles idea produces a long thin tent.

Single hoop tents

These are generally small lightweight tents and as such do not offer a great deal of space.

'Bivvy-bag and tarp'

A gortex bivvy-bag will keep you dry while you sleep, while the lightweight nylon 'tarpaulin' makes an excellent cooking shelter, as well as providing a roof at night. This may sound like 'roughing it', but this system offers the greatest flexibility, especially since not all beaches or river banks offer flat grassy areas suitable for tents. Only the bivvy bag need be kept dry when packed inside the boat thus saving on 'dry-space'. It is a system which, personally, I use quite a lot.

Sleeping bags

Once again, the sleeping bag you have will probably do, provided it is suitable for 'outdoor' use and is not just for use in caravans in high summer. Bulk may be a problem and, this may exclude some designs.

Down

Feather or down sleeping bags can be compacted very small for carrying, which is a great advantage. However, they lose their heat- retaining qualities dramatically if they get wet.

Synthetic

'Holofil' and other similar materials are just as warm as feather or down but are rather bulky. They have the additional advantages that they are warm even when wet, and are easier to clean. Messy eaters take note ! Fibre-pile bags remain comfortable even when damp and salty or sandy inside.

Sleeping mats

Most heat from sleeping canoeists is lost, not upwards into the air but downwards into the ground. Thus a good insulating mat is essential. Traditionally, closed-cell foam 'karrimats' have been used for this purpose. These not only insulate but also iron out some of the bumps. In addition, they do not need to be kept dry during transport since they will dry off in minutes. More recently the introduction of 'thermarest' mats has taken comfort to previously unheard-of limits. They are partially inflated to provide a cross between a karrimat and an old fashioned air-bed. Now even the pebbliest of beaches can be rendered comfortable, but be careful of sharp stones. Be careful too, when packing them inside the boat, that the thermarest's air valve is kept closed, otherwise you will end up with a water-bed.

Plate 18:f
A lightweight nylon sheet forming an effective roof

THE CARGO

Waterproofing

It seems to me that you have two choices: either you put a lot of thought into this knotty little problem or you develop a taste for wet sandwiches. The heart of the problem is not usually the container, it is the seal. Many materials are waterproof. Plastics are excellent. Even neoprene proofed nylon will keep water out, but securing the top is another matter altogether. Not only do you want to seal it, you also need to be able to get into it, and then re-seal it again. Quite a problem!

There are a number of good containers on the market, and we will look at them under two headings: bags and barrels.

Bags are easier to pack and easier to stow. Usually the technique is first to put the bag into the appropriate place inside the craft and then to pack it. Most people like to have a plastic bag liner inside their 'dry-bags' for extra security. Most bags will leak at the seams unless these are regularly checked and re-glued or taped or both. The most effective way to seal the top is to fold the top over several times, then roll or fold this into a scroll and then finally hold it closed by tying or wrapping with a thick hoop of rubber. Even plastic bin liners tied like this will keep water out, but play safe and use two! Knots simply do not work!

A number of American designs now available in the United Kingdom have roll-top rubber or plastic bags with press stud fasteners, which are excellent. Another American variety of bag is sealed with a slider bar, but although these are very waterproof, they are hard to stow. Home-made bags work just as well as the commercial ones, especially if you make them double skinned.

Barrels are usually designed for other purposes - often to keep liquids in - and then borrowed by the paddling world. The smaller ones will fit into kayaks, and

Plate 18:g
Sealing the top of a bag.
Roll, fold into a scroll, tie
or seal with elastic,
rubber band or cord

454

the larger ones are excellent in open canoes. Give some thought, though, as to how you are going to carry these if portages figure in your paddling trips. Whether the lid is screw-on or clip-on, some additional form of rubber-band seal may be necessary. Hoops cut from car inner tubes are still probably the best for this. A neoprene pad fitting just inside the lid, so that it gets squashed when the lid is closed, will also improve your sandwiches' chances.

Packing

Whatever craft you use, be it sea kayak, open canoe or general purpose or other kayak, and whatever length of journey it is to be - from two days to twenty - the same principles for packing apply.

Last in - first out

Whenever possible try to arrange that the things you are going to need first when you arrive at your chosen camp site are easily available. This will usually mean that they are the last things you packed before you set off in the morning. For instance, I like to get into dry clothes as soon as I get off the water so I pack these in the top of the dry-bag which is just behind the seat. Conversely, my sleeping bag is buried in the stern.

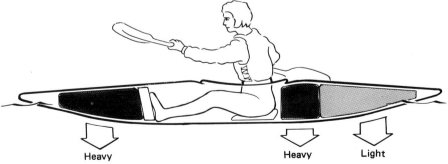

Heavy   Heavy   Light

Fig 18:2
Keep heavy items away from the ends, and remember to trim the boat so that it sits level

455

Trim

Distribute the weight in such a way that the boat will remain level on the water, both side to side and bow to stern. A kayak which is packed nose-heavy, for instance, is very difficult to handle. Also try to arrange that the heavy things are packed close to the mid-point. A boat with all the load at the ends is very difficult to handle. In a kayak, because most of the storage space is behind the seat, a problem is presented. You need to compensate for this by having something small but quite heavy in front of the foot rest.

Securing the load

When packing for a day trip, make sure that in the event of a capsize things do not fall out. Fixtures inside the deck will help a lot.

Buoyancy

Since most of the gear will act as buoyancy, air bags can be reduced or, at times, removed all together. Do not, however, remove foam pillars or other devices which provide structural strength.

CHOICE OF SITE

Sometimes the site will already be known to you or will have been recommended; sometimes you will have checked the area in advance from the land and will have selected a site; sometimes you will spend the latter part of the day checking likely looking possibilities either from the water or by landing, rejecting one in anticipation of a better one; sometimes you do not get any choice !

Once you have chosen your site do not leave setting up camp until too late in the day. If you are aiming for a specific site, allow a couple of hours margin of daylight; looking for a campsite in the dark will possibly be dangerous, will probably be unprofitable and will certainly be more difficult.

The criteria you use for selecting a site will be determined by availability of sites but also by your camping style and equipment. The criteria are:

o *Availability of fresh water.* Of course, you may have anticipated this by bringing your own.

o *Availability of firewood for cooking.* On a number of journeys in which I was involved, this was the most important single factor in deciding where to camp. On the other hand, if you are carrying stoves, then this factor can largely be ignored.

o *Somewhere to sleep.* Most tents require somewhere reasonably large and level and, unless you have a self-supporting dome tent, you will need to be able to get pegs into the ground. Particularly on sea trips, this will limit you considerably. Bivvy bags are much more versatile, and reasonable comfort can be achieved even on a pebbly beach.

o *Access.* Particularly on rivers and, especially in Britain, you will probably need permission to camp. This permission may prove difficult or even impossible to obtain so you would be well advised to check on this in advance. Even on sea journeys, the idea that you have the right to land or even camp on any section of coast is a myth. Above the level of high tide, ie Mean High Water (Mean High Water Springs in Scotland), the land is generally privately owned, be it

456

beach, cliff or anything. The land exposed between high and low tide belongs to the Crown Commissioners. Discretion, however, will often suggest that a particular cove, headland, or beach is unlikely to interfere with anyone. You should still remember, however, that you may not have the right to be there. In practice, if you choose your site considerately, no-one is likely to object.

o *Escape.* Only in periods of very sheltered weather or under equally unusual circumstances should you use a site from which you cannot easily escape to landwards. This is particularly important on sea trips when a storm or even a change in the wind may bring seas crashing onto your beach. This may easily make leaving by that route impossible for your particular group. On rivers, the danger of a rising flood could similarly leave you trapped. Islands

Plate 18:i
PHOTO: ALAN KIMBER

and inescapable caves are attractive places to camp; there is more excitement, more adventure. However, you should always ensure that you are taking on a venture that, collectively, you can cope with, even when things go wrong.

o *Boat security.* Make sure there is somewhere safe to put your canoe or kayak. As we have discussed above, rivers flood and tides come in, and each is well known for sweeping away badly positioned or ill-secured craft.

AND FINALLY . . .

'Despite the lists of equipment and the demoralising tales of not so fortunate associates, the thought of leaving the trappings of civilization for even a short period of time is attractive to many people. Age is not a barrier, nor is canoeing ability, since the standard of the trip is chosen to suit the individuals taking part. Routes and equipment will be chosen in the light of experience; items once considered essential will be discarded in favour of those things found to be more useful. Be ruthless in the amount of equipment taken. Develop the ability to set up or pack up a camp quickly and easily. Enjoy the experience for what it is and by organising your own trips you will soon find that you have tales to tell others . . . should you so choose'.

457

Plate 19:a

19 Surfing

Howard Jeffs and Dennis Ball

Howard Jeffs designs and builds wave skis on Anglesey in North Wales. He is an experienced Sea Coach and has played a significant part in the development of surf coaching in both kayak and ski disciplines. He is still very much an active paddle surfer and is currently a member of the Welsh wave ski team.

Dennis Ball took up serious kayak surfing at the age of 32, and very quickly became one of Britain's elite paddlers. He was a member of the English team, competing on skis and in kayaks. Through his service on the BCU Surf Committee and editorial involvement with Beachbreak magazine, he has been active in shaping both the competitive and non-competitive sides of the sport. He is now the BCU National Surf Coach.

INTRODUCTION

When Captain Cook first sailed into the Hawaiian islands in the late 1700's he was greeted by the local people in or on a variety of craft. As these people made their way towards the shore through the breaking waves, he noted their skills and ability to handle their craft, plus their immense enjoyment of what was thought to be hostile conditions. Whether the origins of the sport involved standing up, lying down, or using a paddle, it will be the source of endless arguments amongst surfers. Paddle surfing as we know it is one of the fastest growing disciplines of canoesport worldwide.

Paddle surfing in Britain became increasingly popular during the mid seventies using slalom kayaks and the specially designed short flat bottomed surf kayaks, which originated in California. With the introduction of the wave ski (probably from Australia) towards the end of the seventies came the demise of the surf kayak and the rise in popularity of a more pure form of surfing derived from the wave ski.

WAVES

Waves are caused by wind and are thus described as 'weather' or 'meteorological' waves (as opposed to the much rarer 'seismic' waves). Generally, it can be said that the stronger a wind blows, the bigger the waves will be, the longer will be the period between them and the faster they will travel through the water. The speed of individual waves is about ten per cent less than the wind speed that created them.

As waves move away from the area in which they were generated, they undergo a process known as 'metamorphosis'. Gradually, they become more

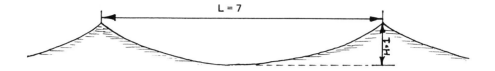

L = 7

H·1

Fig 19:1
Minimum height to length ratio of a wave

sorted-out and regular; waves join up and swell lines become more pronounced, orderly and 'cleaner'. Thus does a confused 'sea' transform itself into regular, parallel lines of swell.

The following definitions will be helpful:

Fetch: The potential distance over which the wind could act in one direction

Period: The time interval between successive passing wave crests

Wave length: The horizontal distance between successive wavecrests

Wave height (amplitude): The vertical distance between the wave crest and the trough

Experience has shown that wave speed, wave length and wave period are in direct relation to each other, as follows:

Individual wave speed (in knots) = 3.1 times period (in seconds)

Deep water wave length (in metres) = 1.5 times period squared (in seconds)

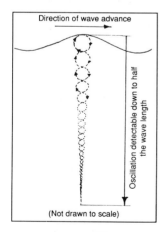

Direction of wave advance

Oscillation detectable down to half the wave length

(Not drawn to scale)

Fig 2:a (left)
Particle oscillation in a deep water wave

Fig 2:b (below)
The particle oscillation becomes elliptical as the wave approaches shallow water

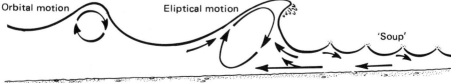

Orbital motion   Eliptical motion   'Soup'

In deep water, the minimum ratio of height of a wave to its length is in theory 1:7. In practice, waves are rarely this short. A ratio of about 1:15 to 1:20 would be a more likely minimum.

Deep water waves

In an unbroken green wave, the body of water within it is not actually moving forward. What actually happens is that when wind blows over the ocean, some of the energy is transferred to the water in the form of a wave. A wave is therefore wind energy travelling through the water.

It is only when a wave meets land and breaks onto a shore that there is a forward rushing of water, as the energy is expended. Although water in a wave does not move bodily forward, water particles in the surface layer move in circular motion (oscillate) with the passing of each wave. The amount of oscillation decreases as depth increases, and becomes negligible at a depth of half the wave length (Fig 19:2a)

For our purposes, water is technically defined as 'deep' when the bottom lies deeper than the oscillations of a particular wave can penetrate. Thus a wave of 300 metres wave length (a very mature swell) will 'feel bottom' in 150 metres of water and start to loose some of its power.

Sets

Very rarely do we experience a simple, or single, swell system. Usually two or more systems are superimposed on each other, each with differing periods and magnitudes. Where the waves of these different systems have peaks that coincide, the resultant waves are larger. Where the peaks of one coincide with the troughs of another, they cancel each other out. This is what gives us 'sets' of larger than average wave size and lulls of smaller than average waves.

It is worth noting that not all the wave systems that arrive on a beach will have travelled from the same source. On any given day, the surf that is arriving may be comprised of a number of swells of differing wave length and having travelled from differing directions. One may have only travelled a few hundred miles whilst another may have travelled thousands. Usually one swell is dominant.

Waves in shallow water

When deep water waves enter shallow waters, they undergo a process of profound modification. Wave speed and length are reduced dramatically, whilst at the same time, wave height increases by a comparable ratio. Finally, upon reaching a certain limiting depth, the waves break onto the shore.

Long wave length swells may start to feel bottom in up to 300 metres of depth whilst small, short wave length 'seas' may feel bottom in as little as one metre.

How much a wave increases in height when it feels bottom depends on the wave length. Where this length is great, the height increase on reaching shallow water may be as much as three times. Those with a small wave length are likely to only double their deep water height. This is why long wave length swells are preferred by surfers, even though their deep water height may be less.

461

Internal motion in shallow water

The particle oscillation in a wave as it reaches shallowing water becomes increasingly elliptical, until a point is reached when the ellipse becomes unstable, the wave becomes critical and breaks, and the energy within the wave is released in a forward rush of water (Fig 19:2b). Other factors which affect the way waves break are the steepness of the beach and off-lying shallows such as sand-bars, shoals and reefs.

Undertows and rips

Up until the moment when a wave breaks, there is no forward movement of water but once this happens, water rushes forward in the form of soup. This water cannot pile up indefinitely on the beach and has to find an escape route back out to sea. It does this in two ways. On steep beaches, the water washes up the slope after the wave breaks and them 'swashes' back down again under the force of gravity. The momentum of this returning mass of water then carries on under the next incoming breaking wave, causing what we know as undertow (Fig 19:3).

On gently sloping beaches, undertow does not occur, instead the water finds its way back out to sea through deep water channels. These are called rips. Rips are often found along the edges of bays where there are rocks. They are sometimes found where a stream running off the land scours out a channel on a beach, or they may create their own escape channels as can be seen on long, sandy beaches. In between rips, the sandy bottom is usually a little higher than the rip channels and this results in an undulating surface across the beach. Once the beach becomes covered by water, these contours in the sand in turn have an effect on the wave shape, creating peaks and giving good surfing waves.

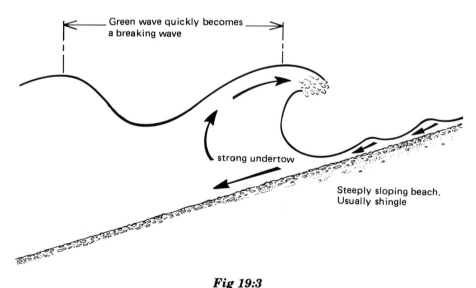

Fig 19:3
Waves breaking on a steeply sloping beach become 'dumpers'. these are powerful, crushing waves, often associated with undertow

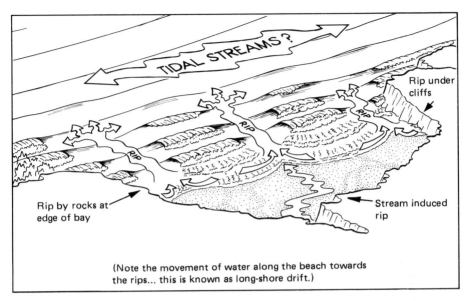

Rip under cliffs

Rip by rocks at edge of bay

Stream induced rip

(Note the movement of water along the beach towards the rips... this is known as long-shore drift.)

Fig 19:4
The possible directions of flow of rips in a small bay

The break line is the area where incoming waves start to break. Rips tend to dissipate once they get beyond the break line, so for good surfers they give a welcome lift out through the break line. For the less experienced, however, and unwary swimmers, they can be death traps, particularly when the surf is large.

Rips flow like a river and it is not uncommon for them to move at several knots. A speed of 12 knots has been recorded in a rip on a Cornish beach during a storm. If caught in a rip as a swimmer, try to remain calm and work out which way it is taking you. Swim at right angles to this and you will soon be out of its influence.

Although rips dissipate outside of the break, they can sweep the unwary paddlers out into strong tidal streams that may be at work just a little way off shore. Be aware of this or a surfing day can easily turn into an unwanted sea trip !

Breaking depth of waves

On average, in no-wind conditions, waves break in a water depth that is 1.3 times the height of the wave at that moment.

On-shore winds tend to make waves break early, ie further out to sea, into water two times the height of the wave at that moment. Offshore winds have the effect of causing waves to break late, into water that is as little as 0.7 times the height of the wave.

Local winds

The direction and strength of local winds are crucial factors when deciding which beach will offer the best surf. Given the choice, it is usually worth seeking out a beach that is not suffering an on-shore wind, even though the surf may be smaller.

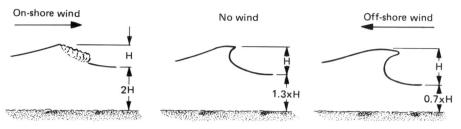

Fig 19:5
The affect of wind on breaking-depth

With a good swell, an on-shore wind above force 1 will soon take the size, power and shape out of it. As wind strength increases, the surf will become less predictable and more 'mushy' and irregular.

An off-shore wind will manicure a swell beautifully, causing it to become steeper, higher, hollower and more powerful. As wind strength increases, the tops will be blow off the waves, eventually reducing the surf size and making wave riding very difficult.

Cross-shore winds can do several things, depending on strength. They can set up strong long-shore drifts and exert powerful rips at the down-wind end of beaches. They can hollow out up-wind shoulders into magnificent tubes or destroy the surf with small wavelets running across the swell.

Any wind above force 4 can make it difficult to stay in the surfing area and under these conditions, leaders supervising groups can have serious problems.

Refraction
When a swell crosses a sea bed of varying depth, those parts which cross shallower waters will be slowed up more than those in deep water. This causes a change in direction of some parts of the swell and is known as refraction.

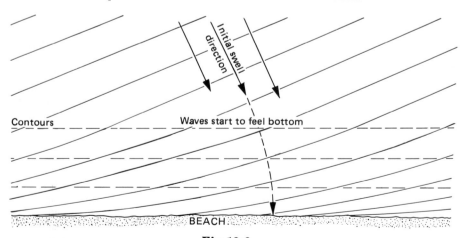

Fig 19:6a
Refraction of an angled swell onto a straight beach

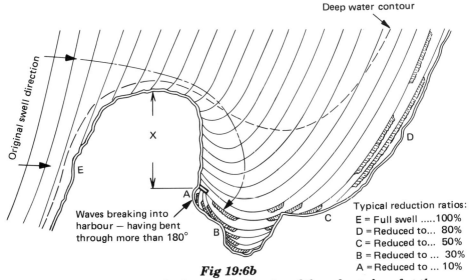

Fig 19:6b

Typical refraction around a headland. The size of the refracted surf at the various points indicated is dependant upon the distance 'X'. The greater this distance, the greater the amount of refraction, and the smaller the surf

If a swell approaches a coastline at an angle of say 30 degrees, those parts which reach shallow water first will start slowing down, causing the swell lines to bend and align more parallel to the shore, as in Fig 19:6a. Refraction can turn swells around headlands, into bays and onto beaches which face away from the original approaching swell. During the process of refraction, swell loses size and power in proportion to the distance over which the refraction has taken place (Fig 19:6b).

Convergence and divergence

Where a swell meets irregular depth contours as it approaches shore, different parts of each swell line are subject to differing degrees of refraction. The parts which feel bottom first are the first to slow down, causing parts of the swell to variously converge and diverge as in Fig 19:7a. Not all refraction results from such close-inshore features. Sometimes off-lying shoals (shallows) can refract swells enough to cause convergence and divergence closer in-shore where no wave bending features exist (Fig 19:7b).

The perfect wave

Surfers look for waves which have the break running along their length rather than those where the whole wave breaks at one time. The point on the wave where the break meets the green wave face is called the shoulder. It is the steepest, unbroken area on the whole wave and it is the position which surfers strive to reach and retain. It is from the steep wall of the shoulder that a surfing craft gathers the energy for manoeuvring.

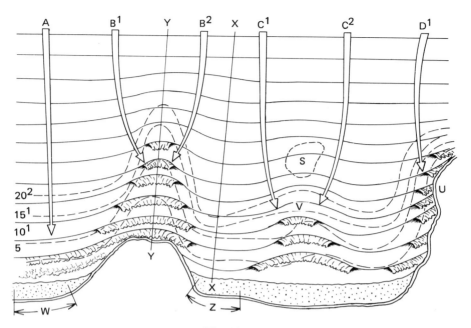

Fig 19:7a

Convergence and divergence
The long arrows show the extent of refraction at various points.
Swells at A meet contours which lie parallel to the shore, thus suffering little or no
refraction.
Swell direction B1 and B2 is much modified, resulting in a major convergence along Y-Y
Swell between B2 and C1 is also modified, with a major zone of divergence occurring along
X-X (no surf at all at Z)
Swell at D is slightly refracted to U

Estimating wave size

Judging the height of waves must be one of the most controversial issues amongst the surfing fraternity. Being caught on the edge of the break line as a large wave is about to descend on you can be a very intimidating experience so the following method can be used as a guide. If you sit on the water's edge and the wave peaks just break the horizon, the surf is small (less than 1m). If you kneel up and they just break the horizon, the surf is getting bigger (about 1 - 1.5m). If you stand up and they break the horizon they are very big waves (over 2m). Remember, as the tide rises and falls the wave height will vary, and it always looks much bigger when you are out there than it does from the beach.

Bores

Tidal bores are a unique phenomenon on which to surf. Luckily in Britain we have one of the world's classics on the River Severn, and they also occur on the Dee, Trent, Kent, and other rivers.

A bore is caused by a larger than normal tide (usually in spring or autumn) forcing its way up an estuary. As the banks slowly get narrower and the bottom shallower, a funnelling effect is created until the bore is formed as an advancing

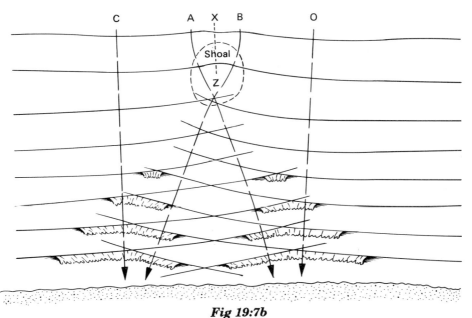

Fig 19:7b

Convergence and divergence from an off-shore feature

*The off-shore shoal has caused swells at A and B to refract and bend around it, resulting in
convergence along X-X. At Z the refracted swells meet, cross through each other, and
continue in their new direction. In shallower water, they meet the unrefracted swells from C
and D and break as swells on the beach*

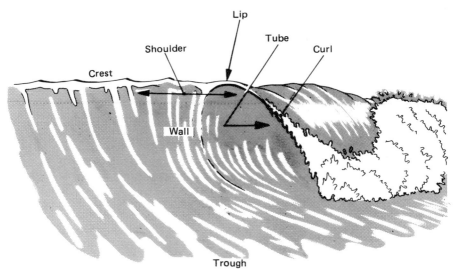

Fig 19:8
The shoulder of a wave

Plates 19:b (above) and 19:c
The Severn Bore

wave. As the bore works its way upstream it usually increases in height and speed (up to 3m on the Severn) until, as on the Severn, it reaches a weir or loses its energy over a long distance. A bore is a great sight to see, but to surf one is an experience not to be missed. Finding out where to put in and at what time the bore occurs is all part of the fun. A strong, stable surf kayak or long wave ski, is the ideal craft to use. You will also need a helmet and buoyancy aid for protection. The penalty for a mistake is a long, fast and muddy swim !

CRAFT AND EQUIPMENT

General purpose kayaks

Polyethylene kayaks have a durability that makes them attractive to the surfer but unfortunately few of the designs have a shape which lends itself to good

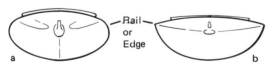

Fig 19:9a and b
The typically broad, rounded gunwale line of a polyethylene kayak (left) and the sharper edges more likely with a grp boat (right). These sharp edges are important for precise handling of the boat in surf

surfing technique. This is because the kayak's edges are usually broad and round, especially to the rear. Grp kayaks are more likely to have lines appropriate for surf use (Fig 19:9 a, b). A design with a sharp rear gunwale line allows the kayak to be 'edged,' or 'railed,' into the wave face, making it easier to track across the wave face. Some surfers experienced

468

Plate 19:d
A general purpose kayak modified for surfing. The flange on the rear edge and turned up nose can be clearly seen

Plate 19:e
The kayak, as opposed to the surf ski, lends itself well to acrobatic looping

in competition use a modified form of kayak which has a turned up nose and a flange that protrudes along the seam line on the rear gunwales (Fig 19:10). This acts as a fin or sharp rail and allows the kayak to surf very high along the wave face.

Surf kayaks

Surf kayaks were used extensively during the seventies (Fig 19:11) with the ultimate manoeuvre being the 360 degree spin. Their shorter length and low buoyancy stern made them difficult to paddle out through surf, and prone to reverse looping, making rolling an essential skill. Although fun to paddle, they are now seen less, due to the emergence of the wave ski.

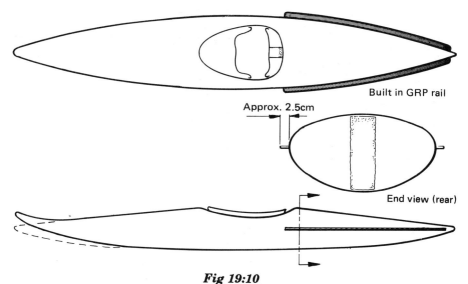

Fig 19:10
The way in which conventional kayaks are modified to improve performance in surf

Wave skis

Wave skis come in an infinite number of shapes, sizes and constructions (Fig 19:12). They differ from a kayak or surf shoe mainly in that you sit on a ski rather than in it, being held firmly in place by toe loops and a quick-release lap strap. If you capsize you can either roll up, or release the strap, turn the ski over, and climb back on board. Because of this ease of use wave skis have become increasingly popular during recent years, and are by far the quickest and most painless way for the newcomer to learn the art of paddle surfing.

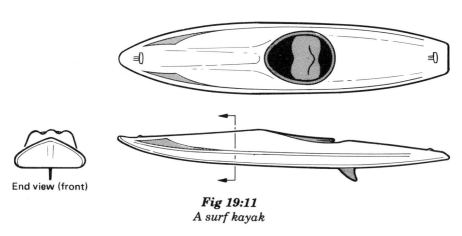

Fig 19:11
A surf kayak

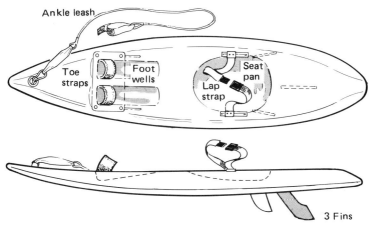

Fig 19:12
A wave ski

3 Fins

Plate 19:f (above) and 19:g
Wave skis

Fins

Fins are a vital piece of equipment for the wave ski and come in all shapes and sizes, each having advantages and disadvantages. The fin, or fins, allow the ski to grip the wave face, rather than letting it skid (spin out) while manoeuvring.

The most common configuration is the thruster/tri-fin system. This consists of two small fins (wings) positioned on each side of the hull under the seat pan area, and one larger central fin. The fins are mounted in fin boxes which allow the rider to adjust them forwards or backwards to the optimum position for the prevailing conditions. Basically, the further forward the fins are, the easier it is for the ski to turn. This is known as 'being loose'. This, however, sacrifices 'grip' on the water. The further back the fins are, the more directional the ski becomes.

471

Paddles

Most dedicated surf paddlers use asymmetric paddles of around 200cm in length, or less. This allows a very high paddle rate for instant maximum speed during take-off or when paddling out. This short paddle also tends to catch less on the wave face during manoeuvres. The only disadvantage is that rolling is slightly more difficult, due to the shortening of the lever.

Leashes

An ankle leash is an important piece of equipment for the ski paddler, especially during the early stages of learning. It consists of a length of strong elastic material which is attached to the ski and the paddler's ankle.

Plate 9:h
Wave ski paddles are short and asymmetric

If the paddler 'bails out' of his ski it cannot be washed away from him and all he has to do is to pull in on the leash and climb back on. Paddle leashes are also now becoming popular. They attach either to the wrist or to the ski.

Wax

Wax is a soft 'sweet smelling' version of ordinary candle wax which is rubbed onto the seat pan and foot wells of the ski to stop you slipping around. A small amount can also be rubbed onto the control-hand side of the paddle shaft for extra grip.

Clothing

A good fitting wet suit, buoyancy aid, spray deck (for kayak paddlers) and helmet will provide not only the necessary insulation and flotation while on the water but also protection in the event of an unexpected collision with another water user. A lot of ski paddlers use a one-piece wet suit, sometimes called a steamer, and sacrifice the buoyancy aid for the freedom of movement thus gained. A full, one-piece wet suit gives a considerable amount of flotation in itself. The decision not to wear a buoyancy aid should take note of your paddling ability and the surf conditions prevailing.

ORGANISATION

When you arrive at a beach, observe the waves for long enough to determine if they are coming in as regular 'sets'. Where does the wave first start to break ? Does it peel off in one particular direction ? Where do you think the rip could be ? Why are all those surfers just in that one spot ? These are some of the questions you

472

should be asking yourself before you get on the water. If you are in charge of a group of beginners then you must give them a thorough briefing before you let them out of your grasp ! This should include :

o 'Buddying up' by splitting the group into pairs with one person paddling whilst the other helps to launch and rescue. Swopping over at regular intervals will help their strength last a little longer.

o Use a set of hand and/or sound signals. The Corps of Canoe Lifeguards have a set of signals laid out for this type of activity or you can invent your own. Either way make sure that your group know what your signals mean. A cheap compressed air horn for attracting attention and a brightly coloured paddle as a pointer will be most useful when working with groups.

o Mark out the area that the group is going to use and make sure everyone stays inside it. This is especially important if the beach is crowded, if there is a cross wind, or a rip is running across the surfing area. You must also observe any lifeguard flags or restrictions that may be in force on the beach at the time.

Use of a pattern shaped like an inverted mushroom (Fig 19:13) is the safest way to organise paddling out and surfing in. It should be stressed to the group that the person surfing in on the wave has 'right of way'. If there is a risk of collision the wisest thing to do to reduce the likelihood of injury is to capsize.

o In the event of taking a swim, a paddler should stay to the seaward side of his craft to avoid being injured by it.

When swimming ashore with a kayak, the easiest method by far is to lie on the upturned hull, across the stern and reaching under the water to grasp the back

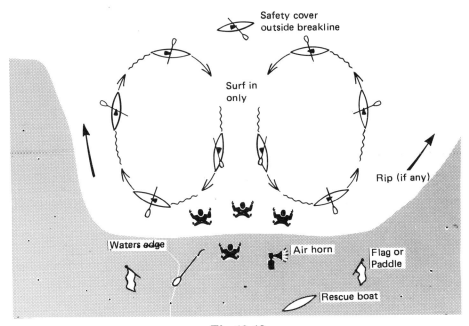

Fig 19:13
Organising a beach for an introductory surfing session

of the cockpit rim. The paddle can be tucked under one arm and the whole thing can be propelled by kicking with the legs. The buddy can wade out to help bring the boat ashore and get it emptied.

It is imperative that a swimmer is not caught on the break line whilst on the shoreward side of the craft, especially if it is a kayak. The enormous weight of a waterlogged kayak can do serious harm.

o Insist that all craft are *carried to the water edge and back again*. Even plastic craft will wear out very quickly if dragged along wet sand. The buddy system works well here especially if it is windy. Wave skis can be carried by one person either 'piggy back' fashion or, if the ski is short, by the lap strap strung over one shoulder.

6 Show courtesy to other surfers. There is always another wave so let everyone get a chance.

A small stove with an endless supply of 'brew' continuously on the boil is a great morale booster. The paddler and buddy can then come in and have a hot drink whenever they wish.

COACHING

With many sports the instructor can go out in front of his pupils, give a demonstration and then set his group to work on the task, calling them in to give advice when necessary. With surfing, the medium in which we are working is continuously changing and so even giving a clear demonstration can be difficult. Surfing alongside pupils and shouting instructions can sometimes work, but conditions have to be good, and the instructor an exceptional handler of his craft.

The use of a video camera, either hand operated, or set up and left running while the session is in progress, works well. The film can be reviewed later in the day in the warmth of the classroom using slow motion (if available) to highlight important coaching points. Video cameras and recorders can now be hired on a daily basis quite cheaply and can be a very effective way of improving your own paddling/coaching technique as well your pupils' performance.

Warm up

Before undertaking any form of physical activity it is important that you warm up thoroughly. Often we arrive at the surf spot in a nice warm car, see the waves breaking perfectly in the bay and then leap into the cold, expecting our bodies to function immediately at maximum efficiency. Breaking surf can be very violent, bending your body into unimaginable positions. If you want your joints and bones to last to a ripe old age it is only fair to spend time before the session on warming up.

Technique

Basic surfing techniques for a kayak and a wave ski are very similar, and once the paddler has mastered these he can then progress into the discipline of his choice, adapting the sound fundamentals to suit the specialised craft.

During the initial sessions it is advisable for ski paddlers not to use fins. The ski will thus be more forgiving, and proper edge control will be developed more quickly. There will also be less risk of damage to the fins, or ski, if it is inadvertently run up the beach.

One of the most important fundamentals of paddle surfing, which many paddlers find difficult to grasp, is the full use of body movement. A board surfer can walk around his board in order to alter its trim, but the paddler is fixed to a single position. He can only alter trim by movement of the upper body from the hips. It is therefore important that he develops the mobility to lean his body throughout a 360 degree radius around the cockpit area.

Launching

Carry the craft down to the water's edge to a point reached only by the larger swells. Climb aboard and fit the ankle leash or spray deck. Wait for the next wave to arrive and then launch out into the water pushing with the paddle on one side and the hand on the other. Once properly afloat the craft is paddled towards the incoming waves. If fins are fitted on a ski then fit the ankle leash first and wade out to thigh depth. Climb aboard leaving the legs in the water for stability while you assemble the lap strap and then slot your feet into the footstraps before tightening the lap strap. During this whole operation you must keep the craft at 90 degrees to the oncoming waves. If the buddy system is being used then the buddy can hold onto the front of the craft and help with the launch once the paddler is ready.

Using a lap strap for the first time can be a little unnerving but correct control of the ski cannot be achieved without it. Test it by paddling out to a safe depth, holding onto the release mechanism, capsizing and releasing yourself. It is important to push with the feet to free them from the toe straps. If you wipe out and try to escape without removing your feet from the toe straps you can injure the ankle joints. Have a buddy stand by when you do capsize practice. Do not use the strap until you are totally confident of releasing it in all situations.

Paddling out

Paddling out through surf can be quite intimidating for the beginner. Many get out beyond the break line and are then reluctant to paddle back in again ! With a little patience and skill the art of getting out will come very quickly. The most important thing to avoid is being hit in the upper body by the full force of a broken wave, unless of course the aim is to reverse loop.

Paddle into oncoming waves at a slight angle rather than at right angles. As the wave approaches the bow lean back and down wave slightly, keeping the paddle high to avoid being hit in the face by the shaft and pull the craft through the wave. As you approach the break line pace yourself so that you can either hold back and let the wave break or put on a quick sprint to get over the top of it. Once you get beyond the break paddle a little further to get your breath back to avoid being caught by any large sets which might come through.

If you are using a ski then the technique is a little different. As the white water approaches the bow lean back and when it hits the hull pull hard on the toe straps and throw your weight forward. Pull through with a deep paddle stroke to shoot the ski up onto the next level of water. Remember, the point where the wave is breaking is the area of greatest power so try to avoid this when paddling out if possible. If there is a rip then use it to your advantage. If conditions are exceptionally difficult the only option you have left is to roll under the waves. As the wall of water approaches you wind up into a screw roll position and capsize just before the water hits the bow. Throw your weight forward to keep the nose of the craft down and pull the paddle close to the body to avoid it being torn out of your grasp. Once the 'washing machine' effect has died down, roll up !

Bongo slide

Before you venture out beyond the break line you must have complete control of your craft in the broken water which is known as the 'soup'. Paddle out to where there are lines of broken waves coming in at regular intervals and turn your craft so that it is sideways-on to the waves. As the water hits you lean well into the wave and apply a high or low brace (in line with the hips) depending on the size of the wave. The wave will push you sideways and bounce you towards the beach in the classic 'bongo slide' position. If you lean forwards and apply the high or low brace in front of the hips the craft will tend to track in the direction the stern is pointing. If you lean back and apply the brace behind the hips the craft will track in the direction the bow is pointing. So by varying your body position you can control the angle of the craft as it slides shorewards. Remember, as with all paddling techniques, to practise on both sides. Once you feel confident at handling your craft in the broken water you can go out beyond the break line to the green waves.

Take off and trim

The point where a wave breaks is the steepest angle it will ever reach. This is the ideal spot to take off from on a wave ride. In the early stages of learning, however, it is best to take off a little to the side of this high point so that you have a less steep platform from which to start the run.

Plate 19:i
The take off

Trunk rotated. Back
towards wave face

Lean back to
slow down

Lean forward
to accelerate

Twist hips into
wave for
grip

Stern rudder at rear.
On shoreward side

Fig 19:14
The diagonal run

As the wave approaches from behind point your craft towards the beach and start paddling. The stern will rise and at this point put in a short sprint, leaning forwards at the same time. The craft will start to fall down the front of the wave face and begin to surf. If you continue to lean forwards then the nose of the craft will start to dig in, the tail will rise and you will loop end over end. So, once the craft starts to surf, lean back and adjust your trim. If you lean forwards the craft will accelerate and fall to the bottom of the wave. If you constantly lean back the craft will 'stall', or slow down and as the wave advances you will climb backwards up the face. By using body movement, fore and aft, you can not only adjust your speed, but also your height on the wave.

Once you have started to run on the wave you will soon notice the craft wanting to turn sideways, parallel to the wave. If it is allowed to do this, it usually results in the wave passing under the craft, leaving the paddler with a feeling of 'falling off the back of the wave'. Sometimes the wave breaks whilst the paddler is sideways-on, in which case he must use a high or low brace as the craft goes into a bongo slide.

The technique of riding an unbroken wave by travelling along its length as well as running shorewards is fundamental to surfing in any craft. It is called a 'diagonal run'.

Get the ski or kayak surfing and then turn away from the break and tilt the craft with the hips into the wave to allow the edge, or rail, to grip the water. Twist the upper body towards the beach and apply a stern rudder on the down-wave (beach) side, prising the stern into the wave to keep the nose down and pointing along the wave (Fig 19:14). Once in this position, alter your trim by moving your

Plate 19:j
The diagonal run is a fundamental wave riding concept which applies to any surfing craft

Plate 19:k

body weight forwards or backwards. With a combination of paddle pressure and hip tilt you should be able to steer a course up and down the wave. This makes for a longer and more interesting ride. If you want to turn back towards the break, roll the hips out to release the rail and to flatten the hull. Slide the paddle out from the stern to a position that is a cross between a low brace and a stern rudder; lean onto the paddle and into the turn, carving what was the beach rail around onto the wave side. Once in this position resume the stern rudder stance again. During the turn you will slow down, so try to maintain speed by leaning forwards.

WHICH WAY ?

At this point in your surfing career you should be looking at waves more closely. Where are they going to break ? When should I get off the wave ? How many turns can I get in ? Wave awareness will only come with practice and many wipeouts ! Now you must choose which path you wish to take: slalom kayak or wave ski. Whatever your choice it is all good fun !

20 Forms of Canoeing Competition

compiled by the Editor

INTRODUCTION

Standards in all sports have been rising consistently for many years. This has lead to specialisation, and craft and techniques have developed in all disciplines of canoeing which in the main are suitable for one purpose only. It is still possible for a performer of high calibre to enjoy good competition and good canoeing in many different ways, but it is less likely now that an individual will rise to the very top in more than one type of event. There is no reason, however, why a canoeist cannot compete at an enjoyable level across the board. Many do, and pursue touring, expeditioning and other recreational pursuits as well. A high proportion of the major white water river expeditions, for instance, have been undertaken by leading slalom and wild water racing paddlers.

During the past decade, greater emphasis has been laid on the importance of training and coaching in order to achieve success. With the continual increase in knowledge about how to attain maximum physical fitness, develop the specific muscles to cope with the power requirement, and the science of psychological preparation to motivate the athlete, it is essential that coaches take the necessary steps to keep themselves informed and up to date.

This chapter does not attempt to provide that specific training or coaching information for competitive canoeists, but reference is made in the Bibliography to the sources from which further information can be obtained.

In general terms, a canoeist needs to develop the cardio-vascular system in order to supply the oxygen required to break down the muscle glycogen which enables them to function. Running, circuit training and swimming are generally reckoned to be the best forms of exercise to achieve this. Cycling is also useful. Interval training, both in the canoe, and when running, is good, because the flat-out burst of effort where high heart beat rates are achieved, followed immediately by a recovery period, has a significant effect. Interval training should not, however, be used with young paddlers (under 16 as a rough guide).

Power training must be specific. There is no point in developing strength in muscles that are not required, nor in ways in which a muscle is not used for canoeing purposes. Various apparatus has been designed to imitate accurately the paddling action, enabling the canoeist to develop his ability to pull with trunk rotation and the lower arm. Heavy weights should not be used by young people until about puberty, because this has an adverse effect on bone growth.

Local muscular endurance is improved by circuit training exercises with weights but again, the routines chosen must be relevant to the use to which the muscles will be put in propelling the canoe. There will be differences between the needs of slalomists and racing paddlers in this respect. In all training routines involving the use of weights, expert advice should be sought before starting. Mobility exercises help to keep muscles supple and extend the range of movement. They should be part of the canoeist's training programme and can be incorporated in a 'warm-up'.

Some coaches feel that diet is important but, generally speaking, properly balanced meals will provide adequate nutritional intake. Women and girls may require iron supplements which should be prescribed by a doctor.

Research has shown that excessive fitness training applied to young people before puberty does not significantly improve performance. Some may enjoy a certain involvement with suitable programmes, but there is no point in pursuing this to any great extent, and the use of heavy weights must be discouraged.

Training in the boat is the most relevant of all, but a proportional balance must be maintained in order to provide variety, and to improve most efficiently those components which together allow maximum performance to be achieved. For juniors, the greatest emphasis should be on developing technique, allied to maintaining interest, having fun, and increasing the ability to cover distances at a steady rate.

HOT DOG CANOEING

Freestyle canoeing, or 'hot dogging', is simply making the canoe perform tricks and stunts. It is mostly done for fun, trying to impress your friends or passers by, although recently canoeists have started organising competitive hot dog events called 'rodeos'. Any stretch of white water has potential for hot dog canoeing, but in the UK the best venues for competitive events are: the big Thames weirs, at Holme Pierrepont, or on the many tide races around the coast.

The best type of boat for learning hot dog canoeing is one with no serious vices in white water. It should be reasonably short, about 2.8 to 3.5 metres in length, and have rounded contours that do not catch the water. A bat or small general purpose plastic kayak is ideal.

When experienced, the choice of a performance kayak is quite wide. Slalom canoes with low volume, sharp edges and high manoeuverability perform well in white water, but are fragile and do not last long. A cut down slalom kayak with rounded ends, or a rotomoulded plastic version of a similar shape works well. Squirt boats are ultra low volume kayaks designed to dip under water with the greatest ease, even on flat water; these are for experts only. Kayaks are available that have been designed purely for hot dog canoeing. They combine the performance of a slalom boat with the toughness of plastic construction, but are normally of higher volume to perform many tricks when airborne rather than underwater. An advantage of hot dog canoeing is that many different types of canoe can compete equally. One rodeo on a tide race even had a class for sea kayaks.

The first basic skill in rodeo canoeing is sitting sideways in a stopper using a low brace support. When happy with that, take your downstream hand off the paddle and plunge it deep into the white water. This provides a surprising amount of support. It is quite easy to balance yourself without a paddle. The tricks then are only limited by imagination. Twirl your paddles like a band leader, throw them away, drink a can of coke, drop your paddles on the upstream side and catch them as they pass beneath the boat with your downstream hand. Learn to hand roll first.

Plate 20:a
Hot dogging in a stopper at Holme Pierrepont

The other skill to master is the loop. Drop into a stopper or wave pointing exactly upstream, and leaning well forward. The bow will dip underwater, and the boat will be thrown upwards and backwards. Either stay leaning forward to let the boat somersault right over, or lean back in the seat to make the boat fly up vertically clear of the water. More advanced tricks involve pirouettes (spinning around the boat's axis when vertical), or looping with the boat tilted on edge, to make it spin round and land back in the stopper facing the other way.

Wild water rodeos are easy to organise, requiring only a few judges and suitable white water. Make the rules as straight forward as possible, rewarding stylish and daring paddling, but keeping an eye on safety. Hot dog canoeing is exciting and very good for your canoeing skills, but try to keep it simple, informal and fun.

MARATHON RACING

The term 'marathon racing' should not deter anyone from entering a local event, whatever their age, or type of kayak or canoe owned. Most people enjoy touring, and marathon racing enables a canoeist to proceed uninterrupted at his own pace, on different and varying waterways.

Racing for fun

A recent revision of the marathon racing scheme has led to the development of a divisional system, in which all types of craft and all ages of people of either sex can compete on equal terms. Known as the Open Racing Scheme, events can be held on any type of water, at club, local, regional and national level, and cater for any number of participants from a minimum of five. The lower Divisions 8 and 9 - race over a *maximum* of only four miles. Full details of how to stage club or local races are available free from the BCU. A network of regional advisers exists to help with enquiries.

Promotion, which from the lower divisions can take place at local level and is organised on a percentage basis. All competitors receive a certificate which entitles them to an entry in a national draw which takes place several times each year. Once a paddler begins to move up the divisions, he will normally compete at regional, and then national level events, but the system enables everyone, in any type of kayak or canoe, to find his level and enjoy continued good competition.

Serious marathon paddlers usually gravitate eventually to international racing K1s or K2s, C1s or C2s and compete over distances which vary between 10 and 80 miles.

The *Racing yearbook* published annually, gives full details of rules and events, with advice to organisers, and shows the ranking lists of paddlers for Divisions 1-8, based on promotion achieved throughout the previous season.

Marathon racing rules

Boats must be rendered sufficiently buoyant to stay afloat and support the crew in rough water when capsized, and adequate spray decks must be worn on open water. Competitors must be competent to swim in the waters on which the race is held, and life jackets or buoyancy aids (minimum inherent buoyancy 6kg) must be worn by all those under 16, and by others at the organiser's discretion.

Plate 20:b
A junior crew competing in Britain's best known canoe marathon, the annual Devizes to Westminster race

Plate 20:c

*Rachel Bland and Jo Turbey, winners of the junior ladies' class in the 1988
Devizes to Westminster race, after one of the many portages*

Competitors may not wash hang on powered craft during a race, nor change
boats. They may receive food and drink, but not other assistance, unless
permitted by the organiser (eg a disabled person whose boat is carried for them
at a portage). Paddles may be changed in the event of a breakage. A code is used
to identify the type of water, and the number of portages involved:

'A' denotes sea, tidal estuary, lake or other open water

'B' denotes fresh water rivers and canals

'P' denotes portages.

A numeral following the symbol shows the length in miles or the number of
portages: eg A5B6P7 indicates a race of five miles on open water, six on closed
water, and seven portages.

Boat designs

Any type of canoe or kayak may be used, but only within the ICF regulations for
length, breadth and weight, as shown:

	Maximum length	*Minimum beam*
Single kayak	520cm (17')	51cm (20")
Double kayak	650cm (21'4")	55cm (21½")
Single canoe	520cm (17')	75cm (29½")
Double canoe	650cm (21'4")	75cm (29½")

Plate 20:d
K2s racing in the Exe Descent

Boats over 460cm in length must not have concave sections. Propulsion shall be by paddle only, the paddle being supported solely by the hands. In essence, the class rules above mean that most canoes or kayaks can race. Obviously, those that conform most closely to the limits are likely to be the most successful in the right hands.

There are different classes of event dependent upon the standard of course and organisation involved, and particular races are nominated to count for various perpetual awards such as the Hasler Trophy, for which the rules are designed to enable any club with an interest in marathon racing to compete on equal terms.

Tactics and portaging

Apart from developing the physical ability to paddle at top speed for the duration of the course, serious competitors pay a great deal of attention to race tactics. The whole concept of marathon is that it should be held on natural waterways, and involve taking whatever steps are necessary to navigate the canoe to the finish. It may be necessary to cross large lakes, or estuaries, shoot weirs, or portage the canoe around obstacles or potentially dangerous situations.

Attention has to be paid to the vagaries of tide and current, reading the water to spot rocks and shallows, and practising techniques to ensure a swift transition at portages. Especially important is the development of 'wash-hanging' skills. By sitting close to another canoe, it is possible to obtain a considerable 'lift' from your opponent's wake. Depending upon the speed of travel, it is usually necessary to place your bow about a third of the way back from his. Thus you are conserving energy for the time when you sprint, and hopefully leave him behind. He, meanwhile, will try to cause you to drop back off the wash, which is invariably extremely difficult to regain.

Most marathons commence with a mass start, and the ability to gain the first portage ahead of the field can be critical. Many paddlers fix foot-rest pumps to enable the boat to be kept dry, and attention needs to be paid to ensure that spray decks keep the water out, but can be quickly removed and fitted when portaging.

National and international competition

A National Championships is held in which all age groups are catered for. The ICF awarded marathon racing international recognition in 1980, and 1988 saw the inaugural World Championships take place in Nottingham. A number of major events between nations now take place, including a European grand prix series. Some races in other parts of the world, notably Australia, South Africa, the USA and Canada, involve hundreds of miles of lake and river, sometimes crossing mountains, and are occasionally of up to a month's duration. The longest race in Great Britain is the annual Devizes to Westminster canoe race, traditionally held at Easter, which is of 126 miles duration and requires 72 portages. Seniors race non-stop, while juniors have three compulsory overnight stops.

Conclusion

Marathon racing has the greatest potential for expansion of all the competitive forms of canoeing. It is now within the scope of any and every local group, club, or individual to stage a low-key event, with a minimum requirement for facilities and organisation. The emphasis is on fun and enjoyment for all the family, but feeding into the national system.

CANOE POLO

A game for teams of five players, who endeavour to pass the ball to each other, avoiding the opposition, until scoring in their opponents goal.

This description does not begin to reveal the excitement and enjoyment that is engendered in having to control a small, unstable craft, propel it at maximum velocity, spin and balance it, while passing the ball, with opponents permitted to capsize the paddler by pushing him off balance when he is in possession, neither does it convey the fierceness with which games are contended at all levels.

Canoe Polo can be played on any area of water that enables a pitch of regulation size to be laid out, and goals - 1.5m long and 1m high with lower edge 2 metres from the water - erected.

In 1989 the ICF Congress accepted Canoe Polo as one of its canoe sports and adopted the new International rules which are now common to all ICF member nations.

The new rules are based on variations of the British, French, and Australian games and provide an excellent basis for international competition.

The Canoe Polo Committee also adopted these ICF rules (with minor alterations) so that one game only would be played at home and abroad.

With the pending acceptance of ICF rules came the introduction of a British Canoe Polo Squad for men based at Luton which since 1987 has been enormously successful winning all but two of the last ten Internationals. Several European countries are now running squads but with a two year start British teams still have the edge in a rapidly developing tactical game. 1990 will see the introduction of a National Ladies Squad and a Youth Squad is likely to be considered by 1993.

Plate 20:e
The wire visor worn in polo to protect the face
PHOTO: TONY TICKLE

Canoe Polo is the fastest growing canoe sport in Great Britain and by far the most successful in International competition. Like other rapidly growing amateur sports however we need the voluntary support of our followers if we are to maintain our position at the top.

Safety

Crash helmets are compulsory, together with full-length buoyancy aids to protect the trunk and lumbar region. Although dangerous use of the paddle is penalised, polo is a close contact game and a wire visor worn to protect the face is a sensible precaution. Paddle blades must not be metal tipped and a minimum thickness at the edge is stipulated. Neither deliberate ramming nor obstruction is permitted.

Contests

Many friendly inter-club games are played, besides local and regional leagues operating. The National League has four Divisions for senior teams, two Divisions for ladies and a further two Divisions for youth teams. In addition there is a National Knockout Competition.

Attracting over 100 entries, the finals of which are held each year at the International Canoe Exhibition at Crystal Palace.

The BCU Canoe Polo Committee run a major international in June each year to which teams from the rest of the world are invited. The venue for this International being either Luton or Crystal Palace.

Coaching and Refereeing

Polo has a well-defined structure for the training and assessing of Coaches and Referees. The details of these, as well as the Polo rules are contained in the BCU Canoe Polo Handbook. The following Coaching points and training games are taken from the booklet *"Canoe Polo, Coaching and Tactics"* available through the BCU supplies department.

Paddle Skills

The paddle is being used more and more in controlling and passing the ball. The advantage of being able to 'play' the ball when it is out of arms reach is obvious but care must be taken not to 'strike' the ball but only to deflect or flick.

In order to pick the ball up out of the water the back of the blade is pushed down on the ball or backwards. The blade is then turned to allow the ball to roll onto the face. This must be a smooth, controlled action without striking the ball. The ball must be submerged sufficiently for it to roll up onto the face of the blade.

Spoon blades are better than curved blades. Flat blades make the action very difficult. If the ball is being moved forwards roll the blade back over the ball. If the ball is being moved backwards roll the blade forwards over the ball.

Small Sided Games

Possession Games

It is important that whatever game is played the team with possession is able to make several passes before losing it. Thus with relative beginners it is usual to play an additional paddler on the side of the attacking team, ie: 2 v 1, or 3 v 2.

Many games are simply possession games without scoring goals, ie: how many passes can you make without losing possession ?

Game 1

The possession game most suited to beginners is 2 v 1

Game 2

3 v 2. The coach can save time by choosing two groups of two; the fifth player plays with the two who have possession at any one time. Thus any player can pass to No. 5 and there are always three with possession against two defenders.

Game 3

1 v 1 possession is a very good game for average player who will enjoy competing on an individual basis.

Game 4

2 v 2 possession is a demanding game and one that involves a wide number of skills and techniques.

Game 5

3 v 3 is the basis of all ball games; with three paddlers you should always have a formation on the pool.

If players cannot play 3 v 3 well a 5 v 5 full game will be of a very low standard.

Game 6

4 v 4 possession demands a large pool and should only be practiced with competent paddlers.

Games involving some form of scoring

There are three basic methods:

Game 7

Rugby type scoring: players score by placing the ball onto the poolside in a designated area (between two sets of steps or the whole of the end of the pool).

Game 8

Shooting to a helper who is standing on the end (or side) of the pool. The helper must catch the ball above his head without moving his feet.

Game 9

Shooting at a goal. Ideally this goal should be 1.5m x 1m, but could be a hoop or something similar.

When using a goal or goals several variations of game are available.

Game 10

One goal is suspended across the centre of the pool. One team score through one side of the goal, the other team through the other side. The game in continuous (except for free throws). The first team to score five goals wins.

It may be necessary to raise the goal to stop players from crowding the area under goal.

Game 11

One goal suspended at the end of the pol. A possession game is played and once a team has made a certain number of consecutive passes they are able to shoot.

Game 12

One goal suspended at the end of the pool. One team defends the goal and the other attacks. Attackers are given four attempts to score., Defenders attempt to score by gaining possession and dribbling the ball to the far end of the pool. Free throws, throw ins, and corners are taken as normal.l The ball may be thrown in at the centre to begin, or given to one side for a goal throw.

Game 13

One goal at each end of the pool. This can either be a 'full' game or restricted in some way to save boat damage, eg: no sprinting for the ball at the centre.

RACING

Previously known as paddle racing, and commonly called sprint, this branch of the sport is a competition for canoes and kayaks over a course as flat and as still as can be obtained of distances up to and including 10,000 metres. Competitions may be organised for any craft, but the normal classes of boat are K1, K2, K4, C1, C2 and C4. The distances are 500 metres, 1,000 metres, and 10,000 metres. Nationally, juniors race 3,000 or 6,000 metres as a distance event, and ladies 6,000 metres.

World championships for seniors are held every year except Olympic year, when canoe racing forms part of the Olympic games. For juniors, a junior world championships is held every two years. Olympic canoe and kayak racing involves 500 and 1,000 metres for men and 500 metres for women. Fig 20:2 shows the usual international and Olympic racing events, while Fig 20:1 identifies the classes of boat and shows their dimensions. For national championships and international purposes, no turns are permitted for distances of 1,000 metres or less, and the start and finish must be at right angles to the course. Where possible there must be at least five metres between boats, which should be able to race in clearly marked lanes. Wash hanging is not permitted for races up to 1,000 metres.

The premier site in Britain for racing is at the National Water Sports Centre at Holme Pierrepont, Nottingham. This purpose-built course accommodates nine buoyed lanes for canoeing and is equipped with modern timing and control equipment, including a photo-finish facility. Local regattas can be held on any river or open area of water which permits a 500 metre straight course. Water should ideally be a minimum of 1.5 metres deep. Full guidance on how to set about staging a regatta is available from the BCU and, whilst there is every reason for the event to be run as well as possible, an approved chief official, when appointed, will be able to advise on the essentials.

Racing registration scheme

When entering a ranking regatta for the first time, paddlers register with the BCU Racing Committee on production of a BCU membership card. A team leader must be identified who is responsible for making all entries and attending the briefing, known as the 'team leaders meeting'. A well-run regatta is an extremely busy affair, with races starting and finishing every few minutes throughout the weekend. As many events may be entered as the competitor wishes, and the greatest headache for organisers is to schedule the classes and distances to ensure that a competitor has a reasonable chance of being able to do so. The annual calendar of events is published in the *Racing yearbook* together with all other necessary information: rules, advice to organisers, names and addresses of officials and coaches, team leaders handbook, and so forth.

Equipment

Until recently, in spite of the advent of fibreglass, wood veneer boats were favoured by most for racing and, with notable exceptions, still are at international level.

However, rigidity and lightness can be combined by using sandwich construction methods, where a lightweight plastic foam honeycomb aluminium or paper core is trapped between two layers of fibreglass. Competition among manufacturers of boats and other equipment connected with racing is intense as, more than in any other branch of the sport when all else is equal, the faster boat will win the day.

Rudders are normally under-stern, for maximum efficiency, and in any case are not included in the maximum length restrictions. Spooned asymmetric paddles are mainly used since these enter more evenly, presenting a balanced face when pulled, and allowing maximum 'grip' of the water. Lifejackets or buoyancy aids are usually unnecessary, except for the very junior classes, as racing is closely supervised by umpire and safety launches.

Skills and tactics

A 'closed skill' is one where an identical movement is repeated consistently in order to achieve the given end, whereas an 'open skill' requires a fluidity of reaction to constantly changing circumstances. Flat water racing is therefore towards the 'closed skill' end of the spectrum so far as canoeing is concerned, and

Plate 20:f
A K4 1,000m event at the 1988 Olympic Regatta in Seoul

great attention must be paid to the development of a strong, efficient and consistent forward paddling technique, that does not break down when the canoeist is under pressure.

Apart from the distance events, where positioning and behaviour on the turns can be vital, tactics largely consist of paddling at the limit of one's capacity.

Getting started

The marathon Open Racing Scheme is probably the best introduction to sprint racing. A K1 or C1 needs to be mastered to the point where it can be comfortably balanced, and so successfully raced for the duration of the course. The Racing Encouragement Tests are a means to this end, and the advice given in chapter 14 is pertinent.

Plate 20:g
Jeremy West and Grayson Bourne, Britain's top racers of the '80s,
training in K2

	World Championship Events			Olympic Events	
	500m	1,000m	10,000m	500m	1,000m
Men					
	K1	K1	K1	K1	K1
	K2	K2	K2	K2	K2
	K4	K4	K4		K4
	C1	C1	C1	C1	C1
	C2	C2	C2	C2	C2
	C4	C4			
Women	500m		5,000	500m	
	K1		K1	K1	
	K2		K2	K2	
	K4			K4	

Fig 20:1
World championships, and Olympic sprint racing distances

Changes have taken place in the organisation of domestic sprint racing at club level, with the policy being to cope with the present expansion and encourage an even greater participation. More competition will be available which will be easily accessible to all at the lower levels.

The Divisional system for Sprint Racing

The racing divisional system for sprint is different from marathon. There are separate races for men, ladies, seniors, juniors, canoe and kayak. The number of divisions at present for each class is shown below. These are being increased as more people take part in the sport. For senior, and junior competitors, the starting point the Senior and Junior 'D' division. Promotion depends on performance.

Class	*Divisions*
Kayak Men	4 Divisions: A, B, C, D.
Kayak Ladies	3 Divisions: A, B, C.
Kayak Junior	4 Divisions: A, B, C, D.
Kayak Junior Girls	4 Divisions: A, B, C, D.
Canoe·	4 Divisions: A, B; and Junior A, B.

Seniors race over 500m, 10,000m. Ladies race over 500m and 6,000m. Junior paddlers race over different distances depending on division - the bottom division distances are 500m and 3,000m. The Division A's race over 500m, 1,000m and 6,000m.

Plate 20:h
Gyulay of Hungary, 1988 Olympic Champion in K1 500 metres

The 10,000 Metre Award

10,000 metres is a standard racing distance, competed over annually in the world championships, and is the longest distance raced under sprint racing conditions. To be able to paddle 10,000 metres in a racing kayak or canoe without stopping is an indication of a fair degree of competence and paddling fitness. A paddler who can do so would feel that he or she could enter a regatta race without being likely to disgrace him or herself. Members of the BCU coaching scheme may assess this test of competence in any racing K1, and may obtain badges and certificates from the Award secretary.

It is suggested that the test should be made something of an occasion, the culmination of a winter's training, perhaps, with spectators, and an interesting course exactly the right length, with notices every 1,000 metres and so on. The assessor must use his experience to ensure safe practice and the proper sort of safety regulations for the 10,000 metre course he is laying out.

Plate 20:i
An International 10 Square Metre Sailing Canoe in full flight

SAILING

The craft

The international 10 square metre canoe is the fastest single-handed sailing dinghy in the world, requiring a combination of skill, fitness and agility unmatched anywhere else in the canoeing or sailing sports.

The 'IC' is a highly sophisticated sea-going craft, sailed in eleven countries throughout the world on open waters; in Britain there are four major fleets at Hayling Island, Stone, Loughton and Scaling Dam with lesser groups to be found across mainland Britain.

The IC has a 5.2 metre long, canoe shaped hull weighing 63kg driven by 10 square metres of sail. The helmsman is provided with a sliding seat on which he perches to counteract the healing force of the wind on the sails. This results in speeds in excess of 30km/h in a good breeze which makes sailing the fastest of all ICF world championship disciplines.

Whilst the shape of the IC's hull is strictly controlled, sailors have the liberty to adjust the rig design to suit their body weights and personal preferences.

Plate 20:k
The World Canoe Sailing Championships at Plymouth, 1987
PHOTO: WESTERN EVENING HERALD

Canoe sailors

The IC is sailed at top championship level by men and women from 69 to 95kg in weight and from 19 to 60 years of age. Older helmsmen offset their lack of vigour with greater skill and cunning as a result of long experience.

To win in competition requires perfect control, tactical exploitation of winds, currents and racing rules, and an ability to prepare and tune the IC to produce maximum performance.

Competition

Racing ranges from weekly events held throughout the year at local club level, through a national and European circuit of about ten events during the summer months, to British (annually) and World Championships (triennially) sanctioned by the BCU and ICF respectively.

Trial and purchase

Detailed information is available from the Secretary of the BCU Sailing Section (address held by BCU headquarters). An information pack is available which includes details of new and secondhand IC's for sale, building plans, hull moulds for hire and further general advice.

Try-outs can be arranged via the information service and the Sailing Section runs occasional training sessions to help new owners.

CANOE SLALOM

Canoe slalom is a time trial event run through a course of obstacles on a wildwater river. This course can consist of up to 25 'gates' hanging over the river through which a paddler must pass in the correct order and direction. Green and white striped poles must be passed through in a downstream direction and double red poles in an upstream direction.

Plate 20:1
Karen Davies, one of Britain's growing band of elite women slalom athletes
PHOTO: TONY TICKLE

The object is to negotiate the course as quickly as possible without incurring any penalty points for touching the gates or doing them out of order. These penalty 'seconds' are added on to the overall running time to produce a total score. Each competitor has two timed runs, only the best total counting in the final results. The course length is normally between 400 - 600 metres.

There are four classes in canoe slalom: mens and ladies kayak, where the paddler sits and uses a double bladed paddle;

canoe singles and doubles where the paddlers kneel up and use single bladed paddles. There are no separate events for men and women in the canoe classes.

There are also team races in each class which involve three boats negotiating the course at the same time and being timed from the first starting to the last finishing, with all penalties being totalled together.

The first canoe slalom in Britain took place in 1937 and, since the first world championships held in Switzerland in 1949, the sport has grown rapidly. There are now over 5,000 registered competitive slalomists in Great Britain, by far the biggest number in Europe and possibly the world.

Plate 20:m
A slalom C2 competing in a Europa Cup
series event at Holme Pierrepont
PHOTO: TONY TICKLE

World championships are held every alternate year and often involve over 25 nations from all over the world. Great Britain is currently established as one of the three leading slalom nations and has won over 20 world championship medals since 1977.

Ranking slaloms are organised by the BCU Slalom Committee or by registered clubs. Each event is directly related to the national ranking and divisional system. At present time, there are five main divisions starting with Premier for the top 150 competitors and going down to 4th division, which contains over 1000 ranked competitors. When taking up the sport, all paddlers enter 'Novice' level slaloms until they are promoted into the divisional system.

Publications

The *Slalom Yearbook* is published each year in February by the Slalom Committee. It contains all the necessary information relating to the rules, entering a slalom, the divisional system and a calendar of the coming year's events. Any rule changes are also published in this handbook. It is issued free to all ranked competitors in Premier Division to Division 4. To obtain a copy contact the Slalom Administrator or the British Canoe Union.

The Slalom Committee also publishes a handbook called *Slalom Canoeing*. This provides all the essential information on entering your first slalom and a section on basic slalom technique written by the National Slalom Coach - Alan Edge. It is essential reading for anyone starting out in canoe slalom. Again, this can be obtained from the Slalom Administrator or direct from the British Canoe Union.

Without doubt, canoe slalom is one of the most attractive of the canoeing disciplines. It is a superb family sport providing exhilarating yet safe competitions for all ages and standards of paddler.

Plate 20:n
A canoe competitor in the men's K1 event at the World Championships at Bourg St Maurice in the French Alps
PHOTO: TONY TICKLE

SURFING

All BCU ranked and International competitions in England and Wales are organised by the BCU Surf Committee (or SCA in Scotland and CANI in Northern Ireland). A calendar of all BCU events is published annually in the *Surfing Yearbook* which also includes guidelines for competition organisation, contest rules, safety and the judging and scoring system.

Each year a number of BCU ranked 'open entry' competitions are organised in England and Wales, with Scotland and Northern Ireland running their own separate competition calenders. An attempt is usually made to spread competitions around the geographical regions although, inevitably there are concentrations in those areas which enjoy the most reliable surf conditions: South West and North East England and South Wales. Some canoe clubs and regional groups also run non-ranking 'friendly' events. There is also an annual 'British Championships', entry to which is achieved through the previous ranking events. A home international competition is also held annually with teams of paddlers selected from England, Scotland, Northern Ireland and Wales.

Competition organisation

Ranked surf competitions are usually held over a weekend and are run on a knock-out basis. Competitors progress through a series of heats, quarter-finals, semi-finals to a final, with a set number going through to the next round at each stage. Ideally each heat comprises four competitors, although up to six has been known where entries are large. Competitors are identified by coloured bibs.

At the moment, there are two main disciplines in surf competition: slalom kayak and ski, with 'open', 'ladies', 'junior' and 'novice' classes in each.

Plate 20:o
Kayak surfing in
North Wales

Safety

All surf competitions are run in accordance with BCU safety regulations for the sport. Thus competitors must wear helmets and buoyancy aids, Ski paddlers must also wear an ankle leash and or a seat belt.

The craft must meet a set of safety standards. Pointed ends, for example, on craft pose a serious threat to other competitors and swimmers and so the surf committee imposes a minimum acceptable end radius for all competing craft. The regulations are also strict on toggles at boat ends and footrests which will prevent the paddler from slipping forwards.

The judging system

Surf competition judging is essentially subjective in its nature, unlike other canoeing disciplines which are simply based on a time comparison. A paddler's performance is evaluated against a set of basic criteria, rather like gymnastics. There is a judging team, usually of six persons comprising: a chief judge, three assistant judges, a spotter, and a scribe. Every competition also has a beach marshall whose responsibility it is to check all craft for safety standards.

Competition heats last 20 minutes during which time every wave ride taken by each competitor is given a score. At the end of each heat, a competitor's five best waves are totalled, giving a score and overall position in the competition. In the event of a tie, a count back of the sixth, seventh, eighth, etc, wave scores is made until the higher placed surfer emerges.

Performance criteria

Judges will be looking for a combination of several factors in a surfer's performance. These would include the following:

o Wave choice; selection of good waves
o Wave reading; positioning on the wave, staying close to the shoulder
o Length of run; on the unbroken wave
o Range and number of manoeuvres; how well the range of manoeuvres performed are linked together.
o Personal flair and style; the overall 'polish' and 'individualisation' of the performance.

International competition

At present, only the home nations have slalom kayak surfing events, but wave ski competitions are held in France, Australia and the USA.

Plate 20:p
*Gill Berrow, of Scotland, British Women's Wild Water Racing Team, at the
World Championships in France*

WILD WATER RACING

The exhilaration felt by the wild water racer when paddling flat out on a race
course is very similar to the feeling of a down hill ski racer on the alpine slopes.
The speed, the control and the freedom to decide one's own path, whilst competing
against the elements and the clock, is the attraction that both events hold for their
participants.

Wild water racing can be described as a combination of the other three major
racing disciplines: the racer's control in the rough water has to be as precise as
that of the slalom paddler through the gates, the distance that is raced demands
the endurance of the marathon paddler and the power to overcome the frequently
changing water conditions requires the same finesse that is needed by the sprint
canoeist leaving the start or putting in a burst in the middle of the 10,000 metre
event.

With races of about 30 minutes in duration over rapids of up to Grade IV or V
in difficulty, the wild water racer needs a perfect combination of strength, speed,
endurance and flexibility. This is why the enthusiasts consider it the ultimate in
canoe and kayak racing.

Controlled by the Wild Water Racing Committee, there are events all over the
country from October through to June for all standards of competitor. There are
separate divisions for the lower ability competitor, and newcomers to the sport
would start in one of these. With many classes and categories of paddler and boat

in all age groups, and with several open and national championship events throughout the season, there is a wonderful opportunity for many paddlers to succeed and be ranked against their peers.

Raced on a time trial basis, the top events often attract in excess of 200 competitors, each of them starting at 1 minute intervals and racing over rapids of varying difficulties. The successful racer negotiates a route that is as rock-free as possible and utilises the best combination of boat and current speed that he can find. Steering and control is almost always maintained by use of strokes that do not impede the forward movement of the boat.

Every two years a world championships is held, attracting hundreds of canoeists from about 18 nations. Britain staged the world championships in 1981 at Bala and we have gained a reputation for being good organisers of world class events. A full international programme is now developing in Britain, with good competition between the home countries also emerging.

Through the Competition Coaching Scheme, the Wild Water Racing Committee offer courses for the prospective trainer or coach and, through the Team Management Group, a highly thoughtful view on development ensures that many paddlers can have training courses provided that are open to all abilities and age. Many training camps and weekends are offered both at home and abroad for the established and prospective wild water racer.

Generally a beginner would only require a boat that is watertight and suitable for both him and the river, a good paddle, buoyancy aid spraydeck and helmet. Bearing in mind that the British climate is very changeable, adequate protective clothing to wear both on and off the water is of major importance.

Joining a club is always a good move, for training, advice and perhaps most important for the newcomer, transport to and from the events. The advice given would be simple but constructive. However, the best way to improve is to get into the boat and paddle it and at the early stage there is little purpose in specialist training schedules. After the necessary skills have been acquired, then it is worth considering training for the sport and, again, the best advice would be 'join a club'.

Plate 20:q
Katie Watt at
the Junior World
Championships

Initially training would take the form of distance and technique work, primarily skill based but resulting in the development of a sound level of endurance from which to base the later speed and strength training.

Covering distances, particularly at a fast pace, would be the best early training in the season, being replaced later by interval and speed training sessions when the weather and water conditions permit. Winter training would consist of race practice on the rivers and a lot of cardio-vascular endurance work: running, swimming, ball games, circuit training and, whenever possible, distance paddling.

Practice in other forms of craft is another very useful tool for the paddler in his efforts to improve and acquire better skills. Big play boats, slalom training and flat water K1 paddling are all useful options for the paddler to consider for gaining confidence and improving technique.

The art of paddling a boat fast on the rough water and negotiating the rocks often takes a long time to perfect. The racer will always want to be in the fastest water, wherever possible, but will also want to take the shortest route. This means choosing where to cut a corner or how far to paddle into the waves and avoid the eddies that may slow the boat down. Going up and down the waves not only means that your boat travels further, but also that your paddling rate is determined by the frequency of the waves: you only pull on the paddle when the boat is going up the wave and rising, not when the bow is going down. You must time the stroke and pick the wave in which to place your paddle rather than place it in the trough. The boat is controlled when the bow is up out of the water and not when it is buried in the trough.

The strokes that are used to control the boat have an order of priority: lean the boat to steer as your first option; if you know it will not be enough, then use a sweep stroke or a bow rudder at the front of the forward stroke and, as a last resort use a reverse stroke. A forward stroke on one side is nearly always better than a reverse on the other to avoid trouble. A very useful skill in the paddler's repertoire is the ability to 'double stroke', this is two or even more strokes on the same side of the boat in quick succession rather than continue paddling on alternate sides all the time. This will get a boat to respond very quickly without losing forward speed.

It is very important that the paddler progresses steadily, without taking on rivers or training sessions that are beyond his or her capabilities. Seek advice wherever possible.

RAPID RACING

Rapid racing is a new event for the wild water racer in Britain, devised with television in mind. Races are over a course of one to two minutes duration taking in the most exciting stretches of a larger wild water race course or racing straight down a slalom course with no gates to negotiate. The event is very exciting to compete in or to watch. The paddlers push themselves to the limit and, because of the intensity of the event mistakes often happen in the most spectacular fashion.

The wild water racer who is used to the longer 20 or 30 minute event is often pushed very hard by the slalom paddlers who have mastered the intricacies of the wild water racing boat. Raced as a time trial, or even 'head to head', rapid racing has proved very popular with paddlers and sponsors alike.

Plate 20:r
Canoe class wild water racers
in action at Holme Pierrepont
PHOTO: TONY TICKLE

In international events around the world, it has been seen that champions from many of canoeing's disciplines can compete against each other on almost equal terms.

Organised by Rapid Racing Limited, with permission from the Wild Water Racing Committee, the events are held all over the country in conjunction with races or slaloms over the same weekend.

Further information on wild water racing is available through the BCU. The *Wild Water Racing Yearbook* contains rules, race dates and other useful addresses.

21 Access to Water

Carel Quaife

Carel Quaife commenced canoeing in 1952 and has been an active participant and organiser in most aspects of the sport from touring to running regattas. He has been a member of Birmingham Canoe Club since 1957, including five years as secretary.

Having served for eight years as regional coaching organiser for the West Midlands, Carel was elected Chairman of the BCU Coaching Committee, steering it through a difficult period of considerable change and growth, before becoming chairman of the Access, Coaching and Recreation Management Committee of Council. Founder Chairman of the BCU West Midlands Regional Group, he served for four years as Chairman of the BCU Access Committee.

In 1985 Carel was appointed to the full time post of National Development Officer of the BCU, within which role the servicing of the Access Commmittee, and access matters generally, have been a major feature.

INTRODUCTION

Access to water has a wide meaning for canoeists. They need to be able to get their canoes to the water, to paddle along the waterway in pleasant, peaceful surroundings without conflict, and then to get their canoes from the water to their transport. In addition, they will often want to practise canoeing skills at specific locations. What is possible physically is frequently challenged on legal grounds. This chapter sets out to clarify access issues and explain why the BCU is pursuing its current policy. The situation is changing constantly so readers are advised to keep abreast of developments since January 1989 when this was written. Regular updates are printed in *Canoe Focus*, which is issued free to BCU members.

Many canoeists assume instinctively that they have the right to canoe wherever it is physically possible. When they find out that this has been restricted by man made laws, it becomes an emotive issue and there is sometimes an unwillingness to accept the current legal reality. This is a significant factor in the slow progress made by the BCU in safeguarding existing access to water and seeking greatly increased access. Without water there will be no canoeing, but as yet not enough canoeists have come forward to assist with access work. This, it must be admitted, is not necessarily the most pleasant voluntary work that a canoeist can undertake for the sport ! There is now cause for optimism because good new access officers are being recruited at an increasing rate. It is to be hoped that this trend will continue as we are still a long way from having an access officer for every river, with several for the longer rivers so that no one officer has too large a task. In the context of access to water, it must be remembered that 'the BCU' is, in fact, its team of voluntary officers. If you feel that 'the BCU' should be doing more, why not join the access team yourself to help make it happen ?

PUBLIC RIGHTS OF PASSAGE BY BOAT

(extracted from the Access Workers Guide)

In England and Wales a sharp distinction is drawn by the law between the sea and tidal waters on the one hand, and non-tidal water on the other.

o On the sea and tidal waters up to the limit of high water mark ordinary spring tides (marked on Ordnance Survey maps), the 'land covered by water' is regarded as belonging to the Crown, which permits public navigation (and fishing), so far as physical conditions allow, unless the Crown has conveyed the bed of the waterway to someone else (eg the Beaulieu River in Hampshire).

o On non-tidal rivers and lakes, the Crown is regarded as having in the long distant past, transferred the bed of the watercourse to the owners of the adjoining land and there is no automatic right for the public to navigate. However, a public right to pass in boats can come into existence in a number of ways:

1 Proof of existence of public use from 'time immemorial'. Proof of existence in 1189 automatically establishes this. If this is not available, proof of a substantial number of years of use openly and without challenge by the public may be held by a court to be sufficient to establish historical use (it need not necessarily be 20 years, and may have been followed by a period of disuse).

2 Express dedication to public use by the owner (unlikely).

3 Presumed dedication by the owner arising from evidence of open and unchallenged use by the public on a sufficient scale and over a sufficient number of years to justify a court in concluding that the owner intended to dedicate it. Because of the difficulty and uncertainty of this, the Rights of Way Act 1932, which has since been consolidated into Section 31 of the Highways Act 1980, which applies to 'land covered by water', as well as to dry land, states that proof of 20 years of such use (prior to the date of challenge) shall be conclusive; but it is still impossible to forecast what would be regarded by a court as sufficient public use.

A notice that there is no public right of way or obstruction for one day every year, would be enough to establish that the owner had no intention of dedicating the way to the public.

4 By Act of Parliament, usually between the 17th and 19th centuries, in conjunction with works to 'make the river navigable' for commercial use, or 'improve' it for that purpose, eg the Suffolk Stour. Some of these Acts have been repealed in later years; in other cases, the artificial works, eg, locks, are unusable.

If the repeal is by a Ministerial order (eg under the Land Drainage Acts to facilitate the construction of weirs or flood prevention works) it is necessary to ascertain whether 'the navigation', ie the commercial undertaking, was simply closed or abandoned, or whether the right of navigation was expressly extinguished.

Acts of Parliament

Once the existence of a public right of navigation has been established, it can only be extinguished by an Act of Parliament or under certain Acts of Parliament by

Ministerial order. Otherwise, the principle 'once a highway, always a highway', applies and obstruction is an offence. Actual passage may, however, still be difficult or impracticable as a result of physical events such as silting up, fallen trees or vegetation, and so forth.

The public right is a right of passage only (either upstream or downstream). It does not entitle canoeists to 'occupy' a stretch of water for a canoeing event. Still less does it give a right for spectators to use the banks. It does not give a right to cross from or to the public highway or to land or launch without permission, except at a public landing place.

In some cases, the public right to navigate is exercisable only after taking out a licence or paying dues authorised by an Act of Parliament, eg on the Thames, Severn, Great Ouse and Nene. Some harbour authorities have power to levy dues on tidal waters. The former right of navigation on canals was extinguished by the Transport Act of 1968, so permission for use is now granted through a licence issued by the British Waterways Board.

Historical use

The Thames and Severn are examples of rivers where a right of navigation is historically established (ie (1) above). There is a statement in Halsbury's Laws of England that 'it has been inferred ..' (by whom it is not stated) .. 'that a section of Magna Carta requiring all weirs and mills obstructing navigation on the Thames and Medway and other rivers throughout England' means that many of the largest rivers were then regarded as 'common streams'; that is, there was a public right of navigation. But to use this argument it would be necessary to produce historical records supporting the existence of actual use. In other words it would be an example of (1).

The 'Spey case' brought out that on the basis of proven public use of the river for log rafts, canoeing by the public was lawful as being a less demanding use (smaller, less draught). It also brought out that the purpose of the public use did not matter. Thus it could be recreational, even though when the public use came into existence, its relevant use was to carry goods. There is no reason to suppose that these considerations would not apply in England.

Riparian rights

The land owner of a river bank , known as the riparian owner, enjoys property rights over the land covered by water to the centre line of the watercourse. He may take fish. He does not own the water, but may use it provided that it does not interfere with the right of the owners lower down to use it when it reaches them. A public right to navigate takes precedence over private rights, and is superimposed on them, but must itself be exercised reasonably, otherwise there is interference that can be trespass. Fishing rights are complicated, but at the risk of over simplification, they are property rights to take fish. The use of the bank for the purpose is a separate property right. Those who enjoy these rights are entitled to do so without interference from others in boats, unless the boaters are exercising a public right of navigation. The law of Scotland is different from that of England and Wales. In consequence, visitors to Scotland should contact the Scottish Canoe Association when planning trips on Scottish rivers.

THE LEGAL POSITION IN PRACTICE

Changing the law

The BCU policy continues to be to seek a change in the law so that canoeists can enjoy more canoeing opportunities as of right. It is to be hoped that one day the Government will implement the principles contained in the Council of Europe 'European Sport for All Charter' (Resolutions (76)41 in September 1976 and R(81)8 in May 1981). These resolutions, encourage member governments, to introduce measures, including legislation, to ensure access to open countryside and water for the purpose of recreation. Any change in the law obviously requires a majority in Parliament. Canoeists have a lot of work to do to win the support of public opinion before they can have any realistic expectation of sufficient parliamentary support to achieve a change in the law.

Such a change will also need the support of many agencies such as the responsible Ministers, the Sports Council, the Countryside Commission, Local Authorities, the Water Authorities and many more. Canoeing is expanding, but the sport is not big enough to go it alone. To secure this support it is necessary that canoeists pursue reasonable and responsible policies. This is the lead being given by the BCU central organisation. Responsible bodies cannot support irresponsible organisations. Introduction of legislation for the specific benefit of canoeists is inescapably a long term objective. The BCU is constantly on the look out for opportunities to seek the introduction of clauses to benefit canoeists in Government Bills, a good example of which is the Union's response to the Government's proposals to privatise the water authorities.

Burden of proof

Canoeists have another legal disadvantage. It is the responsibility of the navigator claiming a public right of navigation to prove the right. If someone with property rights to a stretch of water challenges a canoeist's right of passage on what the canoeist believes to be a public navigation, then the canoeist has the onus in court proceedings to prove his right. This will usually be through the expensive High Court procedure which is also certainly beyond the resources of an individual, bearing in mind that there is no guarantee that he will get his costs reimbursed if he wins and will have to pay the opponent's costs if he loses.

To some readers, the last three paragraphs may seem pessimistic and defeatist. This would not be a fair analysis! It is essential to be realistic and face up to what is and is not achievable based on the present legal framework and the limited resources of canoeists to finance the litigation route. The BCU Access Committee recognises that winning a court case on a specific stretch of water may well relate to that water only, so the cumulative cost of the litigation route (with no guarantee of successes) would be astronomic. Such money as is available could and should be spent in much better ways! Whilst not totally abandoning the legal route, canoeists need a quicker, cheaper and more efficient route to greater access.

Need for research

In case court proceedings are instituted by others, or have to be started by canoeists, it is essential to carry out detailed research to obtain sufficient of the necessary evidence. Such evidence should be collected by canoeists in case it is needed, otherwise there may not be sufficient time for the task when the need actually arises. Canoeists interested in looking for evidence should contact their Local Access Officer, who will be able to give advice on how to go about it. The BCU maintains files of information on rivers and is anxious to add further information to these files as it comes to hand. Historically, canoeists have not actually produced much solid evidence in support of claims that they would like to see pursued. The importance of evidence cannot be over stressed. Having said this, it is to be hoped that canoeists will secure sufficient access to water without resort to costly court proceedings.

ACCESS NEGOTIATION

Factors affecting access

Table 21:1 sets out the four most obvious access factors that are important to canoeists and relates them to five broad categories of waterway. It can be seen that, whether there is a public navigation or not, the best course is to seek agreements by negotiation. This approach will certainly be much cheaper, it has the potential to be much more effective than awaiting changes in the law, and even if progress is slow it will still be a significantly quicker method. That is why the Access Committee is giving priority to this policy. If successes are to be achieved the full support of canoeists is vital.

Table 21:1   Access factors

	Right to Navigate	Right to Launch / Land	Enjoyable Passage	Non-navigation uses	Rating
Public navigations	Yes*	No	Possible	No	1
Public navigations with public launch points	Yes*	Yes*	Possible	No	2
Public navigations with negotiated shared use	Yes*	Yes* or by agreement	Probable	By agreement	4
Private Waters	No	No	Unlikely	No	0
Private waters with negotiated use	By agreement	By agreement	Probable	By agreement	4

May involve tolls
Agreements may involve payment

Developing goodwill

Negotiations do not just happen. The right atmosphere has to be created. There has to be goodwill between parties. Canoeing has a strong moral case as a healthy outdoor sport and recreation appealing to all age groups and all sectors of society, and is totally compatible with the Sports Council's 'Sport for All' policy. If canoeists pursue their objective reasonably and responsibly, the needed goodwill can be earned. There has to be mutual respect between landowners and anglers on the one hand and canoeists on the other. The majority of canoeists do respect anglers and want them to enjoy their sport in the same way that canoeists want to be able to enjoy theirs. The respect of the landowners and anglers has to be earned and recent militant action by a small minority has been counterproductive. Confidence must be built up. This can come from the belief that each interest really wants a negotiated solution, and does not say one thing and then do another. Finally a lot of patience is needed. Progress will be slow and prospects can be quickly jeopardised if anyone expects quick results and then presses for a change of policy if this does not happen.

Statement of Intent

In 1983, landowners, anglers and canoeists agreed the text of a 'Statement of Intent' in relation to canoeists obtaining access to private water by negotiation. Almost immediately anglers drew attention to actions by canoeists which were unacceptable to them. They were then unwilling to recommend negotiations until the BCU had solved the problems. As it involved the control of non-members the BCU found itself in a no-win situation. Consequently, by 1986, frustrations had built up to the point that a pressure group appeared and tried to force the issue. This made the BCU work even more difficult and it was compounded because, although the BCU has no connection with the group and dissociated itself from their provocative statements and actions, the anglers did not believe this to be the case.

Canoeing was in a vicious circle. Lack of agreements had led to the BCU losing credibility with many of its existing and potential members. This created the conditions for the emergence of a pressure group. In this situation, anglers and riparian owners became unhappy about the ability of the BCU to control agreements and, therefore, were unwilling to make new arrangements, thus completing the vicious circle. BCU officers worked very hard behind the scenes to promote the view that the BCU is a responsible organisation and that agreements are in everybody's best interests. In September 1987, the parties to the 'Statement of Intent' met again under the chairmanship of the Sports Council. The atmosphere was cooperative and constructive. It was agreed that there should be regular meetings at national and regional level to promote understanding and agreements, and to iron out any difficulties before they became major issues. The active and patient support of all canoeists is needed to achieve positive results from this opportunity.

Basis for agreement

Negotiation of agreements is not necessarily a matter of dealing with facts or rights. Agreements are made between people, whose decisions are based on their own perceptions and prejudices. Canoeists must promote themselves as people with whom landowners and anglers can live in harmony. Canoeists need to develop their own perceptions so that they are based on reality rather than instinct or the emotive claim to a heritage. If this appears to be a weak approach, consider carefully if it is better to make slow but positive progress or alternatively to risk failure by taking too strong a line, secure in the belief that right is on the canoeist's side ! To put this in perspective, there is a choice between negotiation and litigation. Even the threat of litigation creates bad will on the river. If canoeists prove a navigation right in this way, other interests will certainly close ranks and ensure that it is as difficult as possible for canoeists to get to and from the river. Canoeists have insufficient money for litigation and will find it difficult, if not impossible, to obtain funds for this purpose from other agencies.

The BCU considers it best to secure agreements 'without prejudice' as to whether or not there is a public right of navigation. Otherwise a practical arrangement may never be reached because landowners and anglers may not wish to acknowledge the existence of a right of navigation. As indicated above, landowners and anglers can only be forced into accepting that there is a public right of navigation on a disputed waterway by pursuing the matter through the courts.

The BCU policy is to seek agreements for the benefit of all members and does not favour private agreements made by clubs or small groups for their own exclusive use. Such private agreements are seldom notified to BCU headquarters. They create two problems which the BCU is trying to solve. Firstly, they could result ultimately in no-one being able to canoe on more than the one length of private river for which his group has an exclusive agreement. Secondly, it leads to landowners and anglers believing that there is a large number of agreements in existence and they then have difficulty in understanding why canoeists feel the need for many more agreements. Based on the relatively small number of nationally applicable agreements, it would appear that canoeists are acting as their own worst enemies !

Payment for use

During negotiations, the matter of payment often arises. The perception of many anglers is that they pay large amounts for their sport, while canoeists pay nothing. The BCU policy is that canoeists should be prepared to pay reasonable sums for tangible facilities provided for them at a cost. The cost of such facilities is small compared to the costs of stocking and managing fisheries. When payments for canoeing are agreed, then the BCU will have to devise mechanisms to recover the cost from benefitting canoeists. As more agreements involving payment are entered into, it will rapidly become impossible to meet payments from BCU central funds without raising subscriptions to unacceptable levels. Additionally, many anglers consider that as they have to buy a rod licence, canoeists should buy an equivalent licence to put a canoe on rivers where a licencing arrangement is not in existence. The whole matter of how much should be paid by canoeists, to whom and for what, is very complex The BCU Access Committee is at present considering carefully all the aspects and implications of payments in the field of access.

TRESPASS

The BCU policy is, and always has been, to act only within the law. The BCU expects its members to keep to this policy and recommends all canoeists to do so. However, a canoeist may inadvertantly find himself accused of trespass. The following points, which apply to England and Wales, outline the main relevant legal issues.

509

Trespass is a wrongful act, done in disturbance of the possession of the property of another, or against the person of another, against his will. Trespass is a civil offence (criminal only in exceptional circumstances) that can be committed by mistake, or without malice, or without doing any physical damage. On the other hand, if it is an involuntary and inevitable accident, not arising from negligence, it is not 'trespass'. The owner can require the trespasser to leave his land by the shortest or an agreed route to the nearest public highway or to land where the offender has a right to be, but cannot insist on a route over someone else's private property. If required, the owner can use reasonable force to remove a trespasser.

The alleged trespasser may ask the challenger to identify himself and explain the basis of the trespass. He need not give his own name, and as it is a civil matter he need not give it to a police officer, though it may be sometimes sensible to do so, especially if this might pave the way to a future access agreement. It is important that the trespasser should avoid any action that could be construed as a 'breach of the peace', and thereby give rise to a criminal offence. If it becomes clear that the canoeist is in the wrong, it is better for him to apologise. It is unlikely that the canoeist will have caused any tangible damage, in which case, if damage is minimal, it is best to tender amends of, say, £1 minimum.

Water Authority bailiffs have powers of a constable for the enforcement of the Salmon and Freshwater Fisheries Acts, for example, in relation to poaching or damaging of spawning beds. The landowner or the owner of the fishing rights, if different, may also have a bailiff, who is so authorised will have the powers of the owner as his agent. An ordinary angling club member will not have a bailiff's authority. These matters are mentioned only to avoid misunderstanding, as the watchword in practice should always be courtesy and politeness.

ENVIRONMENTAL CONSERVATION

The preservation and improvement of the countryside and wildlife is important to the canoeist's enjoyment of his sport and recreation. For this reason, the Access Committee has set up an Environmental Conservation Panel. The objectives are to encourage members and others to conserve and care for canoeing environments, to promote scientific research and collect information on any effects that canoeing may have on the environment, and to participate in and encourage projects and schemes which attempt to conserve or improve the canoeing environments. The BCU takes a positive view on conservation matters whereby the maximum number of people can enjoy the countryside through the wise use of resources based on the principle of sustainable yield over time or, to avoid the jargon, this means ensuring that any detrimental effect is within the capability of the environment to regenerate itself.

Additionally the BCU seeks to promote these policies and objectives to bodies concerned primarily with conservation so that they cease to perceive canoeing as a threat to environmental conservation. This perception is an unwelcome and unjustified negative approach tending to exclude people from the countryside. There will be only a limited number of very special sites where exclusion might be justified. The canoe causes no erosion, noise or pollution, and leaves no trace of its passing. All canoeists can help by taking a positive practical interest in conservation matters. Elements of conservation are included in the syllabus for BCU tests of personal performance and coaching awards.

THE BCU ACCESS TEAM

The BCU in cooperation with the Canoe Association of Northern Ireland, the Scottish Canoe Association and the Welsh Canoeing Association has recruited and trained a team of voluntary Local Access Officers. The task of these officers is to get to know all the riparian, fishing and other interests relevant to their stretch of river so as not only to become the local expert but also to be accepted by the other interests as the reliable local canoeing contact. Most access negotiations are conducted on a local basis, so this is the means of providing negotiators and creating the atmosphere conducive to amicable discussions. Wherever possible these officers are recruited from within clubs so that the clubs themselves become closely involved in BCU access work.

Each region has a Regional Access Officer, who sits on the appropriate regional or national committee. The English Regional Access Officers and the National Access Officers from Northern Ireland, Scotland and Wales sit on the policy making British Access Committee. In this way, all access officers can contribute to the determining of policy and the structure exists to enable it to be implemented. Any BCU member can let his views be known to his Local Access Officer. To cover Britain effectively is a large job and there is a need for many more access officers. The team has grown considerably over recent years, but there is still a good way to go ! Canoeists, who do not have enough time themselves to volunteer as access officers, can still make a positive contribution to the access work and help with the cost by joining the BCU and actively supporting its policies. Those who introduce people to canoeing have an important responsibility to make sure that these newcomers understand the main points of the access situation. The so-called 'cowboy' element causes anglers to be slow to talk. The probability is that many 'cowboys' are merely uninformed, but the adverse effect on agreements is the same !

CHECK THE ACCESS SITUATION WHEN PLANNING TRIPS

Before planning a trip on private or disputed waters, be sure to consult the Local Access Officer well beforehand. Send him a stamped, self addressed envelope, quoting your BCU membership number and allow at least 14 days for a reply. BCU members must keep to the terms of access agreements in force. It is also essential to keep to the advice given, even if it means changing the date of the trip or possibly cancelling it. Where there is no agreement under negotiation or in force on a private or disputed waterway, the Local Access Officer will inform enquirers of the position. Canoeists should always abide by the 'Canoeists Code of Conduct'. The name and address of the relevant Local Access Officer can be obtained from the appropriate Regional Access Officer or from BCU (or CANI, SCA, WCA) headquarters. If communicating by letter, please enclose a stamped, self addressed envelope.

LOOKING AHEAD

As an expanding sport and recreation, canoeing may be perceived as a threat to landowners and anglers. This need not be the case if a means of living together can be found by negotiation. Against the background of agricultural surpluses, the farming community is looking for new ways of generating income from their land and is giving attention to the potential of recreation. In all these respects canoeists must work together if the best outcome is to be achieved for canoeing. The BCU is giving the lead and looks to canoeists to join the Union and actively support its policies.

22 Conservation Canoeing

David Gent

David Gent's early canoeing was centred around polo at Leeds Polytechnic where he was studying recreation and the environment. He is currently BCU regional chairman for Yorkshire and Humberside, and secretary of the Union's Environmental Conservation Panel. David's philosophy on conservation is a pragmatic one: help paddlers to become aware of erosion, pollution, disturbance and related factors, and then provide them with the practical information to enable each individual to take appropriate action.

THE CANOEING ENVIRONMENT

Whether you paddle on wild upland rivers, along interesting coastlines, or tour on peaceful canals, without Britain's varied wildlife and landscape much of the pleasure of canoeing would be lost. The reason canoeing remains so popular is that the water environment, both natural and man-made, offers so much interest and challenge to the paddler.

The canoe has great advantages for anyone wishing to explore the water environment as it causes no erosion, noise or pollution and leaves no trace of its passing. That is why the canoe is used throughout the world for exploring wilderness areas and observing wildlife without disturbance.

Your enjoyment of canoeing will be all the more improved and your appreciation of the canoeing environment increased with a basic understanding of your surroundings and how the issues of pollution and conservation affect the sport. This section will briefly help you to recognise some of the major types of wildlife to be encountered when canoeing and how to canoe safely without upsetting any of the environment around you. The major environmental problems associated with each type of canoeing venue are considered.

Plate 22:a
PHOTO: R ROBINSON

INLAND BRITAIN

Fast and slow rivers

For the plants and animals living in a river, the most important feature is the speed of the water . Slow moving and still waters offer plants and animals very different conditions to those found in fast flowing rivers. As the slalomists and wild water racers are swept along in the fast upland river currents, so also will any insect or plant not firmly anchored to the river bed.

Next time as you wait in the eddy for your ride on the stopper, look at the rocks around you and they will most likely be covered in a dark green mat of aquatic moss giving shelter to the larvae of stoneflies and other forms of lowly life. You may also be lucky to see the monkey flower in bloom with its large yellow flowers.

The bird most likely to accompany you on your 'run' or as you shoot a fall is the dipper who is both an excellent swimmer and flier. Like the canoeist, it enjoys playing in and around the falls in a river and chooses to nest close by. It is important then , when inspecting a gate or a fall, especially in the springtime, to be extra careful not to harm this bird's environment.

The slower current of Britain's lowland rivers allows a much more varied waterside environment. Plants with exotic names like water crowfoot, hairy willowherb and purple loosestrife abound, whilst the stoneflies are joined by the may and dragonflies. Pondskaters, whirligig beetles and water boatman all prove that you can not only walk on water but skate and gyrate wildly as well. Typical riverside trees are alders and birches on the upper reaches giving way to willows and poplars as the river heads down stream.

Plate 22:b
'Canoes pass down and away, and leave no evidence of their passing'
PHOTO: DR J WHITEHEAD

From your canoe out on the water, you have an excellent viewpoint to observe the amphibians and reptiles, birds and mammals of lowland river Britain. Frogs and toads are usually found hiding in reed beds or in the muddy margins, only to be seen if they are disturbed.

It is likely that in your canoeing career you will come across the majestic swan at some time, or the moorhen in a hurry amongst the bankside vegetation.

Canoeing quietly and knowing where to look will reward you with glimpses of the kingfisher, the appropriately named pied wagtail and the aerial gymnasts, the sand martins. Mallards and coots paddle in formation along the river's edge, all altering direction in unison.

One of the most easily seen waterside mammals is the water vole, often wrongly called a 'water rat'. They are quite harmless vegetarians which swim along the surface until disturbed, and then with an abrupt 'plop' dive underwater to swim to the safety of their burrows.

Canals

To merely refer to canals as 'man-made waterways for the purpose of drainage and/or navigation' when each canal has its own individual character through its locks, bridges and canalside building, hides much of the interest that they hold for the canoeist. The canal builders laid their canals to connect the new industrial towns of eighteenth century Britain, to 'boldly go where no water had been before'. Consequently, they achieved amazing engineering feats avoiding obstacles, hugging contours, digging deep cuttings and constructing breathtaking aqueducts and tunnels.

So often the canal is used solely for the purpose of training and the paddler, in the rush to gain that extra stamina, fails to appreciate the industrial heritage around him. The buildings and bridges on your local canal may all be an uninteresting 'grotty' eyesore, but a closer look will show they vary both in design and building materials used. Not surprisingly so do the plants and animals which colonise them. Canals are too important a part of Britain's environment to be used solely by the canoeist as a stamina gym.

Plate 22:c
PHOTO: R ROBINSON

Lakes

Lakes come in all shapes and sizes from the dramatic Scottish lochs to the warmer lakes of England. Man's activities also provide lakes by flooding valleys to form reservoirs rich in wildlife, like Rutland Water, or extracting gravel to form the most famous canoeing lake in the world, Holme Pierrepont.

The conditions faced on each type of lake are as different for the canoeist as is the wildlife to be found. The high mountain lakes are striking in that few plants grow, but the yellow flowered bladderwort resembles a 'triffid' digesting insects. Lowland lakes are equally striking in that so much grows with the shoreline often densely clothed in reed bulrush and gypsywort and that plant which gets in all your canoeing gear and is ever nearby, the infamous pondweed.

COASTAL BRITAIN

The coastline and seas of Britain have a magnetic attraction all of their own with their ever changing moods. The sea canoeist is reminded only too quickly of the awesome power of the sea as a sunny blue day of sharp horizons and flat calms, bursts into a menacing slate grey sea of raging white horses with the onset of a storm. The twice daily rise and fall of the sea and Britain's unique geological and climatic conditions mean that the coastline offers the canoeist several distinctive and varied habitats.

Estuaries and muddy waters

Nowhere is the rhythmic movement of the tides more striking than in the estuaries, as the sea ebbs and flows across the estuarine mudflats. The mixture of the fresh river and sea water allows the muddy sediment in both to settle, and gradually the mud builds up to appear above tide level.

A few plants colonise the mudflats, the most common being grasswort, cordgrass and eel-grass. The grasswort is a curious plant as its leaves have been reduced to fleshy scales. The cordgrass is easy to spot as it forms symmetrical islands in the mud while, in the more sheltered estuaries, beds of eel-grass will brush the bottom of your canoe.

A glance from your canoe across a mudflat might not suggest the jungle of subterranean creatures that exist there. The flats are rich in molluscs such as cockles and tellins. They also contain worms such as the ragworm, its presence given away by tell-tale tracks in the mud, radiating from a central hole. June to Christmas is an exciting time for a paddle at low tide, as waders descend on the flats to feed on the rich subterranean food source. There are too many types of waders to list here but the curlew is everybody's favourite with its long downcurved bill. No lowly creature is safe as the curlew probes deep in the mud, reaching even the lugworms in the bottom of their chambers. Meanwhile, the shelduck paddles up and down to force the shellfish and worms to the surface to be eaten.

Sandy shore lines

To many canoeists, the only interest in a beach will be whether or not it has good surf. Even the dedicated sea canoeist may avoid the sandy and shingle beaches to paddle around the more dramatic rocky shores only to use the beach to land and return to the comfort of the car.

Plate 22:d
Sea kayaking off the north coast of Anglesey. Canoeists have agreed to keep away from the cliffs at South Stack during the nesting season in order to minimise disturbance to breeding auks
PHOTO: RAY ROWE

Beaches, especially along the tideline, teem in life both on and underneath the surface. An interesting shellfish to be found on the beach is the razorshell, which in a few seconds can dig into the safety of the sand. Stumbling on the tideline debris as you carry your canoe, the water will send a mass of sandhoppers and kelpflies buzzing and jumping into the air. Thus, rich insect life provides amply food for shoreline birds like ringed plovers.

The canoeist paddling off the quieter sandy beaches will inevitably come across one of the five types of terns often mistaken for gulls, which breed in Britain. The terns live in colonies with their nests no more than shallow hollows in the sand and therefore are quite easily disturbed. So, if you are wishing to land, stay clear of where the terns are nesting, especially if they are arctic terns as they have very sharp beaks and will readily attack you *en masse* if you get too close.

Rocky shores and awesome cliffs

Some of the most spectacular coastal scenery can be enjoyed by the canoeist on the rugged west coasts of Britain, especially the Scottish Islands. Sea cliffs provide a habitat for a wide variety of plants, and during the spring sea birds come to these areas in large numbers to nest. Rocky shores are covered in a luxuriant growth of seaweeds and animal life, especially in the rock pools.

517

The seapink, rock sea lavender and wild cabbage grow in the shallow soil and cracks of the cliffs, whilst kelps of various types crowd the low water shore. Pulling back the bladder wrack will reveal a whole range of sea life.

One such creature is the sea anemone which when submerged waves its flower-like tentacles to catch small fish or crustaceans to eat. Limpets and barnacles are common on the rocky shore, as is the dog whelk which preys on them. All three are capable of withstanding the force of the sea but the oyster catcher, with its strong beak, is expert at penetrating the armour of these creatures.

The cliffs are rich in bird life with the most common being the gulls and fulmars which also venture offshore. The more gentle cliffs will be colonised by puffins, whilst the near vertical faces will often be colonised by incredible numbers of razorbills and guillemots.

The mammals of Britain's coastline, such as grey seals, can be seen on the more remote beaches. Seals often play in the white water overfalls loved by the sea canoeist and the sightings of porpoises and pilot whales are not uncommon by those venturing away from the shoreline.

The best time to visit this type of shoreline is usually in September as tides are reasonably low, the sea is at its warmest, the days are long and a successful breeding season will have produced a large number of the many species to be found.

PURE RIVERS, CLEAN SEAS : THE ENVIRONMENTAL ISSUES

Virtually every day the national newspapers run stories which suggest that neither are the rivers pure, nor the seas clean. Indeed, how often do you tolerate water pollution as you are 'going through the motions' of training on a river, only to suffer an upset stomach the following day.

Water pollution is a great threat since it destroys the canoeing environment and carries harmful pathogens causing illnesses ranging from the 'upset stomach' to the deadly typhoid. These pathogens are released from inadequate sewage disposal systems which in times of flood cannot cope and dump millions of gallons of untreated sewage into the rivers.

Another source of contamination is from the excessive use of nitrogenous fertilizers in agriculture. When these fertilizers are concentrated in the rivers the available supply of oxygen in the river is used up and the river dies. Add to this the damage done by industry through the introduction of heavy metals like mercury and the rivers begin to look more like chemical sinks than sparkling clear brooks. Other threats to the rivers are the massive river management and water conservation schemes, the cooling of industrial plant and acid rain, all of which have serious damaging effects.

The sea and coastline are under no less a threat despite the success of recent campaigns to stop people denuding the coastline of its many attractive animals and plants.

The accidental spillage of oil from tankers and offshore installations around Britain has serious effects. The oil clogs the feathers of seabirds and when it reaches the shore, covers the sand and rocks, killing encrusting organisms by smothering them completely. This effects the food-chain as the higher order species no longer have any food to eat. The canoeing environment is further denuded by the dumping of chemical and radioactive wastes and the water clouded by mining and quarrying. The summer visitors to the coast cause increasing sewage outfall from seaside towns and mudflats are designated as sites for land reclamation.

This presents a depressing picture. You may be wondering if it is still safe to go canoeing, or thinking to yourself, 'is there nothing that I can do ?' Although it may take government legislation to stop water pollution and the dumping of wastes at sea, you can help if, when you see something you do not like happening to your stretch of water, contact the Water and Local Authorities. Do not just accept it.

By canoeing an area regularly and keeping a log of what you see, as well as using your eyes, ears and nose to monitor changes that are happening, you will be able quickly to inform the relevant national and regional bodies to take action.

The BCU has an Environmental Conservation Panel to argue the case for canoeing and the environment. Its success depends on how well local clubs and individuals are informing the panel of what is happening to Britain's waterways. If you want to become involved in the work of the panel or know more about the issues above, contact the panel via the BCU Headquarters.

THE CARING CANOEIST

Whilst all people come into canoeing to paddle and not to build hides or study pollution, we all individually have a clear duty and interest to concern ourselves directly with the care and conservation of the environment where canoeing takes place. Conservation is about the wise use of resources. It is about sharing, partnership and trusteeship for present and future generations of wildlife and people, as well as the environment. It is about caring.

Care and the environment

There are many factors which come into play when planning a river or sea trip, and these are outlined elsewhere in the Handbook. A few extra environment caring factors are included here.

The best way not to disturb the environment is to follow the canoeist's code of conduct as outlined in Appendix IV. The code is designed to ensure that canoeists do not come into conflict with any of the other water users, be they wildlife or other people. PLEASE OBSERVE IT AT ALL TIMES.

Uprooting any wild plant is illegal and, more importantly prevents the plant from reproducing. A rock that makes getting through a slalom gate difficult, may be home to some insect and it would prefer you not to remove it. If by accident you do dislodge a rock, do try and replace it in its original position.

Try not to paddle close to moorhens and ducks with their young in tow, as you may split the family group. The river has predators which enjoy a tasty meal of duckling. Do not approach nesting colonies of birds too closely, as the adults in fright may leave their eggs and young exposed to the dangers of the hungry gulls. In winter, it will also cause them to lose precious energy and fat reserves. Seaweed gives a covering to a whole host of small animals which if exposed will overheat, dry out or be eaten.

A clear plastic bag may be the answer to seeing what is for lunch but underwater it is invisible and traps aquatic animals, killing them. Even the plastic retainers from a pack of beers can strangle birds and trap fish.

By all means observe and enjoy the environment but be careful not to damage or destroy it.

OBSERVING WILDLIFE

If you do observe the canoeists' code carefully, you will be rewarded with some excellent observations of wildlife. As most canoeists write up some form of log, why not record what you see. It may only be a few sketches in the margin, or could provide greater detail giving dates, sizes, colours, numbers, etc.

The best way to 'collect' specimens of wildlife is not to actually remove them but compile a collection of good photographic transparencies and prints. A standard SLR camera with 50mm lens and a set of extension rings will cover most situations with standard 64 ASA film. On the coast you will need polarising and haze filters to cope with the reflections from the sea. A set of 8 x 40 binoculars will help you to observe birds more closely.

A good pair of eyes is the most valuable aid to observing wildlife along with a good nature guide to help with identification. Collins and Hamlyn, the book publishers, both produce excellent field and pocket guides which fit easily into your canoeing gear. A small hand lens is also useful with a magnification of x8 to observe the more lowly forms of life.

Reading a guide before going canoeing and aiming to observe one type of wildlife will be much more successful than trying to identify everything which grows, flies, crawls or swims. Always remember it is important to bring the book to the wildlife and not the other way around. Membership of your local natural history or conservation group will improve your ability to observe and identify wildlife further. The local library will have their address.

Appendix I

British Canoe Union, BCU Coaching Scheme and British Schools Canoeing Association Structure and Policy

INTRODUCTION

The British Canoe Union is a limited company, recognised by the Sports Council and in membership of the Central Council of Physical Recreation, as the governing body of the sport of canoeing in the United Kingdom. It is affiliated to the International Canoe Federation (ICF) and represents the interests of canoeists at home and abroad.

The aims and objectives of the BCU are:

To encourage health, enjoyment, and care of the countryside through the use of canoes and kayaks in competitive and recreational activities.

To promote canoeing in all its forms.

To organise and assist in promoting and organising canoeing meets, regattas, championships, trials, training sessions, tours, rallies, demonstrations, festivals and other competitive and recreational events.

To select, train and administer competitors to represent the United Kingdom.

To give encouragement and support to canoeing expeditions.

To promote international co-operation and friendship by encouraging participation in canoeing activities between nations.

To arrange and provide the holding of courses of instruction and exposition in canoeing skills and techniques, the establishment and conduct of a system of tests and qualifications, and the promotion of safety.

To issue guidelines and make regulations for all forms of canoeing, as appropriate, and to encourage the observance by canoeists of a code of conduct.

To protect the interests of canoeists, and to work for improved facilities and for greater access to waters.

To support administrative or legislative measures which will improve facilities for canoeing and to act to prevent the introduction of such measures injurious to the sport.

To create and promote by publicity and education an informed and interested public opinion on the value and importance of canoeing in all its forms.

To provide and supply information and advice to members by means of books, periodicals and other methods.

To foster technical improvement and development of canoes and equipment.

To investigate and research rights of passage.

To arrange for insurance, travel facilities and the purchase of goods and equipment to be available to members.

To provide services as possible and appropriate for other organisations, clubs and persons interested in or associated with the sport and recreation of canoeing.

Separate Associations exist for Northern Ireland, Scotland and Wales which are recognised through an agreement with the Council of the BCU as the governing bodies of the sport within their respective countries. They have right of representation on the Council, the Management

Committees, and the Specialist Committees of the BCU to ensure their interests are served when matters of a federal (United Kingdom) nature are discussed.

There are full reciprocal rights of membership between the Associations and the BCU.

Membership of the BCU

Membership of the Union is open to organisations within the United Kingdom, and to men, women and young people of any nationality who are interested in canoeing.

Insurance benefits

The insurance policy indemnifies the British Canoe Union and/or its officials, and/or members and/or affiliated clubs (insofar as concerns canoeing and social activities) against claims for legal liability (personal injury and property damage) to third parties up to £1,000,000. Indemnity against third party risks required by many local authorities before canoe surfing is permitted, is covered by this policy. All canoeing and related activities are included and there is member to member liability. It covers the use of swimming pools and other premises hired, except for the first £100 where the damage is not due to fire or explosion. Premises and equipment owned or rented by the club (but not property held in the custody or control of the insured) are covered for third party risks only. The policy also indemnifies members of the Coaching Scheme working in a voluntary capacity, for legal liability arising out of, or caused by, wrongful advice.

The Structure of the British Canoe Union

The affairs of the BCU are managed by a Council who employ a Director, responsible for the general administration of the Union. As Chief Executive of the Secretariat, the Director is responsible for all its activities and directly or indirectly the management of all its staff. He is responsible to the Executive Committee of the Council for management of the Secretariat, and to the Council for achieving the objectives of the BCU and carrying out the policies laid down for him.

The Council consists of:

The President (elected annually at the AGM)

The Chairman (elected annually from within the Council)

The Treasurer (elected bi-annually at the AGM)

10 members (elected for two years at the AGM)

One nominee from each of the National Associations

One nominee from each of the Specialist Committees

One nominee from each of the English regions

Council has over-riding authority in all matters, but delegates its responsibility to the standing committees, formed from its own members, namely:

The Executive Committee - responsible for financial and administrative matters.

The Sports Management Committee - responsible for oversight of the affairs of the specialist sports committees.

The Access, Coaching and Recreation Management Committee - responsible for oversight of the affairs of the other specialist committees.

The Committee for English Affairs - responsible for oversight of the English regional committees, and for endorsing where necessary the selection of English teams.

Further delegation of Council's responsibility for the day to day conduct of its affairs is made to the specialist committees, who are authorised to act in all matters connected with their own branch of the sport, and to draft regulations for the proper management of their discipline.

These specialist committees are for:

Access	Marathon Racing	Slalom
Canoe Polo	Racing	Surf
Coaching	Sailing	Touring and recreation
Corps of Canoe Lifeguards	Sea Touring	Wild Water Racing

The national associations, BCU regions and clubs nominate representatives to the specialist committees, though the qualifying criteria for membership varies between committees. All committee representatives must be full members of the Union.

If every organisation entitled to representation exercised its right to nominate members to every specialist committee, the size of each would be such that it would be quite unmanageable. In practice, organisations tend only to nominate members to those committees in whose activities they are particularly interested. Most, though not all, specialist committees, organise annual general meetings which elect a chairman and executive committee to administer their affairs.

Council has also delegated responsibility for the promotion of canoeing, and the improvement of facilities and access to Regional Committees. These have been established within geographical boundaries based on the Sports Council's regional boundaries for England. Members within the region elect a committee which is responsible to the Council. The constitutions of regions vary, but all are subject to ratification by Council. The regional chairmen form the 'Committee for English Affairs' pending the introduction of a formal federal structure and a separate association for England. The aims of regional associations are:

o   To maintain and establish access rights and facilities for canoeing.

o   To provide a regional programme of activity.

o   To make the services of the Union more direct and meaningful to individual members.

o   To provide a link and encouragement to full membership of the Union to periphery groups and persons.

The Union maintains liaison with and is represented on, a variety of national, regional and local organisations, by voluntary officers, and by members of the headquarters secretariat. These include nominees to the Management Committees of the Plas y Brenin National Centre for Mountain Activities, Regional Councils for Sport and Recreation, the Central Council for Physical Recreation, the National Water Safety Commitee, relevant BSI panels, and many other voluntary and statutory bodies.

COACHING SCHEME

Director of Coaching

A Director of Coaching is employed who is responsible for the proper administration of the whole of the Coaching Scheme. He is supported by National Coaches with special responsibility for the training and qualifying of competition trainers and coaches.

Each region (as previously defined) is sub-divided, for Coaching Scheme purposes, into its county or other administrative area as convenient, each with its own Local Coaching Organiser (LCO). Every qualified member of the Coaching Scheme (including Trainee Instructors and Competition Trainers) is automatically a member of the local coaching panel. The LCO is informed of their name and address, and is kept up to date. He is therefore able to supply names of instructors who may help with training or testing local individuals, groups or clubs as the need arises.

The LCO will know of courses for rolling, introductory and advanced skills, tours, the clubs in the area, and so forth. He is the person to contact for such information - name and address from

BCU Headquarters. Local Coaching Organisers usually circulate periodic newsletters to their panels to keep everyone in touch, and should call occasional meetings. It is advantageous for this workload to be spread by the appointment of District Organisers, willing to call members of the Coaching Scheme together on an even more local basis in order to promote the activity thoroughly, and to ensure that all the needs of the area are being met.

LCOs are elected by their local panels, every three years. Normally the LCOs elect the Regional Coaching Organiser (RCO), who is responsible for representing the view of the region to the National Coaching Committee and the BCU Regional Executive, and National Coaching Committee policy back to the region. Essentially he administers, supports and enthuses LCOs, who in turn should seek to involve and service every member of the scheme within their jurisdiction. The RCO is responsible for authorising all national courses within the region.

The Tests and Awards Structure

The BCU operates a comprehensive system exists of tests of personal performance, and qualifications for those coaching or teaching canoeing. These Tests and Awards cover the wide variety of activities, some related, others unique, which constitute the sport and pastime.

The environment in which canoeing is practiced varies from the comparatively safe to the very hazardous. The particular degree of hazard is, however, identifiable at each level.

Personal performance tests

There are five levels of personal performance tests:

Level	Closed c'pit Kayaks	Open C'pit Kayaks+	Canoes	Life Saving
level I	1 Star	Grade I	1 Star	
level II	2 Star	Grade II	2 Star	Canoe Safety Test
level III	3 Star/Proficiency	Grade III/IV	3 Star/Proficiency	Assistant Lifeguard
level IV	4 Star			
level V	5 Star/Advanced		Advanced Proficiency	

+'Open cockpit' kayaks are kayaks designed for touring or racing where the legs are not engaged under the deck - in the event of a capsize the paddler falls freely out.

Teaching awards

There are four levels of teaching awards:

Level	Relevant test entry level	Closed cockpit Kayak	Open cockpit Kayak	Canoe
level I	II	Supervisor+	PW Teacher~	
level II	III (Star Test)	Instructor+	•	Instructor
level III	III (Proficiency)	Senior Instructor+*	PW Senior	Senior Instructor
level IV	level IV/V	Coach+*	Instructor~	Coach

+Includes use of open cockpit kayaks and canoes within the same terms of reference.
~Includes the use of open cockpit canoes operating within the same terms of reference.
*Separately for inland, sea, and surf.

524

Training courses must be undertaken prior to assessment for Instructor or Senior Instructor. Trainee Instructors, or Trainee Senior Instructors, who possess the relevant life saving test are authorised to teach within the same terms of reference as Supervisors (level I).

The relationship of the awards to different types of water

Relevant Award level	Simple water	White Water	Sea or Surf
level I	Quiet canals / small lakes / slow moving rivers (not weirs)		
level II	Larger lakes / simple rivers		Holiday beaches on nice days
level III	Large lakes / rivers	grade II	Simple coastlines / - up to 3' surf
level IV^		grade III (plus)	Open water / surf

^A Senior Instructor with Advanced Proficiency or relevant experience and knowledge is also competent at this level.

Competition coaching awards
There are three levels of competition coaching award

Level	Award	Purpose	Relevant Teaching Award
level I	Trainer	Club Coach	
level II	Coach	(Regional) Coach	level III*
level III	Senior Coach	National squad	

Entry to Trainer level is available to all.
*Holders of a relevant Teaching Award, or Trainers with sufficient experience, may enter directly for Coach. Others must apply for a letter of exemption.
The competition coaching awards are 'discipline specific' - ie separately for Polo, Racing, Slalom, Surfing, Wild Water Racing; and 'class specific' - ie separately for kayak or canoe.

THE BRITISH SCHOOLS CANOEING ASSOCIATION

The British Schools Canoeing Association was formed in 1970 to encourage, promote and help canoeing in schools. It is concerned with the development of canoeing within the curriculum, with the provision of information, and the staging of events for schools participation.

The BCU recognised the part that canoeing in schools and education centres plays in the overall growth of the sport, and the importance of forging links, so that young people who wish to, may more easily enter the main stream of the activity.

In consequence, a special relationship has been brought about, through which, whilst maintaining the autonomy of the BSCA, the Association as a whole is able to take leaders of youth canoeing groups receive the benefit of both BSCA and BCU club and individual information, by payment of a single fee.

Membership of the BSCA is open to individual school and youth canoeing groups where 85% or more of the membership are under the age of 18 and still undergoing full time education.

The formation of regional and county associations is encouraged, but these do not have direct representation on the Council of the BSCA.

Appendix II

Canoeing Activities of other Organisations

CORPS OF CANOE LIFEGUARDS

Introduction
The main work of the Corps is carried out by members who patrol beaches wherever the general public is likely to get itself into difficulties. The main purpose of the Corps is still to train young people into a state of proficient canoe handling to be able to render assistance to anyone who may be in distress or difficulty in water. Since the risk is not inconsiderable, the training is rigorous and well worthwhile.

The aims of the Corps of Canoe Lifeguards
1   To set a high standard of canoemanship
2   To come to the aid of anyone in difficulties or distress off any beach, or any river, lake or canal, and to this end to work in co-operation with any other rescue organisation or club working for the same purpose.
3   To be available to local authorities or the police, to assist in relief work during times of flood or similar emergencies.
4   To act as a guide or assistant to parties of canoeists who are on more adventurous expeditions, especially parties from schools, youth clubs or youth organisations, both at home and abroad.
5   To teach the skills of canoeing, especially to their fellow club members, and other young people from schools, youth clubs and youth organisations.

Canoe Lifeguard Training
This covers a very wide and varied programme, and is constantly reviewed in the light of experience, changing conditions, new equipment and improved techniques. Initiative and new ideas for training are always welcome. All lifeguards are trained in the following:
1   A high standard of canoeing ability.
2   Surf Life Saving Association and Royal Life Saving Society methods and awards.
3   First Aid.
4   Canoe Lifeguard methods of rescue using a combination of canoeing and lifesaving ability. Techniques vary from Unit to Unit, depending upon local conditions.
5   Methods of patrolling

The Rescue Canoe
The idea of using a canoe for lifesaving is now well established. The skilled Canoe Lifeguard can operate in heavy seas, surf or weirs, and works in conjunction with the Coastguard, RNLI, Police and the Services.

There are times when a lifeguard has to leave his canoe to go to the aid of a patient and a canoe gets filled with water. Because the Rescue canoe has two buoyancy chambers the lifeguard is able to empty his waterlogged canoe single handed and re-enter. In addition it can be used as a stretcher, and even be paddled when it is upside down.

The Rescue Canoe, with red and yellow stripes, is available only to qualified users, but the Instructor Canoe is supplied in plain colours to any canoeist. Both versions are supplied with toggles, handles, towing point, paddle park, hatch and buoyancy. All authorised canoes are registered with the Corps and have a registration certificate glassed into the cockpit.

Awards and Appointments

Canoe Safety Test
An award for all members, testing certain elementary skills. The holder cannot be regarded as a Lifeguard.

The scheme is based upon five awards, each stage being levelled at a particular function within the Corps, and emphasis is placed on gradual progression of knowledge and skill. This should be gained by working with an operational unit. The five awards are:

Assistant Lifeguard
The basic award for all members, giving the basic skills required to enable the holder to work with a Lifeguard or be able to carry out a simple rescue by him/her self if ever required.

Lifeguard Resuscitation
An Advanced Resuscitation Award required an addition the Assistant Lifeguard Award, by some swimming pool managers, and a pre-requisite for the Lifeguard Award.

Lifeguard
This is the desirable award for all operational members, and essential for Patrol Captains. It should enable the holder to co-ordinate, on the scene, a rescue using several canoes, or various rescue craft, and be able to carry out more complex rescues by himself when required.

Senior Lifeguard
This is the desirable award for Patrol Captains and essential for Corps Training Officers or Duty Officers. The Senior Lifeguard
should be able to organise and co-ordinate any rescue, using whatever equipment.

Chief Lifeguard
This award is made by the National Executive Committee to a holder of the Senior Lifeguard Award who has the necessary administrative experience.
In addition to the above awards, the National Executive Committee have the authority to appoint a person, who has sufficient insight into the work of the Corps, coupled with known administrative ability, to the position of *Honorary Chief Lifeguard*.
In recognition of the valuable public service rendered by Canoe Lifeguard Units, the BCU offers honorary membership of the Union - with full affiliation rights as follows: 'That any groups of persons using canoes in their duties as life saving organisations, wherever they may be in the United Kingdom and regardless of whatever organisation to whom they may be affiliated or with whom they may be working, may on application be accepted free of all charge as full member Units of the Corps of Canoe Lifeguards.'

Corps Examiner Grade 1
May examine for the Assistant Lifeguard Award. Requirements:
> Be a BCU Senior Instructor and hold E1 Examiner status.
> Hold the Assistant Lifeguard Award.
> Hold one of the following:
>> Lifeguard resuscitation Award
>> Adult First Aid Certificate.
>> RLSS or SLSA Advanced Resuscitation Award
>> RLSS Grade 2 Examiner
>> Be approved by the COCLG National Coach.

Corps Examiner Grade 2

May examine for Lifeguard Award and Lifeguard Resuscitation.

Requirements:

    Have held Grade 1 Examiner status for two years minimum

    Hold the Senior Lifeguard Award or higher

    Be a full member of the COCLG

    Run an examination in the presence of another Grade 2 Examiner

    Be approved by the COCLG National Coach

A BCU Senior Instructor who is also a RLSS Examiner Grade 1 or SLSA Examiner Grade 1 may apply direct to the National Coach for COCLG Grade 2 status.

A Chief Lifeguard will examine for the Senior Lifeguard Award.

All Examiner Status' must be renewed every three years.

Award for Valour

An Award for Valour has been instituted. The criteria for nomination is as follows: 'The Award shall be made in recognition of any canoeist whose gallantry and devotion in bringing assistance to others in an aquatic situation shall be considered to be of outstanding merit. For the purpose of this Award 'gallantry' and/or 'devotion' shall be seen as an act of quite exceptional quality and perseverance bearing in mind the severity of the climatic or aquatic conditions obtaining at the time. Neither the success of otherwise of the mission, nor the survival or loss of the rescuer or victim shall detract from the qualification. The Award may be made posthumously.'

THE DUKE OF EDINBURGH'S AWARD SCHEME

    Conditions: Age Range 14 to 25

    Minimum starting age: Bronze 14, Silver 15, Gold 16.

    Latest entry date: 23rd birthday.

Sections (Some form of canoeing is applicable to all sections):

o   Service: Corps of Canoe Lifeguards

o   Expeditions (and Explorations)

o   Physical Recreation: BCU tests or Competition or Canoe Marathons

o.   Skills: Canoe Building

Service section

Requiring specific qualifications (group 3),

Corps of Canoe Lifeguards:

    Bronze: Canoe Safety Test

    Silver: Assistant Lifeguard

    Gold: Lifeguard

Conditions complete the appropriate course of specialised training and reach the required standard. In addition, at Gold level, participants are to complete at least 40 hours practical service, related whenever possible to the training undertaken. The combined period of training and practical service is to be at least 12 months,.

The Corps of Canoe Lifeguards Manual, available from the BCU, should be consulted, and is essential reading at Gold level.

Expeditions section

There are three categorise: expeditions, explorations, and other adventurous projects.

Bronze: 2 days, 1 night, min 4 hrs paddling per day, expedition only.

Silver: 3 days, 2 nights, min 5 hrs paddling per day, expedition or exploration

Gold: 4 days, 3 nights, min 6 hrs paddling per day, expedition, exploration or other adventurous project.

Environment: In all cases the water should present an appropriate challenge to the participants. At Silver and Gold it must be unfamiliar to them and can include sheltered coastal waters. (Kayaks only).

Pre-requisites: **Kayaks**: Bronze: pass 3 star or Proficiency test; Silver and Gold: pass Proficiency test; **Open Canoe:** inland water only. On canals and rivers not exceeding BCU grade 2, participants need not train to the above BCU standards but prior to venture they must:

o Present their canoes and equipment for inspection and satisfy the assessors as to their competence.

o Demonstrate that their equipment is adequately waterproof.

Kayak and Canoe: have an understanding of the Water Sports and Seaway codes, as appropriate; be able to recognise and treat hypothermia.

Skills section

Canoe building: This activity should include as much practical work as possible during the stipulated period.

Beginners: familiar with tools, materials, canoe accessories. know names and function of parts of a canoe; have assisted in building a canoe and be able to undertake maintenance and minor repairs. *sSme knowledge:* sharpen and maintain tools, select materials; familiar with more than one method of construction; play a major part in construction of a canoe; present a log book including sketches and notes, *More Advanced::* fully maintain tools, select and prepare materials; familiar with all common types of construction; construct a canoe from plans without guidance; present a detailed log book.

Physical recreation section

Activities with measurable or certified standards (group 1). Points are obtained by participation and standards reached:

Bronze: 24 pts, Silver: 30 pts, Gold: 36 pts.

Participation points may be earned:

weekly one hour session = 2 points (minimum 6 weeks).

Standards points may be earned:

Points	6	12	18	24
Star Tests	1 Star	2 Star	3 Star	4 Star
PW Tests	grade I	grade II	grade III	
Proficiency Tests			Proficiency	Advanced
Competition - % of winner's time	150%	140%	130%	120%
Devizes-Westminster, Junior class	For each		Full completion	
over 19s must compete in	stage completed		of course	
senior event				

Please note that the above is a summary of the conditions, requirement standards etc of the Award. Candidates should consult The Duke of Edinburgh's Award Scheme Handbook for full details.

THE SCOUT ASSOCIATION

Because of the amount of canoeing that takes place within the Scout movement and consequent requirement for the BCU to supply information and advice, and for instructors to train and test its members, a substantial association fee is paid. This entitles Warranted Scout leaders - that is not individual scouts, unless they are members - to take BCU tests at the reduced fee, and to obtain publications and supplies at member rates.

The Scout Association has adopted a grading system for water, and instituted an authorisation scheme. The scheme is based around BCU tests and awards, and is related to the water grading systems.

Throughout the country, Scout Counties are responsible for grading the various stretches of water in the area under their jurisdiction.

The classes of water are:

Class A

Open sea more than 3 miles * from the shore, and other dangerous waters close inshore; inland water BCU Grade IV and above

* The grading system devised by the Scout movement has to cater for all types of boating. For practical purposes insofar as canoeing is concerned, an arbitrary 1-3 or more miles is probably less helpful than the Open Water definition in Appendix III.

Class B3

The sea up to 3 miles off the shore, but excluding more dangerous waters close inshore; busy commercial parts; exposed parts of estuaries; inland water ICF Grade III

Class B2

The sea up to 1 mile off the shore, but excluding more dangerous waters close inshore; more sheltered parts of estuaries; large inland lakes and lochs; inland waters ICF Grade II.

Class B1

Sheltered inland waters and other sheltered waters where currents and tides create no real danger.

Class C

Public boating ponds, etc: some canals and other 'safe' inland waters.

Guidelines on the issue of a District Commissioner's authorisation

General

Canoeing must normally be carried out in groups of three or more. One in every three canoeists should be authorised by the District or County/Area Commissioner or their nominee; or the activity should be under the control of a suitable authorised person. The assessment for these authorisations will be based on the three following areas:

o   The person who wishes to hold authorisation should be in possession of the necessary technical skill and theoretical knowledge relevant to the activity undertaken (eg BCU award)

o   The person applying for authorisation should fully understand the responsibilities of the authorisation and be fully aware of their limits of authority. They should be aware of the need to tailor the activity to the physical and mental need of the young people concerned.

o   The person applying for authorisation should have a good knowledge of the waters that they will operate on and should appreciate specific local hazards.

Technical

The guidance tables below outline the recommended minimum standards of technical ability in canoeing which should be achieved before any authorisation is granted. When authorisation is granted using these technical standards an authorised person should only be allowed to closely supervise two other canoes from a similar craft on the water.

There may be occasions when a person can show considerable experience without necessarily holding a national qualification. In such cases there should be an assessment of the person's technical knowledge and ability against that needed for the national qualification. The person should be encouraged to take direct assessment at their level of competence in order that their standard of instruction will enable young people to enter the national schemes of training. Only in very exceptional circumstances should the authorisation granted be for other than the close supervision of two other canoes on B1 or B2 waters.

Closed cockpit kayaks

Class of water	Suggested technical qualification
C	None required
B1 inland	BCU 2 Star Test
B1 sea	BCU 2 Star Test and tidal knowledge and experience*
B2 inland	BCU Inland Proficiency
	or BCU 3 Star Test
Sea	BCU Inland Proficiency and tidal knowledge and experience*
	or BCU 3 Star Test and tidal knowledge and experience*
	or BCU Sea Proficiency
B3 inland	BCU Inland Proficiency
Sea	BCU Sea Proficiency
A Inland	BCU Advanced Inland Proficiency
Sea	BCU Advanced Sea Proficiency

Note: 'Tidal knowledge and experience' mentioned above in the B2 Charge Certificate should include an appreciation of the effects of tide and its dangers, tidal streams, observation and prediction of tides, tidal ranges, springs and neaps, overfalls, races, the effect of wind on tidal waters, and channels for vessels with deeper draughts.

Open cockpit kayaks

An appropriate qualification for a closed cockpit kayak or:

C	None required
B1	Placid Water Test Grade II
B2	Placid Water Test Grade III
B3 and A	Not applicable

'Open cockpit' kayaks are kayaks designed for touring or racing where the legs are not engaged under the deck - in the event of a capsize the paddler falls freely out.

Canoes

C	None required
B1 Inland	BCU 2 Star Test (Canoe)
B2 Inland	BCU Inland Proficiency (Canoe)
	or BCU 3 Star Test (Canoe)
B3 Inland	BCU Inland Proficiency (Canoe)
A Inland	BCU Advanced Proficiency (Canoe)

When higher technical qualifications and other training experiences have been completed the authorisation granted may be increased to cover more canoes and other forms of supervision. For example:

Qualification	Suggested authorisation
BCU Supervisor Award	Authorised to supervise group activities on B1 waters using closed cockpit kayaks
Completion of Scout Association Leadership and Supervisory Skills Course	Authorised to supervise a specific number of craft closely on B1 or B2 waters depending on technical proficiency held
BCU Instructor	Permitted to authorise activities on B1 waters or B2 waters
BCU Placid Water Teacher	Authorised to supervise group activities on B1 waters using open cockpit kayaks
BCU Senior Instructor	Permitted to authorise activiites on B3 waters
BCU Senior Instructor holding Advanced Proficiency	Permitted to authorise activities on class A water

Lifejackets and buoyancy aids

When canoeing, buoyancy aids are to be worn. On B3 or A class tidal waters all members of the Movement must wear an approved buoyancy aid with a lifejacket of the type with no inherent buoyancy capable of inflation to 16kg, or a lifejacket with inherent buoyancy and capable of inflation to full buoyancy.

A person who is permitted to authorise activities may decide whether a buoyancy aid or lifejacket is to be worn during activities on water for which they are authorised.

When canoeing in swimming pools a lifejacket or buoyanbcy aid is not mandatory.

THE GIRL GUIDES ASSOCIATION

The Girl Guides Association has a grading system for water, similar to that of the Scout Association, based upon the difficulties and hazards. Responsibility for grading rests upon the assistant advisers (boating) in the counties, with regional consultants carrying out a co-ordinating role.

The Association has adopted the BCU's tests and awards system for its instructors. Full details regarding the requirements are obtainable from the Girl Guides Association,

Appendix III

Check list for the guidance of relevant authorities

STUDENTS

All students undertaking canoeing activities should wear a buoyancy aid* or a lifejacket* the fitting of which should be checked by a suitably qualified leader.

Normally canoeists should be able to swim 50 metres in light clothing. Discretion may be exercised, however, in accordance with a coach's training and experience, where special circumstances exist.

Some non-swimmers may, in fact, be safely introduced to canoeing by trained instructors, in a controlled environment, as a means of introducing water confidence.

The BCU recommendation with regard to personal buoyancy is as follows:

It is recommended that buoyancy aids to BCU/BCMA Standard BA 83 be worn by novices for all canoeing activities, and for white water paddling at all levels.

Lifejackets to BSI 3595/81 or buoyancy aids to SBBNF (now known as BMIF) Standards are normally suitable alternatives, but are not permitted for BCU ranking competitions. For canoe polo additional body protection may be required.

QUALIFICATIONS

For canoeing activities, leaders should be qualified as follows:

To undertake initial training with beginners using OPEN COCKPIT ¶kayaks or canoes only on placid water only.
    Placid Water Teacher of the British Canoe Union

To undertake initial 'taster' training with beginners using closed or open-cockpit kayaks or canoes on +very sheltered waters:
    Canoeing Supervisor of the British Canoe Union
    Trainee Instructor / Trainee Senior Instructor of the British Canoe Union

To undertake canoeing activities using closed-cockpit kayaks or canoes on grade I water or equivalent sheltered coastal areas only:*
    Instructor of the British Canoe Union

To undertake proficiency level expeditioning, grade II or above, surfing, or]open water canoeing activities.
    Senior Instructor of the British Canoe Union.

To undertake touring, marathon and sprint racing activities using OPEN COCKPIT kayaks or canoes only.
    Placid Water Senior Instructor of the British Canoe Union.

+ Very sheltered water should be determined by the BCU Coaching Organiser or relevant authority adviser. The rating normally applies from 1 May to 31 October. It implies normal water and weather conditions. The area involved will usually be a stretch of canal, or similar, small gravel pit or lake, or similar, which is not large enough, or does not have difficult landing areas, to allow for problems to occur should there be a sudden change in weather conditions.

* Grade I water is a canal, small lake, sheltered area of larger lake, holiday beach close inshore on a calm day, or quiet river, not involving the shooting of weirs or grade II rapids.

] Open Water is defined as the Sea where it is *possible* to be three miles from land in any direction. For Proficiency Level expeditioning, a simple section of coastline is envisaged, not involving overfalls, tidal races, difficult landings or open crossings. Forecasts should be for winds not in excess of force 4, with moderate 'summer' conditions prevailing.

¶ Open cockpit kayaks are kayaks designed for touring or racing where the legs are not engaged under the deck - in the event of a capsize the paddler falls freely out.

Please Note

Trainee Instructors, Instructors and above are competent to supervise canoeing activities relevant to Placid Water Teachers, but not vice versa.

Senior Instructors are competent to supervise canoeing activities embraced by Placid Water Senior Instructors, but not vice versa. In both instances, however, it is recommended that instructors attend a 'conversion' course in order to make the most of the potential of the Placid Water Scheme.

Staff ratios

The following staff ratios are suggested as ideal for practical teaching purposes. BCU Coaching Personnel are, however, trained to recognise when circumstances allow these guidelines to be safely exceeded, or when lower limits should be applied. The person in charge should always be allowed to exercise discretion.

    a)   For initial training in sheltered water: 1:8

    b)   For surfing, grade II white water activities 1:

Expeditioning

Open Water]

a)   The Expedition Leader should be qualified as stated in 2d.

b)   A ratio of competent canoeists is recommended as follows:

          1 - 4 students: Leader
          5 - 8 students: Leader + 1
          9 -12 students: Leader + 2

c)   Flares or other suitable means of indicating distress should be carried by the leader together with the other equipment listed in the BCU Sea Proficiency test syllabus. A spare split paddle on the deck of the leader and his supporters can be a valuable safety aid.

d)   Canoes ought to possess maximum buoyancy (single pillar buoyancy should be supplemented). Bow and stern toggles are recommended and adequate spray decks. Deck lines, when fitted, must be taut and not able to foul the cockpit area.

534

e)   Each member of the group should carry all the equipment listed in the BCU Sea Proficiency test syllabus, including a hand held flare, at the discretion of the leader taking into account the type of group involved, and the nature of the journey being tackled.

f)   In addition the following should be available to all:

  i)   A waterproof anorak and adequate canoeing clothing
  ii)   A brightly coloured crash helmet
  iii)   A tow line

g)   Spare split paddles carried by other persons in the group is also suggested. These may be in the boats, but should be easily accessible.

White Water Grade II

a)   The expedition leader should be qualified as stated under "Qualifications" (2d).

b)   There should be a ratio of competent canoeists as follows:

  1 - 4 students: Leader
  5 - 8 students: Leader + 1

c)   The leader and each member of the group ought to be fully equipped in accordance with the recommendations in the Inland Proficiency Test Syllabus of the BCU. In addition the leader should carry a suitable length of line and a float.

d)   Where white water training is involved, each student must be equipped with a suitable safety helmet#.

Safety helmets should fit well down on the forehead, and not pull back easily when tugged. Fastenings should not be subject to corrosion, and should remain secure under stress. Helmets which incorporate foam cushioning are particularly recommended.

Size of party
Over-large fleets of canoes on the sea should be avoided. 15 is probably getting towards the maximum size of a party for practical control to be exercised. On rivers, it is better to split groups down into manageable units if this can be achieved while maintaining reasonable staff ratios. Riparian owners and other river users dislike fleets in excess of 10 - 12 canoes.

Advanced level canoeing
For leading competent groups on grade III waters or above inland, or sea conditions in excess of the proficiency level definition Senior Instructors should hold the Advanced Proficiency Test of the BCU, or be able to show equivalent ability and experience.

Escort boats
Priovided staff are appropriately qualified and experienced, the proper equipping, training, gradual building up and reinforcement of experience of the students, renders escort boats unnecessary.

Appendix IV

The canoeist's code of conduct

More and more people are taking to the water. Some do it for recreation, some to earn a living. This code is designed to ensure that canoeists do not come into conflict with any of them. So please observe it at all times.

ON THE RIVER BANK (or beach or lakeside)

o   Obtain permission before using restricted water. Thank those responsible when you leave.

o   Try to avoid overcrowding one site.

o   Park you car sensibly. Avoid overcrowding or obstructing narrow approach roads. Keep off verges. Pay parking fees and use proper car parks.

o   Don't spread yourself and your equipment so that you upset others.

o   Please keep the peace - don't be too noisy

o   Pick up litter. Close gates. Be careful about fires. Avoid damage to land or crops.

o   Obey special instructions such as National Trust Rules, local bye-laws and regulations about camping and caravanning.

o   Changing into or out of paddling clothing in public places can unintentionally cause offense. Please be considerate and discreet under these circumstances.

CCPR GENERAL CODE OF CONDUCT

1   Avoid damaging banks and shoreline vegetation.

2   Avoid using areas important for wintering wildfowl, nesting birds and spawning fish in the appropriate season.

3   Whenever possible, come ashore from boats only at recognised landing places.

4   Do not trespass on private banks or moorings.

5   Do everything possible to avoid pollution. Do not throw litter or rubbish into the water or leave it lying about the banks.

6   Obey the general rules of navigation and any local bye-laws, but remember that, even when you have the right of way, you have an overriding responsibility to avoid collision.

7   Avoid crossing the bows of oncoming craft at close quarters.

8   Give precedence to others when they are engaged in organised competition.

9   Have special regard for the problems of the inexpert or beginner as you have for the learner driver on the road.

10 A hail is often useful to draw a person's attention to a situation which may result in inconvenience, damage to gear, or a collision; but treat a hail as a friendly warning and not as an insult.

11 Know the signs for the marking of areas used by underwater swimmers and divers

12 In shallow waters keep well clear of wading fishermen and leave adequate room both in front of and behind him for his cast. Keep well clear when he is playing a fish.

13 Make sure that your craft is safe and that sufficient safety equipment is carried at all times.

14 It is advisable to be in possession at all times of a Public Liability Insurance Policy. (Note: this is an automatic benefit of BCU membership)

15 All governing bodies of watersports (including the BCU) produce extensive rules for safety and other matters, these should be read and understood before participating in any activity.

CCPR CANOEING CODE

16 a) Keep away from banks from which anglers are fishing

b) Keep well clear of anglers tackle, do not loiter in fishing pools, cause as little disturbance as possible.

c) Keep a sharp look out for fishermen. Comply with any signals they may make to indicate whether they wish you to wait for a moment or to pass. Give a hail if you think your approach has been unnoticed.

d) Be particularly careful not to touch anglers lines.

17 Do not alter course so as to baulk other craft, particularly in narrow waters. Remember that larger boats are less easily manoeuverable and that canoes can use much shallower water than other craft.

18 Keep clear of rowing craft - sculls, fours and eights - particularly when racing or serious coaching is taking place. Remember that it is sometimes difficult for rowing craft to see canoes.

AND FINALLY

Do get the most from canoeing by being a member of the British Canoe Union.

Bibliography

A comprehensive list of books on canoeing was compiled by Brian Skilling for his thesis *British Canoeing Literature* 1866-1966 published by University Microfilming Ltd. The University of Birmingham, supported by the Sports Council, has a sports literature service, known as the National Documentation Centre for Sport, Physical Education and Recreation, and publishes regular bulletins.

Detailed here are most of the major British works, and some from North America. Many of the older journals will be out of print and a few are now collectors' items. In general the titles of these indicate the nature of the content, which is often an account of a journey.

* Available from BCU Supplies

ARCHIVAL BOOKS

A Canoe Ramble on Thames and Medway; F. Hodges; 1968.
A Canoe Voyage in the Pooion; J.H. Hamilton; 1868.
A Cruise Across Europe; D. Maxwell; 1906.
A Cruise through Scotland; F. Hodges; 1868.
A Thousand Miles in the Rob Roy Canoe; J.A. MacGregor; Sampson Low 1867.
Alone at Sea; H. Lindemann; 1958.
An Englishman in Ireland; R.A. Scott-Jones; 1910.
An Inland Voyage; R.L. Stevenson; Chatto & Windus 1890
As the Water Flows; E. Barnes; Grant Richards 1920.
Beacon Six; H. Cundy; 1969.
Camping Voyages on German Rivers; A.A. MacDonnell; 1890.
Canoe Errant; Major R. Raven-Hart; John Murray 1935.
Canoe Errant on the Mississippi; Major R. Raven-Hart; Methuen 1938.
Canoe Errant on the Nile; Major R. Raven-Hart; John Murray 1936.
Canoe in Australia; Major R. Raven-Hart; Georgian House 1948.
Canoe to Mandalay; Major R. Raven-Hart; Frederick Mull 1939.
Canoe Touring Abroad; G. Seal; 1969.
Canoe Travelling; W. Baden-Powell; 1895.
Canoeing; B. Jagger; Arco c1965.
Canoeing; W.G. Luscombe & L.J. Bird; A & C Black 1936.
Canoeing; W.G. Luscombe; Philip Allan 1936.
Canoeing; J.D. Hayward; Bell & Sons 1893.
Canoeing; T.H. McCarthy; Pitmans Game and Recreation Series 1940.
Canoeing; P.W. Blandford; Foyles Handbooks 1957.
Canoeing and Camping Adventures in Northern Waters; R.C.Anderson; Gilbert Wood 1910.
Canoeing Complete; Brian Skilling; Kaye & Ward 1980.
Canoeing Complete; Skilling and Sutcliffe; Nicholas Kaye 1966.
Canoeing Down the Rhone; J. Wilson; Chapman & Hall 1957.
Canoeing for Beginners; Peter Mytton-Davis; Elek Books 1971.
Canoeing in Ireland; Major R. Raven-Hart; Canoe & Small Boat 1938.
Canoeing; P.W. Blandford; Foyles Handbooks 1963.
Canoeing Today; P.W. Blandford; Vawser & Wiles 1964.
Canoeing Waters; P.W. Blandford; Lutterworth 1966.
Canoeing Waters; W. Bliss; Methuen 1934.

Canoeing with Sail and Paddle; J.D. Hayward;1893.
Canoes and Canoe Sailing; W. Baden-Powell; 1871.
Canoes and Canoeing; P.W. Blandford; Lutterworth Press 1962.
Cockleshell Heroes; C.E. Lucas-Phillips; William Heinemann 1956; Pan Books 1957.
Cruise in a Cockleshell; A.H.Reed; 1867.
Cruise of the Ringleader Canoe; J. Inwards; 1870.
Down River; G. Boumphrey; Allen & Unwin 1936.
Down the Jordan in a Canoe; R.J.E. Boggis; 1939.
Down the Nile by Canoe; A. Davy; 1958.
Down the Orinoco in a Canoe; S. P. Train; 1902
Elements of Canoeing; A.V.S. Pulling; Prakken Publishing Co 1933.
Ethiopian Adventure; H. Ritlinger; 1959.
Exploration of the Arroux; P. G. Hamerton 1867 1867.
4,000 Miles of Adventure; A. Davy;Robert Hale 1958.
Gino Watkins; J.M. Scott; Hodder & Stoughton 1935.
God's River Country; M. and B. Ferrier; 1958.
How to Build and Manage a Canoe; A.R. Ellis & Beams; Brown Son & Ferguson 1949 vol.1 text;
    vol.2 plans.
Joe Lavally and the Paleface; B. Wicksteed; 1948.
Kayak to Cape Wrath; J.L. Henderson; MacLellan 1951.
Kingfisher Abroad; T. Rising; Cape 1938.
Log of the Guerf and Rapid; J.A. Godwin & T.S. George; 1872.
Men, Rivers and Canoes; I. Players; 1964.
Canoeing; Major R. Raven-Hart; 1939.
Canoeing; Charles Sutherland; Faber and Faber 1964.
My Canoe; C.M. Chenu; Eric Partidge 1931.
Nanook of the North; Robert Flaherty; Windmill Books 1971.
Our Canoe Voyage; M. Black; 1876.
Ouse's Silent Tide; C. Frederick; 1921
Paddles and Politics Down the Danube; P. Bigelow; 1892.
Practical Canoeing; Tiphys; Norie & Wilson 1883.
Quest by Canoe; Glasgow to Skye; A.M. Dunnett; Bell & Sons 1950.
Rapid Rivers; W. Bliss; Witherby 1935.
Starting Canoeing; Russell; Adlard Coles c1960.
Tackle Canoeing This Way; P.W. Blandford; Stanley Paul 1964.
The Book of Canoeing; D.J. Davis; Arthur Baker 1969.
The Book of Canoeing; A.R. Ellis; Brown Son & Ferguson 1935.
The Boys Book of Canoeing; E. Jessup; Dutton & Co. 1926.
The Canoeing Manual; Noel McNaught; Nicholas Kaye 1956.
The Cockleshell in Ireland; A.H. Reed; 1872.
The Commodore's Cruise; G. Heavside; 1871
The Dangerous River; R.M. Paterson; Allen & Unwin 1954.
The Danube Flows through Fascism; W. Van Til; 1938.
The Heart of England by Waterway; R. A. Downie; Witherby 1934
The Lonely Land; S.F. Olson; 1961.
The Rob Roy on the Baltic; J. MacGregor; Sampson Low 1872
The Rob Roy on the Jordan; J. MacGregor; Murray 1869.
The Unknown River; P. G. Hamerton; 1871
The Waterway to London; Anonymous; 1869
Three in Norway; J.Arth & W.J. Clutterbuck; 1882.
Two Canoe Gipsies; M. Chater; 1933
Under Sail through Red Devon; R. Cattell; 1937.
Voyage in a Paper Canoe; N. Bishop; 1878.
Water Music; Sir J.Squire; Heinemann 1939.
Watery Wanderings Mid Western Locks; T.H. Holding; E. Marlborough & Co 1886.
You and Your Canoe; O.J. Cock; Ernest Benn 1956.
Your Book of Canoeing; B. Jagger; Faber & Faber 1963.

MODERN BRITISH BOOKS

A Broadland Canoe Club; K.D. Millican; New Horizon 1980.
Adventure Weekends; A Pearce; W Foulsham & Co Ltd 1986.
*A Practical Guide to Sea Canoeing; H N Jeffs; BCU 1986.
All About Wave Skis; R Shackleton; Surfside Press 1986; ISBN: 0 9589 385 0 4
Angmagssalik Round Britain; J Clarke; BCU/Geoffrey Hunter 1985.
*Barty; J. Collins; Blackie; ISBN: 0-216-91840-5.
Better Canoeing; Alan Harber; Kaye & Ward 1973
Blazing Paddles; M Corfield; 1989
Blue Water Summer; D Johnston & K Nicholson; Orca Publ 1987; ISBN: 0-951 1842 0 2
Canoe Building in Glass Reinforced Plastic; Black;1977.
*Canoe Games; D. Ruse; A & C Black 1986; ISBN: 0 7136-5612-3
Canoeing; Dennis Davies; Hodder & Stoughton Teach Yourself Books 1981. .
Canoeing; Peter Little and David English; Puffin Books 1981.
*Canoeing; John Brailsford and Stephen Baker; Oxford Illustrated Press 1977.
Canoeing; Franklin Watts; Norman Barrett; ISBN 0 863 13 156 1; 1987.
Canoeing; Peter Williams; Pelham Books 1977.
*Canoeing; Picture Library Service; 1988
*Canoeing Down Everest; M. Jones; Hodder & Stoughton 1979. Written by the inimitable Dr
  Mike Jones, later drowned on a similar attempt on K2, the full story of a dramatic first in
  canoeing history is unravelled, revealing a fresh and almost cavalier approach to major
  expeditions, capturing the personality of this extraordinary paddler.
Canoeing Skills and Canoe Expedition Technique for Teachers and Leaders; Sqn Ldr P.F.
  Williams; Pelham Books 1976;
*Canoeing Skills and Techniques; Neil Shave; The Crowood Press 1985.
*Canoeing The Fladbury Way: Getting Started; D Train; Glen Villa 1983.
Canoeing Through Life; Nick Inman; Find Horn Press 1985.
Cosmic Kayak Tours; Cosmic Kayak Tours; Foxy 1984.
*Eskimo Rolling for Survival; D Hutchinson; 1989
Getting about in the Great Outdoors; Anthony Greenbank; Penguin Books Ltd 1985.
*Godwin's Saga; K Macksey; Brassey's 1987; ISBN 0-08-034742-8.
Guide to Sea Kayaking; Derek C. Hutchinson; Pacific Search Press; ISBN 0931397 006; 1986.
*Iceland Breakthrough; Paul Vander Molen; BCU 1986; ISBN: 0-94660-924-1.
Kayak Canoeing; E.P. Publishing Know the Game Series 1977.
Little Kayak Book; J Brand; Bramble Tye 1984
Living Canoeing; Alan Byde; A & C Black 1969.
Marsyandi; Alan Barber; BCU 1985.
Outdoor Pursuits; I Lockren; 1988
On the River; Walter Magnes Teller; 1988
*Paddling Progressions; P Rawlings Jackson ; 1987.
*Raging Rivers, Stormy Seas; T Storry, M Bailie, N Foster; 1989
*Sail Your Canoe; J Bull; 1989
Science of Surfing; R. Abbott; John Jones Cardiff Ltd 1972.
*Sea Canoeing; Derek Hutchinson; A & C Black 1979.
*Sea Touring; John Ramwell; J. Ramwell 1978.
Small Boats Down the Years; R Pilkington; 1987
Start Canoeing; Anne Williams & Debbie Piercey; Stanley Paul 1980.
The Adventure Alternative; Colin Mortlock; Cicerone Press 1984.
*The Black Hole (Cartoon); A. F. Fox; Foxy 1986.
The Complete Book of Canoeing and Kayaking; Gordon Richards; B.T. Batsford Ltd 1981.
The Spur Book of Wild Water Canoeing; F. Barlow; Spurbooks 1978.
*Up the Creek - An Amazon Adventure; J. Harrison; BCU 1986; ISBN: 0-946983-04-6; 1986.
Victorian and Edwardian Boating; W. Wigglesworth; B. T. Batsford Ltd; 1987; ISBN: 0-7134-
  5510-1.
Water Sports for the Disabled; EP Publishing Ltd 1983; 0 7158 0864 8.
Weir Wisdom; Tony Ford; White Water Publications 1987.

White Water Kayaking; R Rowe; 1988
White River; Brown Water; A Holman; Hodder & Stoughton 1985.
Wild Water Canoeing; R. Steidle; E.P. Publishing 1977.

TECHNICAL HANDBOOKS

The following books are written for the budding serious competitor and give advice on technique and training methods for the discipline.

Canoe Polo - Coaching and tactics; Brian Barfoot; BCU 1985/6.
Competing Abroad; F. Dick & R. Holman; Sport Nutrition Division 1984.
On Tow; N Flack; 1989
Slalom Canoeing: An Introduction; Garry D Nevin; Slalom Committee of the BCU 1987.
Slalom Handbook; Peter King; BCU Slalom Committee 1983.
The Expedition Cookbook; Carolyn Gunn; 1988.
Wild Water Racing Handbook; David Llewellyn; BCU Wild Water Racing Committee 1980.
Sports Injuries; Dr M Reed (with Paul Wade); Breslich & Foss 1984; 1 85004 001 7.
The Ultimate Run; Bill Endicott; W.T. Endicott 1983.
To Win the Worlds; Bill Endicott; Reese Press, Baltimore, USA 1980.

TRAINING AND OTHER MANUALS

Canoe Building - Glass Fibre
Canoe Building - Soft Skin
Canoeing for Schools and Youth Groups
Coaching Study Packs: The Coach in Action; The Body in Action; Safety and Injury; Improving Techniques; Mind Over Matter; Planning and Practice; National Coaching Foundation
Duke of Edinburgh Award Expedition Guide; W Keay BCU 1987; ISBN: 905425014.
Expeditions and Explorations; Nigel Gifford; MacMillan London 1983.
Expedition Pack; P Knowles; BCU 1987.
First Aid for Canoeists; B Sheen; BCU 1984.
How to Build a Glassfibre Canoe; Trylon Ltd 1983.
Hypothermia, Frostbite and other cold Injuries; Wilkerson, Bangs and Hayward; The Mountaineers, Seattle 1987; ISBN: 0-89886-024-5.
NCF Coaching Manuals: Stretching, B Anderson; *Sports Injuries,* Dr M Read; *Coach at Work; Safety First for Coaches; Physiology and Performance;* National Coaching Foundation
Rafting and Canoeing Expeditions: A Planning Guide; Peter Knowles; Expeditions Advisory Centre 1985.
Resuscitation and First Aid; A.J. Handley; Royal Life; Saving Society (RLSS) ISBN 090.7082 31 9;1986.
Saving Life;A Handley; 1989
Survival; M. Forrester; Sphere Books Ltd 1988.
The Chest Harness and its Use in White Water Canoeing; R. Rowe & G.Wardle; BCU 1986.
The Inner Game of Kayaking; R Cunnington; BCU 1988
The Throwline and its Use in White Water Canoeing; R. Rowe; BCU 1987.

RIVER GUIDES

A Boater's Guide to the Waterways; 1989
A Canoe Guide to Northern Ireland; CANI 1986.
A Scottish White Water Guide.
Alpine White Water; T Storry; Jim Hargreaves (Marine) Ltd; 1983.
Austrian and Bavarian River Guide.

*British Waterways Board Map
*Broadlands Map
Canal Companion; Warwickshire Ring; Pearsons; 1985; Llangollen and Shropshire Union; Pearsons; 1986
*Canoe Touring in East Anglia.
*Canoeists Guide to East Anglia; 1988
*Canoeists Guide to the River Wye.
*Canoeists Map of French Rivers
Cheshire Ring Canal Walk; Cheshire County Council Countryside & Recreation Dept; 1986.
Elvepadling; N Flastad & L Orgstad; Norges Kajakk OG Kanoforbund; 1988; ISBN: 82-90674-00-7.
*France: River Allier Guide; River Eyre and Leyre Guide; River Dordogne Guide; River Cele Guide; River Charente Guide; River Yonne Guide.
*French River Notes
*Guide to the Waterways of the British Isles; British Canoe Union.
    This is the only full guide to the waterways of Britain written from a canoeist's point of view, giving itineraries for every significant river. Regretfully, the itineraries have not been updated since 1961 and the situation is now complicated by the current access problems. Reprinted in 1980 it is still very useful in locating rivers and giving factual information as to their practical canoeability. For information on the current legal or licensing situation on a given waterway reference must be made to the BCU river advisory service.
Nicholson / Ordnance Survey Inland Waterways Map of Great Britain; David Perrott; 1987.
North Wales White Water; Jim Hargreaves, Terry Storry; Cascade Press 1981.
*Guide to the Rivers of the West Midlands; Mike Nicholls & Mike Hubbard; BCU West Midlands Region 1987.
A Guide to Scottish Rivers; Scottish Canoe Association 1981. Visitors to Scotland should contact the SCA, 18 Ainslie Place, Edinburgh before canoeing on Scottish rivers.
Handbook and River Guide of the East Midlands Regional Group of the BCU; BCU East Midlands Region; 1983.
*Holme Pierrepont Artificial Slalom Course: A Users Guide; Frank Goodman & George Parr; Valley Canoe Products Ltd 1986.
In Canoa; A Fortis; Centro Documentazione Alpine 1984.
Inland Waterways of Great Britain; : A Edwards; 1985
Illustrated Guide to Britain's Coast; Drive Publications Ltd; Automobile Association 1984, amended 1985.
Rail, Water & Tramways; Cheshire County Council Countryside & Recreation Dept 1986; 0 906 759 21 8.
*River Severn Map.
*River Thames Map - Lechlade to Richmond.
*River Wye Map.
*Rivers of Cumbria; Mike Hayward; 1988
Rutas Deportives; Ministero de Cultura 1984.
*Snowdonia White Water Sea and Surf; T. Storry; BCU 1987.
*The Lakeland Way; S Bowles; 1987
*Where to Launch your Boat; Barnacle Marine 1986; ISBN: 09487888 00 3.
The Floaters Guide to Colorado; D. Wheat; Falcon Press 1983.
The Lost Rivers of London; N. Barton; Historical Publications Ltd 1983.

NAVIGATION AND WEATHER FORECASTING

*Coastwise Navigation; G.G. Watkins; Butler & Tanner 1977.
*Exercises in Coastwise Navigation; G.W. White; Stanford Maritime Ltd 1980.
Weather Forecasting for Sailors; Frank Singleton; Hodder & Stoughton 1981.

SOME BOOKS FROM NORTH AMERICA

The following are published in USA or Canada . 'Canoeing' means that the subject is open or decked canoes (Canadians).

An Innocent on the Middle Fork; Eliot Dubois; The Mountaineers 1987; 0 89886 125 x; 1987.

Baidarka; George Dyson; Alaska Northwest Publishing Co 1986; 0 88240 315 x

Basic River Canoeing; Robert E. McNair; American Camping Association Inc 1972.

Boat Builders Manual; Charles Walbridge; American Canoe Association.

Canoe Craft; Ted Moores and Marilyn Mohr; 1988

*Canoeing; American National Red Cross; 1985. ISBN 0-385-08313. This is the comprehensive handbook on the open canoe.

Canoeing: An Olympic Sport; A Toro; BCU; 1987.

Canoeing with the Cree; Eric Savareid; Minnesota Historical Society 1968 (Reprint of 1935 edition)

Freshwater Saga; E. W. Morse; ISBN: University of Toronto Press 1988: ISBN: 0-8020-6657 7.

From Start to Finish; George P. Sipos; 1965.

Fundamentals of Kayaking; Jay Evans; Ledyard Canoe Club 1964.

Kayaking; the new Whitewater Sport for Everyone; R.R. Anderson and J. Evans; American Canoe Association.

Kayaks to Hell; W Nealy; 1982; ISBN: 0 89732 010 7.

Keep It Moving; Valerie Fons; The Mountaineers 1987; 0 89886101 Man and the Sea; Phillip Banbury;* Book Club Associates 1975.

Master Canoe Builder; N Nickels; 1986.

On the River; Walter Magnes Teller; Rutgers University Press 1976.

*Paddle to the Amazon; D Starkell; 1989

Pole, Paddle, Portage; Bill Riviere; Van Nostrand Reinhold 1974.

River Gods; R Bangs and C Kallen; 1989

River of the Sacred Monkey; D. Krustev; Wilderness Holidays 1970.

River Rescue; L Bechdel & Slim Ray; Appalachian Mountain Club 1985; 0 910146 55 1.

River Runners Recipes; P Chambers; Pacific Search Press 1984.

Rushton and His Times in American Canoeing; Atwood Manley; Syracus University Press 1978.

*Sea Kayaking; John Dowd; Douglas & MacIntyre, Vancouver, 1988.

Survival of the Bark Canoe; John McPhee; Straus and Girox 1975.

The Coastal Kayaker; R Washburne; Pacific Search Press 1983.

The Canoe; K G Roberts & P Shackleton; Macmillan of Canada 1988; 0 7715 9582.

The Canoe and White Water - from Essential to Sport; C S Franks; University of Toronto Press 1977.

The Canoe Campers Handbook; Roy Bearse; Winchester Press 1974.

The Canoe Paddling Thumb Video; We-no-nah Canoe Company; Mobile Adventure Ltd 1988.

The Complete Wilderness Paddler; J.W. Davidson and J. Rugge; Alfred Knopf 1976.

The Entry Level Guide to Canoeing and Kayaking; J Vichman; New England Publications 1983.

The Little Kayak Book; Part II 1987; Part III 1988

*The Path of the Paddle; Bill Mason; Van Nostrand Reinhold 1980. A superb, comprehensive book of the open canoe.

The Sound of White Water; Hugh Fosburgh; Belmont Books 1971.

The Starship and the Canoe; K. Brower; Holt Rinehart and Winston 1978.

The White Water River Book; R Watters; Pacific Search Press 1982.

To the Arctic by Canoe; C. Stuart Houston; McGill Queens University 1974.

*US White Water Handbook; Appalachian Mountain Club; J.T Urban 1986; ISBN 0 910 146 28 4.

Where Rivers Run; G and J McGuffin; 1988

White Water - (Running the Wild Rivers of North America); Bart Jackson; Walker & Co 1979.

White Water Handbook for Canoe and Kayak; Appalachian Mountain Club 1981.

White Water Racing, Eric Evans and J. Burton; Burton Nantahala Outdoor Centre 1980.
Whitewater Tales of Terror; Menasha Ridge Press 1983; 0 89732 024 7.
White Water Trips; Betty Pratt-Johnson; Adventure/Pacific Press 1986.
White Water Trips Poster/Roadmap for British Columbia; Adventure Publishing (Betty Pratt-Johnson) Ltd; 0 92100902 Pacific Search Press 0 931397 09 x ; 1987.
Yukon Solo; Karel Dohnal; BCU 1985; ISBN: 0-8323-0421-2.

CLASSICAL WORKS

The Bark Canoes and Skin Boats of North America; Adney and Chapelle; Smithsonian Institute, United States National Museum Bulletin No 230 1964.
British Coracles and Irish Curraghs; James Hornell; Society for Nautical Research.
Nunaga: Ten years of Eskimo Life; Duncan Pryde; MacGibbon & Kee 1972.
The Eskimos; Birket-Smith; Methuen 1959.
The Exploration of the Colorado River and its Canyons; John Wesley Powell; Dover 1895.

MAGAZINES

Canoe Focus - BCU House Journal (free to members)
Canoeist - Stuart Fisher
Ceufad - Welsh Canoe Association (free to WCA members)
SCAN- Scottish Canoeing Association (free to SCA members)

BOOKS FROM OVERSEAS

Bergriviergids van de Ardennen; G Haesendonck; 1984.
Canoeing - 50 years in the Olympic Games; Hans Egon Vesper; International Canoe Federation 1987.
Kanu 84; J Gerlach & H Machatschek; 1983.
Il Reste Encore des Rivieres (There are still some rivers); Claude Roggero; Serre Editions 1980.
The Kayaking Book; J Evans; Stephen Greene Press 1985; ISBN: 0-8289-0501-0.
*This is Canoeing; Jane & Roy Farrance; BCU 1985.

Index

High brace: 170
High recovery: 147, 148, 164, 173
Hip flick: 303, 312, 314-315, 321, 336
Hogging wrap arounds: 236
Holes: 88, 89, 227
Holme Pierrepont National Watersports
   Centre: 9
Hot dogging: 480, 481
Hydraulic jump: 88
Hyperventilation; 85
Hypothermia: 91

Indian canoe: 59, 121, 122, 404
Indian stroke: 419
Inherent stability: 29
Initial stability: 29, 250
Inner game: 352-353
Inside pivot turn: 417
International Canoe Exhibition: 4, 21, 104
International Ten Square Metre: 12

Jet: 194, 221
J stroke: 194, 221

Karabiner: 234
Keyel range: 68-69
Kevlar: 59, 74, 75
Klepper: 23
Knee lift: 158

Laminar flow: 34
Landing: 257-258
Lapstrake canoes: 65
Lateral stability: 30, 45
Lath and canvas: 66
Launching: 255-256, 408, 475
Laying up: 75-76
LCO: 524
Leading on white water: 245-246
Leaning: 151, 200
Leash: 472
Ledges: 188-189, 190, 229
Lifejacket: 87, 104
Linear polyethylene: 79, 81-82
Lining and tracking: 423, 424
Lining up: 197
Long River Canoeists Club: 24
Longtitudinal stability: 30, 45
Loom: see Paddle shaft
Low brace: 170, 414
Low brace turn: 137, 151, 152, 165, 169,
   174, 195, 202
Low Recovery: 147, 149 164 173

MacGregor: 60, 65, 122, 124
Manouevrability: 28

Marathon and open racing scheme: 441,
   481-485
Marathon Racing: 18
Marathon Racing Committee: 20
Medical enquiry form: 369, 388
Mental disability: 372
Moving draw: 170
Morphology, river: 179

National Access Officer: 24
National Coach: 6, 14
National Coaching Committee: 6
National White Water Centre: 15, 16
Navigation: 282, 542
Neoprene: 108, 113
Night paddling: 272
Non-swimmers: 356

Observing wildlife: 520
Open canoe: 125
Outside pivot turn: 420, 421

Packing equipment: 455-456
Paddle
   awareness: 157
   brace: 262
   blade feather: 428
   float: 267
   grip: 126, 428
   length: 428, 434
   mitts: 109
   park: 113
   shaft: 56, 427
   wing: 10, 53, 267, 432-433
   wooden: 56-57
Paddles: 51-58, 136, 251-252, 380-383,
   395, 427, 472
Paddling cycle: 138
Part method of learning: 354
Pawlata: 4, 312
PBK: 23, 66, 122, 124
Period: 460
Piggy back method of boat retrieval: 235
Pilots and cruising guides: 275, 276
Pitch stroke: 415
Pivot turn: 200
Placid Water Teacher Award: 121
Placid Water Scheme: 123, 133, 379
Planing: 39
Planning a journey: 359, 363
Poling: 404
Polo: 485-488
Polo kayak: 50
Polyethylene: 46, 78-83, 395
Polyurethene: 395
Polyurethene foam: 58

Standing waves: 151, 185, 186, 194, 208,
    226-227
Static resistance: 34
Stern carry for swimmer: 306
Stern rudder: 130, 137, 149-151, 164, 165,
    173, 208, 261, 412
Stopper, rescue from: 239, 242-244
Stoppers: 88, 89, 183-184, 185, 186, 191,
    194, 224-226
Stopper slot: 225
Stopper technique: 210-215
Stopping: 129, 137, 141, 142, 162
Stoves: 447-449
Strainer: 229
Stretching exercises: 160
Stripwood boats: 67
Stroke linking: 168-171
Stroke timing: 210, 218, 219
Styrene fumes: 76
S-turn: 220, 221, 222
Support stroke: 131
Surf: 36
Surf Committee: 22
Surfing: 496-497
Surf kayaks: 469
Surf ski: 22
Swedish form: 33
Sweep stroke: 129, 137, 142, 143, 144,
    162, 169, 170, 172, see also forward and
    reverse sweep
Switching: 422, 423, 438

Take off and trim: 476-477
Teaching checklist: 355
Tents: 450-452
Thermal wear: 106
Throw bag: 233, 237-238
Throw line: 243
Through-the-air recovery: 145
Tidal streams: 275
Tide races and overfalls: 275-277
Tides: 273-274
Tide tables: 274, 283
Tillering: 150
Toggles: 111
Tongue: 194
Towing: 115-117, 270-272
Traditional canoes and kayaks: 63-67
Trailer: 118
Training for competition: 442
Transits: 286-287
Trees: 229, 230, 239
Trespass: 509
Trimming: 419, 456
Trough: 194

Trunk rotation: 138, 139, 140, 142, 143,
    144, 145, 154, 157, 160, 168, 171, 172,
    173, 174
Tumblehome: 405
Turbulent flow: 34
Turning: 137

Undertows and rips: 462

Vacuum bagging: 76
Vacuum formed canoes: 83-84
Veering: 116
Ventricular fibrillation: 93
Visibility: 278
Visualisation: 351-352
V's, upstream and downstream: 179, 185,
    186, 187, 188

Water flow rate: 179-181
Waterproofing equipment: 454-455
Watkins, Gino: 4, 312
Wave
    convergence: 465, 467
    divergence: 465, 467
    length: 36
    particle oscillation: 462
    refraction: 464-466
    shoulder: 467
    size estimation: 466
    skis: 470-471
Waves: 35, 36, 38, 459-462
Waves in deep water: 461
Waves in shallow water: 461
Weather: 277-280
Weather forecasts: 279
Weil's disease: 100
Weirs: 88-90, 189-190, 211, 224, 228-229,
    363
Welsh Canoe Association: 6
Wet Suit: 107, 252
White water
    dangers: 228-311
    kayak: 50, 330
    rescue techniques: 234-244
    terminology: 194
    training programmes: 217
'Whole' method of learning: 354
Wild Water Racing: 498-501
Wild Water Racing kayak: 49
Wind: 277
Windchill: 94, 95
Wood and epoxy construction: 67
Wrap-around (folding): 47, 67, 236
Wrist roll: 144, 149, 150, 154, 163, 169,
    173, 261